T0379477

"*Adult Learning, Second Edition* is a meticulously organized book that thoroughly explores the field of adult education, offering clear insights into the frequently asked question: What constitutes adult education? This book serves as a comprehensive guide for an introductory course in any adult education program or as an adult learning course for students of other disciplinary programs."

—**Dr. Mary V. Alfred,** Professor Emerita Adult Education and Human Resource Development Texas A&M University

"*Adult Learning, Second Edition* serves as a vital resource, highlighting the importance of grounding adult education in theory, practice, as well as an understanding of the interconnected socio-cultural, political, economic, technological, and historical realities of the people we serve. Using reflexive practices, Bierema, Fedeli, and Merriam situate the learner/teacher within an educational context or environment and provide resources and tools to create and develop strategies and activities based on certain factors."

—**Vanessa Sheared,** EdD (Retired) Board President, Closing the Gap Foundation Board of Directors, United Way, California Capital Region

"This new edition is an exemplary text that continues to make a significant contribution to the field of adult education. It offers a rich and comprehensive synthesis of the major theories, concepts, and frameworks that inform how adults learn, while simultaneously emphasizing the practical implications of these ideas for educators working in diverse settings. It remains an essential text for anyone teaching or studying in this field."

—**Mitsunori Misawa,** PhD, Associate Professor Adult and Continuing Education University of Tennessee

ADULT LEARNING

ADULT LEARNING

Linking Theory and Practice

Second Edition

Laura L. Bierema, Monica Fedeli,
Sharan B. Merriam

JB JOSSEY-BASS™
A Wiley Brand

Published by John Wiley & Sons, Inc., Hoboken, New Jersey.
Published simultaneously in Canada.

For general information on our other products and services or for technical support, please contact our Customer Care Department within the United States at (800) 762-2974, outside the United States at (317) 572-3993 or fax (317) 572-4002.

Wiley also publishes its books in a variety of electronic formats. Some content that appears in print may not be available in electronic formats. For more information about Wiley products, visit our web site at www.wiley.com.

Library of Congress Cataloging-in-Publication Data:

Names: Bierema, Laura L. (Laura Lee), 1964- author | Fedeli, Monica author | Merriam, Sharan B. author
Title: Adult learning : linking theory and practice / Laura L. Bierema, Monica Fedeli, Sharan B. Merriam.
Description: Second edition. | Hoboken, New Jersey : Jossey-Bass, [2025] | Previous edition: 2014. | Includes bibliographical references and index.
Identifiers: LCCN 2025015888 (print) | LCCN 2025015889 (ebook) | ISBN 9781394265329 hardback | ISBN 9781394265343 adobe pdf | ISBN 9781394265336 epub
Subjects: LCSH: Adult education | Adult education—Research | Education and globalization | Activity programs in education
Classification: LCC LC5215 .M524 2025 (print) | LCC LC5215 (ebook) | DDC 374—dc23/eng/20250515
LC record available at https://lccn.loc.gov/2025015888
LC ebook record available at https://lccn.loc.gov/2025015889

Cover Design: Paul McCarthy
Cover Art: © Getty Images / Zpagistock

SKY10116832_061225

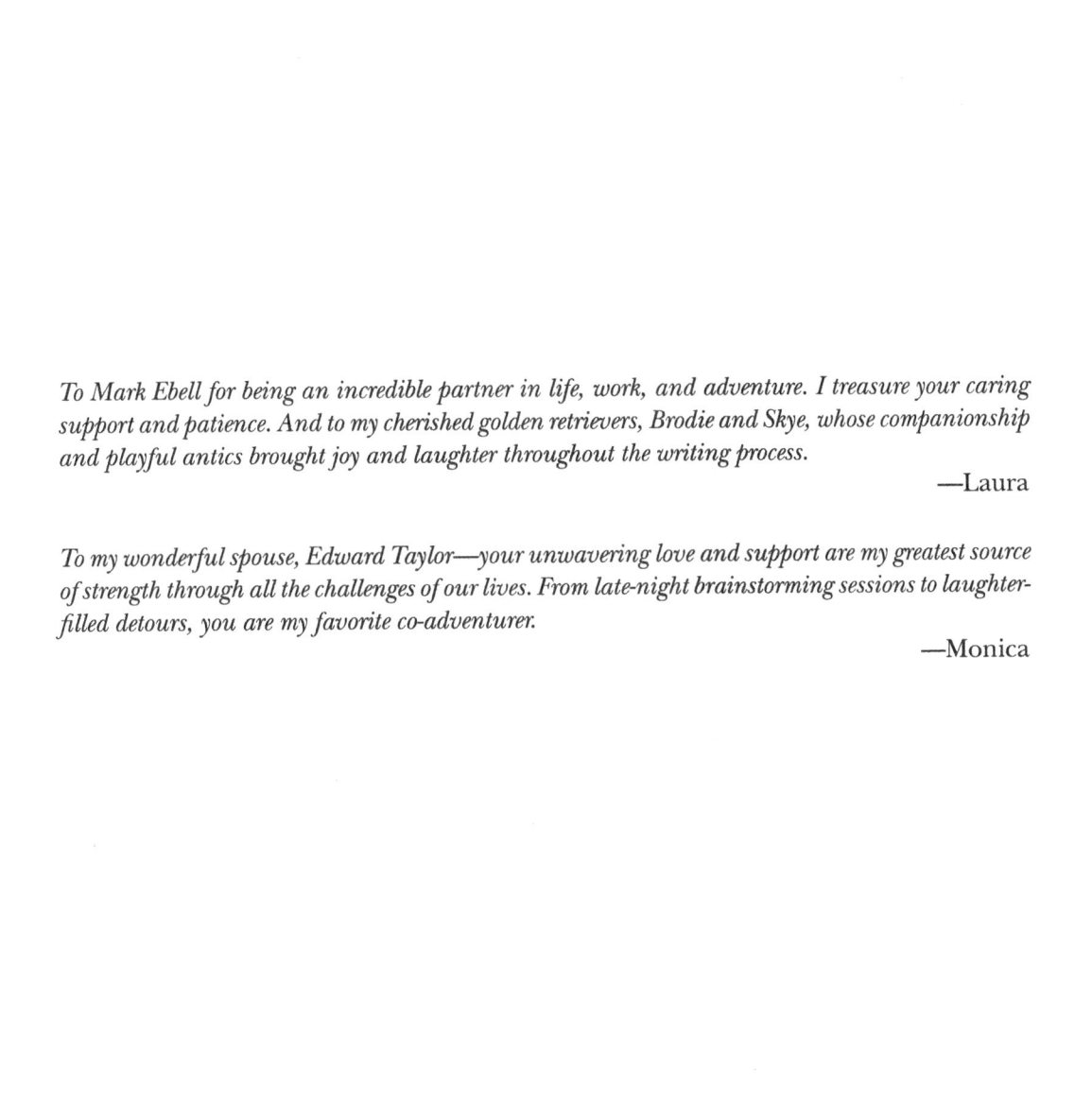

To Mark Ebell for being an incredible partner in life, work, and adventure. I treasure your caring support and patience. And to my cherished golden retrievers, Brodie and Skye, whose companionship and playful antics brought joy and laughter throughout the writing process.

—Laura

To my wonderful spouse, Edward Taylor—your unwavering love and support are my greatest source of strength through all the challenges of our lives. From late-night brainstorming sessions to laughter-filled detours, you are my favorite co-adventurer.

—Monica

CONTENTS

PREFACE

Introduction to the Book

As an adult, you are constantly learning. You might search the Internet to plan a vacation, hear about a new book you want to read on the radio, ask a co-worker to explain a new reporting procedure, or sign up for a class to earn a certificate or a degree. Learning infiltrates your daily activities in family, work, and community life. Learning can occur anywhere, anytime, from human resource development programs at work to seminars and workshops sponsored by libraries, museums, religious organizations, hospitals, and other institutions to more formal programs offered by schools, colleges, and universities. Learning is also accessible in multiple formats, such as in-person, online, or hybrid. The field of **adult education**—adults engaging in systematic, sustained learning activities to gain new knowledge, skills, attitudes, or values—is dedicated to the diverse and varied ways adults learn throughout their lives. You, *the adult learner*, are what unites practitioners and scholars of adult education and learning. Adult educators strive to understand their own learning to better design and facilitate meaningful adult learning activities.

Most likely, you are reading this book to discover more about adult learning. However, unlike Malcolm Knowles, who, as Director of Adult Education at the Boston YMCA in the 1940s, lamented his inability to "find a book that would tell me how to conduct a program of this sort" (Knowles, 1984, p. 2), and realized "that although there was general agreement among adult educators that adults are different from youth as learners, there was no comprehensive theory about these differences" (Knowles, 1984, pp. 3–4), this information exists for your benefit as a learner, educator, or both. Today, the literature on adult learning is vibrant and voluminous, serving both practitioner and scholarly audiences. This book will give you a solid foundation of adult learning theory and tangible ways to apply the ideas presented.

Purpose and Audience

The inspiration behind the first edition of *Adult Learning: Linking Theory and Practice* (Merriam & Bierema, 2014) was based on a survey of adult learning literature in the 2010s, revealing that it primarily focused on a particular aspect of adult learning, such as motivation (Wlodkowski, 2008; Wlodkowski and Ginsberg, 2017), **andragogy**—the art of teaching adults—and its application to workplace learning and human resource development (Knowles et al., 2011), critical thinking (Brookfield, 2012), experiential learning, (Fenwick, 2003), dialogic education (Vella, 2000), and transformative learning (Taylor & Cranton, 2012). At that time, many other textbooks were highly theoretical (Jarvis, 2006; Illeris, 2004) or theory and research-intensive (Merriam et al., 2007). What was missing from the literature on adult learning was a book that provides an overview of the major theories and research in adult learning in language that those new to adult education can understand and, at the same time, point out applications of these ideas to practice.

The first edition of *Adult Learning: Linking Theory and Practice* presented adult learning theory, mindful that *you*, the reader, are yourself an adult learner. The first edition was also intended for adult learning practitioners who design and facilitate educational programs for adults. As authors, a driving goal of the first edition was to create a reader- and practitioner-friendly book with included activities and resources at the end of each chapter for personal and instructional use. We have improved this aspect of the book significantly in this second edition, as explained later in this preface.

Today, adult learning is of crucial social importance, particularly in a time of globalization, **VUCA** (volatile, uncertain, complex, and ambiguous) social, environmental, and economic challenges, the rise of artificial intelligence, shifts as a consequence of the COVID-19 pandemic and Great Resignation, and an aging society. Many of these changes have occurred in the last decade, making revising *Adult Learning: Linking Theory and Practice* timely.

The intended audiences for this book are students, faculty, and anyone interested in deepening their knowledge of the theory and practice of adult learning.

The primary audience for this book is students and faculty in adult education, human resource development, and other programs dedicated to understanding and facilitating effective adult learning in any context. Usually, these academic programs have a core required course in adult learning. Whether these are undergraduate, master's, or doctoral-level programs, typically, this course is the student's first introduction to adult learning. Another audience for this book is graduate students in professional preparation programs whose work may involve the education and training of adults, such as school administrators, public health personnel, social workers, corporate consultants and trainers, counselors, government administrators, higher education faculty, and administrators. Across the globe, academic programs dedicated to adult learning may have different names, such as Lifelong Learning, Social Education, Adult and Professional Education, Community Education, and others. Still, most have a course on adult learning. Of course, this book is also appropriate for anyone interested in adult learning.

Overview of Book Organization and Features

Adult learning theory emerged in the mid-20th century and has evolved with the development of theory and practice to understand how adults learn to be contributing family members, workers, and citizens. Several theories, models, and practices have been developed over the decades, making the landscape of adult learning and education theory rich and daunting. Partelow (2023) explained that **disciplinary frameworks** articulate a set of assumptions, values, concepts, and practices and provide a basis for inquiry, underscoring, "Frameworks are positioned within a theory of science. Understanding this positioning can guide scholars in comprehending how their engagement with frameworks contributes to the overall advancement of their field" (p. 512).

Inspiration for the design of the second edition of *Adult Learning: Linking Theory and Practice* came from Merriam and Caffarella's (1999) premise that "Learning in adulthood can be distinguished from childhood in terms of the learner, the context, and to some extent the learning process" (p. 389). Their "configuration of context, learner, and process" (p. 399) inspired Bierema's (2008, 2019) framework of the context, educator, learner, process, and method, which was briefly introduced in the first edition of this book (Merriam & Bierema, 2014). According to this framework, the second edition of *Adult Learning: Linking Theory and Practice* represents a comprehensive exploration of adult learning.

The Framework for Adult Learning summarizes its key components, including the: (1) Adult learning *context*, (2) Adult *educator*, (3) Adult *learner*, (4) Adult learning *process*, and (5) *Methods* for adult learning facilitation, essentially considering the *where, who, how,* and *what* of adult learning, presented in Figure P.1. The framework melds key issues and ideas in adult learning and education, bridges theory and practice, and provides the organizing structure for the book. The adult learning framework captures the context or *where* learning occurs and how social dynamics impact individuals, groups, and learning systems. It considers the *who,* including adult educators, and how their values and approaches affect learning and learners and how best to honor their learning goals, motivations, and challenges. It also tackles the learning process or *how* learning unfolds in people's heads, hearts, and bodies. Finally, the framework addresses *what* is required to effectively integrate the context, educator, learner, and process in methods for planning and facilitating meaningful adult educational programs.

The practical focus of *Adult Learning: Linking Theory and Practice* is its distinguishing feature. Many adult education and learning books are mired in theory with inadequate explanations of the applications. The second edition of *Adult Learning: Linking Theory and Practice* builds on the strong foundation of the first edition and introduces a new framework and features. As noted, the book is organized according to five adult learning domains introduced as a framework for understanding the field in the first edition. Further, the book has recurring feature boxes embedded in each chapter. Although the first edition incorporated helpful tips for practice and instruction at the end of each

FIGURE P.1 FRAMEWORK FOR ADULT LEARNING

The Adult Learning **Context**	•Appreciating the social system where learning occurs and the learner is situated, including learner positionality, physical environment, and the psychological environment.
The Adult **Educator**	•Examining the role of persons trained in adult learning principles, practices, and facilitation who engage in ongoing examination and adjustment of practice.
The Adult **Learner**	•Understanding what motivates adult participation in educational activities, and how they prefer to learn so they can be effective members of their family, workplace, and community.
The Adult Learning **Process**	•Probing what goes on in the learner's head, heart, body, and soul that leads to change in behavior or perspective.
The **Methods** for Adult Learning Facilitation	•Putting the theories and concepts of adult learning into action to create relevant, timely, and engaging learning experiences for diverse learners.

FIGURE P.2 CHAPTER FEATURES

 **Chapter Overview and Learning Objectives**

This box provides a short summary of the chapter and what readers will learn by the end of the chapter.

 **Recommendations for Further Learning**

This box recommends resources for readers to continue their learning and investigate topics further.

 **Reflective Practice**

This box contains reflective activities and offers a chance to pause and consider the implications of a specific idea, theory, or practice as it relates to learning in adulthood and facilitating adult learning.

 **Adult Learning and Teaching Cases**

Adult learning and teaching case studies are included in several chapters to help readers think about the nuances of issues that arise when adults are learning and changing.

 SoTL: The Scholarship of Teaching and Learning

This box contains summaries of the best evidence available to inform the facilitation of effective adult learning.

 **Adult Learning by the Numbers**

This box contains statistical and demographic information on adult learning.

chapter, this edition has expanded that feature by integrating these activities throughout the text. The book features integrated boxes to provide chapter overviews, prompts for reflective practice, connections of evidence to practice, and tips and tools for teaching and learning to enhance the learning experience for readers and help them apply their knowledge in good adult education form. Figure P.2 illuminates the new features in this edition.

There are some changes in content from the first edition. The content is organized into sections based on the five foci of the second edition's framework, beginning with context and culture rather than ending with those topics. A new section (Section 2) on *The Adult Educator* explores the careers and competencies of people doing this work. We added a new chapter on "Connecting Learning and Change in Adulthood," as learning and change processes are interwoven and mutually reinforcing. We expanded the "Transformative Learning" chapter to "Learning for Transformation" to reflect the theoretical developments in this area. We have integrated the chapter on "Body and Spirit in Learning" throughout the book, as embodied, spiritual, and narrative learning are excellent methods for fostering all types of adult learning. We created a new section with three chapters titled *Developing and Delivering Adult Learning Programs—The What* to help educators and learners use effective tools and strategies to design new programs in online, hybrid, and face-to-face formats using active learning. All chapters have been updated based on advances in theory and practice. We (the authors) hope you find this book user-friendly and relevant to your thinking and practice as adult educators and learners.

References

Bierema, L. L. (2008). Principles of instructional design and adult learners. In. V. Wang (Ed.), *Strategic approaches towards curriculum development for adult learners in the global community* (pp. 7–33). Krieger.

Bierema, L. L. (2019). Adult learning theories and practices. In M. Fedeli, & L. L. Bierema (Eds.). *Connecting adult learning and knowledge management: Strategies for learning and change in higher education and organizations* (pp. 3–26). Springer.

Brookfield, S. D. (2012). *Teaching for critical thinking: Tools and techniques to help students question their assumptions.* Jossey-Bass.

Fenwick, T. (2003). *Learning through experience: Troubling orthodoxies and intersecting questions.* Krieger.

Illeris, K. (2004). *Adult education and adult learning.* Krieger.

Jarvis, P. (2006). *Towards a comprehensive theory of human learning.* Routledge.

Knowles, M. S. (1984). *The adult learner: A neglected species* (3rd ed.). Gulf.

Knowles, M. S., Holton, E. F. III, & Swanson, R. A. (2011). *The adult learner* (7th ed.). Gulf

Merriam, S. B., & Bierema, L. L. (2014). *Adult learning: Linking theory and practice.* John Wiley & Sons.

Merriam, S. B. & Caffarella, R. (1999). Learning in adulthood. *A comprehensive guide.* Jossey-Bass.

Merriam, S. B., Caffarella, R. S., & Baumgartner, L. M. (2007). *Learning in adulthood* (3rd ed.). Jossey-Bass.

Partelow, S. (2023). What is a framework? Understanding their purpose, value, development and use. *Journal of Environmental Studies and Sciences, 13*(3), 510–519. https://doi.org/10.1007/s13412-023-00833-w.

Taylor, E. W., & Cranton, P. (Eds.) (2012). *The handbook of transformative learning.* Jossey-Bass.

Vella, J. (2000). A spirited epistemology: Honoring the adult learner as subject. *New Directions for Adult and Continuing Education, 2000*(85), 7–16. https://doi.org/10.1002/ace.8501.

Wlodkowski, R. J. (2008). *Enhancing adult motivation to learn: A comprehensive guide for teaching all adults* (3rd ed.). Jossey-Bass.

Wlodkowski, R. J. & Ginsberg, M. B. (2017). *Enhancing adult motivation to learn: A comprehensive guide for teaching all adults* (4th Ed.). Jossey-Bass.

ACKNOWLEDGMENTS

It is with heartfelt gratitude we recognize and appreciate the people who supported our writing journey. This book would be impossible to write without the outstanding adult learners we work with in classes, workshops, and seminars, as well as on research. You challenge us to do our best work. We have written this book for you and hope it enhances your thinking and practice in adult education. We acknowledge our Editor, Samuel Offman; Managing Editor, Ashirvad Moses; and their colleagues at John Wiley & Sons, who were highly supportive and helpful throughout writing and production. We also thank friends and family, including Mark Ebell, Phillip Holmes, and Ed Taylor, who read chapter drafts and provided invaluable feedback. A special appreciation goes to University of Georgia PhD Candidate and Graduate Research Assistant Eunbi Sim and University of Padova Research Assistant Marica Liotino. Eunbi served as an expert library researcher and proofreader, finding excellent resources, chasing references, and tending to the technical issues as we neared publication. Marica supported technical issues, actively searched for relevant resources, and carefully proofread the content to ensure accuracy and clarity. We are indebted to you for your contributions. We thank all of you, including our family, friends, and colleagues, for your support and encouragement.

—Laura L. Bierema
Athens, Georgia
February 2025

—Monica Fedeli
Padova, Italy
February 2025

THE AUTHORS

Laura L. Bierema is a professor of adult learning, leadership, and organization development at the University of Georgia, Athens, Georgia, United States. Her research interests include workplace learning, career development, women's development, organization development, executive coaching, leadership, and critical human resource development. She holds bachelor's and master's degrees from Michigan State University and a doctorate in adult education from UGA. She has published over 200 book chapters and articles in research and professional publications and authored, co-authored, or edited 12 books. She was a 2018 US Fulbright Research Scholar at the University of Padova, Italy.

Dr. Bierema has won multiple research, teaching, mentoring, and leadership awards, including the Academy of Human Resource Development's (AHRD) Outstanding Scholar, Forward, and Human Resource Development Scholar Hall of Fame Awards; AHRD's Book of the Year for *Adult Learning: Linking Research and Practice, 1st Edition* (2014) and *Human Resource Development: A Critical Perspective* (2024); the University, Professional, and Continuing Education Association's Phillip E. Frandson Award for Literature for *Adult Learning: Linking Theory and Practice, 1st Edition* (2014); and she was inducted into the Adult and Continuing Education Hall of Fame (2022).

Monica Fedeli is a professor in the Department of Philosophy, Sociology, Pedagogy, and Applied Psychology at the University of Padova, Italy. She holds leadership roles as Vice-Rector for Outreach and Relations with the Territory and Advisor for Innovative Teaching and E-Learning at the university.

Fedeli's research focuses on adult learning, faculty development, and organizational change, particularly emphasizing active learning methodologies, employability, and transformative learning. She has contributed extensively to higher education innovation, developing new teaching strategies and promoting faculty training programs. Her scholarly work includes the authorship and co-authorship of multiple books and over 80 journal articles on adult education, knowledge management, and innovative pedagogies. She has served as an editor and board member for international journals such as *Excellence and Innovation in Learning and Teaching* and *Reflective Practices.*

Fedeli has been recognized internationally for her contributions to adult education, including collaborations with Fulbright research programs, Erasmus+ projects, and multiple international teaching fellowships at institutions across Europe and the United States. Her notable publications include *Connecting Adult Learning and Knowledge Management* (2019) and *Teaching4Learning@Unipd* (2020), exploring strategies for enhancing higher education learning and organizational development.

Fedeli remains a leading voice in faculty development and innovative learning, continuously working to bridge the gap between research, policy, and educational practice.

Sharon B. Merriam is a professor emerita of adult education and qualitative research at the University of Georgia in Athens, Georgia, United States. Merriam's research and writing activities have focused on adult and lifelong learning and qualitative research methods. She was co-editor of *Adult Education Quarterly*, the primary research and theory journal in adult education. She has published 26 books, several translated into Chinese, Korean, Japanese, and French, and over 100 journal articles and book chapters. She is a four-time winner of the prestigious Cyril O. Houle World Award for Literature in Adult Education for books published in 1982, 1997, 1999, and 2007. Based on her widespread contributions to adult education, Merriam has been inducted into the International Adult and Continuing Education Hall of Fame and was the first to receive the American Association of Adult and Continuing Education's Career Achievement Award. She has conducted workshops and seminars on adult learning and qualitative research throughout North America and overseas, including countries in southern Africa, Southeast Asia, the Middle East, and Europe. She has been a Fulbright Scholar, a Senior Research Fellow in Malaysia, and a Distinguished Visiting Scholar at universities in South Korea and South Africa.

THE ADULT LEARNING CONTEXT

Context is *where* learning occurs, and it affects every learning exchange. **Context** is the social system that permeates the thinking and actions of all human beings within a particular situation, such as a classroom, school, organization, community, or nation. Context may incorporate physical conditions, political conditions, economic conditions, power dynamics, and other influences that impact those occupying that space. **Learning context** is "the social system that affects the thinking and actions of people within a particular social situation such as a classroom, school, organization, community, or nation . . . [that] incorporates culture, privilege, and power" (Merriam & Bierema, 2014, p. 241).

As an adult educator or learner, consider the context where you live, study, or work. Who are the members? What are the dynamics? Is there trust? What is the culture? The world is complex, changing, and unpredictable, and adults need to effectively cope with how these forces affect life and work. Global diversity is increasing, and learners and educators must also respond to how culture, privilege, and power shape society. This section explores how the VUCA (volatile, uncertain, complex, and ambiguous) shapes teaching and learning. It also examines how culture, privilege, and power affect teaching and learning.

Educators are responsible for being aware of context and working to make their classroom an environment that values diversity, equity, and inclusion, where learners can safely and bravely voice their ideas, share, and question assumptions. The physical or psychological learning context may also require inhabitants to modify their thinking and actions when occupying the space. This responsibility means that adult educators need to create an atmosphere conducive to the emergence of a learning community centered on equity and respect.

Chapter 1, "Introducing *Adult Learning: Linking Theory and Practice*," introduces key adult learning concepts and terms. Chapter 2, "Understanding Adult Learning in Contemporary Social Context and Culture," situates adult learning today, considering how social, technological, economic, cultural, and global dynamics affect every aspect of adulthood. Chapter 3, "Applying Critical Perspectives to Adult Learning in Social Context," explores the role of scrutiny in adult learning by describing what being critical as an adult learner or educator means, including understanding criticality as a philosophy, thinking process, and agenda for mindful and timely action on social problems and challenges.

Reference

Merriam, S. B., & Bierema, L. L. (2014). *Adult learning: Linking theory and practice.* John Wiley & Sons.

CHAPTER ONE

INTRODUCING *ADULT LEARNING: LINKING THEORY AND PRACTICE*

 **Box 1.1 Chapter Overview and Learning Objectives**

Learning is a fundamental process that is continual and lifelong. An African proverb captures this sentiment about adult learning:

> Anyone who fails to learn. . .is regarded as *oku eniyan* (the living dead).
> (Avoseh, 2001, p. 483)

Learning—acquiring knowledge, skills, and attitudes—is as natural as breathing and vital to life. As an adult, you constantly learn throughout your day and life, whether or not you are conscious of it. You learn about breaking news from your smartphone. You decide to try a new recipe you scanned in the newspaper. You discover a new route across town due to an unexpected detour. You encounter a moment to question an assumption when a friend tells you how they shifted their thinking about a shared value. Your concern for a struggling child prompts you to identify ways to help them navigate the situation that sends you to other parents, their teacher, or your therapist. You decide to make a major life change that creates significant upheaval. These moments are learning opportunities in adulthood, largely unplanned and informal, and sometimes surprising.

This chapter introduces the second edition of *Adult Learning: Linking Theory and Practice* and provides an overview of the book with advice on how to read it. This book is written for you: an adult learner, an adult educator, a person interested in learning, or all three. The chapter and book contain key terms and ideas about adult education and learning. The chapter begins with an introduction to the book and its features, introduces key terms and definitions, and provides an overview of its framework. The boxes throughout the book include *Chapter Overview and Learning Objectives, Adult Learning and Teaching Cases, SOTL: The Scholarship of Teaching and Learning, Reflective Practice,* and *Tips and Tools for Teaching and Learning, Adult Learning by the Numbers,* and *Recommendations for Further Learning.*

As a result of reading this chapter and completing the exercise boxes, you, the reader, should be able to:

1. Understand the aims of *Adult Learning: Linking Theory and Practice* and how to read this book.
2. Define key adult learning concepts and terms.
3. Understand the book's framework.

Adult Learning in Turbulent Times

Globalization, the knowledge age, technology, and demographic changes characterize today's learning context. This chapter describes the world where adults learn. Most people have heard the adage attributed to Greek philosopher Heraclitus of Ephesus (535–475 BCE) that "Change is the only constant." The axiom has never been truer, with change at an exponentially higher rate than ever throughout history. Learning has been adults' proven response to change, and as action learning advocate Reg Revans (2017) said, "There can be no learning without action, and no action without learning" (p. 53).

When you, the reader, think about learning, what flashes into your mind? It is likely a formal classroom with rows, pupils, materials, and a teacher. Yet, the majority of learning in adulthood is informal—not organized or taught by a teacher—and often incidental in that it is a byproduct of another experience, such as shifting to remote work and realizing life is more or less stressful or listening to the news and trying to understand geopolitical conflict. Learning happens as you navigate and negotiate daily life in your communications with others, face personal and interpersonal challenges, care for family members, engage in work or a career, participate in your community, and adjust to unexpected changes and catastrophes like the COVID-19 pandemic. Jarvis (1987) observed that adult learning rarely occurs in isolation but in the context of life and the world. The editors of the 2023 *Handbook of Adult and Continuing Education* began the book by observing the field of adult education as "a forward-looking domain of practice and scholarship" (Mizzi et al., 2023, p. 1), describing the time as tumultuous:

> Adult and continuing education should not simply respond to rapidly changing social, economic, technological, and political environments across the globe, but should lead the way in preparing adults to become informed, globally connected, critical citizens who are knowledgeable, skilled, and open and adaptive to change and uncertainty. (p. 7)

We (the authors) wrote the second edition of *Adult Learning: Linking Theory and Practice* deeply committed to providing you, as an adult or educator, with theoretically sound applied ways to enhance your learning and that of others. As adults muddle through a global pandemic, learn new technology, grapple with a health change, or travel to a new place, their learning is embedded within the social context, affected by the people, places, and current events they encounter.

Volatility or "VUCA"

The acronym "VUCA" represents conditions that are V-volatile, U-uncertain, C-complex, and A-ambiguous (van der Steege, 2017; Yoder-Wise, 2021). The United States Army War College devised VUCA to describe and study perplexing, shifting, confusing, and multifaceted conditions (US Army Heritage and Education Center, 2018; Whiteman, 1998). VUCA circumstances prevail: The world grapples with the aftermath of the global COVID-19 pandemic and how it is reshaping work and career conditions; brutal wars rage and people are displaced, wounded, and killed, with little evident movement toward resolution; global poverty and hunger plague many nations; police violence against Black and Brown humans continues in the United States and elsewhere, although the wave of demands for equity and justice following the murder of George Floyd and others are being doused by conservative voices and initiatives to weaken or destroy diversity, equity, and inclusion (DEI) efforts in the workplace and educational settings; voters are electing populist leaders who are creating global conflict and unrest; and severe weather conditions have become the norm, causing destruction and human suffering as a result of climate change. These VUCA challenges capture what Rittel and Webber (1973) called **"wicked problems"**—obtuse, incomprehensible situations that are difficult for people to understand, predict, control, or address and require different mindsets and approaches than easily solved problems.

Living and Learning Amid Volatility

Learning in a VUCA world puts new demands on adults who must create meaning and make decisions with incomplete, changing information. Hawley et al. (2023) underscored, "The pandemic and the continued devaluation of Black lives are the backdrop for two of the major challenges resulting during this unprecedented time: economic and social disruption" (p. 453). They noted further that adult and continuing education is critical in helping people and nations confront these challenges. For example, Canzittu (2022) explained that in today's context, employers expect workers to flex amid complexity by facilitating learning and leveraging knowledge to respond effectively to problems and derive appropriate solutions. Further, organizations grapple with capacity building to create, maintain, and share knowledge to address wicked problems. Table 1.1 describes VUCA concepts in adult learning terms using the COVID-19 pandemic as an example of a VUCA situation.

VUCA circumstances present continual opportunities for learning and change while simultaneously creating conditions that create resistance to both. The COVID-19 pandemic was unusual because change was compulsory and immediate once lockdowns began. Although few changes are as extreme, the situation proved that humanity could change radically and quickly (Korten, 2020).

Most people dislike or resist change, so living in a VUCA world can create anxiety and frustration. Finding resilience and staying focused can be difficult. Adopting a learning orientation—asking "What is new or different now?" or "What can I learn from this situation?"—is a healthier coping mechanism than feelings of helplessness or exasperation. It also helps to talk about change and uncertainty with others to make collective meaning and perhaps take collective action. Box 1.2 applies VUCA.

The research and scholarship in adult learning are extensive, and this book provides a solid introduction and firm grounding in the theories and research that inform evidence-based practice. One of the book's features highlights SoTL—the scholarship of teaching and learning. Box 1.3 defines this concept.

Defining Adult Education and Learning Concepts and Terms

Adult education and the process of adult learning have several important concepts and terms to understand in order to be conversant in the field. Table 1.2 provides a summary of commonly used terms and a definition. Review the table to discover how many terms are familiar to you as a learner or educator.

The book will use these terms to introduce theory and research and tie them to best practices for facilitating effective adult learning.

TABLE 1.1 ADULT LEARNING IN VUCA TERMS

VUCA Term	Definition	Adult Learning Examples	Learning Strategies for Coping with Change	Reflective Questions
V **Volatility**	Unstable change, even in situations that are understandable and identifiable.	The COVID-19 pandemic injected volatility into life and work overnight globally. Even though people knew how to live and work, the disruption caused immediate shifts in how people lived, worked, and learned, demanding new ways of being and knowing. The lines blurred between home and work life, creating life balance challenges; formal learning suddenly became remote and technology-driven for all ages; jobs were reconfigured for remote work; anxieties prevailed about safety; social distancing became the norm, and new ways of connecting were discovered; and many people began reassessing their values and life goals, especially related to work.	**Find balance, be agile, and be open to new learning:** When the world is unpredictable, find a space, practice, or community that feels safe and centering. Ask questions about new challenges and learning. Accept change as a constant and develop flexibility to maneuver and change with the fluctuating demands. Create a vision for your next steps in life and help others do the same.	• What do I understand about this situation? • What do I not understand about this situation? • What scares me about this situation? • What am I learning about myself? Others? • How can I support others in this moment? • How do I want to show up in this moment?
U **Uncertainty**	The present is unclear, and the future is uncertain. A lack of knowledge about the implications or consequences of a situation prevails, even when its causes and effects are anticipated and recognizable.	The COVID-19 pandemic created a health risk situation that required immediate changes in daily life and work. It was unclear how long the pandemic would last and how it would affect lives in the future.	**Learn:** Seek to understand and build knowledge about the situation. Work on environmental scanning to assess the current reality and anticipate future needs, opportunities, and challenges. Reflect on what you do well and how you can improve. Use the situation to enhance your learning and knowledge. Keep perspective and attempt to control what is in your sphere of influence. Take care of yourself and your loved ones.	• What is known about the situation? • What is unknown? • What do I know that can be useful right now? • What can I control? • How can I support others in navigating the uncertainty?

(Continued)

TABLE 1.1 (*Continued*)

VUCA Term	Definition	Adult Learning Examples	Learning Strategies for Coping with Change	Reflective Questions
C Complexity	Multiple factors within a system come into play that create confusion and chaos.	How COVID-19 vaccines were developed and administrated was a global, confusing, and chaotic task. On a more individual level, how families decided to organize their lives was a new learning territory. Similarly, work teams and organizations had to deal with the upheaval and awkwardness of remote work.	**Communicate:** Clearly and often. Whether engaging with family and friends or peers, supervisees, customers, or the boss, transparent exchanges help create alignment on the next steps. Communicating and ensuring people understand expectations also enhances collaboration and results.	• How might I cultivate a growth or learning mindset? • What scares me about not knowing? How can I lean into the confusion? • What are different ways of looking at this situation? Who else should I be talking with? • How am I affected by this situation? How can I influence this situation?
A Ambiguity	Little or no clarity exists about the situation.	When the COVID-19 pandemic began, there was little clearness about personal safety measures like masking or social distancing. There was a blurring of personal and professional work for remote workers. Once some organizations began returning to in-person work, many CEOs made and continue making missteps in their policies and communication.	**Experiment and foster resilience and flexibility:** When the situation is unclear, you may have to try different things. Sometimes, that means making an individual decision. Another may mean negotiating the appropriate situation and learning new coping skills. Talking about coping with others can also be helpful and therapeutic.	• What is known? • How can I remain calm in the face of the unknown? • Who seems to manage ambiguity well? What can I learn from them? • What happens if I make the wrong decision?

Source: Adapted from Bierema, 2024, pp. 22–23.

Box 1.2 Reflective Practice

Applying VUCA to Life's Challenges

VUCA gives you, as an adult learner or educator, the language to make meaning of abstruse and fluctuating situations and find ways to be resilient during uncertainty. Referring to Table 1.1, picture a taxing situation you have encountered or are currently trying to solve. Review the definitions, examples, and coping strategies and consider how you might handle it from a VUCA perspective. Jot your reflections in this box:

VUCA Term	Definition	Coping Strategies
V Volatility	Unstable change, even in situations that are understandable and identifiable.	Find balance and be agile by:
U Uncertainty	The present is unclear, and the future is uncertain.	Learn by:
C Complexity	Multiple factors within a system come into play that create confusion and chaos.	Communicate by:
A Ambiguity	Little or no clarity exists about the situation.	Experiment and foster resilience and flexibility by:

Source: Adapted from Bierema, 2024, p. 24.

Box 1.3 SoTL: The Scholarship of Teaching and Learning

What Is the Scholarship of Teaching and Learning?

The scholarship of teaching and learning (SoTL) began with Boyer's (1990) work, *Scholarship Reconsidered: Priorities of the Professorate*, in which he advocated reframing traditional scholarship to reflect the range of faculty work. Boyer proposed expanding scholarship beyond conventional or basic research to include integrative scholarship that compiles and interprets original research and insights from existing research, the scholarship of application or bridging of theory and practice, and the scholarship of teaching to profile effective, evidence-based teaching methods.

Fanghanel et al. (2015) explained:

> SoTL covers concepts as diverse as reflection and inquiry on learning and teaching practices, strategies to enhance teaching and learning, curriculum development, the promotion of research-informed teaching, undergraduate research, and student engagement in disciplinary or SoTL research. SoTL is also fundamentally linked to, and informs, visions of, and practices for, strategic professional development, career planning, promotion and recognition (Chalmers, 2011; Fanghanel, 2013; Hutchings et al., 2011; Mårtensson et al., 2011). (pp. 8–9)

Adult education scholar Roger Boshier (2009) criticized SoTL, arguing that the concept has become a synonym for non-teaching–related activities, the definition has conceptual confusion, SoTL is difficult to operationalize, SoTL discourse is anti-intellectual, and it over-relies on peer review to determine effectiveness.

This book will profile research that provides evidence for effective adult learning practice, where the information is available, and share contrary views and evidence.

A Framework for Adult Learning

This edition of the book applies a framework to organize the major sections of the book. Merriam et al. (2020) offered a scaffold for adult learning that distinguishes it from child learning according to the characteristics of the learner, process, and context that inspired the current framework. The first edition of *Adult Learning: Linking Theory and Practice* expanded the scaffolding to consider the additional variables of the educator and the design and facilitation of the learning itself. The framework has evolved and become the organizing framework for this book: the educational context, the educator, the learner, the process, and the method. This section briefly introduces the framework.

The Adult Learning Context—The Where. *Context* is *where* learning occurs, and it affects every learning exchange. **Context** is the social system that permeates the thinking and actions of all human beings within a particular situation, such as a classroom, school, organization, community, or nation. Context may incorporate physical conditions, political conditions, economic conditions, power dynamics, and other influences that impact those occupying that space. For example, the context of the

TABLE 1.2 COMMON ADULT LEARNING AND EDUCATION TERMS

Term	Definition
Adult Education	Adults engage in learning or educational activities to develop new knowledge, skills, or attitudes, encompassing everything from basic literacy to advanced graduate work to activities not associated with academic institutions or formal instruction. Adult education is considered distinctive from the education of children.
Adult Educator	A person who teaches, supports, and facilitates adult education and learning on various topics.
Adult Learner	Any person holding roles with adult-like responsibilities (e.g., worker, parent, responsible citizen) who is engaged in acquiring new knowledge, whether formal, informal, or nonformal (see definitions in this table).
Adult Learning	When adults engage in systemic, sustained activities to gain new knowledge to meet a desired goal, such as learning, connecting with others, or advancing at work, adult learning can be formal, informal, or nonformal.
Andragogy	Contrasted with pedagogy, andragogy is typically learner-centered education where learners define their learning goals and have input and control over the learning process, even when engaged in formal education.
Chautauqua	A late-19th and early 20th century adult education and social movement in the United States that provided community-based entertainment and cultural learning. Some are still active today, such as The Chautauqua Institution in New York State, the original Chautauqua, or the Athens Chautauqua Society in Athens, Georgia.
Critical Pedagogy	Education that questions power relationships and who in society creates knowledge. This approach teaches learners to think critically and question their knowledge and the material others try to teach them. The intent of critical pedagogy is learning and action that promotes social change, equity, and justice.
Critical Thinking	Pondering about the information one consumes through observation, experience, reflection, reasoning, or communication by conducting analysis, interpretation, and evaluation about the quality of the information and using good judgment and discernment in the information one believes and accepts as knowledge.
Digital Literacy	Adults' ability to responsibly use and consume digital information with confidence, critique, and safety.

(Continued)

TABLE 1.2 (*Continued*)

Term	Definition
Formal Learning	Structured, organized education usually depends on a teacher presenting planned lessons. This type of learning often leads to some kind of credentialing, such as degrees or certificates.
Informal Learning	Learning occurring in the course of daily activities and experiences that is unplanned, unstructured, and not organized, but instead happens as an adult encounters other people, challenges, or opportunities. Informal learning can also be incidental or learning as a byproduct of doing something else. For example, incidental learning might be learning what annoys the boss during a meeting—a consequence of the activity that was neither intended nor planned.
Nonformal Learning	Learning that occurs through planned learning activities where some support of the learner is available, but the learning is not part of the formal education and training system, such as vocational education, continuing education, or apprenticeship training.
Lifelong Learning	Learning in all its forms (formal, informal, nonformal) occurs across a person's lifespan and may encompass formal education, job training, life experiences, and cultural, civic, and social activities.
Literacy	The ability to read, write, speak, and listen that allows a person to effectively communicate with others and make sense of their world.
Lyceum	A loose collection of adult education programs popular in the mid-19th century in the United States, before and after the Civil War. They were traveling programs that included lectures, drama, classes, and debates by well-known entertainers and scholars. The lyceum movement influenced the development of adult education in the United States. Similar programs are common across the globe such as the Scottish Mechanics' Institutes, the Workers Educational Association (WEA) in the United Kingdom, Danish folk high schools (Folkehøjskoler), German people's high schools (Volkshochschulen), the Latin American Pedagogical Movement (Movimiento Pedagógico Latinoamericano), the Tawjihi movement in the Middle East, and community learning centers in Asia.
Pedagogy	Contrasted with andragogy, pedagogy is typically teacher-centered education with the goal of filling learners' empty minds with knowledge. Freire (2011) referred to this type of teaching as "banking education," where the teacher would "deposit" knowledge into the learner's head.
Training	The process of increasing an adult's knowledge and skills for a particular task, job, or desired level of performance, productivity, or capacity.

COVID-19 pandemic radically affected how people lived, worked, and learned worldwide. The physical or psychological context may also require inhabitants to modify their thinking and actions when occupying the space. For example, the physical context, such as a classroom setup and format, affects the learning exchange. A traditional in-person lecture format with all learners facing the front will create very different interpersonal dynamics than a room where learners can sit around a table and face each other or a room with only chairs but no tables. Of course, learners from more teacher-centered cultures may be uncomfortable with a room setup that turns their gaze away from the teacher and toward their peers. The psychological environment, such as one marked by interpersonal conflict, creates very different dynamics from one where there is collaboration and respect. Online learning contexts have other influences on learning as they change the nature of human interaction that might occur in a classroom.

The Adult Educator—The Who. Oftentimes, scholars and practitioners overlook the *educator* in discussions of teaching and learning in adult education. We, the authors, believe this is a mistake as helping adults learn begins with the well-being and mindset of the educator, where one is involved in the learning. Throughout this book, we address both the educator and learner since the roles are intertwined. We also think it is essential to acknowledge that all educators are learners first. Being an educator is an honor and responsibility and striving to improve as a teacher is a lifelong learning endeavor. Outstanding educators embody Schön's (1983) notion of the reflective practitioner stance in which one is engaged in an ongoing examination and adjustment of practice. This reflective practice gives the educator a keen sense of self and how their values translate into educational thought and action. Educators are continually creating and testing theories and practices as they strive to meet learner needs. Both non-Western and Western teaching approaches have much to offer learners. Educators can more effectively reach diverse learners across cultures by using multiple methods and embracing multiple perspectives and worldviews.

The Adult Learner—The Who. The *learner* tends to get most of our attention as educators, and for good reason. This book addresses many aspects of the learner, from who participates in adult education to what motivates learners to how learners can thrive in a constant state of ambiguity and social upheaval. Early theoretical work in adult education focused on describing the learner. These contributions dominated from the 1960s through the 1980s and include Houle's (1961) work on understanding learner goals, Knowles's (1970) popularization of the Andragogy concept, the advancement of self-directed learning as a key feature of adult learning (Knowles, 1975), and the development of lesser-known theories such as McClusky's (1950) Theory of Margin. Adults participate for multiple reasons, although work-related learning remains a significant focus. Adults are also engaged in English as a second language (ESL), adult basic education (ABE), general education development (GED), credential programs, apprenticeship programs, continuing professional education, and personal development courses. Adults have high expectations for timely and relevant learning. Although adult learning has common characteristics, the diversity of learning needs and varied cultures of learners must be acknowledged and valued in the learning process. Adulthood is full of multiple demands, so most adults seek learning when it is relevant to a life issue or problem. The learning must also be about something adults care about and find useful. Adult motivation to learn is likely intrinsic; adults learn to meet unmet needs, resolve unwanted conditions, or reach desired goals. Box 1.4 summarizes work-based adult learning.

The Adult Learning Process—The How. Educators and learners are key stakeholders in the *learning process.* Just how does the learning happen? The **learning process** concerns what goes on in the learner's head, heart, body, and soul, leading to a change in behavior or perspective. The learning process is culturally bound, and change is often a significant catalyst for learning. Adulthood is characterized by constant change that may prompt an identity crisis, challenge relationships, and impact a person's sense of legacy—what they will leave for the next generation. Learning helps adults cope with change, whether it is expected or unanticipated. For example, people might anticipate leaving home for the first time, becoming a college student, committing to a relationship, joining a cause, starting a family, taking a new job, or assuming an important community role. All of these foreseen life events are learning opportunities. Adults are less prepared for life's unexpected changes, such as the breakup of a relationship, sudden death of a loved one, loss of a job, change in financial circumstances, or new insights gained from events, travel, or relationships. Some of these changes could evoke **transformative learning** that provokes shifting one's way of thinking and being in the world. Change often requires people to reframe their understanding of circumstances and ideas. Adults learn by making meaning of life situations, reorganizing their understandings of ideas, and, at times, changing their behaviors and beliefs due to learning. The chapters in this book explore various aspects of this learning process, including motivation, the role of experience, self-directed learning, transformative learning, brain and cognitive functioning, embodied and spiritual learning, and critical thinking.

 ## Box 1.4 Adult Learning by the Numbers

Adult Learning in the Workforce

This box contains summaries of research on AL from the National Center for Educational Statistics (NCES—see https://nces.ed.gov/).

The NCES conducts periodic surveys on *Participation in Adult Education and Lifelong Learning*. Results from the 2001 survey concluded:

> In 2001, the overall participation rate in formal AE during the 12 months before the interview was 46 percent. About 92 million adults participated in one or more types of formal educational activities during this period (p. vi).

The rate shifted from 40% to 45% during the 1990s, which is the most recent data.

During 2005, the breakdowns of adults taking specific programs, classes, or courses included (see https://nces.ed.gov/programs/digest/d19/tables/dt19_507.40.asp):

- Informal learning activities for personal interest: 70.5%
- Career or job-related courses: 27%
- Personal interest courses: 21.4%
- Basic skills/General Educational Development (GED) classes: 1.7%
- Part-time post-secondary education: 5%
- Apprenticeship programs: 1.2%
- English as a second language (ESL) classes: 0.9%

Informal learning is common among adults and occurs outside traditional, formal settings like a classroom. Much of AL is self-directed, planned, and controlled by the learner. Work-related learning is the second highest area, where activities like workplace training occur.

Workplace training is a thriving industry, with *Training* magazine reporting in its annual Training Industry Report that US expenditures were $10.1 billion in 2023, averaging $954 per employee (Freifeld, 2023).

The Method of Facilitating Adult Learning—The What. Effective learning for adults is cognizant of the intersecting roles of the context, educator, learner, and process in designing and facilitating **learning**—creating and delivering learning experiences that help adults develop and demonstrate their understanding of knowledge, skills, or attitudes. The design and facilitation of learning is the bridge between theory and practice in adult education. It is the moment we, as educators, must take our theories and concepts of adult learning and put them into practice to create relevant, timely, and engaging learning experiences for diverse learners. No single formula exists for creating robust programs to optimize learners' learning. Yet, as discussed throughout this book, there are several things that educators can do to ensure that each participant has an opportunity to learn from the experience.

The impact of culture continues to be essential for educators and learners as we strive to appreciate diverse ways of knowing. Although the traditional theories of adult learning are here to stay, such as andragogy, self-directed learning, and transformative learning, the field is focusing on more contemporary emerging understandings of learning, such as holistic learning, embodied learning, spirituality, non-Western ways of knowing, technology, and generative knowing. We, as authors, would like to think that these perspectives are a result of our increasingly globalized and technologically connected world. Smith (2010) suggested that holism is the most effective means of facilitating learning as it promotes a "natural state of the human being. . .[an] interconnectedness within the human being (mind, body, spirit), between humans, and between humans and the universe" (p. 150). Smith explained that the technical, rational Western approach to learning fails to honor the intellectual, emotional, physical, social, aesthetic, and spiritual aspects important in many non-Western cultures. She noted that Western approaches privilege the intellect over other ways of knowing and value autonomy and independence over collective ways of learning. On the other hand, holism is experiential, interdependent, community-oriented, and culturally responsive. It values using the learner's culture within her learning context while inviting the learning community to engage in the learning.

It is our hope as authors that the second edition of *Adult Learning: Linking Theory and Practice*'s framework and features will provide a path through the vast and voluminous research, theory, and practice of adult education and adult learning and equip readers with the necessary understanding to accomplish their goals whether they be learners, educators, or both. Box 1.5 offers an opportunity to apply the learning framework to your learning and teaching as an educator or learner.

 **Box 1.5 Reflective Practice**

Applying the Framework for Adult Learning

This chapter described the organizing framework for the book to include:

1. The adult learning context
2. The adult educator
3. The adult learner
4. The adult learning process
5. The method of facilitating adult learning

Considering yourself as the learner, how have you been affected by each domain of the five-part framework?

Chapter Summary

This chapter introduced the second edition of *Adult Learning: Linking Theory and Practice* by providing an overview of the book. The book contains integrated features as an interactive tool for connecting research and theory to practice. The chapter also defined key concepts and terms in adult education and learning. The chapter concluded with an overview of the book's framework. We, the authors, welcome you to this second edition and hope you find the information interesting and applicable to your life and work as a learner, educator, or both!

Key Points

- The chapter establishes the foundation for understanding adult learning using a five-part framework of the context, adult educator, adult learner, adult learning process, and method, emphasizing the importance of adaptability and lifelong education.
- Historical and theoretical foundations shaping adult learning were discussed, examining how they have evolved.

- Adult learners face challenges, including inequitable access to education, motivation, work-life balance, and technology adaptation.
- Adult learning and education challenge traditional pedagogy that relies on banking education.
- Economic conditions, social structures, and systemic inequalities impact adult learning opportunities and outcomes.
- Lifelong learning is essential for adults' continuous skill development, adaptability, and the integration of learning into daily life.

References

Avoseh, M. B. M. (2001). Learning to be active citizens: Lessons of traditional Africa for lifelong learning. *International Journal of Lifelong Education, 20*(6), 479–486. https://doi.org/10.1080/02601370110088454.

Boshier, R. (2009). Why is the scholarship of teaching and learning such a hard sell? *Higher Education Research & Development, 28*(1), 1–15. https://doi.org/10.1080/07294360802444321.

Boyer, R. (1990). *Scholarship. Reconsidered: Priorities of the Professoriate.* Princeton, NJ: Carnegie Foundation for the Advancement of Teaching.

Brookfield, S. D. (2012). *Teaching for critical thinking: Tools and techniques to help students question their assumptions.* Jossey-Bass.

Canzittu, D. (2022). A framework to think of school and career guidance in a VUCA world. *British Journal of Guidance & Counselling, 50*(2), 248–259. https://doi.org/10.1080/03069885.2020.1825619.

Chalmers, D. (2011).Progress and challenges to the recognition and reward of the scholarship of teaching in higher education. *Higher Education Research & Development 30*(1), 25–38. https://doi.org/10.1080/07294360.2011.536970.

Fanghanel, J., McGowan, S., Parker, P., McConnell, C., Potter, J., Locke, W., & Healey, M. (2015). *Literature Review. Defining and Supporting the Scholarship of Teaching and Learning (SoTL): A sector-wide study.* York: Higher Education Academy. https://research.brighton.ac.uk/files/384315/literature_review.pdf.

Fenwick, T. (2003). *Learning through experience: Troubling orthodoxies and intersecting questions.* Krieger.

Freire, P. (2011). The banking concept of education. In E. B. Hilty (Ed.), *Thinking about schools: A foundations of education reader* (pp. 117–127). Routledge.

Hawley, J. D., Merriweather, L. R., Smith, C., Mizzi, R. C., & Rocco, T. A. (2023). Epilogue: Considerations of the COVID-19 Pandemic and Black Lives Matter. In T. S. Rocco., M. C. Smith, R. C. Mizzi, L. R. Merriweather, & J. D. Hawley (Eds.), *The handbook of adult and continuing education* (pp. 453–456). Taylor & Francis.

Houle, C. O. (1961). *The inquiring mind.* University of Wisconsin Press.

Hutchings, P., Huber, M. T., & Ciccone, A. (2011). *The scholarship of teaching and learning reconsidered: Institutional integration and impact* (Vol. 21). John Wiley & Sons.

Illeris, K. (2004). *Adult education and adult learning.* Krieger.

Jarvis, P. (1987). *Adult education in the social context.* Croom Helm.

Jarvis, P. (2006). *Towards a comprehensive theory of human learning.* Routledge.

Knowles, M. S. (1970). *The modern practice of adult education: Andragogy versus pedagogy.* Cambridge Books.

Knowles, M. S. (1975). *Self-directed learning: A guide for learners and teachers.* Association Free Press.

Knowles, M. S. (1984). *The adult learner: A neglected species* (3rd ed.). Gulf.

Knowles, M. S., Holton, E. F. III, & Swanson, R. A. (2005). *The adult learner* (6th ed.). Gulf.

Knowles, M. S., Holton, E. F. III, & Swanson, R. A. (2011). *The adult learner* (7th ed.). Gulf

Korten, D. (2020, March 19). *Why coronavirus is humanity's wakeup call.* YES! Magazine. https://www.indianz.com/News/2020/03/19/david-korten-why-coronavirus-is-humanity.asp.

Mårtensson, K., Roxå, T., & Olsson, T. (2011). Developing a quality culture through the scholarship of teaching and learning. *Higher Education Research & Development, 30*(1), 51–62. https://doi.org/10.1080/07294360.2011.536972.

McClusky, H. Y. (1950). *Theory of margin: A framework for understanding adult learning.* [Unpublished manuscript]. University of Michigan.

Merriam, S. B., & Bierema, L. L. (2014). *Adult learning: Linking theory and practice.* John Wiley & Sons.

Merriam, S. B., Caffarella, R. S., & Baumgartner, L. M. (2007). *Learning in adulthood* (3rd ed.). Jossey-Bass.

Merriam, S. B., Baumgartner, L. M., & Caffarella, R. S. (2020). *Learning in adulthood: A comprehensive guide* (4th ed.). Jossey-Bass.

Revans, R. (2017). *ABC of action learning.* Taylor & Francis.

Rittel, H. W. J., & Webber, M. M. (1973). Dilemmas in a general theory of planning. *Policy Sciences, 4*(2), 155–169. https://doi.org/10.1007/BF01405730.

Schön, D. A. (1983). *The reflective practitioner: How professionals think in action.* Basic Books.

Smith, R. O. (2010). Facilitation and design of learning. In C. E. Kasworm, A. D. Rose, & J. M. Ross-Gordon (Eds.), *Handbook of adult and continuing education: 2010 edition* (pp. 147–155). Jossey-Bass.

Taylor, E. W., & Cranton, P. (Eds.) (2012). *The handbook of transformative learning.* Jossey-Bass.

US Army Heritage and Education Center. (2018). *Who first originated the term VUCA (Volatility, Uncertainty, Complexity and Ambiguity)? USAHEC ask us a question.* The United States Army War College. https://usawc.libanswers.com/faq/84869.

Van der Steege, M. (2017). Introduction. In M. Van der Steege, R. Elkington, & J. Glick-Smith (Eds.), *Visionary leadership in a turbulent world: Thriving in the new VUCA context* (pp. 1–12). Emerald Publishing.

Vella, J. (2000). A spirited epistemology: Honoring the adult learner as subject. *New Directions for Adult and Continuing Education, 2000*(85), 7–16. https://doi.org/10.1002/ace.8501.

Whiteman, W. E. (1998). *Training and educating army officers for the 21st century: Implications for the United States military academy.* USAWC Strategy Research Project, US Pennsylvania: Army War College.

Wlodkowski, R. J. (2008). *Enhancing adult motivation to learn: A comprehensive guide for teaching all adults* (3rd ed.). Jossey-Bass.

Yoder-Wise, P. S. (2021). From VUCA to VUCA 2.0: Surviving today to prosper tomorrow. *Nursing Education Perspectives, 42*(1), 1–2. https://doi.org/10.1097/01.NEP.0000000000000774.

UNDERSTANDING ADULT LEARNING IN CONTEMPORARY SOCIAL CONTEXT AND CULTURE

 **Box 2.1 Chapter Overview and Learning Objectives**

The world is complex and unpredictable, facing wicked problems like political polarization, climate change, global pandemics, war and violence, and economic instability, which can seem impossible to address. Eleanor Roosevelt reminded people that they can make meaningful change in their own context:

> *Where, after all, do universal human rights begin? In small places, close to home—so close and so small that they cannot be seen on any maps of the world. Yet they are the world of the individual person; the neighborhood he [sic] lives in; the school or college he [sic] attends; the factory, farm, or office where he [sic] works. Such are the places where every man, woman, and child seeks equal justice, equal opportunity, equal dignity without discrimination. Unless these rights have meaning there, they have little meaning anywhere. Without concerted citizen action to uphold them close to*

home, we shall look in vain for progress in the larger world. (Eleanor Roosevelt, 1958, in Malhotra, 2012, p. 9)

Roosevelt urged people to pay attention to their communities and make changes there, hoping such social action would become global. Learning is a fundamental response to life's challenges, and the context of learning is continually shifting. Perhaps you, as an adult learner or community member, can think of times you took an interest or became involved in issues in your community through a neighborhood group, parent-teacher organization, political party, church, or non-profit organization. How were you able to affect change?

The purpose of this chapter is to situate adult learning in contemporary context and culture. Although the topics covered in this chapter can be daunting—like globalization and technology—they are issues people can relate to in their daily lives in their communities through the products and services they consume, the people they live and work with, and the ways they interact with digital information.

As a result of reading this chapter and completing the exercise boxes, you, the reader, should be able to:

1. Discuss issues of life and learning in turbulent times.
2. Define terms like *globalization, capitalism, neoliberalism, hyperconnectivity, capitalism,* and *consumerism* and understand how they affect adult learners and their learning.
3. Recognize how the knowledge society affects life, learning, and work.
4. Consider how technology affects every aspect of life.
5. Appreciate global demographic shifts.
6. Engage in applied and reflective activities related to the chapter content.

This chapter situates adult learning in contemporary society among its volatility and vulnerability. Adult learning occurs in an unpredictable and changing world where learning is one of the first defenses in functioning and addressing seemingly intractable problems. When adult education was in its infancy in the mid-20th century, its early goals were to educate people to be effective family members, workers, and citizens. Although this role remains crucial, the meaning and challenges of adulthood are constantly shifting and evolving, and today, individuals, communities, and nations grapple with complex challenges that demand continual learning, followed by mindful action.

Global Capitalism and Neoliberalism

Education is a **commodity**—knowledge or skills sold or exchanged as inputs to produce goods and services. Page (2019) observed,

> In an increasingly competitive environment that positions students as consumers, universities have become ever more marketised, responding to policy contexts that foreground value for money, consumer choice and competition. The intensity of marketisation is argued to have profoundly affected the nature of academic work and scholars themselves, recreating academics as commodities to be weighed and measured, becoming corporatised, alienated and inauthentic in their practice. (p. 585)

Wong (2016) reported that "colleges and universities have become a marketplace that treats student applicants like consumers" (para. 1) and questioned the value of university classification systems like the *US News & World Report* (n.d.) annual ranking. Marketers view students as customers who "shop" the global academic marketplace to find the educational program that best fits their needs, budget, and desired results. There is even a growing area of research and writing on what is being called **"academic capitalism."** Here, higher education institutions become commercial enterprises in "the pursuit of market and market-like activities to generate external revenues" (Slaughter & Rhoades, 2004, p. 11). So, while students may "shop" for their education, colleges and universities also "shop" for students. Neoliberalism and globalization fuel these dynamics in higher education, which are present across the global economy.

Neoliberalism

Neoliberalism values free-market capitalism, minimal governmental interference, and deregulation based on the conviction that economic freedom fosters economic and social progress. It is an economic principle typically espoused by conservative and right-libertarian organizations and politicians. Neoliberalists disdain governmental scrutiny and presuppose that individuals are answerable for their own financial and social standing, with little regard for systemic forces such as racism that create discrimination in employment and life. Smith et al. (2023) noted that neoliberalist educational practices have caused education to be "increasingly viewed as a private rather than a public good, or a choice rather than a right" (p. 447). The devaluation of adult education programs in the United States is an artifact of neoliberalist policies. Yet, Smith et al. urged,

> All of these contemporary political, economic, and societal issues provide a context and a backdrop for the consideration of adult and continuing education and how the field might respond and offer leadership and potential solutions. Without question, adult and continuing education must be prepared to lead the way in educating adults to become informed, globally connected, capable citizens who are knowledgeable, skilled, and open and adaptive to change in uncertainty. (p. 448)

Neoliberal policies have increased corporate power, known as **corporatocracy,** that shifts wealth to society's wealthier citizens, who also make economic policy further swing benefits to the rich (Wolff, 2012). These practices are particularly evident in billionaires' political behavior in the 2024 US presidential election by donating to Donald Trump's presidential campaign and pressuring for policies and legislation to make them richer. Neoliberal policies and politics create monopolistic growth where companies like Amazon or McDonald's dominate global markets. These policies also cause economic inequity, job insecurity due to outsourcing, and apathy toward individual suffering that amplifies social injustice. **Social injustice** is "the repression of a person's individual and civil rights [that] could hinder their capacity to achieve full potential to learn and perform (Byrd, 2014)" (Byrd, 2018, p. 3). **Social justice** is a "vision of equity, fairness, dignity, and respect across lines of difference" that "balances the scale between privilege (decreasing the force exerting power) and marginalization (pushing back to gain power)" (Byrd, 2018, p. 3).

How does neoliberalism affect adult learning and education and create injustice? Gouthro (2022) explained, "Embracing neoliberal values means educators and students need to adapt to the values of a marketplace that celebrates individualism and the so-called freedom of choice to make personal decisions about how to best situate oneself in a competitive position" (p. 113). Further, when learners decide where to seek education, this approach to education and learning factors in market demands and employability. Neoliberalist views of education assume people have choices and freedom to choose from an array of opportunities that, in reality, many learners lack access to. Some for-profit universities promise exciting, lucrative careers that never materialize for students in debt, degreeless, and unemployed (Armona et al., 2022; Eaton, 2022). The structure of education itself breeds social injustice, as does global capitalism.

Globalization

Capitalism is an economic system where private entities own and control property and use it for profit generation, like an automotive manufacturing company with a production facility in a community. **Globalization** is the movement of goods, services, people, and ideas across national borders. It incorporates organizations' scaling activities and initiatives to internationalize their workforce, products, services, and production facilities to influence the industry. Ford Motor Company, for example, was founded in Detroit, Michigan, in 1903. The company introduced the assembly line and large-scale production of vehicles. Today, Ford is one of the largest automotive companies operating in 125 countries, self-described on its website as "truly a global brand" (Ford, n.d., para. 2). Box 2.2 invites reflection on the extent to which learning activities have a global focus.

Friedman (2011) described globalization as moving from "connected to hyperconnected" (para. 4). However, **hyperconnectivity**—the use of digital systems to engage with others through social networks and other information sources—created what anthropologist and MIT computer culture scholar Sherry Turkle (2011) wrote about in her book, *Alone Together: Why We Expect More from Technology and Less from Each Other*. Turkle critiqued social network relationships as lacking essential aspects of human interaction. Candiotto

---

 **Box 2.2 Reflective Practice**

Reflect on a Recent Learning Activity

As an adult learner or educator, describe a learning activity you recently experienced. Reflect on the following questions:

1. To what extent did the activity relate to the global context? For example, if you attended a session on "planting a resource-friendly garden" sponsored by the local botanical garden, did climate change or water preservation come up as topics?
2. Did your learning involve technology?
   a. Did you become familiar with the botanical garden's website?
   b. Did you use the Internet to learn about specific plants and shrubs?
3. If the session lacked a global focus, how might you improve it?

(2022) explored what she termed "extended loneliness," or the lack of meaningful social connections that can result from an abundance of hyperconnectivity. Yet, hyperconnectivity has fueled global capitalism in every sphere of life.

Global capitalism is when private owners control economic and political systems to profit at the expense of citizens and communities on a scale that transcends nations. However, communities have little power over corporations' governance (Sklair, 2001) due to the transnational nature of global capitalism. For example, the Russian War in Ukraine has caused several nations to pump billions of dollars into military spending. McDonald's restaurants, Coca-Cola beverages, and iPhones are just a few globally dominant products that span the globe. When you, as a customer, speak to a representative for your airline or hotel reservation or make a customer service complaint, it is likely the company they represent has outsourced the call center to another country where labor costs are lower. Of course, it is also likely that you were first routed to an artificial intelligence (AI) bot to troubleshoot your problem and determine if human interaction was necessary. Although a social construction, global capitalism has tangible effects on policy, politics, education, and economics. Centeno and Cohen (2013) depicted capitalism as "a 'deep institution'—a socially constructed, politically contentious and deeply habituated way of understanding and practicing economic life" (p. 4), noting global capitalism is composed of trade, finance, and consumption that create challenges of governance, inequality, and the environment. Global capitalism is problematic because policy and enforcement occur at community or country levels. Yet, the transactions in the global economy occur in spaces that extend beyond local or national control. Further, global capitalism creates unfairness between nations in the quest for money, market share, and growth, which destroys people, communities, and the environment.

Fueled by globalization, **consumerism** values increasing market consumption of goods and services. Social media accounts often market goods that people show interest in as a way to create more demand. Global capitalism pushes unsustainable consumerism that damages people's health, pollutes the environment, and destabilizes weaker economies. Box 2.3 provides an opportunity to see articles, charts, and other data on globalization according to individual interests.

Global Capitalism, Coca-Cola, and Its Impact on Community, Environment, and Health. Coca-Cola, or Coke, is the largest soft drink producer in the world, with over 500 products in distribution. The corporation markets what some describe as unhealthy, sugary beverages and is also one of the largest producers of plastic pollution worldwide (Bleich & Vercammen, 2018; Bolt-Evensen et al., 2018;

 ## Box 2.3 Adult Learning by the Numbers

The World in Data

Visit the website Our World in Data, which aims to publish "research and data to make progress against the world's largest problems" (para. 4). The site charts multiple global phenomena over time, such as poverty, disease, hunger, climate change, and inequality. Try adding some terms related to adult learning and adult education that interest you as a learner or community member, and you will discover interesting data and charts.

https://ourworldindata.org/

Question for reflection: How is your life and work affected by globalization?

Gower et al., 2020). Coca-Cola is an example of how global capitalism has a far-reaching impact on global communities, affecting almost everyone. Crawford et al. (2021) wrote:

> In 2019, the brand consultancy Interbrand ranked the world's most important brands. Based on the perception of the brand across the world, the value that the brand adds to the company, and the brand's future plans, Interbrand positioned Coke as the fifth most important brand in the world. Despite declining sales over the last five years, Coke's worth was estimated at US$63.4 million, a figure that outranked Disney, McDonald's, and Facebook (Khan, 2019). The salience of Coke is testament to the degree to which Coca-Cola has successfully constructed, cultivated, and sustained its brand for over 135 years. (p. 11)

Pendergrast (2013), author of a history of the company, described the brand: "Coke has achieved the status of a substitute modern religion that promotes a particular, satisfying, all-inclusive worldview espousing perennial values such as love, peace, happiness, and universal brotherhood" (p. 472).

Although Coke's product marketing has a tone of healthfulness and community, the products are unhealthy, and the company's presence has not necessarily been good for communities, environments, or nations where they do business. Wood et al. (2021) explained, "Market power and corporate wealth and income distribution in the global soft drink market negatively impact public health and health equity" (p. 138) and are concentrated in low- and middle-income countries (Singh et al., 2015). Citing Coca-Cola and PepsiCo, Wood et al. further asserted the corporations "operate across an extensive patchwork of highly concentrated markets. Both corporations control vast amounts of wealth and resources and are able to allocate relatively large amounts of money to potentially harmful practices, such as extensive marketing of unhealthy products" (p. 138). Health effects of Coca-Cola and similar products include dental decay, obesity, and heavy users are more prone to diabetes. Sugar-sweetened beverages were estimated to claim 184,000 lives annually and create 8.5 million disability-adjusted life years worldwide (Mullee et al., 2019; Singh et al., 2015). Wood et al. further argued that market power, corporate wealth, and income distribution negatively impact public health and health equity. Global capitalism also creates social inequity:

> Capitalism is a racialised global system of value production with a capitalist class that owns the means of production and an exploited and alienated working class. That across the world the most exploited peoples are Black, Indigenous, and other People of Color (BIPOC) is not an accident. (Heinemann & Monzó, 2021, p. 67)

According to Heinemann and Monzó (2021), capitalism has historically depended on stealing labor from the non-Western world, exploiting people and the environment. They explored language learning among adult migrants in the United States and Germany to explore the effects of capitalism. They concluded that adult education could provide a "support structure for global racialised capitalism" (p. 65) since "the majority of those who enter adult education programs are those who have been 'failed' by the opportunity structures that [are] supposed to support social mobility within the basic school education system" (p. 66).

Global Capitalism and Adult Learning. What does capitalism have to do with adult education and learning? Jacobson (2016) put it this way:

> Increasingly, the provision of adult education (including literacy and training programs) is influenced by a rhetoric of workforce development that tasks education with closing a supposed "skills gap" between the skills that workers have and what employers are looking for. This deficit model of education blames adult learners for their own condition, as well as for larger problems in the economy. In addition to arguing for broader goals for adult education, those in the field also need to question the economic premises of this rhetoric. A review of current economic conditions points to fundamental aspects of capitalism as the

source of instability, which means that education and training programs have a limited ability to move large numbers of people out of poverty. For this reason, students and teachers in adult education should focus on developing structural analyses of the situation and push for substantive changes in the economy. (p. 3)

Capitalism is also evident in education in for-profit schools and universities where money is primary in decision-making and management. Pressure is on university faculty to seek external funding at the expense of teaching, research, and service. The rise of adjunct faculty has been steady, as has higher education's reliance on precarious workers such as adjuncts, graduate students, and staff (Sim & Bierema, 2025). That capitalism is associated with racism is no surprise since the slave trade was one of the earliest forms of global capitalism that influenced modern management practices (Bohonos & James-Gallaway, 2022). Globalization creates opportunities for some people to travel. Box 2.4 describes how travel can be a powerful learning experience in a globalized context.

 ## Box 2.4 SoTL: The Scholarship of Teaching and Learning

Planning a Vacation Abroad? It Might Shift Your Worldview and Identity

Yelich Biniecki and Conceição (2014) conducted a phenomenological study with 10 adult learners who had travel and living experiences in countries outside their native homeland to understand how the experience influenced participants' worldviews and personal identity. They defined worldview as "how an individual sees the world at a point in time, which is influenced by culture and experiences" (p. 40), viewing a person's worldview as unique and culturally based. They found that these travel experiences increased awareness of multiple worldviews by changing, confirming, or broadening participants' personal beliefs, often simultaneously, about their own and other cultures. The travel also impacted how the learners perceived themselves and helped foster a transnational identity, which is how one sees oneself after experiencing another culture concerning self and social position.

Reflect for a moment on your travels and as an adult learner:

1. How were the ways you see the world challenged?
2. What surprised you about yourself?
3. How did the travel change how you see yourself or the world?

Travel expands adults' perspectives on the world, compatible with a primary goal of adult learning and education to help adults raise their consciousness about how values, rhetoric, beliefs, products, or social forces influence them within their social contexts. Freire (1973) defined this as **conscientization,** or how people acquire critical awareness through reflection, assumption testing, and action. Powerful people and entities attempt to convince adults that their service, beliefs, candidacy, or product is good for them when, in reality, the opposite is true. Convincing a person that something terrible is good for them is **hegemony,** discussed further in Chapter 3. Realizing the influence of hegemony on one's life is essential learning for adults, as it can transform their mindsets, thoughts, and actions through conscientization. For example, learning sugary beverages are harmful to one's health and the environment may cause a person to cut back or stop their consumption—they hear new information about the product, reflect on its consequences or use, and decide to act.

The Knowledge Society

Global capitalism, technological advances, and correspondingly quickly expanding knowledge are impacting every aspect of life and work across the globe. The knowledge society grew out of the knowledge economy. It contributes to the VUCA condition by accelerating change amid perplexing world problems. The implications of the knowledge society affect educational models and delivery, as well as what learners need to learn and how they engage with learning and education.

The Knowledge Economy

Globalization has historically involved outsourcing low-wage production to countries with low-income workers. Today, businesses and individuals broker goods and services globally and exchange intellectual capital by sharing information and ideas, a phenomenon known as the "knowledge economy." Florida and Kenney (1993) defined the **knowledge economy:** "Capitalism is undergoing an epochal transformation from a mass production system where the principal source of value was human labour to a new era of 'innovation-mediated production' where the principal component of value creation, productivity and economic growth is knowledge" (p. 637). Brinkley (2006) concluded in a report that "Defining the knowledge economy is challenging precisely because the commodity it rests on—knowledge—is itself hard to pin down with any precision" (p. 29). The report adopted the OECD/Work Foundation industry definition of the knowledge-intensive industries being high- to medium-tech manufacturing, finance, telecommunications, business services, education, and health, although pointed out in the conclusion that the definition was not final as they would continue to develop measures and definitions of the knowledge economy.

The knowledge society has replaced the industrial society, characterized by manual labor and manufacturing, with significant implications for learning and educational systems across the globe and throughout the lifespan. Dumont and Istance's (2010) predictions for the 21st-century competencies remain relevant: "21st-century competencies" include "deep understanding, flexibility and the capacity to make creative connections" and "a range of so-called 'soft skills' including good teamwork. The quantity and quality of learning thus become central, with the concern that traditional educational approaches are insufficient" (p. 20). They further emphasized the role of knowledge as a key economic driver, with expertise valued as capital.

The Complexity of the Knowledge Society

The knowledge society is complicated, inundating people constantly with bits and pieces of information that only become useful and meaningful after they are weighed, organized, and structured into meaningful units of knowledge. It is with the knowledge that you, as an adult learner or educator, build new insights, new understandings, and even new products, all of which can contribute to a more enriching context for learning. Yet, the knowledge society is not a utopia. Some places in the world are so torn by strife, poverty, illiteracy, and other calamities that a knowledge society has not evolved, leaving these countries far behind and noncompetitive compared to countries that foster knowledge creation and sharing. Some groups of citizens, discriminated against because of gender, race or ethnicity, disability, or age, are marginalized in their own societies and bared from meaningfully participating in the knowledge society. Although the knowledge society is a promising proposition, global literacy rates differ, depending on the country and region, as described in Box 2.5.

According to Azcona et al. (2023), living a long and healthy life is inequitable by gender or geography. For example, a girl born in Lesotho today is predicted to live 54.2 years on average, compared to a girl born in Japan who is

 ## Box 2.5 Adult Learning by the Numbers

Global Literacy and Education Rates

According to O'Neill (2024),

> In the past five decades, the global literacy rate among adults has grown from 67 percent in 1976 to 87.01 percent in 2022. In 1976, men had a literacy rate of 76 percent, compared to a rate of 58 percent among women. This difference of over 17 percent in 1976 has fallen to just seven percent in 2020. (para. 1)

The World Population Review (n.d.) described the global literacy rate in 2024 as high, with the average for women and men who are at least 15 years old at 86.3%. The discrepancies appear in country-by-country comparisons. For example, the literacy rate in the Ukraine, Russia, and Cuba is 100% compared to 27% in Chad and 37% in Afghanistan. Poverty and literacy compound each other as education is less available in poverty-stricken areas, and education helps people get out of poverty. There is also a gender gap in literacy, with over two-thirds of the approximately 781 million adults worldwide unable to read or write being women, primarily due to social expectations for them to care for the household and children.

When it comes to higher education, the National Center for Education Statistics (NCES) (2024) reported that across the Organization for Economic Cooperation and Development (OECD) countries (30 countries collaborating to promote trade and economic growth), "the average percentage of 25- to 64-year-olds with any postsecondary degree increased from 32 percent as of 2012 to 41 percent as of 2022. In the United States, during the same period, the percentage increased from 43 to 50 percent" (para. 1). The percentage of people earning postsecondary degrees is highest in Canada (63%) and lowest in Italy (20%).

OECD countries report an 80% high school graduation rate, with the lowest being Mexico (44%) and the highest in the Czech Republic (94%).

How does this scaling of the global population affect how and where you see yourself as a learner?

predicted to live 86.9 years. They further noted that survey data for 47 countries confirmed "that older women aged 65 and older spend, on average, NEARLY TWICE THE TIME performing unpaid care and domestic work tasks as men" (emphasis in original, p. 6). Azcona et al.'s report also documented that income insecurity, food insecurity, and violence disproportionately affect women. Although access to education is rising among girls and boys, girls and women do not engage with the educational system in conflict-affected areas, like Afghanistan, where, as of September 2022, authorities prohibited girls from attending school or university. In addition to formal schooling, women and girls are disproportionately excluded from opportunities to build employability skills. "Globally in 2022, 32.1 percent of young women aged 15 to 24 were not in education, employment or training . . . compared to 15.4 percent of young men" (Azcona et al., 2023, p. 11). Finally, women's careers are disrupted by care responsibilities and wage discrimination, meaning women earn only about one-third of global labor income, according to Azcona et al. (2023), who explained:

> Women's right to participate equally and fully in the economy remains unrealized. Globally, less than two thirds (61.4 percent) of prime working-age women (aged 25 to 54) were in the labour force in 2022 compared to 90.6 percent of prime working-age men. In 2019, for each dollar men earned in labour income, women earned only 5 cents. In other words, in 2019, women's share of total earned labour income was a mere 34 percent. (p. 18)

One might assume that a knowledge society creates more equity in society. Although it has not, its pace is unrelenting.

The Pace of Change and Disruption. The pace of change is usually lamented as constant and unrelenting. Sorokin (2019) explained:

> In 1982, futurist and inventor R. Buckminster Fuller estimated that up until 1900, human knowledge doubled approximately every century, but by 1945 it was doubling every 25 years. And by 1982, it was doubling every 12–13 months. In retrospect, this may sound a little quaint since experts now estimate that by 2020, human knowledge will double every 12 hours. But the real question is, "How is it making us smarter?" (para. 1)

Futurist Jim Carroll (2022) called the pace of change **"knowledge velocity,"** arguing that knowledge acceleration would continue to define organizations and their challenges. He cited fellow futurist Ray Kurzweil, who claimed knowledge doubles every 12 hours, thanks to the Internet. Kurzweil (2004) proposed that historically, technological change is exponential, meaning humanity would not experience 100 years of progress during the 21st century but rather 20,000 years, based on today's rate. He also predicted machine intelligence would exceed human intelligence, and in 2023, ChatGPT became widely available, changing how people live, work, and learn. Accenture (2024a) surveyed 3,400 leaders in their "Pulse of Change: 2024 Index," ranking six factors of change affecting businesses: Technology, Talent, Economic, Geopolitical, Climate, and Consumer and Social. Technology was rated as most disruptive in 2023 due to advances in generative AI. The survey found that overall, across the six factors, change has risen 183% since 2019. Accenture's (2024b) CEO, Jack Azagury, said,

> The most significant source of change and disruption—technology—is also the key to this structural change. We believe that the companies that will succeed in the next decade are those that embrace a strategy of continuously reinventing every part of their business using technology, data and AI, including harnessing the power of generative AI, and ensuring their people are at the center of their transformations. (para. 6)

Despite technological advances, nearly 50% (47%) of surveyed leaders indicated they were unprepared for the accelerating rate of change.

Knowledge Sharing and Management. Within the knowledge economy are knowledge workers, a focus on learning in organizations, and knowledge management. Hislop (2013) defined **knowledge management** as:

> An umbrella term which refers to any deliberate efforts to manage the knowledge of an organisation's workforce, which can be achieved via a wide range of methods including directly, through the use of particular types of ICT, or more indirectly through the management of social processes, the structuring of organisation in particular ways or via the use of particular culture and people management practices. (p. 56)

Castaneda and Cuellar (2020) systematically reviewed knowledge sharing and innovation. They described knowledge sharing as a prevalent research topic that explores human interactions around the raw material of knowledge. Citing Hogel et al. (2003), they defined **knowledge sharing** as "the exchange of experience, skills, and tacit and explicit knowledge among employees" (p. 159).

In a PEW Trust Trend Article, Parker and Rainie (2020) reviewed how the "knowledge-focused age" affects people's view of necessary skills and training to meet their goals. They explained, "job growth has been more robust in occupations that rely most heavily on social, fundamental, and analytical skills" (para. 3). The occupations showing robust growth from 1980 to 2018 were those where social skills such as negotiating and instructing, fundamental skills such as critical thinking and writing, and analytical skills such as complex problem solving and programming were required. A 2016 PEW Research Center survey reported that in the United States, people see personal upgrading as a constant necessity, with most learning and development job-focused. This focus on self-learning might be due to worries about outsourcing and the rise of contract or temporary workers. Adults view the responsibility for preparing and excelling in the workforce as starting with themselves. Adults are also weighing the value of a college degree. The knowledge society is now deeply entrenched, extended by technology.

Technology

Globalization and the knowledge society depend on communications technology and the Internet. From multinational companies' use of technology to conduct business and facilitate remote work to friends on different continents chatting over Zoom to social media enabling social movements, technology has irrevocably affected how we live, work, learn, and interact with friends, colleagues, and strangers. Since publishing the first edition of *Adult Learning: Linking Theory and Practice*, new educational innovations include virtual and augmented reality, artificial intelligence, cloud computing, learning analytics, 3D printing, gamification and educational games, micro-learning, online learning, learning via social media platforms such as YouTube or LinkedIn, flexible instructional models, and higher-quality remote learning with the accessibility of virtual platforms and improved online learning platforms. Technological advances are the norm in a VUCA context where new gadgets and innovations have changed how people monitor their health and fitness, control their money, communicate, learn, work, and shop.

Smartphone ownership shows the global reach of capitalism and technology adoption, with 86% of the world's population owning one (GilPress, 2024). The projected smartphone will reach 7.1 billion by the end of 2024. Smartphone use has been increasing by approximately 5% annually, with China having the highest number of smartphones. Nearly half of the US population's 132.13 million users spend approximately five to six hours on their smartphones daily (GilPress, 2024). Taherdoost (2023) urged that keeping current with new technology is essential if individuals and organizations wish to maintain a competitive edge. These new technologies include cloud computing, the Internet of Things (IoT), artificial intelligence, blockchain, big data analytics, virtual and augmented reality, a 5g network, and more. Table 2.1 presents brief explanations of these technologies.

As pointed out earlier in the chapter, technology is inseparable from globalization and the knowledge society. Adult learners have specific needs as technology transforms their work and personal lives. Trenerry et al. (2021) conducted an integrative review of research on digital transformation, finding that workers are often overlooked during the transition. They need support for adopting new technology, developing perceptions and attitudes toward technological change, gaining skills and training, building workplace resilience and adaptability, and cultivating work-related well-being. Groups need help with team communication and collaboration, workplace relationships, team identification and adaptability, and resilience. Organizations need leadership, human resources, and organizational culture/climate support. Technology affects adults' lives beyond work and can support their lifelong learning, well-being, and management of routine tasks. Yet, the **digital divide** represents the chasm between people who can easily access computers and the Internet and those who do not. Fang et al. (2019) explored the social inequities of the digital divide among seniors to understand who accesses and benefits from the digital landscape. They concluded that although age contributes to the digital divide, other factors contribute to inequity, including education, income, gender, and generational status. There is still much to do to address marginalized people's and nations' basic needs before all can participate in this digitalized, globalized, knowledge society.

Demographic Shifts

The dynamic global context of adult learning creates opportunities and challenges for learning and education. Ramdeholl et al. (2023) urged that adult education is a human right:

> Adult education has a long history of people coming together to struggle toward a more equitable society—from Highlander Folk School in

TABLE 2.1 EMERGING TECHNOLOGIES AND THEIR APPLICATIONS

Technology	Definition	Applications
Artificial Intelligence (AI)	A computer system able to perform tasks requiring human intelligence, such as speech recognition, decision-making, visual perception, and language translation.	• Manufacturing robots (e.g., iRobot/Roomba) • Self-driving cars (e.g., Tesla) • Smart assistants (e.g., Grammarly, Apple's Siri) • Healthcare management (e.g., Well) • Automated financial investing (e.g., Liberty Mutual Insurance) • Virtual travel booking agents (e.g., Google Maps) • Social media monitoring (e.g., Slack, Meta) • Marketing/Retail chatbots (e.g., Instacart, Amazon)
Augmented Reality	Amplifies surroundings digitally, making them available through a camera or smartphone.	• Google Translate® to navigate in a different language while traveling • IKEA's furniture app to see how furniture configurations look in the home • Toyota's AR vehicle visualization and test drive • BMW i Visualizer • Augmented reality mirrors
Big Data Analytics	Converting raw data into usable information helps discover hidden patterns, improve decision-making, analyze trends, and draw conclusions.	• Uber or other rideshare companies to predict demands and driver availability • Netflix to identify series investments and how to market them to subscribers
Blockchain	A distributed digital ledger that immutably and transparently records transactions across many computers to protect transactions from being altered after the transaction has occurred because it would require consensus across the network.	• JPMorgan Chase • Cash App • DHL
Cloud Computing	Using a network of remote servers on the Internet to store, manage, and access data.	• Adobe Creative Cloud • Dropbox • Google Drive • Netflix, Slack • Zoom

Technology	Definition	Applications
5g Network	It stands for the fifth-generation mobile network of cellular technology that allows faster upload and download speeds, more consistent connectivity, and improved capacity that can potentially transform how the Internet is used and accessed.	• University internet access at home • Autonomous vehicle updates • Public transportation fleet tracking • Municipal surveillance • Public internet access
The Internet of Things (IoT)	Objects containing sensors, software, and other technology that connect and share data with other devices and systems between the device and the cloud, as well as device-to-device.	• Vehicle systems that locate the vehicle or connect it with a car service network • Alexa or Google Home systems • Smartwatches that share data between family members or remote home security systems
Virtual Reality	A computer technology that immerses the user in a simulated experience so that it seems real even though it is synthetic or virtual.	• Virtual patients to train health workers • Work simulation for training • Gaming • Three-dimensional home tours • Mona Lisa: Beyond the Glass at the Louvre Museum, Paris

Appalachia to the Occupy Movement to Fees Must Fall to the Landless Workers' Movement to Prison Abolition (and countless other movements nationally and globally). Now is the time for adult education scholars and activists to stand up and speak out about emerging challenges due to increasingly rapid erosion of human rights. Adult educators have an important role to play in resisting this erosion, and in doing so, to reclaim their roots. Documenting the narratives of struggle is critical in a moment when the erasure of racial and social justice is all around us. (p. 343)

Chapter 2 concludes by examining how the world population is shifting, compounded by other contextual variables. Box 2.6 explores culturally responsive teaching research, a crucial competency in today's context.

Box 2.6 SoTL: The Scholarship of Teaching and Learning

Culturally Responsive Teaching Research with Adult Learners

Rhodes (2018) reviewed the literature of research on culturally responsive teaching (CRT) with adults. They found that many participants eschewed the culturally responsive framework in various learning environments with adults. Educators seemed to choose selected aspects focused on learners' cultural identities, the need to explore self-cultural identity as educators, and the role of diverse curriculum materials in building inclusive learning environments.

Jenkins and Alfred (2018) used a qualitative research methodology to explore White culturally responsive professors' motivation to become culturally inclusive in their teaching with adult learners. They interviewed three men and four women aged 50–60. All were US-based except one faculty from England. Their fields represented adult education, educational leadership, educational psychology, and teacher education. All participants had published work on cultural responsiveness. There were four major themes of findings, including (1) personal convictions about pedagogy, desires to create a better society, and the value of CRT; (2) processes for transformation that influenced changes leading the educators to CRT; (3) components of CRT, including learner centeredness, curriculum, and professor; and (4) the internal and external challenges of CRT. The authors noted that the participants did not label themselves as culturally responsive regarding theoretical models such as Ginsberg and Wlodkowski (2009).

Utilizing Ginsberg and Wlodkowski's (2009) culturally responsive framework, they found they had a sense of moral rightness in their work and felt obligated to teach in culturally sensitive ways. The faculty reported complex considerations in implementing culturally responsive teaching that created challenges. They urged faculty interested in culturally responsive teaching to garner administrative and moral support from similarly minded colleagues.

Today, five generations comprise the workforce: Traditionalists, Baby Boomers, Generation X, Millennials, and Generation Z. Some adults' careers span six or more decades (Collinson & Hodin, 2023), making this the first time in history such a generational span has worked side-by-side. As an employee, how many generations do you work with? Engaging with multigenerational work or community colleagues allows people to learn new ideas and skills and share expertise and life experiences (Collinson & Hodin, 2023; Hastwell, 2023).

Yet, **ageism** or age-based discrimination grounded in ageist stereotypes and prejudice causes devaluation and non-inclusion of older workers in organizations (Cebola et al., 2023).

Gerhardt et al.'s (2021) *Gentelligence* and OECD's (2020) "Promoting an Age Inclusive Workforce" offered detailed analyses of the intergenerational labor force, underscoring the benefit of multiple perspectives and experiences and also posing challenges for organizations to operate in ways sensitive across generations (Hastwell, 2023). Tension between generations may arise due to conflicting priorities, often life-stage-related. Generations tend to stereotype and make assumptions about each other that breed misunderstanding, miscommunication, and conflict. Communication styles also differ by generation, making it wise for organizations to communicate using various methods such as virtual and in-person meetings, email, and text messaging. When communicating across generations, it is also a good idea to avoid using "us versus them" perspectives, which quickly diminish when people have opportunities to develop trusting relationships with each other, regardless of age.

Global Population

Demographics are changing globally, and age is not the only factor. The United Nations (2024a) updates its largest dataset every two years, and the "World Population Prospects 2024" report predicted that the global population would peak in 2084 with around 10.4 billion people. Population rates differ by region and country, and the analysis of the UN report by Ritchie and Rodés-Guirao (2024) on the "Our World in Data" website offers population charts by continent. Falling fertility rates are also a global trend, with the global fertility rate dropping more than 50% since the 1960s from 5 children per parent to 2.3. Part of the reason for the decline is women's ability to exercise greater control over their reproductive health, according to the United Nations Population Fund (2023). Other reasons for the decline include the cost of children and the reality that "Women's desire for motherhood [is] undermined by relentless gender discrimination" (p. 7). Life expectancy is also returning to pre-pandemic levels. Six million people fled the Ukraine during 2022–2023, with even more displaced within the Ukraine. Box 2.7 provides a proportional exploration of the world population.

In the United States, the US Census Bureau predicted that by 2030, all baby boomers will be over age 65, and one in every five Americans will be of retirement age. This same year is also significant because immigration will exceed the natural population increase as the primary population growth variable. Older adults will likely outnumber children by 2034. These changes could make the 2030s a "transformative decade for the US population" (Vespa et al., 2020, p. 1).

 **Box 2.7 Adult Learning by the Numbers**

If the Word Were a Village of 100 People . . .

Globalization and all that it entails has enabled people everywhere to see the diversity of the world's eight billion people. As a global citizen, the world's rich diversity is visible on your television and computer screens, travel, and local communities. When exploring global diversity, it is much more challenging to be inward-looking and ethnocentric, seeing yourself as the center of and superior to the rest of the world. Rosenberg (2019) provided statistics through an analogy of presenting the world as a community of 100 people, keeping all of the proportions the same as in our world of over eight billion. Imagining over 8 billion people to appreciate differences is an impossible task. With this number of 100, global differences are more understandable, especially with the world facing intractable problems. Here are the highlights from the article:

If the world were a village of 100 people . . .

- 61 villagers would be Asian (of that, 20 would be Chinese, and 17 would be Indian).
- 14 would be African.
- 11 would be European.
- 9 would be Latin or South American.
- 5 would be North American.
- None of the villagers would be from Australia, Oceania, or Antarctica.
- At least 18 would be unable to read or write, 33 would have cellular phones, and 16 would be online.
- Twenty-seven would be under 15 years of age, and 7 would be over 64 years old.
- There would be an equal number of females and males.
- There would be 18 cars in the village.
- Sixty-three would have inadequate sanitation.
- Thirty would be unemployed or underemployed.
- Fifty-three villagers would live on less than two US dollars a day.

How does this scaling of the global population affect how and where you see yourself in the world?

The United States is becoming more diverse, and according to the US Census Bureau, Generation Z will be the last American generation with a White majority (de Visé, 2023). "The nation's so-called majority-minority arrived with Generation Alpha, those born since about 2010" (de Visé, 2023, para. 1). By approximately 2045, non-Hispanic White people will represent less than half of the US population. Box 2.8 highlights demographic shifts in the United States.

 # Box 2.8 Adult Learning by the Numbers

Demographic Shifts in the United States 2020–2060

Vespa et al. (2020) reported on the US Census Bureau's population projections from 2020 to 2060. The year 2030 is predicted to be a transformative turning point for US demographics. Here are the highlights:

- 21% of the population will be 65 or older in 2030 and 23% by 2060. The nation will shift from a youth-dependent to an elder-dependent population.
- Net international migration will surpass natural increases (the number of births minus deaths) in the population. Deaths of the Baby Boomer population will outnumber births.
- The number of people aged 85 and older is expected to double by 2035 (from 6.5 million to 11.8 million) and triple by 2060 (19 million).
- The non-Hispanic White population is projected to shrink from 199 million in 2020 to 79 million people in 2060.
- People of two or more races are predicted to be the fastest-growing racial or ethnic group in the coming decades, followed by Asians and Hispanics.
- The foreign-born population is expected to rise from 44 million in 2016 to 69 million in 2060, or growth from 14% to 17% of the population. The previous historical high was in 1890 when approximately 15% of the population was foreign-born.
- Older women will continue to outnumber men, although the gap is narrowing as men's life expectancy is projected to rise.
- The nation will see growing racial and ethnic pluralism. One in three Americans, or 32% of the population, is predicted to be a race other than White.
- The US population will continue growing, but the rate will be slower.

How do you see these data in your life, education, or work as an adult learner or educator?

Global Migration

Another worldwide demographic trend is the movement of people across borders, usually related to employment opportunities, but also in search of a better life and, in some cases, escaping war and violence. The phenomenon created by the knowledge society wherein people with specialized training are in demand, irrespective of national borders, is **brain drain,** where highly trained individuals leave their home country to seek more lucrative positions or better living conditions. Mucci et al. (2019) argued that "Migrant workers show an increase in the incidence of serious, psychotic, anxiety, and post-traumatic disorders due to a series of socio-environmental variables, such as loss of social status, discrimination, and separations from the family" (p. 120). They conducted a systematic review and highlighted the prevailing psychological pathologies and risks these workers experience, analyzing 127 articles published from 2009 to 2019. They found migrants susceptible to depressive syndrome (poor concentration at work, feeling down, or anger and somatization), anxiety, alcohol or substance abuse, and poor sleep quality. These conditions create poor living conditions intensified by social marginalization, strenuous work, and, in some cases, verbal or physical abuse, and employment in dangerous, unhealthy jobs. The authors advocated the role of occupational medicine in promoting the well-being of migrant workers. Reid et al. (2021) reported how globally migrant and immigrant workers shouldered the burden of the COVID-19 pandemic as essential workers, many of them becoming infected with the virus and experiencing precarious employment with no sick leave, Social Security, or compensation for undertaking risks during the pandemic. They argued for improving the working and living conditions of migrant workers as a positive outcome of the aftermath of the pandemic.

Migration has consequences for adult learners; as Alfred (2015) argued, "A review of the adult education literature reveals the glaring neglect of issues that affect the rapidly increasing number of foreign-born adults who take up residence in other countries, either through voluntary or through forced migration" (p. 87). She advocated the teaching of **diaspora**—the challenges of "forced migration from one's country of origin, maintenance of a national identity in the new homeland, and a dream of return to the home of origin" (p. 88), within the discourse of adult education to develop

> an agenda for the deconstruction of assumptions that equate globalization primarily with progress and economic empowerment and, instead, replace it with new ways of understanding structure, agency, and social change as they relate to human development and the quest for identity and place of belonging. (p. 95)

 **Box 2.9 Tips and Tools for Teaching and Learning**

Local Demographic Changes and Your Observations

As an adult educator or learner, consider the following activity to assess your local community.

1. Explore how demographics are changing in your community. Most munici-palities have information about the population. See what information you can find.
2. Regarding changing demographics, informally survey your immediate commu-nity for learning opportunities designed for immigrants, English language learn-ers, and/or older adult learners.
   a. Have these opportunities increased over the last five years?
   b. What about participation?

Box 2.9 offers a tip for teaching and learning about demographic change. Khan (2021) synthesized qualitative literature over two decades (2000–2020) to understand the phenomenon of academic brain drain from European countries. They identified five factors responsible for European academics seeking careers elsewhere including: (1) attractive salaries outside Europe, (2) short-term fixed contracts for early career researchers, (3) unfair recruitment procedures, (4) attractive migration policies, and (5) the indi-rect role played by internationalization policies to encourage permanent mobility (p. 265).

Lexicons of Adult Learning in a Global Context

A globalizing, multicultural world has created opportunities to learn about **DEI**—diversity, equity, and inclusion—and **DEIB**—diversity, equity, inclusion, and belonging, or other combinations of these values and actions to make cultures more welcoming and just. **EDID**—equity, diversity, inclusion, and decolonization—acknowledges that Western ideologies represent particular biases, values, and practices that shape knowledge construction (Bermúdez et al., 2016). Although initiatives to promote justice and equity are under attack in the United States, the world and workplace are highly diverse, and the need to help people understand and work with people who are different from themselves is a constant learning opportunity. Bierema et al. (2024) illuminated, "As understandings of how power structures exclude participation and silence marginalized individuals and groups progress, new labels for these terms emerge to capture what kinds of practices organizations seek to emphasize" (p. 87). Table 2.2 summarizes lexicons or key vocabulary to appreciate diversity and embrace equity and justice.

TABLE 2.2 KEY LEXICONS FOR A GLOBAL, JUST CONTEXT

Term	Definition
Diversity	The existence of variations in race, gender identity and expression, ethnicity, sex, social class, (dis)ability, indigeneity, age, religion or spirituality, and other identities and positionalities.
Equity	The achievement of fairness and justice with considerations of imbalances in identity and positionality and provision of needed resources and opportunities to people depending on their needs.
Inclusion	The embrace of difference and efforts to validate the value of all people and identify similarities while simultaneously valuing uniqueness and individuality. People feel welcome, a sense of belonging, and respected.
Decolonization	Understanding **colonialism**—typically the Western world's forcing of its own cultural, ideological, and economic systems on less powerful countries. Decolonization resists colonialism by reinforcing local and national culture, customs, and values.
Cultural Competence	The appreciation of diverse cultures with little or no openness to learning and changing when exposed to other cultures and their members (Lekas et al., 2020).
Cultural humility	Engaging with new cultures with an ethic of care and self-reflection to understand reactions to new cultures. It is also an appreciation for the new culture and receptivity to learning about it and from the people in the culture. Cultural humility is the opposite of cultural competence.
Epistemic humility	The capacity to recognize the confines of one's knowledge and willingness to identify situations when one's ignorance may be potentially harmful or dangerous. Additionally, it focuses on how people relate to the truth or rationality of their own beliefs relative to experts' knowledge, recognizing that some situations resist knowability, and this non-knowing is an enduring and central condition in decision-making (Parviainen et al., 2021).
Belonging	Feelings of security, acceptance, inclusion, value, and support within a social group.

 **Box 2.10 Tips and Tools for Teaching and Learning**

Culturally Responsive Teaching

Gloria Ladson-Billings (1994) introduced **culturally responsive teaching** based on a culturally relevant pedagogy framework recognizing the role of culture in shaping how learners see themselves and the world around them. Rhodes (2018) noted that much culturally responsive teaching research has focused on K–12 settings. Guy (1999) advocated embracing culturally responsive teaching to create more effective learning environments for adult learners from minority backgrounds, emphasizing that culture is at the heart of everything in education. Key assumptions of culturally responsive learning for adults highlighted in Rhodes's (2018) work:

1. Learners and educators bring their cultural identities into the learning setting (Guy, 2009).
2. Cultural strategies people bring to the learning environment may or may not serve learners well, depending on the learning activity.
3. The learner is at the core of the learning process and draws on their cultural knowledge, prior experiences, frames of reference, and performance styles (Gay, 2010, in Rhodes, 2018).
4. Historically excluded or marginalized learners due to cultural identity and experience may encounter a cultural mismatch between their culture and the culture of the learning environment, especially when dominant cultures stigmatize their culture's group norms and values.
5. Culturally relevant pedagogy addresses the mismatch by centering learners and their values, beliefs, and experiences in the learning process.
6. The Motivational Framework for Culturally Responsive Teaching (Ginsberg & Wlodkowski, 2009; Wlodkowski, 2004; Wlodkowski & Ginsberg, 2017) "dynamically combines the essential motivational conditions that are intrinsically motivating for adults in culturally diverse learning environments" (Wlodkowski & Ginsberg, 2017, p. 97). Here are the components of the framework with questions posed by Wlodkowski & Ginsberg (2017, pp. 100–101):
   a. **Establish inclusion** by creating norms of respect and connection among learners that value the co-construction of knowledge using strategies like jigsaw or peer teaching activities (Rhodes, 2018). When planning the lesson, ask,

"How do we create or form a learning atmosphere in which we feel respected and connected?"

b. **Develop attitude** by addressing the *relevance and creation of student volition* in the learning environment (emphasis in the original, Rhodes, 2018, p. 35). Volition involves having learners create classroom norms for problematic terms and labels and inviting student input into formulating course goals and outcomes. Learning assessment invites problem-solving activities that yield a variety of possible solutions. When planning the lesson, ask, "How do we create or affirm a favorable disposition toward learning through personal relevance and learner volition?"

c. **Enhance meaning** by inviting deep reflection and critical inquiry into issues related to the course content, such as simulations, role-playing, or games (Rhodes, 2018). Ask throughout the lesson, "How do we create engaging and challenging learning experiences that include learners' perspectives and values?"

d. **Engender competence** using assessments sensitive to learner backgrounds with multiple ways of demonstrating learning. These might include reflective learner self-assessments, dialogue, focused reflections, or journals (Rhodes, 2018). Ask throughout and at the end of the lesson, "How do we create or affirm an understanding that learners have effectively learned something they value and perceive as authentic to their real world?"

Consider the points and strategies as an adult learner or educator.

1. What have you experienced or integrated into your teaching?
2. How might this information change how you approach learning and teaching in the future?

Adult learners and educators engage with multicultural communities regularly. Building the capacity to engage in meaningful dialogue, provide mutual support, and bridge understanding helps adults function effectively in the complex social context of learning and living. Box 2.10 highlights strategies for culturally responsive teaching.

Chapter Summary

Chapter 2 touched on several significant trends influencing adult learning in contemporary context and culture. Each topic has stacks of book-length treatments, reports, and articles. The VUCA nature of the world is shaped by global capitalism, neoliberalism, knowledge society, technology, and changing demographics, and they are so interconnected that it is taxing to ponder one without considering the others. Adults' learning reflects and responds to these forces prevalent in the context where people live, work, and learn. Learning gives adults the capacity to change and vice versa. As George Bernard Shaw (1856–1950), an Irish poet, critic, playwright, and political observed, "Progress is impossible without change; and those who cannot change their minds, cannot change anything" (1944, p. 330). Learning builds adults' capacity to change, creating new avenues for learning.

Chapter Highlights

- Globalization is the movement of goods, services, people, and culture across national boundaries. The intensity and speed of this movement characterize globalization today in a volatile environment influenced by global capitalism and neoliberalism.
- The knowledge society brokers intellectual capital, fueled by rapid increases in knowledge and the capacity to share it digitally.
- Changing demographics, particularly concerning cultural and ethnic diversity and an aging population, characterize most societies today.

References

Accenture. (2024a). *Pulse of Change: 2024 Index.* Accenture Newsroom. https://www.accenture.com/us-en/about/company/pulse-of-change.

Accenture. (2024b). *Businesses anticipate unprecedented rate of change in 2024, new Accenture 'pulse of change index' shows.* Accenture Newsroom. https://newsroom.accenture.com/news/2024/businesses-anticipate-unprecedented-rate-of-change-in-2024-new-accenture-pulse-of-change-index-shows.

Alfred, M. V. (2015). Diaspora, migration, and globalization: Expanding the discourse of adult education. *New Directions for Adult and Continuing Education, 2015*(146), 87–97. https://doi.org/10.1002/ace.20134.

Armona, L., Chakrabarti, R., & Lovenheim, M. F. (2022). Student debt and default: The role of for-profit colleges. *Journal of Financial Economics, 144*(1), 67–92. https://doi .org/10.1016/j.jfineco.2021.12.008.

Azcona, G., Bhatt, A., Fillo, G. F., Min, Y., Page, H., & You, S. (2023). *Progress on the sustainable development goals: The gender snapshot 2023.* United Nations Women and United Nations Department of Economic and Social Affairs. https://www.unwomen.org/en/digital-library/ publications/2023/09/progress-on-the-sustainable-development-goals-the-gender-snapshot-2023.

Bermúdez, J. M., Muruthi, B. A., & Jordan, L. S. (2016). Decolonizing research methods for family science: Creating space at the center. *Journal of Family Theory & Review, 8*(2), 192–206. https://doi.org/10.1111/jftr.12139.

Bierema, L. L. (2024). *Rethinking adult career development: A critical perspective.* Edward Elgar.

Bierema, L. L., Callahan, J. L., Elliott, C. J., Greer, T. W., & Collins, J. C. (2024). *Human resource development: Critical perspectives and practices.* Routledge.

Bleich, S. N., & Vercammen, K. A. (2018). The negative impact of sugar-sweetened beverages on children's health: An update of the literature. *BMC obesity, 5,* 1–27. https://doi .org/10.1186/s40608-017-0178-9.

Bohonos, J. W., & James-Gallaway, A. (2022). Enslavement and the foundations of human resource development: Covert learning, consciousness raising, and resisting antiBlack organizational goals. *Human Resource Development Review, 21*(2), 160–179. https://doi .org/10.1177/15344843221076292.

Bolt-Evensen, K., Vik, F. N., Stea, T. H., Klepp, K. I., & Bere, E. (2018). Consumption of sugar-sweetened beverages and artificially sweetened beverages from childhood to adulthood in relation to socioeconomic status—15 years follow-up in Norway. *International Journal of Behavioral Nutrition and Physical Activity, 15,* 1–9. https://doi.org/10.1186/s12966-018-0646-8.

Brinkley, I. (2006). *Defining the knowledge economy.* London: The work foundation, 19. https:// www.seeda.co.uk/_publications/Defining_the_Knowledge_Economy_2007.pdf.

Byrd, M. Y. (2014). Re-conceptualizing and re-visioning diversity in the workforce: Toward a social justice paradigm." In M. Y. Byrd & C. L. Scott (Eds.), *Diversity in the workforce: Current issues and emerging trends* (pp. 334–346). Routledge.

Byrd, M. Y. (2018). Does HRD have a moral duty to respond to matters of social injustice? *Human Resource Development International, 21*(1), 3–11. https://doi.org/10.1080/13678868 .2017.1344419.

Candiotto, L. (2022). Extended loneliness. When hyperconnectivity makes us feel alone. *Ethics and Information Technology, 24*(4), 47. https://doi.org/10.1007/s10676-022-09669-4.

Carroll, J. (2022, December 12). *23 trends for 2023: #8—Knowledge velocity.* Jim Carroll. https:// jimcarroll.com/2022/12/23-trends-for-2023-8-knowledge-velocity/.

Castaneda, D. I., & Cuellar, S. (2020). Knowledge sharing and innovation: A systematic review. *Knowledge and Process Management, 27*(3), 159–173. https://doi.org/10.1002/kpm.1637.

Cebola, M. M. J., dos Santos, N. R., & Dionísio, A. (2023). Worker-related ageism: A systematic review of empirical research. *Ageing & Society, 43*(8), 1882–1914. https://doi.org/10.1017/ S0144686X21001380.

Centeno, M. A., & Cohen, J. N. (2013). *Global capitalism: A sociological perspective.* John Wiley & Sons.

Collinson, C., & Hodin, M. (2023, October 23). *Best practices for engaging a multigenerational workforce.* Harvard Business Review. https://hbr.org/2023/10/best-practices-for-engaging-a-multigenerational-workforce.

Crawford, R., Brennan, L., & Khamis, S. (2021). Introduction: Unpacking coke. In R. Crawford, L. Brennab, & S. Khamis (Eds.), *Decoding Coca-Cola: A biography of a global brand* (pp. 1–10). Routledge.

De Visé, D. (2023, August 7). *America's white majority is aging out.* The Hill. https://thehill.com/homenews/race-politics/4138228-americas-white-majority-is-aging-out/.

Dumont, H., & Istance, D. (2010). Analysing and designing learning environments for the 21st century. In H. Dumont, D. Istance, & F. Benavides (Eds.), *The nature of learning: Using research to inspire practice* (pp. 19–34). OECD Publishing: Organisation for Economic Co-operation and Development.

Eaton, C. (2022). Agile predators: Private equity and the spread of shareholder value strategies to US for-profit colleges. *Socio-Economic Review, 20*(2), 791–815. https://doi.org/10.1093/ser/mwaa005.

Fang, M. L., Canham, S. L., Battersby, L., Sixsmith, J., Wada, M., & Sixsmith, A. (2019). Exploring privilege in the digital divide: Implications for theory, policy, and practice. *The Gerontologist, 59*(1), e1–e15. https://doi.org/10.1093/geront/gny037.

Florida, R., & Kenney, M. (1993). The new age of capitalism: Innovation-mediated production. *Futures, 25*(6), 637–651. https://doi.org/10.1016/0016-3287(93)90105-3.

Ford. (n.d.). *Locations.* Ford. https://corporate.ford.com/operations/locations.html#:~:text=During%20our%20first%20year%2C%20Ford,125%20countries%20around%20the%20world.

Friedman, T. L. (2011, August 13). *A theory of everything (Sort of).* The New York Times Sunday Review. http://www.nytimes.com/2011/08/14/opinion/Sunday/Friedman-a-theory-of-everyting-sort-of.html.

Freire, P. (1973). *Education for critical consciousness* (Vol. 1). Bloomsbury Publishing.

Gay, G. (2010). *Culturally responsive teaching: Theory, research, and practice.* Teachers College Press.

Gerhardt, M., Nachemson-Ekwall, J., & Fogel, B. (2021). *Gentelligence: The revolutionary approach to leading an intergenerational workforce.* Rowman & Littlefield.

GilPress. (2024, January 31). *How many people own smartphones (2024–2029).* Whats The Big Data. https://whatsthebigdata.com/smartphone-stats/.

Ginsberg, M., & Wlodkowski, R. (2009). *Diversity and motivation: Culturally responsive teaching in college.* Jossey-Bass.

Gouthro, P. A. (2022). Lifelong learning in a globalized world: The need for critical social theory in adult and lifelong education. *International Journal of Lifelong Education, 41*(1), 107–121.

Gower, R., Green, J., & Williams, M. (2020). *The Burning Question: Will companies reduce their plastic use?* Tearfund. https://policycommons.net/artifacts/12290133/2020-tearfund-the-burning-question-en/13184173/.

Guy, T. (2009). Culturally relevant curriculum development for teachers of adults: The importance of identity, positionality, and classroom dynamics. In V. C. X. Wang (Ed.), *Curriculum development for adult learners in the global community* (pp. 9–38). Krieger.

Guy, T. (1999). Culture as context for adult education: The need for culturally relevant adult education. In T. C. Guy (Ed.), *Providing culturally relevant adult education* (pp. 5–18). Jossey-Bass.

Hastwell, C. (2023, January 18). *Engaging and managing a multigenerational workforce*. Great Place To Work. https://www.greatplacetowork.com/resources/blog/engaging-and-managing-multigenerational-workforce.

Heinemann, A., & Monzó, L. (2021). Capitalism, migration, and adult education. Toward a critical project in the second language learning class. *European Journal for Research on the Education and Learning of Adults, 12*(1), 65–79. https://doi.org/10.25656/01:21963; 10.3384/rela.2000-7426.ojs3464.

Hislop, D. (2013). *Knowledge management in organisations: A critical introduction* (3rd ed.). Oxford University Press.

Hogel, M., Partboteeah, K., & Munson, C. (2003). Team level antecedents of individuals knowledge networks. *Decision Sciences, 21*(1), 40–51. https://doi.org/10.1111/j.1540-5414.2003.02344.x.

Jacobson, E. (2016). Workforce development rhetoric and the realities of 21st century capitalism. *Literacy and Numeracy Studies, 24*(1), 3–22. http://dx.doi.org/10.5130/lns.v24i1.4898.

Jenkins, C., & Alfred, M. (2018). Understanding the motivation and transformation of White culturally responsive professors. *Journal of Adult and Continuing Education, 24*(1), 81–99. https://doi.org/10.1177/1477971417738793.

Khan, J. (2021). European academic brain drain: A meta-synthesis. *European Journal of Education, 56*(2), 265–278. https://doi.org/10.1111/ejed.12449.

Khan, Y. (2019, October 18). *These are the Top 10 Brands in the World in 2019*. Business Insider. https://www.businessinsider.com.au/interbrand-top-10-brands-inthe-world-2019-10?r=US&IR=T.

Kurzweil, R. (2004). The law of accelerating returns. In C. Teuscher (Ed.) *Alan Turing: Life and legacy of a great thinker* (pp. 381–416). Springer. https://doi.org/10.1007/978-3-662-05642-4_16.

Ladson-Billings, G. (1994). *The dreamkeepers. Culturally responsive teaching.* Jossey-Bass.

Lekas, H. M., Pahl, K., & Fuller Lewis, C. (2020). Rethinking cultural competence: Shifting to cultural humility. *Health Services Insights, 13*, 1178632920970580. https://doi.org/10.1177/1178632920970580.

Malhotra, R. (2012). *Human rights indicators: A guide to measurement and implementation*. United Nations Human Rights, Office of the High Commissioner. https://www.ohchr.org/sites/default/files/Documents/Publications/Human_rights_indicators_en.pdf.

Mucci, N., Traversini, V., Giorgi, G., Tommasi, E., De Sio, S., & Arcangeli, G. (2019). Migrant workers and psychological health: A systematic review. *Sustainability, 12*(1), 120. https://doi.org/10.3390/su12010120.

Mullee, A., Romaguera, D., Pearson-Stuttard, J., Viallon, V., Stepien, M., Freisling, H., . . . & Murphy, N. (2019). Association between soft drink consumption and mortality in 10 European countries. *JAMA Internal Medicine, 179*(11), 1479–1490. https://doi.org/10.1001/jamainternmed.2019.2478.

National Center for Education Statistics. (2024). *International educational attainment. Condition of education.* US Department of Education, Institute of Education Sciences. https://nces.ed.gov/programs/coe/indicator/cac.

OECD. (2020). *Promoting an age-inclusive workforce: Living, learning and earning longer.* OECD Publishing, Paris. https://doi.org/10.1787/59752153-en.

O'Neill, A. (2024, February 2). *Global adult literacy rate aged 15 years and older from 1976 to 2022 by gender.* Statista. https://www.statista.com/statistics/997360/global-adult-and-youth-literacy/#:~:text=Global%20literacy%20rate1976%2D2022&text=In%20the%20past%20five%20decades,of%2058%20percent%20among%20females.

Page, D. (2019). The academic as consumed and consumer. *Journal of Education Policy, 35*(5), 585–601. https://doi.org/10.1080/02680939.2019.1598585.

Parker, K., & Rainie, L. (2020, April 13). *Americans and lifetime learning in the Knowledge Age.* PEW: Trend Magazine. https://www.pewtrusts.org/en/trend/archive/spring-2020/americans-and-lifetime-learning-in-the-knowledge-age.

Parviainen, J., Koski, A., & Torkkola, S. (2021). 'Building a ship while sailing it.' Epistemic humility and the temporality of non-knowledge in political decision-making on COVID-19. *Social Epistemology, 35*(3), 232–244. https://doi.org/10.1080/02691728.2021.1882610.

Pendergrast, M. (2013). *For God, country and Coca-Cola: The definitive history of the great American soft drink* (3rd ed.). Basic Books.

Pew Research Center. (2016, October 6). *The state of American jobs.* PEW Research Center. https://www.pewresearch.org/social-trends/2016/10/06/the-state-of-american-jobs/.

Ramdeholl, D., Gnanadass, E., Merriweather, L., & St. Clair, R. (2023). Adult education as a human right/Adult education for human rights. *Adult Education Quarterly, 73*(4), 343–344. https://doi.org/10.1177/07417136231198375.

Reid, A., Ronda-Perez, E., & Schenker, M. B. (2021). Migrant workers, essential work, and COVID-19. *American Journal of Industrial Medicine, 64*(2), 73–77. https://doi.org/10.1002/ajim.23209.

Rhodes, C. M. (2018). Culturally responsive teaching with adult learners: A review of the literature. *International Journal of Adult Vocational Education and Technology (IJAVET), 9*(4), 33–41.

Ritchie, H., & Rodés-Guirao, L. (2024, July 11). *Peak global population and other key findings from the 2024 UN World Population Prospects.* Our World in Data. https://ourworldindata.org/un-population-2024-revision.

Rosenberg, M. (2019, January 5). *If the world were a village. . ..* ThoughtCo. https://www.thoughtco.com/if-the-world-were-a-village-1435271#:~:text=If%20the%20world%20were%20a%20village%20of%20100%20people,Australia%2C%20Oceania%2C%20or%20Antarctica.

Shaw, B. (1944). *Everybody's political what's what.* Dodd, Mead.

Sim, E., & Bierema, L. L. (2025). Intersectional precarity in academia: A systematic literature review. *Equality, Diversity and Inclusion.* Advanced Online Publication. https://doi.org/10.1108/EDI-09-2023-0306.

Singh, G. M., Micha, R., Khatibzadeh, S., Lim, S., Ezzati, M., & Mozaffarian, D. (2015). Estimated global, regional, and national disease burdens related to sugar-sweetened beverage consumption in 2010. *Circulation, 132*(8), 639–666. https://doi.org/10.1161/CIRCULATIONAHA.114.010636.

Sklair, L. (2001). Capitalism: Global. *International Encyclopedia of the Social and Behavioral Sciences, 2001,* 1459–1463. https://doi.org/10.1016/B0-08-043076-7/01831-3.

Sorokin, S. (2019, April 5). *Thriving in a world of "knowledge half-life."* CIO. https://www.cio.com/article/219940/thriving-in-a-world-of-knowledge-half-life.html.

Slaughter, S. & Rhoades, G. (2004). *Academic capitalism and the new economy*. The Johns Hopkins University Press.

Smith, M., Mizzi, R. C., Hawley, J. D., Rocco, T. A., & Merriweather, L. R. (2023). Conclusion: Reflecting on struggles, achievements, and cautions in complex times. In T. S. Rocco, M. C. Smith, R. C. Mizzi, L. R. Merriweather, J. D. Hawley (Eds.), *The handbook of adult and continuing education* (pp. 445–451). Taylor & Francis.

Taherdoost, H. (2023). An overview of trends in information systems: Emerging technologies that transform the information technology industry. *Cloud Computing and Data Science*, 1–16. https://doi.org/10.37256/ccds.4120231653.

Trenerry, B., Chng, S., Wang, Y., Suhaila, Z. S., Lim, S. S., Lu, H. Y., & Oh, P. H. (2021). Preparing workplaces for digital transformation: An integrative review and framework of multi-level factors. *Frontiers in Psychology*, *12*, 620766. https://doi.org/10.3389/fpsyg.2021.620766.

Turkle, S. (2011). *Alone together: Why we expect more from each other and less from technology*. Basic Books.

United Nations. (2024). *Population division: World Population Prospects 2024*. https://population.un.org/wpp/.

United Nations Population Fund. (2023). *The problem with 'too few.'* United Nations Population Fund. https://www.unfpa.org/swp2023/too-few.

US News & World Report. (n.d.). *US News Best Colleges*. US News & World Report. https://www.usnews.com/best-colleges.

Vespa, J., Medina, L., & Armstrong, D. M. (2020, February). *Demographic turning points for the United States: Population projections for 2020 to 2060*. Current Population Reports, P25-1144, The United States Census Bureau, Washington, DC. https://www.census.gov/content/dam/Census/library/publications/2020/demo/p25-1144.pdf.

Wlodkowski, R. J., & Ginsberg, M. B. (2017). *Enhancing adult motivation to learn: A comprehensive guide for teaching all adults*. John Wiley & Sons.

Wlodkowski, R. J., & Galbraith, M. W. (2004). Creating motivating learning environments. In M. W. Galbraith (Ed.), *Adult learning methods: A guide for effective instruction*, *3*, 141–164. Krieger.

Wolff, R. D. (2012). *Democracy at work: A cure for capitalism*. Haymarket books.

Wong, A. (2016, March 30). *The commodification of higher education*. The Atlantic. https://www.theatlantic.com/education/archive/2016/03/the-commodification-of-higher-education/475947/.

Wood, B., Baker, P., Scrinis, G., McCoy, D., Williams, O., & Sacks, G. (2021). Maximising the wealth of few at the expense of the health of many: A public health analysis of market power and corporate wealth and income distribution in the global soft drink market. *Globalization and Health*, *17*, 1–17. https://doi.org/10.1186/s12992-021-00781-6.

World Population Review. (n.d.). *Literacy rate by country 2024*. World Population Review. https://worldpopulationreview.com/country-rankings/literacy-rate-by-country.

Yelich Biniecki, S. M., & Conceição, S. C. (2014). How living or traveling to foreign locations influences adults' worldviews and impacts personal identity. *New Horizons in Adult Education and Human Resource Development*, *26*(3), 39–53. https://doi.org/10.1002/nha3.20071.

CHAPTER THREE

APPLYING CRITICAL PERSPECTIVES TO ADULT LEARNING IN SOCIAL CONTEXT

 ## Box 3.1 Chapter Overview and Learning Objectives

Anand Giridharadas (2023) started his *New York Times* best-selling book, *The Persuaders: At the Front Lines of the Fight for Hearts, Minds, and Democracy,* with a prologue about how Russian troll farms attempted to disrupt the 2020 United States Presidential Election:

> In June 2014, Aleksandra Krylova and Anna Bogacheva arrived in the United States on a clandestine mission. Krylova was a high-ranking official at the Internet Research Agency in St. Petersburg, Russia, an ostensibly private company that was known to work on behalf of Russian intelligence. Bogacheva, her road buddy, a researcher and data cruncher, was more junior. Their trip had been well planned: a transcontinental itinerary, SIM cards, burner phones, cameras, visas obtained under the pretense of personal travel, and, just in case, evacuation plans.

The women made stops in California, Colorado, Illinois, Louisiana, Michigan, Nevada, New Mexico, New York, and Texas, according to a federal indictment issued years later. Beyond that, their activities are not well known, though their mission is: to gather evidence of conditions in the United States for a project to destabilize its political system and society, using the rather improbable weapon of millions of social media posts. (p. 3)

The project was a risky foreign intelligence service to inflame other Americans into writing off people they disagreed with, "assuming they would never change their minds or ways, dismissing them as hopelessly mired in identities they couldn't escape, viewing those who thought differently as needing to be resisted rather than won over" (Giridharadas, 2023, p. 4). These dismissals became inescapable, "taking different guises on the left and the right, showing up among regular citizens and in the marble corridors of power" (Giridharadas, 2023, p. 4). It is likely that you, as an unassuming consumer or concerned US citizen, used the Internet or social media during these years and that you received messages from one or more of hundreds of workers putting in 12-hour shifts to promote bogus messages on social media using fake accounts. The initiative worked to deepen existing divisions in US public discourse. "The troll farm wanted Americans to regard each other as immovable, brainwashed, of bad faith, not worth energy, disloyal, repulsive" (Giridharadas, 2023, p. 7). United States spy agencies have determined continued threats, announcing "A broad effort to push back on Russian influence campaigns in the 2024 [presidential] election, as it tries to curb the Kremlin's use of state-run media and fake news to sway American voters" (Barnes et al., 2024, para. 1). That such rancor broadly infects society seems preposterous, but it was not and remains a threat, as Giridharadas (2023) carefully documented in his book exploring how persuasion occurs and why being open to it matters to democracy.

Engaging in conversations and learning that challenge your knowledge as an adult learner, educator, or citizen can feel intimidating and even threatening. Yet, being curious and "willing to be disturbed" is what Wheatley (2002) described as "Our willingness to have our beliefs and ideas challenged by what others think" (p. 34). She further emphasized that everyone needs other views and perspectives beyond their own to address today's challenges, and the best way to begin that process is by "admitting we don't know" (p. 34).

This chapter explores the role of critical perspectives in adult learning by describing what being critical as an adult learner or educator means, including understanding criticality as a philosophy, thinking process, and agenda for mindful and timely action on social problems and challenges. As a result of reading this chapter and completing the exercise boxes, you, the reader, should be able to:

1. Understand key tenets of critical perspectives and adult learning.
2. Define key concepts and terms contributing to critical adult learning and education perspectives.
3. Apply these perspectives to your learning and life.

As humans, we all have moments that compel us to stop and reconsider our beliefs. When the opportunity arises, we might dismiss the information, as became common in the opening example. The COVID-19 pandemic played out differently and became a rare moment where most of the world took a collective pause from life as we knew it to shelter and learn how to cope in the face of a frightening virus that was initially poorly understood and had no vaccination. There were divisions and dismissals along that journey, often fueled by misinformation. Although human dilemmas are not usually as dramatic as a presidential election or global pandemic, many of us can relate to questioning the political party, religious views, gender-role expectations, or cultural attitudes we grew up accepting without a second thought. What makes us stop and question, and perhaps change, our beliefs? When you pause and rethink something, the process is known as critical thinking, a central goal of adult education.

Critical thinking is the process of questioning, analyzing, evaluating, judging, or interpreting what you believe or what others might say, do, write, or advocate. For example, you might have accepted your family's political views without question. Still, as you learn more about the issues and what the favored political party stands for, you assess whether the platform matches your evolving values. Or you might be listening to the radio while driving home from work, and someone is offering opinions or research results that cause you to doubt their truth or accuracy. These moments of misgiving and discernment are critical thinking and markers of effective learning.

Being Critical

As adult learners or educators, what do we really mean when we talk about critical thinking? Brookfield (2012), in his book *Teaching for Critical Thinking*, began by defining what it is *not*. Critical thinking does not require a college education or an advanced understanding of philosophy, nor is it problem-solving or creativity. It does not mean you criticize persons or things, nor is it associated with age or IQ. Critical thinking is a practice everyone can do. Yet, as busy adults, we may not consciously evaluate our assumptions or think about how the broader social environment influences them as we go about daily life. This chapter considers what it means to be "critical." **Being Critical** is not synonymous with being negative, disparaging, or unsympathetic toward others; instead, it is a process of being curious, mindful, reflective, analytical, astute, and contemplative about the ideas and realities swirling around your family, workplace, community, and world. Criticality in our learning, thinking, and acting shifts our focus from ourselves to the broader social structures that shape our interactions and experiences in various settings. This chapter locates critical thinking in its broader context, as discussed in Chapter 2, considering its philosophical underpinnings and contemporary counterparts. The chapter begins with a discussion of what it means to be critical. The following sections introduce critical theory, critical thinking, and critical action as a framework for learning, teaching, and living.

Critical education has been the foundation of social and liberation movements such as Freire's (1970/1988) work with sugar cane workers in Brazil, Horton's (1989) work with the Highlander School on civil rights issues in the United States, and the more recent Black Lives Matter and #MeToo movements to protest racial and gender inequality. There has been global outrage about the War in Gaza and the treatment of citizens, protests of Hamas's attacks on Israeli citizens and the humanitarian crisis in Gaza, and abhorrence over Russia's war on Ukraine, evidenced by many countries pledging financial and military support. Social media makes it easy for social movements to organize. "The potential for liberation always exists when students are encouraged to step outside of their individual world, to develop empathy, to think historically, and to think critically" (Zamudio et al., 2008, p. 216).

Promoting adults' capacity for being critical holds excellent promise for adult education, yet do adults know what it is or how to do it? A systematic literature review found that teachers tend to focus on content instead of helping learners build capacity for critical thinking (Alsaleh, 2020). Bellaera et al. (2021) surveyed 176 UK and US university faculty and asked them to rank 10 critical thinking skills. The top three were analysis, evaluation, and interpretation, with the lowest ranked including creativity, deductive reasoning, description, and problem-solving. Research indicates that an overwhelming majority (89%) of university faculty claimed that promoting critical thinking is a primary objective of their instruction (Paul et al., 1997). "Yet only 19% could define critical thinking, and 77% had little or no conception of how to reconcile content coverage with the fostering of critical thinking" (Mandernach, 2006, p. 41).

More recently, a nonprofit dedicated to elevating critical thinking—Reboot—conducts surveys of public attitudes toward critical thinking using

MTurk Prime. During 2020, 1,152 respondents completed the general survey, and 499 teachers completed the teaching survey. Reboot (2020) concluded that many people lacked sufficient skills by relying on inadequate information sources, making decisions based on poor research, and avoiding people with conflicting viewpoints. They also raised alarm about the proliferation of online misinformation that seems today's dominant forum for public discourse—a forum that amplifies cognitive biases and "where groupthink and filter bubbles proliferate" (p. 3). Correspondingly, political polarization has deepened and become more personal. Awareness of racial inequities has grown, but journalism has shifted in ways hurting critical thinking, such as incentivizing clickbait and offering sensationalized, siloed content. The report concluded (1) support for critical thinking is high, but skepticism remains that people are getting needed help to improve their capacity to reason; (2) both worrisome trends and promising signs exist in critical thinking habits and daily practices with most people not engaging enough with people with whom they disagree; and (3) three leading causes cited for deficits in critical thinking skills: technology, shifting social norms, and the educational system (Reboot, 2020). Reboot also surveyed teachers who rated critical thinking as "extremely important" or "very important" 94% of the time but harbored misconceptions about how to teach it and need more support in this area. The report also concluded that media literacy education should be taught more widely.

Being critical in adult learning and education has at least three components. The first is **critical theory**, the philosophy underlying critical perspectives and approaches. Critical theory gives you, as an adult learner, a basis for critical thinking. The second is **critical thinking**, a reflective process of assessing what you believe or do. The third, **critical action**, is making timely and mindful

TABLE 3.1 ASPECTS OF BEING CRITICAL

Critical Theory—A Philosophy	Critical Thinking—A Thought Process	Critical Action—A Mindful and Timely Intervention

• Critiques social conditions and how they create unequal power relations based on attributes like race, gender, class, age, sexual orientation, physical ability, and other identities.
• Challenges "truth" that is advanced by dominant groups
• Seeks emancipation and elimination of oppression in society
	• Reflects on assumptions and beliefs
	• Critiques self-thought and action
	  • Hunts assumptions
	  • Checks assumptions
	  • Sees things from different viewpoints
	• Connects individual experience to broader social conditions
		• Takes informed action
		• Monitors and corrects the self/group
		  • Clarifies or changes thought
		  • Changes behavior
		  • Makes timely intervention
		• Justifies our actions

interventions once you have critically evaluated your thoughts, past behaviors, and future options. This framework is outlined in Table 3.1 and discussed in the following sections.

Critical Theory

Critical theory is a philosophical tradition that developed out of the Frankfurt School—a group of scholars seeking to analyze the conditions that created the Holocaust during World War II as a means of avoiding such heinous oppression in the future. The imprisonment and killing of Jewish people during World War II shows how powerful and credulous a dominant belief or ideology can be when it is advanced by those in power (in this case, Hitler's Germany). The events surrounding the Holocaust involved nations disregarding the overt torture, murder, and oppression of a particular ethnic group.

Critical theory, as implied by its name, critiques social conditions based on a Marxist goal of "relentlessly criticizing all existing conditions." Brookfield (2012) explained it as "describ[ing] the process by which people learn to recognize how unjust dominant ideologies are embedded in everyday situations and practices. These ideologies shape behavior and keep an unequal system intact by making it appear normal" (p. 48). Certainly, the dismissal of people and ideas on social media aligns with this ideology. **Dominant ideologies** are broadly accepted beliefs and practices that usually work to perpetuate an economically unequal, racist, homophobic, and sexist society with negligible resistance (Brookfield, 2012). To be a critical person from a critical theory perspective, you would "take action to create more democratic, collectivist, economic, and social forms" (Brookfield, 2012, p. 49). Adult education has embraced critical theory as an important lens for analyzing learning dynamics and environments. Critical theory helps us, as adult learners, do three crucial things: (1) critique prevailing social conditions, (2) challenge universal truths or dominant ideologies, and (3) seek social emancipation and the elimination of oppression. Imagine how relationships might have been different if people rejected the culture of dismissal during the 2020 presidential election. Box 3.2 describes ideology.

Hegemony

Critical theorists talk about **"hegemony,"** or the process of the dominant group creating "truths" that become accepted as the natural and proper way to think about something. Hegemony is when those in power either coerce or convince others to fall under their influence. The term derives from the

 **Box 3.2 Tips and Tools for Teaching and Learning**

Teaching About Ideology

Ideology is a belief system people are often steeped in yet unable to see. Ideology becomes reified as truth through mass media, religious teachings, schools, the government, and other outlets. People participate in what Brookfield (2001) described as "investing in our unhappiness," emphasizing: "*Because capitalism will do its utmost to convince us that we should live in ways that support its workings, we cannot be fully adult unless we attempt to unearth and challenge the ideology that justifies this system*" (p. 16, italics in original). Brookfield suggested that people must critique the more visible social conditions accompanying their underlying ideology of capitalism, which most leave unquestioned.

When critical theorists critique social conditions, they seek to expose "truths" or underlying ideologies people accept without question that function to hurt them. In the examples presented, when consumers accepted the economic conditions as "true," it allowed the moneyed stakeholders in the economy to retain power. At the same time, those less fortunate faced financial trauma but took actions that ultimately hurt them, like taking out unaffordable loans. Brookfield (2001) suggested that a critical theory of adult learning must explore how adults learn to resist ideological manipulation, or in other words, they need to question truths that seem immutable. Yet this "truth" about corporate profits being good for America results in individuals losing power and income as corporations and CEOs become richer and more powerful at the taxpayers' expense. Corporate power is not in the interest of most Americans, yet few question this particular ideology. When we, as informed consumers, begin to doubt and ultimately reject unquestioning support of corporate growth and excess (or any dominant ideology), we shift away from blind acceptance of the status quo to become more emancipated in how we think about and participate in capitalism or other "isms" we previously did not question.

Greek term *hēgemonia*, meaning "dominance over." For example, considering what has become a US truism, "What's Good for General Motors is Good for America," can help describe hegemony. During the 20th century, American corporations became more and more powerful, ignoring changing market conditions, and enjoying more rights than individual citizens. General Motors has a long history of mismanagement, such as not anticipating the demand for fuel-efficient cars, over-incentivizing purchases, halting electric car innovation, and not anticipating the demand for trucks that culminated in the corporation going bankrupt and needing an $85 billion government bailout by the Obama administration in the early 2000s. GM was also not attentive to civil rights as the company created working-class neighborhoods in the United States for White-only families. "In putting its muscle behind segregation, GM helped create patterns of inequality that remain with us today" (Clark, 2019, para. 15), including disinvestment in Black communities. The company also has played a role in anti-union practices that resulted in decentralized production, White flight, and manufacturing outsourcing to other countries. Clark continued, "It is a challenge to compile a detailed balance sheet for all of the ways General Motors helped and hurt the nation that it did so much to define" (para. 21). Today, with the first woman CEO of a major automotive company and now in its 11th decade, the company is working toward safer, more environmentally friendly cars.

Critical theorists are interested in power and how the powerful shape what people accept as knowledge and truth in society by creating ideologies people believe in, even when harmful, like doubting the Holocaust or trusting "What is good for GM is good for America." Critical theory acknowledges that the social world creates structures that confer privilege to some and marginalize others based on race, ethnicity, gender, age, sexual orientation, religion, class, physical ability, and other identities. Box 3.3 shows how hegemony can affect critical thinking.

Critical Perspectives

Before moving on to *Critical Thinking* and *Critical Action*, the two other dimensions of the *Being Critical Framework*, it is essential to note that there are other critical perspectives besides critical theory. These perspectives, drawn from many disciplines, seek to change inequitable social, organizational, and educational systems by recognizing and challenging ideological domination and manipulation. Critical approaches "urge us to find ways of naming, knowing, and being in the world that move outside sites of revolutions and into spaces of transformation" (Fox, 2002, p. 198). A brief list of definitions of these critical perspectives typically found in critical studies and relevant to adult learning and education follows.

Critical Disability Theory. Critical disability theory, also referred to as critical disability studies (CDS), "analyze[s] disability as a cultural, historical, relative, social, and political phenomenon" (Hall, 2019, para. 1) in ways that challenge

 # Box 3.3 Tips and Tools for Teaching and Learning

Teaching About Hegemony

Hegemony can seem like an intimidating concept to understand. This box features two examples to illustrate its power and ordinariness in everyday life. Understanding this principle gives you, as a learner or educator, the tools to assess social conditions that evade scrutiny. Critical theorists ask questions about these situations to prompt reflection and critique, such as "Who benefits from these arrangements?" and "Who says X is true?" Asking these essential questions is a citizen's best defense against hegemony when people present rhetoric as fact.

Hegemony and Financial Crisis

People's failure to critique the social conditions (neoliberal global capitalism as described in Chapter 2) of the economy fueled the financial crisis at the beginning of the 21st century. Many of us, as consumers, participated in running up credit far above our means by taking out unrealistic mortgages, convinced by the "truths" of "More and Bigger Is Better" and "Charge It." The banking system allowed and encouraged participation in these "truths" that were bad for everyone, except some banks, who profited handsomely from people taking out loans they could not afford. It is not difficult to find a person adversely affected by this fiscal crisis through loss of income, a mortgage underwater, decline of investments, unemployment, reorganization at work, explosive debt, or foreclosure. Yet, averting financial disaster might have been possible with a strenuous critique of the social conditions creating the situation. Instead, it was much more comforting to believe in unstoppable growth, escalating real estate prices, and unlimited credit—until the bubble popped. The banks claimed they were neutral and never talked people into loans they could not afford. Still, from a critical perspective, the banking industry was not innocent—although it likely had bought into its ideology just as vigorously as the people it hurt.

Hegemony and White Supremacy

The brutal murder of George Floyd, a Black man, by a White police officer created global rage and protests against the ideology of systemic racism and fueled the Black Lives Matter movement. These powerful affronts to the social reality of systemic racism have created backlashes of the powerful, evident in recent attacks on diversity, equity, and inclusion, claiming that critical race theory is part of the K–12 curriculum in the United States, even though this allegation is untrue. Critical race theory (CRT) began as a theoretical approach in legal studies to explain racial inequities. Gloria Ladson-Billings, the originator of CRT in the 1990s, explained how it has become scrutinized and heavily politicized, making it grossly misunderstood and a catch-all term for things that are not CRT. The attacks on CRT began with the former president and candidate Donald Trump arguing it would destroy democracy and how he would refuse to fund any education that mentioned CRT if re-elected, which he is working toward with a vengeance as president. He also paired CRT and anti-racism, although they are unlinked in the literature or practice. Ladson-Billings explained,

> It's like if I hate it, it must be critical race theory. . . . You know, that could be anything from any discussions about diversity or equity. And now it's spread into LGBTQA things. Talk about gender, then that's critical race theory. Social-emotional learning has now gotten lumped into it. And so, it's fascinating to me how the term has been literally sucked of all of its meaning and has now become "anything I don't like."
> (Anderson, 2022, para. 3)

Other efforts came from influential people who have worked to render CRT toxic so that Americans would associate it with negativity and craziness (Ladson-Billings in Anderson, 2022). Benson (2022) described the fervor over CRT as fueled by the erosion of news media within a capitalist society where more and more Americans "consume news through hyper-partisan cable news networks" combined with "social media that comports with their individual ideological preference; the decrying of CRT in schools as the latest iteration of historically-reliable White Backlash; and a highly-effective conservative messaging apparatus skilled in fomenting White Rage based on disinformation" (p. 1). Benson (2022) continued, "The modern conservative media machine push[es] fake news highlighting the (non-existent) issue of CRT in primarily suburban public schools as an exemplification of White Rage to protect whiteness and its hegemony for political gain" (p. 1). The CRT example shows how quickly the rhetoric of the powerful can become accepted as truth. What has followed is the shuttering of DEI offices in both public and private institutions and a sanitizing of equity-related language in many organizations from universities, with 25 states passing legislation regulating DEI (Gretzinger et al., 2024), to corporations like the Tractor Supply Company that cut back its DEI and climate goals after a conservative pressure campaign (Treisman, 2024).

how people think about disability as not a medical construct, but rather a social construct. Hall (2019) described it as calling for social justice and emancipation commitment. Kwon (2024) urged human resource development to be more inclusive of people with disabilities in research and practice, where it is viewed as a broader diversity concern, integrated into the curriculum, creating disability-friendly cultures in academia and the profession, and expanding advocacy globally. He offered a vision of a "world where disability is not treated as disability but as one of many forms of human diversity" (p. 157).

Critical Human Resource Development (CHRD). Critical human resource development (CHRD) emerged in the early 2000s and shares goals similar to critical management studies (CMS), focusing on human resource activities and how they can create inequity and injustice in organizations. **Critical human resource development** challenges the concept of HRD practice that privileges managers and profits over people. CHRD advocates for HRD to be socially conscious, responsible, and just to multiple stakeholders. Some key problems CHRD addresses are treating workers more like commodities than humans; privileging management and shareholder interests above all others, such as employees, communities, families, customers, and the environment; unquestioning acceptance of managerial power and dominance; and adopting traditional organization structures and reward systems (Bierema, 2010). Bierema et al. (2024) offered a theoretical and practical discussion of CHRD in their textbook.

Critical Management Studies (CMS). Emerging in 1992, Critical Management Studies (CMS) evaluates management theory and practice and questions the "truths" that tend to preserve power among managers and executives, typically White men (Alvesson & Willmott, 1992). Its goals include fostering insight, providing critique, and creating a "transformative redefinition" of organization practices, cultures, and structures (Alvesson & Deetz, 1996). Critical theory informs CMS's effort to "challenge the legitimacy and counter the development of oppressive institutions and practices" (Alvesson & Willmott, 1996, p. 13), and its vision is to emancipate workers and create more accountability for managers whose acts impact the lives of employees and other stakeholders (Alvesson & Willmott, 1996). Within this perspective, management and business are privileged above all other interests, sometimes called **managerialism**. CMS is concerned with marginalized people in organizations and management relationships.

Critical Race Theory (CRT). Critical race theory (CRT) was introduced earlier in this chapter and emerged from a 1970s legal movement to critique and protest the languishing progress of the 1960s US Civil Rights Movement. Delgado and Stefancic (2023) defined **critical race theory** as "a collection of activists and scholars engaged in studying and transforming the relationship among race, racism, and power" (p. 3). The key tenets of CRT are (1) racism is ordinary, occurring in day-to-day life; (2) racism benefits the dominant group, also known as White supremacy; (3) race and races are socially constructed phenomena that are invented, manipulated, or retired when convenient; (4) society engages in differential racialization at different times, for example, the demand for migrant workers, disfavor of Japanese during World War II and internment in camps in the United States, Japanese colonization of Korea during World War II that forced women into sexual slavery as "Comfort Women," or the distrust of Middle Easterners as security threats post 9/11; (5) people are complex and have intersectional identities that cannot be essentialized (e.g., assuming Black people all have similar tastes); and (6) people of color have a unique voice and experience to discuss the effects of race and racism (Delgado & Stefancic, 2023).

CRT challenges us as learners and citizens to confront the role of law in upholding White supremacy. Today, CRT has become a movement in other disciplines, such as education, sociology, and women's studies, that seeks to promote understanding of the social and experiential context of racism. It is considered *oppositional scholarship*; that is, it challenges the experience of Whites as the normative standard. Zamudio et al.'s (2010) explanation remains relevant today:

> As a society, we like to believe that racism is no longer a salient social problem since it has been illegal for over 50 years. Most of us have never lived in a society where slavery was accepted, land was stolen, and segregation was legally enforced. Critical race theorists believe that not only does racial inequality continue to be embedded in the legal system . . . but that racial inequality permeates every aspect of social life. (p. 3)

White privilege is a "truth" that goes unchallenged by Whites, who often live unaware of the advantages conferred by their skin color: "Whites don't see their viewpoints as a matter of perspective. They see it as truth" (Taylor, 1998, p. 122). Box 3.4 highlights a famous article and accompanying video about racism.

Decoloniality. **Decoloniality** is a perspective and practice that strives to create justice by dismantling injustices created by colonialism—when a country occupies another country and foists its culture and traditions on the new context (see, for example, de Sousa Santos, 2015; Maldonado-Torres, 2008; Mignolo, 2011; Quijano, 2000; Wa Thiong'o, 1998). The process involves

 ## Box 3.4 Tips and Tools for Teaching and Learning

Exploring White Privilege: Unpacking the Invisible Knapsack by Peggy McIntosh (1988)

As an adult learner or educator,

1. Read this classic anti-racist article at http://www.nymbp.org/reference/WhitePrivilege.pdf.
2. View Peggy McIntosh describing the transformation that led her to write this piece: http://www.youtube.com/watch?v=DRnoddGTMTY.

Questions for Discussion:

1. How did this article or video help you reflect on your assumptions?
2. How will this information influence future thought and action?

examining asymmetrical power relations created by colonialism and reclaiming indigenous knowledge and culture lost in the imposition of colonial rule. For example, slavery in the United States was a product of colonization. Slavery was outlawed after the Civil War, yet artifacts of racism and slavery continue to shape every aspect of American society, including educational, economic, social, political, and cultural systems.

Feminism and Feminist Pedagogy. **Feminism** concerns women and other marginalized social groups, highlighting inequality in politics, economics, and society. Feminism is not only concerned with the individual experience of women but also how social forces create marginalizing conditions for women, such as being segregated into gendered jobs or receiving less pay than men for comparable skill and work. **Feminist pedagogy** seeks to create learning environments where learners can critique social conditions and understand how their gender, race, sexuality, class, or other identities affect their personal, work, and social lives. Feminist pedagogy (hooks, 1994) principles parallel good adult education. When educators teach from this perspective, as a learner, you can expect them to: Share authority and decision-making with learners, candidly discuss how power dynamics affect the topic, honor the experience of you and other learners, analyze the effects of background and status on social life, empower learners through creating respectful environments where they have multiple opportunities to be heard, help learners develop voice, address power relations and authority as they arise in the classroom, challenge learners to think critically, raise issues related to sexism and heterosexism, and consider how society can be transformed. See Maher and Tetreault (1994, 2001) for a classic discussion of feminist pedagogy and Almanssori (2020) for a genealogical literature review.

Intersectionality. **Intersectionality** is how people's multifaceted, overlapping identities mold how they experience the world and how others perceive and treat them (Crenshaw, 1989). Intersectionality emerged from Black feminism to convey the complex and unique experiences of women of color that could not be explained by separately analyzing either gender or race. Intersectionality was born out of Black women's exasperation that feminist theory and activism centered on White middle-class women. Black feminism emphasizes Black or African American women's experiences and how they are affected by the interlocking forces of racism, sexism, and other isms. Black feminism (Collins, 1990, 2022) is also called womanism, Afrocentric feminism, and Africana womanism (Collins, 1990, 2022). Collins (1990) advanced Black Feminist Thought, advocating the diversity of Black women yet providing a shared basis for examining and understanding Black women's experiences. The meaning of intersectionality has been broadened to acknowledge the existence of people's multiple social identities and the complex ways they intertwine, interconnect mutually, and are socially constructed (Bowleg, 2008; Collins & Bilge, 2020). Intersectionality plays out in adult learning in the multiple ways people learn and make meaning of their experiences across the lifespan.

Inquiry-based Meaning-making and Research Approaches. There are excellent critical **cooperative** or **collaborative inquiry tools** where a learning community works together to critically reflect on their assumptions and practices to make better-informed decisions or jointly conduct research to address challenges. Call-Cummings et al. (2023) defined **critical participatory inquiry** (CPI) as "a form of inquiry that questions the status quo and oppressive systems, all for the purpose of co-constructing equitable knowledge systems and pushing for transformative change" (p. 7). **Participatory action research (PAR)** connects critical emancipatory action research and participation (Stephen & Robin, 2000). "PAR claims to further change processes in constructive, nonviolent ways due to its emphases on awareness-building processes, although it does anticipate revolutionary action in cases of collective frustration or belligerent reactionary violence applied at base levels and groups" (Fals-Borda, 1987, p. 329). Call-Cummings et al. (2023) described **critical participatory action research (CPAR)** as "a 'disciplined' way of making change because many of the kinds of changes that occur in our lives are imposed, apparently random, or ill considered" (p. 18). They viewed it as a vehicle for dialogue and conversation to make meaning. Kemmis et al. (2014) noted engaging in CPAR "expresses a commitment to bring together broad social analysis, the self-reflective collective self-study of practice, and transformational action to improve things" (p. 12). When change is compulsory, it can frustrate adults and foster dissatisfaction and alienation in life and work. Call-Cummings et al. (2023) offered CPAR to reshape life and work to actively and thoughtfully change problematic conditions.

Multiculturalism. **Multiculturalism** is a perspective that values diverse and multiple cultures within a society. Rather than seeking the "melting pot" status where many cultures meld together into one, multiculturalism respects the unique identities and contributions of individuals and their cultures. Multicultural education is concerned with providing strategies for educators to create democratic, inclusive learning environments that honor the cultural diversity of learners. Multicultural education recognizes that curricular decisions are political and that material selection is influenced by the instructor's philosophical outlook and own culture. Educators who take a multicultural perspective reflect on the consequences of their philosophical outlook and chosen pedagogy and develop an awareness of how their social status affects how they address multicultural issues. Multiculturally sensitive educators will strive to provide a range of readings by diverse authors rather than those who represent dominant groups. They will also honor diverse perspectives and create opportunities for learners to share their voices. An important outcome of multicultural education is the creation of inclusive learning environments for adult learners (see Tisdell (1995) for a discussion of inclusion and Sheared et al. (2010) for an extensive discussion of multiculturalism in adult education).

Postmodernism and Post-Postmodernism. Postmodernism, like critical theory, emerged in the 20th century. **Postmodernism** critiques what are considered "absolute truths" or "metanarratives" (Lyotard, 1984). Postmodernism arose as a reaction to **modernism,** or the early 20th-century rejection of traditional culture focused on experimentation, abstraction, and the subjective experience of the individual. A metanarrative is a grand story or shared historical account of unquestioned events. Postmodernism questions the validity of these metanarratives. An example of a metanarrative in the United States is that everyone has an equal chance to succeed or that over-the-top consumerism and consumption are indicators of success. Brookfield (2000) noted metanarratives impacting adult education with the following postmodernist critique: "Adult education grand narratives of self-direction, andragogy or perspective transformation are seen as illusory, representative chiefly of our desire to impose a fictional, conceptual order on the chaotic fragmentation of learning and practice" (p. 34). His postmodern analysis rejected the belief that educational meaning is transparent or shared. Bierema et al. (2024) identified key metanarratives in human resource development, such as the "learning versus performance" debate, which holds true neither in research nor practice.

Postmodernists believe knowledge can emerge from a particular context or event and shift as the context, learner, or events change. Postmodernists acknowledge that a person's experience of a specific context or event will differ from the next person's. Correspondingly, postmodernists do not believe there is a single rule for judging the validity of knowledge and will question anything presented as knowledge. Postmodernists deconstruct "knowledge" to discover discourses or assertions about what is right, good, or normal. For example, postmodernists question the use of binaries such as good/bad, right/wrong, boy/girl, and teacher/student in which the *order* of the terms (note which terms are first) conveys which term is more powerful and preferred. Postmodern critique looks for distortion of meaning as a means to gain or retain power, with the understanding that power is present in relationships, not held by one individual. **Post-postmodernism** criticizes the "anything goes" ethos of post-modernism and is an emergent attempt to connect faith, trust, dialogue, performance, and sincerity, especially in a social context dictated by digital communication and the lack of authentic connection between people.

Post-structuralism. **Post-structuralism** (Derrida, 1976, 1981) emerged in the late 20th century to challenge structuralism—the belief in a single, objective truth, which simplified human experience across the lifespan to the most basic of components with no appreciation for complexity or diversity or the questioning of "truths" professed by the powerful, as have been detailed throughout this chapter. Post-structuralism is the process of questioning binaries' essentialist identities—important in understanding intersectionality, which is a foregrounded emphasis in the second edition of *Adult Learning: Linking Theory and Practice* as adults grapple with learning and change in a VUCA context as discussed in Chapter 1. Post-structuralism questions widely accepted beliefs that reinforce power dynamics, such as "your gender identity is the sex (female or male) you were born with." It highlights marginalized voices, as is evident in the #MeToo and Black Lives Matter movements. From the current backlash against transgender people and insensitivity toward gender identity to "gender reveal parties," the clash between structuralist and post-structuralist interpretations of gender is unmistakable.

Queer Studies. Different from Queer Theory (an analysis within queer studies that challenges how we socially construct categories of sexuality), queer studies emerged approximately 40 years ago. It is a multidisciplinary field grounded in critical theory that explores power relations related to sexuality and gender identity with a focus on LGBTQIA+ (lesbians, gays, bisexuals, transgender individuals, queers, intersex individuals, asexuals, and others). The development of this critical perspective has been influenced by Judith Butler (1990) and Michael Foucault (1978), as well as Gayle Rubin, Leo Bersani, and Eve Kosofsky Sedwick, among many others (Warner, 2012). Similar to critical theory's critique of social conditions and challenging truths, queer studies confront how ideologies of sexuality have developed to privilege heterosexuality as the norm. Queer studies examines queer influences in society and is also concerned with their relationship to the social and political oppression of marginalized people based on gender, race, and class.

So far, this chapter has discussed what it means to be critical, defined critical theory, and identified some key critical perspectives influenced by critical theory. Next, the focus returns to the *Being Critical Framework* to understand how critical thinking and action relate to adult learning and education.

Critical Thinking

The notion of critical thinking is traceable to ancient Greece, where intellectuals generally believed that immutable "truths" existed and that it was the task of great minds to discover them. For Plato (427–347 BC) and his followers, truths were universal, eternal, remote from ordinary life, and accessible only to privileged men philosophers. Conversely, falsehoods "were commonplace and could, when unmanaged, cause untold mischief, especially when generally believed by citizens in that worst of all political systems, democracy" (Doughty, 2006, p. 1), not unlike today. Another Greek philosopher, Socrates (470–399 BC), "spent his time bantering with a local audience . . . . He could be expected to undo the errors of his colleagues by the use of brisk 'Socratic' cross-examination. By these lights, critical thinking meant the exposure of foolishness by someone wise enough to engage winningly in discussion" (Doughty, 2006, p. 2). A more modern take on critical thinking is that it is not the sole province of the elite, nor are there universal "truths," as Plato believed. Further, there are more educational methods to stimulate critical thinking than just the Socratic method of questioning learners through vigorous discussion. Box 3.5 provides critical thinking resources for further study.

Defining Critical Thinking

Critical thinking—the ability to assess your assumptions, beliefs, and actions as an adult learner—is imperative to survival; failure to engage in it makes you a target of those who may wish to harm or manipulate you (Brookfield, 2012).

> Intellectually engaged, skillful and responsible thinking that facilitates good judgment, critical thinking requires the application of assumptions, knowledge, competence and the ability to challenge one's own thinking. Critical thinking skills require self-correction, monitoring to judge the reasonableness of thinking, and reflexivity. (Behar-Horenstein & Niu, 2011, p. 26)

 **Box 3.5 Tips and Tools for Teaching and Learning**

Critical Thinking Resources

If you, as an adult learner or educator, wish to take a deeper dive into critical thinking, check out these resources.

Critical Thinking.NET | http://www.criticalthinking.net/

This site provides a rigorous collection of critical thinking resources and information developed by Robert H. Ennis and Sean F. Ennis.

The Foundation for Critical Thinking | https://www.criticalthinking.org/

The Foundation and Center for Critical Thinking homepage is where you can find resources, books, professional development opportunities, research, conferences, assessment and testing, and online learning related to critical thinking. Here you can also find the Critical Thinking Assessment: http://www.criticalthinking .org/pages/critical-thinking-testing-and-assessment/594

If you are unable to think critically, you will not be able to defend yourself or ultimately get the outcomes you desire. Effective critical thinking is vital to making good decisions throughout life such as relationship choices (friendships, dating), career selection, political orientation, dietary options, financial strategies, living situation, and child rearing (Brookfield, 2012). Brookfield (2012) defined critical thinking in education:

> Critical thinking describes the process by which students become aware of two sets of assumptions. First, students investigate the assumptions held by scholars in a field of study regarding the way legitimate knowledge is created and advanced in that field. Second, students investigate their own assumptions and the way these frame their own thinking and actions. Thinking critically requires us to check the assumptions that we hold, by assessing the accuracy and validity of the evidence for these assumptions and by looking at ideas and actions from multiple perspectives. A person who thinks critically is much better placed to take informed actions; actions that are well grounded in evidence and that are more likely to achieve the results intended. (p. 157)

Although researchers and educators agree on the importance of teaching critical thinking (Roth, 2010), there is less agreement on the best ways to promote it through teaching (Tsui, 2002). The first edition of *Adult Learning: Linking Theory and Practice* introduced a framework for being critical as a way to make these concepts more accessible to the reader. The second edition builds on that framework.

Brookfield (2012) defined critical thinking as incorporating four activities: (1) hunting assumptions, (2) checking assumptions, (3) seeing things from different viewpoints, and (4) taking informed action. He emphasized that the heart of critical thinking effectiveness is *not* the first three steps but the fourth—taking action grounded in analysis and evidence. Box 3.6 explains this thinking approach.

Without the final step—taking informed action—you have engaged in critical reflection but have not taken the key action step toward development or change. The last step is crucial to applying critical thinking to reality. Box 3.7 provides an alternative way to understand critical thinking or the lack thereof.

Critical thinking "is a way of living that helps you stay intact when any number of organizations (corporate, political, educational, and cultural) are trying to get you to think and act in ways that serve their purposes" (Brookfield, 2012, p. 2). This chapter featured several examples of this phenomenon, including the Holocaust, the Civil Rights Movement, economic crisis, corporate

 **Box 3.6 Reflective Practice**

Applying the Four Steps of Critical Thinking

Brookfield (2012) explained that critical thinking has four key aspects. This box defines each one with examples and questions you might ask yourself as an adult learner who is thinking critically. The examples and questions involve how someone might think critically while attending a leadership seminar (a formal adult education activity). During the workshop, several ideas and new concepts about leadership are presented, causing the learner to wonder.

Aspect of Critical Thinking	Definition	Asks	Example	Questions: The learner begins to wonder . . .
1. Hunting Assumptions	Questioning taken-for-granted beliefs about the world.	*"What do I believe?"*	The speaker is talking about key leadership definitions and points.	*"What does the speaker really believe about leadership?"* *"What do I believe about it?"*
2. Checking Assumptions	Naming and questioning the beliefs that underlie how you make sense of the world.	*"Are these assumptions valid and reliable?"*	The speaker is talking about the behaviors of effective leaders.	*"Is what the speaker is telling me logical? Do I agree with their perspective?"*
3. Seeing Things from Different Viewpoints	Considering a situation or idea from an alternative perspective.	*"How else could I think about this?"*	The speaker introduces a leadership model you were unfamiliar with.	*"What would happen if I tried that leadership strategy?"*
4. Taking Informed Action	Deciding how your learning and information available will shape your subsequent behaviors, choices, or plans.	*"Now that I have thought about it, I am going to . . ."*	The speaker has inspired you to change your leadership behavior when you return to your workplace or community.	*"The first thing I am going to do when I return to my office is to . . ."*

Now that you have the examples in this box, work on applying critical thinking to yourself using an assumption, new learning, or firmly held belief, and work through the four steps of critical thinking. The point is not necessarily to change your beliefs or actions but to contemplate them and decide whether to change.

 ## Box 3.7 Adult Learning and Teaching Cases

Jake the Yellow Labrador and Being Critical

This case study features one of the authors (Laura) who has a story that puts hegemony and being critical in perspective. See if you can relate the story to yourself or others as an adult learner and observer of behavior.

I was sitting in my upstairs home office working one afternoon in Ann Arbor, Michigan. My next-door neighbor, Kent, was hosting his mother for several days and working on renovations in his kitchen. His spouse was traveling, and his daughter, Kelly, who was at work, had a yellow lab named Jake—a big, lovable pup. Kelly's grandmother was instructed not to walk the dog because she was a slight woman without much strength or dog savvy who likely weighed less than the dog. Kent's mother was hovering over his repairs, and he finally told her to leave the kitchen and find something else to do while he finished his work. So, the grandmother decided, perilously, to walk the dog. She leashed Jake and headed out the back door, unbeknownst to Kent.

Immediately upon getting outside, Jake began pulling, which was too much for her to handle. Meanwhile, while still working in my office, I heard a commotion and thought someone was trying to break into my house. Moments later, I saw Kent, a proud couch potato, racing down the street barefooted. I ran downstairs to see what was wrong and came upon his mother standing in my yard sobbing so hard I could not understand a word. Eventually, the story came out: Upon getting outside with the dog, Kent's mom knew it was a mistake and decided to attach his leash to a Weber grill for a minute to get Kent's help. Within seconds, Jake pulled on his leash, the grill toppled over, and he was spooked. Jake took off racing down the middle of the street, clanging grill in tow. Kent found poor Jake after he had run down our street, across four lanes of traffic, through downtown, winding up on the University of Michigan Campus Diag. Several students came to the rescue, trying to calm Jake and remove what little was left of the grill from the leash. Poor Jake's foot pads were raw and bloodied, and Kent carried him home, later walking back down the street to retrieve the broken bits of the Weber grill scattered along the way. Jake healed, the grandmother bought a new grill, and everyone had grilled steak that night. Jake was never quite the same, though.

So, how does Jake the Dog's debacle relate to being critical?

1. When the grill toppled over, Jake assumed it was attacking him, so he decided to run. Perhaps the thought "A grill is chasing me!" ran through his mind.
2. Jake did not hunt assumptions. Although Jake is a dog, people behave similarly and react to their immediate conclusion without pausing to investigate further.
3. Because there was no hunting of assumptions, they could not be checked, weighed, or result in any action other than bolting, which was a hazardous reaction.
4. Jake's action put him in harm's way, even though he thought the safe thing to do was run away from the grill, which equates to a hegemonic act.

Questions for Reflection:

1. When did you or someone you know behave like Jake?
2. Have you had a thought or ideology that ultimately caused you to see a situation incorrectly? What was it? How did it influence your thoughts and actions?
3. What might have been different if there had been critical thinking in the moment?
4. How can you deliberately incorporate critical thinking into your decision processes?

mismanagement and mis-messaging, and social movements. Issues that require critical thinking may be as personal as deciding what brand of coffee is most environmentally sustainable, to joining a local political campaign to elect a candidate who supports community issues, to demonstrating in national protests such as the "Black Lives Matter" and "#MeToo" movements, to supporting international protests over war. Box 3.8 illuminates what sets critical thinkers apart from others.

What does critical thinking look like? The next sections follow the characteristics introduced in Box 3.5 and discuss how critical thinking is grounded in reflection, involves a critique of thought and action, and connects our individual experiences to broader social conditions as adult learners and educators.

Reflecting on Assumptions and Beliefs

Critical thinking begins with examining your assumptions as a learner, educator, or citizen. An **assumption** is a deeply held belief that guides your thoughts and actions. Brookfield (2012) classified assumptions into three categories: prescriptive, paradigmatic, and causal. **Prescriptive assumptions** are our beliefs

 ## Box 3.8 Reflective Practice

Things Critical Thinkers Do That Set Them Apart from Noncritical Thinkers

Ennis (1989) posited that critical thinkers possess particular abilities that distinguish them from those not exhibiting critical thinking. These include the following:

- Assume a position or change it based on the evidence
- Remain relevant to the point
- Seek information and precision in the information sought
- Exhibit open-mindedness
- Consider the big picture
- Focus on the original problem
- Search for reasons
- Orderly consider complex components of problems
- Seek a clear statement of the problem
- Search for options
- Show sensitivity to others' feelings and knowledge
- Use credible sources

How well are you emulating these behaviors in your learning or teaching as an adult learner or educator? What do you need to work on next?

about how we should behave. As educators, we may have certain prescriptive beliefs about teaching ("I *should* be able to facilitate group conflict," "I *need* to treat everyone equally," and so on). What are some prescriptive assumptions you hold? **Paradigmatic assumptions** are deeply held beliefs or mental models that shape how we view the world, like the ideologies discussed earlier in this chapter. These assumptions are so deeply embedded that it may be difficult to articulate them or surprising once we discover what they are. A mental model or paradigmatic assumption that has permeated adult education is **humanism—** the belief in all people's inherent good and potential. This paradigm underlies much modern-day adult education practice, such as andragogy, self-directed learning, experiential learning, and transformational learning. Patriarchy is another example of a dominant paradigmatic assumption. All of us participate in this system that protects White masculine power. As educators, we may be shocked to discover that we call on men more often in the classroom, yet this is one unconscious way teachers, whether women or men, preserve masculine power and protect what has been described as a "chilly climate" in university classrooms (see Hall & Sandler, 1982; Lee & McCabe, 2021; Seifried 2000). Students rate men higher than women professors when they teach identical courses, further illustrating this sexist culture (Mitchell & Martin, 2018).

We, as authors, are all surprised in our own teaching how often women students defer power to the men in the classroom (even when men are a distinct minority). Students are usually shocked and embarrassed when we point out that they just engaged in a patriarchy-preserving act with their deference to the men learners. **Causal assumptions** allow us to both explain and predict circumstances. For instance, if I do "X," then "Y" will occur. Most of us have been told, "Do Unto Others as You Wish to Have Done Unto You." Yet, through trial and error, we have probably learned that doing good deeds does not always mean they return to you. What are some causal assumptions you hold? How comfortable are you discussing them with others? Box 3.9 summarizes how to see dialogue as a reflexive practice.

Box 3.9 Tips and Tools for Teaching and Learning

Engaging in Dialogue as a Critically Reflective Practice

The art of deep, meaningful conversation seems lost most days when we turn on the radio or news as interested citizens. Often, we hear people interrupting, dismissing, and dissing each other in their advocacy for their point of view over any other. If explored linguistically, discussion came from the Latin *discutere,* literally translated as "smash to pieces." When you get into a heated discussion, you are likely advocating your opinion to get others to agree. You might tend to dig in your heels and defend it even more vigorously when they do not. The discussion is like a boxing match between ideas, with each boxer angling to win and throwing punches whenever possible. Yet, agitated discussion is not the only model of discourse. Neither is it conducive to effective communication because it puts us, as listeners or learners, in a defensive stance.

One alternative to combative discussion is **dialogue** or listening to create new understandings or meanings about the issue. When you enter into dialogue, your goal is not to prove a point or get others to agree with you. Instead, it is an inquiry or exploration of questions and assumptions with the goal of learning and creating new meaning. It respects competing perspectives and invites people to hunt assumptions about their thinking or issues.

Paulo Freire described dialogue as "the encounter between [people], mediated by the world, in order to name the world." This Infed entry describes his notions of dialogue and learning: http://www.infed.org/biblio/b-dialog.htm

Dialogue is easy to practice, and one of the authors (Laura) shares a module on effective dialogue with every class she teaches. Here are the basic principles of dialogue:

1. Suspend judgment of ideas and their rightness or wrongness.
2. Identify assumptions behind ideas.
3. Listen more than you talk.
4. Inquire into others' views and reflect on the information.
5. Practice the "Edge of the Seat Test":

> When you are poised (either physically or mentally) on the edge of your seat, waiting for the speaker to either take a breath or stop talking so you can insert your "superior" point of view, that means YOU ARE NOT LISTENING! Sit back, take a deep breath, and listen. Get off the edge of your seat!

Here are some tips for how you can start practicing dialogue:

- Practice listening and asking questions instead of offering opinions for one week. Assess results.
- Read about learning.
- Look up learning and dialogue websites.
- Target one person with whom you rarely have dialogue, and practice dialogue strategies with them for one month. Assess results.
- Visit a therapist and critique their ability to dialogue.
- Practice dialogue with a family member regularly.
- Have a dialogue with yourself (or your dog).
- Make a list of people who are effective at dialogue and identify why.
- Challenge discussant's to dialogue.
- Have a discussion followed by a dialogue on the same issue. Compare results.
- Identify films with great dialogue scenes.
- Start a collection of great quotes about dialogue and learning.
- Identify and be aware of your assumptions.

- Observe silence.
- Ask questions from a "place of genuine not knowing." Work on increasing skills of inquiry. Ask or State:
  - *"Say more about that . . ."*
  - *"Why?"*
  - *"Help me understand your thinking . . ."*
  - *"What questions do you have about this . . . ?"*
  - *"What questions does this idea raise?"*
  - *"Tell me what assumptions underlie your thinking."*
  - *"I understand."*
  - *"I never thought about it that way before."*
  - *"What other ways could we look at this?"*
  - *"What collective assumptions do we share?"*
  - *"I like your thinking."*
  - *"I wonder . . ."*
  - *"Where I am on this issue now is . . . . Where are you?"*
- Assume a viewpoint opposite of yours. Live it for a day.
- Breathe instead of speaking. Close your eyes and listen.
- Change your mind.
- Help other people learn to practice dialogue and action learning.
- Notice your internal responses and learning that coexists with them. Silently reflect on these without feeling you must verbalize them.
- Give up seeking blame.
- Think and act counter to a society addicted to speed. Slow down.
- Listen deeply. Neither fix, nor counter, nor argue the issue.
- Keep a learning journal.
- Teach someone about dialogue.

Critiquing Thought and Action

The next important aspect of critical thinking is to shift critique to thought and action as a learner or educator. Brookfield (2012) offered an excellent framework that includes hunting assumptions, checking assumptions, seeing things from different viewpoints, and taking informed action. **Hunting assumptions** involves trying to identify what underlies our thoughts and actions. Hunting assumptions is an effort to unearth what you believe and determine its accuracy. We spend our days acting on assumptions that are grounded in our experience. These actions are often embedded in deeply socialized gender roles. Imagine a woman's dog barking and pacing near his dish. She assumes the dog is hungry, so she feeds him. You may not think that making assumptions about pet care is as deeply embedded as those linked to dominant ideology, like patriarchy. Yet perhaps the woman has internalized feeding the dog as part of her role in the home. Like many other women, there are probably dozens of actions this woman takes daily that are deeply embedded in patriarchy that she does not stop to question, such as caregiving, unpaid labor in the home, playing a nurturing role in relationships, deferring to her spouse when it comes to career decisions. Brookfield refers to this behavior as **"instrumental reasoning"** (p. 8) or figuring out how to fix something without questioning whose interests are served by the fixing.

Next is **checking assumptions.** Once we become aware of assumptions as learners, educators, or citizens, we need to assess their accuracy. We may seek evidence from experience, authorities, or even disciplined research. We can consider another gendered home care example: mowing the lawn. This home maintenance activity is overwhelmingly considered "men's work." Suppose we are in the critical thinking mode of checking assumptions. In that case, we might ask how other men (and women) expect men to unquestioningly accept and adopt the home-maintenance roles in their families. The third step is **seeing things from different viewpoints.** hooks (2010) suggested that an open mind is essential for critical thinking and asked her students to embrace "radical openness" (p. 10) because we become overly attached to our own ideas and discount other ideas without even assessing them. Taking a different viewpoint in the lawn mowing example might involve seeking out other men who do not play this role in their families or women who mow their lawns and understanding their perspectives and behaviors. Finally, **taking informed action** is the last step and key goal0 of critical thinking. The man who mows the lawn may decide it is time to renegotiate tasks in his home or discuss assumptions about his role with his family, as does the woman shouldering the responsibility of feeding the dog and providing significant amounts of dependent care. Taking informed action will be more extensively discussed later in this chapter.

Connecting Individual Experience to Broader Social Conditions

Critical thinking might make you, as an adult learner, think of someone deep in thought as they contemplate ideas or events, whether at work, school, or home. Although this is often the case, individual critical thinking can be shared and sometimes merged into collective reflection on assumptions and beliefs. That is not to say that everyone will agree at the end of the collective dialogue, but that conditions were created for joint assessment of assumptions.

Critical thinking becomes powerful when we understand how our individual experience is not unique to us but that others may be caught in the same dominant ideology that is hurting them. Brookfield (2012) emphasized "critical thinking is a social learning process" (p. 229). hooks (2010) advocated, "Critical thinking is an interactive process, one that demands participation on the part of the teacher and students alike" (p. 9). She also argued that it requires everyone to engage fully. Box 3.10 shares hooks's legacy.

As adult educators, we often seek to create these collective critical thinking conditions in our classrooms, where we raise challenging issues for learners to consider. Critical thinking becomes most powerful when we connect our

---

 Box 3.10 SoTL: The Scholarship of Teaching and Learning

The Contributions of bell hooks to Critical Thinking and Critical Feminist Pedagogy

bell hooks (1952–2021) has been described as "one of the preeminent feminist voices of our time" (Berea College, n.d., para. 1), writing over 30 books, including a book influential in adult education and critical pedagogy circles, *Teaching to Transgress* (hooks, 1994). She wrote:

> To educate as the practice of freedom is a way of teaching that anyone can learn. That learning process comes easiest to those of us who teach who also believe that there is an aspect of our vocation that is sacred; who believe that our work is not merely to share information but to share in the intellectual and spiritual growth of our students. To teach in a manner that respects and cares for the souls of our students is essential if we are to provide the necessary conditions where learning can most deeply and intimately begin. (p. 13)

Teaching to Transgress offers reflections and strategies for reimagining education as liberation, challenging dominant narratives, enhancing critical thinking and creativity, and using education as a tool of social change.

bell hooks died in 2021. Her institution, Berea College, has this tribute on its website: https://www.berea.edu/centers/the-bell-hooks-center/about-bell and a video of people discussing her impact on their lives and work: https://youtu.be/m6ZL-YxSrDQ.

ideas and experiences to broader social issues. For instance, one of the authors—Laura—once worked in corporate America. At the time, she was not a feminist and did not put much stock in the cause. Then, she started constantly bumping up against patriarchy by being invisible, harassed, questioned, and singled out as representative of all women. She felt isolated and alone for a long time and thought something was wrong with her. When she finally discovered feminist critique and learned that there were philosophies that questioned social conditions and truths like critical theory, it was cathartic. Suddenly, she could connect her individual experience with social situations and see how her participation in this culture was harmful. She has never been quite the same, embarking on a new academic career aimed at exposing inequities in the workplace—thinking critically and taking action for social change. Box 3.11 presents a critical thinking activity.

 ## Box 3.11 Tips and Tools for Teaching and Learning

Quotes to Affirm and Challenge

Adult education scholar Steven Brookfield recommended the "Quotes to Affirm and Challenge" activity in his textbook *Teaching for Critical Thinking* (pp. 114–118). The activity engages adult learners in a dialogue about positionality, privilege, context, and power. You can do this activity as an educator or learner interested in practicing critical thinking. Steps:

1. The purpose of this assignment is to invite learners to critically reflect on the readings and experience a "critical thinking" activity intended to help them unearth assumptions.
2. Learners review the assigned readings and:
   a. Choose one quote they wish to affirm.
   b. Choose one quote they want to challenge.
3. During class, students share their quotes in small groups (with appropriate credits to the source) and a brief rationale for their selections.
4. Learners discuss the quotes.
5. Next, learners engage in a reflective audit by discussing the following questions:
   a. What quotes did you select, and why did you originally pick them?
   b. If you had to do this exercise again using the same text, would you still choose these quotes?

c. If "yes," explain. If "no," what altered your original choice?

d. What was the pair of quotes posed by another person that you chose to discuss, and why did you select them? As you dialogued with other students, what new information or perspectives did you learn about the topic? If nothing new to you emerged, what parts of your thinking were confirmed?

e. What does your participation in this exercise tell you about your own thinking patterns on this topic? What arguments or what kinds of evidence are you drawn to, what constitutes good research or scholarship on this topic, and what constitutes poor research or scholarship?

Resource for Further Learning:

Brookfield, S. (2012). *Teaching for critical thinking: Tools and techniques to help students question their assumptions.* Jossey-Bass.

A comprehensive text on facilitating critical thinking with adult learners with activities for beginning, intermediate, and advanced critical thinking.

Dr. Stephen Brookfield's Website | https://www.stephenbrookfield.com/
A website portal for Dr. Brookfield's work, books, articles, interviews, critical incident questionnaires, visuals, papers, and workshop materials.

Critical Action—Mindful and Timely Intervention

The crux of critical thinking is not simply engaging in it. It is using new insights to inform future actions. Without acting on new knowledge, all we have—as learners, workers, and citizens—is a collection of thoughts. Critical action emerges in three ways: (1) taking informed action, (2) monitoring and correcting ourselves, and (3) justifying our actions.

Taking Informed Action

Brookfield (2012) viewed informed action as basing our actions, as learners or educators, on some evidence that supports taking them. Of course, the quality of evidence you rely on will be important in how accurate your assumption was in the first place. Take medical doctors, for example. Most of us would assume that since they are knowledgeable and highly trained, they would be excellent critical thinkers. Not necessarily so. Overusing antibiotics for infections most likely caused by a virus is common, even though antibiotics do nothing to treat a viral infection. Rather than considering the best available evidence, decision-making may be motivated by patient expectations, an imperative to "don't just stand there, do something," and fear of undertreating a bacterial infection. If a patient is given an antibiotic but returns a few days later feeling no better, the critical thinker should question the underlying assumption that an antibiotic is appropriate. Instead, physicians too often fail to think critically and prescribe a different (more potent) antibiotic that is even more inappropriate for a likely viral infection (Ebell & Radke, 2015). A more critical approach would be to seek out the best research available in making treatment decisions.

What does it mean to take informed action? To break it down, **informed** means being knowledgeable, up-to-date, and conversant about personal, professional, community, and world concerns, usually based on the person's interests, responsibilities, and roles. **Action** requires mental or physical activity with the assumption that something will be done in response to a stimulus. For example, imagine you were walking through your neighborhood and witnessed a homeless person sitting on a curb with a sign asking for help. Being informed about homelessness means not simply making judgments about the circumstances the person is in but understanding how homelessness manifests. A misconception about homelessness is that it is a choice people make that might cause some people to blame people experiencing homelessness (Williamson & Brunjes, 2024). However, homelessness is a symptom of a systemic social problem caused by the decreasing availability of affordable housing and gentrification (Rukmana, 2020) and the deinstitutionalization of state mental hospitals, along with cuts in public welfare expenditures (Dear & Wolch, 2014). Although homelessness is a systemic problem, what do you do when you encounter a homeless individual in your community? When people ignore, make disparaging remarks toward, or harass the homeless, they are taking *uninformed action*. According to an opinion piece in the *New York Times*,

> Living in the city—especially in metropolises where homelessness is an unsolved, unending crisis—means that at some point in your day, or week, a person seeming (or claiming) to be homeless, or suffering with a disability, will ask you for help. You probably already have a panhandler policy. You keep walking, or not. You give, or not. Loose coins, a dollar, or just a shake of the head. Your rule may be blanket, or case-by-case. If it's case-by-case, that means you have your own on-the-spot, individualized

benefits program, with a bit of means-testing, mental health and character
assessment, and criminal-background check—to the extent that any of
this is possible from a second or two of looking someone up and down.
(The Editorial Board, *New York Times*, 2017, paras. 4–7)

What the editorial described is likely *uninformed action* toward people experiencing homelessness. While on a visit to New York in 2017 Pope Francis
offered the following advice when approached by panhandlers: "Giving something to someone in need is 'always right'" (para. 9). The editorial further
paraphrased the Pope, who elaborated on the *appropriate action*:

The way of giving is as important as the gift. You should not simply drop
a bill into a cup and walk away. You must stop, look the person in the
eyes, and touch his or her hands. The reason is to preserve dignity, to
see another person not as a pathology or a social condition, but as a
human, with a life whose value is equal to your own. (paras. 11–12)

The article called for actions of compassion and seeing the other person.
Acknowledgment is a basic humanity, and not doing so creates an inhuman
action toward a human in difficult times. The article spurred many people to
take more informed actions in their interactions with people in need.

Monitoring and Correcting Ourselves

"**Monitoring** is a self-regulatory process involved in making changes to behavior.
Monitoring involves a person, group, or organization taking stock of the current
situation, comparing this to some goal or reference value, and identifying
whether or not there is a discrepancy" (Webb & de Bruin, 2020, p. 537). Monitoring is a process of clarifying or changing thoughts and altering behavior and
doing so promptly. **Correcting** is an act to amend or counteract a faulty or
harmful perspective or action with a more constructive intervention.

Discrepancies between desired and actual actions can impel an adult learner
or educator to intervene to improve the next time. A challenge is that people
often fail to monitor their effectiveness at taking informed actions, creating "the
ostrich effect," essentially a cognitive bias that prevents people from processing
negative information or feedback that would help them improve future actions.
Failing to clarify thought or change behavior means there was ineffective monitoring. Returning to the homeless encounter in your neighborhood, imagine
you avert your eyes or pretend to be looking at your smartphone when you pass
the person. You feel a pang of guilt, but the next time you encounter another

homeless person, you do the same thing—your action remains unchanged. To effectively monitor and correct yourself means you must reflect on what you did, determine how you want to alter your behavior next time, and then act on it with timeliness.

Justifying Our Actions

What are other ways we, as aspiring critical thinkers, can take action on our critical thinking and justify or rationalize them? Being present or mindful in the moment of acting is one way. If you want to know whether you are doing this well as an adult learner or educator, assess how calm you can remain when things go awry. Critiquing your intentions, ideologies, and actions is another way to check how your mindful and timely intervention is going. Effective critical thinkers and actors monitor and correct themselves and their family, friends, coworkers, and neighbors when appropriate. Opportunities for such correction are plentiful in a classroom setting. Simple things like thinking out loud or articulating assumptions go a long way in opening up reflection and dialogue on our ideas. Brookfield (2012) stressed that it is essential for instructors to model these behaviors to foster critical thinking in learners. Once people become mindful of their assumptions, they can move into Brookfield's process of hunting, checking assumptions, and entertaining different viewpoints. When people do this, it creates conditions for individual and collective clarification of ideas and sometimes changes in ideology and behavior. Another key aspect of critical action is making timely interventions. Once critical thinkers have completed the critical thinking process, it is time to put our new perspectives into action in a way that does the most social good.

Critical thinking is not a neutral process because it asks you, as a learner, educator, or citizen, to question values and who benefits from your actions. Brookfield (2012) emphasized that "part of critical thinking is making sure that the actions that flow from our assumptions are justifiable according to some notion of goodness or desirability" (p. 15). The act of critical thinking becomes more complicated when we begin to understand the power relations tied to it. He further observed, "If critical thinking is understood only as a process of analyzing information so we can take actions that produce desired results, then some of the most vicious acts of human behavior could be defined as critical thinking" (p. 16). We cannot separate critical thinking from our morals and values. This connection is where it becomes crucial that the action be both mindful and timely: mindful in the sense that it has a moral or ethical basis and timely in that we do not wait to overthink acting when intervention is needed.

Chapter Summary

This chapter explored the process of "being critical" and the role of critical perspectives in adult learning by describing criticality as a philosophy, thinking process, and agenda for mindful and timely action on social problems and challenges. The chapter introduced key tenets of critical perspectives and adult learning, defined key concepts and terms, and applied these ideas to adult learning and life. Being critical is central to adulthood. As French mathematician, physicist, and philosopher Jules Henri Poincare observed, "To doubt everything or to believe everything are two equally convenient solutions; both dispense with the necessity of reflection" (1902/2017, Author's Preface).

Chapter Highlights

- Critical theory is a philosophical stance that critiques social conditions and challenges ideologies adults have come to accept as "truth" as a means of ending oppression and promoting emancipation.
- Critical thinking is a thought process of evaluating and critiquing assumptions.
- Critical theory and critical thinking help adult learners connect individual experiences to broader social conditions.
- Critical theory has influenced the development of critical perspectives across disciplines, including: postmodernism, feminist pedagogy, critical race theory, queer studies, multiculturalism, critical management studies, critical human resource development, and others.
- Being critical is grounded in critical theory and involves facilitating critical thinking and helping learners take timely action.

References

Almanssori, S. (2020). Feminist pedagogy from pre-access to post-truth: A genealogical literature review. *Canadian Journal for New Scholars in Education/Revue canadienne des jeunes chercheures et chercheurs en éducation, 11*(1), 54–68.

Alsaleh, N. J. (2020). Teaching critical thinking skills: Literature review. *Turkish Online Journal of Educational Technology-TOJET, 19*(1), 21–39. https://files.eric.ed.gov/fulltext/EJ1239945.pdf.

Alvesson, M., & Deetz, S. (1996). Critical theory and postmodernism approaches to organizational studies. In S. Clegg, C. Hardy, and W. Nord (Eds.). *Handbook of organizational studies* (pp. 191–217). Sage.

Alvesson, M., & Willmott, H. (Eds.). (1992). *Critical management studies.* Sage.

Alvesson, M. and Willmott, H. (1996). *Making sense of management: A critical introduction*. Sage.

Anderson, J. (2022, February 23). *The state of critical race theory in education: The pioneer of critical race theory in education discusses the current politicization and tension around teaching about race in the classroom*. Harvard Graduate School of Education. https://www.gse.harvard.edu/ideas/edcast/22/02/state-critical-race-theory-education.

Barnes, J. E., Thrush, G., & Myers, S. L. (2024, September 4). *US announces plan to counter Russian influence ahead of 2024 election*. The New York Times. https://www.nytimes.com/2024/09/04/us/politics/russia-election-influence.html.

Behar-Horenstein, L. S., & Niu, L. (2011). Teaching critical thinking skills in higher education: A review of the literature. *Journal of College Teaching & Learning, 8*(2), 25–41. https://core.ac.uk/download/pdf/268111091.pdf.

Bellaera, L., Weinstein-Jones, Y., Ilie, S., & Baker, S. T. (2021). Critical thinking in practice: The priorities and practices of instructors teaching in higher education. *Thinking Skills and Creativity, 41*, 100856. https://doi.org/10.1016/j.tsc.2021.100856.

Benson, K. E. (2022). Crying, "Wolf!" The campaign against critical race theory in American public schools as an expression of contemporary white grievance in an era of fake news. *Journal of Education and Learning, 11*(4), 1–14. https://doi.org/10.5539/jel.v11n4p1.

Berea College. (n.d.). *Getting to know bell hooks*. Berea College. https://www.berea.edu/centers/the-bell-hooks-center/about-bell.

Bierema, L. L. (2010). *Implementing a critical approach to organization development*. Krieger.

Bierema, L. L., Callahan, J. L., Elliott, C. J., Greer, T. W., & Collins, J. C. (2024). *Human resource development: Critical perspectives and practices*. Routledge.

Bowleg, L. (2008). When Black + lesbian + woman ≠ Black lesbian woman: The methodological challenges of qualitative and quantitative intersectionality research. *Sex Roles, 59*(5–6), 312–325. https://doi.org/10.1007/s11199-008-9400-z.

Brookfield, S. (2000). The concept of critically reflective practice. In A. L. Wilson & E. R. Hayes (Eds.), *Handbook of adult and continuing education* (pp. 33–49). Jossey-Bass.

Brookfield, S. (2001). Repositioning ideology critique in a critical theory of adult learning. *Adult Education Quarterly, 51*(1), 7–22. https://doi.org/10.1177/07417130122087368.

Brookfield, S. D. (2012). *Teaching for critical thinking: Tools and techniques to help students question their assumptions*. Jossey-Bass.

Butler, J. (1990). *Gender trouble: Feminism and the subversion of identity*. Routledge.

Call-Cummings, M., Dazzo, G. P., Hauber-Özer, M. (2023). *Critical participatory inquiry: An interdisciplinary guide*. SAGE Publications.

Clark, A. (2019, September 21). *The General Motors century*. The New York Times. https://www.nytimes.com/2019/09/21/opinion/general-motors-history.html.

Collins, P. H. (1990). *Black feminist thought: Knowledge, consciousness, and the politics of empowerment*. Routledge.

Collins, P. H. (2022). *Intersectionality as critical social theory* (2nd ed.). Duke University Press.

Collins, P. H., & Bilge, S. (2020). *Intersectionality* (2nd ed.). Polity Press.

Crenshaw, K. (1989). Demarginalizing the intersection of race and sex: A Black feminist critique of antidiscrimination doctrine, feminist theory, and antiracist politics. *University of Chicago Legal Forum, 1989*(1), 139–167.

Dear, M. J., & Wolch, J. R. (2014). *Landscapes of despair: From deinstitutionalization to homelessness* (Vol. 823). Princeton University Press.

Delgado, R., & Stefancic, J. (2023). *Critical race theory: An introduction* (Vol. 87). NYU press.

Derrida, J. (1976). *Of grammatology*, trans. G. C. Spivak. Johns Hopkins University Press.

Derrida, J. (1981). *Dissemination*, trans. B. Johnson. University of Chicago Press.

Dong, M., Li, F., Chang, H. (2023, June 15). Trends and hotspots in critical thinking research over the past two decades: Insights from a bibliometric analysis. *Heliyon, 9*(6):e16934. https://doi.org/10.1016/j.heliyon.2023.e16934. PMID: 37441412; PMCID: PMC10333430.

Doughty, H. A. (2006). Critical thinking vs. critical consciousness. *College Quarterly, 9*(2), 1–54.

Ebell, M. H., & Radke, T. (2015). Antibiotic use for viral acute respiratory tract infections remains common. *Am J Manag Care, 21*(10), e567–e575. PMID: 26295356; PMCID: PMC8085714.

Ennis, R. H. (1989). Critical thinking and subject specificity: Clarification and needed research. *Educational Researcher, 18*(3), 4–10. https://doi.org/10.3102/0013189X018003004.

Fals-Borda, O. (1987). The application of participatory action-research in Latin America. *International Sociology, 2*(4), 329–347. https://doi.org/10.1177/026858098700200401.

Fanon, F. (1963). *The wretched of the earth.* Grove Weidenfeld.

Foucault, M. (1978). *The history of sexuality: An introduction, volume 1* (R. Hurley, Trans.). Pantheon Books.

Fox, C. (2002). The race to truth: Disarticulating critical thinking from whiteliness. *Pedagogy: Critical Approaches to Teaching Literature, Language, Composition, and Culture, 2*(2), 197–212.

Freire, P. (1970/1988). *Pedagogy of the oppressed.* Continuum.

Giridharadas, A. (2023). *The persuaders: At the front lines of the fight for hearts, minds, and democracy.* Vintage.

Gretzinger, E., Hicks, M., Dutton, C., & Smith, J. (2024, August 2). *Tracking higher ed's dismantling of DEI.* The Chronicle of Higher Education. https://www.chronicle.com/article/tracking-higher-eds-dismantling-of-dei.

Hall, M. C. (2019). Critical disability theory. In E. N. Zalta (Ed.), *The Stanford Encyclopedia of Philosophy* (Winter 2019 Edition). https://plato.stanford.edu/archives/win2019/entries/disability-critical/.

Hall, R. M., & Sandler, B. R. (1982). *The campus climate: A chilly one for women?* Washington, DC: Association of American Colleges. (Report of the Project on the Status and Education of Women).

hooks, b. (1994). *Teaching to transgress: Education as the practice of freedom.* Routledge.

hooks, b. (2010). *Teaching critical thinking: Practical wisdom.* Routledge.

Horton, M. (1989). *The Highlander Folk School: A history of its major programs.* Carlson.

Kemmis, S., McTaggart, R., & Nixon, R. (2014). *The action research planner: Doing critical participatory action research.* Springer.

Kwon, C. K. (2024). Why HRD needs to do more in relation to disability: Recommendations and future directions. *Human Resource Development International, 27*(1), 152–159. https://doi.org/10.1080/13678868.2023.2205073.

Lee, J. J., & Mccabe, J. M. (2021). Who speaks and who listens: Revisiting the chilly climate in college classrooms. *Gender & Society, 35*(1), 32–60. https://doi.org/10.1177/0891243220977141.

Lugones, M. (2016). The coloniality of gender. *Feminisms in movement,* 35.

Lyotard, J. (1984). *The postmodern condition: A report on knowledge.* University of Minnesota Press.

Maher, F. A., & Tetreault, M. K. T. (1994). *The feminist classroom: A look at how professors and students are transforming higher education for a diverse society.* Basic Books.

Maher, F. A., & Tetreault, M. K. T. (2001). *The feminist classroom: Dynamics of gender, race and privilege. Expanded edition.* Rowman & Littlefield Publishers.

Maldonado-Torres, N. (2008). *Against war: Views from the underside of modernity.* Duke University Press.

Mandernach, B. J. (2006). Thinking critically about critical thinking: Integrating online tools to promote critical thinking. *InSight: A Journal of Scholarly Teaching, 1,* 41–50.

McIntosh, P. (1988). *Working Paper 189, White Privilege and Male Privilege: A Personal Account of Coming to See Correspondences through Work in Women's Studies.* http://www.nymbp.org/reference/WhitePrivilege.pdf.

Mignolo, W. (2011). *The Darker Side of Western Modernity: Global Futures, Decolonial Options.* Duke University Press.

Mitchell, K. M., & Martin, J. (2018). Gender bias in student evaluations. *PS: Political Science & Politics, 51*(3), 648–652. https://doi.org/10.1017/S104909651800001X.

Paul, R., Elder, L. & Bartell, T. (1997). *California teacher preparation for instruction in critical thinking: Research findings and policy recommendations.* The Foundation for Critical Thinking: Dillon Beach, CA.

Quijano, A. (2000). Coloniality of power and Eurocentrism in Latin America. *International Sociology, 15*(2), 215–232. https://doi.org/10.1177/0268580900015002005.

Reboot. (2020, November). *The state of critical thinking 2020.* Reboot. https://reboot-foundation.org/the-state-of-critical-thinking-2020/.

Roth, M. S. (2010, January 3). Beyond critical thinking. *The Chronicle of Higher Education.* http://chronicle.com/article/Beyond-Critical-Thinking/63288/.

Rukmana, D. (2020). The causes of homelessness and the characteristics associated with high risk of homelessness: A review of intercity and intracity homelessness data. *Housing Policy Debate, 30*(2), 291–308. https://doi.org/10.1080/10511482.2019.1684334.

Seifried, T. J. (2000). The chilly classroom climate revisited: What have we learned, Are male faculty the culprits? *PAACE Journal of Lifelong Learning, 9,* 25–37.

Sheared, V., Johnson-Bailey, J., Colin, S. A. J., Peterson, E., & Brookfield, S. D. (Eds.). (2010). *The handbook of race and adult education: A resource for dialogue on racism.* Jossey-Bass Higher Education.

de Sousa Santos, B. (2015). *Epistemologies of the South: Justice against epistemicide.* Routledge.

Stephen, K., & Robin, M. (2000). Participatory action research: Communicative action and the public sphere. In N. K. Denzin & Y. S. Lincoln (Eds.). *Handbook of qualitative research* (pp. 559–603). Sage Publications.

Taylor, E. (1998). A primer on critical race theory: Who are the critical race theorists and what are they saying? *The Journal of Blacks in Higher Education, 19,* 122. https://www.proquest.com/scholarly-journals/primer-on-critical-race-theory-who-are-theorists/docview/195567578/se-2.

The Editorial Board. (2017, March 3). *The Pope on panhandling: Give without worry.* The New York Times. https://www.nytimes.com/2017/03/03/opinion/the-pope-on-panhandling-give-without-worry.html.

Tisdell, E. J. (1995). *Creating inclusive adult learning environments: Insights from multicultural education and feminist pedagogy, Information series No. 361.* ERIC Clearing House on Adult, Career and Vocational Education.

Treisman, R. (2024, June 28). *Tractor Supply slashes its DEI and climate goals after a right-wing pressure campaign.* NPR. https://www.npr.org/2024/06/28/nx-s1-5022816/tractor-supply-dei-climate-backlash.

Tsui, L. (2002). Fostering critical thinking through effective pedagogy: Evidence from four case studies. *Journal of Higher Education, 73*(3), 740–763. https://doi.org/10.1080/00221546.2002.11777179.

Wa Thiong'o, N. (1998). Decolonising the mind. *Diogenes, 46*(184), 101–104. https://doi.org/10.1177/039219219804618409.

Warner, M. (2012, January 1). *Queer and then?* The Chronicle of Higher Education. http://chronicle.com/article/QueerThen-/130161/.

Webb, T. T., & de Bruin, M. (2020). Monitoring interventions. In M. S. Hagger, L. D. Cameron, K. Hamilton, N. Hankonen, & T. Lintunen (Eds.). (2020). *The handbook of behavior change* (pp. 537). Cambridge University Press.

Wheatley, M. J. (2002). *Turning to one another: Simple conversations to restore hope to the future.* Berret-Koehler.

Williamson, A. E., & Brunjes, M. (2024). Homelessness is not a personal choice or inevitable. *BMJ, 384.* https://doi.org/10.1136/bmj.q247.

Zamudio, M., Rios, F., & Jamie, A. M. (2008). Thinking critically about difference: Analytical tools for the 21st Century. *Equity and Excellence in Education, 41*(2), 251–229. https://doi.org/10.1080/10665680801957378.

Zamudio, M., Russell, C., Rios, F., & Bridgeman, J. L. (2010). *Critical race theory matters: Education and ideology.* Routledge.

THE ADULT EDUCATOR—THE *WHO* AND THE *WHY*

Adult learning literature is skewed toward learners and developing pedagogy that resonates with their goals and needs for good reason. Oftentimes, the *educator* is overlooked in discussions of teaching and learning in adult education. As authors, we believe this is a mistake as helping adults learn begins with the well-being and mindset of the educator, where one is involved in the learning. Although the *why* for learners is learning, for educators, it is both learning and teaching.

This book addresses the adult educator and learner since the roles are intertwined. We also think it is essential to acknowledge that all educators are learners first. Being an educator is an honor and responsibility, and striving to improve as a teacher is a lifelong learning endeavor. Adult learners are the people who motivate the theory and practice of the field. Yet, adult learners represent only part of the "who" of the field, and much learning depends on the education, training, mindsets, and practices of the *educators* themselves, who significantly impact adult learners in terms of the design and facilitation of learning experiences. Despite the importance of educators, they tend to be ignored in discussions of teaching and learning.

Section 2 has two chapters. Chapter 4, "Pursuing a Career in the Adult Education Field," explores adult education's broad and diverse landscape and considers what it means to build a career in this field. Chapter 5, "Becoming an Adult Educator," aims to transcend the technical aspects of being an adult educator and examine four crucial mindsets that differentiate excellent teachers of adults.

PURSUING A CAREER IN THE ADULT EDUCATION FIELD

 **Box 4.1 Chapter Overview and Learning Objectives**

Adult education scholar Jerry Apps (1996) wrote,

> Teaching from the heart comes from the depths of the teacher as a person. It is not only what the teacher knows, but *who the person is* that makes a difference. Teaching from the heart is an authentic endeavor. The teacher constantly asks, "Is what I am doing truly an expression of who I am? And if it is not, why is it not?" Teachers strive to touch the hearts of learners, to form a connection. The teacher encourages people to take responsibility for their own learning. Teaching from the heart, rather than replacing well-known teaching approaches adds to them. It builds on them and takes them deeper. It provides another perspective, an opportunity to work beneath the surface of the obvious to help people get in touch with additional components of their lives. (pp. 16–17, italics in original)

Teaching is a complex and rewarding endeavor. Chapter 4 explores adult education's broad and diverse landscape and considers what it means to build a career in this field. As a result of reading this chapter and completing the exercise boxes, you, the reader, should be able to:

1. Recognize the contested and fragmented boundaries of the adult education field.
2. Discuss your identity and those of others as adult educators.
3. Understand career options and preparation in the field of adult education.
4. Explore adult education philosophy, principles, and perspectives.

Chapter 4 asks, "Who is the adult educator?" and also that you, as an aspiring or accomplished adult educator, take a moment to step back and reflect on your professional identity—your own and that of the field. What does it mean to be an adult educator? How do learning and development fit into individual, organization, and community schema? How does your position as an adult education professional fit into the structure of your organization? How do you fit into the field of adult education? Did you even know there was a field?

When people think of learning, they likely picture a classroom full of young learners. They probably remember certain teachers fondly. But do they think about who the teacher really is or how they became one? Considering the adult educator is Chapter 4's focus: an exploration of the role of people trained in adult learning principles, practices, and facilitation and how they embody and adjust their teaching practice. This chapter will explore the field of adult education and how people build a career in this work, whether or not they consider themselves adult educators.

Adult Education and Adult Educators

Houle (1972) defined **adult education** as

> The process by which men and women alone, in groups, or in institutional settings seek to improve themselves or their society by increasing their skill, knowledge, or sensitiveness; or it is any process by which individuals, groups, or institutions try to help men and women improve in these ways. The fundamental system of practice of the field,

if it has one, must be discerned by probing beneath many different surface realities to identify a basic unity of process. (p. 32)

Adult education encompasses "activities intentionally designed for the purpose of bringing about learning among those whose age, social roles, or self-perception define them as adults" (Merriam & Brockett, 2007, p. 8).

Although identifying the adult learner is somewhat straightforward, What about the adult educator? Who is an adult educator? Who stands out to you as an adult learner or educator? **Adult educators** facilitate adults' learning by delivering formal instruction, training, providing support such as coaching, mentoring, or advising, and creating conditions conducive to learning. Bierema (2010) described adult educators this way:

We call ourselves "Adult Educators," yet that term holds different meanings for each of us. You may mean that you are a literacy teacher, continuing education instructor, continuing professional educator, labor educator, non-profit staff, instructional designer, human resource developer, K–12 educator, corporate trainer, higher education administrator, extension agent, prison educator, organization development consultant, college professor, career development counselor, community activist, health educator, public official, or something else. The dizzying array of adult education occupations and contexts is what makes our field dynamic and diverse, yet difficult to define. Adult education occurs in a range of contexts where professional boundaries may be blurred or contested. The field's breadth means it is fair to assume that what I mean by referring to myself as an "adult educator" may not necessarily be what you mean. Or you may not even consider yourself an "adult educator." (p. 135)

English (2005) lamented that the adult education "field [was] flooded with practitioners of every sort—intuitive practitioners (Atkinson & Claxton, 2000), deliberative practitioners (Forester, 1999), practitioner-researchers (Jarvis, 1999), OpenSpace practitioners (Owen, 1992), reflective practitioners (Schön, 1983), and contemplative practitioners (Miller, 1994)" (p. 86).

Ioannou (2023) regarded adult educators as playing an essential role in facilitating adult learning and in society in general since they ensure the quality of learning and are "considered to be a critical pillar of adult education" (p. 379). Unfortunately, according to their analysis of policy documents in the European context,

Despite a consensus about the importance of quality adult education, over the past two decades little attention has been given to the initial training and continuous professional development of adult educators in practical terms. Due to a lack of opportunities, the professional development seems weak and still faces many challenges. (p. 379)

Fejes and Nylander (2019) mapped the research in the field of adult education and learning in their edited book, noting in their introduction that the field is multidisciplinary and that the key concepts denoting the field are shifting, such as the model of adult education and *Bildung* (the German tradition of becoming through self-education and self-cultivation that leads to personal and cultural maturity), which became replaced by the notion of **lifelong learning**—the practice of continuing to develop knowledge and skills throughout the lifespan. Their book is an excellent resource to explore the historical emergence and transformation of adult education and learning.

Sheared (2023) explained the **adult educator career path**,

Unlike other careers, adult education is one that most people enter, often by happenstance and not because of one saying that "When I grow up, I want to become an adult educator." In fact, many of us, as the editors and authors in this publication share, did not even know that a career in adult education was even possible. (p. xii)

Happenstance is not uncommon for a career educating adults. One of the authors (Laura) gravitated to educational roles throughout her life and work. In her words:

I had no idea there was a field of adult education until I was working in automotive manufacturing in rural Georgia, and a local literacy educator and professor from the University of Georgia visited me to see if the company would support an in-plant literacy program. The company decided to support the program, and I was astonished when approximately 60 workers out of 200 showed up for the informational session. I decided it was essential to learn more about this "adult education thing"; a month later, I enrolled in a doctoral program! To say that discovery was life-changing would be accurate, as it led me on a new career path that shifted from corporate human resources to academia. (Laura Bierema, personal communication)

How did you discover this field as an adult educator? How did you learn to become one? What do you value about the field? How do you develop professionally? Which adult educators serve as your role models or mentors? The answers to these questions will depend on where you work, how you were trained, and what you believe about learning and teaching.

Boundaries of Adult Education

Lindeman (1926), in his introduction to *The Meaning of Adult Education*, wrote,

> A fresh hope is astir. From many quarters comes the call to a new kind of
> education with its initial assumption affirming that *education is life*—not
> merely preparation for an unknown kind of future living. Consequently
> all static concepts of education which relegate the learning process to
> the period of youth are abandoned. The whole of life is learning;
> therefore education can have no endings. This new venture is called
> *adult education* not because it is confined to adults but because
> adulthood, maturity, defines its limits. (p. 6)

Adult education is as limitless as how adults learn and make meaning from
their experiences. It is a diverse, fragmented field that seeks multiple goals in
various settings. Jeris and Daley (2004) explained a field's boundaries "are held
strongly in place by theoretical premises, philosophical foundations, language,
the practice arena, and the codification of knowledge in graduate programs"
(p. 101). Boundary ambiguity emerges when the diverse subfields of adult
education explore philosophical bases and values, define knowledge and practice, and both set and resist boundaries (Jeris & Daley, 2004). As an adult educator, how do you determine the boundaries of your work?

The boundaries of adult education are extensive, some complementary, some
contested. The explicit social justice and change agenda of the US Highlander
Center contrasts with continuing professional education aimed at individual
compliance with legislation or policy. Teaching someone to read is a more individualized process than educating to inspire social activism such as the #MeToo
or Black Lives Matter movements. Corporate learning and development may
embrace goals and values different from environmental activism. These adult
education programs' various types, settings, and goals are weakly threaded
together to form a highly decentralized and fragmented "field" of adult education.

Roth (2004), musing on divisions between adult education and human
resource development, observed how boundaries in adult education evolved
"at arm's length from one another. Historically, scholars from both camps
have been content to fertilize within fenced-in yards rather than explore and
nurture common ground" (p. 9). Heaney (2000) considered the complex and
sometimes contradictory social visions pursued by adult educators in multiple
contexts where one might find literacy workers helping individual learners
improve their job prospects and community functioning, while other educators seek to create dramatic shifts in social class through social movements,
or corporate trainers who help organizations achieve performance goals,

while labor educators teach workers to resist management, or military educators versus peace educators working at apparent odds. Heaney asked how adult education can create a vision without conflict in purposes. He cautioned that adult education's polarized foci can put the field at risk:

> An adult education practice that, despite a multiplicity of visions, does not engender strategies for action across the borders of our now divided terrain is destined to reproduce uncritically and indiscriminately both the best and the worst of the world's conditions. (Heaney, 2000, p. 570)

It is helpful to identify the boundaries of the field and understand the robust and diverse ways adult education and learning occur across the spheres of family, work, and community life. The literature base, graduate study, and professional associations have helped establish adult education as a field (Imel et al., 2000). However, not all adult educators participate in these activities. This section explores the delivery of adult education to learners and grapples with the professional identity of the field.

Adult Education Delivery Systems

Regardless of a particular adult education program's goals or boundaries, Merriam and Brockett (1997) suggested that most adult education falls into three general delivery systems: institutional, content area, and personnel. See Table 4.1 for descriptions of institutional delivery systems. These delivery systems contribute to the fragmentation of the adult education field.

Major content areas of adult education include continuing professional education, remedial or basic skills education, human resource development, recreational or leisure learning, citizenship, and technology. There are likely many more content areas than listed here, particularly given the range of contexts where adult learning occurs across the levels of individuals, organizations, and communities and in institutions that range from healthcare to education, business, nonprofit, technology, religious organizations, government, and so on.

The third major delivery system of adult education is personnel: the people who deliver and receive adult education. Houle (1956) discussed adult educators' roles as comprising three pyramid tiers, as represented in Figure 4.1, which provides a helpful metaphor for adult education's delivery personnel. Houle's typology would include, at the top, individuals who focus primarily on adult education as their paid work and career identity, such as professors, researchers, and scholars. The middle also represents paid work in the field, including work by practitioners and professionals in educational activities with adults. The base

TABLE 4.1 INSTITUTIONAL ADULT EDUCATION DELIVERY SYSTEMS

Adult Education Institutional Delivery System	Institutional Focus
Independent Adult Education Organizations that provide adult education as their primary function, including:	• Community-based (learning exchanges and grassroots organizations) • Private (e.g., Pro Literacy) • Proprietary schools and residential centers, such as the Highlander Center for Research and Education
Educational Institutions that provide formal education across the lifespan:	• Public Schools • Postsecondary Institutions • Cooperative Extension Service
Quasi Educational Organizations are private or public and view education as an important part of their mission.	• Libraries • Museums • Mass Media • Community Organizations • Religious Organizations
Noneducational Organizations are similar to quasi-educational organizations but do not include education as a primary part of their mission.	• Learning and development in business and industry • Consulting organizations

FIGURE 4.1 ADULT EDUCATION (AE) PYRAMID

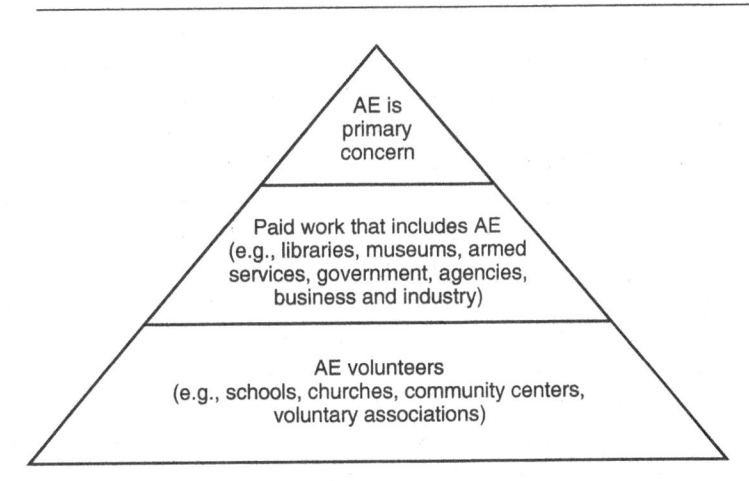

AE is primary concern

Paid work that includes AE (e.g., libraries, museums, armed services, government, agencies, business and industry)

AE volunteers (e.g., schools, churches, community centers, voluntary associations) is individuals working in adult education, although not in paid or full-time positions. People at each level of the pyramid likely identify differently with the field and how they see their roles given the range of institutions, content, and personnel involved in adult education, developing both an individual and collective sense of professional identity.

Professional Identity

Identity is "what it means to be who one is" (Burke, 2003a, p. 1), conveyed through worldviews, love, and work (Arnett, 2015). Gedro (2017) defined professional identity as "internalization of one's occupational status and role" (p. 27). Professional identity includes a person's self-concept, personality development, individuation, and continuity over time (Goltz & Smith, 2014). Forging an identity is a lifelong, shifting process that occurs through assuming roles, having multiple identities, experiencing identity conflict, and resolving identity conflicts. Professional socialization is a learning process of acculturation into a field that involves the outside world recognizing one's assumed professional identity and the person's internalization or self-recognition of the identity (duTont, 1995). Professional socialization causes a new identity to emerge through academic training and experience. Yet not all adult educators have received such training or would identify themselves as such.

When you, as an adult educator, are asked what you do for a living, what do you say? You will likely receive quizzical looks if you reply, "I am an adult educator." If you say that, many people immediately assume you do literacy work, and even more have never heard of the field. One of the authors (Laura) often replies with something like, "I help adults learn and change in their work or community context," and then the next reply is something like, "Oh, then you do training?" Working in a fragmented field that is not immediately obvious to some people raises questions worth considering: What is the scope of professional identity in adult education? How did you form a professional identity as an adult educator or perhaps another role? Is there a collective sense of professional identity within the field itself? These questions persist from Jarvis (1999), who wrote, "Adult education knowledge is a complex and ever-changing phenomenon, overlapping, and subdividing" (p. 5) to Imel et al. (2000), who concluded in the 2000 *Handbook of Adult and Continuing Education*, "Many who practice adult education do not identify with adult education as a field because they do not see its relevance to their work and the learners they serve" (p. 632).

Bierema wrote about the professional identity of the field in the 2020 *Handbook of Adult and Continuing Education*, although the recent 2023 edition (Rocco et al., 2023) does not include a similar chapter. Collins (2023) discussed the interdisciplinarity of the field in their chapter in the 2023 volume, noting the field has historically been "intertwined with other formal academic disciplines" (p. 31) and that "adult education has never been seen as a single field of practice or scholarly focus" (p. 32). They concluded that the interdisciplinarity of adult education "demonstrates the diversity within the field and the integration and numerous disciplines, but this leads to an erosion of identity when divided into specializations and enmeshed with other disciplines" (p. 35). Adult education knowledge passes between generations, but perhaps with little consideration by the field:

> The adult education knowledge base is taught through graduate programs to new members, who then participate in professional activities, which in turn solidifies a sense of belonging to the profession. Those who identify themselves with the profession, or are seen by others as members, generally represent formal, institutionalized, mainstream adult education. (Merriam & Brockett, 1997, p. 239)

Considering that graduate training programs, research activities, and professional associations serve as the significant socialization gatekeepers into the adult education field, it is fair to assume that a large majority of those delivering adult education are excluded from this process, particularly since only 14.4% of the US population holds a master's degree or higher (US Census Bureau, 2022). Box 4.2 explores definitions related to professional identity in adult education.

Careers and Roles in Adult Education

Monaghan et al. (2023), in their edited book, *Career Pathways in Adult Education*, showcased the possibilities for a career in the field, covering the primary skills of adult educators, focusing on the work of practitioners from adult basic education/ English as a second language/family literacy to correctional education to corporate training. They explored the activities of adult educators, career paths, educational preparation, and the knowledge, skills, and abilities required to pursue a career in the field.

According to Ross-Gordon et al. (2016), categorizing adult educator roles has remained relatively constant over the decades. They noted:

> Houle's (1956) notion of a field that consists of vast numbers of individuals working as educators of adults, with a more limited number of individuals engaged full time as adult educators, and a still more limited number who hold professional identities as adult educators, still makes sense today. (p. 76)

 **Box 4.2 Tips and Tools for Teaching and Learning**

Defining Your Professional Identity and Field

The breadth of the adult education field is immense, paralleling the diversity of learners and learning in adulthood. Distinctions have been made between adult educators and educators of adults (Griffith, 1989; Merriam & Brockett, 1997). Griffith classified **educators of adults** as those concerned with specific and practical educational goals compared to **adult educators** as those with a vision for the field that includes professionalization, academic programs, and interest in a collaborative field. Brockett (1991) differentiated between adult educators and those who conduct adult education. These distinctions may help adult education practitioners understand the difference between identity development at the individual versus field level, especially since people who deliver adult education may not have formalized training or professional affiliation in adult education.

The academic field of adult education is well established, giving faculty and graduates of these programs a more cohesive identity than practitioners who may lack formal training or identification with the field. The reality is many people working in an educational capacity with adults may or may not identify themselves as "adult educators." Merriam and Brockett (1997) suggested that the part of the field that challenges assumptions about "what is an adult educator" or "what is the profession" exists in that it does not fit how adult education is defined or how people are trained to practice within the field.

Professional identity in adult education takes two forms.

1. **How do you conceive of your own professional identity as an adult educator or something else?** What is your identification with and adaptation to the field and culture of adult education? Since there are many types of adult education, you might be more inclined to identify yourself in ways that are not an "adult educator," such as:
   a. Literacy teacher
   b. Health educator
   c. Human rights activist
   d. Human resource developer
   e. Instructional designer
   f. Other . . .

2. **How the field itself creates, maintains, and changes its professional identity. In other words, adult education has a public face with a relatively agreed-upon discourse, research, and practice.** This "profession" is more straightforward to trace by identifying the many professional groups and conferences that are concerned with adult education, such as:

   a. The American Association for Adult and Continuing Education
   b. The Adult Education Research Conference
   c. The Standing Conference on University Teaching and Research in the Education of Adults
   d. The Council on Adult Basic Education
   e. The Council for Adult and Experiential Learning
   f. The Academy of Human Resource Development
   g. The University Continuing Education Association
   h. The National Association of State Judicial Educators
   i. The Association for Talent Development (formerly The American Society for Training and Development)
   j. Dozens and dozens of others

3. Many associations and conferences also exist on a state-by-state level. Given this range of professional associations, it is no wonder that forging an individual or collective professional identity is challenging for adult education since each of these subsets has its own professional identity.

   How would you define your professional identity and field as an adult educator and learner?

Fenwick (1996) offered metaphors of adult educators' roles from an analysis of 65 adult educators taking courses at the University of Alberta as follows:

1. Adult Educator as Tour Guide: Functioning as experts on a journey.
2. Adult Educator as Firestarter: Igniting the learner's motivation.
3. Adult Educator as Outfitter: Equipping learners with the necessary tools and confidence building but not participating in their journey.
4. Adult Educator as Caregiver: Helping people grow and develop as caretakers or parents might do.
5. Adult Educator as Dispenser: Supplying helpful information.
6. Adult Educator as Good Host: Welcoming learners.

Fenwick observed that the adult educators in her study tended to focus on learning as an individual engagement, with little discussion of group learning or educational context. Fenwick's (2004) later research on the same theme accounted for the work context more and framed it as ecological learning theory, describing learning as nimbler in response to today's VUCA conditions of organization learning. Her metaphors shifted to:

1. Noisemakers: Assume a voice highlighting contradictions and injustices in the organization's life.
2. Interpreters: Naming realities unfolding and changing the discourse to shift from dominant discourses.
3. Mapmakers: Creating pathways for disrupting prevailing power relations and creating learning opportunities.
4. Facilitators: Helping adult learners find equilibrium as they experience imbalanced systems.

Ross-Gordon et al. (2016) listed the roles of adult educators appearing in the *Handbooks of Adult and Continuing Education* from 1936–2010. These roles included:

- Teacher, Facilitator, or Trainer
- Program Developer or Program Development
- Administrator or Administration
- Individual Learner: Counseling or Guidance, Advising, Coaching, Mentoring
- Professor or Researcher
- Media Use or Distance Education

They describe these roles in detail in Chapter 3 of their book.

Adult educators' roles and work contexts are diverse, and many do not have formal training. Academic programs in adult education have standards to guide the curriculum. See Box 4.3 for an overview.

Key Competencies of Adult Educators

Wahlgren (2016) observed that the competencies of adult educators are broad, heterogeneous, and complex and must meet the demands of national and cultural contexts. However, the key competencies fall into the areas of (1) communicating subject knowledge, (2) considering students' prior learning, (3) creating a supportive learning environment, (4) reflecting on one's performance as an adult educator, and (5) enabling learners' ability to apply and transfer their new

Box 4.3 SoTL: The Scholarship of Teaching and Learning

Professional Preparation in Adult Education

The *Standards for Graduate Programs in Education* specify topics for doctoral-level study in the field, including:

- Advanced study of adult learning and development (theory and research)
- Historical, philosophical foundations of Adult Education
- Study of leadership, including theories of organizational leadership, administration, and change
- The changing role of technology in Adult Education
- Policy issues concerning Adult Education
- Globalization and international issues or perspectives in Adult Education
- Social, political, and economic forces that have shaped the foundations and discourse of Adult Education
- Diversity and equity in Adult Education
- Advanced specialty courses relevant to unique program and faculty strengths (e.g., continuing professional education, workplace learning, social movement learning, etc.)
- Qualitative and quantitative research methodology coursework to support dissertation research and ability to utilize existing literature

The complete *Standards for Graduate Programs in Education* are available here:

> https://www.aaace.org/resource/resmgr/Engage/Commissions/CPAE/cpae_2014_standards_update.pdf

Activity:
Review the standards and self-assess how well your preparation as an adult educator aligns with the recommended curriculum and competencies.

knowledge to their life, community, or work contexts. Table 4.2 summarizes general competencies for you to develop and hone as an adult educator.

Deep reflection and analysis of what it means to educate adults are scant in the literature, so Monaghan et al.'s (2023) book is a welcome contribution and the first textbook focusing on the profession since Merriam and Brockett's 1997 and 2007 editions of *The Profession and Practice of Adult Education: An*

TABLE 4.2 ADULT EDUCATOR COMPETENCIES

Competency	Definition	Teaching Examples
Understanding How Adults Learn	Being attuned to the needs, experiences, and motivations of adults.	• Valuing and using learners' experience as a basis for teaching and learning. You might ask learners: *How does this idea align with your experience?* • Focusing learning on life-based problem-solving and immediate relevance. You might ask learners: *How might you apply this idea in practice?* • Honoring of adults' propensity to be self-directed in their learning. You might ask learners: *What steps do you want to take to learn?* • Recognizing that adults' internal drive motivates learning. You might ask learners: *What is meaningful to you?*
Developing Effective Facilitation Skills	Capacity to lead a group of adult learners in building safe, brave learning spaces.	• Communicating effectively using active listening. • Effectively managing group dynamics by setting communication agreements, mediating disagreements, and addressing interpersonal challenges. • Linking learning to expected results and helping learners apply lessons. • Building learning communities or communities of practice. • Creating intuitive instructional design by creating relevant, understandable, applicable lessons. • Aligning learning to capability and meeting learners where they are.
Acquiring Program Planning Skills	Strategically developing educational classes, workshops, conferences, and other activities.	• Engaging stakeholders in dialogue about the purpose and objectives of educational programs. • Conducting needs assessment. • Designing an educational experience. • Developing educational materials. • Delivering the program. • Evaluating the program.
Developing Assessment, Evaluation, and Educational Research Skills	Systematically collecting and analyzing educational data.	• Research involves collecting qualitative and quantitative data about learners and programs and analyzing it. • Assessment is reviewing data about adult learners through tests, observation, projects, portfolios, or other methods. • Using the results to inform future educational decisions and actions.
Building and Adapting Technology Skills	Ability to interact with and adapt to the digital world.	• Honing computer skills such as typing and being proficient with using software programs. • Knowing how to use AI (artificial intelligence) effectively. • Integrating technology into teaching through audio-visual use.

Introduction. You will find this a helpful resource as an adult educator to delve into this topic and consider: What drives me to this work? What do I believe about teaching adults? How are my beliefs and values about teaching adults translated into my practice? As you mull a career in adult education as an aspiring or active adult educator, Box 4.4 shares a glimpse of the size and scope of the business of educating adults.

 ## Box 4.4 Tips and Tools for Teaching and Learning

State of the Industry Reports for Learning, Training, and Development

One way to stay abreast of the diverse adult education and learning field is through the annual State of the Industry reports published by various entities. This box lists reputable ones. Some complete reports require association membership or a fee, although they tend to make the abstracts and highlights available for free. The report associations, titles, links, and highlights are featured in this box.

Training Magazine: *2023 Training Industry Report* (Freifeld, 2023) https://trainingmag.com/2023-training-industry-report/

- 42-year history
- US Training expenditures in 2022–2023: $101.8 billion
- Training average expenditure per learner: $954.00

Association for Talent Development (formerly known as the American Society for Training and Development). *2023 State of the Industry: Talent Development and Benchmark Trends* https://www.td.org/product/p/192311

- Training average expenditure per learner: $1,220.00

Chartered Institute of Personnel and Development—CIPD *Learning at Work 2023 Survey Report* (Overton, 2023)
https://www.cipd.org/globalassets/media/knowledge/knowledge-hub/reports/2023-pdfs/2023-learning-at-work-survey-report-8378.pdf

- Organizations are prioritizing efficiency, productivity, talent retention, and well-being.
- Professionals are battling with workloads, a lack of capacity, a lack of organizational priority, and a lack of insight about what is needed and what has worked.

- Face-to-face learning continues to decline, and digital learning continues to rise, with 48% reporting increased usage.
- A significant number do not feel skilled at designing. Regarding delivering learning, only 50% have a process for using feedback for continuous improvement.
- Sixty-three percent of L&D practitioners agree to collaborate with other functions to deliver business-critical priorities.
- 65% of respondents agree that the LND profession offers a meaningful career.

Activity: Review these reports for yourself, drawing your own conclusions about the state of adult learning, learning and development, and training and development.

Exploring Philosophy, Principles, and Perspectives of Adult Education

Apps (1996) explained, "Teaching from the heart comes from the depths of the teacher as a person. It is not only what the teacher knows, but *who the person is* that makes the difference" (p. 16, italics in original). To begin discovering the core of who we are requires work to become aware of our beliefs and values. He offered an exercise for educators to connect with their beliefs and values, as profiled in Box 4.5.

Teaching is an expression of an educator's values and beliefs. Learning is a complex phenomenon inspiring centuries of research inquiry. Merriam and Caffarella (1999) emphasized, "Learning defies easy definition and simple theorizing" (p. 248) and illustrated how Plato and Aristotle influenced the early investigation of learning through Plato's "rationalism" evident in Gestalt and cognitive psychology and Aristotle's "empiricism" evident in early behavioral psychology. The scientific investigation of learning began during the 19th century by exploring the mind, knowing, and behavior. Assessments are available for adult educators and learners wishing to learn more about the values and beliefs they bring to education.

Philosophy concerns the general principles of any phenomenon, object, process, or subject matter (Elias & Merriam, 1995). Philosophy: (1) helps practitioners and researchers identify issues and make good decisions; (2) demands reflective practice, inquiry into thought and action, and a holistic systems perspective; (3) incorporates political and social dimensions; and (4) is often ignored

 **Box 4.5 Reflective Practice**

Apps' (1996) Teaching Beliefs and Values Exercise (pp. 63–64)

As an adult educator, reflect on your practice as you complete the exercise.

1. At the top of a blank paper, write, "When I teach, I . . ."
   Write statements that describe your present teaching.
2. Once you have developed a list, consider what beliefs and values lie beneath your statements. If you are doing this exercise in a group or even with one other person, share your list and encourage this person to write what beliefs and values seem foundational to your statements about teaching.
3. What beliefs and values underlie the statements you wrote down?
4. How closely do your actions match your values and beliefs about teaching?

by adult educators. Philosophy is not something most people stop to think about on any given day, even though it operates constantly in the background.

> The educator is generally more interested in skills than in principles, in means than in ends, in details than in the whole picture. The philosophy of adult education does not equip a person with knowledge about what to teach, how to teach, or how to organize a program. It is more concerned with the why of education and with the logical analysis of the various elements of the educational process. (Elias & Merriam, 1995, p. 8)

Elias and Merriam (1995) argued that understanding **educational philosophy** distinguishes professional educators from paraprofessionals and beginning teachers. True professionals not only know what to do but why they do it. They seamlessly merge theory and practice and embody truly reflective practice.

Elias (1982) recognized that one of the most challenging problems philosophers address is the relationship between philosophy and action or between theory and practice. A key process in bridging the theory-to-practice gap is understanding the *why* in our practice as adult educators. Philosophy offers an opportunity to reflect on the *why*. Why should we, as adult learners and educators, care about philosophy? Merriam and Brockett (1997) provided several reasons.

1. Developing awareness of underlying values and assumptions provides guidelines for making decisions and creating policy.
2. Recognizing the connection between assumptions and values and their impact on curriculum and instruction is essential.
3. Understanding individual philosophy helps one to communicate it more effectively in interpersonal relationships.
4. Articulating a philosophical standing also allows educators to contribute to the field by raising questions about ethics and practices.
5. Articulating a philosophy separates professionals from paraprofessionals.
6. Bridging theory and practice.

Philosophical frameworks of adult education have been proposed by Apps (1973), Beder and Carrea (1988), and Elias and Merriam (1995). Validated tools are available to help you make meaning of your values, beliefs, and practices as an adult educator or learner. Each is briefly described, with instructions on accessing them, in the following sections.

Philosophy of Adult Education Inventory (PAEI)

Educators interested in assessing their philosophy should refer to Zinn's (1983, 1991) PAEI, Philosophy of Adult Education Inventory. Zinn developed this assessment from her dissertation research, following the philosophical framework proposed by Elias and Merriam (1995). The PAEI assessment is available via this URL: http://www.labr.net/paei/inventory.html. The assessment, based on Elias and Merriam's five philosophies of adult education, include: (1) Liberalism, (2) Progressivism, (3) Behaviorism, (4) Humanism, and (5) Radical adult education. Table 4.3 summarizes the five philosophical approaches to teaching and learning.

Elias and Merriam (2005) added two additional philosophical perspectives in their 3rd Edition of *Philosophical Foundations of Adult Education*: Analytic and postmodern. **The analytic philosophy of adult education** focuses on the conceptual analysis of linguistics, such as seeking to define and clarify key terms in the field like *adult*, *learning*, and *teaching* and understand how language is used to describe the field. The approach, as explained by the authors, "is concerned with the grounds for knowledge, beliefs, actions, and activities that make up human life" (p. 194). Although this approach can help educators clarify the terms, goals, and methods of the field, it is an abstract, disconnected approach that may leave educators unclear about how to apply it in their classrooms. Proponents of analytic philosophy favor liberal education, although its devaluing of pragmatic and utilitarian education contradicts the justice ethos of adult education. Elias and Merriam (2005) concluded that the value of neutrality professed by philosophers in this tradition may be impossible in actual practice.

The **postmodern philosophy of adult education** challenges traditional views of knowledge, truth, and power, questioning universal truths, metanarratives, and subjectivity that influence learning and life. Counter to the analytic view, postmodernism eschews liberal education as elitist. They concluded the book by examining how the postmodern view considers each of the five philosophical views presented in Table 4.3 and critiques all approaches. Elias and Merriam (2005) concluded their book by asking, "The final question to be considered in this book might be the most important one: what stance should the adult educator adopt as his or her personal philosophy of adult education?" (p.251). They suggested that whatever philosophy is embraced, "it must be held critically" (p. 251). They urged professional adult educators to be "constantly examining, evaluating, and perhaps rejecting or modifying what has been received in the past. A study of philosophies of adult education should produce professionals who question their own theories, practices, institutions, and assumptions, as well as those of others" (p. 251).

Principles of Adult Learning Scale (PALS)

Conti (1998) developed the Principles of Adult Learning Scale (PALS) based on the proposition that the actions of educators impact student achievement. The assessment is available via this URL: http://www.conti-creations.com/Online_Page.htm. Conti developed and tested the PALS in a study involving 29 teachers and 837 students in an adult basic education program. The instrument asks adult educators to respond to the frequency with which they engage in certain educational activities. It yields a score to indicate how collaborative the person is in their teaching. High scores on the instrument indicate the instructor uses initiation, progressive, and learner-centered techniques, including informal evaluation, collaborative teaching, and expecting learners to take responsibility for their own learning. Low scores on the PALS indicate constructs of responsive, traditional, and teacher-centered behaviors that focus on formal testing, encouraging learners to accept middle-class values, favoring quiet desk work and discipline, and teaching most students similarly. Table 4.4 summarizes the PALS Factors.

TABLE 4.3 PHILOSOPHY OF ADULT EDUCATION INVENTORY DESCRIPTIONS

Characteristics	Liberal (Arts) Education	Progressive Adult Education	Behavioral Adult Education	Humanistic Adult Education	Radical Adult Education
Purpose(s)	Develops intellectual powers of the mind to facilitate the broadest sense of learning and provide a general, "well-rounded" education.	Supports responsible participation in society as a citizen, family member, and worker and gives learners practical knowledge and problem-solving skills.	Promotes competence, skill development, and behavioral change. To ensure compliance with standards and societal expectations.	Enhances personal growth and development to facilitate individual self-actualization.	Brings about fundamental social, cultural, economic, and political change through education.
Learner(s)	A "Renaissance person" always learning, seeking knowledge, and expecting to gain conceptual and theoretical understandings.	The learner's needs, interests, and experiences drive learning, and the learner takes an active role in education.	Learners are not involved in setting objectives but are expected to master one step before another through practice behaviors to build skills.	The learner is highly motivated and self-directed. They assume responsibility for learning and are very involved in planning learning projects.	Learners and teachers collaborate equally in learning processes where the learner has autonomy and is empowered as a voluntary participant.
Educator Role	An expert transmitter of knowledge who teaches students to think and directs the learning process.	A guide or coach who organizes learning processes, provides real-life learning applications, and guides collaborative learning.	A manager, controller, "boss," or authoritative supervisor who sets expectations, predicts, and directs learning outcomes.	A facilitator, mentor, helper, and partner in teaching-learning exchange who supports the learning process.	Coordinator who convenes as an equal partner who contributes to but does not direct the process.

Key Concepts and Terms	Liberal arts, learning for its own sake, comprehensive or general education, critical thinking, traditional knowledge, cultural literacy, and academic excellence.	Problem-solving, practical learning, experience-based, learner-centered, needs assessment, transfer of learning, active inquiry, collaboration, social responsibility.	Standards-based, mastery learning, competence, behavioral objectives, performance, feedback, and reinforcement. Accountability.	Andragogy, freedom, autonomy, individuality, entrepreneurialism, self-directedness, teaching-learning exchange, openness, interpersonal communication, personal meaning, authenticity.	Critical perspectives (e.g., critical theory, feminist theory, critical race theory, etc.), liberation, radical social reorganization, empowerment, social action, and social justice.
Methods	Lecture, reading and critical analysis, question-and-answer, teacher-led discussion, individual study, essay testing, "bell-curve" grading.	Projects, scientific or experimental methods, simulations, group investigation, cooperative learning, portfolios, pass/no-pass grading.	Competency-based instruction and lock-step curriculum. Technical skill training, demo, and practice, standardized and criterion-reference testing.	Experiential learning, discovery learning, open discussion, individual projects, collaborative learning, independent study, and self-assessment.	Conscientization, consciousness-raising, transformative learning, non-compulsory learning, autonomy, critical discussion and reflection, problem posing, media analysis, and social action theater.
People	Aristotle. Plato. Rousseau, Piaget, Hutchins. Adler. Houle, Hirsch.	Dewey, Tyler, Whitehead, Lindeman.	Thorndike, Skinner, Mager, Nadler.	Rogers, Maslow, Knowles, Tough, Mezirow, Stanage.	Freire, Illich, Kozol, Shor, Habermas, Olinger, Collins, Perelman, Kendi.
Programs	Great Books Program, Paideia Program, Center for the Study of Liberal Education, Chautauqua, Elderhostel.	Citizenship education, cooperative extension programs, university without walls, academic credit for prior learning, community schools, environmental.	Human performance technology, ASTD, vocational training, management-by-objectives, certification exams, military training, religious indoctrination.	Self-directed learning, popular education, diversity education, personal growth and development programs, assertiveness training.	Free School Movement, Freedom Schools, feminist studies, Highlander Folk Center, socialist worker education, social justice education.

Source: Adapted from Elias and Merriam (1995).

TABLE 4.4 PALS FACTORS AND EXAMPLES

PALS Factor	Examples
Personalizing Instruction	• Includes personalized learning, self-paced instruction, minimal lecturing, and cooperation (not competition) to meet students' needs. • Students identify knowledge gaps they hope to address.
Relating Learning to Experience	• Activities account for students' experiences. • Learning is made relevant to the students' experiences and context.
Assessing Student Needs	• Holding individual conferences and informal counseling. • Assist students in developing short-, mid-, and long-term goals.
Climate Building	• Dialogue and interaction are encouraged. • Build breaks into instruction. • Risk-taking in learning is encouraged.
Participation in the Learning Process	• Student determines content. • Students develop assessment criteria. • Students are actively engaged.
Flexibility in Personal Development	• Low: Provider of knowledge, not facilitator, rigid objectives, well-disciplined classrooms, avoid issues related to value judgments. • High: Personal fulfillment is the goal of education, and flexibility to meet students' changing needs, issues, and values are discussed.

Teaching Perspectives Inventory

Pratt (Pratt, 1998; Pratt & Smulders, 2016) proposed adult educators prefer one of five teaching perspectives based on interviews, observations, and re-interviews of over 250 educators in over 100 countries, which led to the development of the Teaching Perspectives Inventory (TPI). The TPI assesses adult educators' teaching orientations. To take the TPI, visit the URL: https://www.teachingperspectives .com/tpi/ and take the free assessment. The five perspectives of the TPI are:

1. Transmission—Teaching as delivering content efficiently.
2. Apprenticeship—Teaching as modeling and coaching.
3. Developmental—Teaching as developing ways of thinking.
4. Nurturing—Teaching as supporting students' self-efficacy and confidence.
5. Social Reform—Teaching as a means of promoting social change.

Each perspective represents a different "good teaching" type and combines to create a profile.

Table 4.5 presents the perspectives.

TABLE 4.5 SUMMARY OF PRATT'S TPI PERSPECTIVES

Perspective	Transmission	Apprenticeship	Developmental	Nurturing	Social Reform
Educator	**Commit to the Subject** Master subject matter and strive to represent it with accuracy, efficiency, enthusiasm, and presentation flair.	**Create Opportunities for Learners to Perform Authentic Tasks within their "Zone of Development"** Highly skilled at translating and teaching the topic in any context and recognized for it.	**Plan Learning from the Learner's Viewpoint** Understand their learners' reasoning and thinking and help them develop the capacity to approach the content with sophistication.	**Long-term, Hard, Persistent Effort Comes from the Heart (not Head) in a Supportive, Accountable Environment** Remove the fear of failure from the learning process.	**Teaching the Collective to Critique and Take Timely, Mindful Action** Strive to help learners achieve conscientization. Critique is the focus, but not the end; action is.
Learner	Learn legitimate and authorized forms of the content.	Engage with the content at their developmental level with the guidance and direction of the instructor. Learners take on more responsibility as they learn and become independent.	Challenge the learner to move from simple to complex thinking and bridge between simple and more complex ways of understanding the topic.	Encourage learners that they will succeed by trying, which is a product of their own effort and ability.	Awaken to values and ideologies embedded in discourse and practices within context and how they are positioned socially. Take critical stances.
Teaching Activities	Provide clear learning objectives; moderate lecture pace, use class time effectively, correct errors, hold reviews, share summaries, provide timely feedback, direct students to resources, set high standards, and assess learning fairly.	They know their learners and how to build instruction from simple to complex in accessible language and scaffolded learning activities.	Questions, case studies, examples, and adaptive pedagogy, depending on the learner's development.	Nurture learners, create safe, trusting spaces, build a community of support by teachers and peers, and help learners set achievable yet challenging goals but accept no excuses. Assess individual growth along with course achievement.	Challenge the status quo, analyze and deconstruct common, taken-for-granted practices, text interrogation for messages and omissions, and consider who has a voice in the dominant discourse.

Appreciate Pedagogical Validity

Pratt et al. (2019) offered that the intersection of an adult educator's pedagogy, educational goals, and underlying values and assumptions comprises their "**pedagogical validity**'—who they are as a teacher and why they teach the way they do" (p. 638). They emphasized that for educators' reflection, judgment, and improvement to have an impact, they need to respect the tents of pedagogical validity and that people use four types of pedagogy to make meaning out of their teaching. These teaching frames help justify "good teaching" and are usually all present in any given educator's repertoire, although most people prefer one or two over the others. They noted the four types are: (1) Intellectual validity—claims to truth and evidence that use reasoning; (2) Relational validity—learning is influenced through relationships with others; (3) Moral validity—teaching involves moral judgments, decisions, and actions that are complex and ambiguous; and (4) Cultural validity—awareness of cultural values and social norms shape how a person teaches. The authors argued that an educator's **pedagogical identity** incorporates the four types. Pratt et al.'s (2019) tips for using pedagogical validity (p. 638):

1. Good teaching depends on more than a set of pedagogical skills.
2. Good teaching depends on an alignment of pedagogical skills and pedagogical validity.
3. Good teaching requires interpreting and responding to dynamic patterns of significance.
4. Patterns of significance are interpreted through frames of reference and habits of mind.
5. Frames of reference and habits of mind arise from a teacher's pedagogical validity.

Challenging the Teacher-as-Helper Paradigm

Brookfield (2021) challenged whether educators prefer one teaching perspective given the range of activities and fluidity they exhibit when teaching over a period of time where they might need to draw on multiple perspectives to serve learners best. The heart of Brookfield's critique is that if adult educators focus on helping learners learn, they engage in:

> planning instruction, creating a positive learning environment, overcoming resistance to learning, and building motivation. . . . This helping-people-learn perspective emphasizes continually shifting roles and methodologies. It places learners and learning at the conceptual

heart of teaching and emphasizes teachers arriving at a particular strategy only after getting to know learners. (Brookfield, 2021, p. 154)

Brookfield (2021), in the *Handbook of Adult and Continuing Education*, also disputed the value neutrality of the "teaching-as-helping-adults-learn" paradigm as being value neutral in that it "flattens curriculum, assigning everything a moral equivalency" (p. 154). He continued, "Teaching, when conceived as the technical task of helping adults learn, risks perpetuating broader asymmetries of power and privilege" (p. 155). He also critiqued the helping paradigm as failing to problematize the positional power and authority of the teacher, which can be implicitly authoritarian or oppressive. Brookfield concluded with a point that speaks to the diversity and fragmentation of the adult education field:

The paradigm of teacher as helper of adult learning will probably continue to hold sway in adult education. It has a necessary malleability that appeals to a field that, as this handbook shows, exhibits widely varying sites of practice period equally comma however comma its internal contradictions and its tendency to leave wider inequities in place will continue to be explored. (p. 156)

Chapter Summary

Chapter 4 explored "Pursuing a Career in the Adult Education Field," discussing adult education's broad and diverse landscape and considering what it means to build a career in this field. The chapter reviewed the conceptual, instrumental, technical, and interpersonal aspects of being an adult educator. Chapter 5 explores the inner life of an educator, considering how things like critical thinking and cultural humility influence their work.

Key Points

- Adult education is a broad range of activities to enhance skills, knowledge, or personal growth among adults in various contexts, from literacy programs to corporate training and community activism.
- Adult educators may work as literacy teachers, corporate trainers, instructional designers, and health educators. Their roles are diverse and often tailored to specific community, organizational, or individual needs.

- Building a professional identity as an adult educator is challenging due to the field's fragmentation. This identity is shaped by personal beliefs, values, and experiences and may or may not involve formal education in adult learning principles.
- The field spans a range of delivery systems, including formal educational institutions, community-based programs, and corporate learning environments, each with distinct goals, from social activism to workforce development.
- Effective adult educators must develop competencies in understanding adult learning processes, creating supportive learning environments, planning programs, assessing learners, and integrating technology.
- Many adult educators enter the field by chance and may lack formal training or clear professional boundaries, which can affect the coherence of their professional identity.
- Chapter 4 introduced tools to help adult educators reflect on their teaching philosophies and roles, including the Philosophy of Adult Education Inventory and Teaching Perspectives Inventory.

References

Apps, J. W. (1973). *Toward a working philosophy of adult education.* Syracuse University.

Apps, J. W., (1996). *Teaching from the heart.* Krieger.

Arnett, J. J. (2015). Identity development from adolescence to emerging adulthood: What we know and (especially) don't know. In K. C. McLean & M. U. Syed (Eds.), *The Oxford handbook of identity development* (pp. 53–64). Oxford University Press.

Association for Talent Development. (2023). *2023 State of the Industry: Talent development and benchmark trends.* ATD. https://www.td.org/product/p/192311.

Atkinson, T. A., & Claxton, G. L. (2000). *The intuitive practitioner: On the value of not always knowing what one is doing.* Open University Press.

Beder, H., & Carrea, N. (1988). The effects of andragogical teacher training on adult students' attendance and evaluation of their teachers. *Adult Education Quarterly, 38*(2), 75–87. https://doi.org/10.1177/0001848188038002002.

Bierema, L. L. (2010). *Implementing a critical approach to organization development.* Krieger.

Brockett, R. G. (1991). Professional development, artistry, and style. In R. G. Brockett (Ed.), *Professional development for educators of adults.* New Directions for Adult and Continuing Education, No. 51 (pp. 5–13). San Francisco: Jossey-Bass.

Brookfield, S. D. (2021). Teaching perspectives. In T. S. Rocco, M. C. Smith, R. C. Mizzi, L. R. Merriweather, & J. D. Hawley (Eds.), *The handbook of adult and continuing education* (pp. 150–157). Routledge.

Burke, P. J. (2003a). Introduction. In P. J. Burke, T. J. Owens, R. T. Serpe, & P. A. Thoits (Eds.), *Advances in identity theory and research* (pp. 1–7). Kluwer Academic/Plenum.

Collins, R. A. (2023). Interdisciplinarity. An adult and continuing education. In T. S. Rocco, M. C. Smith, R. C. Mizzi, L. R. Merriweather, & J. D. Hawley (Eds.), *The handbook of adult and continuing education* (pp. 31–37). Routledge.

Conti, G. J. (1998). Identifying your teaching style (Ch. 4). In M. W. Galbraith (Ed.), *Adult Learning Methods* (2nd ed., pp. 73–84). Krieger.

duTont, D. (1995). A sociological analysis of the extent and influence of professional socialization on the development of a nursing identity among nursing students at two universities in Brisbane, Australia. *Journal of Advanced Nursing, 21*, 164–171. https://doi.org/10.1046/j.1365-2648.1995.21010164.x.

Elias, J. L. (1982). The theory-practice split. *New Directions for Continuing Education, 15*, 3–11. https://doi.org/10.1002/ace.36719821503.

Elias, J. L., and Merriam, S. B. (1995). *Philosophical foundations of adult education* (2nd ed.). Malabar, FL: Krieger.

Elias, J. L., and Merriam, S. B. (2005). *Philosophical foundations of adult education* (3rd ed.). Malabar, FL: Krieger.

English, L. M. (2005). Third-space practitioners: Women educating for justice in the global south. *Adult Education Quarterly, 55*(2), 85–100. https://doi.org/10.1177/0741713604271851.

Fejes, A., & Nylander, E. (Eds.). (2019). *Mapping out the research field of adult education and learning*. Cham: Springer. https://doi.org/10.1007/978-3-030-10946-2.

Fenwick, T. (1996). *Firestarters and outfitters: Metaphors of adult education*. http://eric.ed.gov/?id=ED400463 (ERIC Reproduction Document No. ED 400463).

Fenwick, T. (2004). Learning in complexity: Work and knowledge in enterprise cultures. In P. Kell, S. Shore, & M. Singh (Eds.), *Adult education@21st century* (pp. 253–267). Peter Lang.

Forester, J. (1999). *The deliberative practitioner: Encouraging participatory planning processes*. MIT Press.

Freifeld, L. (2023, November 14). *2023 training and industry report*. *Training* magazine. https://trainingmag.com/2023-training-industry-report/.

Gedro, J. (2017). *Identity, meaning, and subjectivity in career development: Evolving perspectives in Human Resources*. Springer.

Goltz, H. H., & Smith, M. L. (2014). Forming and developing your professional identity: Easy as PI. *Health Promotion Practice, 15*(6), 785–789. https://doi.org/10.1177/1524839914541279.

Griffith, W. S. (1989). Has adult and continuing education fulfilled its early promise? In B. A. Quigley (Ed.), *Fulfilling the promise of adult and continuing education*. New Directions for Continuing Education, No. 44 (pp. 5–13). San Francisco: Jossey-Bass.

Heaney, T. W. (2000). Adult education and society. In A. L. Wilson & E. R. Hayes (Eds.) *Handbook of adult and continuing education* (pp. 559–572). Jossey-Bass.

Houle, C. O. (1956). Professional education for educators of adults. *Adult Education Quarterly, 6*(3), 131–150. https://doi.org/10.1177/074171365600600301

Houle, C. O. (1972). *The design of education*. Jossey-Bass.

Imel, S., Brocket, R. G., & James, W. B. (2000). Defining the profession: A critical appraisal. In A. L. Wilson & E. R. Hayes (Eds.), *Handbook of adult and continuing education* (pp. 628–642). San Francisco: Jossey-Bass.

Ioannou, N. (2023). Professional development of adult educators: A European perspective. *International Review of Education, 69*(3), 379–399. https://doi.org/10.1007/s11159-023-10014-0.

Jarvis, P. (1999). *Practitioner-researcher: Developing theory from practice*. Jossey-Bass.

Jeris, L., & Daley, B. (2004). Orienteering for boundary spanning: Reflections on the journey to date and suggestions for moving forward. *Advances in Developing Human Resources, 6*(1), 101–115. https://doi.org/10.1177/1523422303260420.

Lindeman, E. (1926). *The meaning of adult education.* New Republic, Incorporated.

Merriam, S. B., & Brockett, R. G. (1997). *The profession and practice of adult education: An introduction.* Jossey-Bass.

Merriam, S. B., & Brockett, R. G. (2007). *The profession and practice of adult education: An introduction.* Jossey-Bass.

Merriam, S. B., & Caffarella, R. (1999). *Learning in adulthood. A comprehensive guide.* Jossey-Bass.

Miller, J. P. (1994). *The contemplative practitioner.* Bergin & Garvey.

Monaghan, C. H., Isaac-Savage, E. P., & Putman, P. G. (Eds.). (2023). *Career pathways in adult education: perspectives and opportunities.* Taylor & Francis.

Overton, L. (2023). *Learning at work 2023 survey report.* London: Chartered Institute of Personnel and Development. https://www.cipd.org/globalassets/media/knowledge/knowledge-bhub/reports/2023-pdfs/2023-learning-at-work-survey-report-8378.pdf.

Owen, H. (1992). *Open space technology: A user's guide.* Abbott.

Pratt, D. D. (1998). *Five perspectives on teaching in adult and higher education.* Krieger.

Pratt, D. D., & Smulders, D. (2016). *Five perspectives on teaching: Mapping a plurality of the good.* Krieger.

Pratt, D. D., Schrewe, B., & Pusic, M. V. (2019). Pedagogical validity: The key to understanding different forms of "good" teaching. *Medical Teacher, 41*(6), 638–640. https://doi.org/10.1080/0142159X.2018.1533242.

Rocco, T. S., Smith, M. C., Mizzi, R. C., Merriweather, L. R., & Hawley, J. D. (Eds.). (2023). *The handbook of adult and continuing education.* Taylor & Francis.

Ross-Gordon, J. M., Rose, A. D., & Kasworm, C. E. (2016). *Foundations of adult and continuing education.* John Wiley & Sons.

Roth, G. (2004). CPE and HRD: Research and practice within systems and across boundaries. *Advances in Developing Human Resources, 6*(1), 9–19. https://doi.org/10.1177/1523422303260417

Schön, D. A. (1983). *The reflective practitioner: How professionals think in action.* Basic Books.

Sheared, V. (2023). Foreword. In C. H. Monaghan, E. P. Isaac-Savage, & P. G. Putman (Eds.). *Career Pathways in Adult Education: Perspectives and Opportunities* (pp. xi–xiii). Taylor & Francis.

US Census Bureau. (2022, February 24). *Census Bureau releases new educational attainment data.* US Census Bureau. https://www.census.gov/newsroom/press-releases/2022/educational-attainment.html.

Wahlgren, B. (2016). Adult educators' core competences. *International Review of Education, 62,* 343–353. https://doi.org/10.1007/s11159-016-9559-4.

Zinn, L. M. (1983). *Development of a valid and reliable instrument to identify a personal philosophy of adult education.* The Florida State University.

Zinn, L. M. (1991). Identifying your philosophical orientation. In M. W. Galbraith (Ed.), *Adult learning methods* (pp. 39–77). Krieger.

CHAPTER FIVE

BECOMING AN ADULT EDUCATOR

 **Box 5.1 Chapter Overview and Learning Objectives**

Michelle Obama (2021) wrote,

> Becoming isn't about arriving somewhere or achieving a certain aim. I see it instead as forward motion, a means of evolving, a way to reach continuously toward a better self. The journey doesn't end. (p. 419)

Chapter 5 is about becoming an adult educator, and Obama's notion of forward-evolving movement applies to becoming an adult educator and sustaining excellence as a teacher. The chapter takes a big-picture approach to considering what makes adult educators excellent. Becoming an effective teacher requires engagement in continuous learning and reflection to help learners achieve their goals effectively. The purpose of this chapter is to transcend the technical aspects of being an adult educator and examine four crucial mindsets that differentiate excellent teachers of adults. As a result of reading this chapter and completing the exercise boxes, you, the reader, should be able to:

1. Understand how to cultivate a global, adaptive stance.
2. Think critically about your work as an adult educator.

3. Understand the importance of equity and justice in effective teaching.
4. Define an adult learning leader.

The first section of educator Parker Palmer's (1998) book *The Courage to Teach* began with the header "We Teach Who We Are" (p. 1). Palmer wrote,

> I am a teacher at heart, and there are moments in the classroom when I can hardly hold the joy. When my students and I discover unchartered territory to explore, when the pathway out of the thicket opens up before us, when our experience is illuminated by the lightning-life of the mind—then teaching is the finest work I know.

> But at other moments, the classroom is so lifeless or painful or confused—and I am so powerless to do anything about it—that my claim to be a teacher seems a transparent sham. Then the enemy is everywhere: in those students from some alien planet, in that subject I thought I knew, and in this personal pathology that keeps me earning my life this way. What a fool I was to imagine that I had mastered this occult art—harder to divine than tea leaves and impossible for mortals to do even passably well! (p. 1)

Palmer's unvarnished reflections on the joys and travails of teaching capture the ups and downs and existential experiences of becoming an educator. His central premise in the book is that educators must know themselves: "*Good teaching cannot be reduced to technique; good teaching comes from the identity and integrity of the teacher*" (p. 10, italics in original). As an adult learner and educator, you have daily career experiences available as a learning repository, but do you use them? You take actions—doing things with particular aims in mind—multiple times daily. Perhaps you think about your actions, although probably not as a general rule or in a structured way.

Learning is a life force constantly in motion—discovering new ideas, boldly challenging the known, probing the unknown, making meaning, questioning reality, continually evolving, and developing the self and others. Learning is mostly informal; that is, it happens without structure or planning and maybe even in spite of educators or organizations. Without learning, people would struggle to survive. Learning gives an edge, whether it is to individuals who are gaining special training or making sense of information that is assaulting their senses during every waking hour or to organizations that value learning, create space and support for it, and pass on learning from generation to generation.

When there is no learning, people dig in their heels and refuse to budge from their much cherished and protected ideas, and conflict and unpleasantness ensue (Headlee, 2017). Nichols (2017) argued that the hyper-connected, information-rich society is perpetuating the "death of expertise," where a preference for 24–7 news programs and easy Internet access emboldens people to proudly reject the opinions and research of experts. Why pay attention to professionals who have worked their entire lives developing theory and practice around a topic when surfing an internet site puts them on equal footing with doctors and diplomats? Suddenly, expert knowledge is not as valued as it once was. Effective learners do not fall into this trap of opinion advocacy and ad hominem attacks, but rather, they stop and question and find appreciation for alternative views, even when they do not change their own.

A challenging and complex culture of deep political divisions and divisiveness characterizes the current social context. People seem less interested in learning about different views and are hopelessly polarized around key political, economic, and cultural values and beliefs. There is a sense of hopelessness and resignation around healing the wounds and scars that now characterize social, economic, cultural, and political landscapes worldwide. However, what is needed is to bring people together to work on the problems they collectively confront or even to find common ground. As authors, we often lament that the world needs more adult learning, especially among politicians and policymakers whose deep political divisions seem to render them incapable of learning or legislating and offering terrible examples of how to live a reflexive life of inquiry in community.

The field of adult education is continually changing in response to national and global trends, such as economic (in)stability, technological developments, political dynamics, and workforce needs. Nicolaides (2022) inquired, "How can adult learning make new worlds for self and society real?" (p. xxv) in her quest to understand "how adults learn and to make meaning, especially in the face of the unknown" (p. 1). Nicolaides (2022) stressed "the field of AE is grappling with how adults learn in a world being recomposed by a global pandemic and the *Ruptures* that have emerged from its influence" (p. 8, italics in the original). She advocated generative learning for learners to contend with the brisk pace of change and describing it as *"learning to become"* (p. 8).

Professionals in adult learning must adapt to these complexities and learn how they might change their priorities and their organization's needs. These dynamics mean it is helpful for adult educators to stay abreast of current events around the world and in their field, anticipate what will be required of them, and play an active role in educating others.

Yet, an effective adult educator is not simply a content expert who keeps up with current events, nor is it being an accomplished adult educator who meets the technical requirements for working in the field, as presented in Chapter 4. Becoming an excellent adult educator means you are knowledgeable about how adults learn and imaginative about designing experiences that make learning applicable, relevant, memorable, just, and equitable. You are deeply engaged in your own learning pursuits and inquiry into your teaching practices, philosophy, and values.

Chapter 4 detailed careers in adult education, the field's boundaries, teaching perspectives and philosophies, and the key competencies necessary for doing the work. Adult education is broad and an enduring challenge for the field is many people doing the work of adult education do not necessarily identify themselves as adult educators. Perhaps there is a need to rebrand the title "adult educator" to something more inspiring and illustrative of the crucial work of this field. People who facilitate the learning of adults serve a vital role to individual learners and society in that they catalyze lifelong learning; help people develop skills, mindsets, knowledge, and capacity to function in a VUCA context; support the growth and development of individuals, groups, organizations, and communities; provide valuable mentoring, coaching, and advising; design innovative, active learning experiences for learners; and empower people to see themselves as knowers and knowledge creators and potentially create transformation. Although this chapter may not suggest a perfect new title for the vital work of the adult education field, it focuses on the mindsets and capacities of excellent adult educators.

Effectiveness as an adult educator is a way of being and helping others in their learning quests. It is a privilege and a serious undertaking. This chapter transcends the technical aspects of pursuing a career in adult education and focuses on four crucial mindsets that distinguish excellent teachers of adults: (1) cultivating a global, adaptive stance; (2) thinking critically about your work as an adult educator; (3) committing to equity and justice; and (4) becoming an adult learning leader.

Cultivating a Global, Adaptive Stance

Adult educators are pivotal in helping adults learn to think critically, participate effectively in society, and create meaningful change. Given the politically divisive global context, many countries around the world are confronting myriad social issues that seem difficult, if not impossible, to solve, such as social injustice; intractable wars causing displacement of and senseless violence against civilians; environmental crises such as climate change and weather catastrophes; food and water insecurity; lack of access to health care; and economic and political instability. These thorny problems and conflicts are described as **"wicked problems"** (Rittel & Webber, 1973), also known as "divergent problems" (Schumacher, 1995), "ill-structured problems" (Mitroff et al., 2004), or "social messes" (Ackoff, 1973; Horn, 2001). Resolving these challenges will require many people to change their mindsets and behaviors and collaborate with others to address problems and implement change. Adult educators can be pivotal in helping learners and organizations learn through these abstruse challenges.

Understanding "Wicked Problems"

VUCA—shorthand for volatile, uncertain, complex, and ambiguous—was introduced in Chapter 2 and has been adopted broadly to describe the current and future state of the world as it grapples with the megatrends of globalization, technology, individualization, demographic change, digitization, political uncertainty, economic instability, and environmental crisis, where a state of VUCA is the new normal (van der Steege, 2017). Prior to entering the VUCA age, social problems were defined as "tame," as noted by Rittel and Webber (1973):

> The professional's job was once seen as solving an assortment of problems that appeared to be definable, understandable and consensual. He [sic] was hired to eliminate those conditions that predominant opinion judged undesirable. His [sic] record has been quite spectacular, of course; the contemporary city and contemporary urban society stand as clean evidences of professional prowess. The streets have been paved, and roads now connect all places; houses shelter virtually everyone; the dread diseases are virtually gone; clean water is piped into nearly every building; sanitary sewers carry wastes from them; schools and hospitals serve virtually every district; and so on. The accomplishments of the past century in these respects have been truly phenomenal, however short of some persons' aspirations they might have been. (p. 156)

This book uses the term "wicked problems" to refer to these seemingly intractable social issues.

Addressing wicked problems requires mitigating their negative impacts and redirecting learners and organizations in more sustainable and life-enhancing ways. It also requires a systems perspective, multi-collaborative approaches, and the development and application of interdisciplinary knowledge and skills. *An essential consideration for adult education is equipping practitioners and the field to address the individual, organizational, and community learning needs inherent in these complex social issues.* Understanding wicked problems is a key aspect of cultivating a global adaptive mindset. Box 5.2 further defines the concept of wicked problems.

Becoming Adaptable and Resilient and Helping Learners Do the Same

The adaptive leadership literature offers insights for considering the role of facilitating learning amid VUCA conditions. Adult educators functioning in complex and ambiguous contexts cannot succeed by applying the exact instrumental, technical solutions that have not worked in solving the same problems repeatedly, in much the same way these approaches are ineffective for education. VUCA context and wicked problems demand a more flexible approach typical of **adaptive leadership**—"the practice of mobilizing people to tackle tough challenges and thrive" (Heifetz et al., 2009, p. 14). Adaptive thinkers and educators need to distinguish between adaptive challenges and technical problems, and the failure to do this is the most common cause of leadership failure (Heifetz et al., 2009), and we, as authors, would add learning failure. **Technical problems,** also described by Rittel and Webber (1973) as "tame," can be complicated and important to resolve, but they have known solutions that can be implemented using current knowledge by an authoritative figure (you have a flat tire and need to repair or replace it).

On the other hand, **adaptive challenges** or wicked problems require learning to define and solve and rely on motivating stakeholders to change their priorities, beliefs, habits, and loyalties (e.g., creating a self-driving or electric vehicle). Consider women leaders for a human contrast of technical and adaptive problems. Technical solutions such as hiring more women, offering sensitivity training, or putting token women in high-profile positions do not address inhospitable culture, challenge leadership stereotypes, develop new identities for women leaders, or diminish implicit bias against women. An adaptive approach would address systemic bias and discrimination and intervene to change policy and culture to make the organization more welcoming for women's advancement.

Cseh et al. (2013) conducted a qualitative study to understand how leaders developed global mindsets. They found that these leaders cultivated transcendence, plasticity of the mind (flexibility, thinking differently, rebalancing, openness, having multiple frames of reference), mindfulness, curiosity, and humility. The leaders learned these skillsets through informal learning as they went about their work and personal lives and reported the value of learning from

 ## Box 5.2 Tips and Tools for Teaching and Learning

Wicked Problems

The VUCA state generates "wicked problems," defined by Rittel and Webber (1973) as difficult or seemingly impossible challenges due to the lack of a single solution and their incomplete, contradictory, and shifting characteristics. Existing knowledge and theory prove inadequate for accurate forecasting and action about wicked problems, and political pluralities make achieving unified aims arduous, if not impossible. Rittel and Webber defined 10 characteristics of wicked problems as being:

1. There is no definitive formulation of a wicked problem because understanding of the problem is fleeting.
2. Wicked problems have no stopping rule; there is no correct answer. Stopping work on wicked problems usually means running out of time, money, or patience.
3. Solutions to wicked problems are not true or false but good or bad.
4. There is no immediate and ultimate test of a solution to a wicked problem. "Solutions" often have unintended consequences with repercussions that may be difficult to measure, particularly in the short term.
5. Every solution to a wicked problem is a "one-shot operation" because there is no opportunity to learn by trial and error. Every attempt counts significantly.
6. Wicked problems do not have an enumerable (or an exhaustively describable) set of potential solutions, nor is there a well-described set of permissible operations that may be incorporated into the plan—for example, efforts to stop crime or drug usage.
7. Every wicked problem is essentially unique.
8. Wicked problems are symptoms of another problem. Conflicting evidence only makes it more challenging to pinpoint the problem and take action to solve it.
9. The existence of a discrepancy representing a wicked problem can be explained in numerous ways. The choice of explanation determines the nature of the problem's resolution.
10. The planner has no right to be wrong (pp. 161–166).

What wicked problems have you encountered as an adult educator or learner?

mistakes, learning from the self and others, and learning through self-reflection. Cseh et al. concluded that self-reflection and reflection with others are fundamental to developing a global mindset. Doing the deep work of learning to lead requires a commitment to learning that relies on reflective practice, openness, and humility, which are rarely discussed in management literature and tend to be performative, masculine, and instrumental. Given the VUCA context and wicked problems, adult educators need to be comfortable with ambiguity and risk, develop themselves, and help others develop ease in working in this VUCA context with challenging issues. They must also cultivate critical thinking and reflexivity about their role, values, and work as educators.

Developing Resilience in Teaching and Learning

Cultivating an adaptive stance requires resiliency. People who demonstrate **resilience** "possess three defining characteristics: They coolly accept the harsh realities facing them. They find meaning in terrible times. And they have an uncanny ability to improvise, making do with whatever's at hand" (Coutu, 2002, p. 46). Resilience is one of four psychological constructs of **positive organization behavior** (hope, efficacy, resilience, and optimism)—"the study and application of positively oriented human resource strengths and psychological capacities that can be measured, developed, and effectively managed for performance improvement in today's workplace" (Luthans, 2002, p. 59). Eliot (2020) wrote about the importance of human resource development in building the resiliency capacity of individuals and organizations. Gichuhi's (2021) systematic literature review of shared leadership and organizational resilience recognized that the "great man" view of leadership (an all-powerful man, usually white, influences people and the organization through their power, position, and heroic actions) is outdated in a shifting global and turbulent context. Shared leadership is more egalitarian and depends on resilience to face tumultuous times. Gichuhi's review linked shared leadership with resilience to result in crisis-aware organizations capable of sharing and assimilating knowledge to better respond to crisis, effectively absorb challenges, and develop transformative capacity through shared leadership and employee commitment. The review also found that people were inclined "towards soft-skilled leaders who demonstrate self-awareness, motivation, empathy, and self-regulation, as opposed to an exhibition of purely hard leadership skills such as intelligence, technical prowess, and rigor" (p. 81).

Bertella (2022) argued that resiliency links to learning, evident in the capacity of a community and its citizens to learn to adapt in the face of crisis, noting resiliency's characteristics of elasticity, hysteresis, and malleability

(Westman, 1986). **Elasticity** is how quickly a community or system can restore stability after a disturbance, likened by Bertella to **single-loop learning** that seeks to correct routine errors by modifying behaviors (Argyris and Schön 1997). **Hysteresis** is the extent to which recovery patterns do not reverse the original situation but instead retain a memory of the original state and accommodate the change to deal with the challenge. **Malleability** is how easily systems alter permanently. Bertella surmised that systemic and malleable resilience relates to multiple loop learning as posed by Argyris and Schön (1997) that extends beyond single loop learning to question assumptions, focus on learning to learn, consider how the social context affects learning, and result in deep or transformative learning.

Thinking Critically About Your Work as an Adult Educator

Palmer wrote about the identity and integrity of teachers. As an adult educator, you can develop these attributes by cultivating a curious mind, practicing reflexivity, engaging in action inquiry, and developing conscientization.

Cultivating a Curious Mind

Curiosity is "the motivation to learn, be open to new ideas, and explore novel environments and situations" (Chamorro-Premuzic, 2023, para. 2) or the desire to acquire cognitive knowledge and sensory experiences that promote exploratory behavior (Berlyne 1966). Reio et al. (2006) defined curiosity as information seeking or cognitive inquisitiveness that motivates information seeking, plus sensory exploration that causes people to seek out sensation through cognitive and sensory exploratory behavior. For example, imagine a person visiting Italy and strolling through a bustling outdoor market, where they encounter food, textiles, and home accessories. They begin exploring different produce stands to discover unfamiliar fruits and vegetables. They look up translations of the produce names on their smartphone or ask the vendor about their products (cognitive curiosity through information seeking about the produce). They also reach out to smell the fruit and touch the produce to experience the physical aspects of new fruits and vegetables (sensory exploration through direct physical interaction of touch, smell, and sight). This example illustrates curiosity in both information-seeking and sensory exploration. Curiosity also enables a person to continue learning, which is essential for effectiveness as an adult educator and learner and is a highly sought-after attribute when organizations seek workers (Chamorro-Premuzic, 2023).

In their review of curiosity measures, Wagstaff et al. (2021) concluded that curiosity matters in contexts where learning occurs. Excellent adult educators are curious about cognitive and sensory experiences that improve their teaching capacity. Although curiosity is important, perhaps it is not always a priority of educators. Gouthro (2019) explored reasons why educators may not spend as much time teaching and learning, lamenting, "Within a neoliberal context, we are not encouraged to reflect on broader social issues of equity, inclusion, or citizenship" (p. 70). They further emphasized,

> Becoming a good adult educator involves being able to delve into assumptions that we have about teaching and learning, and helping learners reflect on their beliefs as well. With a well-grounded understanding of theory to inform our teaching, we may be better able to draw on the most appropriate pedagogical strategies in response to situations that can occur in various teaching contexts.
> (Gouthro, 2019, p. 70)

As adult educators and learners go about their lives, they juggle family, organization, and community roles. They may not always have time to improve their capacity to teach and learn, as observed by Gouthro (2019):

> As we become exposed to a wider array of theories, we realize that as educators, we have the choice to be better informed about our teaching practices. Sometimes as educators, we struggle, of course, working against indifference, stifling administrative structures, or dealing with fractious colleagues. . . . Most of us believe that the work that we do does have meaning, and so the meaning-making purpose of theory is an important resource to sustain us in striving to be our best, and to help our students engage in valuable learning that will help them develop their own contributions to the field. (p. 73)

Gouthro emphasized "slow learning," borrowing from the slow food movement that embraces enjoying things at one's own pace, experimenting, and asking questions. They suggested "apply[ing] these principles to our own work as adult educators to engage in careful scholarship and reflect on the values and beliefs that shape our work" (Gouthro, 2019, p. 73). Box 5.3 features strategies for being more curious.

Practicing Reflexivity. The average person has more than six thousand thoughts per day (Tseng & Poppenk, 2020). Yet, how many of these thoughts are

 **Box 5.3 Tips and Tools for Teaching and Learning**

Building Curiosity

Have you ever felt like you get into the same rut with your teaching as an adult educator? Most educators lead full lives and have multiple roles. Chamorro-Premuzic (2023), in their *Harvard Business Review* article, "How to Strengthen Your Curiosity Muscle," offered the following strategies for becoming more curious in life and work. Try some of these out if you would like to approach life with more curiosity:

1. Intentionally Practice Activities that Enhance Curiosity:
   a. Schedule 20–30 minutes daily to cultivate curiosity intentionally. You might try journaling, visiting a museum, calling someone to chat, or taking a meditative walk.
   b. Seek colleagues to share ideas and brainstorm about life or work issues and how you might think about them in new ways.
   c. Make asking "Why?" a regular habit so that you can go deeper in your exploration of your life and work and conversations.

2. Self-reflect on the Following Questions:
   a. What do I want to know more about?
   b. Where do I want to build my expertise?
   c. What questions keep me up at night?

3. Change your Routine:
   a. Collaborate with people you don't usually collaborate with.
   b. Switch the route you take to work.
   c. Eat new foods or try a new restaurant.
   d. Try something new on the weekends.
   e. Set out to learn or experience something new.

4. Experiment:
   a. Find opportunities for new experiences where you might learn a new skill or idea or have the chance to have a deep conversation or visit new places.
   b. Play with generative AI.
   c. Switch to a new activity when you find yourself getting bored.
   d. Find a curiosity buddy or a person and mutually challenge each other to be more curious.

Source: Adapted from Chamorro-Premuzic (2023).

introspective—inwardly scrutinizing one's thoughts, feelings, and actions? Self-scrutiny, examination, or soul searching about one's work life is known as **professional reflexivity** or **reflection**—a practice of critical self-examination that probes one's beliefs, assumptions, choices, and behaviors to assess how they influence one's work, in this case, teaching and educating. Reflection involves learning from and within an experience. The skills of reflexivity must be honed continuously as an adult educator. It is not a new concept as Dewey (1933) advocated the importance of an "ability to 'turn things over,' to look at matters deliberately, to judge whether the amount and kind of evidence requisite for decision is at hand" (pp. 66–67). Dewey believed that reflection began with an experience that beckoned the opportunity to learn from it. The action-learning cycles typical in action learning echo this belief. Dewey also argued that reflection prevented people from falling into routinized thought and action influenced by an external authority to engage in a more careful and critical consideration of taken-for-granted knowledge within the self.

Schön (1983) distinguished between reflection-on-action and reflection-in-action in his work on professional learning. **Reflection-on-action** involves retrospectively evaluating a decision, event, or action by contemplating what happened, why it happened, and how future thinking and acting might be improved. For instance, as an adult educator, you might assess your teaching after the class has ended and consider how your curricular decisions about the lesson and its delivery mode impacted learning or how class dynamics influenced learners and might be challenged or changed next time. **Reflection-in-action** occurs when you rely on a tacit knowing-in-the-moment, or "thinking on your feet," which involves spontaneously making decisions and acting on them almost simultaneously. For example, you might assess a student who is overtalking during class and determine the behavior requires you to intervene on behalf of another student or the entire class, and you do so during the class. You might call for a break and speak with the student instead of calling on them during the class remark, "I see you have another comment, and let's hear from someone who has not yet spoken on this issue." Reflection-in-action relies on the individual, group, and institutional knowledge and practice you have amassed over time and the ability to apply this knowledge to the context and situation. Box 5.4 lists strategies to bolster reflection in your own life as an adult learner or educator.

Engaging in Action Inquiry. Torbert (2004) offered additional ways of approaching reflection, or "action inquiry." **Inquiry** is engagement in reflection, listening, speaking, and leading with mindfulness and integrity. **Action** results from your reflections, learning, mistakes, and consultations with others. Ideally, it is mindful,

Box 5.4 Reflective Practice

Reflection Strategies

How can you build more reflection and introspection into your life and work as an adult learner or educator? Here are 20 strategies to try:

1. Devote time to reflective activities regularly by practicing reflective meditation, journaling, or discussing issues with trusted confidantes.
2. Assess yourself by reflecting on your teaching, seeking assessment instruments, or asking someone else to give you feedback.
3. Tune into your emotions. Ask yourself, "How did I feel when X happened in class?"
4. Ask open-ended questions like *"How could I think about this differently?"*
5. Journal.
6. Make art.
7. Try deep breathing exercises.
8. Dialogue with trusted colleagues or friends.
9. Meditate.
10. Seek feedback.
11. Practice reflective writing: Engage in self-analysis of an experience, opportunity, or challenge. Write in the first person.
12. Write a letter to yourself for some date in the future.
13. Reflect with a peer.
14. Think out loud. Consider capturing your thoughts on audio.
15. Try something new and reflect on the experience.
16. Take a retreat.
17. Take a walk.
18. Practice gratitude by reviewing people and things you are thankful for.
19. Assess your behaviors or actions and consider what you might change.
20. Think about what you do not know.

timely, and just. After reflecting, you decide to shift how you go about the work as an educator or learner. Inquiry follows Torbert's (2004) three levels of reflection being first person, second person, and third person, or essentially (1) pondering individual thought and action as an adult learner or educator—critiquing an activity you facilitated in class, (2) being mindful of your interactions with others—considering how you advised a student, and finally, (3) considering how your thought and action affects larger systems like organization and communities—connecting how your engagements with the educational program create a particular culture or outcomes.

Inquiry seeks information or meaning where you can be "simultaneously productive and self-assessing" (Torbert, 2004, p. 13). How often do you seek meaning in your teaching decisions and actions? Likely, you do when something goes wrong, but engaging in this type of learning is always available, and if you are to be a good learning role model, it is necessary for mindful practice. Action inquiry is a powerful approach to learning from life, particularly your career as an adult educator.

Torbert (2004) defined **action inquiry** as "a way of simultaneously conducting action and inquiry as a disciplined leadership practice that increases the wider effectiveness of our actions" (p. 1). The value of action inquiry is it is free, always available, and anyone can do it. Torbert continued, "Action inquiry becomes a moment-to-moment way of living whereby we attune ourselves through inquiry to acting in an increasingly timely and wise fashion for the overall development of the families, teams, and organizations in which we participate" (pp. 1–2). Torbert (2004) urged "conscious living" by paying careful attention to our interactions "from the inside-out to the experience we have, hoping to learn from them and modify our actions and even our way of thinking as a result" (p. 4). Another way to think about action inquiry is as a reflexive practice of correcting errors while engaging with others during your work. This practice demands that you be highly aware of the present situation and respond accordingly. Torbert posed action inquiry as a collaborative process where people co-create and support the inquiry process.

What is the value of action inquiry? Torbert (2004) identified three primary aims as (1) generating effectiveness and integrity by exploring the gaps between the results that were intended versus the outcomes that were realized; (2) generating a critical and constructive mutuality in relationships where there is inquiry into power dynamics and how it plays out between people to allow them to more creatively construct shared vision, strategy, and collaboration; and (3) generating sustainability that results in effectiveness, integrity, mutuality, and transformation to greater social good and justice, principles constituting core adult learning activities. As Torbert mused,

> Action inquiry represents an approach to powerful action that is
> fundamentally different from modern political/organizational action
> because it treats mutually transforming power—a kind of power that few

people today recognize or exercise—as more powerful than unilateral power. . . . The special power of action inquiry—transforming power—comes from a combination of dedication to our intent or shared vision; alertness to gaps among vision, strategy, performance, and outcomes in ourselves and others; and a willingness to play a leading role with others in organizational or social transformations, which includes being vulnerable to transformation ourselves. (pp. 8–9)

Torbert introduced three levels of inquiry as a structure for becoming more mindful and aware of how one's engagement in relationships affects them, others, and their system, known as first, second, and third person. Table 5.1 offers definitions and career implications.

As an adult learner and educator, you will find reflecting on these three levels of interactions beneficial to promoting learning. Inquiry is engagement in reflection, listening, speaking, and leading with mindfulness and integrity. Having another colleague, coach, mentor, or friend who can help you inquire into your mindsets, emotions, and ideas and debrief with you when things go awry is helpful. Action results from your reflections, learning, mistakes, and consultations with others. Ideally, it is a mindful, timely, and just response to the activities and ideas you have been reflecting on in your own teaching and learning. Reflecting on action and change helps ensure career events within your control are constructive.

Torbert (2004) asked how people can "become more aware of, and less constrained by, [their] own implicit and often untested assumptions about situations [they] find [themselves] in?" (p. 21). He suggested the first step is to

TABLE 5.1 THREE LEVELS OF ACTION AS ADULT EDUCATOR REFLECTION

Step	Definition	Adult Educator Application
First Person	Reflect on your thoughts and actions.	Now that I am leading adult learners, I have to make decisions and engage people in them or explain what I decided and why. I am not always feeling confident in this new role.
Second Person	You are mindful of your interactions with others.	Sometimes, my unsureness and lack of confidence mean I am not detailed or patient enough in my requests for input or giving of explanations.
Third Person	You consider how your thoughts and actions affect larger systems like organizations and communities.	My mindset of insecurity is not helping me build trusting relationships with my students, team, or boss, which hurts our ability to do our work.

 **Box 5.5 Reflective Practice**

Strategies to Practice Noticing

Torbert (2004, p. 56) offered strategies for recognizing the limits of ordinary attention and awareness. Practice noticing these things as you go about your day as an
adult learner or educator.

1. Set an alarm to go off every 60 minutes. When your alarm rings, spend 10 seconds
   noticing how you feel mentally, emotionally, and physically when the alarm goes
   off. This state might include being irritated when the alarm rang.
2. When you transition from one activity to another, focus on the transition and
   notice how you feel about ending the previous activity and beginning the next one.
3. Check-in with yourself periodically every day, for example, at mealtime or bedtime, to identify the most satisfying moment since the last check in. Stop to recognize what was least satisfying since the last check in and why. Reflect on whether
   you were aware of these reactions when the events occurred.
4. Develop a habit of noticing how you feel after each meaningful interaction with
   other people.

practice noticing—realize how limited the human attention and awareness span
is. The next step is to exercise awareness in new ways amid challenges. Torbert
recommended reflective practice as an important tool to recognize the limits
of ordinary attention by journaling about significant personal, professional, or
community incidents, people, and unsatisfactory outcomes. The beauty of
action inquiry is it foregrounds learning as a key process for change, interpersonal collaboration, and growth. Box 5.5 offers activities to practice noticing.

Developing Conscientization

Brazilian educator Paulo Freire, author of the widely acclaimed *Pedagogy of the
Oppressed*, highlighted the humanity of learning: "For apart from inquiry, apart
from the praxis, [individuals] cannot be truly human. Knowledge emerges only
through invention and re-invention, through the restless, impatient, continuing,
hopeful inquiry human beings pursue in the world, with the world, and with each
other" (Freire, 1970, p. 58). Freire valued transformational learning for its role in

fostering social change. Learning here is viewed as emancipatory: Through learning, unequal forces of power can be challenged, and oppression is diminished. As people recognize their own power to influence change, they go through a process of "conscientization," achieved through a mixture of action and reflection.

Adult education aspires to inspire learners to discover a Freirean (Freire, 1973a, 1973b) **"critical consciousness,"** which refers to recognizing how structural oppression and social marginalization due to racism, sexism, ableism, colonization, or lack of access to education or opportunity create inequities in work and life. Diemer and Blustein (2006) described critical consciousness as "the capacity to recognize and overcome sociopolitical barriers" (p. 220). For instance, understanding how structural racism and inequitable access to resources create educational inequities and how people can take individual or collective action can change the system through learning. **Conscientization**—the process of becoming critically alert to social and cultural context through reflection and action—was introduced by Freire, who developed a critical pedagogy to teach impoverished, poorly educated Brazilians how to challenge the system. Box 5.6 captures some of Freire's key ideas about teaching adults.

Dialogue is the basis of conscientization—a process of naming the world (McKillican, 2020) where people mutually question assumptions behind their thinking, explore new ideas and concepts, and seek to create an understanding of the topic of conversation. McKillican (2020) investigated Irish adult educators' use of Freirean concepts in their teaching practice and how their experiences shaped their pedagogy, philosophy, and practice. They found that personal and collective awareness were essential to developing conscientization, concluding,

> Adult education research should not only embrace those aspects of
> Freire's theory which focus on the socio-economic, functional or political
> aspects of education, adult education research should also focus on those
> elements of Freire's theory that allow us to formally analyze aspects such
> as how adult education can bring us to a closer understanding of
> ourselves in our relationships with other people. (p. 137)

Conscientization is a vital tool for addressing social inequity. Byrd (2018) challenged the human resource development field to confront social injustice by speaking about organizational injustices and helping learners develop mindsets dedicated to advancing social justice and fostering strong human relations. She recommended social justice as a progressive workplace norm that honors inclusivity, safety, and security, access to developmental opportunities, and promoting workplace democracy. Supporting conscientization requires learning.

Box 5.6 Reflective Practice

Breaking the Bank

Paulo Freire (1970) was a vocal critic of education and pedagogies such as lecture with its consequence of habituating students into becoming passive recipients of information deposits provided by the teacher. Freire called this transaction "banking education" as a metaphor of the teacher making knowledge deposits into the learner's head, which the learners were supposed to accept without question. The problems with banking education include that it locks learners into subordination to the teacher and prevents them from developing critical thinking skills. Banking education depends on reinforcing polarities that bolster the teacher-learner hierarchy:

- Teachers teach, and students are taught.
- Teachers are experts, and students are inexpert.
- Teachers talk, and students listen (and take notes).

The big-picture impact of banking education is its reinforcement of social power binaries.

Freire proposed shifting education to a process of problem-posing and dialogue where teachers and learners collaboratively explored concepts as an alternative to banking education. Through intellectual engagement with learners, the teacher is no longer a detached "dominating" figure telling learners what to think. Instead, learners and teachers are mutually answerable for learning.

Consider your experience as an adult learner or educator:

1. Have you experienced what Freire (1970) called "banking education"?
2. How is education and learning complicit in teaching students to depend on the teacher for their learning?
3. What strategies might you employ to design education to encourage more learner self-directedness?
4. What have been some of your most engaging and autonomous learning experiences? Would you rank them as "banking education" or more mutual dialogue and exploration?

Source: Adapted from Bierema et al., 2024, p. 141.

Committing to Equity and Justice

Thinking critically about adult learning and education means becoming attuned to power and marginalization dynamics to practice more equitably and justly as an adult educator. Applying critical perspectives, as introduced and defined in Chapter 3, helps adult educators in this quest. It involves understanding how your positionality shapes your teaching and how your biases manifest. Over the past three decades, views on diversity, equity, equality, justice, inclusion, decolonization, and decoloniality have garnered increased attention. Power relations function to exclude participation and silence marginalized individuals based on **positionality** or identities such as gender, race, age, physical ability, gender identity and expression, religion, language, social class, and other identities. Many organizations have undertaken initiatives aimed at being more just and equitable, captured under some familiar acronyms such as: DEI (diversity, equity, and inclusion), DEIB (diversity, equity, inclusion, and belonging), EDI (equality, diversity, and inclusion), EDID (equity, diversity, inclusion, and decolonization), EDIR (equality, diversity, inclusion, and respect), or JEDI (justice, equality/equity, diversity, and inclusion). Unfortunately, these initiatives are under political attack in the United States and elsewhere, as discussed in Chapter 3. Committing to equity and justice involves appreciating intersectionality, and practicing cultural humility for optional learning that honors diversity, equity, and inclusion. Learners and educators can begin this process by assessing diversity intelligence, as described in Box 5.7.

 ## Box 5.7 Tips and Tools for Teaching and Learning

Assessing Diversity Intelligence®

Hughes and Liang (2020) defined diversity intelligence (DQ) as "the capability of individuals to recognize the value of workplace diversity and to use this information to guide thinking and behavior" (Hughes, 2018, p. 374). To assess your level of DQ, you can visit this website (note there is a cost): https://www.diversityintelligencellc .com/. The instrument measures diversity knowledge, workplace training and education perceptions, individual behavior, and an overall DQ score.

Appreciating Intersectionality

Intersectionality, coined by Kimberlé Crenshaw (1989), denotes women of color's distinctive and complicated life experiences that are not explainable by analyzing them through the lens of gender or race. Intersectionality was shaped by Black feminism (Collins, 1990, 2022) and Black women's frustration over the short-comings of feminist theory and its associated activism for how it centered on White middle-class women's experience. Black feminism emphasizes the experiences of Black or African American women, illuminating how racism and sexism intersect to marginalize and oppress them. For example, Black women experience a more significant pay gap than White or Asian women (Belli, 2018; Ketkar et al., 2021; Payscale, 2023). Black Feminist Thought (Collins, 1990) recognizes the diversity of Black women and provides a common ground for interpreting Black women's experience of entwined oppressions of gender and race.

Although the interlinking positionalities of gender and race served as the initial impetus for exploring Black women's subordination, scholars broadened its scope beyond gender and race (Cho et al., 2013) to capture the multiple social identities shaping people and the countless ways they interlace, and are socially created (Bowleg, 2008; Collins & Bilge, 2020). Intersectionality unfolds in adult education in the diverse ways people learn, process information, and make meaning across their life span. Inequity and injustice based on intersectionality occur when adult learners have unequal access to education or are marginalized in the learning process by the educator, other learners, or the institution. Recently, Sim and Bierema have published scholarship linking intersectionality with pedagogy, leadership, and adult education research (see Sim & Bierema, 2023; Sim et al., 2023; Sim & Bierema, 2024). Box 5.8 offers an opportunity to assess individual bias.

Practicing Cultural Humility

Understanding intersectionality helps adult educators become more aware of the dynamics that shape educational experiences and environments. Awareness is essential, and there are additional tools to help educators navigate social structures that perpetuate inequity, such as colonization and discrimination. **Colonization** is when one nation exerts political and economic power over other countries or groups, seizing their land and resources, and the colonizer enlists the colonized entity's people:

> In oppositional relations of domination and subordination in which each is convinced and complicit in their role. This oppositional relationship is maintained through a cultural, educational, and psychological hegemony in which the colonized come to believe in their own inferiority and that

Box 5.8 Reflective Practice

The Implicit Bias Association Test (IAT)

The Implicit Bias Association Test (IAT) was developed to measure brain associations when associating various images. This tool can help you become more aware of your implicit bias as an adult learner or educator. If you discover something you did not expect as you work through these exercises, try asking yourself questions about it from a place of curiosity. Questions such as, "What is behind this result?" or "Where did I learn this?" might be effective starting points.

According to the website:

The Implicit Association Test (IAT) measures attitudes and beliefs that people may be unwilling or unable to report. The IAT may be especially interesting if it shows that you have an implicit attitude that you did not know about. For example, you may believe that women and men should be equally associated with science, but your automatic associations could show that you (like many others) associate men with science more than you associate women with science. (Project Implicit, para. 2)

You can learn more and use the tool here:
https://implicit.harvard.edu/implicit/takeatest.html

they must become Whiter (Fanon, 1967); they gain self-worth and prestige to the degree they come to adopt the culture of the colonizers. (Hanson & Jaffe, 2023, p. 341)

Bierema et al. (2024) defined **colonialism** as the Western world's foisting of cultural, ideological, and economic structures on less powerful countries. **Decolonization** is a counter-response to challenge the injustices of colonization and a process where adult education to inspire and facilitate social change is crucial, especially to resist colonizing educational practices (Hanson & Jaffe, 2023; Nyerere, 1968). Hanson and Jaffe argued although Western education has made significant advances, it must also be challenged for creating epistemic injustices from colonizing practices that subordinate other Indigenous populations through educational institutions that construct colonized people as "intrinsically different, threatening, superstitious, and incorrect" (p. 342). Decolonizing education involves scrutinizing "who speaks for whom; [and] how knowledge about others is expressed, understood and valued . . . and how knowledge is embedded in colonial systems of meaning and power. . . . Decolonizing methodologies involve confronting positionality" (Hanson & Jaffe, 2023, p. 342). Hanson and Jaffe (2023) further emphasized "decolonizing [adult and continuing education] involves deconstructing colonial systems of knowledge by rewriting, rethinking, and reassessing how we teach, learn, and conduct research" (p. 342). They also urged constant reflexivity and the development of decolonizing pedagogies. Decolonizing for adult educators is reviewing and reversing the structural mechanisms that sustain educational systems that have created "'Othering,' the marginalization of minoritised epistemology and racially driven human rights violations" (Anka, 2024, p. 1).

Challenging colonization requires educators to develop epistemic and cultural humility (Ewuoso, 2023). These can be better understood by first defining **epistemic injustice** as "the silencing of a person's knowledge, their capacity to speak as a knower and the psychological harm caused by the silencing" (Anka, 2024, p. 8). There are two types of epistemic injustice, according to Fricker (2007): testimonial and hermeneutical. **Testimonial injustice** is the silencing or not acknowledging a knower's capacity to speak or the prejudicial unwillingness to give the person credibility or respect. **Hermeneutic injustice** is "when a gap in collective interpretive resources puts someone at an unfair disadvantage when it comes to making sense of their social experiences" (Fricker, 2007, p. 1). **Epistemic humility** is when a person realizes the limits of their knowledge and is willing and able to discern instances when their ignorance can cause potential injury.

Further, epistemic humility is the extent to which people prioritize the truth of their own beliefs over experts' knowledge. Their capacity to acknowledge some circumstances resist knowability, and this ambiguity permeates much of decision-making (Parviainen et al., 2021). **Cultural humility** is a person's capacity to engage with new cultures using an ethic of care stance (privileging relationships) and self-reflexivity (capacity to self-reflect). They appreciate experiencing new cultures and demonstrate genuine curiosity to learn about the new culture from its members. Cultural humility is contrasted with **cultural competence,** which is the appreciation of diverse cultures but not necessarily the openness to learn and shift individual beliefs and customs once exposed to other cultures and their members (Lekas et al., 2020). Anka (2024) noted:

> Cultural humility involves a lifelong process of self-reflection about how one comes to know and an openness to learn. Self-reflexivity, humility and an acknowledgment that we don't know it all, an appreciation of other people and communities' knowledge, flexible thinking, a desire to learn and to address power imbalance and privilege are considered important attributes of cultural humility, as is being respectful of other cultures. (p. 8)

Box 5.9 offers an opportunity to assess cultural humility.

 ## Box 5.9 Reflective Practice

Assessing Cultural Humility

Hook et al. (2013) developed a Cultural Humility Scale based on their definition of the construct as "Having an interpersonal stance that is other-oriented rather than self-focused, characterized by respect and lack of superiority toward an individual's cultural background and experience" (p. 353). The instrument was developed to measure a therapist's cultural humility as assessed by the client. Hook et al. provided evidence for the client-rated measure's estimated reliability and construct validity. The researchers concluded that "client perceptions of their therapist's cultural humility are positively associated with developing a strong working alliance" (p. 353).

Clients were asked to rate the following statements from strongly disagree to strongly agree:

Regarding the core aspects of my cultural background, this staff member. . .

1. Is respectful.
2. Is open to explore.
3. **Assumes they already know a lot.**
4. Is considerate.
5. Is genuinely interested in learning more.
6. **Acts superior.**
7. Is open to seeing things from my perspective.
8. **Makes assumptions about me.**
9. Is open-minded.
10. **Is a know-it-all.**
11. **Thinks they understand more than they actually do.**
12. Asks questions when they are uncertain.

Note that the negative behaviors that are not considered to exhibit cultural humility are highlighted in bold.

From: Hook et al. (2013), p. 366.

As an adult educator or learner, reflect on each question and self-assess your level of cultural humility. You could do this exercise with a trusted colleague or invite students to complete it.

Becoming a Learning Leader

Adult educators tend to care about learning and development in organizations, workplaces, and communities. As authors who have merged adult learning with organization change processes, we contend that leadership *and* learning are imperative for the challenges now and in the future and that transdisciplinary collaboration and creation are needed for meeting and effectively functioning in the VUCA context full of wicked problems. Chapter 9 further explores this idea by examining the mutuality of learning and change.

Defining the Learning Leader

Being an effective teacher of adults requires much more than the rather instrumental competencies discussed in Chapter 4. In many ways, it requires adult educators to regard themselves as *learning leaders* who help learners face ambiguous, wicked challenges and build adaptable, resilient mindsets so they can learn through equitable, just processes and apply their knowledge and skill sets in ways that address crucial social challenges and potentially transform themselves, others, and society. Marky Parker Follett was a management consultant and social worker who advanced innovative ideas in organization behavior and theory, known for emphasizing people in organizations over the industrial technical aspects. Follett's ideas translate easily to the work of adult educators as she regarded the titles of "leader" and "teacher" as synonymous. "A great leader is he [sic] who is able to integrate the experience of all and use it for a common purpose" (Follett, in Metcalf & Urwick, 2013, p. 268). She observed that "leadership appears in many places" (p. 266) and urged leaders to build leadership capacity among what she termed as "under executives" so that they could fully use their capacities. She advocated that leaders must clearly define purpose, take the long view, and benefit the good of the community. Through these actions, leaders transform the experience of their workers into power.

Viewing Leadership as Teaching and Teaching as Leadership. Follett (1927) discussed leadership and how leaders should relate to the organization (in Metcalf & Urwick, 2013). She named the fundamental leadership behaviors as "evoking, interacting, integrating, and emerging" (p. 267) or highly adaptive behaviors that draw out the fullest potential of every person with the responsibility for the education and training of everyone. Follett's sense of these ideas was to evoke needed change through inquiry and disclosure, interacting through collaboration, and integrating desires. Hence, everyone wins and emerges with new solutions—which is effective, just teaching pedagogy. Although Follett's writing dates back to the early 20th century, it is relevant to the VUCA challenges of today. Follett's urging that "leadership is teaching" parallels adult educators' work and viewing learning as a strategy to tackle wicked problems. Follett (1924) observed, "When leadership rises to genius it has the power of transforming, of transforming experience into power. And that is what experience is for, to be made into power. The great leader creates as well as directs power" (Follett, 1924, as cited in Graham, 2003, p. 169).

Learning Leaders Take Mindful Action that Fosters Collective Capacity to Learn. Learning leaders do more than think critically. They apply their critical reflection (Schön, 1983), articulating their intentions, ideologies, and actions, as Cseh et al. (2013) noted in their study on global mindsets. Learning leaders are willing to self-critique, admit mistakes, and create a culture where it is acceptable to fail, err, and question. They are also effective at having conversations where there is disagreement and can respectfully listen and learn (Headlee, 2017). They also ask difficult questions about who benefits from learning, who gets to participate, and who decides, and ensures that learning is for everyone.

Mindful action also demands that learning leaders are cognizant of the values at play and who benefits from the organization's decisions and actions. Taking mindful action based on critical reflection becomes more complicated when we, as learners and educators, begin to understand the power relations tied to it, and making thoughtful, timely interventions is not the popular route. Merriam and Bierema (2013) advocated in the first edition of this book that mindful action, grounded in critical thinking, occurs when leaders self-monitor and self-correct and help others to do the same. They are capable of clarifying and changing thoughts and behavior. They make timely interventions using the best data available and can justify them.

Helping Learners Embrace Improvisational Expertise. Bateson (1994) used the metaphor of a spiral to describe learning across the lifespan with a notion of expanding larger and circling back when perhaps learners did not understand something the first time or the lesson was irrelevant until another passage by the learning. Bateson also advocated the "improvisational base" of learning—creating meaning through storytelling, learning from experience, playing, imagining, and questioning. Dealing with ambiguity is central to her premise, as educators and learners must constantly learn how to face the unknown, test assumptions, and continually re-invent themselves. Bateson also referred to the need for being adaptive, particularly learning and living in a diverse society in ways that honor and expose people to new cultural traditions.

Of course, as adult educators functioning as learning leaders, we must refine the capacities we hope to generate in others, much in the way Bateson (1994) characterized learning as "spiraling," envisioning learners as continually building capacity and knowledge each time they circle back to prior learning and ideas that were not fully realized or understood the first (or second) time:

> Spiral learning moves through complexity with partial understanding, allowing for later returns. For some people, what is ambiguous and not immediately applicable is discarded, while for others, much that is unclear is vaguely retained, taken in with peripheral vision for possible later clarification, hard to correct unless it is made explicit. (Bateson, 1994, p. 31)

Bateson further observed, "Sometimes change is directly visible, but sometimes it is apparent only to peripheral vision, altering the meaning of the foreground" (p. 6).

Adaptive leadership and teaching require leaders to move beyond their current know-how and form new types of what Heifetz et al. (2009) call **improvisational expertise,** or ways of experimenting with untried relationships, communication methods, and interactions that transcend the current wisdom. Practicing learning leadership in this vein involves two key processes: diagnosis and action. Diagnosis happens first and occurs with both the system and the self, followed by action on both the system and the self, and then the cycle repeats. Diagnosis is a step often skipped or given short shrift as the tendency to jump quickly into action is embedded in many cultures, particularly Western. Adaptive learning leaders are willing to step back and consider what is really occurring in the classroom, organization, or community. This step requires the learner to put some distance between the self and the challenge. Mary Parker Follett valued controversy for its "revealing nature" that helps issues surface and creates the possibility of reconciliation, as she noted,

> There are three ways of dealing with difference: domination, compromise, and integration. By domination only one side gets what it wants; by compromise neither side gets what it wants; by integration we find a way by which both sides may get what they wish. (In Metcalf, 2003, p. 200)

Adult educators are uniquely positioned to help learners build the capacity to adapt, relate, and foster meaningful, timely change in their lives.

Chapter Summary

This chapter, "Becoming an Adult Educator," has taken a big-picture approach to the crucial mindsets and learning leadership we, the authors, feel is imperative for adult educators to consider in their teaching, development, and action. The key points of Chapter 5 emphasize the importance of a continuous journey in teaching, mirroring Michelle Obama's growth concept of "forward motion."

Key Points

Chapter 5 stresses four primary mindsets essential for effective adult educators. These mindsets support educators in evolving within their role, aligning teaching with values of social change, inclusivity, and lifelong learning:

- **Global, Adaptive Stance:** Adult educators need to develop resilience and adapt to global challenges, described as "wicked problems," which require systems thinking and collaborative solutions.
- **Critical Reflection:** Educators should cultivate curiosity, engage in reflexive practices, and apply critical thinking to their teaching approaches. Techniques like reflexivity and action inquiry were highlighted for improving self-awareness and teaching effectiveness.
- **Commitment to Equity and Justice:** Emphasizing social justice, the chapter explored the importance of understanding diversity, equity, intersectionality, and cultural humility in teaching practices to foster inclusive and fair educational environments.
- **Adult Learning Leadership:** Effective educators are also leaders who inspire learning beyond technical competencies, adapting to ambiguous challenges and empowering learners to address complex social issues through transformative learning.

References

Ackoff, R. L. (1973). Science in the systems age: Beyond IE, OR, and MS. *Operations Research*, *21*(3), 661–671. https://doi.org/10.1287/opre.21.3.661.

Anka, A. (2024). Using the concept of epistemic injustice and cultural humility for understanding why and how social work curricular might be decolonized. *Social Work Education*, *43*(9), 1–17. https://doi.org/10.1080/02615479.2023.2299245.

Argyris, C., & Schön, D. A. (1997). Organizational learning: A theory of action perspective. *Reis*, (*77/78*), 345–348.

Bateson, M. C. (1994). *Peripheral visions: Learning along the way.* Harper Perennial.

Belli, G. (2018, October 1). *Here's how many years you'll spend at work in your lifetime.* Payscale. https://www.payscale.com/career-news/2018/10/heres-how-many-years-youll-spend-work-in-your-lifetime.

Berlyne, D. E. (1966). Curiosity and exploration. *Science, 153*(3731), 25–33. https://doi.org/10.1126/science.153.3731.25.

Bertella, G. (2022). Discussing tourism during a crisis: Resilient reactions and learning paths towards sustainable futures. *Scandinavian Journal of Hospitality and Tourism, 22*(2), 144–160. https://doi.org/10.1080/15022250.2022.2034527.

Bierema, L. L., Callahan, J. L., Elliott, C. J., Greer, T. W., & Collins, J. C. (2024). *Human resource development: Critical perspectives and practices.* Routledge.

Bowleg, L. (2008). When Black + lesbian + woman ≠ Black lesbian woman: The methodological challenges of qualitative and quantitative intersectionality research. *Sex Roles, 59* (5–6), 312–325. https://doi.org/10.1007/s11199-008-9400-z.

Byrd, M. Y. (2018). Does HRD have a moral duty to respond to matters of social injustice? *Human Resource Development International, 21*(1), 3–11. https://doi.org/10.1080/13678868.2017.1344419.

Chamorro-Premuzic, T. (2023, November 3). *How to strengthen your curiosity muscle.* Harvard Business Review. https://hbr.org/2023/11/how-to-strengthen-your-curiosity-muscle.

Cho, S., Crenshaw, K. W., & McCall, L. (2013). Toward a field of intersectionality studies: Theory, applications, and praxis. *Signs: Journal of women in culture and society, 38*(4), 785–810. https://doi.org/10.1086/669608.

Collins, P. H. (1990). *Black feminist thought: Knowledge, consciousness, and the politics of empowerment.* Routledge.

Collins, P. H. (2022). *Black feminist thought: Knowledge, consciousness, and the politics of empowerment.* Routledge.

Collins, P. H., & Bilge, S. (2020). *Intersectionality* (2nd ed.). Polity Press.

Coutu, D. L. (2002). How resilience works. *Harvard Business Review, 80*(5), 46–56. https://hbr.org/2002/05/how-resilience-works.

Crenshaw, K. (1989). Demarginalizing the intersection of race and sex: Black feminist critique of antidiscrimination doctrine, feminist theory and antiracist politics. *University of Chicago Legal Forum, 1989*, 139–168.

Cseh, M., Davis, E. B., & Khilji, S. E. (2013). Developing a global mindset: Learning of global leaders. *European Journal of Training and Development, 37*(5), 489–499.

Dewey, J. (1933). *How we think: A restatement of reflective thinking to the educative process.* Heath (DC).

Diemer, M. A., & Blustein, D. L. (2006). Critical consciousness and career development among urban youth. *Journal of Vocational Behavior, 68*(2), 220–232. https://doi.org/10.1016/j.jvb.2005.07.001.

Eliot, J. L. (2020). Resilient leadership: The impact of a servant leader on the resilience of their followers. *Advances in Developing Human Resources, 22*(4), 404–418. https://doi.org/10.1177/1523422320945237.

Ewuoso, C. (2023). Decolonization projects. *Voices in Bioethics, 9*, 1–7. https://philpapers.org/rec/EWUDPW.

Fanon, F. A. (1967). *Dying colonialism,* trans. Haakon Chevalier. Grove Atlantic.

Follett, M. P. (1927). Management as a profession. In *Management and organizational behavior classics.* Boston, MA: Richard D. Irwin, 7–17.

Follett, M. P. (1924). *Creative experience* (vol. 7). Longmans, Green.

Freire, P. (1970). *Pedagogy of the oppressed.* Continuum.

Freire, P. (1973a). *Pedagogy of the oppressed: Ethnics, democracy and civic courage.* Seabury Press.

Freire, P. (1973b). *Education for critical consciousness* (Vol. 1). Bloomsbury Publishing.

Fricker, M. (2007). *Epistemic injustice: Power and the ethics of knowing.* Oxford University Press. https://doi.org/10.33844/ijol.2021.6 536.

Gichuhi, J. M. (2021). Shared leadership and organizational resilience: A systematic literature review. *International Journal of Organizational Leadership, 10*(1), 67–88. doi:org/10.33844/ijol.2021.60536.

Gouthro, P. A. (2019). Taking time to learn: The importance of theory for adult education. *Adult Education Quarterly, 69*(1), 60–76. https://doi.org/10.1177/0741713618815656.

Graham, P. (Ed.). (2003). *Mary Parker Follett: Prophet of management: A celebration of writing from the 1920s.* Beard Books.

Hanson, C., & Jaffe, J. (2023). Decolonizing adult education. In T. S. Rocco, M. C. Smith, R. C. Mizzi, L. R. Merriweather, & J. D. Hawley (Eds.), *The handbook of adult and continuing education* (pp. 341–349). Routledge.

Headlee, C. (2017). *We need to talk: How to have conversations that matter.* Hachette UK.

Heifetz, R. A., Heifetz, R., Grashow, A., & Linsky, M. (2009). The practice of adaptive leadership: Tools and tactics for changing your organization and the world. Harvard Business Press.

Hook, J. N., Davis, D. E., Owen, J., Worthington Jr, E. L., & Utsey, S. O. (2013). Cultural humility: measuring openness to culturally diverse clients. *Journal of Counseling Psychology, 60*(3), 353. https://psycnet.apa.org/doi/10.1037/a0032595.

Horn, R. E. (2001, July). *Knowledge mapping for complex social messes.* A speech to the Packard Foundation Conference on Knowledge Management. http://www.stanford.edu/rhorn/SpchPackard.html.

Hughes, C. (2018). Conclusion: Diversity intelligence as a core of diversity training and leadership development. *Advances in Developing Human Resources, 20*(3), 370–378. https://doi.org/https://doi.org/10.1177/1523422318778025.

Hughes, C., & Liang, X. (2020). *Hughes and Liang Diversity Intelligence®(DQ) Scale© 2020.* https://www.diversityintelligencellc.com.

Ketkar, S., Puri, R., & Chowdhury, S. R. (2021). Bridging the gender pay gap. *Empirical Economics, 61*(2021), 2237–2263. https://doi.org/10.1007/s00181-020-01950-z.

Lekas, H. M., Pahl, K., & Fuller Lewis, C. (2020). Rethinking cultural competence: Shifting to cultural humility. *Health Services Insights, 13,* 1178632920970580. https://doi.org/10.1177/1178632920970580.

Luthans, F. (2002). Positive organizational behavior: Developing and managing psychological strengths. *Academy of Management Perspectives, 16*(1), 57–72. https://doi.org/10.5465/ame.2002.6640181.

McKillican, A. (2020). The educational ontology of Paulo Freire and the voices of Irish adult educators. *Adult Learner: The Irish Journal of Adult and Community Education, 121,* 140. https://eric.ed.gov/?id=EJ1272416.

Merriam, S. B., & Bierema, L. L. (2014). Adult learning: Linking theory and practice. John Wiley & Sons.

Metcalf, H. C., & Urwick, L. (2004). *Dynamic administration: The collected papers of Mary Parker Follett.* Routledge.

Metcalf, H. C., & Urwick, L. (2013). *Dynamic administration: The collected papers of Mary Parker Follett.* Martino Fine Books.

Mitroff, I. I., Alpaslan, M. C., & Green, S. E. (2004). Crises as ill-structured messes. *International Studies Review, 6*(1), 175–182. https://doi.org/10.1111/j.1521-9488.2004.393_3.x.

Nichols, T. M. (2017). *The death of expertise: The campaign against established knowledge and why it matters*. Oxford University Press.

Nicolaides, A. (2022). *Generative knowing: Principles, methods, and dispositions of an emerging adult learning theory*. Myers Education Press.

Nyerere, J. K. (1968). Education for self-reliance. *CrossCurrents, 18*(4), 415–434. https://www.jstor.org/stable/24457417.

Obama, M. (2021). *Becoming*. Crown.

Palmer, P. J. (1998). *The courage to teach. Exploring the inner landscape of a teacher's life*. Generic.

Parviainen, J., Koski, A., & Torkkola, S. (2021). 'Building a ship while sailing it.' Epistemic humility and the temporality of non-knowledge in political decision-making on COVID-19. *Social Epistemology, 35*(3), 232–244. https://doi.org/10.1080/02691728.2021.1882610.

Payscale. (2023). *2023 Gender pay gap report*. Payscale. https://www.payscale.com/research-and-insights/gender-pay-gap/.

Reio, T. G., Petrosko, J. M., Wiswell, A. K., & Thongsukmag, J. (2006). The measurement and conceptualization of curiosity. *The Journal of Genetic Psychology, 167*(2), 117–135. https://doi.org/10.3200/GNTP.167.2.117-135.

Rittel, H. W. J., & Webber, M. M. (1973). Dilemmas in a general theory of planning. *Policy Sciences, 4*(2), 155–169. https://doi.org/10.1007/BF01405730.

Schön, D. A. (1983). *The reflective practitioner: How professionals think in action*. Basic Books.

Schumacher, E. F. (1995). *A guide for the perplexed*. Random House.

Shaw, B. (1944). Everybody's political what's what. Dodd, Mead.

Sim, E., & Bierema, L. L. (2023). Infusing intersectional pedagogy into adult education and human resource development graduate education. *Adult Education Quarterly*. https://doi.org/10.1177/07417136231198049.

Sim, E., & Bierema, L. (2024). A systematic literature review of intersectional leadership in the workplace: The landscape and framework for future leadership research and practice to challenge interlocking systems of oppression. *Journal of Leadership & Organizational Studies*. https://doi.org/10.1177/15480518241292214.

Sim, E., Nicolaides, A., & Bierema, L. L. (2023). Intersectional research in adult education: A diffractive gaze. *New Directions for Adult and Continuing Education, 2023*(180), 11–23. https://doi.org/10.1002/ace.20508.

Torbert, W. R. (2004). *Action inquiry: The secret of timely and transforming leadership*. Berrett-Koehler.

Tseng, J., & Poppenk, J. (2020). Brain meta-state transitions demarcate thoughts across task contexts exposing the mental noise of trait neuroticism. *Nature Communications, 11*(1), 1–12. https://doi.org/10.1038/s41467-020-17255-9.

Van der Steege, M. (2017). Introduction. In M. Van der Steege, R. Elkington, & J. Glick-Smith (Ed.), *Visionary leadership in a turbulent world: Thriving in the new VUCA context* (pp. 1–12). Emerald Publishing.

Wagstaff, M. F., Flores, G. L., Ahmed, R., & Villanueva, S. (2021). Measures of curiosity: A literature review. *Human Resource Development Quarterly, 32*(3), 363–389. https://doi.org/10.1002/hrdq.21417.

Westman, W. E. (1986). Resilience: concepts and measures. In B. Dell, A. J. M. Hopkins, B. B. Lamont (Eds.) *Resilience in mediterranean-type ecosystems*. Tasks for vegetation science, vol 16. Springer, Dordrecht. https://doi.org/10.1007/978-94-009-4822-8_2.

Wlodkowski, R. J., & Galbraith, M. W. (2004). Creating motivating learning environments. In M. W. Galbraith (Ed.), Adult learning methods: A guide for effective instruction, (3), 141–164. Krieger.

SECTION THREE

THE ADULT LEARNER—THE *WHO*

The *learner* tends to get most of our attention as educators, and for good reason. This book addresses many aspects of the learner, from who participates in adult education to what motivates learners to how learners can thrive in a constant state of ambiguity and social upheaval. Early theoretical work in adult education focused on describing the learner. The systematic study of adult learning began in the 1920s, and the professional field of adult education was founded in 1926 (Merriam & Brocket, 1997, 2007). Yet, no comprehensive theory of adult learning exists. Merriam (2001) used the metaphor of a mosaic to describe what she termed "borrowed" theory. The mosaic represented other disciplinary influences in adult education, including feminism, situated cognition, critical and postmodern theory, emotion, neuroscience, and embodied learning. Merriam suggested these borrowed theoretical mosaics completed the field's understanding of adult learning and built on traditional adult learning theories of andragogy, self-directed learning, transformative, and informal and incidental learning.

Adults participate in learning for multiple reasons, although work-related learning is a significant focus. Adults are also engaged in English as a second language (ESL), adult basic education (ABE), general education development

(GED), credential programs, apprenticeship programs, continuing professional education, and personal development courses. Adults have high expectations for timely and relevant learning. Although adult learning has common characteristics, the diversity of learning needs and varied cultures of learners must be acknowledged and valued in the learning process. Adulthood has multiple demands, so adults seek learning when it becomes relevant to a life issue or problem. The learning must also be about something adults care about and find useful. Adult motivation to learn is likely intrinsic; adults learn to meet unmet needs, resolve unwanted conditions, or reach desired goals.

Section 3 includes three chapters and delves into adult learning. Chapter 6, "Understanding Adult Learners' Motivation," focuses on understanding the theoretical foundations of motivation as applied to adult learners and the barriers adults encounter preventing them from learning. The chapter also considers how educators can foster adult motivation to learn. Chapter 7, "Applying Andragogy—The Art and Science of Helping Adults Learn," covers the history of adult learning, including andragogy and its core principles. Chapter 8, "Valuing Adults' Self-Directedness in Learning," discusses self-directed learning, including definitions, characteristics, facilitation and assessment, myths, and critiques.

References

Merriam, S. B. (2001). Andragogy and self-directed learning: Pillars of adult learning theory. *New Directions for Adult and Continuing Education, 89*, 3–14.

Merriam, S. B. and Brockett, R. G. (1997). *The profession and practice of adult education: An introduction.* Jossey-Bass.

Merriam, S. B., & Brockett, R. G. (2007). *The profession and practice of adult education: An introduction.* San Francisco: Jossey-Bass.

CHAPTER SIX

UNDERSTANDING ADULT LEARNERS' MOTIVATION

 **Box 6.1 Chapter Overview and Learning Objectives**

Wlodkowski and Ginsberg's (2017) sentiment reflects the key foci of this chapter:

> Motivation and learning are inseparable—attention, interest, and inspiration are emotional points along a continuum of learning, integral to the process itself. (p. ix)

Chapter 6 focuses on understanding the theoretical foundations of motivation as they apply to adult learners. The chapter explores barriers to adult education and reviews contemporary issues in motivation across various contexts. Additionally, strategies for fostering motivation for teaching and learning and how to incorporate motivation into the planning of adult learning and teaching activities will be discussed.

The chapter examines applications of motivation-enhancing techniques for adult learners, including how motivation drives participation and engagement in diverse settings, including a series of activities to provide adult learners and educators with opportunities to reflect on applying specific ideas, theories, and practices related to enhancing motivation in adult teaching.

As a result of reading this chapter and completing the exercises, you should be able to:

1. Understand the theoretical foundations of motivation and their applications to adult learners.
2. Identify the role of motivation in adult education and for adult learners.
3. Recognize the importance of motivational thinking for adult learners and in planning activities.
4. Reflect on assumptions about learning and motivation.
5. Apply Wlodkowski's and Ginsberg's (2017) integrated levels of adult motivation in AL settings.

Before diving into this chapter on motivation, take a few minutes to reflect on your reasons for reading this book, as an adult learner or educator. Understanding your motivations can enhance your learning experience and help you apply the concepts more effectively. Box 6.2 offers an activity to delve more deeply into your motivations.

After this activity, you might find yourself with a list of many items, as motivation is a complex and fluid phenomenon. Asking what motivates learning is an important question to contemplate. Several factors impact learners' stamina to continue. As adult educators and learners, how can learners' engagement be enhanced, not eroded, while teaching and learning?

Motivation and Its Definitions

The word "motivation" comes from the Latin *motivus*, meaning "a moving cause" (Ahl, 2006, p. 387). Motivation is the drive and energy people put into accomplishing something they want to do. Motivation cannot be seen or touched, but it is ever present in our thoughts and actions as adults (Wlodkowski & Ginsberg, 2017), suggesting that motivation is basic to survival and that it means being purposeful. Wlodkowski and Ginsberg (2017) described its signs—"effort, perseverance, completion—and we listen for words: 'I want to . . .,' 'We will . . .,' 'You watch . . .,' 'I'll give it my best!'" (p. 2). Motivation can also be described as educational engagement or "the time and energy students devote to educationally sound activities inside and outside the classroom, and

Box 6.2 Reflective Practice

Reflective Activity: Understanding Your Motivation

Consider the following questions to reflect on your learning motivation.

Self-Reflection Questions:

- Why did you choose to read this book?
- Did someone recommend it?
- Did the topic catch your interest?
- Are you looking to solve a specific problem or answer a question?

What are your goals for reading this book?

- Are you aiming to gain knowledge for personal growth?
- Do you need this information for a project, work, or academic purpose?
- Are you preparing for an upcoming exam or trying to improve your skills?

By completing this activity, you will have a clearer understanding of your motivations and goals, which will help you stay focused and engaged as you read the chapter on motivation. Happy reading!

the policies and practices that institutions use to induce students to take part in these activities" (Kuh, 2003, pp. 24–25). Wlodkowski and Ginsberg (2017) defined motivation to learn "as the tendency to find learning activities meaningful and worthwhile and to benefit from them" (p. 5). Motivation connects with educational and learning paradigms and influences learning achievement (Hulleman & Barron, 2015).

Motivation can be extrinsic or intrinsic to you as an adult educator or learner. **Extrinsic motivation** usually provides a means to an end derived from factors outside yourself, such as seeking approval or attaining credentials. External motivators might be receiving recognition from your teachers or classmates, getting a promotion, earning a certificate or diploma, or achieving another goal. **Intrinsic motivation** is usually an end, internal to you. Intrinsic motivation tends to be grounded in challenge, curiosity, and mastery (Pintrich et al., 1991). Intrinsic motivators might be learning for the love of the intellectual challenge or desiring to achieve mastery of a topic or practice for the satisfaction it brings you. Motivation also involves initiating and sustaining behavior (Linnenbrink-Garcia et al., 2016; Schunk & Di Benedetto, 2020).

In his influential book *Drive*, Daniel Pink (2009) challenged conventional views on motivation, asserting that many widely accepted beliefs about human potential and performance are misguided. He critiqued the effectiveness of short-term incentive plans and pay-for-performance models, highlighting that they often fail to enhance motivation. Instead of viewing individuals merely as extrinsically motivated profit maximizers, Pink posited that people are also intrinsically motivated purpose maximizers. Increasingly, people desire work where they can be creative, intellectually stimulated, and self-directed rather than suffer monotony and external control.

Pink summarized his argument by advocating for a shift in understanding motivation in the modern workplace. He suggested that the traditional "carrots and sticks" approach is outdated and called for an upgrade to focus on three core elements: **autonomy, mastery,** and **purpose.** These elements are essential for fostering intrinsic motivation and enhancing productivity and fulfillment in various contexts, including work and education (Oudeyer & Kaplan, 2007; Pink, 2011). Box 6.3 offers an opportunity to reflect on and understand its role in everyday life.

Research on the effectiveness of intrinsic versus extrinsic motivation supports Pink's assertion that intrinsic motivation is more effective for complex tasks. Findings suggested that environments fostering autonomy, opportunities for mastery, and a sense of purpose lead to higher engagement and satisfaction (Pink, 2011). Therefore, organizations should prioritize these intrinsic factors to cultivate a motivated workforce, driving greater innovation and performance. **Autonomy** is the yearning to direct our own lives as educators or learners, or in other words, to control tasks, time, team, and technique (what we do, when we do it, whom we do it with, and how we do it). Autonomy is synonymous with self-directedness. Key components of self-regulated learning are recognizable in implicit theories of intelligence (Bråten & Strømsø, 2004). **Mastery** represents the drive to develop and enhance skills in significant areas. Pink (2009) described it as a mindset that perceives abilities as infinitely improvable rather than limited. Achieving mastery requires substantial effort, determination, and intentional practice, and it embodies a goal that can never be fully attained, leading to both frustration and attraction for individuals engaged in the process (Oudeyer & Kaplan, 2007). This perspective aligns with findings linking mastery to cognitive control and individual motivation (Winget & Persky, 2022; Brett & Dubash, 2023), emphasizing fostering a growth and continuous improvement mindset.

Pink's concept of **purpose,** the third element in his motivation framework, emphasized working toward goals beyond personal gain. He criticized businesses for prioritizing profit maximization over cultivating a sense of purpose,

Box 6.3 SoTL: The Scholarship of Teaching and Learning

Learning and Mastering New Knowledge: Strategies for Sustaining Motivation

Pink's book *Drive: The Surprising Truth About What Motivates Us*, published in 2009, offered several suggestions for individuals and organizations to sustain motivation. Here are some particularly relevant to learning and mastering new knowledge and skills:

Give yourself a "flow" test. Based on the creative work of Csikszentmihalyi (1990), set an alarm or reminder on your computer or smartphone to go off randomly 40 times during the week. Each time the alarm rings, write down what you are doing, how you are feeling, and whether you are in **"flow,"** a state of consciousness where you experience deep enjoyment, creativity, and a complete engagement with what you are doing. Record your observations and see if you can decipher patterns. At the end of the week, consider the following questions:

1. Which moments produced a feeling of "flow"? Where were you? What were you doing? Who were you with?
2. Do you have certain times of day that are more "flow friendly" than others? How might you restructure your time based on your findings?
3. How might you increase the opportunities to be in "flow"?
4. What insights has this exercise given you about your work, studies, or other activities?
5. What does this exercise tell you about your true source of motivation? (adapted from Pink, 2009, pp. 153–154).

arguing that these two objectives are interconnected. Pink proposed a "purpose motive," aligning goals, language, and policies to promote purpose and profitability (Pink, 2009). To better understand the meaning of purpose, explore the simple exercise in Box 6.4 to reflect on your priorities as an adult learner or educator and ways of identifying and managing behaviors and activities that drain your energy without a clear purpose.

Although Pink's (2009) advice reflects workplace contexts, his ideas readily transfer to educational settings. By deliberately connecting learners' sense of purpose with their learning objectives, educators can create intentional learning environments that foster **autonomy, mastery,** and **purpose** (Machynska &

 **Box 6.4 Tips and Tools for Teaching and Learning**

Identifying Your Priorities: Reflecting on Your Everyday Activities and Behaviors

Just Say No—With a List is a good starting point for identifying the activities that unnecessarily distract you.

We all have to-do lists. Pink (2009) recommended following management guru Tom Peters' advice and creating a "to-don't" list—an inventory of behaviors and activities that drain your energy and distract your focus. In essence, you should make an agenda of avoidance to keep yourself away from things draining your motivational energy. "To-don'ts" might involve ending unimportant or unnecessary obligations or eliminating time-wasting distractions such as meetings or email.

If you are an adult educator, we recommend this as a practical learning activity to better understand priorities and essential things for you and your learners.

Boiko, 2020; Wang & Hansman, 2017). These environments aim to enhance student's motivation and engagement by aligning learning experiences with intrinsic motivators, which research suggests is more effective than relying solely on extrinsic rewards (Ryan & Deci, 2020). Box 6.5 offers reflective questions about learning motivation.

After this reflection activity, you, as an adult learner and educator, should be more informed about motivation and how it can contribute to developing learning. Box 6.6 provides further resources to involve learners in the learning process using creativity.

Much research on motivation is conducted on traditional-age undergraduate students (18–22 years old) engaged in formal education. However, the number of **nontraditional students** is increasing, with learners over 25 years becoming North America's fastest-growing group of undergraduates (Bye et al., 2007). Bye et al. (2007) surveyed 300 traditional and nontraditional undergraduates aged 18–60 on intrinsic and extrinsic motivation to learn. Not surprisingly, nontraditional students reported higher intrinsic learning motivation. Given adults' interest in learning what is relevant and timely to their lives, it seems fitting that there would be a more substantial internal drive to learn. Learners' drive is related to self-determination (Deci & Ryan, 1985): People are led to change and grow by innate needs, competence, autonomy, and relatedness. Bye et al. (2007) advocated balancing intrinsic

Box 6.5 Reflective Practice

Reflective Practices on Motivation and Learning

This activity invites you to consider Pink's (2009) questions about motivation as an adult educator or learner.

1. What is most important to you as you think about your best work? Autonomy over what you do (task), when you do it (time), how you do it (technique), or with whom you do it (team)? Why? How much autonomy do you have in your learning or teaching right now? Is that enough?
2. Does education today put too much emphasis on extrinsic rewards? What is the best way to build intrinsic motivation into the accountability equation?
3. What really motivates you? Make a list. Now, jot down how you spent your time last week. How many of those 168 hours were devoted to those things? How might you do better?

Box 6.6 Tips and Tools for Teaching and Learning

Motivation Resources

If you are interested in more resources on motivation, try this activity: **Get Unstuck by Going Oblique.** Pink (2009) offered this activity as a fun way to curb a creativity drought or writer's block. You can create your index cards with a question or statement to jolt you out of your mental rut, such as "What would your closest friend do? Your mistake was a hidden intention. What is the simplest solution? Repetition is a form of change. Don't avoid what is easy" (p. 157). You can purchase a deck of these cards at http://www.enoshop.co.uk/product/oblique-strategies or follow a Twitter account that touts the strategies at http://twitter.com/oblique_chirps.

You will find creative suggestions that may help you change your perspective and act differently and more innovatively.

and extrinsic learning motivators when teaching. They also suggested validating nontraditional students as active partners in a shared learning experience to increase intrinsic motivation and positive affect.

Motivation Theories

You have probably studied motivation theory in a psychology course as an adult educator or learner. These same theories apply to learning. Ahl (2006) provided a thorough overview of classical motivation theories, as depicted in Table 6.1.

Economic—Rational Motivation Theory

Economic or rational motivation theory is traceable to Adam Smith's *The Wealth of Nations* (1776/2000). Economic motivation theory views humans as rational actors who seek to maximize self-interest and outcomes, yielding the highest economic returns. Economic motivation theory became popular from Frederic Taylor's *Scientific Management* (1911) published during the Industrial Revolution. **Scientific management** is visible in work and reward systems designed to maximize productivity through specialization and piecemeal work. Educationally, economic motivation might mean you select a college major that promises a good income (business) rather than something you are more interested in and passionate about (art). You might enroll in a training seminar that gives you better chances of a promotion at work, or you might be motivated to get good grades to avoid the consequences of not doing so. Economic or rational motivation is also extrinsically oriented. Smith's exploration of self-interest is evident in modern interpretations, highlighting the balance between individual motivations and societal benefits. For instance, Ashraf et al. (2005) argued that

TABLE 6.1 CLASSICAL MOTIVATION THEORIES

Humans As	Are Motivated By
Economic/Rational	Rewards and Punishments
Social	Social Norms, Groups
Responsive to Stimuli (behaviorism)	Stimuli and/or Rewards
Need-Driven	Inner Needs
Cognitive	Cognitive Maps

Source: Adapted from Ahl, 2006, p. 387.

while self-interest is a driving force, it coexists with concerns about fairness and altruism, suggesting a more nuanced understanding of economic interactions (Salinas, 2023). This dual perspective aligns with Smith's assertion that individuals, while pursuing their interests, inadvertently contribute to the greater good of society, a concept famously illustrated by the "invisible hand" metaphor (Smith, 1776/2000). He stated that individual motivation is the main force that motivates human economic activity and serves social interests and people's well-being.

Social Motivation Theory

Social or human motivation theory emerged as a reaction to scientific management through the work of Elton Mayo and Hawthorne Studies. Mayo and his collaborators (1933) concluded that factors other than pay and physical working conditions, such as social and emotional aspects of working in well-functioning groups, impacted work motivation. Their work challenged the economic model that assumed workers rationally sought profit maximization and instead argued that workers were social beings motivated by relationships. The Human Relations School emerged from these discoveries and served as a precursor to the rise of Human Resource and Organization Development. The influence of social motivation theory in education is evident in the humanist philosophy that underlies several AL models and theories, such as andragogy, self-directed learning, and social learning.

Behavioristic Motivation Theory

Behavioristic motivation theory, popularized by Pavlov, Thorndike, and Skinner, assumed that behavior and learning were based on providing a stimulus to provoke a desired response. The learner would then be conditioned through punishments and rewards. Learning occurs when appropriate stimuli are presented, and the learner is subsequently rewarded for exhibiting the desired behavior. These views dominated through the 1960s (Ahl, 2006) and still influence many education and training programs.

Need-driven Motivation Theory

Need-driven motivational theories grew out of Abraham Maslow's (1943) hierarchy of needs. Maslow contended that although humans are partially motivated by external factors, innate, intrinsic human needs are the main drivers of human behavior. He created a hierarchy of needs, with the lowest being physiological needs, such as safety and sustenance. As individuals meet these fundamental needs, they progress to higher-order needs, which include belonging, recognition, cognitive, and aesthetic needs, culminating in self-actualization (Maslow, 1943). Humanistic educational philosophy and practice fall under this theory, assuming learners would not be motivated by things that already satisfy basic needs and requirements but relatively higher-order needs. In other words, as a prospective homeowner, you would probably have little interest or motivation in a course on financing your first home if you have already done so (safety needs) but would be more enthusiastic about a course on how to improve your landscaping (aesthetic). Humanism has significantly influenced adult education through models and practices such as andragogy, self-directed learning, and learner-centered teaching.

Cognitive Motivation Theory

Cognitive motivation theory concerns people's thoughts and how they influence our actions as adult learners and educators. These models assume that there is not one unequivocal reality that affects our thoughts and actions but perceptions of reality that vary between individuals. Kurt Lewin (1935) and Victor Vroom (1964/1995) were early theorists in this area. These theories dominate motivation research today. According to cognitive motivation theory, a reward for learning will have different meanings and be of varying importance from person to person. History is also a key factor in how you conceive of reality today, which depends on how you thought of it yesterday and how you interpret it tomorrow. You might also liken this perspective to critical and postmodern understandings of learning that regard knowledge as fluid, changing, and dependent on the learner.

Classical motivation theory provides insight into adult motivation to learn and how it affects adults' access to and participation in learning activities. It also serves as a historical glimpse into how adult education has evolved from rational models that assumed external motivation was the impetus to learn to social models that explain how group dynamics and relationships influence motivation and learning. Next came behavioristic explanations of motivation that are interested in providing the best stimuli to provoke a learning response, to the more humanistic or need-driven models that undergird much of adult education practice today, to more cognitive understandings of motivation, and how adults create and interpret knowledge differs. The following section explores how motivation influences adults' educational endeavors.

Motivation in Adult Education

The literature discussing adult motivation to learn is diverse, drawing on psychology, educational psychology, anthropology, and sociology (Schlesinger, 2005). Houle's 1961 publication of *The Inquiring Mind* initiated motivation research of adult learning, and around the same time, needs-driven and cognitive motivation theories gained popularity. Houle's book reported an in-depth study of 22 adults engaged in continuous learning. He interviewed adults about their learning experiences and self-perceptions of themselves as learners. He identified three types of learning orientations in his analysis. *Goal-oriented learners* engage in learning to attain a desired aim and tend to be extrinsically and economically motivated. For instance, a person might attend a training program to become competitive for a promotion or learn woodworking to start a cabinet-making business. *Activity-oriented learners* participate for the opportunity to socialize with other learners and for the sake of the activity. They might attend a photography class to meet new people and engage in conversation or join a book club to meet new friends with similar interests. Activity-oriented learning might be extrinsically or intrinsically motivated and driven by social and need-driven motivation. Finally, *learning-oriented learners* focus on developing new knowledge. For example, a person might devour everything available in the US Civil War based on a love of the subject. Learning-oriented learners are likely intrinsically and cognitively motivated. Motivation is fluid, and people's motivations for learning activities can include multiple goals. They might take a watercolor painting class to learn it, then discover they are good at it and start a business selling paintings. In this scenario, a primary "learning" motivation becomes "goal oriented."

Boshier (1991), building on the work of Houle, developed the most extensive instrument to measure adult motivation to learn with his Education Participation Scale (EPS). It measures six factors related to adult engagement in learning. Several general motivation theories can account for these factors, as noted in Table 6.2.

Boshier and Collins (1985) also tested Houle's original typology (goal, social, and learning orientations) by analyzing responses from 13,442 learners from Africa, Asia, New Zealand, Canada, and the United States. They reported results like Houle's.

Dia et al. (2005) evaluated the Boshier and Collins measurement model and theory underlying the Educational Participation Scale—Modified (EPS-M). They surveyed 225 licensed social workers in Maryland, finding the EPS-M a valid and reliable measure for identifying motivational orientations of social workers who pursue continuing professional education. Participants often cited

TABLE 6.2 COMPARISON OF BOSHIER'S ADULT LEARNING MOTIVATIONAL FACTORS WITH CLASSICAL MOTIVATION THEORY

Boshier's Factor	Example	Links with Classical Motivation Theory
1. Communication improvement of verbal and written skills	ESL course Writing workshop Toastmasters	Economic/Rational Behaviorism Cognitive
2. Social contact	Meeting people Making friends Continuing Education	Social Need-Driven
3. Educational preparation and remediation of past educational deficiencies	GED Education GRE Test Preparation	Economic/Rational Behaviorism Need Driven Cognitive
4. Professional advancement	Promotion New career opportunities	Economic/Rational Need Driven
5. Family togetherness	Relationships across generations	Social Need-Driven
6. Social stimulation	Escaping boredom	Social Need-Driven
7. Cognitive interest	Learning for the sake of learning	Cognitive

professional knowledge as their primary motivator, consistent with interest and participation in work-related learning among other occupational groups.

Motivation theory helps explain what drives people to pursue activities such as learning. It does not account for the many variables that affect access to and participation in education. For instance, a person might be economically motivated to attend learning that improves their job prospects but cannot attend due to financial or family constraints. Motivation is not always enough if other variables prevent us from pursuing education. McClusky's Theory of Margin (1963, 1970, 1971), a lesser-known theory of adult learning, illustrates the complex dynamics adults face when attempting to learn.

Recent studies emphasized the critical role of motivation in adult education, noting that personal characteristics such as age, education level, and literacy skills significantly impact motivation to learn (Yamashita et al., 2022). Such insights underscore the necessity of considering intrinsic and extrinsic motivational factors to foster effective adult learning environments.

In 2023, the World Economic Forum researched motivating older workers in their professional activity in 19 countries, involving 40,000 participants (Schwedel, 2023). According to the analysis, 150 million jobs will shift to workers aged 55 and older by the end of this decade. As people live better and longer, the world is entering a new phase of demographic development. Investing in this new trend of research on motivation and aging is essential, as it can enhance the performance of older workers and create better work conditions for employees. The study outlines three key steps for firms to motivate older workers: (1) retain and recruit, (2) **reskill,** and (3) respect their strengths. Workers' motivation evolves with age. When people are under 60, the primary retention strategy is compensation. Around 60 and beyond, motivation is more likely to be driven by autonomy, flexibility, and leadership opportunities. Regarding reskilling, most older workers believe they do not need new skills, and only 22% of older workers think they need tech skills. New training programs for companies need to be designed to reskill older workers. Finally, older workers bring respect to the workplace, and this can strengthen the culture and the sense of belonging of everyone.

Another significant area of research in the field of motivation is the cultural diversity and the multicultural perspectives. Different cultures impact the interpretation of the external world, and motivation is considered a factor of success in learning (Wlodkowski & Ginsberg, 2017). It seems that the challenges for educators are increasing, and they are responsible for creating equal and inclusive learning environments for all learners. Box 6.7 highlights motivation and gender differences.

Box 6.7 SoTL: The Scholarship of Teaching and Learning

The Effects of Motivation on Learners' Success: The Role of Gender

Zaccone and Pedrini (2019) investigated the relationship between intrinsic and extrinsic motivation on students' learning effectiveness. The research considered a sample of 1,491 students attending a computer science course in three different countries: Burundi, Morocco, and India.

Intrinsic motivation, which involves enjoyment and interest in the activity, positively impacts learning effectiveness for both genders. However, this positive effect is stronger for men than for women. Men, who are socialized to be more agentic (self-assertive and motivated to perform), benefit more from intrinsic motivation in terms of learning effectiveness.

Women socialized to be more communal (selfless and concerned with others) do not experience the same level of enhancement in learning effectiveness from intrinsic motivation.

Extrinsic motivation, which involves external rewards and pressures, negatively impacts learning effectiveness. This negative effect is more pronounced for women than men. Women may experience greater psychological distress and feel more burdened by societal stereotypes and discrimination, which undermines their learning effectiveness when motivated extrinsically.

Men, being more focused on career and success, are less negatively affected by extrinsic motivation regarding their learning effectiveness.

This study highlights how societal expectations shape different roles based on gender, which in turn influence learning processes. According to social role theory, gender behaviors are modeled through society's structure, leading to different motivational and learning patterns based on gender.

Based on this article's findings, reflect on the following questions as an adult learner or educator:

1. How might the findings on intrinsic and extrinsic motivation in the study by Zaccone and Pedrini (2019) influence the design of educational programs in diverse cultural contexts?
2. How can educators address the different impacts of intrinsic and extrinsic motivation on men and women students to enhance learning effectiveness?
3. How can understanding the moderating role of gender in motivation and learning effectiveness help create more inclusive and effective educational strategies?
4. What strategies can be implemented to mitigate the adverse effects of extrinsic motivation, particularly for women students, as highlighted in Zaccone and Pedrini's (2019) research?

Considering the role of motivation in teaching and learning, the next section presents the different theories of human development and how they relate to motivation and engagement in learning.

McClusky's Theory of Margin

McClusky (1963) believed that humans had unlimited potential during their lifetime and viewed adulthood as a dynamic process of continuous development, change, and challenge requiring energy and resources for addressing daily life. His major contribution to adult education was the 1963 Theory of Margin, also known as the power-load-margin (PLM) formula. The formula, a conceptual model, addresses motivation as a measure of how many resources (power) the learner has to offset the demands (load) that potentially diminish motivation for learning. Reporting the author's definition:

> Margin is a function of the relationship of load to power. By load we mean the self and social demands required by a person to maintain a minimal level of autonomy. By power we mean the resources, i.e., abilities, possessions, position, allies, etc., which a person can command in coping with load. (McClusky, 1970, p. 27)

McClusky posited that adults need enough margin to handle life's load of challenges, changes, and crises. A low margin might indicate the adult is under undue stress or illness. An excessive margin might indicate a life with too little load where the adult is not fulfilling their potential (Stevenson, 1982). Although McClusky never developed an instrument to study his formula, Stevenson (1982) constructed an instrument for her research in nursing and identified six key areas for measuring margin, including self, family, religiosity/spirituality, body, extra-familial relationships, and environment.

Load and power are affected by the interacting internal and external variables such as those depicted in Table 6.3 (Baum, 1978; Main, 1979). *Load* might be family commitments, occupational responsibilities, or goals. *Power* is the ability to deal with the load, such as economic wealth, physical health, social contacts, or coping skills. *Margin* is the dynamic relationship between load and power.

TABLE 6.3 LOAD AND POWER

Load	Power
Self and Societal Demands on Learner	Learner's Resources to Cope with Load
• External Motivators	• External Resources and Capacity
o Family Commitments	o Physical Health
o Occupational Responsibilities	o Economic Wealth
o Social Obligations	o Social Abilities
o Civic Duties	o Social Contacts
• Internal, Personal Motivators	• Internal Skills and Experiences
o Expectations of Self	o Resiliency
o Ideals	o Coping Skills
o Goals	o Personality
o Values	
o Attitudes	

Margin is surplus power or power available to a person over and beyond that required to handle. . .load. . .. Margin is essential to the mental hygiene of the adult. . . .. *A margin allows a person to invest in life expansion projects and experiences including learning experiences* (Main, 1979, p. 23, italics in original).

An adult will be more motivated to learn by maintaining a power surplus and less motivated with a load surplus (Infed, n.d.). Main (1979) offered illustrations of the PLM Formula in *Adult Education Quarterly* to clarify the principles of the model. Here are some examples based on his work:

$$\frac{2 \text{ (Power)}}{4 \text{ (Load)}} = 0.5 \text{ (Margin)} \qquad \frac{\text{Deficit of Power to Handle Load}}{\text{Crisis of Excess Load Pressures}}$$

$$\frac{7 \text{ (Load)}}{7 \text{ (Power)}} = 1.0 \text{ (Margin)} \qquad \frac{\text{Breaking Even}}{\text{Barely Holding On}}$$

$$\frac{4 \text{ (Power)}}{2 \text{ (Load)}} = 2.0 \text{ (Margin)} \qquad \frac{\text{Surplus of Power to Handle Load}}{\text{Space to Maneuver}}$$

Adults can carry a high load, presuming they have comparable power resources to handle it. For example, many adults continue their higher education while holding down full-time jobs, managing households, juggling children's needs and activities, and participating in their communities. Successfully managing this load requires power, such as a supportive spouse, internal drive, physical health and stamina, economic stability, and a supportive work environment. The load would be very different for a single parent working two jobs with little familial or workplace support to continue their education. In this scenario, the load would likely exceed power, making perseverance and success in higher education more difficult. McClusky (1971) also identified barriers to learning related to adult life stages, including the unexpected loss of margin (job loss, relocation, illness, loss of spouse), time allocation (finding scarce time to engage in learning), resistance to learning (time pressures, personality, unwillingness to admit need for change, fear of risk, inability to reorder life commitments), viewing the self as a "non-learner," and a declining sense of discovery.

McClusky's Theory of Margin (1971) is also relevant in teaching. Hiemstra and Sisco (1990) pointed out that instructors can unknowingly create a surplus "load" for learners by assuming a traditional, authoritarian stance and not respecting learners' opinions or experiences. Other instructor behaviors contributing to learner load might be disorganization, distracting mannerisms, inappropriate assignments, or unclear evaluation guidelines. They suggest that it is imperative for instructors to carefully craft the learning environment to avoid creating additional load for learners. Following good adult education practices that honor and respect the learner is vital for giving learners more power to engage in educational activities.

Masden et al. (2004) studied the relationship between an individual's margin in life (MIL) and their readiness for change (RFC) across four organizations. Using a scale to assess MIL, their survey of 464 employees found that employees who have higher MIL levels (meaning they feel more energy, strength, joy, and power from their work and nonwork lives and environments) may be more open and ready for changes the organization may require of them. Furthermore, employees who feel good and are not burdened down by various work (job in general, job demands, relationship with boss, workplace social support, job knowledge and skills, and commitment to the organization) and possibly nonwork (family, balancing work and family, physical and mental health) appear to be ready to make the changes that may be needed by the organization (Masden et al., 2004, p. 765).

They suggested interventions that might help employees deal with MIL and RFC, such as supporting employees' life balance needs with flextime, childcare assistance, and job sharing. They also recommend offering wellness programs, improving management-employee communications, providing development to enhance job knowledge and skills, and programming to enhance employee commitment. Box 6.8 provides a chance to calculate PLM.

 ## Box 6.8 Tips and Tools for Teaching and Learning

McClusky's Power Load Margin Formula: Calculating Margin

Calculating Margin is an activity that you, as an adult learner and educator, can offer while teaching. McClusky's Power-Load-Margin formula can be used to assess how personal circumstances affect motivation, as described in this chapter.

1. Now that we have considered how margin affects learning, take a moment to figure out yours by creating your own formula.
2. Write down the elements making up your "load" on a scale of 1-to-5.
3. Then, write down the elements of your "power" on a scale of 1-to-5 to counter it.
4. Calculate your margin. What does it say about your motivation toward reading this book?

Wlodkowski and Ginsberg's Integrated Levels of Adult Motivation

Wlodkowski and Ginsberg (2017) offered one critical assumption about adults and learning related to their motivation: "Adults want to be successful learners" (p. 85). In their view, instructors should plan a very-well-designed lesson that motivates learners. Instructors and learners should develop a significant relationship to increase learning and motivation. Relationships impact not only student learning but also the well-being of the teacher and are potentially transformative for both students and teachers as they engage with each other within an educational experience (Taylor, 2019).

According to the authors, the five pillars for motivating teaching and learning are *expertise, empathy, enthusiasm, clarity,* and *cultural responsiveness* (Wlodkowski & Ginsberg, 2017, italics in original, p. 48). These pillars can be translated into skills for educators who should be able to teach their knowledge and competencies, develop a significant relationship with the learners, and show passion and enthusiasm for their job and the knowledge. Furthermore, they should be able to explain what they know with practical examples and actions and create activities for the learners. Finally, they must be aware of cultural differences and their impact on learning processes.

Wlodkowski and Ginsberg (2017) presented the most comprehensive exploration of motivation in their book *Enhancing Adult Motivation to Learn.* They suggested their framework's value is that it provides both a model of motivation and an aid for instructional design. They cited four intersecting motivational conditions essential to attend to when teaching adults and being culturally responsive. These conditions are inclusion, attitude, meaning, and competence.

Inclusion. Establishing inclusion involves creating an atmosphere that promotes a learning community "in which they and their instructor are respected by and connected *to* one other" (Wlodkowski & Ginsberg, 2017, p. 88). The same authors suggested that connectedness and respect create the conditions for adults to share their experiences, develop conversation and dialogue, and give meaning to their personal histories and narratives (Wlodkowski & Ginsberg, 2017). Connecting experiences and stories generates emotions and feelings across learners, and these are factors that increase connections in the neuronal networks (Barrett, 2017). To better understand:

> The nature of the emotion, we must also model the brain systems that
> are necessary for making meaning of the physical changes in the body
> and in the world . . . A more holistic approach based on the connections
> among brain, physical changes and body, generates the so-called theory
> of constructed emotion. (p. 16)

Box 6.9 features inclusion strategies to move toward connecting experiences, feelings, and connections with learners.

Attitude. The second condition of the motivation framework, also recommended for attention at the start of the lesson, is *developing an attitude* of favorability toward the learning by helping learners see its relevance to their experience.

 ## Box 6.9 Tips and Tools for Teaching and Learning

Establishing Inclusion: Strategies for Teaching

Introduce Yourself and the Learners

One strategy for establishing inclusion is introducing yourself and the learners. This vital activity builds relationships, trust, and care and even lowers anxiety at the beginning of a lesson. Making introductions and building connections is time well spent as it facilitates learning for the class duration.

Building Opportunities for Multidimensional Sharing

Another inclusion strategy is building opportunities for multidimensional sharing, such as introductory exercises, personal anecdotes, potlucks, or other activities both inside and outside the classroom. Wlodkowski and Ginsberg (2017) advocated taking the fear out of learning for learners by being available through office hours, during breaks, or at other times to partner with learners in ways that make it okay for them to ask for help.

Wlodkowski and Ginsberg offered several pedagogical strategies that help promote learner inclusion, including using **collaborative and cooperative learning;** clearly communicating learning goals and objectives, and connecting learning to the learners' personal lives and experience; conducting a needs analysis to ensure course relevance for learners; establishing course ground rules; providing solid rationale when giving mandatory assignments; and acknowledging different ways of knowing and being in the classroom.

Reflective questions for educators:

- How do you introduce yourself and your learners to build rapport and trust at the beginning of a lesson? Could you think of an example of an introduction activity that you find compelling?

- What strategies do you use to create opportunities for multidimensional sharing in your classroom? Could you reflect on a specific example of an activity or exercise that encourages personal connections among students?
- How do you make yourself available to students outside of regular class hours to reduce their anxiety and encourage them to seek help?
- What techniques do you employ to communicate learning goals and objectives to your students?
- What ground rules do you establish in your courses, and how do you ensure these rules support an inclusive learning environment?

"Attitudes affect human behavior and learning. . . . They help people to make sense of their own world" (Wlodkowski & Ginsberg, 2017, p. 90). The authors maintained that *relevance* and *volition* help develop positive attitudes among learners (Wlodkowski & Ginsberg, 2017, italics in original, p. 91). The learning has to be meaningful and connected with some personal or professional relevant experiences or needs of the learners. They look for challenges and a sense of relevance in their learning related to their beliefs, values, and desires for improvement and change. Promoting positive learner attitudes is facilitated by providing physically and psychologically favorable conditions in the classroom, presenting lessons at a reasonable pace, providing ample notice on assignments and tests (in other words, no pop quizzes), and creating a safe learning environment that is free from humiliation or shame when students do not know the answer or are unfamiliar with the subject. Wlodkowski and Ginsberg offered a pedagogy supportive of positive attitudes, which includes diversifying instruction to promote learning, providing clear expectations and evaluation criteria, scaffolding complex learning tasks, giving learners control over their learning, using **learning contracts,** and helping them with their own accountability for their learning successes.

Meaning. The third motivational condition is *enhancing meaning* through creating challenging and engaging experiences that value the learners' viewpoints and values. "Meaning is at the core of motivation and learning for adults because it is where ideas and emotions join to fulfill their personal, cultural and spiritual commitment" (Wlodkowski & Ginsberg, 2017, p. 94).

Making meaning may involve cognitively connecting previous and new knowledge or connecting experiences with values and purposes. By engaging learners' experiences and giving meaning to their experience, learning may become meaningful for adults, and "they will learn more about something they care [about]" (Wlodkowski & Ginsberg, p. 94). Tisdell (2003) in her book *Exploring Spirituality and Culture in Adult and Higher Education,* sustained the idea that adults create meaning through cognitive experiences but also through representations of their experiences in a symbolic, cultural, and spiritual way: "Trying to teach adult learners in a way that is culturally relevant to their own lives in a culturally pluralistic teaching context is a challenge" (p. 3).

Wlodkowski and Ginsberg recommended strategies such as providing frequent opportunities for learners to respond to the content through Q&A, sharing opinions, reflecting on practice, solving problems, demonstrating concepts, reviewing research, **role-playing,** simulating the learning issue, engaging in service learning, studying cases, and reacting to feedback. Keeping learning active and inventive is a key focus of many recommendations of adult educators and scholars in this area. It is also a good idea to vary your **presentation style, type of instruction,** and the learning materials when engaging learner attention. Learners must also see how the learning relates to their own individual interests and values. Box 6.10 highlights addition motivational strategies for learning.

 ## Box 6.10 Tips and Tools for Teaching and Learning

Implementing Strategies for Teaching Enhancing Motivation

Based on the conditions evoked by Wlodkowski and Ginsberg (2017), educators can foster a positive and motivating learning environment by implementing the following strategies:

Develop positive attitudes toward learning:

1. **Connect learning to personal experiences:** Help learners see the relevance of the material by relating it to their personal or professional experiences and needs.
2. **Create a positive classroom environment:** Ensure the classroom is physically and psychologically comfortable by avoiding humiliation or shame when learners are unfamiliar with the subject matter.
3. **Pace lessons appropriately:** Present reasonably paced lessons and provide ample notice for assignments and tests to reduce anxiety and allow for thorough preparation.
4. **Diversify instruction:** Use various teaching methods to cater to different learning styles and keep students engaged.

Enhance meaning through engagement:

1. **Create challenging and engaging experiences:** Design activities that are both challenging and engaging, valuing the learners' viewpoints and experiences.
2. **Use meaningful learning strategies:** Implement Q&A, opinion sharing, reflective practice, problem-solving, concept demonstrations, research reviews, role-playing, simulations, service learning, case studies, and feedback reactions.
3. **Vary presentation styles:** Keep learners' attention by varying your presentation style, instructional methods, and learning materials.
4. **Relate learning to learners' interests:** Ensure that learners see the connection between their learning and their interests and values.

Competence. The fourth motivational condition is *engendering competence.* Wlodkowski and Ginsberg (2017) sustained that "*as* adults, we most frequently view competence as the desire to be *effective at what we value*" (italics in original, p. 95). Educators can contribute to this by supporting learners in being successful at their learning, whether according to their personal and/or social standards. Key ways of promoting learner **self-efficacy** in this condition are providing timely feedback that avoids cultural bias and making assessment tasks and criteria explicit to learners before completing assignments. Carefully selecting tasks and activities ensures they are authentic—as close to real-life context as possible. **Authentic and realistic assessment** allows learners to integrate their knowledge in real contexts and self-assess their progress, creating the conditions for developing **competencies** and engendering confidence.

Box 6.11 highlights strategies to promote new knowledge and competencies using authentic tasks and enhancing motivation.

Wlodkowski and Ginsberg (2017) laid out a comprehensive framework for motivating adult learners and included multiple planning strategies in diverse settings. Their methods are summarized in Table 6.4. You may find them helpful for your instructional design planning as an adult learner and educator.

Motivation in Online Settings

It is now undeniable that knowledge and training are readily accessible online, with most nontraditional learners turning to the internet to acquire new skills and information. So, what motivates these learners to engage in online education? You might reflect on your own experience as a learner. What is your first

Box 6.11 Tips and Tools for Teaching and Learning

Implementing Strategies for Teaching Enhancing Confidence

Based on the condition evoked by Wlodkowski and Ginsberg (2017) to engender competence and support self-efficacy following a short presentation of some teaching strategies for educators:

Real-Life Scenario Projects:

- **Activity Description:** Design projects that simulate real-life scenarios relevant to the learners' personal or professional lives. For instance, a business course could include a project where learners develop a business plan for a startup.
- **Objective:** To provide authentic, real-world contexts for learners to apply their knowledge and skills.
- **Implementation:** Break the project into stages with clear criteria and provide detailed rubrics for each stage. Offer timely feedback at each stage to guide learners toward successful completion.

Peer Review and Self-Assessment:

- **Activity Description:** Incorporate structured peer review and self-assessment sessions where learners can evaluate each other's work using predefined criteria.
- **Objective:** To develop learners' ability to assess their own and others' work, fostering self-efficacy and competence.
- **Implementation:** Provide training on how to give constructive feedback and use rubrics. After the review sessions, have learners reflect on the feedback received and create action plans for improvement.

These activities are designed to help learners develop competence, see the relevance of their learning, and build self-efficacy through authentic and meaningful educational experiences.

thought when you think about online learning? Can you recall a specific instance when you felt highly motivated to learn something online? What was the topic, and what drove your motivation? How does the flexibility of online learning impact your motivation and ability to complete courses or training programs?

TABLE 6.4 SUMMARY OF WLODKOWSKI AND GINSBERG'S (2017) MOTIVATIONAL STRATEGIES (2017)

Major Motivational Condition	Motivational Purpose	Motivational Strategy
Inclusion (beginning learning activities)	To engender an awareness and feeling of connection among adults	• Allow for introductions. • Provide an opportunity for multidimensional sharing. • Concretely indicate your cooperative intentions to help adults learn. • Share something of value with adult learners. • Use collaborative and cooperative learning. • Clearly identify the learning objectives and goals for instruction. • Emphasize the human purpose of the learning and its relationship to the learners' personal lives and current situations.
	To create a climate of respect among adults	• Assess learners' current expectations, needs, goals, and experiences related to your course or training. • Explicitly introduce important norms and participation guidelines. • Create a clear, inviting, and inclusive course syllabus. • Acknowledge different ways of knowing, different languages, and different levels of knowledge or skill among learners.
Attitude (beginning earning activities)	To build a positive attitude toward the subject	• Eliminate or minimize any adverse conditions that surround the subject. • Positively confront the erroneous beliefs, expectations, and assumptions that may underlie a negative learner attitude. • Use differentiated instruction to enhance successful learning of new content. • Use assisted learning to scaffold complex learning.
	To develop self-efficacy for learning	• Promote learners' control of learning. • Promote a growth mindset by helping learners believe they can improve to enhance their capability, effort, and knowledge. • Help learners understand that reasonable effort and knowledge can help them avoid failure at learning tasks that suit their capability. • Use relevant models to demonstrate expected learning. • Encourage the learners.
	To establish challenging and attainable learning goals	• Make the criteria of assessment as fair and transparent as possible. • Help learners understand and plan for the time needed for successful learning. • Use goal-setting methods. • Use learning contracts.
	To create relevant learning experiences	• Use the entry points suggested by multiple intelligences theory as ways of learning about a topic or concept. • Make the learning activity an irresistible invitation to learn. • Use the K-W-L strategy to introduce new topics and concepts (learners identify what they KNOW, what they WANT TO KNOW, and what they have LEARNED).

Meaning (during learning activities)	To maintain learners' attention	• Provide frequent response opportunities for all learners. • Help learners realize their accountability for what they and their peers are learning. • Provide variety in personal presentation style, modes of instruction, and learning materials. • Introduce, connect, and end learning activities attractively and clearly. • Selectively use breaks, settling time, and physical exercises. • Relate learning to adults' interests, concerns, and values. • Clearly state or demonstrate the benefits of a learning activity.
	To evoke and sustain learners' interest	• While instructing, use humor liberally. • Use examples, analogies, metaphors, and stories. • Invite learners to anticipate and predict. • Use concept maps to develop interest and deepen understanding of ideas and information. • Use critical questions to engage in challenging reflection and discussion. • Use relevant problems, problem-based learning, and collaborative inquiry to deepen engagement and learning.
	To deepen learners' engagement and challenge	• Use project-based learning to deepen understanding and to engage in challenging, authentic topics. • Use case study methods to deepen learning and to engage in challenging, authentic topics. • Use role-playing to embody new learning within a more realistic and dynamic context. • Use simulations and games to embody the learning of multiple concepts and skills that require a real-life context and practice.
	To enhance learners' engagement, challenge, and adaptive decision-making	• Use visits, internships, and service-learning to raise awareness, provide practice, and embody new concepts and skills in authentic settings. • Use invention, artistry, imagination, and enactment to render deeper meaning and emotion in learning.

(Continued)

TABLE 6.4 *(Continued)*

Major Motivational Condition	Motivational Purpose	Motivational Strategy
Competence (ending learning activities)	To engender competence with assessment	• Provide effective feedback. • Use formative assessments to improve learning and instruction essential to course or training goals. • Promote equity in assessment procedures. • Use authentic performance tasks as part of assessments so learners will know they can proficiently apply new learning to their real lives. • Provide opportunities for adults to demonstrate their learning in ways that reflect their strengths and multiple sources of knowledge. • When using rubrics, ensure they assess the essential features of performance and are fair, valid, and straightforward. • Use self-assessment methods to provide insights and deepen learning. • Use grading practices that enhance learner motivation. • Foster the intention and the capacity to transfer learning. • When necessary, use constructive criticism.
	To engender competence with transfer	• Effectively praise and reward learning.
	To engender competence with communications and rewards	• Use incentives to develop motivation for valued learning that is initially unappealing. • Emphasize that learning has natural consequences and help learners be aware of them and their impact. • Provide positive closure at the end of significant units of learning.

Source: Adapted from Wlodkowski and Ginsberg (2017), pp. 362–370.

Today, online programs have changed people's ideas of learning and, above all, the idea of having access to knowledge. COVID-19 significantly impacted teaching and education. Education is experiencing a unique opportunity in terms of pedagogical commitment to innovation and transformation of teaching from face-to-face to online. We are now in the post-digital era, thinking about teaching that integrates technologies into a pedagogical design built on the dimensions of flexibility, **sustainability,** attention to diversity, promotion, and development of globalization. Box 6.12 shares numbers on online learning.

Box 6.12 Online Learning by the Numbers

Online Learning by the Data

Adult online is increasing tremendously. In 2022 in Europe, 47% of the adults aged 25–64 participated in education in the last 12 months (Eurostat, 2024a).

Younger people were more likely to participate in training than older people. Employed people are far more likely to join than the unemployed. Those with a low level of education were the least likely to participate. These patterns are almost identical in most countries (Eurostat, 2024b, 2024c, 2024d).

Visit the Adult Learning Statistics website of the European Commission for further explanation on Eurostat (2024e) statistics. Other relevant data on online education worldwide are published by Statista (n.d.).

Finally, as higher education online programs increase, consider the impact of the transformation from face-to-face programs to online programs. The statistics reveal that in the US, more than 10 million students enrolled in online programs in 2022 (Carlton, 2024).

Questions for Reflection:

1. How have your personal and professional life as an adult educator been affected by online learning, and do you feel that your previous educational experiences have prepared you well for online learning, or do you face unique challenges?
2. Given the significant increase in online education enrollment, especially in higher education in the US, how do you see the future of online learning evolving? How will this shift from traditional face-to-face to online programs impact your educational and career aspirations?

Motivation in online learning contexts presents unique challenges and opportunities compared to traditional educational settings. Online learning environments necessitate a nuanced adaptation of established motivational principles to ensure adequate student engagement and achievement. According to Haasio and Kannasto (2024), the asynchronous nature of online courses can influence students' motivation by necessitating self-regulation and time management skills, which are crucial for maintaining engagement and performance. As the authors reported on their results:

> Students' motivation increased when they could study via the internet. Many felt that online studies saved money and enabled more efficient time use. Thus, the students' life situation significantly impacted how online teaching was reacted to and how motivating it was perceived (Haasio & Kannasto, 2024, p. 415).

The principle of self-determination theory, which emphasizes autonomy, competence, and relatedness, remains integral but requires specific adaptations in online settings where direct social interactions are limited (Deci & Ryan, 2012). For instance, McLoughlin and Lee (2010) highlighted that fostering a sense of community through online forums and collaborative tools is essential for enhancing students' feelings of relatedness and support. Additionally, incorporating personalized feedback and adaptive learning technologies can address individual differences in motivation and learning styles, promoting a more tailored educational experience (Brusilovsky & Millán, 2007).

However, it is also critical to address potential pitfalls, such as the risk of decreased motivation due to reduced face-to-face interaction and the challenge of maintaining a consistent sense of presence and immediacy (Joksimović et al., 2015). Therefore, while the foundational principles of motivation apply, their implementation in online learning contexts requires careful adaptation to accommodate the distinct characteristics of digital education environments.

With their study, Fedeli et al. (2022) demonstrated how Massive Open Online Courses (MOOCs)—open web-based educational courses—designed according to adult learning theories can be a valuable tool for developing new knowledge and skills in higher education. Also, the high levels of engagement, learner interaction, and learner retention achieved in the first run of the MOOC provide robust evidence of the effectiveness of the proposed activities (Fedeli et al., 2022). Moreover, embedding the MOOC in a blended university course encouraged interaction between students from different countries and between students and professionals in an international online environment (Fedeli et al., 2022). MOOC-based blended university courses provided a fertile space for reflection and asynchronous discourses (Araneta et al., 2024). Thus, it is important to intentionally and carefully integrate reflective activities into the course design to enable students to engage in critical thinking, develop communication skills, and gain new perspectives (Araneta et al., 2024). MOOCs provide learners with time and space for reflection, enhancing the class learning experience in higher education settings and promoting meaningful learning (Araneta et al., 2024).

Related to online learning, Wlodkowski and Ginsberg (2017) showed adopters of their motivational framework found it useful and applicable in online settings "to explore which motivational conditions (inclusion, attitude, meaning and competence) relate[d] to student learning in online courses" (p. 110). Their framework has also been used with different aims for better understanding students' readiness to learn online, how the model works for instructional design of online courses, and most frequently, as a tool to design motivating experiences for adult learners.

Adult motivation to learn is affected by many variables and contexts. It is important to take a holistic view that considers the learner and their social context, incorporating other learners, instructors, and the macro dynamics in society and how these variables intersect to influence the context of learning.

Ahl (2006) challenged the assumption that motivation is a phenomenon existing only within the individual learner because it suggests a deficit. Ahl took issue with the notion that adult learners must be recruited and kept, thus assuming they are neither easily recruited nor retained. She contended that adult learners do not have motivational problems. Still, the problem lies in the relationship between the learner and those providing learning opportunities with their own motives. Through the motivation discourse, Ahl (2006) argued the "unwilling adult learner" has been created:

> The "unwilling adult learners" are both the reasons for and the solutions
> to societal problems, while those who formulate the problems, and the
> basis for the formulation of the problem remain invisible. They are made
> invisible because they represent normality, the ideology in power, and
> knowledge that is always taken for granted. (p. 401)

Ahl's critical assessment of adult learning motivation literature shows how motivation theory stigmatizes people we regard as "unmotivated" because motivation problems are only attributed to the individual. Ahl advocated reconceptualizing motivation as a relational phenomenon, not just within the individual. She urged, "Instead of asking what motivates adults to study, research should focus on *who states that this is a problem, and why, and the reasons for this conclusion*" (Ahl (2006), italics in original, p. 385). Ahl suggested that her approach would reveal power relations and show how the discourse of lifelong learning constructs adults as inadequate. She also noted that the majority of motivational recommendations in the adult education literature are pedagogical, putting much confidence in educators to counteract the many variables that can affect motivation to learn that have little to do with teaching. Ahl offers a critical counter-narrative to the dominant discourse about unmotivated learners. Presumably, she would not agree with Wlodkowski's (2008) approach, given its overreliance on pedagogy and teacher behaviors as the keys to unlocking learner motivation.

Chapter Summary

Motivation is key to adult learning, influencing engagement and persistence. This chapter explores intrinsic motivation (curiosity and mastery) and extrinsic motivation (rewards and recognition), along with theories explaining why adults learn. McClusky's Theory of Margin highlights the balance between life's demands and resources, while Houle's learner types categorize motivation as goal-driven, social, or knowledge-seeking.

Daniel Pink emphasizes autonomy, mastery, and purpose over traditional incentives. Wlodkowski and Ginsberg's framework outlines four motivational conditions: inclusion (respect), attitude (relevance), meaning (engagement), and competence (confidence). The chapter also examines online learning, highlighting self-regulation and engagement strategies.

Finally, it challenges the idea of "unmotivated learners," arguing that motivation is shaped by personal and societal factors. Educators can foster lasting motivation through inclusive, engaging, and meaningful learning experiences.

Key Points

- Motivation is the drive and energy we put into accomplishing something we want to do. We cannot see or touch it, but it is ever present in our thoughts and actions.
- Motivation can be either extrinsic or intrinsic.
- Houle identified three types of learning orientations in his analysis. *Goal-oriented learners* engage in learning as a means to attain another goal. *Activity-oriented learners* participate for the opportunity to socialize with other learners and for the sake of the activity. *Learning-oriented learners* are focused on developing new knowledge for the sake of learning.
- McClusky's Theory of Margin posits that motivation to learn is a function of how adults can balance the load of life by offsetting it with power or resources, a ratio known as Margin in Life.

- Wlodkowski and Ginsberg (2017) offer two critical assumptions of learning and motivation: "*If something can be learned, it can be learned in a motivating manner . . . every instructional plan also needs to be a motivational plan*" (p. 44, italics in original).
- At least three key contexts affect adult motivation to participate in education: personal, societal, and learning.

References

Ahl, H. (2006). Motivation in adult education: A problem solver or euphemism for direction and control? *International Journal of Lifelong Education, 25*(4), 385–405. https://doi.org/10.1080/02601370600772384.

Araneta, M. G., Liotino, M., Olatunji, T. I., & Fedeli, M. (2024). Leveraging massive open online courses to foster reflective practice in blended university courses. *Innovations in Education and Teaching International*, 1–13. https://doi.org/10.1080/14703297.2024.2320697.

Ashraf, N., Camerer, C. F., & Loewenstein, G. (2005). Adam Smith, behavioral economist. *Journal of Economic Perspectives, 19*(3), 131–145. https://doi.org/10.1257/089533005774357897.

Barrett, L. F. (2017). The theory of constructed emotion: An active inference account of interoception and categorization. *Social cognitive and affective neuroscience, 12*(1), 1–23. https://doi.org/10.1093/scan/nsw154.

Baum, J. (1978). An exploration of widowhood: Implications for adult educators. In *Proceedings of the Annual Adult Education Research Conference*. San Antonio, TX. ED157989.

Boshier, R. (1991). Psychometric properties of the alternative form of the education participation scale. *Adult Education Quarterly, 41*(3), 150–167. https://doi.org/10.1177/0001848191041003002.

Boshier, R., & Collins, J. B. (1985). The Houle Typology after twenty-two years: A large-scale empirical test. *Adult Education Quarterly, 35*(3), 113–130. https://doi.org/10.1177/0001848185035003001.

Bråten, I., & Strømsø, H. I. (2004). Epistemological beliefs and implicit theories of intelligence as predictors of achievement goals. *Contemporary Educational Psychology, 29*(4), 371–388. https://doi.org/10.1016/j.cedpsych.2003.10.001.

Brett, G., & Dubash, S. (2023). The sociocognitive origins of personal mastery. *Journal of Health and Social Behavior/Journal of Health & Social Behavior, 64*(3), 452–468. https://doi.org/10.1177/00221465231167558.

Brusilovsky, P., Millán, E. (2007). User models for adaptive hypermedia and adaptive educational systems. In P. Brusilovsky, A. Kobsa, W. Nejdl (Eds.) *The Adaptive Web. Lecture Notes in Computer Science*, vol. 4321 (3–53). Springer. https://doi.org/10.1007/978-3-540-72079-9_1.

Bye, D., Pushkar, D., & Conway, M. (2007). Motivation, interest, and positive affect in traditional and nontraditional undergraduate students. *Adult Education Quarterly, 57*(2), 141–158. https://doi.org/10.1177/0741713606294235.

Carlton, G. (2024, August 23). *2024 Online learning Statistics*. Forbes Advisor. https://www.forbes.com/advisor/education/online-colleges/online-learning-stats/.

Csikszentmihalyi, M. (1990). *Flow: The psychology of optimal experience*. Harper & Row.

Deci, E. L., & Ryan, R. M. (1985). *Intrinsic motivation and self-determination in human behavior*. Plenum.

Deci, E. L., & Ryan, R. M. (2012). Motivation, personality, and development within embedded social contexts: An overview of self-determination theory. In R. M. Ryan (Ed.), *Oxford handbook of human motivation* (pp. 85–107). Oxford University Press. https://doi.org/10.1093/oxfordhb/9780195399820.013.0006.

Dia, D. Smith, C. A., Cohen-Callow, A., Bliss, D. L. (2005). The education participation scale–modified: Evaluating a measure of continuing education. *Research on Social Work Practice, 15*(3), 213–222. https://doi.org/10.1177/1049731504273543.

Eurostat. (2024a, August 20). *Participation rate in education and training by sex.* https://doi.org/10.2908/TRNG_AES_100. https://ec.europa.eu/eurostat/databrowser/view/trng_aes_100/default/table?lang=en.

Eurostat. (2024b, December 12a). *Participation rate in education and training (last 12 months) by sex and age.* https://ec.europa.eu/eurostat/databrowser/view/trng_lfs_17/default/table?lang=en.

Eurostat. (2024c, December 12b). *Participation rate in education and training (last 12 months) by sex, age and educational attainment level.* https://ec.europa.eu/eurostat/databrowser/view/trng_lfs_18/default/table?lang=en.

Eurostat. (2024d, December 12). *Participation rate in education and training (last 12 months) by sex, age and labour status.* https://ec.europa.eu/eurostat/databrowser/view/trng_lfs_19/default/table?lang=en.

Eurostat. (2024e). *Adult learning statistics.* https://ec.europa.eu/eurostat/statistics-explained/index.php?title=Adult_learning_statistics.

Fedeli, M., Liotino, M., Taylor, E. W., Araneta, M. G. (2022). Enhancing learning in higher education using MOOC: The experience of the University of Padua. In G. Casalino, et al. *Higher Education Learning Methodologies and Technologies Online. HELMeTO 2021. Communications in Computer and Information Science*, vol 1542. Springer. https://doi.org/10.1007/978-3-030-96060-5_16.

Ginsberg, M. B., & Wlodkowski, R. J. (2010). Access and participation. In C. E. Kasworm, A. D. Rose, and J. M. Ross-Gordon (Eds.), *Handbook of adult and continuing education.* Sage.

Haasio, A., & Kannasto, E. (2024). Motivational factors of online learning in higher education. *European Journal of Applied Sciences, 12*(1), 405–419. https://doi.org/10.14738/aivp.121.16497.

Hiemstra, R., & Sisco, B. (1990). *Individualizing instruction.* Jossey-Bass.

Houle, C. O. (1961/1988). *The inquiring mind.* Madison: University of Wisconsin Press & Norman Oklahoma Research Center for Continuing Professional Higher Education. (Original work published 1961).

Hulleman, C. S., & Barron, K. E. (2015). Motivation interventions in education: Bridging theory, research, and practice. In L. Corno & E. M. Anderman (Eds.), *Handbook of educational psychology* (pp. 174–185). Routledge.

Infed. (n.d.). Howard McClusky and educational gerontology. *Infed: The encyclopaedia of informal education.* http://www.infed.org/thinkers/mcclusky.htm.

Joksimović, S., Gašević, D., Loughin, T., Kovanović, V., & Hatala, M. (2015). Learning at distance: Effects of interaction traces on academic achievement. *Computers and Education, 87*, 204–217. https://doi.org/10.1016/j.compedu.2015.07.002.

Keller, J. M. (1983). Motivational design of instruction. In C. M. Reigeluth (Ed.), *Instructional-design theories and models: An overview of their current status* (pp. 383–434). Lawrence Erlbaum Associates.

Kim, K., Hagedorn, M., Williamson, J., & Chapman, C. (2004). National Household Education Surveys of 2001: Participation in adult education and lifelong learning: 2000-01.

US Department of Education Institute of Education Sciences NCES 2004-050. http://nces.ed.gov/pubs2004/2004050.pdf.

Kuh, G. D. (2003). What we're learning about student engagement from NSSE: Benchmarks for effective educational practices, *Change: The Magazine of Higher Learning, 35*(2), 24–32. https://doi.org/10.1080/00091380309604090.

Lewin, K. (1935). *A dynamic theory of personality*. McGraw-Hill.

Linnenbrink-Garcia, L., Patall, E. A., & Pekrun, R. (2016). Adaptive motivation and emotion in education: Research and principles for instructional design. *Policy Insights from the Behavioral and Brain Sciences, 3*(2), 228–236.

Machynska, N. & Boiko, H. (2020). Andragogy = The science of adult education: Theoretical aspects. *Journal of Innovation in Psychology, Education and Didactics, 24*(1), 25–34.

Main, K. (1979). The power-load-margin formula of Howard Y. McClusky as the basis for a model of teaching. *Adult Education 30*(1), 19–33. https://doi.org/10.1177/074171367903000102.

Masden, S. R., John, C., Miller, D., & Warren, E. (2004). The relationship between an individual's margin in life and readiness for change. *Proceedings of the Academy of Human Resource Development, USA*, (pp. 759–766). Austin, TX.

Maslow, A. H. (1943). A theory of human motivation. *Psychological Review, 50*(4), 370–396. https://doi.org/10.1037/h0054346.

Maslow, A. A. (1987). *Motivation and personality*. Addison Wesley Longman.

Mayo, E. (1933). *The Human Problems of an Industrial Civilization*. MacMillan.

McClusky, H. Y. (1963). The course of the adult life span. In W. C. Hallenbeck (Ed.), *Psychology of adults*. Adult Education Association of the U.S.A.

McClusky, H. Y. (1970). Dynamic approach to participation in community development. *Journal of the Community Development Society, 1*(1), 25–32. https://doi.org/10.1080/15575330.1970.10877417.

McClusky, H. Y. (1971). The adult as learner. In R. J. McNeil & S. E. Seashore (Eds.), *Management of Urban Crisis* (pp. 27–39). The Free Press.

McLoughlin, C., & Lee, M. J. (2010). Personalised and self-regulated learning in the Web 2.0 era: International exemplars of innovative pedagogy using social software. *Australasian Journal of Educational Technology, 26*(1), 28–43. https://doi.org/10.14742/ajet.1100.

Oudeyer, P., & Kaplan, F. (2007). What is intrinsic motivation? A typology of computational approaches. *Frontiers in Neurorobotics, 1*, 108. https://doi.org/10.3389/neuro.12.006.2007.

Pink, D. H. (2009). *Drive: The surprising truth about what motivates us*. Riverhead Books.

Pintrich, P. R., Smith, D. A., Garcia, T., & McKeachie, W. J. (1991). *A manual for the use of the Motivated Strategies for Learning Questionnaire (MSLQ)*. Ann Arbor: University of Michigan, National Center for Research to Improve Postsecondary Teaching and Learning.

Ryan, R. M., & Deci, E. L. (2000). Intrinsic and extrinsic motivations: Classic definitions and new directions. *Contemporary Educational Psychology, 25*(1), 54–67. https://doi.org/10.1006/ceps.1999.1020.

Ryan, R. M., & Deci, E. L. (2020). Intrinsic and extrinsic motivation from a self-determination theory perspective: Definitions, theory, practices, and future directions. *Contemporary Educational Psychology, 61*, 101860. https://doi.org/10.1016/j.cedpsych.2020.101860.

Salinas, A. (2023, March 1). *Adam Smith as behavioral economist?* Adam Smith Works. https://www.adamsmithworks.org/documents/adam-smith-as-behavioral-economist.

Schlesinger, R. (2005). Better myself: Motivation of African Americans to participate in correctional education. *The Journal of Correctional Education, 56*(3), 228–252. http://www.jstor.org/stable/23282589.

Schunk, D. H., & Di Benedetto, M. K. (2020). Motivation and social cognitive theory. *Contemporary educational psychology, 60*, 101832.

Schwedel, A. (2023, September 15). 3 ways organizations can empower older workers amid an ageing global workforce. World Economic Forum. https://www.weforum.org/agenda/2023/09/how-organizations-can-embrace-older-workers-amid-an-ageing-workforce/.

Smith, A. (1776/2000). *The wealth of nations.* Random House.

Statista. (n.d.). *Online Education - Worldwide | Statista market forecast.* https://www.statista.com/outlook/emo/online-education/worldwide.

Stevenson, J. S. (1982). Construction of a scale to measure load, power, and margin in life. *Nursing Research, 31*(4), 222–225.

Taylor, F. W. (1911). *The principles of scientific management.* Jossey-Bass.

Taylor, E. W. (2019). Student–teacher Relationships: The elephant in the classroom. In M. Fedeli & L. L. Bierema, (Eds.) *Connecting Adult Learning and Knowledge Management. Knowledge Management and Organizational Learning,* vol 8. (pp. 69–83) Springer, Cham. https://doi.org/10.1007/978-3-030-29872-2_4.

Tisdell, E. J. (2003). *Exploring spirituality and culture in adult and higher education.* John Wiley & Sons.

US Department of Education, National Center for Educational Statistics. (2007). The condition of education 2007 (NCES 2007-064). Washington, DC: US Government Printing Office. http://nces.ed.gov/programs/coe/indicator_aed.asp.

Vansteenkiste, M., Lens, W., & Deci, E. L. (2006). Intrinsic versus extrinsic goal contents in self-determination theory: Another look at the quality of academic motivation. *Educational Psychologist, 41*(1), 19–31. https://doi.org/10.1207/s15326985ep4101_4.

Vroom, V. H. (1964/1995). *Work and motivation.* Jossey-Bass.

Wang, V. C. X., & Hansman, C. A. (2017). Pedagogy and andragogy in higher education. In V. C. X. Wang, (Ed). *Theory and practice of adult and higher education* (87–111). Information Age Publishing, Inc. https://books.google.it/books?hl=it&lr=&id=2AcoDwAAQBAJ&oi=fnd&pg=PA87&dq=Wan,+V.C.X.+and+Hansman,+C.A.+(2017)&ots=SNfLJQDKp_&sig=APr_NNHpSq3hoCK7QjFjnRt0a7k&redir_esc=y#v=onepage&q&f=false.

Winget, M., & Persky, A. M. (2022). A practical review of Mastery learning. *American Journal of Pharmaceutical Education, 86*(10), ajpe8906. https://doi.org/10.5688/ajpe8906.

Wlodkowski, R. J. (2008). *Enhancing adult motivation to learn: A comprehensive guide for teaching all adults* (3rd ed.). Jossey-Bass.

Wlodkowski, R. J. & Ginsberg, M. B. (2017). *Enhancing adult motivation to learn: A comprehensive guide for teaching all adults* (4th ed.). Jossey-Bass.

Yamashita, T., Smith, T. J., Sahoo, S., & Cummins, P. A. (2022). Motivation to learn by age, education, and literacy skills among working-age adults in the United States. *Large-Scale Assessments in Education, 10*(1), 1. https://doi.org/10.1186/s40536-022-00119-7.

Zaccone, M. C., & Pedrini, M. (2019). The effects of intrinsic and extrinsic motivation on students learning effectiveness: Exploring the moderating role of gender. *International Journal of Educational Management, 33*(6), 1381–1394. https://doi.org/10.1108/IJEM-03-2019-0099.

CHAPTER SEVEN

APPLYING ANDRAGOGY—THE ART AND SCIENCE OF HELPING ADULTS LEARN

 **Box 7.1 Chapter Overview and Learning Objectives**

Andragogy is one of the most applied adult learning frameworks, described by Knowles as "The art and science of helping adults learn" (Knowles, 1980, p. 43). This model is focused on procedures and resources aiding a learner in developing information and skills (Knowles, 1990).

The purpose of this chapter is to describe andragogy by introducing the history of adult learning before andragogy and the development of its theoretical framework, highlighting key scholars and their scientific contributions. The assumptions of andragogy and their implications for instruction and program design for adult learners will be analyzed, explained, and critiqued. Next, the core principles of andragogy will be presented: the learner's self-concept, the value of experience, readiness to learn, problem-centered orientation, internal motivation, and the need to know. Finally, the application of andragogy in contemporary settings will be explored through case studies, providing you, the reader, with the best available evidence to inform understanding of how to facilitate learning and teach adults.

As a result of reading this chapter and completing the exercises, you, the reader, should be able to:

1. Identify the characteristics of adult learners within the framework of andragogy.
2. Understand the andragogical approach to planning instruction for adults.
3. Recognize the value of experience and the diverse needs of adult learners.
4. Evaluate the assumptions about adult learners and their implications for program design.
5. Apply andragogical principles in various adult learning settings.

Andragogy and the Development of Adult Learning

As a human being, you have always engaged in learning—learning to survive, live in a social group, and understand the meaning of your experiences. Interestingly, "All the great teachers of ancient times were teachers of adults, not children" (Ozuah, 2005, p. 84). Savicevic (2008) pointed out that "Plato's Academy and Aristotle's Lyceum were adult education institutions" (p. 366) and that these teachers, as well as Chinese, Hebrew, and Christian educators, used dialogue, parables, and what today would be referred to as problem-based learning activities with adults. It was not until the monasteries established schools for children in the seventh century that the term "pedagogy" came into use. Pedagogy, Knowles (1973) explained, "spread to the secular schools of Europe and America and, unfortunately, was much later applied even to the education of adults" (p. 42). Nevertheless, scholars of antiquity offered the seeds of an approach to adult learning that differed from child pedagogy.

While stories of these ancient adult educators exist, there was no systematic investigation of adult learning until the late 19th and early 20th centuries. Behavioral and social scientists from Pavlov and Skinner to Piaget and Freud, and humanists Maslow and Rogers used the investigative tools of their day to try to understand the nature of learning. In 1928, *Adult Learning* by Thorndike et al. was the first publication from this period to report on "scientific" studies with adult learners rather than animals or children.

Early Adult Education Research

Aside from Thorndike's work, much of the writing on adult learning in the early decades of the 20th century was socially and philosophically oriented. In his classic *The Meaning of Adult Education* in the United States, first published in 1926, the same year as the founding of the American Association for Adult Education, Lindeman wrote of the dual purpose of adult education: to change individuals and society. He also identified the learner's experience as "the resource of highest value in adult education" and "the adult learner's living textbook" (Lindeman, 1926, pp. 9–10). Further, Lindeman proposed that adult learning be built around "needs and interests" that are embedded in an adult's situation—"his [sic] work, his [sic] recreation, his [sic] family life, his [sic] community life . . . Adult education begins at this point" (Lindeman, 1926/1961, pp. 8–9). Interestingly, Lindeman, who used the term "andragogy" in an article published in 1926 in *The Meaning of Adult Education*, presented it as a method for teaching adults (Henschke, 2011). Knowles was apparently unaware of his early usage of the term.

Until the 1970s, adult educators relied on Lindeman and other social philosophers and behavioral and cognitive research in learning, memory, and intelligence to understand and design instruction for adult learners. Knowles (1984) himself talked about his unease teaching adults in the 1930s and 1940s:

> I tried to find a book that would tell me how to conduct a program of
> this sort, and I couldn't find one. So, I sought out people who were
> directing adult education programs . . . and formed an advisory council
> to give me guidance. (p. 2)

Knowles (1984) admitted being enlightened by Lindeman's book "about the unique characteristics of adults as learners and the need for methods and techniques for helping them learn" (p. 3).

Only gradually did resources on adult learners and adult learning appear, which helped move the field toward identifying how learning in adulthood differed from learning in childhood. Two critical studies researched adult learners and the development of andragogy. Houle's *The Inquiring Mind*, published in 1961, reported on an analysis of 22 adult learners and their motivations for learning. He found some were goal-oriented in that they had clear-cut objectives in their learning. Some were activity-oriented, where the primary motivation was human interaction, and others were learning-oriented, wherein the adult sought knowledge for knowledge's sake. Tough's *The Adult's Learning Projects* (1971) built on Houle's work in this study of 66 adults' learning projects inspiring a line of inquiry still viable today—self-directed learning. He found that self-directed learners often spend hundreds of hours on learning projects, which they plan, implement, and evaluate independently.

Global Discussions and Critiques of Andragogy

In the 1950s, numerous publications on andragogy emerged from Germany, Switzerland, the Netherlands, and later Yugoslavia (Reischmann, 2004). This surge in interest was driven by the desire to develop educational frameworks that fostered social justice and peace, demonstrating that Europe had learned from the horrors of World War II. These educational approaches aimed to move beyond the racial hatred and intolerance that had marked the wartime era (Loeng, 2018).

In 1967, Yugoslavian adult educator Dusan Savicevic attended one of Knowles's workshops on adult learning and introduced him to the term "andragogy," which was widely used in Europe to describe the growing body of knowledge and technology related to adult learning (Knowles, 1984). Knowles first wrote about andragogy in a 1968 article and, by 1970, published the first edition of *The Modern Practice of Adult Education: Andragogy Versus Pedagogy*. Savicevic (2008) expressed ambivalence about Knowles's popularization of andragogy, stating that Knowles "reduced andragogy to a prescription, recipes for teachers' behavior in the process of education and learning" (p. 374).

Giroux (2000) underscored the pivotal role of culture in shaping political discourse, while Moll (2023) argued that andragogy is misleading due to its inherent bias toward White people, failing to account for differences in race, gender, and culture.

In alignment with this critique, Dantus (2021) and Duff (2019) emphasized in recent debates on the decolonization of adult learning that andragogy is entrenched in the ideologies of universality and individualism, reflecting the dominant White men's culture of the Global North. Scholars argued that andragogy grew from mid-20th-century individualistic norms modeled on a White, middle-class American man portrayed as a self-motivated, autonomous, and resourceful problem-solver. In recent years, the 2030 Agenda for Sustainable Development (UN, 2015) has elevated issues such as social justice and gender equality within adult education. The 2030 Agenda emphasizes the significance of inclusive and equitable quality education, promoting lifelong learning for all. Box 7.2 addresses policy.

Despite the significance of the andragogical approach in teaching adults across both formal and nonformal education settings, Pratt (1993) underscored two significant concerns regarding andragogy: "First, knowledge is assumed to be actively constructed by the learner, not passively received from the environment; and second, learning is an interactive process of interpretation, integration, and transformation of one's experiential world" (p. 17). According to Pratt, andragogy lacks clarification of the beliefs and values underpinning the

Box 7.2 SoTL: The Scholarship of Teaching and Learning

Learning and Social Justice: Challenging Policy and Social Issues

Acharya et al. (2020) highlighted how the field of adult education globally addresses issues related to policy environments, learning, and social justice, especially concerning Indigenous women in Nepal. This study illustrated adult education's multifaceted role in promoting social justice and gender equality. The analysis revealed that Indigenous women are marginalized and not involved in the political debate and representation (Acharya et al., 2020).

For indigenous women in Nepal, adult education enhances literacy and vocational skills and is a powerful tool for empowerment and social change. It helps overcome traditional gender role barriers and provides a platform for these women to engage in community leadership and advocacy (Acharya et al., 2020).

Reflect for a moment on one of your best learning experiences as an adult learner and try to answer the following questions:

1. How has the learning challenged your perspective of the world?
2. What social issues were you able to face thanks to your best learning experience?
3. What discoveries about yourself and your worldview have surprised you most?

learning process. Additionally, it does not critically question the learning process if learning occurs under certain circumstances without further examination (Pratt, 1993).

In any case, andragogy, as promoted by Knowles, is considered the first systematic formulation laying out the differences between children and adult learners. Andragogy contributed to the development of adult education when adult educators struggled to establish their own identity separate from childhood education. It helped "professionalize" the field of adult education by establishing a knowledge base unique to adult learners.

Assumptions about Adult Learners

"A new label and a new technology" of adult learning is how Knowles introduced andragogy to American educators in 1968 (p. 351). Pedagogy comes from the "Greek word 'paid,' meaning child (plus 'agogus' meaning leader of)" (Merriam & Bierema, 2014, p. 46). Literally, **pedagogy** means the "art and science of teaching children" (Knowles, 1973, p. 43), while **andragogy** comes from the Greek word *aner*, meaning man, so andragogy refers to helping *adults* learn (Knowles, 1973). Having a term to differentiate adult learning from pedagogy was insufficient to establish a robust theory of adult learning. At this point, Knowles drew heavily from Lindeman's ideas regarding adult learning being situation-motivated and experience-centered. Knowles (1973) was perhaps less concerned with a definition of andragogy than with "differentiating between the *assumptions* about learners that have traditionally been made by those who practice pedagogy in contrast to the assumptions made in andragogy" (italics in original, p. 43). The following box allows you, as an adult learner and educator, to understand the assumptions about adult learners and how to link these principles to andragogy. Box 7.3 features andragogy.

Roessger et al. (2022) focused their study on assessing the validity of the pedagogical assumptions across cultures. This study, relevant at the international level, considered data from the Program of the International Assessment of Adult Competencies (PIAAC) collected between 2011 and 2015. The questionnaire was administered to over 160,000 learners aged 16–65 in 32 countries of the Organization for Economic Cooperation and Development (OECD) and aimed to assess adults' motivations and preferences in selecting teaching strategies. The findings revealed that cultural factors significantly influenced adults' andragogical learning preferences. Specifically, the study identified that each of the six cultural dimensions correlated with a distinct learning preference: "whereas countries with dominant masculine values, a focus on future-oriented aims, and preferences for the free expression of human desires have learners with lower preferences for pedagogical learning. Interestingly, no country perfectly fit this profile" (p. 33). Moreover, the study concluded that andragogical learning preferences emerge only after meeting more basic needs, as discussed in Chapter 6.

Each of Knowles's assumptions has implications for program design and instruction. Although a pedagogical model emphasizes content—lessons determined, organized, delivered, and evaluated by the teacher—an andragogical model emphasizes process. In andragogy, the facilitator sets a climate for learning that physically and psychologically respects adult learners and then involves the learners in planning, delivering, and evaluating their learning (Knowles & Associates, 1984). A more detailed discussion of the assumptions underlying andragogy and their application to practice follows.

Box 7.3 SoTL: The Scholarship of Teaching and Learning

The Practice of Teaching and Learning: Principles of Andragogy

Understanding andragogy and adult learning hinges on grasping the underlying assumptions and linking these principles to the practice of teaching and learning adults. Knowles defined andragogy as "the art and science of helping adults learn" (Knowles, 1980, p. 43). Andragogy is based on assumptions about adult learners, influencing how educators teach and promote learning. Knowles developed these assumptions in two phases: The first four appeared in earlier works (1980) and the last two in later publications (1984). The complete set of assumptions about adult learners includes:

1. **Self-concept:** As a person matures, their self-concept moves from that of a dependent personality toward one of a self-directing human being; adults are responsible for their own decisions and learning.
2. **Experience:** Adults' accumulated experiences are a rich resource for learning.
3. **Readiness to learn:** Adults learn when they perceive it necessary for personal or professional development; their readiness to learn is closely related to the developmental tasks of their social role.
4. **Problem-centered orientation:** Learning helps adults solve real-life and professional problems. There is a change in time perspective as people mature—from future application of knowledge to immediacy of application. Thus, an adult is more problem-centered than subject-centered in learning (Knowles, 1980, pp. 44–45).
5. **Internal motivation:** Internal motivation is crucial for effective adult learning.
6. **Need to know:** Adults need to understand the reason for their learning and how it can improve their lives or careers (Knowles & Associates, 1984, p. 12).

Understanding these principles helps educators design and organize learning processes that engage and motivate adult learners.

Reflection

Reflect for a moment on your learning process:

1. How have you encountered or applied these principles in your teaching and learning experience as an adult learner or educator?

2. How have your accumulated experiences contributed to your learning process? Can you recall a time when your past experiences enriched your learning?
3. How have you applied your learning to solve real-life or professional problems? Can you provide an example of a problem you solved through your learning?
4. What role has internal motivation played in your learning? How do you stay motivated when faced with challenging material?

The Learner's Self-concept

This first assumption posits that people become more independent and self-directing as they mature. An infant, for example, is dependent on others for survival. Children slowly learn to do things for themselves but still rely on adults for most aspects of their lives. The teen years bring more independence, and people take responsibility for their own lives by young adulthood.

This difference in self-concept between a child and an adult reflects how people treat children versus adults. People ask children their age or what grade they are in at school because they assume children's primary role is a full-time student. With adults, people are more likely to ask about their family, work, or community engagement—reflecting the adult roles of being independent, contributing members of society. Because adults see themselves as independent and self-directing, they develop "a deep psychological need to be perceived by others, and treated by others, as capable of taking responsibility for ourselves" (Knowles & Associates, 1984, p. 9) and if "others are imposing their wills on us without our participating in making decisions affecting us, we experience a feeling, often subconsciously, of resentment and resistance" (Knowles & Associates, 1984, p. 9).

Feelings of "resentment and resistance" happen when an instructor uses pedagogical strategies with adult learners (Knowles & Associates, 1984, p. 9). Adults who make decisions daily regarding family, work, and community life suddenly find they have no voice in what and how they learn something. Knowles pointed out that this is a "special problem" for adult educators because even though most adults are self-directing in major areas of their lives:

> The minute they walk into a situation labeled "education," "training," or any of their synonyms, they hark back to their conditioning in school, assume a role of dependency, and demand to be taught. However, if they really are treated like children, this conditioned expectation conflicts with their much deeper psychological need to be self-directing. (Knowles & Associates, 1984 p. 9)

Educators can address this dependency gradually, working with adults in ways that allow for increased self-direction in their learning.

The fact that adult learners can be presumed to have a more independent self-concept than a child and, therefore, be more self-directed in their learning does not imply that all adults are always self-directing and can plan their learning or that all children are always teacher dependent. Even Knowles and Associates (1984) eventually conceded that there are situations where an adult encountering a new area of learning will, of necessity, be more dependent on a teacher and, similarly, children who are naturally curious and "very self-directing in their learning *outside of school* . . . could also be more self-directed in school" (italics in original, p. 13).

What does this assumption that adult learners have independent self-concepts and are self-directed in their learning imply for adult educational programs? Knowles (1996) emphasized the importance of "climate setting" as a fundamental condition for effective learning. Creating a supportive learning environment requires attention to two key aspects: the broader institutional climate and the specific atmosphere of the training setting (Knowles, 1996). In his process model of instruction, the physical environment must be comfortable and adult oriented. Second, there should be a psychological climate of mutual respect and trust and an atmosphere of collaboration. Atmospheres where adults are respected as adults embolden participants to contribute to course content planning and engage in self-directing their learning.

This first assumption underlying Knowles's promotion of andragogy converged with Houle's typology (1961) of adult learners and Tough's research (1971) on adult learning projects. Tough's finding that more than 90% of adults engaged in self-directed learning launched an entirely new program of research and theory-building in self-directed learning. Knowles contributed to this line of research with a book on self-directed learning published in 1975.

The Learner's Experience

The second assumption of andragogy is that an adult's accumulated life experiences are a "rich resource for learning" (Knowles, 1984, p. 45). As people age, they have a variety of life experiences that can be drawn on in a learning situation but also stimulate the need for learning.

The vital role of experience in learning is well-documented in the learning literature. Cognitive psychologists such as Piaget, Bruner, and Ausubel firmly acknowledged the role of experience in a person's ability to process information (Merriam & Bierema, 2014). Developmental psychologists and educators also saw development as the processing of life experiences. Erik Erikson's

(1963) famous eight-stage theory of psycho-social development is a good example. At each stage of life, from infancy to old age, one deals with a central issue important to development. The adult issues are all connected to adult life experiences, such as dealing with intimacy in young adulthood or generativity (caring for others) in middle age. Box 7.4 provides an opportunity to reflect on developmental experiences and how they influence adult learning.

The link between learning and development is perhaps most clearly evident in the work of psychologist and educator Robert Havighurst. In 1952, he published *Developmental Tasks and Education,* laying out developmental tasks to be accomplished at each life stage, such as finding a mate and getting started in an occupation in young adulthood. These "life situations," as Lindeman might have called them, presented what Havighurst termed "the teachable moment" (Havighurst, 1952, p. 7). For example, the teachable moment to learn about parenting is when one has young children. Learning about retirement becomes relevant when one is bringing full-time work life to a close. Knowles (1980) acknowledged that these developmental tasks created "'a readiness to learn' which at its peak presents a 'teachable moment'" (p. 51).

An adult accumulates life experience just by engaging in the roles of adult life. This life experience makes each individual unique, for no two life trajectories are alike. Thus, experience is integral to an adult's identity or self-concept. Knowles et al. (2011) explained:

> Young children derive their self-identity largely from external definers—who their parents, brothers, sisters, and extended families are; where they live; and what churches and schools they attend. As they mature, they increasingly define themselves in terms of the experiences they have had. To children, experience is something that happens to them; to adults, their experience is who they are. This fact for adult education implies that in any situation in which the participants' experiences are ignored or devalued, adults will perceive this as rejecting not only their experience but rejecting themselves as persons. (p. 65)

Because adults are defined largely due to accumulated life experiences, rejecting or ignoring their experiences threatens their independent self-concept, the first assumption of andragogy. The self-concept and life experience assumptions further intersect when one considers the number and variety of life experiences of the typical adult. The implication is that a group of adult learners is likely to differ from a group of children. Because of this variety, not only is it imperative to use these experiences in learning, but it is also crucial for adults to take control of their learning and become independent, self-directed learners.

 ## Box 7.4 Reflective Practice

Integrating Identity Crisis, Adult Development, and Career Development

Your ability as an adult to construct meaning in the face of developmental tasks and challenges is an essential marker of adulthood. Adulthood has at least three recurring developmental themes across the lifespan. Erikson (2001) identified these developmental quandaries as related to identity, collegial intimacy, and generativity.

(Re)Interpreting Identity: Who Am I?

The term **identity crisis** or **midlife crisis** refers to the developmental challenge of identity. **Identity** is a person's unique traits and characteristics influencing their self-concept, self-image, self-esteem, and individuality. Identity crises arise from any major life event that forces a person to resolve identity issues, such as getting promoted, graduating, losing a job, or dealing with a personal catastrophe. Adults effectively resolve identity issues by:

- Articulating qualities most central to the self, especially during change. For example, being able to state, "I am _____."
- Developing a core self-image that provides continuity and sameness.
- Building a sense of "inner firmness" or resolve in one's individuality.
- Realizing strong values and beliefs that relate to social and work roles.
- Finding a vocation.
- Resolving the central identity learning dilemma: Identity is called into question during change, which raises the question, "Can I be faithful or live up to my identity?"

Developing Collegial Intimacy: How Is My Interpersonal Competence?

Collegial intimacy effectively builds high-quality, trustful relationships with others in one's personal life, workplace, or community. Characteristics of collegial intimacy include:

- Respecting other people's identity without imposing the self.
- Willingness to take risks, compromise, sacrifice, and keep commitments.
- Working cooperatively, seeking, and offering help.
- Having influence and being influenceable.
- Forming sustained, trusting relationships.

Fostering Generativity: Am I Ready to Care for and Nurture the Next Generation?

Generativity is the desire to give back or leave a legacy by participating in activities supporting future generations' well-being and sustainability. This aspect of adult identity is often associated with aging, although it is not linked to chronological age. Most people hope their lives have meaning and importance to the people and communities they care about. Characteristics of generativity include:

- Contributing to a cause or organization.
- Ensuring the future sustainability of ideas and institutions one cares about.
- Passing along ideas and values to the next generation.

Reflect on these three learning dilemmas of adulthood. What have you experienced as an adult learner?

Source: Adapted from Bierema, 2024, pp. 123–125.

The nature of life experience in adult learning also has its downside. Adults can become dogmatic and closed-minded about learning something new because their prior knowledge and experience have worked for them, and they see no need to know something else. Also, a traumatic life experience might function as a barrier to learning (Merriam et al., 1996), nor does the amount of experience necessarily equate with the quality of experience. At the same time, some children may have had a range and depth of experience that was more intense and powerful than some adults.

Life experience as a resource for learning applies to adult education practice in several ways. A facilitator can begin with an adult student's experiences and then assist the learner in connecting those experiences with new concepts, theories, and experiences. Many adult educators tap into adult learners' experience as an instructional starting point. Discussion, role play, simulations, field experiences, problem-based learning, case studies, and projects enable learners to draw on their life experiences as resources for learning.

Finally, this connection between life experience and learning is at the heart of several theoretical frameworks explaining learning, particularly adult learning. From Dewey's classic *Experience and Education* (1938) to Kolb's experiential learning cycle (1984), to Schön's notion of reflective practice (1983), to communities of practice where participants' experiences form the basis for learning (Fenwick, 2003), the learner's experiences are front and center. (For more on experiential learning, see Chapter 9.) The following tip in Box 7.5 provides activities to engage the learner in reflecting on good and bad learning experiences.

Box 7.5 Reflective Practice

Engaging Adults to Learn: Reflecting on Your Learning Experiences

A good starting point for engaging with andragogy is for you as an adult learner or educator to examine your learning. You can do this by recalling good and bad learning experiences, as recommended in the previous section of this chapter.

1. Write out a short narrative description of each, then stand back and compare the two incidents.
2. What was different?
3. What assumptions of andragogy were present in the good experience and absent in the bad experience?
4. What could have been done to turn the bad experience into a good one?

If you are an adult educator, we recommend this as an effective learning activity for teaching about andragogy and effective learning facilitation.

Together with the experience and the reflection on it, the need to learn plays a significant role. Most of the learning needs are related to the developmental tasks of adults who want to improve their position and professional role.

The Learner's Readiness to Learn

The assumption that an adult's learning agenda is closely related to developmental tasks and social roles of adult life connects to the previous assumption that life experiences are a resource for learning. The main emphasis in this assumption is that the *social roles* of adulthood create a need for learning. As mentioned earlier, the child's main social role in life is that of a student. Much of children's learning is subject-centered and in preparation for future learning—learning the alphabet so they can read, learning basic math to move on to algebra, and so on. Conversely, adults are engaged in multiple social roles, such as worker, spouse, parent, and community member. The demands of each of these roles also change as people age. A young adult may be preparing for work or experimenting with various career options. In contrast, a middle-aged adult may be managing or supervising other workers or looking to change careers, and the older adult may be trying to figure out how to stay up to date to keep a job or to plan for retirement.

Ideally, readiness to learn intersects with the "teachable moment" mentioned earlier in this chapter. Adult social roles create teachable moments, and adult education programs can be entirely planned around these needs. Forrest and Peterson (2006) offered an example from management education:

> A newly promoted manager may have had little interest in learning about giving performance feedback when holding a nonmanagement position. However, such an individual can be eager to learn such information because the knowledge has relevance once the individual is promoted to a management position. (p. 119)

Although all social roles and changes in these roles throughout the life span provide myriad learning opportunities, the social role of the worker drives adults' engagement in formal learning activities. When adults in national surveys were asked for their reasons for participation in formal adult education activities, 85–90% of those surveyed cited career- or job-related reasons for participation (Merriam et al., 2007). However, these studies focus on formal programs sponsored by educational institutions, businesses, and industry. Even more prevalent than learning in formal settings is the learning embedded in everyday life—informal or nonformal learning. Although considered more prevalent, this kind of learning is more challenging to capture. However, studies on informal and self-directed learning (see Chapter 8) indicate that personal development related to social and work roles is a decisive motivating factor.

Though it seems obvious that readiness to learn is related to adult development and social roles, much of this learning, especially in formal settings, emphasizes preparation for future roles rather than responding to an immediate need. One trick for adult educators is to create the readiness for learning through experiential instructional techniques. For example, using a natural disaster in the news can be a real-life stimulus for learning about community organizations or disaster relief management. Industry downsizing can lead to learning activities focusing on updating employee skills or career development activities. Knowles (1973) discussed professional reskilling preparation:

> It is my observation that a good deal of professional education is totally out of phase with the students' readiness to learn. For example, . . . the new social work student needs to have some direct experience with clients with problems before he [sic] is ready to learn about public welfare legislation and policy, casework principles and techniques, theory and practice of

 ## Box 7.6 Tips and Tools for Teaching and Learning

Taking or Administering a Learning Inventory

An effective way of exploring learning as an adult educator or learner is to inventory your own or your students' orientation to learning, such as whether it is more pedagogical or andragogical. Several instruments are available (see a review by Holton et al., 2009). We, the authors of this book, used Conti's (2004) Principles of Adult Learning Scale (PALS). This 44-item instrument assesses the extent to which your teaching style is more learner-centered than teacher-centered and, thus, more andragogical. The PALS assesses knowledge of learner-centered instructional activities, climate-setting, relating learning to real-life problems and experiences, and the extent to which students are encouraged to participate in planning and evaluation. The PALS is available in a chapter written by Conti (2004).

After administering or taking the PALS, reflect on these questions:

1. What influenced the development of my teaching style?
2. What are the strengths of my teaching approach?
3. What are the limitations of my teaching approach?
4. How will I use this assessment to further my development as an adult learner or educator?

> administration, concepts of community organization, group work, and research methods. He'll [sic] be ready to inquire into these areas of content as he [sic] confronts problems to which they are relevant. (p. 47)

The key aspects of readiness to learn highlight the need for learning and its connection to personal and professional goals. This necessity centers on addressing and investigating problems or needs that adults face in their lives. Box 7.6 contains tips for considering your teaching style as an adult educator.

The Learner's Problem-Centered Orientation

Imagine that you have just been diagnosed with a serious health problem such as cancer. You want to find out about this form of cancer, what the treatment options are, where to get the best care, and what you can do in terms of diet and exercise to maximize your chances of survival. You consult with healthcare professionals, family, and friends and go online to learn all you can. You might even attend a cancer self-help group. Your learning is problem-centered; your cancer diagnosis is the problem. It is not subject-centered; you are not interested in learning about cancer in general, and you would not have investigated this topic at all if it had not become a problem for you. Further, if you are interested in immediate application, what can you learn to apply to your situation now, not later? Immediacy is the essence of the fourth assumption—that adults are problem-centered, not subject-centered, and desire immediate, not postponed, application of the knowledge learned.

The fourth assumption of andragogy is logically related to the previous three. Most adults are motivated to learn to deal with an issue or problem of immediate concern. Often, these issues are related to their social roles, intertwining with their life experiences. Again, as with the other three assumptions above, there are a couple of caveats to consider. First, some adults learn for the sheer joy of learning, for the sense of accomplishment in learning something outside one's comfort zone, and not to deal with an immediate problem. On the other end of the continuum, not all childhood learning needs to be subject centered with postponed application. **Service learning,** which engages students in addressing real issues in their community, is very problem-centered (Savery, 2015). Conversely, the **flipped classroom** approach is subject-centered and focuses on developing knowledge on specific topics while enhancing various soft skills (Green & Schlairet, 2017).

Nevertheless, adult learning, more often than not, is problem-centered with a desire for immediate application. Most continuing education programs and community-based nonformal offerings are of this nature. An interesting example is Taylor's studies (2005, 2012) of learning activities offered by home-improvement stores. These stories provide short sessions on topics related to problems that arise for homeowners, such as fixing a leaky faucet or laying floor tile.

Adults prefer problem-centered learning because it is more engaging and provides immediate application, solidifying the learning. Indeed, this is the rationale behind some forms of professional preparation, such as problem-based learning in medical training and just-in-time teaching in management education. Students tackle a real-world business problem with an organization as their "clients" (Watson & Temkin, 2000, p. 763). Finally, professional graduate education has become open to students engaging in action research where they and their organization define a real problem to study, design, implement, and evaluate the solution (Manfra, 2019; Watkins et al., 2023). Empirical studies on andragogy related to the adult learning environment, teaching and learning strategies, classroom interactions, and course assignments seem necessary to connect andragogy to these learning factors and to give evidence of the relevance of this approach (Ekoto & Gaikwad, 2015). Box 7.7 explains how to integrate andragogy into courses.

Using active learning and learner-centered strategies creates more engaging contexts for adults to learn. **Active learning** "is the process of engaging learners with the topic and each other where they are talking, doing, and creating together" (Bierema, 2019, p. 30). **Learner-centered teaching** (Weimer, 2013) is defined as teaching with a focus on learning, and what the learners are doing is central to the process more than the content (p. 15). These approaches foster innovation and creativity, enabling learners to develop competencies essential for professional success. By emphasizing practical application and personal relevance, these strategies (e.g., interactive lecturing, small collaborative learning groups, project-based learning, problem-based learning, classroom feedback technology) enhance learning experiences and better prepare individuals to compete in professional environments. The benefits of such methods are

---

 ## Box 7.7 Tips and Tools for Teaching and Learning

Andragogical Overhaul of a Topic or Course

As an adult learner or educator, consider a topic or course that you have taken or taught or would like to take or teach that has traditionally been taught in a teacher-centered, lecture format mode. How might you redesign the course to employ some, if not all, of the six assumptions of andragogy? Here are some tips:

1. Vary the instructional format.
2. Consider low, medium, and high interaction activities. For example, a low interaction activity might be to watch a movie clip or listen to a reading. A medium activity might be a small group discussion. A high activity might be a simulation.
3. Test yourself on the six principles of andragogy:
   a. How can you make the topic or course more self-directed?
   b. How can you build on your learners' experiences?
   c. How can you tie the learning to your students' social or professional roles?
   d. How can you adopt the content to be more problem-centered than subject-centered?
   e. How can you tap into adults' internal motivation to learn?
   f. How can you ensure the topic or course is relevant to the learners' needs?

well-documented in recent studies (Bierema, 2019; Fedeli & Taylor, 2023), highlighting their importance in modern adult education.

Internal Motivation

In light of the above four assumptions, it is no surprise that the most potent motivators for adults to learn are internal rather than external. In other words, increased job satisfaction with one's work, enhanced self-esteem, improved quality of life, and personal fulfillment lead adults to learn beyond what might be required by some agency or institution. An adult is free to choose to learn, which is quite a bit different from pre-adult learning, where others determine what the student needs to know. Chapter 6 explored motivation and its relationship to learning.

Andragogy is firmly rooted in humanistic psychology, as this assumption about internal motivation demonstrates. From this perspective, human nature is intrinsically good, and humans can choose how they behave and what they want to learn. There is also the potential for growth and development, as well as self-actualization in Maslow's terms (1970), which enables adults to realize their potential by using their skills to implement their tasks and activities. Adults are internally motivated, and self-actualization is the goal of learning. Rogers (1969) also felt learning needed to be self-initiated and that the goal was to develop a fully functioning person. Indeed, internal motivation and the other assumptions of andragogy place this theory squarely in a humanistic framework where the individual is at the center of the learning transaction, self-direction and independence are valued, and learning seeks personal growth and fulfillment.

Of course, not all adult learning is internally motivated. There are times when employers require workers to participate in workplace training programs, when a degree or certificate is necessary to engage in certain activities or professional work, or when an educational program is mandated by a governmental or social agency (for example, to retain one's driver's license or access unemployment benefits). Even in these situations, efforts by the facilitator to link the content to the needs and interests of the learners might result in participants becoming more internally motivated.

The Need to Know

Adults want to know why they need to learn something and how what they learn will apply to their immediate situation. This assumption goes hand in hand with the aforementioned assumption about intrinsic motivation. If adults can see why it is important to learn something before they begin a learning activity, their motivation will be much stronger. Of course, much of the "need to know"

Box 7.8 Tips and Tools for Teaching and Learning

Watching the Movie "Renaissance Man"

An entertaining activity to engage learners in understanding andragogy would be to watch the movie *Renaissance Man*. Danny De Vito plays an unemployed marketing executive hired to teach English comprehension to recruits at an army boot camp. In the process, De Vito discovers how to engage the recruits in their own learning by performing a Shakespeare play. He stumbles upon andragogical principles that viewers of the film will readily recognize.

arises from encountering life situations and developmental changes in social roles. For example, a childless adult has no "need to know" about raising children. However, it may become necessary if that adult decides to raise a child. People involved in a corporate merger may find themselves unemployed; they may need to know how to prepare a resume and compete in the job market. A person who becomes a caregiver for a family member with a newly diagnosed disease has a great need to know about the disease and how best to care for the affected person. In these examples, it is clear that these adults need to see this information and that the knowledge will have immediate application. Box 7.8 recommends a movie to illustrate andragogical principles.

As with the other assumptions, there are situations where learning is mandated or where the learning is in preparation for some future application. These situations challenge the adult educator, who cannot rely on the learners' internal motivation or need to know to facilitate their learning effectively. Knowles et al. (2011) addressed this situation in a business environment:

> The first task of the facilitator of learning is to help the learners become aware of the "*need to know.*" At the very least, facilitators can make an intellectual case for the value of the learning in improving the effectiveness of the learners' performance or the quality of their lives. Even more potent tools for raising the level of awareness of the need to know are real or simulated experiences in which the learners discover for themselves the gaps between where they are now and where they want to be. Personnel appraisal systems, job rotation, exposure to role models, and diagnostic performance assessments are examples of such tools. (p. 63)

In summary, these six assumptions make up the andragogical adult learning model. Andragogy draws primarily on a humanist philosophy wherein the individual is central, internally motivated, and self-directed and engages in learning for self-fulfillment, problem-solving, and greater competency in life roles.

Andragogy Today

As explained in the previous section, andragogy came into use first in Europe and then in North America in the mid-20th century as the field of adult education emerged. Andragogy enabled adult educators to claim a knowledge base by identifying what was unique about adult learners. Today, the term andragogy applies in several ways in Central and Eastern European countries. There are some academic departments of andragogy and some places where andragogy and pedagogy are subdivisions under education (Savice-vic, 1991, 2008). In other countries, andragogy is equivalent to the North American term *adult education*, which signifies a professional field of practice. In North America, andragogy prevails as a framework to differentiate adult learners from children.

Over half a century has passed since Knowles first introduced andragogy to North America. Enthusiasm for andragogy persists, evident in academic programs preparing people to work in adult education and human resource development, as well as professionals planning and implementing programs for adults. The durability and appeal of andragogy are evident among educators who encounter it readily, relating to its assumptions and finding it a helpful framework for planning meaningful instruction for adults. Henschke (2011) pointed out that although there is no consensus on whether andragogy is a theory, a philosophy, a teaching description, a scientific discipline, a mechanical tool or technique, or a strategy to help adults learn, this imprecision has not inhibited enthusiasm for andragogy.

Despite its intuitive appeal to practitioners working with adults in all settings, from literacy programs to leisure activities to continuing professional education, to higher education, to business and industry, scholars have critiqued andragogy from several positions. An early question was whether andragogy was a theory of adult learning; Knowles (1989) ceased calling it a theory and instead called it "a model of assumptions about learning or a conceptual framework that serves as a basis for an emergent theory" (p. 112). While most can accept that andragogy is a model of assumptions about adult learners that can guide practice, a second question is whether the assumptions are valid for adults only and not children. When Knowles first presented it in his 1970 book *Modern Practice of Adult Education,* the subtitle was *Andragogy Versus Pedagogy.* After educators pointed out that the assumptions did not necessarily apply to all adults and that some children could be self-directed in their learning, Knowles revised the subtitle in the 1980 edition of the book *From Pedagogy to Andragogy.* He proposed thinking of andragogy as one end of a continuum; that is, there was a range between being teacher-directed, as in pedagogy, and being learner-directed, as in andragogy. It depends on the situation: sometimes adults know so little about the subject that the teacher has to take the lead; conversely, some young people can take the lead depending on their experience and knowledge of the content area.

Although most adult learning scholars and practitioners are content to acknowledge that andragogy describes what adult learners are like most of the time, the actual research supporting these assumptions is mixed at best. As pointed out in the previous discussion, each assumption seems somewhat situation-dependent. For example, there are times when adults receive external pressure to learn something and do not feel remotely intrinsically motivated, or adults sometimes learn something for the sheer joy of learning and not because they "need" to learn it or have a problem to solve. Some studies find support for some assumptions; others are inconclusive. Rachal's (2002) review of 18 experimental or quasi-experimental theses and dissertations of andragogy reported a mix of results supporting andragogy. He attributed the ambiguous findings to several factors that need to be addressed for future research to establish the validity of andragogy for adult learners. For example, participation in the learning activity should be voluntary, objectives and instruction should be collaboratively determined, and learners should be adults, not traditional college-age participants (Rachal, 2002). Rachal also pointed out that assessing the effectiveness of andragogy is hindered by the fact that tests and grades are anathema to andragogy, which assumes adults can self-evaluate their own learning.

Research has shown that many studies claiming to evaluate andragogical effectiveness often fail to operationalize its principles adequately. For example, Rachal (1994) reviewed numerous studies and found that many did not meet essential criteria for assessing andragogy, such as including adult learners and measuring learning outcomes effectively. These shortcomings highlight a persistent issue: the difficulty in clearly defining and measuring the constructs of andragogy in research settings (Clardy, 2005).

Moreover, the literature points out that while andragogy posits that adults are inherently self-directed learners, this assumption may not always hold (Clardy, 2005). Critics argue that the radical subjectivism in andragogical theory can undermine the objective standards of knowledge crucial in specific educational contexts, particularly in vocational training where expertise is paramount (Clardy, 2005). Houde (2006) also examined the principles of andragogy through two motivation theories, validating andragogy as an approach to adult learning. However, some researchers feel that the way to assess the validity of andragogy is through developing and using a valid and reliable instrument.

Taylor and Kroth (2009) conducted a meta-analysis exploring three key areas surrounding andragogy: (1) its concept and history, (2) its assumptions, and (3) its primary criticisms. They suggested using a panel of experts to develop a Likert-scale questionnaire based on the six assumptions of andragogy. Taylor and Kroth (2009) felt that an instrument evaluating andragogical concepts' incorporation into instruction would help "overcome the major criticism that has plagued [andragogy] for the last 30 years: finding empirical data" (p. 10). Holton et al. (2009) addressed this challenge by developing a survey instrument to assess the effects of andragogical principles and design elements on learner satisfaction and outcomes. They report that their initial testing of the instrument with a convenience sample of graduate students "holds promise for advancing research on andragogy" (Holton et al., 2009, p. 169).

Recent studies highlight the historical development of andragogy and its implications for contemporary adult education. For instance, Henschke's (2016) research emphasized the importance of understanding the role of the educator and the learner's context in applying andragogical principles effectively. He identified key factors contributing to a productive learning environment, such as respect, intellectual freedom, and regular feedback, all enhancing adult learning outcomes.

Additionally, research has explored the validity of coaching assessment tools derived from adult education principles, further illustrating the versatility of andragogical concepts across different domains (Young et al., 2020). These studies employed rigorous validation methods, including content and factorial validity assessments, to ensure the reliability of the tools developed (Young et al., 2020).

Recent advancements have focused on developing reliable assessment tools based on andragogical principles—for instance, Zainuddin et al. (2024) introduced the Gamification for Adults Questionnaire (GAQ), which was validated through exploratory factor analysis and demonstrated high reliability (Cronbach's alpha of 0.97). This tool aims to evaluate gamification strategies in adult learning environments, showing promise in bridging theoretical and practical applications of andragogy (Zainuddin et al., 2024).

Also, Knapke et al. (2024) were the first to apply the theoretical principles of Malcolm Knowles's theory of andragogy to evaluate data collected from learners who participated in team science training workshops in a biomedical research setting. The deductive analysis in this study demonstrated that approximately 85% of the qualitative data connected to at least one andragogical principle (Knapke et al., 2024). Participant responses to positive evaluation questions were related mainly to learning readiness and problem-based learning orientation. Participant responses to negative questions centered on two different principles: the role of experience and self-direction. The study findings demonstrated that andragogy could be a valuable construct to integrate into developing effective team science training for biomedical researchers (Knapke et al., 2024).

Summarizing, the recent literature on andragogy underscores a dual focus: the need for robust empirical assessments of andragogical principles and the development of reliable tools to measure their effectiveness in practice. Significant strides toward validating andragogical concepts have occurred, but ongoing challenges remain in operationalizing these principles in diverse educational contexts. Future research should continue to address these gaps, ensuring that andragogy remains a relevant and effective framework for adult education.

Andragogical Principles and Learning Experiences

This section begins by featuring four case studies in Box 7.9, highlighting andragogical principles applied to different learning experiences in various contexts.

The preceding case studies highlight the differences between good and bad adult learning experiences. Laura wanted to learn what other staffing managers were doing in their practice and how to recruit and retain a diverse workforce. Unfortunately, the instructors lectured nonstop, never asking questions or creating opportunities to interact with other participants. The physical setting was uncomfortable in the tax class and staffing training, and the instructors had no idea what the learners needed. In contrast, Monica's experience in the champagne-tasting event fully engaged the participants through various activities, valued the participants' contributions, and enabled participants to learn from each other and gain personal expertise. Andragogy is all about creating good learning experiences for adults. Thinking about a good learning experience and how to engage learners in activities actively, Box 7.10 offers examples of reflective practice promoting active learning.

Box 7.9 Learning and Teaching Cases

Memorable Learning Experiences

The following case studies highlight the differences between good and bad adult learning experiences. These case studies offer you, the reader and adult learner, the opportunity to analyze different situations and contexts in which learning is happening and allow you to critically reflect on the assumptions of andragogy and how these assumptions can influence the learning process. Authors and adult educators Laura, Monica, and Sharan tried to make sense of their learning experiences as follows:

Laura-Case Study 1: A memorable worst experience for me was attending a week-long training on diversity staffing sponsored by a nationally prominent human resource management society. Participants sat for the entire week, being lectured by a parade of prominent White men (for example, vice presidents of staffing and diversity at Fortune 500 corporations). The importance of recruiting and retaining a diverse staff was lost on the program planners. Not only was the importance of diverse staffing not modeled by the presenters, but also the speakers addressed diversity in a cursory fashion. In addition to poor role modeling, the pedagogy was instructor-centered. There were no opportunities to compare notes about staffing challenges with other human resource managers. The instructors never sought feedback on whether the participants' needs were being met. Participants struggled to stay awake, visibly checking their watches, shifting in their seats, and not paying attention.

Laura-Case Study 2: A favorite learning experience of mine was spending a week learning the theories behind the Learning Organization at MIT under the guidance of Peter Senge. Although there were 100 participants, there were multiple opportunities for engagement. All learners sat in a very comfortable leather executive chair with wheels that were adjustable for comfort. There were no tables, allowing learners to move into new groups quickly. Each day began with a silent meditation and was varied with brief lectures, simulations, embodiment exercises, games, themed meals, movies, application exercises, and opportunities for individual and group reflection. Learners had opportunities to meet and work with different learners, challenging each other to "think outside the box." The sessions were visually compelling, with art displayed throughout the training room, inspirational quotes, music during breaks, and toys to play with. Not only was the experience highly engaging, but also very educational. I still refer to my journal from that session almost 30 years later!

Monica-Case Study 3: One of the best nonformal adult learning experiences I had was when I went to Champagne, France. My husband and I decided to take a champagne-tasting class. This session involved a tour of the caves and an explanation of the phases of champagne production. After the tour, the guide brought us into a room, and we sat around a nicely organized table. In front of each of us were 10 cards (images representing the different phases of champagne production), 10 little glass jars with a different liquid aroma (representing different favors for describing various champagnes), and 5 glasses of different types of champagne. The tour guide invited us to correctly order the 10 cards for the different phases of champagne production, from harvest to dosage and corking. This activity was a way to evaluate and remind us of the lesson on champagne production. Then she asked us to individually smell the different liquid aromas, trying to match each flavor of champagne. After reflecting on our own, we discussed our matching with others. Finally, she asked us to rate which of the five champagnes was best according to our test. Even if the taste is a very personal issue, the guide made an excellent point at introducing the group to a discourse based on the smell of the aroma, used to identify the various characteristics of different varieties of champagne, its quality based on age, color, type of grapes, dosage, and perlage. After this amazing experience, we had lunch together, drank champagne, and talked in a very informal and lovely atmosphere, trying to learn from each other's tastes and choices.

Sharan-Case Study 4: One of my worst adult learning experiences was a six-week community education course on "How to Figure Your Own Income Taxes." The room was too small for the number of people who had signed up, forcing us to sit in rows on small desk chairs. After taking attendance, the instructor sat at the teacher's desk and talked nonstop for three hours about the new tax codes and regulations. She never asked us why we had signed up, what we wanted to learn, or what questions we had. I decided to give it one more try. The second week, she again sat on the desk and talked about retirement-related tax issues (although no one appeared to be of retirement age) and how to deal with operating a business out of your home. I left and never returned.

Questions for Reflection and Dialogue:

1. What key factors contributed to positive learning experiences in the case studies?
2. How did the environment and teaching methods negatively impact the learning experiences in the examples above?
3. What role do engagement and interaction play in adult learning?
4. How can educators better meet the needs of adult learners based on these examples?

 **Box 7.10 Reflective Practice**

Reflective Practices to Promote Active Learning

This box contains reflective activities and offers a chance to pause and consider the implications of a specific idea, theory, or practice related to learning in adulthood and facilitating adult learning. Andragogy, as promoted by Malcolm Knowles, outlines key characteristics of adult learners: active learning and reflective activities.

Active Learning: Adult learners are characterized by an independent self-concept, a reservoir of experience, developmental tasks related to adult social roles, a desire for immediate application, internal motivation, and a need to know.

Reflective Activities: Given its effectiveness in identifying adult learner characteristics, andragogy is widely embraced by educators and trainers in various instructional settings.

Here are some reflective activities designed to engage adult learners in class and online based on the principles of andragogy:

1. **Reflective Journaling**
   Purpose: To encourage self-awareness and critical thinking by allowing learners to connect their experiences with the learning material.
   Activity: At the end of each session or module, ask learners to write a journal entry reflecting on what they learned, how it relates to their prior experiences, and how they plan to apply it in their professional or personal lives. The writing might occur in a physical journal, online blog, or discussion forum.
   Outcome: Learners can track their growth over time, identify areas where they need further development, and articulate the relevance of the content to their lives.

2. **Peer Reflection Circles**
   Purpose: To enhance collaborative learning and provide multiple perspectives on a topic or experience.
   Activity: Organize learners into small groups and have them share personal experiences related to the studied topic. Each learner then reflects on how their peers' experiences relate to their own, discussing similarities, differences, and any new insights gained. Reflections can be facilitated either in-person or through virtual breakout rooms.
   Outcome: Learners gain a broader understanding of the topic, develop empathy by seeing how others interpret similar experiences, and improve their communication and critical thinking skills.

These activities are rooted in the principles of andragogy, encouraging active participation and deep reflection, which are essential for effective adult learning.

Some interesting and useful resources connected to andragogy and teaching adults are:

- *Methods for Facilitating Adult Learning* (Coryell et al., 2024).
- *Connecting Adult Learning and Knowledge Management. Strategies for Learning and Change in Higher Education and Organizations.* Springer International Publishing (Fedeli & Bierema, 2019).
- *Becoming a Critical Reflective Teacher* (Brookfield, 2019).
- *Powerful Techniques for Teaching Adults* (Brookfield, 2013).

Chapter Summary

Despite the lack of research documenting the assumptions of andragogy and the criticism that it ignores the sociocultural context of learning, andragogy continues to be a significant theory, model, or approach to understanding and planning instruction for adult learners. For those new to adult education, the assumptions about adult learners make intuitive sense, and the instructional practices accompanying them acknowledge the experience and needs of many adult learners. Knowles (1984) compiled 36 case examples of andragogy applied in practice in business and government, postsecondary education, professional education, health education, religious education, K–12, and remedial education. From these 36 cases, he drew several lessons about applying andragogy to practice: It is flexible, and the whole or parts can be applied; climate setting is the most common and easiest starting point; both teachers and learners need to orient to an andragogical approach; and many practitioners "have found imaginative ways to adapt to traditional systems without sacrificing the essence of the andragogical model" (Knowles & Associates, 1984, p. 419). Finally, some publications attest to the continued broad applicability of andragogy to numerous settings including agriculture (Gharibpanah & Zamani, 2011), nursing (Riggs, 2010), e-learning (Muirhead, 2007), engineering (Winter et al., 2009), criminal justice (Birzer, 2004), management (Forrest & Peterson, 2006), human resource development (Holton et al., 2009; Knowles et al., 2011), just to mention a few. In recent years, above all after COVID, andragogy was applied in online settings to enhance learning outcomes, redesign program online, and involve learners in online programs (Harrison & Barber, 2021; Ladwig et al., 2021; Lemoine et al., 2021).

Key Points

- Andragogy, promoted by Malcolm Knowles, is the first learning model to identify adult learners' characteristics.
- Adult learners are characterized by an independent self-concept, a reservoir of experience, the developmental tasks of adult social roles, a desire for immediate application, internal motivation, and the need to know.
- Because of its validity in identifying adult learner characteristics, andragogy is popular with educators and trainers of adults in all types of instructional settings.
- Due to these characteristics, definitive research on andragogy is complex and inconclusive in results.

References

Acharya, S., Jere, C. M., & Robinson-Pant, A. (2020). Indigenous adult women, learning and social justice: Challenging deficit discourses in the current policy environment. In S. Aikman & A. Robinson-Pant (Eds.), *Indigenous women and adult learning* (pp. 136–157). Routledge.

Birzer, M. L. (2004). Andragogy: Student centered classrooms in criminal justice programs. *Journal of Criminal Justice Education, 15*(2), 393–410. https://doi.org/10.1080/10511250400086041.

Brookfield, S. D. (2013). *Powerful techniques for teaching adults.* John Wiley & Sons.

Brookfield, S. (2019). *Becoming a critically reflective teacher* (2nd ed.). Jossey-Bass.

Clardy, A. (2005). *Andragogy: Adult learning and education at its best?* ERIC ED492132 Online Submission.

Conti, G. J. (2004). Identifying your teaching style. In M. W. Galbraith (Ed.), *Adult learning methods: A guide for effective instruction* (3rd ed.) (pp. 75–91). Krieger.

Coryell, J. E., Baumgartner, L. M., & Bohonos, J. W. (Eds.). (2024). *Methods for facilitating adult learning: Strategies for enhancing instruction and instructor effectiveness.* Taylor & Francis.

Dantus, S. J. (2021). A Triadic Worldview? The Misconception and Bias of Universality in Knowles' Andragogy. Commission for International Adult Education.

Dewey, J. (1938). *Experience and education.* Collier Books.

Duff, M. C. (2019). Perspectives in AE—Adult Black males and andragogy: Is there a goodness of fit. *New Horizons in Adult Education and Human Resource Development, 31*(4), 51–58.

Ekoto, C. E., & Gaikwad, P. (2015). The impact of andragogy on learning satisfaction of graduate students. *American Journal of Educational Research, 3*(11), 1378–1386. https://doi.org/10.12691/education-3-11-6.

Erikson, E. H. (1963). *Childhood and society* (2nd ed., rev.). Norton.

Fedeli, M., & Bierema, L. L. (2019). *Connecting adult learning and knowledge management.* Springer.

Fedeli, M., & Taylor, W. E. (2023). The impact of an active learning designed development program: A students' perspective of an Italian University. *Tuning Journal for Higher Education, 11*(1), 151–174., https://doi.org/10.18543/tjhe1112023.

Fenwick, T. (2003). *Learning through experience: Troubling orthodoxies and intersecting Questions.* Krieger.

Forrest III, S. P. & Peterson, T. O. (2006). It's called andragogy. *Academy of Management Learning & Education, 5*(1), 113–122. https://doi.org/10.5465/amle.2006.20388390.

Gharibpanah, M. & Zamani, A. (2011). Andragogy and pedagogy: Differences and applications. *Life Science Journal, 8*(3), 78–82.

Giroux, H. A. (2000). Public pedagogy as cultural politics: Stuart Hall and the "crisis" of culture. *Cultural Studies, 14*, 341–360. https://doi.org/10.1080/095023800334913.

Green, R. D., & Schlairet, M. C. (2017). Moving toward heutagogical learning: Illuminating undergraduate nursing students' experiences in a flipped classroom. *Nurse Education Today, 49*, 122–128. https://doi.org/10.1016/j.nedt.2016.11.016.

Harrison, R., & Barber, W. (2021). Online learning: The need for critical reflection as a result of the COVID-19 pandemic. *EDULEARN21 Proceedings*, 1522–1527.

Havighurst, R. J. (1952/1972). *Developmental tasks and education* (3rd ed.). McKay.

Henschke, J. A. (2011). Considerations regarding the future of andragogy. *Futures Column, Adult Learning, 22*(1–2), 34–37. https://doi.org/10.1177/104515951102200109.

Henschke, J. (2016). A history of andragogy and its documents as they pertain to adult basic and literacy education. *The PAACE Journal of Lifelong Learning, 25*, 1. https://irl.umsl.edu/adulteducation-faculty/42.

Holton, E. F. III, Wilson, L. S., & Bates, R. A. (2009). Toward development of a generalized instrument to measure andragogy. *Human Resource Development Quarterly, 20*(2), 169–193. https://doi.org/10.1002/hrdq.20014.

Houde, J. (2006). Andragogy and Motivation: An Examination of the Principles of Andragogy through Two Motivation Theories. *Online Submission ERIC ED492652.*

Knapke, J. M., Hildreth, L., Molano, J. R., Schuckman, S. M., Blackard, J. T., Johnstone, M., Kopras, E. J., Lamkin, M. K., Lee, R. C., Kues, J. R., & Mendell, A. (2024). Andragogy in practice: Applying a theoretical framework to team science training in biomedical research. *British Journal of Biomedical Science, 81*. https://doi.org/10.3389/bjbs.2024.12651.

Knowles, M. S. (1968). Andragogy, not pedagogy. *Adult Leadership, 16*(10), 350–352, 386.

Knowles, M. S. (1970). *The modern practice of adult education: Andragogy versus pedagogy.* Cambridge Books.

Knowles, M. S. (1973). *The adult learner: A neglected species.* Gulf Publishing.

Knowles, M. S. (1975). *Self-directed learning: A guide for learners and teachers.* Association Press.

Knowles, M. S. (1980). *The modern practice of adult education: From pedagogy to andragogy* (2nd ed.). Cambridge Books.

Knowles, M. S. (1984). *The adult learner: A neglected species* (3rd ed.). Gulf Publishing Company.

Knowles, M. S. (Ed.). (1989). *The making of an adult educator: An autobiographical journey.* Jossey-Bass.

Knowles, M. S. (1990). *The adult learner. A neglected species* (4th ed.). Gulf Publishing.

Knowles, M. S. (1996). Wherefore Pedagogy? In American Society for Training and Development. *The ASTD Training and Development Handbook: A Guide to Huma Resource Development* (pp. 253–265) McGraw-Hill.

Knowles, M. S. & Associates. (1984). *Andragogy in action: Applying modern principles of adult learning.* Jossey-Bass.

Knowles, M. S., Holton, E. F. III, & Swanson, R. A. (2011). *The adult learner* (7th ed.). Gulf Publishing.

Kolb, D. A. (1984). *Experiential learning: Experience as the source of learning and development.* Prentice Hall.

Ladwig, A., Berg-Poppe, P. J., Ikiugu, M., & Ness, B. M. (2021). Andragogy in graduate health programs during the COVID-19 pandemic. *Distance Learning, 18*(3), 31–44.

Lemoine, P. A., Garretson, C. J., Waller, R. E., Mense, E. G., & Richardson, M. D. (2021). Online learning for the adult learners using andragogy. In *Ensuring adult and non-traditional learners' success with technology, design, and structure* (pp. 37–58). IGI Global.

Lindeman, E. (1926/1961). *The meaning of adult education.* New Republic.

Loeng, S. (2018). Various ways of understanding the concept of andragogy. *Cogent Education, 5*(1),1–15. https://doi.org/10.1080/2331186X.2018.1496643.

Manfra, M. M. (2019). Action research and systematic, intentional change in teaching practice. *Review of Research in Education, 43*(1), 163–196. https://doi.org/10.3102/0091732X18821132.

Maslow, A. H. (1970). *Motivation and personality* (2nd ed.). HarperCollins.

Merriam, S. B., & Bierema, L. L. (2014). *Adult learning: Linking theory and practice.* John Wiley & Sons.

Merriam, S. B., Mott, V. W., & Lee, M. (1996). Learning that comes from the negative interpretation of life experience. *Studies in Continuing Education, 18*(1), 1–23. https://doi.org/10.1080/0158037960180101.

Merriam, S. B., Caffarella, R. S. & Baumgartner, L. M. (2007). *Learning in adulthood.* Jossey-Bass.

Moll, I. (2023). A critique of andragogy in the South African TVET context. *Journal of Vocational, Adult and Continuing Education and Training, 6*(1), 145–163.

Muirhead, R. J. (2007). E-learning: Is this teaching at students or teaching with students? *Nursing Forum, 42*(4), 178–184. https://doi.org/10.1111/j.1744-6198.2007.00085.x.

Ozuah, P. O. (2005). First, there was pedagogy and then came andragogy. *Einstein Journal of Biology and Medicine. 21*(2), 83–87. https://doi.org/10.23861/EJBM20052190.

Pratt, D. D. (1993). Andragogy after twenty-five years. In S. Merriam (Ed.), *Adult learning theory: An update.* Jossey-Bass, 15–25.

Rachal, J. (1994). *Andragogical and pedagogical methods compared: a review of the experimental literature.* ERIC ED 380 566.

Rachal, J. (2002). Andragogy's detectives: A critique of the present and a proposal for the future. *Adult Education Quarterly, 52*(3), 210–227. https://doi.org/10.1177/0741713602052003004.

Reischmann, J. (2004). *Andragogy. History, meaning, context, function.* http://www.andragogy.net.

Riggs, C. J. (2010). Taming the pedagogy dragon. *The Journal of Continuing Education in Nursing, 41*(9), 388–389. https://doi.org/10.3928/00220124-20100825-02.

Roessger, K. M., Roumell, E. A., & Weese, J. (2022). Rethinking andragogical assumptions in the global age: How preferences for andragogical learning vary across people and cultures. *Studies in Continuing Education, 44*(1), 14–38.

Rogers, C. R. (1969). *Freedom to learn.* Merrill.

Sandlin, J. (2005). Andragogy and its discontents: An analysis of andragogy from three critical perspectives. *PAACE Journal of Lifelong Learning, 14*, 25–42.

Savery, J. R. (2006). Overview of problem-based learning: Definitions and distinctions. *Interdisciplinary Journal of Problem-Based Learning, 1*(1). https://doi.org/10.7771/1541-5015.1002.

Savery, J. R. (2015). Overview of problem-based learning: Definitions and distinctions. In W. Andrew, L. Heather, C. Hmelo-Silver, & P. Ertmer (Eds.), *Essential readings in problem-based learning: exploring and extending the legacy of Howard S. Barrows* (pp. 5–15). Purdue University Press. https://doi.org/10.2307/j.ctt6wq6fh.6.

Savicevic, D. (1991). Modern conceptions of andragogy: A European framework. *Studies in the Education of Adults, 23*(2), 179–201. https://doi.org/10.1080/02660830.1991.11730556.

Savicevic, D. (2008). Convergence or divergence of ideas on andragogy in different countries. *International Journal of Lifelong Education, 27*(4), 361–378. https://doi.org/10.1080/02601370802051504.

Schön, D. A. (1983). *The reflective practitioner: How professionals think in action.* Basic Books.

Taylor, E. W. (2005). Teaching beliefs of nonformal consumer educators: A perspective of teaching in home improvement retail stores in the United States. *International Journal of Consumer Studies, 29*(5), 448–457. https://doi.org/10.1111/j.1470-6431.2005.00462.x.

Taylor, E. W. (2012). *Teaching adults in public places: Museums, parks, consumer education sites.* Krieger.

Taylor, B. & Kroth, M. (2009). Andragogy's transition into the future: Meta-analysis of andragogy and its search for a measurable instrument. *Journal of Adult Education, 38*(1), 1–11.

Thorndike, E. L., Bregman, E. O., Tilton, J. W., & Woodyard, E. (1928). *Adult learning.* Macmillan.

Tough, A. (1971). *The adult's learning projects: A fresh approach to theory and practice in adult learning.* Ontario Institute for Studies in Education.

UN. 2015. *The 2030 Agenda for Sustainable Development* (UN, New York, 2015). http://bit.ly/TransformAgendaSDG-pdf.

Watkins, K. E., Nicolaides, A., & Gilbertson, E. (2023). *The action research dissertation: Learning from leading change.* Myers Education Press.

Watson, C., & Temkin, S. (2000). Just-in-time teaching: Balancing the compelling demands of corporate America and academe in the delivery of management education. *Journal of Management Education, 24*(6): 763–778. https://doi.org/10.1177/105256290002400608.

Weimer, M. (2013). *Learner-centered teaching: Five key changes to practice.* John Wiley & Sons.

Winter, A. J., McAuliffe, M. B., Hargreaves, D. J., & Chadwick, G. (2009). *The transition to academagogy.* Paper presented at the Philosophy of Education Society of Australasia (PESA) Conference Brisbane, Queensland. http://eprints.qut.edu.au/17367/1/17367.pdf.

Young, B. W., Rathwell, S., & Callary, B. (2020). Testing a coaching assessment tool derived from adult education in adult sport. *Psychology of Sport and Exercise, 47*, 1–10. https://doi.org/10.1016/j.psychsport.2019.101632.

Zainuddin, Z., Chu, S. K. W., & Othman, J. (2024). The evaluation of gamification implementation for adult learners: A scale development study based on andragogical principles. *Education and Information Technologies*, 1–30. https://doi.org/10.1007/s10639-024-12561-x.

CHAPTER EIGHT

VALUING ADULTS' SELF-DIRECTEDNESS IN LEARNING

 **Box 8.1 Chapter Overview and Learning Objectives**

Merriam and Bierema (2013) captured the essence of learning overseen by learners:

> At the heart of Self-Directed Learning is the notion that the learner takes control of his/her own learning; that is, the learner decides what and how to learn. (p. 62)

This chapter opens by defining Self-Directed Learning (SDL), describing the goals of SDL in adulthood, examining SDL as a process and an attribute, considering the context where SDL occurs, discussing SDL assessment, exploring myths about SDL, and raising critiques.

Learning Objectives: As a result of reading this chapter and completing the exercises, you, the reader, should be able to:

- Identify the characteristics of SDL and value self-direction in adult learners.
- Understand the goals of SDL.
- Reflect on the process of SDL in the different contexts.
- Build your knowledge and apply it in your teaching practices.

Think of a time as a learner or educator when you set out to learn something on your own, perhaps a new hobby, sport, or professional quest where you hunted information, asked friends, and scoured the Internet. You were engaged in **self-directed learning** (SDL)—a learning process you managed from start to finish. Given the VUCA and rapidly changing environment, it is no longer possible to learn everything we need to know in formal educational settings; therefore, one of the essential roles of adult educators is to support self-directed learning.

You are in good company if you have identified one or more SDL projects. Tough (1971) found that 90% of the 66 adults in his study were involved in at least one learning project and that the learners themselves planned 70% of all learning projects. Subsequent studies have confirmed that over 90% of adults are engaged in some kind of informal learning project (Livingstone, 1999, 2002). Knowles (1975) believed adults become increasingly self-directed with maturity (see Chapter 7) and viewed SDL as a hallmark of adult learning. SDL does not necessarily mean that you sit in a room alone and learn something; indeed, you may decide to take a course, consult with others, or find materials on the Internet to support your learning. The key is taking responsibility for what is learned and how you learn it. Box 8.2 guides you through an SDL reflection activity.

You may think it is obvious that we are constantly learning as adults. Indeed, this kind of informal SDL characterizes adulthood and shapes us as individuals (Loeng, 2019; Owen, 2002). Sometimes SDL is taken for granted as a key learning process, regarded as little more than self-study (Doo & Zhu, 2024; Silen & Uhlin, 2008; Song & Bonk, 2016). Tough (1967), building on the work of Houle (1961), provided the first comprehensive model of SDL, initially calling it **"self-teaching."** SDL is sometimes used interchangeably with independent learning, autonomous learning, self-study, learning projects, self-teaching, self-education, and self-regulated learning (Ahammad, 2023; Cronin-Golomb & Bauer, 2023; Leach et al., 2005; Rager, 2006). This interchangeability reflects the multifaceted nature of SDL, which encompasses different approaches and contexts. Several authors have conducted reviews and analyses of SDL, contributing to its theoretical and practical base (Brockett et al., 2000; Brockett & Hiemstra, 1991, 2018; Broek et al., 2023; Caffarella, 1993, 2000; Garrison, 1997; Loeng, 2019; Long, 1998; Merriam & Baumgartner, 2020; Munas-inghe et al., 2019; Owen, 2002). Recent literature emphasized that SDL is an individual endeavor influenced by social contexts and collaborative learning environments (Charungkaittikul & Henschke, 2018; Silén & Uhlin, 2008). Therefore, educational institutions and academic staff are responsible for fostering educational settings in which SDL is encouraged:

> Educators and institutions need to promote it as an educational
> approach, incorporate it into students' learning experiences, and

Box 8.2 Adult Learning and Teaching Cases

Engaging Adults to Learn: Reflecting on Your Learning Experiences

A good way to start with self-directed learning (SDL) is to recall and analyze a learning experience. When was your last attempt to learn a new skill, tackle a home improvement project, address a life issue, or make a personal change?

One of the authors (Laura) took up sourdough bread making as an SDL project during the COVID-19 pandemic. She consciously sought to learn bread baking to recreate the loaves she found on European trips. She planned her learning, which included making a starter, reviewing recipes, watching YouTube videos, talking to other bakers, and trial and error. Her family can attest to many "hockey-puck-like" loaves that looked awful but usually tasted okay. Today, she is turning out beautiful, delicious loaves. She is still learning, trying new techniques, and perfecting her process, which puts her learning in an ongoing, lifelong learning endeavor.

Take a moment and think of an example of an SDL experience in your life:

1. What was the project?
2. How did you learn?
3. What resources did you use?
4. How did you know you were making progress?
5. How did you evaluate it?

Chances are, your project was SDL if you intentionally sought the learning, planned your learning, took responsibility for your learning, monitored your learning, and evaluated the outcome. Your learning may have been short-term, lasting a few hours, or it may have been an ongoing, perhaps lifelong project.

If you are an adult educator, we recommend this as an effective learning activity for teaching about SDL and for effective learning facilitation.

> evaluate its effectiveness. While addressing the factors necessary for SDL's success, guidance, resources, and structured opportunities are provided. (Dahal & Bhat, 2024, p. 113)

Although most adults can be self-directed learners, the willingness, motivation, and life circumstances necessary for self-direction can vary widely (Cronin-Golomb

& Bauer, 2023; Doo & Zhu, 2024; Loeng, 2019; Owen, 2002). Factors influencing SDL include: language proficiency, interest in the subject matter, accessibility of learning resources, teaching methods and teaching styles (Munasinghe et al., 2019), and social relationships and support (Broek et al., 2023; Munasinghe et al., 2019).

Motivation is a key SDL driver, with intrinsic motivation being fundamental (Broek et al., 2023). Self-determination theory emphasizes the role of autonomy, competence, and relatedness in promoting self-directed and intrinsically motivated learning in adulthood (Broek et al., 2023). Therefore, factors such as personal goals, life experiences, and external support systems play a critical role in shaping an adult's ability to engage in SDL (Doo & Zhu, 2024). Additionally, the emergence of technology and online learning platforms has transformed SDL by providing new tools and resources facilitating self-directed educational experiences (Doo & Zhu, 2024; Merriam & Baumgartner, 2020). For example, AI-based writing tools, such as ChatGPT, support SDL by increasing learner engagement and providing personalized feedback (Morris & Rohs, 2023; Doo & Zhu, 2024).

Furthermore, the concept of SDL has evolved to include considerations of how learning occurs within the context of work and life, often referred to as "learning in the flow of work" (Ferrario, 2020). This model emphasizes the seamless integration of learning into daily activities, allowing individuals to acquire new skills and knowledge without interrupting their workflow (Ferrario, 2020). However, challenges remain, including the need for guidance, content relevance, and technology barriers that can hinder effective SDL (Ferrario, 2020).

Defining Self-Directed Learning

SDL has been a focus of research, theory, and practice for over 60 years, with significant contributions from scholars such as Brockett and Hiemstra (1991, 2019; Hiemstra & Brockett, 2012), Candy (1991), Houle (1961), Knowles (1975), and Tough (1967, 1971, 1978). SDL is both a personal attribute and a process.

SDL emphasizes an individual's predisposition toward autonomous learning when viewed as a personal attribute. This perspective emphasizes motivation, self-efficacy, and comfort with independence in the learning process. Recent studies suggested learners with higher levels of self-directedness tend to perform better academically and are more likely to engage in lifelong learning (Stockdale & Brockett, 2011; Tekkol & Demirel, 2018). For example, the development of the **Self-Directed Learning Readiness Scale (SDLRS)** by Guglielmino (1977) was instrumental in assessing personal attributes facilitating SDL, including creativity, initiative, and independence in learning. The **Personal Responsibility Orientation to Self-Directed Learning Scale (PRO-SDLS)** assesses these learner characteristics, showing a strong correlation between self-direction and academic success (Stockdale, 2003). As a process, SDL is an approach to learning that the learner controls. Knowles is well known for his definition of the process of SDL, "in which individuals take the initiative, with or without the help of others, in diagnosing their learning needs, formulating learning goals, identifying human and material resources for learning, choosing and implementing appropriate learning strategies, and evaluating those learning outcomes" (1975, p. 18). Knowles (1975) also delineated a six-step process that can serve as a framework for both learners and instructors in planning SDL experiences:

1. Climate Setting: Creating an atmosphere of mutual respect and support.
2. Diagnosing Learning Needs: Identifying what the learner needs to know.
3. Formulating Learning Goals: Setting clear and achievable objectives.
4. Identifying Resources: Recognizing both human and material resources available for learning.
5. Choosing and Implementing Strategies: Selecting appropriate methods for achieving the learning goals.
6. Evaluating Learning Outcomes: Assessing the effectiveness of the learning process and outcomes. (p. 18)

These steps reflect a philosophy that empowers learners to take charge of their educational experiences. Garrison (1997) further expanded on the steps by introducing a comprehensive model of SDL that includes three overlapping dimensions: self-management (task control), self-monitoring (cognitive responsibility), and motivation (entry and task). Garrison's model emphasized that personal attributes play a crucial role in self-management, including the effective use of resources and motivation (Garrison, 1997; Bosch et al., 2019). Box 8.3 highlights an SDL project.

Tough (1978) studied SDL from the perspective of learning projects, which he defined as deliberate efforts to build knowledge, develop skills, or make changes—efforts that took at least seven hours. He also outlined a process similar to Knowles's. Learners proceed through a series of steps to decide what to learn, what resources they need (time? money? materials?), where to learn, and how to maintain the motivation to learn (see Chapter 6). The steps also include setting goals and timetables, determining the pace, and assessing current knowledge and skills. Self-directed learners also evaluate their learning to determine what might hinder it and adjust accordingly.

Brandt (2020) highlighted several factors of SDL in a literature review study illustrating its complexity and multifaceted characteristics, including self-regulation, motivation, personal responsibility, and autonomy. **Self-regulation**

Box 8.3 Adult Learning and Teaching Cases

Planning for Teaching and Learning: Identify the Steps for a Personal Change

Monica's Personal Transformation Project

One of the authors (Monica) embarked on a personal change project to begin a consistent exercise routine to improve her physical fitness and overall health. Her plan included the following steps:

1. Define your change goal: Regularly exercise to improve physical fitness and overall health.
2. Determine why this goal is important: Improving physical fitness will increase her energy levels, reduce stress, and improve her overall well-being, contributing to a healthier lifestyle.
3. Develop specific strategies: Plan to exercise thrice weekly, alternating between cardio and strength training. Join a fitness class or find a workout buddy for motivation. Track daily food intake to ensure a balanced diet. Set small milestones, such as increasing the duration or intensity of the workout every two weeks.
4. Measure your progress: Keep a log to record exercise sessions, duration, and feelings after each session. Monitor physical changes, such as increased endurance, weight management, and muscle tone. Use a fitness tracker to measure daily steps and heart rate.
5. Track and adjust: Review the progress each Sunday evening. Reflect on what worked well and what didn't. Adjust the workout plan or diet as needed to stay on track. Celebrate small wins and set new weekly goals to keep the momentum going.

By following these steps, Monica effectively pursued her personal change project and stayed motivated and on track to achieving her fitness and health goals.

If you are an adult educator, ask your learners to apply these steps to a goal or change they wish to make as an effective learning activity for teaching about SDL and for effective learning facilitation.

is "the ability to plan, direct, and control one's emotions, thoughts, and behaviors during a learning task" (Brandt, 2020, p. 4). **Motivation** represents the learner's intention to engage in a task or activity. Learners with a growth mindset tend to be more curious, open-minded, and persistent in their learning (Duckworth, 2016; Dweck, 2006). **Personal responsibility,** also called **ownership,** involves accountability for one's actions and individual learning choices. The last of the four factors is **autonomy,** representing the ability to control learning choices based on the context, environment, and personal and social dynamics (Brandt, 2020, p. 4). Autonomous learners manage their lives, make decisions about their learning process, and monitor and evaluate their progress.

SDL is a broader concept that includes **self-regulated learning** (SRL). SRL involves a deep sense of responsibility and autonomy in the learning process, including monitoring and evaluating one's own progress. With the rise of online learning and instructional technologies, SDL and SRL have become increasingly important. As a result, more studies and experiences are emerging within the context of online learning (Merriam & Baumgartner, 2020, p. 140). Box 8.4 discusses SDL promotion research.

Box 8.4 SoTL: The Scholarship of Teaching and Learning

SDL: Factors to Promote SDL in Educational Institutions

Vaičiūnienė and Kazlauskienė (2023) conducted a systematic international literature review on SDL, analyzing factors in three key dimensions: the learning environment, prior knowledge and abilities, and learner proactivity. The authors undertook a careful selection process, ultimately including 27 papers from 16 countries in their review. Of these, 14 papers focused on comprehensive education, 13 on higher education, and 1 on vocational training.

Their learning environment analysis revealed categories sustaining SDL, including support, innovative learning, teaching and learning strategies, assessment, collaboration, and the emotional environment. They also found learner abilities and knowledge important in SDL, including self-efficacy, problem-solving, critical reflection, time management, and meta-learning abilities. A third aspect of their findings examined learner proactivity, identifying learner needs, collaboration, seeking learning support, and asking questions. Finally, the authors identified an oppressive dimension at learner, teacher, and educational institution levels. Key oppressive factors included learning load, teaching and learning strategies, teacher authority, and anxiety. At the institutional level, oppressive factors involved teacher support, learning environment and learning culture, and institutional support (pp. 6–10).

Understanding these various factors can help you, both as an adult educator and learner, to better navigate and support the learning process within educational institutions.

As you reflect on this study, which factors have you experienced in your learning journey? How have these factors influenced your knowledge, skills, or approach to learning as a learner and an adult educator?

The following section explores the goals of SDL and how you can design your teaching and learning related to SDL goals.

Goals of Self-directed Learning

Merriam and Baumgartner (2020) categorized SDL into three main goals. The first goal focuses on motivating learners to actively engage in SDL, emphasizing individual responsibility and autonomy in achieving personal goals. The second goal focuses on the process, specifically promoting transformational learning and change. This transformational learning is enhanced when critical reflection is integrated into the learning process, as Mezirow (1985) highlighted. The third goal goes beyond individual learning to promote social change, incorporating **emancipatory learning** and supporting social justice and political action (Merriam & Baumgartner, 2020, p. 140).

These three goals are interrelated. The critical reflection component of the second goal is fundamental to achieving the third goal of promoting social action through SDL. Brookfield (1986, p. 38) supported this view, stating that "the most complete form of SDL occurs when process and reflection are married in the adult's pursuit of meaning." This way, SDL fosters personal growth and empowers individuals to contribute to broader social transformation.

The Process of Self-Directed Learning

Since Tough's (1971) and Knowles's (1975) pioneering work on SDL, many others have added to understanding this approach to adult learning according to the linear, interactive, and instructional models.

The Linear Model of SDL

Tough's and Knowles's model is linear (following a step-by-step process) and includes a planning phase followed by a series of steps to help learners achieve their goals. To facilitate this structured approach, Knowles (1986) introduced the **learning contract**—a written agreement between the learner and the instructor specifying the steps and intended outcomes of an SDL. This tool is widely used in various contexts to promote SDL. Box 8.5 presents learning contract steps.

Box 8.5 Tips and Tools for Teaching and Learning

Using Learning Contracts: Planning Your Steps

This worksheet helps you plan your independent study as an adult learner. Your project should be based on the amount of time and effort you would spend in a typical graduate class. A general guideline is that each **credit** requires 15 hours of "contact" (time you would spend in class) and usually about twice that amount outside the class contact hours. Thus, one independent study credit would be approximately 45 hours of work. Your learning contract should be based on a typical course workload based on the number of credits you take. The terms of the contract are negotiated between you and the instructor.

Here is an example of a contract. See how you can apply it to your course.

General Information:
Name:
Semester Enrolled:
Contact Information:
Number of Credits:
Contract:

1. Describe the overall title and focus of the learning project.
2. Outline the objectives or learning outcomes you hope to achieve for the project.
3. Describe the activities you will undertake to achieve these objectives:
   a. Time frame and duration of the project
   b. Where it will take place
   c. What will you be doing?
   d. And so on.

4. List the resources and materials (books, articles, etc.) you expect to use in pursuing these objectives.
5. Anticipate the number of meetings you would like to have with me for planning and counseling.
6. Explain the basis upon which you expect a grade. What products will you turn in as a basis for a grade?

Student's Signature   Date
Professor's Signature   Date

This worksheet is valuable for guiding learners as they plan their independent studies. They can manage their time effectively and achieve meaningful learning outcomes by aligning their projects with typical course workloads.

The Interactive Model of SDL

Spear (1988) and Spear and Mocker (1984) questioned the step-by-step linear processes outlined by Knowles and Tough. They interviewed 78 self-directed learners with less than a high school education about their experiences and concluded that pre-planning SDL is uncommon. Rather, SDL is mediated by opportunities learners find in their environment, prior or new knowledge, and serendipity, and all SDL projects have elements of these factors. Spear and Mocker called the influence of the immediate environment the **"organizing circumstance,"** that is, "self-directed learners, rather than preplanning their learning projects, tend to select a course from limited alternatives which occur fortuitously within their environment, and which structures their learning projects" (p. 4). Spear disputed that SDL projects occurred in a linear, lock-step fashion, suggesting instead that the learning spiraled between multiple sets of activities or clusters, eventually coalescing into a coherent whole. The interactive model focuses not only on the step-by-step development of the process but also on other factors shaping the process, including the environment, personal characteristics, cognition, and the learning context (Merriam & Baumgartner, 2020). See Box 8.6.

The Instructional Model of SDL

Based on interest in how learners construct SDL, Brockett and Hiemstra (1991, p. 26) developed the **Personal Responsibility Orientation (PRO)** model of self-direction in learning, which considers both instructional methods (or process) and learner personality attributes. Stockdale and Brockett (2011) tested a 25-item

 ## Box 8.6 Adult Learning and Teaching Cases

Exploring the Interactive Model of SDL: Two Learning Experiences

The following learning experiences provide you, as an adult learner or educator, an opportunity to reflect on the interactive learning model. In this model, learning occurs in a non-linear, more spontaneous way, where each step is not necessarily directly related to the previous or subsequent steps.

Marianne's experience: While searching in the library for information on cybersecurity and cyberspace, Marianne discovered a new concept. Deciding to explore the topic further, she searched the Internet and found a virtual community and a blog. She gained new insights and understanding of the topic as she interacted with the online community. Finally, while exploring the new idea in cyberspace, Marianne unearthed an interesting way to connect her new learning to her ongoing research.

Marica's experience: Marica was engaged in a garden landscaping learning project, reading about which plants adapted to her regional climate. During a neighborhood block party, she overheard a conversation about deer eating her neighbors' flowers. She listened and learned that deer like certain plants and flowers. Later, she consulted with a cooperative extension agent about which plants to avoid and which are "safe" to plant. After Marica had completed landscaping, she discovered that some flowers were still attracted by deer. She then searched the Internet and consulted with neighbors about which deer repellants work.

In Spear's (1988) model, Marianne's and Marica's learning projects spiraled from one cluster of activity to another, circumstances organizing their learning. Bateson (1994) described interactivity as "Spiral learning moves through complexity with partial understanding, allowing for later returns" (p. 31), suggesting that learning amplifies as adults move through experience, grasping what is immediately applicable, and later when new meanings become relevant, they return for further learning.

Reflection on the interactive model: both Marianne and Marica's learning experiences illustrated the non-linear, spontaneous nature of learning in Spear's interactive model. How do these examples challenge traditional views of learning as a step-by-step process, and how might this affect your approach as an adult educator or learner?

How did your environment, knowledge, and serendipitous encounters influence your SDL experiences?

PRO to Self-Direction in Learning Scale (PRO-SDLS) and found the instrument highly reliable in measuring SDL among college students. In the instructional process, the learner takes primary responsibility for planning, implementing, and evaluating learning. The *personal attributes* aspect of SDL in this model depends on the learner's propensity to be self-directed and take responsibility for learning. Box 8.7 applies the instructional SDL model.

In 2012, Brockett and Hiemstra updated their PRO model in response to confusion over terminology. They explained that the term "personal responsibility" created confusion, noting that it has been "politically co-opted" by the political right in the United States by "blaming the victim for their circumstances in life because they did not take responsibility to avoid getting into their difficulties" (p. 158). They also attempted to address criticisms that their model was too humanistic, ignored social and cultural influences, and did not fully address metacognitive learning. In response, they proposed the Person, Process, Context (PPC) model as an intersecting dynamic between the *person* (personal characteristics such as creativity, critical reflection, enthusiasm, life experience, life satisfaction, motivation, prior education, resilience, and self-concept), the *process*

 ## Box 8.7 Adult Learning and Teaching Cases

Exploring the Instructional Model of SDL

As you read the following experience, as an educator and learner, reflect on a similar experience that happened to you, considering the instructional model.

Monica's experience: Monica wanted to learn how to sail. She decided to ask her neighbor Carlo, an experienced sailor, to teach her. Carlo was an educational agent skilled at providing resources and facilitating learning. A clear assessment of her learning was whether she could sail effectively and independently.

The *personal attributes* aspect of SDL in this model depends on the learner's propensity to be self-directed and take responsibility for learning. In other words, if Monica had not determined to learn to sail and was unwilling to manage the process, she would not do it.

Brockett and Hiemstra (1991, 2019) also emphasized that context influences SDL. The learning context in this sailing example might be affected by the sailboat she uses, the weather, her relationship with her neighbor Carlo, available resources, or proximity to the sea and access to a boat.

(the teaching-learning transaction including facilitation, learning skills, learning styles; planning, organizing, and evaluating skills; teaching styles, and technological skills), and the *context* (the environmental and sociopolitical climate such as culture, power, learning environment, finances, gender, learning climate, organizational policies, political environment, race, and sexual orientation).

Building on Knowles's definition of SDL, Garrison (1997) suggested that SDL was influenced by self-management, self-monitoring of the knowledge construction process, and intrinsic and extrinsic motivation. **Self-management** situates the learner in the social context and is the degree to which the learner takes control of the environment to achieve goals. Self-management involves using learning materials and maintaining communication to build shared understanding. For example, Monica, who was learning to sail, used her environment (resources) and the people in it (her neighbor Carlo) to test and validate her learning. Self-monitoring and motivation are the cognitive aspects of the model. Self-monitoring is the learner's ability to gauge cognitive and metacognitive processes in many ways, like double-loop (reflecting on assumptions) and triple-loop (reflecting on the learning itself) learning (Argyris, 1991). Self-monitoring is also closely related to reflective practice and critical thinking. Monica might have drawn on her previous boating experience and knowledge to learn how to sail and critique her learning process as she attempted to navigate the boat. Motivation is what drives the learner to engage in SDL. Monica may have been motivated by spending time with her neighbor, watching as others enjoy sailing, or hearing from a friend about how much fun sailing is.

Grow's model (1991, 1994) described how educators can help learners become more self-directed in their SDL. It has four stages, depicted in Table 8.1. In this model, problems occur when the instructor does not meet the learners' stage. It is the educator's job to continually monitor and adapt the learning to the individual. For example, if the learner is not self-directed, as might be when learning something completely new and unfamiliar, the educator's role must be more directive, perhaps using lectures and immediate feedback. At the other end of the continuum is a highly self-directed learner. In this case, the educator is more of a consultant and resource person, encouraging independent projects and discovery learning. Table 8.1 identifies some appropriate instructional strategies for effective teaching and learning at each stage of Grow's model.

Reflecting on the three models, can you think of a match or mismatch that affected your SDL as a learner? How has it affected your learning? How has it impacted your work as an educator? Which of the models best describes your SDL? Why?

TABLE 8.1 GROW'S SELF-DIRECTED LEARNING STAGES

Stage	Learner Status	Educator Role	Teaching Strategies for Stage
1	• Dependent • Lacking self-direction	• Authority • Direct learning • Coach • Teacher-centered	• Providing introductory material • Giving few choices • Lecturing—subject centered • Drilling • Helping the learner see the immediate connection between concepts and application • Giving immediate feedback • Tutoring
2	• Interested • Confident	• Motivator • Guide	• Inspiring learning • Helping learners set goals • Assisting with the development of learning strategies • Lecturing inspirationally with guided discussion • Applying the basics in an interesting way • Providing close supervision
3	• Involved • Engaged as self-directed learners • Possess knowledge and self-efficacy for SDL	• Facilitator • Partner	• Applying the material • Facilitating discussion • Applying learning to real problems • Developing group projects or presentations • Providing learning strategies • Encouraging critical thinking • Promoting collaborative learning
4	• Self-directed learner • Able to plan, execute, and evaluate learning	• Consultant • Delegator • Mentor	• Encouraging independent projects and learner-led discussions • Learning through discovery • Offering expertise, consulting, and monitoring as needed • Providing autonomy • Creating opportunities for learners to share their learning • Focusing on both the process and product of learning • Using service learning • Coaching learners

Source: Adapted from Grow (1991, 1994).

SDL as a Personal Attribute

Much of the focus on SDL has been on the process, but SDL as a learner attribute has received comparable attention (Guglielmino, 1977). Knowles (1975) viewed self-directedness as an outcome of learner maturity, increasing with age. Furthermore, the tendency to be self-directed is one of the significant andragogy assumptions outlined by Knowles (see Chapter 7). Brockett and Hiemstra (1991) also supported learners taking responsibility for learning. They suggested that SDL is positively associated with high self-efficacy, meaning the more responsibility you take for learning, the more confident you will be. Using the sailing example above, Monica could start by sailing a sunfish and then build up the confidence to try a catamaran or a larger boat. Research to understand SDL as an attribute has examined learning style, education level, life satisfaction, and readiness; however, clear conclusions about defining attributes are elusive (Merriam et al., 2007; Merriam & Baumgartner, 2020).

Self-Directed Learning in Various Contexts

SDL is both a process and an attribute. The importance of context—the psychological, social, political, cultural, and economic environment—is widely discussed because learners may be more comfortable and capable of SDL in an area or environment where they have some experience (Candy, 1991). The importance of learning context has dominated adult education research for the past 30 years. Understanding how learner characteristics such as age, gender, race, or socioeconomic status play out within a learning environment is essential to effective learning and teaching. Box 8.8 considers these factors.

SDL can occur in a variety of contexts for a variety of reasons. Life context generates much learning. You may want to learn how to cook a new dish, understand a medical condition, improve your parenting skills, or get a promotion. You initiate a learning program to meet your learning needs. For example, Rager studied how a diagnosis of breast cancer (2004) and prostate cancer (2006) shaped patients' SDL. Roberson and Merriam (2005) shed light on how SDL is used to manage life changes in older adults. They interviewed 10 rural older adults about their SDL. They found that they used it to negotiate life transitions, particularly those related to late-life family transitions, such as becoming a grandparent, and losses, such as having to leave the family home or the death of a spouse or other loved one. Their findings also highlighted the importance of understanding how an adult's position in the lifespan intersects with and shapes learning needs. Wilson and Halford (2008) examined the

 **Box 8.8 Adult Learning and Teaching Cases**

Understanding How Different Learning Characteristics Can Impact Learning

An African American man is interested in learning how to use a new software system, so he attends a continuing education class offered at a community college. All the other learners are White, and they treat him as if he were invisible. His sense of self-efficacy and motivation to return to that context is likely low and may affect his learning motivation. On the other hand, imagine he returns to the class the following week. This time, the mix of learners is different, and they include him and value his knowledge and experience.

His learning experience will be very different—this time in the same environment but with different people. SDL learning contexts include personal, professional, organizational, educational, and online environments.

Reflective questions:

1. Can you think of a time when the dynamics of a learning group either enhanced or hindered your ability to participate and learn fully?
2. How did this experience affect your willingness to return to that learning context?
3. How can educators make learning environments more welcoming for all learners?

process of change in self-directed relationship education for couples. Fifty-nine couples completed a self-directed program that included a DVD and manual with telephone-based coaching sessions with a professional relationship educator. Couples completed an average of 96% of the learning tasks and implemented a wide range of self-change with continued implementation of learning strategies at a six-month follow-up interview. They concluded SDL is an effective approach to couple education.

SDL is also becoming prominent in continuing professional education in many social, health, and medical fields (Karas et al., 2020; Koskimäki et al., 2021), including physical therapy (Musolino, 2006), dental education (Hendricson et al., 2006, Luu & Da Silva, 2024; Syed & Ashar, 2020), veterinary and medical education (Raidal & Volet, 2009; Ricotta et al., 2021), pharmacy education (Huynh et al., 2009; Murry et al., 2024; Yao et al., 2023), in ICT work (Lemmetty & Collin 2020, 2021; Lemmetty, 2021), and library science (Oladokun & Mooko, 2022; Quinney et al., 2010). These professions recognized the need for continuous, lifelong learning and incorporated it into the curriculum. For example, recognizing a generational technology gap in the skills of its librarians and users, the Library at Brigham Young University implemented a self-directed training program to improve librarians' technology skills and develop their lifelong learning skills (Quinney et al., 2010).

Self-directed training has also been used in business and organizational settings to compete in a globalizing and changing environment (Hutasuhut et al., 2021). As Oh and Park (2012) stated, "With rapidly continuing changes in organizations and globalization, it is important for organizations to support workers by promoting SDL which is more adaptable and responsive to change" (Lee, 2001, as cited in Oh & Park, 2012, p. 269).

Higher education is another place SDL has taken hold (Fedeli et al., 2013). Long common in adult education programs, it is now used in service-learning projects (Butin, 2010) and problem-based learning (PBL), considering the impact of cooperative learning on SDL, especially in medical education (Silen & Uhlin, 2008; Taylor et al., 2023) and project-based based courses (Larson et al., 2020) and instructional design (Adinda & Mohib, 2020). Integrating SDL into higher education can be challenging, as evidenced by Raidal and Volet (2009), who examined 128 preclinical students' attitudes toward social and SDL (key elements of problem-based and case-based learning used in medical education). They found that students preferred external teacher regulation and individualized forms of learning—a mismatch with the type of learning required in practice. They concluded that guiding students toward greater learning autonomy is necessary for social, SDL, and continued lifelong learning after graduation.

García Botero et al. (2018) investigated the effectiveness of SDL in informal settings by analyzing how Duolingo enhanced the language skills of 118 higher education students. The study found that Duolingo can effectively support language learning by fostering motivation and providing a conducive learning environment. However, the results also show that some students need additional support and training to become more self-directed. Another study highlighted the significant impact of COVID-19 on the learning process, particularly in informal contexts, where SDL played a crucial role in times of uncertainty (Roberson et al., 2021).

SDL in online contexts is a growing phenomenon with implications for both the learning process and learner attributes (Song & Hill, 2007). **Virtual Learning Environments** (VLEs) characterize these learning contexts, including online training or e-learning, as gaining popularity for their convenience and cost-effectiveness (Simmering et al., 2009). Chu and Tsai (2009) surveyed 541 Taiwanese adults enrolled in adult education institutes to measure their preference for VLEs. A key finding was that SDL readiness was a decisive factor in predicting preferences for online learning environments, especially for highly intellectual challenges. The higher the SDL readiness, the greater the need to construct ideas, solve problems, and create learning activities online. One of the problems with VLEs is the lack of instructor guidance. SDL is almost a given for this type of learning, which can leave some learners lost and frustrated. To pursue online SDL, new ways of understanding and facilitating it are needed. Song and Hill contended that existing frameworks focus primarily on SDL as a process and personal attributes in face-to-face settings. They suggested current models might be poorly suited to the online learning context.

Al-Adwan et al. (2022) explored the factors that influence e-learning and its potential benefits as a supplement to traditional learning methods. The study involved 590 undergraduate students from three different universities in Jordan. The results showed that the quality of the service and the information system significantly impacted online usage and the intention to use e-learning plat-forms. Interestingly, SDL negatively impacted both satisfaction and intention to use e-learning. The study identified three primary factors influencing the effectiveness of e-learning systems: The quality of information, the quality of service, and SDL. By understanding these factors, adult educators and learners can more effectively navigate and support e-learning in educational environ-ments. Box 8.9 explores using generative artificial intelligence (GAI) in SDL.

 ## Box 8.9 SoTL: The Scholarship of Teaching and Learning

The Role of SDL Using ChatGPT: AI-Assisted Writing

Wang et al. (2024) investigated how higher education students use ChatGPT to enhance their SDL in writing assignments. Through 384 surveys and 10 interviews, the study revealed that students primarily used ChatGPT for brainstorming, gen-erating new ideas, and satisfying curiosity to complete academic assignments. The findings showed that students were responsible and highly motivated, using various SDL strategies. However, opinions varied as to whether ChatGPT improved stu-dents' writing skills. Nevertheless, the ability to receive immediate feedback allowed students to devote more time to writing practice. This study invited further explo-ration of how AI influences teaching, learning, and the development of SDL.

How might AI tools like ChatGPT better integrate into the writing classroom to enhance students' learning experiences?

Reflecting on your teaching practice, how might you integrate AI tools like ChatGPT to support writing skills and foster greater student autonomy?

The following section analyzes the SDL assessment process, which is usually challenging for educators and teachers who want to use SDL and help learners improve, especially in formal settings.

Assessing Self-Directed Learning

The **Oddi Continuing Learning Inventory** (OCLI) and the **Self-Directed Learning Readiness Scale** (SDLRS) are widely used to measure learners' tendency toward self-direction. The OCLI is a 24-item scale that measures self-directedness as a personality trait (Oddi, 1986; Oddi et al., 1990). The more widely used SDLRS developed by Guglielmino (1977) measures *readiness* to engage in SDL. According to Guglielmino, SDL is a mixture of attitudes, values, and abilities predisposing learners to SDL. Psychological traits contributing to readiness include initiative, independence, persistence in learning, responsibility, self-discipline, curiosity, independence in and enjoyment of learning, goal setting, and problem-solving orientation.

The SDLRS has been heavily relied upon; however, Stockdale and Brockett (2011) criticized it for being used in empirical studies without revision and despite challenges to its validity. Nevertheless, it is the most widely used instrument in SDL research (Merriam et al., 2007; Merriam & Baumgartner, 2020). Researchers have attempted to link various factors, such as learning style, educational level, and life satisfaction, to an individual's propensity for SDL. However, the results of these studies have been largely inconclusive (Merriam & Baumgartner, 2020).

Assessment Strategies for Self-Directed Learning by Costa and Kallick (2004) is full of strategies. Self-assessment begins with goals that are appropriate and attainable. Effective self-directed learners take ownership of their learning goals, set criteria for their learning, and can modify their process based on feedback and self-awareness. They identified the attributes of self-directed learners as self-managing, self-monitoring, and self-modifying and suggested that the key to SDL is becoming effective at self-assessing learning. Table 8.2 presents their criteria for assessing effective SDL for educators and learners. For example, in self-managing your SDL, as a learner you might use prior knowledge to manage your learning and organize your time effectively. You might ask others to share their perspectives on your project to self-monitor your learning progress. To self-modify your SDL, you might seek feedback from others, reflect on your performance, and adjust your SDL accordingly. Costa and Kallick (2004) described what makes an individual effective at self-direction and how to cultivate SDL in other people and organizations. They also provided a self-assessment to help learners evaluate their SDL competency.

TABLE 8.2 COSTA AND KALLICK'S CRITERIA FOR SELF-DIRECTED LEARNER ASSESSMENT

Self-Managing	Self-Monitoring	Self-Modifying
• Draws from prior knowledge, sensory data, and intuition to guide, hone, and refine actions. • Displays internal locus of control. • Thoughtfully plans and initiates actions. • Manages time effectively. • Produces new knowledge through research and experimentation. • Uses clear and precise language. • Balances solitude and togetherness, action and reflection, and personal and professional growth. • Displays a sense of humor.	• Seeks perspectives beyond self and others to develop thoughtful responses. • Generates new and innovative ideas and problem-solving strategies. • Pursues ambiguities and possibilities to create new meanings. • Manages oneself concerning the group. • Is aware of what is known and not known and develops strategies to fill in the gaps. • Evaluates, corrects, and adjusts work to improve its quality.	• Explores choice points between self-assertion and integration with others. • Seeks feedback from appropriate sources for improved performance. • Reflects on and learns from experience. • Continues to learn new skills and strategies. • Thoughtfully receives feedback and acts on it.

Source: Adapted from Costa & Kallick, 2004.

The assessment strategies outlined by Costa and Kallick (2004) emphasize the importance of reflection and self-assessment in learning. Key strategies include holding debrief sessions with peers or the instructor to review learning goals, track progress, and make necessary adjustments. As an adult educator or learner, you might consider using a set of reflective questions during these conferences, such as: What is working well with your project? What challenges are you facing? What has surprised you?

They also recommended creating checklists of key steps or competencies related to the learning task and offered several examples. **Portfolios,** a collection of the learner's work, are also effective for project documentation and assessment. When using portfolios, devote class time to sharing portfolios in small groups as a valuable exercise as learners compare notes on their learning journeys. Furthermore, the same authors identified factors discouraging and reducing SDL, such as too much reliance on the instructor, for instance, when the instructor has all the answers or fails to push learners to find their answers. If learners have an unclear vision for their projects, focusing on and maintaining them can also be challenging (Costa & Kallick, 2004). Using learning contracts with students when planning SDL projects helps ensure clear goal-setting and accountability.

Taylor et al. (2023) conducted a literature review study to analyze the assessment practices of SDL in undergraduate health professions. They highlighted the importance of using multiple assessment tools with different measures to assess students. They used an expanded seven-step SDL framework to assess activities and interventions. They found that most studies used more than one assessment method and recommended evidence-based best practices for assessing SDL.

Myths of SDL

Although adults have always been learners, it was not until the late 1960s that adult educators and researchers began to focus systematically on adult learning. Andragogy (see Chapter 7) and SDL were the two earliest and most robust conceptualizations of the nature and characteristics of adult learning. Although andragogy identifies assumptions or characteristics of adult learners, SDL is more about the process by which adults engage in their learning that respects adult learner characteristics. SDL immediately resonated with adult educators and researchers, resulting in a burgeoning body of writings, publications, and applications. Along with the growing body of research and writing, some misconceptions, or what Brockett (1994) and Brockett and Hiemstra (2012) refer to as *myths* of SDL, developed that sometimes cloud understanding of this type of learning. Examining these 10 myths (Brockett & Hiemstra, 2012) and their refutations is helpful when integrating SDL.

Myth 1: *Self-directedness is an all-or-nothing concept*—A false notion since every learner is different and prefers varying levels of self-directedness. It is more accurate to view SDL as a continuum, "a characteristic that exists, to a greater or lesser degree, in all persons and in all learning situations" (Brockett & Hiemstra, 1991, p. 11).

Myth 2: *Self-direction implies learning in isolation*—An inaccurate stereotype that places the learner in isolation from other learners. Although learners may engage in periods of intense, individualized learning, their learning is enhanced by sharing it with others and asking other adults or instructors about their questions, insights, and reflections.

Myth 3: *Self-direction is just another adult education fad*—refuted over time and likely tied to SDL emerging during the 1970s and 1980s, a time known as the "me" generation where "hedonism and self-centeredness" prevailed (Brockett & Hiemstra, 1991, p. 12).

Myth 4: *SDL is not worth the time required to make it work*—It depends on a cost-benefit analysis of the learning goals versus the time and resources available. Indeed, not all learning unfolds with SDL. However, investing in SDL preparation, learning needs assessment, learning plan design, and learning evaluation engages the learner in meaningful ways that often result in deeper learning than teacher-led approaches, making it well worth the time.

Myth 5: *SDL activities are limited primarily to reading and writing*—This view overlooks the informal nature of learning and the reality that adults cannot meet all learning goals from reading books or writing, like improving a golf swing, speaking a language, building a deck, or training a dog. SDL works best when it is experiential and embedded in the context of an adult's life (see Chapter 6).

Myth 6: *Facilitating self-direction is an easy way out for teachers*—A pervasive myth, according to Brockett and Hiemstra (1991). Helping learners become self-directed requires educators to take a very active, individualized approach with learners to communicate the process and support the development of their SDL plan. Learners come to SDL with different needs and capabilities, making facilitation just as challenging as, if not more demanding than, traditional instruction.

Myth 7: *SDL is limited primarily to those settings where freedom and democracy prevail*—Assumes that ideal conditions must exist for SDL to occur. However, SDL certainly occurs in very controlling social and educational environments. Think of the SDL done by people in prison, by protesters in the Arab Spring revolutions, or by women and girls continuing their learning in hiding under Taliban rule in Afghanistan. People learning under duress may need more time and support to engage in and take ownership of SDL experiences.

Myth 8: *SDL is limited primarily to white, middle-class adults*—Suggests that this learning method reflects the dominant culture. While this is one of the main criticisms of SDL, Brockett and Hiemstra (2019) noted that there are examples of SDL in diverse social groups and societies outside of North America and Western Europe.

Myth 9: *SDL will erode the quality of institutional programs*—Does not occur when learners assume more control over their learning. The only risk to quality is poor management of SDL. Many institutions do not believe it is the best approach to learning and, therefore, do not support it in the organizational context.

Myth 10: *SDL is the best approach for adults*—It causes problems if learners' individual needs and goals are not considered when structuring learning activities. As with any approach, we need to be realistic about the limitations of SDL and use it appropriately. These myths can help you to reflect on and improve your teaching and learning design.

Critiques of Self-Directed Learning

Although many have embraced SDL, it is not without its problems. First, the assumption that all adults desire self-direction in their learning is problematic on developmental, technical, economic, and cultural levels. Developmentally, not all adults desire or are capable of SDL. Readiness to engage in SDL varies from learner to learner. Tailoring SDL to learner needs involves recognizing and being sensitive to different readiness levels. Brookfield (1984) raised concerns about educators' ability to facilitate SDL's goal setting, instructional design, and evaluation of SDL without questioning its validity or value compared to other options. Not all adult learners have the resources to engage in SDL activities, and some cultures may be reluctant to rely on such learning techniques.

Brookfield (2013) suggested that SDL describes how the dominant majority learns and may ignore essential aspects of culture and context. For example, SDL tends to be a Western teaching method that may be culturally at odds with some learners. Confucius asserted that students would need a competent teacher to guide them and believed students would better spend time absorbing structured ideas than thinking independently (Confucius, 479 BC). In contrast, the goal of educational institutions and universities "is creating self-directed, self-motivated, independent learners who are able to critique and direct their own work with critical thinking and rational judgment" (Lee, 2012, p. 395). Wang and Farmer (2008) surveyed Chinese adult teachers. They found that they preferred to teach lower-level thinking skills associated with the first three levels of Bloom's Taxonomy (knowledge, comprehension, and application), confirming their hypothesis that a teacher-centered, information-based, test-driven instructional format characterizes Chinese education. However, when Chinese learners enroll in Western universities, professors may expect them to immediately acculturate to new learning processes (including SDL) that may threaten their expectations of how they should behave in an educational context.

An important question for us to consider as adult educators is whether SDL remains a relevant, robust area of research. Some adult education texts have omitted the topic (Drago-Severson, 2009; Foley, 2004; Merriam, 2011; Merriam et al., 2006; Merriam & Grace, 2011). Historically, adult and continuing education handbooks are published once a decade to assess the field. Although discussions of self-directed learning occur in these volumes, SDL has not warranted a chapter in the past 40 years (Kasworm et al., 2010; Merriam & Cunningham, 1989; Rocco et al., 2023; Wilson & Hayes, 2009). Do these omissions mean the field has exhausted the topic? Conner et al. (2009) analyzed the citations of the SDL literature from 1980 to 2008 and concluded that the current state of the research is strong. In addition, a website (www.sdlglobal.com), a journal (*International Journal of Self-Directed Learning*), and an annual conference for over 35 years attest to the continued relevance of SDL to the understanding of adult learning. However, longevity alone is not synonymous with relevance and innovation. Going forward, Brockett and Hiemstra (2019) advocated for more research on the foundations of SDL, new measures of self-directedness, new research methods such as phenomenology and critical theory, and connections to other fields to build a richer understanding of SDL.

Chapter Summary

Self-Directed Learning (SDL) is a foundational concept in adult education, emphasizing learner autonomy, motivation, and self-regulation. Knowles (1975) defined SDL as a process in which individuals take initiative in diagnosing their learning needs, setting goals, identifying resources, implementing strategies, and evaluating outcomes. Researchers like Tough (1971) highlighted SDL as a significant aspect of adult learning, revealing that most learning projects are self-planned. Assessment tools such as the Self-Directed Learning Readiness Scale (SDLRS) have been widely used despite criticisms regarding their validity (Stockdale & Brockett, 2011). Costa and Kallick (2004) provided a framework for assessing SDL, categorizing it into self-managing, self-monitoring, and self-modifying behaviors. Effective SDL involves goal setting, self-assessment, feedback-seeking, and reflection. Myths about SDL, as identified by Brockett and Hiemstra (2012), include misconceptions that SDL occurs in isolation, is exclusive to Western culture, or is the best learning approach for all adults. These myths often overlook the diverse ways learners engage in SDL across various contexts. Despite its widespread adoption, SDL faces critiques regarding its accessibility, cultural relevance, and the assumption that all adults prefer self-direction (Brookfield, 1984; Wang & Farmer, 2008). Some educational systems emphasize teacher-led instruction, making SDL challenging to implement globally. While SDL remains a significant research area, its prominence in academic discussions has fluctuated. However, continued research, conferences, and publications highlight its enduring relevance and the need to explore further its foundations, assessment methods, and cross-cultural applications (Brockett & Hiemstra, 2019).

Key Points

- SDL involves planning, organizing, controlling, and assessing individual learning in a process initially described by Tough as "self-teaching."
- SDL is not necessarily a solitary activity. Learners may consult with peers, experts, or instructors during the quest.
- You may even enroll in a class. SDL is both a process of instruction and an attribute of the learner.
- SDL can be integrated into highly structured, formal, controlled learning environments through activities and assignments.
- In formal settings, SDL requires the active involvement of the instructor to guide the learners in identifying goals and strategies and in assessing their learning.
- Learners exhibit varying degrees of self-direction along a continuum from high dependence on the instructor to independent SDL that may rely on the instructor as a consultant or mentor.
- Self-directed learning helps adults learn in personal, professional, organizational, educational, and online contexts.

References

Adinda, D., & Mohib, N. (2020). Teaching and instructional design approaches to enhance students' self-directed learning in blended learning environments. *Electronic Journal of eLearning, 18*(2), 162–174. https://doi.org/10.34190/EJEL.20.18.2.005.

Ahammad, F. (2023). Self-directed learning: A core concept in adult education. *The Online Journal of Distance Education and e-learning, 11*(3), 2952–2962.

Al-Adwan, A. S., Nofal, M., Akram, H., Albelbisi, N. A., & Al-Okaily, M. (2022). Towards a sustainable adoption of e-learning systems: The role of self-directed learning. *Journal of Information Technology Education: Research, 21.* https://doi.org/10.28945/4980.

Argyris, C. (1991, May–June). Teaching smart people how to learn. *Harvard business review,* 99–109.

Bateson, M. C. (1994). *Peripheral visions: Learning along the way.* HarperCollins.

Bosch, C., Mentz, E. & Goede, R. (2019). Self-directed learning: A conceptual overview, in P. B. Bergamin, C. Bosch, A. Du Toit, R. Goede, A. Golightly, D. W. Johnson, et al. *Self-directed learning for the 21st century: Implications for higher education* (pp. 1–36), AOSIS. https://doi.org/10.4102/aosis.2019.BK134.01.

Brandt, D. W. C. (2020). *Measuring student success skills: A review of the literature on self-directed learning.* PBLWorks.

Brockett, R. G. (1994). Resistance to self-direction in adult learning: Myths and misunderstandings. *New Directions for Adult and Continuing Education, 64,* 5–12.

Brockett, R. G., & Hiemstra, R. (1991). *Self-direction in adult learning: Perspectives on theory, research, and practice.* Routledge, Chapman, and Hall.

Brockett, R. G., & Hiemstra, R. (2018). *Self-direction in adult learning: Perspectives on theory, research, and practice*. Routledge, Chapman, and Hall.

Brockett, R. G., Stockdale, S. L., Fogerson, D. L., Cox, B. F., Canipe, J. B., Chuprina, L. A., et al. (2000). Two decades of literature on self-directed learning: A content analysis. https://eric.ed.gov/?id=ED449348.

Broek, S., Van Der Linden, J., Kuijpers, M. A. C. T., & Semeijn, J. H. (2023). What makes adults choose to learn: Factors that stimulate or prevent adults from learning. *Journal of Adult and Continuing Education, 29*(2), 620–642. https://doi.org/10.1177/14779714231169684.

Brookfield, D. S. (1984). Self-directed adult learning: A critical paradigm. *Adult Education Quarterly, 35*(2), 59–71. https://doi.org/10.1177/0001848184035002001.

Brookfield, D. S. (2013). *Powerful techniques for teaching adults*. Jossey Bass.

Brookfield, S. (1986). *Understanding and facilitating adult learning: A comprehensive analysis of principles and effective practices*. McGraw-Hill Education (UK).

Butin, D. W. (2010). *Service learning in theory and practice: The future of community engagement in higher education*. Palgrave Macmillan.

Caffarella, R. S. (1993). Self-directed learning. *New Directions for Adult and Continuing Education, 57*, 25–35.

Caffarella, R. S. (2000). Goals of self-directed learning. In G.A. Straka (Ed.), *Conceptions of self-directed learning: Theoretical and conceptual considerations* (pp. 37–48). Waxmann.

Candy, P. C. (1991). *Self-direction for lifelong learning: A comprehensive guide to theory and practice*. Jossey-Bass.

Charungkaittikul, S., & Henschke, J. (2018). Applying an andragogical approach to foster lifelong self-directed learning in the 21st century higher education classroom settings. *Journal of Educational Leadership in Action, 5*(2), 5. https://doi.org/10.62608/2164-1102.1040.

Chu, R. J-C., & Tsai, C-C. (2009). Self-directed learning readiness, Internet self-efficacy, and preferences towards constructivist Internet-based learning environments among higher-aged adults. *Journal of Computer Assisted Learning, 25*(5), 489–501. https://doi.org/10.1111/j.1365-2729.2009.00324.x.

Conner, T. R., Carter, S. L., Dieffenderfer, V., & Brockett, R. G. (2009). A citation analysis of self-directed learning literature: 1980–2008. *International Journal of Self-directed Learning, 6*(2), 53–75.

Costa, A. L., & Kallick, B. (2004). *Assessment strategies for self-directed learning*. Corwin Press/Sage.

Cronin-Golomb, L. M., & Bauer, P. J. (2023). Self-motivated and directed learning across the lifespan. *Acta Psychologica, 232*, 103816. https://doi.org/10.1016/j.actpsy.2022.103816.

Dahal, A., & Bhat, N. (2024). Self-directed learning, its implementation, and challenges: A review. *Nepal Journal of Health Sciences, 3*, 102–115. https://doi.org/10.3126/njhs.v3i1.63277.

Doo, M. Y., & Zhu, M. (2024). A meta-analysis of effects of self-directed learning in online learning environments. *Journal of Computer Assisted Learning, 40*(1), 1–20. https://doi.org/10.1111/jcal.12865.

Drago-Severson, E. (2009). *Leading adult learning: Supporting adult development in our schools*. Corwin, a SAGE Company.

Duckworth, A. (2016). Grit: The power of passion and perseverance. New York: Scribner/Simon & Schuster.

Dweck, C. S. (2006). *Mindset: The new psychology of success*. Random house.

Fedeli, M., Giampaolo, M., & Coryell, J. E. (2013). The use of learning contracts in an Italian university setting. *Adult Learning, 24*(3), 104–111. https://doi.org/10.1177/1045159513489113.

Ferrario, M. (2020). *The limits of informal learning in companies.* DynDevice. https://www
.dyndevice.com/en/news/the-limits-of-informal-learning-in-companies-ELN-2035/.

Foley, G. (Ed.). (2004). *Dimensions of adult learning: Adult education and training in a global era.*
Open University Press.

García Botero, G., Questier, F., Cincinnato, S., He, T., & Zhu, C. (2018). Acceptance and
usage of mobile assisted language learning by higher education students. *Journal of
Computing in Higher Education, 30,* 426–451.

Garrison, D. R. (1997). Self-directed learning: Toward a comprehensive model. *Adult
Education Quarterly, 48*(1), 18–33. https://doi.org/10.1177/074171369704800103.

Grow, G. (1991). Teaching learners to be self-directed: A stage approach. *Adult Education
Quarterly, 41*(3), 125–149. https://doi.org/10.1177/0001848191041003001.

Grow, G. (1994). In defense of the staged self-directed learning model. *Adult Education
Quarterly, 44*(2), 109–114. https://doi.org/10.1177/074171369404400206.

Guglielmino, L. M. (1977). *Development of the self-directed learning readiness scale.* Unpublished
doctoral dissertation. University of Georgia.

Hendricson, W. D., Andrieu, S. C., Chadwick, D. G., Chmar, J. E., Cole, J. R., et al. (2006).
Educational strategies associated with development of problem-solving, critical thinking,
and self-directed learning. *Journal of Dental Education, 70*(9), 925–936. https://doi.org/
10.1002/j.0022-0337.2006.70.9.tb04163.x.

Hiemstra, R., & Brockett, R. G. (2012). *Reframing the meaning of self-directed learning: An updated
model.* Adult Education Research Conference, pp. 155–162. https://newprairiepress.org/
aerc/2012/papers/22.

Houle, C. O. (1961). *The inquiring mind.* University of Wisconsin Press.

Hutasuhut, I., Ahmad Zaidi Adruce, S., & Jonathan, V. (2021). How a learning organization
cultivates self-directed learning. *Journal of Workplace Learning, 33*(5), 334–347. https://doi
.org/10.1108/JWL-05-2020-0074.

Huynh, D., Haines, S. T., Plaza, C. M., Sturpe, D. A., Williams, G., De Bittner, M. A. R., &
Roffman, D. S. (2009). The impact of advanced pharmacy practice experiences on students' readiness for self-directed learning. *American Journal of Pharmaceutical Education,
73*(4). https://doi.org/10.5688/aj730465.

Karas, M., Sheen, N. J., North, R. V., Ryan, B., & Bullock, A. (2020). Continuing professional
development requirements for UK health professionals: A scoping review. *BMJ Open,
10*(3), e032781. https://doi.org/10.1136/bmjopen-2019-032781.

Kasworm, D. E., Rose, A. D., & Ross-Gordon, J. M. (Eds.). (2010). *Handbook of adult and continuing education.* Sage.

Knowles, M. S. (1975). *Self-directed learning: A guide for learners and teachers.* Association
Free Press.

Knowles, M. S. (1986). Using learning contracts.

Koskimäki, M., Lähteenmäki, M. L., Mikkonen, K., Kääriäinen, M., Koskinen, C., Mäki-Hakola, H.,
et al. (2021). Continuing professional development among social-and health-care educators.
Scandinavian Journal of Caring Sciences, 35(2), 668–677. https://doi.org/10.1111/scs.12948.

Larson, J., Jordan, S. S., Lande, M., & Weiner, S. (2020). Supporting self-directed learning in
a project-based embedded systems design course. *IEEE Transactions on Education, 63*(2),
88–97. IEEE Transactions on Education. https://doi.org/10.1109/TE.2020.2975358.

Leach, J., Ametller, J., Hind, A., Lewis, J., Scott, P. (2005). Designing and evaluating short
science teaching sequences: Improving student learning. In K. Boersma, M. Goedhart,
de O. Jong, H. Eijkelhof (Eds.) *Research and the quality of science education.* Springer.
https://doi.org/10.1007/1-4020-3673-6_17.

Lee, H. J. (2012). Rocky road: East Asian international students' experience of adaptation to critical thinking way of learning at U.S. universities. In J. Buban & D. Ramdeholl (Eds.), *Proceedings of the 53rd Annual Adult Education Research Conference* (pp. 395–397). SUNY Empire State College.

Lemmetty, S. (2021). Employee opportunities for self-directed learning at technology organisations: Features and frames of self-directed learning projects. *Studies in Continuing Education, 43*(2), 139–155. https://doi.org/10.1080/0158037X.2020.1765758.

Lemmetty, S., & Collin, K. (2020). Self-directed learning as a practice of workplace learning: Interpretative repertoires of self-directed learning in ICT work. *Vocations and Learning, 13*(1), 47–70. https://doi.org/10.1007/s12186-019-09228-x.

Lemmetty, S., & Collin, K. (2021). Self-directed learning in creative activity: An ethnographic study in technology-based work. *The Journal of Creative Behavior, 55*(1), 105–119. https://doi.org/10.1002/jocb.438.

Livingstone, D. W. (1999). Exploring the icebergs of adult learning: Findings of the first Canadian survey of informal learning practices. *Canadian Journal for the Study of Adult Education, 13*(2), 49–72.

Loeng, S. (2019). Self-directed learning: A core concept in adult education. *Education Research International, 2020*(1), 3816132. https://doi.org/10.1155/2020/3816132.

Long, H. B. (1998). Theoretical and practical implications of selected paradigms of self-directed learning. In H. B. Long & Associates (Eds.), *Developing paradigms for self-directed learning* (pp. 1–14). University of Oklahoma.

Luu, K., & Da Silva, K. (2024). An evaluation of dental continuing professional development programs in the USA and Canada. *Journal of Dental Education, 88*(3), 269–277. https://doi.org/10.1002/jdd.13425.

Merriam, S. B. (Ed.). (2011). *Third update on adult learning theory*. New directions for adult and continuing education, no. 119. John Wiley & Sons.

Merriam, S. B. and Baumgartner, L. M. (2020). *Learning in adulthood: A comprehensive guide.* (4th ed.). Jossey-Bass.

Merriam, S. B., & Bierema L. L. (2013). *Adult learning: Linking theory and practice.* Jossey-Bass.

Merriam, S. B., & Cunningham, P. M. (1989). *Handbook of adult and continuing education.* The Jossey-Bass Higher Education Series. Jossey-Bass.

Merriam, S. B., & Grace, A. P. (Eds.). (2011). *The Jossey-Bass reader on contemporary issues in adult education.* Jossey-Bass.

Merriam, S. B., Courtenay, B. C., & Cervero, R. M. (Eds.). (2006). *Global issues and adult education: Perspectives from Latin America, Southern Africa, and the United States.* Jossey-Bass.

Merriam, S. B., Caffarella, R. S., & Baumgartner, L. M. (2007). *Learning in adulthood: A comprehensive guide.* (3rd ed.). John Wiley & Sons.

Mezirow, J. (1985). A critical theory of self-directed learning. *New Directions for Adult and Continuing Education, 1985*(25), 17–30. https://doi.org/10.1002/ace.36719852504.

Morris, T. H., & Rohs, M. (2023). The potential for digital technology to support self-directed learning in formal education of children: A scoping review. *Interactive Learning Environments, 31*(4), 1974–1987. https://doi.org/10.1080/10494820.2020.1870501.

Munasinghe, D. S., Sutha, J., & Perera, K. J. T. (2019). A study of factors influences on self-directed learning of undergraduates (with special reference to Sri Lankan universities). *Journal of Management and Tourism Research, 2*(2) 55–70.

Murry, L. T., Whittington, B., & Travlos, D. V. (2024). Continuing professional development activities provided by continuing pharmacy education providers. *American Journal of Pharmaceutical Education, 88*(4), 100685. https://doi.org/10.1016/j.ajpe.2024.100685.

Musolino, G. M. (2006). Fostering reflective practice: Self-assessment abilities of physical therapy students and entry-level graduates. *Journal of Allied Health, 35*(1), 30–42.

Oddi, L. F., (1986). Development and validation of an instrument to identify self-directed continuing learners. *Adult Education Quarterly, 36*(2), 97–107. https://doi.org/10.1177/0001848186036002004.

Oddi, L. F., Ellis, A. J., & Roberson. J. E. A. (1990). Construct validity of the Oddi continuing learning inventory. *Adult Education Quarterly, 40*(3), 139–145. https://doi.org/10.1177/0001848190040003002.

Oh, J. R., & Park, C. H. (2012). *Self-directed learning in the workplace: Implications for the legislation of trade union education in South Korea.* Adult Education Research Conference. pp. 265–271. https://newprairiepress.org/aerc/2012/papers/38.

Oladokun, O., & Mooko, N. P. (2022). Academic libraries and the need for continuing professional development in Botswana. *IFLA Journal, 49*(1), 117–131. https://doi.org/10.1177/03400352221103901.

Owen, T. R. (2002). Self-Directed Learning in Adulthood: A Literature Review. ED 461 050.

Quinney, K. L., Smith, S. D., & Galbraith, Q. (2010). Bridging the gap: Self-directed staff technology training. *Information Technology and Libraries, 29*(4), 205–213. https://doi.org/10.6017/ital.v29i4.3131.

Rager, K. B. (2004). A thematic analysis of the self-directed learning experiences of thirteen breast cancer patients. *International Journal of Lifelong Education, 23*(1), 95–109. https://doi.org/10.1080/0260137032000172088.

Rager, K. B. (2006). Self-directed learning and prostate cancer: A thematic analysis of the experiences of twelve patients. *International Journal of Lifelong Education, 25*(5), 447–461. https://doi.org/10.1080/02601370600911982.

Raidal, S. L., Volet, S. E. (2009). Preclinical students' predispositions towards social forms of instruction and self-directed learning: A challenge for the development of autonomous and collaborative learners. *Higher Education, 57*, 577–596. https://doi.org/10.1007/s10734-008-9163-z.

Ricotta, D. N., Richards, J. B., Atkins, K. M., Hayes, M. M., McOwen, K., et al. (2021). Self-directed learning in medical education: Training for a lifetime of discovery. *Teaching and Learning in Medicine, 34*(5), 530–540. https://doi.org/10.1080/10401334.2021.1938074.

Roberson, D. N., & Merriam. S. B. (2005). The self-directed learning of older, rural adults. *Adult Education Quarterly, 55*(4), 269–287. https://doi.org/10.1177/0741713605277372.

Roberson, D. N., Zach, S., Choresh, N., & Rosenthal, I. (2021). Self-directed learning: A long-standing tool for uncertain times. *Creative Education, 12*(5), 1011–1026.

Rocco, T. S., Smith, M. C., Mizzi, R. C., Merriweather, L. R., & Hawley, J. D. (Eds.). (2023). *The handbook of adult and continuing education.* Taylor & Francis.

Silen, C., & Uhlin, L. (2008). Self-directed learning—A learning issue for adults and faculty! *Teaching in Higher Education, 13*(4), 461–475. https://doi.org/10.1080/13562510802169756.

Simmering, M. J., Posey, C., & Piccoli, G. (2009). Computer self-efficacy and motivation to learn in a self-directed online course. *Decision Sciences Journal of Innovative Education, 7*(1), 99–121. https://doi.org/10.1111/j.1540-4609.2008.00207.x.

Song, D., & Bonk, C. J. (2016). Motivational factors in self-directed informal learning from online learning resources. *Cogent Education, 3*(1). https://doi.org/10.1080/2331186X.2016.1205838.

Song, L., & Hill, J. R. (2007). A conceptual model for understanding self-directed learning in online environments. *Journal of Interactive Online Learning, 6*(1), 27–42.

Spear, G. E. (1988). Beyond the organizing circumstance: A search for methodology for the study of self-directed learning. In H. B. Long & others, *Self-directed learning: Application and theory.* University of Georgia.

Spear, G. E., & Mocker, D. W. (1984). The organizing circumstance: Environmental determinants in self-directed learning. *Adult Education Quarterly, 35,* 1–10. https://doi.org/10.1177/0001848184035001O.

Stockdale, S. (2003). Development of an instrument to measure self-directedness. Doctoral Dissertation, University of Tennessee.

Stockdale, S. L., & Brockett, R. G. (2011). Development of the PRO-SDLS: A measure of self-direction in learning based on the personal responsibility orientation model. *Adult Education Quarterly, 61*(2), 161–180. https://doi.org/10.1177/0741713610380447.

Syed, I. B., & Ashar, A. (2020). A query about continuous professional development from dental teachers. *Pakistan Armed Forces Medical Journal, 70*(2), 549–554. https://pafmj.org/PAFMJ/article/view/4227.

Taylor, T. A. H., Kemp, K., Mi, M., & Lerchenfeldt, S. (2023). Self-directed learning assessment practices in undergraduate health professions education: A systematic review. *Medical Education Online, 28*(1). https://doi.org/10.1080/10872981.2023.2189553.

Tekkol, I. A., & Demirel, M. (2018). An investigation of self-directed learning of undergraduate students. *Frontiers in Psychology, 9.* https://doi.org/10.3389/fpsyg.2018.02324.

Tough, A. (1967). *Learning without a teacher.* Ontario Institute for Studies in Education.

Tough, A. (1971). *The adult's learning projects: A fresh approach to theory and practice in adult education.* Ontario Institute for Studies in Education.

Tough, A. (1978). Major learning efforts: Recent research and future directions. *Adult Education, 28*(4), 250–236. https://doi.org/10.1177/074171367802800403.

Vaičiūnienė, A., & Kazlauskienė, A. (2023). Liberating and oppressive factors for self-directed learning: A systematic literature review. *Education Sciences, 13*(10), 10. https://doi.org/10.3390/educsci13101020.

Wang, C., Li, Z., & Bonk, C. (2024). Understanding self-directed learning in AI-Assisted writing: A mixed methods study of postsecondary learners. *Computers and Education: Artificial Intelligence, 6,* 100247. https://doi.org/10.1016/j.caeai.2024.100247.

Wang, V. & Farmer, L. (2008). Adult teaching methods in China and Bloom's Taxonomy. *International Journal for the Scholarship of Teaching and Learning, 2*(2), 1–15. https://doi.org/10.20429/ijsotl.2008.020213.

Wilson, K. L., & Halford, W. K. (2008). Processes of change in self-directed couple relationship education. *Family Relations, 57*(5), 625–635. https://doi.org/10.1111/j.1741-3729.2008.00529.x.

Wilson, A. L., & Hayes, E. (Eds.). (2009). *Handbook of adult and continuing education.* John Wiley & Sons.

Yao, X., Li, H., Wen, L., Tian, Y., Zhang, Y., Zhang, X., Du, S., Li, J., Fu, H., & Yin, Z. (2023). What learning strategies are commonly used by hospital pharmacists in the process of self-directed learning? A multicentre qualitative study. *BMJ Open, 13*(4), e069051. https://doi.org/10.1136/bmjopen-2022-069051.

SECTION FOUR

THE ADULT LEARNING PROCESS—THE *HOW*

So far, *Adult Learning: Linking Theory and Practice* has discussed the *where* (context) and the *who* (adult educators and adult learners), and next, Section 4 delves into *how* adults learn. "The *process* of adult learning transpires in the learner's head, heart, body, and soul that leads to new knowledge, behaviour change, or perspective transformation" (Bierema, 2019, p. 13, italics in original). Educators and learners are key stakeholders in the **learning process,** which concerns what goes on in the learner's head, heart, body, and soul, leading to a change in behavior or perspective.

The learning process is culturally bound, and change is often a significant catalyst for learning. Constant change characterizes adulthood, prompting identity crises, challenging relationships, and impacting a person's sense of legacy—what they leave for the next generation. Learning helps adults cope with change, whether it is expected or unanticipated. For example, people might anticipate leaving home for the first time, becoming a college student, committing to a relationship, joining a cause, starting a family, taking a new job, or assuming a vital community role. All of these foreseen life events are learning opportunities. Adults are less prepared for life's unexpected changes, such as the breakup of a relationship, sudden death of a loved one, loss of a job, change in financial circumstances, or new insights gained from events, travel, or relationships. Some of these changes could evoke transformative learning that provokes shifting one's way of thinking and being in the world. Change often requires people to reframe their understanding of circumstances and ideas. Adults learn by making meaning of life situations, reorganizing their understandings of ideas, and, at times, changing their behaviors and beliefs due to learning.

Section 4 has four chapters. Chapter 9, "Connecting Learning and Change in Adulthood," explores learning and change across the lifespan and how these processes are mutually reinforcing. Chapter 10, "Experiencing Learning in Adulthood," investigates learning and experience in adulthood and how adults learn both within and from life situations. Chapter 11, "Learning for Transformation," considers learning for transformation (L4T) by defining it and exploring its role for individuals, groups, organizations, communities, and social systems. Chapter 12, "Connecting Neuroscience and Adult Learning," discusses adult learning and the brain, including the development of intelligence and wisdom.

Reference

Bierema, L. L. (2019). Adult learning theories and practices. In M. Fedeli, & L. L. Bierema (Eds.), *Connecting adult learning and knowledge management: Strategies for learning and change in higher education and organizations*, (pp. 3–26). Springer.

CHAPTER NINE

CONNECTING LEARNING AND CHANGE IN ADULTHOOD

 **Box 9.1 Chapter Overview and Learning Objectives**

Viktor Frankl wrote, in his poignant 1959 book, *Man's Search for Meaning*, about surviving a Nazi Germany death camp,

> When we are no longer able to change a situation . . . we are challenged to change ourselves. (p. 112)

Frankl found himself in a situation that was difficult, if not impossible, to change, so he decided to shift how he coped with the problem and found meaning in it. Although few adults will find themselves in such dire circumstances, Frankl's words are an inspiration and essential for any adult needing to understand their situation and make a change.

The purpose of Chapter 9 is to explore learning and change in adulthood and how these mutual processes reinforce each other. The chapter begins with a discussion of adult learning and change. It explores different types of change and organization theorist Lewin's (1947) three-step change model. Next, it considers the dynamic between adult learning and change and how the pace, planning, and scale of change affect adults. The chapter connects change and learning to systems dynamics theory and finally offers strategies for how adults can cope with change in various situations.

As a result of reading this chapter and completing the exercises, you, the reader, should be able to:

1. Recognize how the characteristics of adult learners have implications for how they will experience change.
2. Relate adult learning processes to change processes.
3. Explore the pace, planning (or lack thereof), and scale of change and how it affects adult learning.
4. Identify coping strategies for change.

Bierema (2019) observed, "Adult learning might be the most overlooked learning process across the lifespan" (p. 4), emphasizing how children's learning is privileged in society. Adults' lives are changing constantly, from issues they face in their family, work, and community roles to social, political, and environmental shifts, crises, and other events. Adults often cope with change by learning; correspondingly, learning frequently leads to change. For example, imagine a person who aspires to advance to a leadership role in their organization. They receive encouragement and feedback that they need to learn how to lead and develop a team. This feedback causes the person to seek out formal learning through a leadership development program and work with a coach, and in turn, they begin to change how they see themselves and interact with others in their work.

Appreciating How Change Relates to Adult Learning

Change is the process of altering or modifying something, which sometimes results in a new state. It is also an adult's constant adjustment to the environment, which usually requires learning. As an adult learner or educator, you have probably changed your mind about something, your life or work circumstances shifted, or you experienced upheavals in life and work. Beard (2023) explained, "The term *learning* relates to change, or transformation, in a person, community, or organization, resulting from the acquisition of knowledge, ideas, skills, behaviors, or attitudes derived from experiences" (p. 194, italics in original). People resist and sometimes fear changes even though they cannot always control it. Most people grudgingly accept change, and a typical response is resistance, such as not wanting to relocate when a family member needs to for their work or resentfully adjusting one's lifestyle as a doctor recommends.

Planned change is an anticipated, altered state, such as switching jobs, moving into a new house, or complying with doctor's orders. Whether relocating or changing lifestyle habits, adults must learn as they adjust to a new community, make new friends, start new jobs, or accommodate medically recommended lifestyle changes such as exercising more and eating healthfully. **Unplanned change** is an unforeseen shift, such as an unexpected crisis or swing in the economy, politics, or culture, like the COVID-19 pandemic or a weather catastrophe.

Change might be temporary, transitional, reversible, or permanent. **Temporary change** is an impermanent modification of something. It might mean taking a detour on the way to work due to construction or becoming a caretaker while a family member recovers from an illness or surgery. Temporary caretaking change, for example, requires learning to abide by doctor's orders, helping family members in new ways, and considering how being a caretaker affects one's self-image and perhaps thoughts about how they would handle a similar situation if they were the patient. Transitional change occurs in life and work. As an educator, you might take on a new teaching assignment that gradually evolves into a new focus over time, or it might involve assuming a new role in one's community, child's school, or work. **Reversible change** is a shift that can easily be undone, such as serving in an interim position and then returning to a former station. **Permanent change** is irreversible and unending: A loved one dies, a child leaves home, students graduate, a position ends, colleagues come and go, or a natural disaster changes life irrevocably. Adults must learn to cope and live with these situations.

Finally, **transformational change,** similar to transformative learning, shifts how adults see themselves in the world. The pandemic created conditions for many adults to live and work in new ways, allowing them to consider how well their previous situation aligned with their values and needs. Many adults transformed their relationship with work and sought circumstances, allowing them more autonomy and balance than pre-pandemic. The COVID-19 pandemic offered an important lesson in change because it demonstrated that humanity can drastically shift personal and professional behavior instantly, countering the rhetoric that change requires time and planning. The world went into lockdown and remote work almost overnight, made transformative change, and experienced transformative learning. Change is part of life. Box 9.2 details some global changes that affect people's lives.

 ## Box 9.2 Adult Learning by the Numbers

Adults and Change

Change punctuates adulthood. Here are some statistics on how adulthood has changed over the years. As you read about these changes, consider how they might align with your current experience as an adult learner or educator.

- According to the most recent United States Census Bureau (2024) data, 64% of households were classified as family households in 2024, marking a significant change from 50 years ago when 79% were family households. Relatedly, 29% of households were one-person households in 2024, which increased from 19% in 1974.
- The global population is expected to peak around 10.3 billion in the mid-2080s, up from 8.2 billion in 2024 (United Nations, 2024).
- One in four people globally lives in a country whose population has already peaked in size (United Nations, 2024).
- Women today bear one child fewer on average than they did around 1990, with the global fertility rate at 2.25 live births per woman, down from 3.31 births (United Nations, 2024).
- After the COVID-19 pandemic, global life expectancy is again rising (United Nations, 2024).
- By 2080, people aged 65 or older will outnumber children under 18 (United Nations, 2024).
- People aged 20–29 years old in 2022 reported living with challenges due to several global crises, including COVID-19, climate change, cost of living increases, and economic insecurity. These social, environmental, and cultural factors have resulted in young people needing to live with their parents for financial reasons, feeling concerned about job loss, and not being in either employment or education and training programs (OECD, 2024).
- According to the US Bureau of Labor Statistics (2024), remote work rose dramatically during the COVID-19 pandemic, raising the total factor productivity of remote workers across 61 industries in the private business sector.

Types of Change

The type of change is directly related to the scale of change, which Ackerman (1986) described as developmental, transitional, or transformational. **Developmental change** denotes the learning and growth people experience when acquiring new skills and knowledge, building interpersonal relationships, and undertaking new roles and tasks. When people gradually work toward a goal over time, they are engaged in **transitional change.** Transitional change might involve an adult joining a support group to deal with grief and making small, incremental shifts over time to process their loss and loneliness, or a family that embarks on training a new puppy together and attends obedience training and works with a dog trainer to learn how to provide supportive, affirming corrections and praise on the dog as they grow and develop. Transitional change tends to minimize disruption as the adult or group shifts to a new way of thinking, being, or doing. The grieving widowed person slowly reframes their loss and makes small steps toward building a new life without their spouse. The family adjusts how they behave around the dog to reinforce calmness and desired behaviors from the pet.

A change that creates an extraordinary shift in thinking, being, or doing is **transformational change.** This type of change tends to be irreversible because it alters how adults view themselves in the world. Perhaps you can think of a significant learning experience that changed you as an adult. Once an adult experiences transformational change, they see themselves and the world differently. Bierema (2019) offered adult learning principles, as denoted with implications for learning and change in Table 9.1.

Lewin's 3-Step Change Model

Kurt Lewin, known as "the intellectual father of contemporary theories of applied behavioral science" (Schein, 1988, p. 239), is often credited with originating the field of organization development (OD). However, this assertion contradicts the social, collective ethos of action research (Glassman et al., 2012). Still, Lewin is known for devising tools that facilitate change, such as his three-step change model. Lewin's (1947) model described the change process as requiring three events: (1) unfreezing, (2) moving, and (3) refreezing. As you read about the model, imagine a change you have made as an adult learner and assess how you moved through the phases, as represented in Figure 9.1.

The first step of the model is **unfreezing,** or recognizing a need to change. Unfreezing metaphorically represents thawing or shifting to a new state created by problems, opportunities, crises, new knowledge, or feedback. For example, if a person faces a life-threatening illness, they are often forced to make lifestyle changes. Suddenly, they may have to adjust their diet,

TABLE 9.1 CHARACTERISTICS OF ADULT LEARNERS AND IMPLICATIONS FOR ADULT LEARNING AND CHANGE

Adult Learning Characteristic	Definition	Adult Learning and Change Implications
Adult Learning is Distinguishable from Children's Learning	Adult learning is distinguishable from children's learning in at least three ways: (1) **Reflective capacity**—An adult's ability to hold contrary thoughts and examine them simultaneously; (2) **Experience**—Adults have a rich repertoire of experiences that have taught them lessons and helped them develop values and assumptions about the world; and (3) **Critical thinking**—The ability to recognize and test assumptions, beliefs, and actions, and possibly change mindsets, thoughts, or actions.	Adults are likely to approach challenges and problems in three ways: (1) **Reflective capacity**—Assessing the pros and cons of the decisions they face and their relationships and assumptions. Questioning oneself about a decision might involve asking, *"How open am I to this change?"* or *"What am I afraid of?"* These thoughts are hallmarks of reflection. (2) **Experience**—Adults build knowledge through interactions with others and engagement with projects and challenges. Yet, this same deep knowledge may prevent them from seeing new ways of doing things, leading to a bad or no decision, thus little learning and change. (3) **Critical thinking**—Rethinking values, mindsets, or behaviors related to a change or new learning.
Learning Helps Adults Cope with Change	Change tends to stimulate learning in adulthood, and few changes can be tackled without learning, and few lessons can endure without change. Change is either planned or unplanned. Change potentially creates identity shifts or crises and may compel adults to question who they are, what they want, and whom they can trust. Change can spur introspection about values, goals, and relationships.	Planned change: An adult pursues a graduate degree or credential for career advancement or job change. Unplanned change: A person experiences job change or loss; their family dynamic changes (marriage, birth, divorce, death); they have an unanticipated crisis; or they experience a natural disaster.

Adult Learning Characteristic	Definition	Adult Learning and Change Implications
Adult Learning Is Life-Centered	Adults' motivation to learn is higher when the learning is relevant to their lives or work. The focus of learning is on life-centered issues rather than subject-centered ones. For instance, few adults would sign up for a painting workshop unless they were interested in developing skills as a painter or understanding artists' techniques.	A person recently promoted and newly responsible for supervising a team had no interest in learning how to lead teams until they decided to pursue advancement and received a promotion. Although leadership development was likely available in their organization, the motivation to take advantage of it did not occur until it became clear that they would need this skill to achieve career goals. Adults' learning motivation will be low unless they can relate it to their lives.
Experience Is a Key Learning Asset	The encounters, challenges, relationships, travels, and work of adults provide them with a rich learning resource. Experience can also hinder learning new ways of thinking and being when it is at odds with adults' current knowledge, mindsets, and behaviors.	Life experience is a vast resource for adults to tap for learning and sharing with others. For example, when many adults shifted to remote work during the COVID-19 pandemic, the change allowed them to draw on their work knowledge and employ it in a new, virtual context. Unfortunately, some CEOs dismiss people's pandemic learning in their advocacy or demand that workers return to the office. These insensitive mandates might also indicate that the CEOs' pre-pandemic expectations for how people work have become impediments to relearning how work can be different and often more effective remotely.
Adult Learners Tend to Be Risk-averse	Adults may be hesitant in learning situations, particularly when they feel threatened. Typical reactions include preserving self-esteem and self-efficacy. Adults fear publicly making blunders and appearing inept in front of their peers. When adults are uneasy in learning situations, they will likely clam up and withdraw, which makes meaningful learning more difficult.	Adults tend to play it safe by avoiding risk-taking in learning situations where they feel unsafe or unsure. For example, many learners may have the same question but stay silent.

(Continued)

TABLE 9.1 (*Continued*)

Adult Learning Characteristic	Definition	Adult Learning and Change Implications
Learning Should Be Active and Self-Directed	When adults are involved in conversations, practice, or teaching their peers, they are engaged in active learning. This pedagogical practice has been proven more effective than passive learning activities such as lectures, reading, or demonstrations. When learners actively participate in the learning process, they retain more of the lesson and transfer it to their lives or work environments.	Most adults create self-directed learning projects where they plan, control, adjust, and evaluate their learning themselves. For example, consider an adult who wants to improve their parenting skills. They might seek out books, videos, podcasts, and classes, or observe other parents and solicit their tips. As learners, they have designed and executed their learning plan.
Learning Is Potentially Transformational	Learning changes how one sees oneself in the world, known as transformative learning. The learning does not shift what a person knows; it alters their self-perception. Transformative learning can be gradual or sudden. This type of learning differs from learning where adults build on their existing skills or knowledge. Transformative learning alters how people see themselves in the world. Transformative learning is grounded in change and change-producing learning.	A woman might not be conscious of gendered power relations in society until she realizes her reproductive health choices are diminishing. Suddenly, she begins to observe other women's treatment and how sexist the culture is. She becomes interested in women's health rights and challenging the patriarchal culture. The woman, who was never interested in feminist causes or considered herself a feminist, is now shifting her priorities and identity.

FIGURE 9.1 LEWIN'S 3-STEP CHANGE MODEL

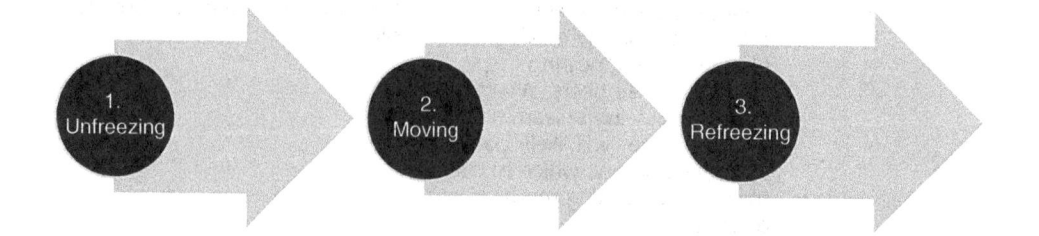

consent to medical testing and procedures causing fatigue and discomfort, or take new drugs to treat the condition that have side effects to manage. They may have to adjust work and family life to cope with the illness. **Moving,** step two, is making a change. The person diagnosed with a threatening illness opts to learn everything they can about the disease and treatment options. They may also undergo personal transformation in how they view their relationships, priorities, and mortality. Moving is when the adult is taking steps to shift their thinking and behavior and measures to sustain the change. Although one might assume moving is the hardest step of the change model, it is step three, refreezing, which requires maintaining the change over the long term. **Refreezing** involves measures to reinforce and uphold the change to ensure it is permanent. Although the person with illness has shifted their outlook and lifestyle, they may also need to ensure they do not put themselves at risk in the future for complications or a relapse. Box 9.3 features a tool Lewin developed to ensure moving and refreezing happen by identifying factors supporting and impinging on change.

Box 9.3 Reflective Practice

Lewin's Field Theory

Lewin (1947) considered the complexity and social context of change and imagined change processes as occurring in a field with competing forces that simultaneously propel and prevent the change. He felt having a clear grasp of the conditions affecting change was crucial. The change "field" is in flux, adapting constantly as some forces support the change and others resist it.

The Force Field Analysis emerged from Lewin's thinking that if a change is to be effective, it is vital to bolster the forces propelling or driving it and to minimize the forces preventing or restraining it. For example, many adults change their diet or exercise routine. Imagine you were striving to eat a more healthy diet. Driving factors might be not buying new clothes, self-image, energy level, lowering cholesterol, or meeting a weight goal. Restraining forces might be pressure from family to eat foods you should not, lack of time to prepare healthy meals, lack of healthy cooking know-how, or desire to eat unhealthy foods.

Consider a change you would like to make personally or one you are trying to make at work as an adult educator or learner. Identify forces driving the change and those resisting the change, as depicted in the following activity.

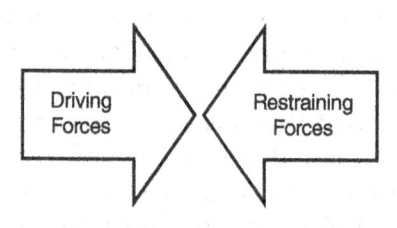

Understanding Adults' Learning and Change Dynamic

Learning and change are deeply intertwined, affecting each other throughout life, especially adulthood. Carl Rogers (1995) declared, "The only person who is educated is the one who has learned how to learn and change" (p. 134). Physicist turned action learning aficionado Reg Revans (2017) explained, "There can be no learning without action, and no action without learning" (p. 53). What these theorists were advocating is the mutuality of learning and change processes. Learning enables adults' capacity for change and adaptability to uncertainty. Change animates adult learning. Together, adult learning and change are iterative, complimentary processes that shape and define adulthood, as symbolized in Figure 9.2.

Herbert Simon (1996) explained, "Learning is any change in a system that produces a more or less permanent change in its capacity for adapting to its environment" (p. 100). Simon's quote captures the dynamism between learning and change processes. Figure 9.2 represents a feedback loop where learning

FIGURE 9.2 THE ADULT LEARNING AND CHANGE FEEDBACK LOOP

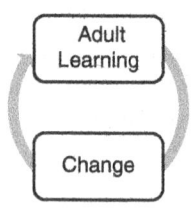

stimulates change, and the resulting change creates new situations that kindle further learning. For example, acquiring leadership skills might lead to a promotion, necessitating learning how to manage larger teams and new priorities. Change can bring about stress, and Box 9.4 highlights the Holmes and Rahe (1967) Stress Scale.

The learning-change dynamic also affects adults emotionally. Change, especially unplanned, can be stressful, although when adults learn to cope with uncertainty and change effectively, they can be remarkably resourceful and resilient during transitions and transformations. On the other hand, change can also adversely affect people's emotional well-being and sense of self-efficacy. When this happens, people resist change, which stymies learning and further change. As Yep (1995) explained, "You can learn to change the world or go on being changed by it" (p. 35). Bateson (1994) likened learning to spiraling, as presented in Chapter 4. A virtuous learning and change spiral is how learners

---

 **Box 9.4 Tips and Tools for Teaching and Learning**

The Holmes and Rahe Stress Management Quiz

As an adult learner or educator, you may feel stress or work with other stressed-out people. To pinpoint key life stressors, you can take the Holmes and Rahe stress management quiz (https://www.stress.org/holmes-rahe-stress-inventory). Many of the stressors are typical changes adults face throughout their lives. Table 9.2 has information to help interpret scores.

TABLE 9.2 HOLMES AND RAHE STRESS MANAGEMENT QUIZ SCORES AND RISK

Score	Chance of Illness or Accident within 2 Years
Below 150	35%
From 150 to 300	51%
More than 300	80%

As you work with this quiz, consider how change affects stress and how learning might be an appropriate de-stressor for adult learners.

move through learning cycles and change, whereby the learning becomes richer with each loop of the spiral. For example, imagine a person working with a coach. They learn they do not listen effectively to their team and attempt to change. They change by practicing new tools to listen more intentionally at work, which inspires further learning about listening and communication and, eventually, a transformation in how the person interacts with others at work and in life.

Learning Enables Capacity to Change and Adaptation to VUCA Contexts

When you learn as an adult, you become equipped with new knowledge, skills, and attitudes that support adapting to new situations and shifting circumstances. Essentially, learning helps you prepare for and make changes. For example, many adults have begun experimenting with generative artificial intelligence (AI) on platforms such as ChatGPT, which helps them keep up with shifting technology and learn how to integrate AI into their lives and work. The learning helps protect their job relevancy as work will likely change as technology advances. Other adults have committed to learning how to be an ally to transgender and nonbinary people by learning their pronouns and how to provide safety and support. Learning also helps adults change their minds when exposed to opportunities to challenge their own assumptions and people with different views, like questioning values passed down by one's family, trying a new process at work and discovering new ways of approaching common issues, or assessing political platforms and shifting identification with political parties or candidates.

When adults are open to exploring new ways of thinking, they free themselves to see the world differently, and through that learning comes the capacity for change. When adult learners encounter new ideas challenging their existing beliefs, they can change through personal and professional growth that accompanies questioning assumptions. Sometimes, this learning can be transformative, leading to profound mindset shifts, like a worker realizing they are not valued in their organization, which changes their attitude toward their workplace and perhaps even chosen vocation. Learning in the face of change can also lead to adults adopting new habits and behaviors. The person who realizes they are not valued might go into more self-advocacy, find a mentor in their current workplace, or leave and seek to self-advocate and find a new workplace where they are valued and belong. It might also cause them to mentor other workers in similar predicaments. Another example would be someone who works with an executive coach who shifts how they listen, delegate, and support their staff or decides to join a social cause. Learning in anticipation of change can also reinforce a person's resiliency in the face of VUCA conditions, as explained in Table 1.1 in Chapter 1.

Change Animates Learning

Management and women's leadership scholar Rosabeth Moss Kanter (1984) observed, "Change demands new learning" (p. 123). Just as the previous section illustrated how learning builds change capacity, change also animates learning in several ways. Change generates opportunities for adult learning. For example, the COVID-19 pandemic shifted how people live and work almost overnight when the globe went into lockdown. People learned to use their time differently and work remotely in many cases. They also had to juggle living under one roof where people lived, learned, and worked. The change also opens new possibilities for learning. For instance, when adults assume a new role in their community or workplace, they have to learn how to show up differently in the new role, navigate new contexts, work with new people, and use different tools than needed previously.

Change can also motivate adult learners to seek new learning and knowledge they previously did not know or care about, such as when people moved to remote working during the pandemic. Suddenly, they needed to learn to navigate virtual meeting platforms as participants and facilitators. Think about a time when your life changed, and you had to seek learning as an adult for which you had no motivation until the change loomed or occurred. It might have been a new job, birth, divorce, death, accomplishment, or other life event that precipitated learning. Change can also demand new learning by adults. An organizational restructuring might require people to work with new teams, learn new personalities and group dynamics, or learn new processes. Change is often disruptive, forcing adults out of their comfort zones. Although discomforting at first, change can also spark creativity and critical thinking. Understanding this symbiotic relationship between learning and change is key in adult education, workplace training, and personal development programs. It highlights the need for adaptable, learner-centered approaches that align with the complexities of adult life.

Understanding the Pace, Planning, and Scale of Change and Applying It to Adult Learners

Most books on adult learning may casually refer to change but not explicitly tie it to learning or consider the reciprocal nature of the processes. The pace, planning (or lack thereof), and scale of change help understand change (Senior & Fleming, 2006), an ongoing process for individuals, teams, organizations, communities, and nations.

The Pace of Change

Change can be sporadic and episodic or continuous. **Discontinuous or episodic change** happens when a change event creates shifts or transformations. Consider periodic events interrupting daily life, like the COVID-19 pandemic, natural disasters, or personal illness or loss. When these sporadic change events occur, learning follows naturally as a coping mechanism, and sometimes, the change is so dramatic that it might change a person's point of view. For instance, many adults realigned their values with different work paces or career paths in the wake of the pandemic. **Continuous change** is the opposite of discontinuous or episodic and occurs through perpetual, perhaps slight, adaptations that result in significant shifts over time. Technology provides a good example here, where the notion of a handheld device that could be used as a telephone, play music, take photos, and provide navigation would have once seemed impossible, yet technological innovation is a constant. The once improbable idea of a smartphone finds today that there are over 7 billion smartphones in the world, and nearly 90% of the world's population owns one (Howarth, 2024). Adults depend on smartphones to retain their schedules and contacts, keep their pets and homes under surveillance, track fitness, watch movies, read the news, pinpoint family members' locations, navigate trips, request dinner reservations, play games, shop, and many other activities. Reliance on virtual, digital, or AI (artificial intelligence) assistants is becoming mainstream. These voice-activated services report the weather, cue requested music, answer questions, and give directions. For people who conduct research, visiting the library and pulling books and other sources from the stacks is no longer necessary. Conducting a library search is easy from the comfort and convenience of one's home computer.

The Planning (or Lack Thereof) of Change

Change can be planned or unplanned. **Planned change** is engaging in an intentional and anticipated transition or transformation organized in advance, such as planning a vacation or relocation. When organizations plan change, it can cause workers stress and worry since it can disrupt workflows, increase uncertainty, and threaten job security. **Unplanned change** is unanticipated, occurring without forewarning or planning. Unexpected change can be gradual based on incremental shifts, such as global warming. It can also be sudden and dramatic, such as Hurricane Helene destroying mountain communities in the North Carolina mountains, where some people moved to escape violent weather due to climate change. Change may also occur due to unpredicted events that force adults and organizations to react to VUCA conditions requiring immediate action and adjustment, such as the COVID-19 pandemic that forced working, learning, and living online overnight.

The Scale of Change

The **scale of change,** or the magnitude of the situation, ranges from moderate disruptive changes, such as adjusting to technology that is constantly innovating, to wide-ranging transformations, such as the push for remote work schedules and increased flexibility by workers in the aftermath of the COVID-19 pandemic. Moderate change is also known as **first-order change,** where business carries on as usual with modifications to a change's intensity, pace, or extent. For example, a leader learns new listening strategies and commits to listening more intently with their colleagues about their key concerns and ideas. Or, upon the urging of a doctor, a person works on eating better and exercising regularly. Moderate or first-order changes are implemented relatively easily and tend to be reversible. The leader may discover their listening adjustments are increasing the length of meetings and modifying where and when they engage in listening with colleagues. The person attempting healthier choices might be in a hurry and make poor dietary choices or opt not to go to the gym. The leader might also regress to former lousy listening habits. Because of the nature of first-order change, it is not always lasting or effective, as it is easy to regress to former ways of doing things.

Transformative change is a radical alteration that permanently refashions ways of thinking, being, and doing, which makes reverting to old ways impossible. The COVID-19 global pandemic necessitated adjustments in every aspect of human life, generating new challenges that forced change and adaptation on individual, organization, community, and national levels. Transformative change is a **second-order change** that compels new learning and thinking by adults, often transformative learning. This type of change is also known as **adaptive,** "the practice of mobilizing people to tackle tough challenges and thrive" (Heifetz et al., 2009, p. 14). Returning to the leader listening example, perhaps they decide to fundamentally restructure how they communicate, shifting not only the frequency but also the content and delivery mode through using technology and more dialogical ways of interacting and listening that significantly improve their relationships and team functioning, or the person seeking to live more healthfully commits to learning how to prepare healthy meals and signs up for a virtual class, and they find a workout partner.

Adult Learning and Change and Systems Theory

Although many adults eschew change, they are engaged in it constantly and capable of navigating change processes. General systems theory provides a theoretical and practical grounding to understand change, as introduced by Ludwig von Bertalanffy (1950, 1968) during the 20th century and applied to organizations. Systems theory presumes that social entities are intricately interconnected and independent structures such as families, schools, organizations, communities, or nations. Each entity is composed of stakeholders who have varying and sometimes competing interests.

Essentially, any shift within the system alters other parts of the system. Von Bertalanffy (1950, 1968) explained how systems behave in ways to guarantee survival, where their assorted subsystems impact each other and influence the system's ability to achieve its intended purpose. Figure 9.3 illustrates five properties of systems per Von Bertalanffy: (1) **Semipermeable boundaries,** the first system principle, are fluid edges that filter inputs and outputs to the system (e.g., physical, time, and social borders). Consider how this might work for you as an adult learner. For example, imagine you are in a graduate program in adult education and recognized as a student, representing one type of social boundary. A time boundary might be the hours the university is open, class times, or the start and finish of the semester. (2) **Inputs** are the external raw materials and resources that allow the production of outputs in the form of

FIGURE 9.3 SYSTEM PROPERTIES

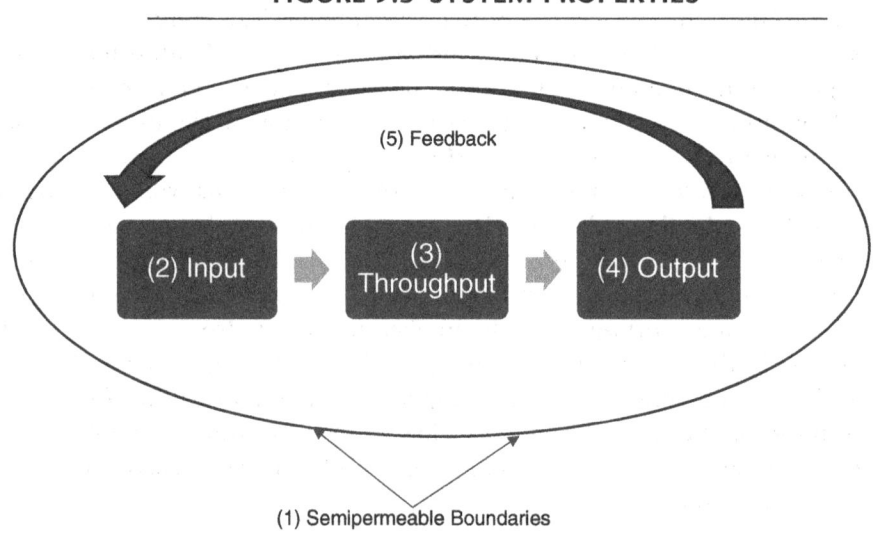

the system's goods and services. Inputs as a graduate student might include coursework, collaboration with other students and faculty, conferences, and the overall context of the academic program and university shaping the system. (3) **Throughputs** involve transforming inputs into goods and services (outputs). Throughput might be your reflection and learning as a student. (4) **Outputs** typically are the goods and services produced by the organization and desired by the community. Regarding graduate education, goods and services are employable skills and capacities to impact one's family, community, and work. (5) **Feedback loops** within the system provide data to the organization indicating how effectively the system functions to meet its purpose. For you as an adult learner, they might be in the form of grades, comments on a paper, or a diploma. Figure 9.3 illustrates the principles of systems, and Box 9.5 provides an opportunity to explore membership in various social systems.

 **Box 9.5 Reflective Practice**

Pinpoint Your Systems

As an adult learner or educator, think of systems you belong to, for instance, a family, social group, school, community, church, workplace, or digital community, and see if you can identify the five elements:

1. Semipermeable boundaries
2. Inputs
3. Throughputs
4. Outputs
5. Feedback loops

For example, consider a professional association like the American Association for Adult and Continuing Education—AAACE. All AAACE members are **bound** by their work in the field and participation in annual meetings and other events such as webinars, committees, or special interest group meetings occurring throughout the year. Association members' **boundaries are semipermeable** as the members interact as members of other systems, including their organizations, networks, or other professional associations like the Academy of Human Resource

Development—AHRD. Still, the boundary for this group is AAACE. **Inputs** to the professional association would be the research, practices, and developmental relationships shared among AAACE members. **Throughputs** might be the knowledge, meanings, and collaborations between members in AAACE events. **Outputs** might be how members learn about the field and collaborate to develop articles, chapters, presentations, and other scholarly and professional products. The **feedback loops** would transfer into future conferences, meetings, and collaborations created among the AAACE members.

Think about other systems you belong to and see if you can identify the five elements of systems.

Coping with Change in Adulthood

Change in adulthood is diverse and may entail cultural change, work disruption, political struggles, a global pandemic, natural disaster, and a host of planned and unplanned changes. When change occurs at any level (e.g., community, organization, individual), it can be planned or unplanned and evoke various responses. Sometimes, the trust of people leading the change is affected negatively or positively, depending on how they implement it. Implementing change with little stakeholder input, minimal communication, or inept leadership heightens resistance. Difficulty in making change is also likely when change implementors dismiss the human side of change, people's emotional reactions, or the necessity of learning. The strength of relationships and trust levels also influence willingness to change throughout the process. Change is often done hurriedly, with inadequate planning and communication, increasing its risk of being done poorly or failing. When people disregard change as a learning process, they are unlikely to see the desired change occur. What can you do as an adult learner or educator to lessen the stress and sting of change? The following sections outline tips for approaching change with a healthy perspective and constructive actions.

Community and Organization Strategies for Coping with Change

If you are a community leader implementing change, clearly explain the anticipated change. For example, one of the authors (Laura) recently participated in a pilot curbside composting program offered by the local government where she lives. The community introduced the program with a full explanation and call for volunteers. The pilot leaders regularly communicated with a weekly newsletter and email reminders about composting and placing your bin in the pickup area, which both informed and educated participants about the change. The community evaluated the composting pilot with regular opportunities to give input. Once the program ended, the pilot leaders shared the results of a survey they conducted among pilot participants. Overall, it was a good experience, and if the community adopts the program more broadly, it will have a cadre of people already supporting it who participated in the pilot. What made this change work was the change leaders communicated regularly and provided multiple opportunities for participants to share input and suggestions. The leaders invited people from various neighborhoods representing diversity in housing, income, education, and race to understand how the change affected multiple stakeholders. They took time to involve the community, answer questions, communicate how the pilot was going, and problem-solve. They also invited critiques and listened to problems people encountered using the program. For example, the community provided large, cumbersome bins that were heavy and difficult to handle and admitted they did not work, even though the program was overall successful. When the program ended, the change leaders thanked the participants and recognized the waste management employees involved in the effort. In this case, the pilot leaders did several things right, including sharing ongoing communication, seeking diverse stakeholders to participate, listening and responding to feedback, and recognizing and thanking people for participating. These are essential tips for leading a community or organization-level change.

Leaders' Strategies for Coping with Change

As a change leader, there are several things you can do to help implement effective change with the teams and groups you are working with. Communication is of utmost importance, and making yourself available to regularly discuss the change and encourage people to share their feelings and reactions to the change can address fears and worries early in the process. You can leverage change initiatives to build trusting relationships with people affected by the change by inviting their input and involvement and showing appreciation. Listening to people's concerns about the change and helping them feel safe during times of uncertainty is also important. Ensuring people are engaged and invited to collaborate and problem-solve during the change process also helps improve buy-in and support of the change and makes it more sustainable in the long term. Thanking people for their work on the change is a crucial way of showing you are aware of and appreciative of their efforts to support the initiative. For example, leaders, like New Zealand's Prime Minister Jacinda Ardern's leadership during the COVID-19 pandemic, modeled these leader coping strategies. She was particularly effective at inspiring citizens to prepare for and accept the lockdowns brought on by the crisis. Her communication was straightforward, honest, and compassionate, sometimes on video with her in her sweats at home, talking to her country about her concerns and experiences and encouraging them to stay safe and care for their loved ones. Her parting words became a national mantra: "Please be strong, be kind, and unite against COVID-19" (Kerrissey & Edmondson, 2020, para. 10).

Group and Team Strategies for Coping with Change

As an adult learner or educator, you likely belong to groups or teams in your community, work, or personal relationships that have experienced change. Groups and teams can lean on each other during uncertain, difficult times to provide support, determine what they can control, and act on it as appropriate. Communication is essential among groups affected by change, and opening dialogue to talk about feelings, worries, assumptions, expectations, and hopes is an important coping mechanism. Regular communication is always a good strategy, especially during change. Not only can the group or team use their conversations to make meaning about the situation, but also to learn from each other about how to better navigate the change or challenge. During the COVID-19 pandemic, Zoom meetups became a way for people to stay connected with groups in their personal, work, and community lives, which became a form of support, problem-solving, and collegiality.

Individual Strategies for Coping with Change

Few people claim to love change, especially since most adults abhor and resist it. Yet, change is a perpetual in life and work. Adults can try to anticipate and plan for its emotional, professional, and financial consequences to lessen the sting of change. **Environmental scanning** or studying your context as an adult learner or educator to understand what is happening can help you anticipate changes on the horizon. Embracing a growth mindset is also a strategy by viewing change as a learning opportunity rather than something to be avoided, feared, or resisted. You can ask yourself, "*What scares me about this change?*"

or *"What might be good about this change?"* Be mindful that the *only* thing you control during change is yourself. Approaching change with a growth mindset presents opportunities to challenge assumptions, try new things, and learn. Partaking in self and community care also helps keep you from becoming overwhelmed by the change. Making time for play, rest, and non-work-related happenings is necessary.

Chapter Summary

Chapter 9, "Connecting Learning and Change in Adulthood," explored the interconnection between adult learning and change, emphasizing how these processes mutually influence and drive one another throughout adulthood. Change is constant in adulthood in every aspect of life, often necessitating learning. The chapter introduced organizational change theory and types and levels of change. It framed learning as a tool to cope with and adapt to change, stimulating further learning. Discussions of adult learning imply change, although the absence of it as a theoretical construct in adult education literature is odd. For example, the 2020 edition of the *Handbook of Adult and Continuing Education* (Rocco et al., 2020) contains only two index entries on change related to assessment and management. As authors, we believe the neglect of change and its relationship to learning is problematic, hence our decision to add a chapter on the topic in this edition of the book. We hope to inspire more discussion of this reciprocal relationship between adult learning and change in both theory and practice.

Key Points

1. Change can be planned (e.g., career development) or unplanned (e.g., crises like the COVID-19 pandemic).
2. Types of change include developmental (skills acquisition), transitional (small, gradual shifts), and transformational (irreversible changes in worldview or behavior).
3. Kurt Lewin's 3-Step Change Model (unfreezing, moving, refreezing) and Force Field Analysis highlight the importance of understanding and managing forces that drive or resist change.
4. Systems theory explains how changes within one part of a social system affect the entire structure, requiring adaptive learning and feedback loops to maintain system efficacy.

5. Change evokes varying emotional and professional responses. Effective coping strategies include: clear communication and stakeholder involvement, embracing a growth mindset to view change as a learning opportunity, and employing support structures at individual, team, and community levels.

References

Ackerman, L. S. (1986). Change management: Basics for training. *Training & Development Journal, 40*(4), 67–68.

Bateson, M. C. (1994). *Peripheral visions: Learning along the way.* HarperCollins

Beard, C. (2023). Experiential learning. In A. Belzer, & B. Dashew (Eds.), *Understanding the adult learner: Perspectives and practices,* pp. 193–211. Taylor & Francis Group.

Bierema, L. L. (2019). Adult learning theories and practices. In M. Fedeli, & L. L. Bierema (Eds.), *Connecting adult learning and knowledge management: Strategies for learning and change in higher education and organizations* (pp. 3–26). Springer.

Frankl, V. E. (1959). *Man's search for meaning.* London: Hodder & Stoughton.

Glassman, M., Erdem, G., & Barthomolew, M. (2012). Action research and its history as an adult education movement for social change. *Adult Education Quarterly, 63*(3), 272–288. https://doi.org/10.1177/0741713612471418.

Heifetz, R. A., Heifetz, R., Grashow, A., & Linsky, M. (2009). *The practice of adaptive leadership: Tools and tactics for changing your organization and the world.* Harvard Business Press.

Holmes, T. H., & Rahe, R. H. (1967). The social readjustment rating scale. *Journal of Psychosomatic Research 1*(2), 213–218. https://psycnet.apa.org/doi/10.1016/0022-3999(67)90010-4.

Howarth, J. (2024, June 13). *How many people own smartphones? (2024–2029).* Exploding Topics. https://explodingtopics.com/blog/smartphone-stats#smartphone-top-picks.

Kerrissey, M. J., & Edmondson, A. (2020, April 13). *What good leadership looks like during this pandemic.* Harvard Business Review. https://hbr.org/2020/04/what-good-leadership-looks-like-during-this-pandemic.

Lewin, K. (1947). Frontiers in group dynamics: Concept, method and reality in social science; social equilibria and social change. *Human Relations, 1*(1), 5–41. https://doi.org/10.1177/001872674700100103.

Moss Kanter, R. (1984). *Change masters.* Simon and Schuster.

OECD. (2024, June 20). *Society at a glance 2024: OECD social indicators.* OECD. https://www.oecd.org/en/publications/society-at-a-glance-2024_918d8db3-en.html US Bureau.

Revans, R. (2017). *ABC of action earning.* Routledge.

Rocco, T. S., Smith, M. C., Mizzi, R. C., Merriweather, L. R., & Hawley, J. D. (Eds.). (2020). *The handbook of adult and continuing education.* Taylor & Francis.

Rogers, C. (1995). *A way of being.* Houghton Mifflin Harcourt.

Schein, E. H. (1988). *Organizational psychology* (3rd ed.). Prentice Hall.

Senior, B., & Fleming, J. (2006). *Organizational change.* Pearson Education.

Simon, H. (1996). *The sciences of the artificial* (3rd ed.). The MIT Press.

United Nations. (2024). *World Population Prospects 2024: Summary of Results* (UN DESA/POP/2024/TR/NO. 9). https://www.un.org/development/desa/pd/.

United States Bureau of Labor Statistics. (2024, October). *The rise in remote work since the pandemic and its impact on productivity.* United States Bureau of Labor Statistics. https://www.bls.gov/opub/btn/volume-13/remote-work-productivity.htm.

United States Census Bureau. (2024, November 12). *Nearly two-thirds of US households are family households.* United States Census Bureau. https://www.census.gov/newsroom/press-releases/2024/families-and-living-arrangements.html.

Von Bertalanffy, L. (1950). An outline of general system theory. *British Journal for the Philosophy of Science, 1,* 134–165. https://doi.org/10.1093/bjps/I.2.134.

Von Bertalanffy, L. (1968). *General system theory: Foundations, development, applications.* George Braziller.

Yep, L. (1995). *Dragon's gate.* Harpertrophy.

CHAPTER TEN

EXPERIENCING LEARNING IN ADULTHOOD

 **Box 10.1 Chapter Overview and Learning Objectives**

Author Minna Thomas Antrim (1902) wrote, "Experience is a good teacher, but she sends in terrific bills" (p. 99), capturing the truth that learning happens in experience, which can be challenging, unsettling, life-changing, and costly.

The purpose of Chapter 10 is to explore learning and experience in adulthood and how adults learn both within and from life situations. The chapter begins by discussing experience and learning and their mutually reinforcing nature, including profiles of learning experiences according to Dewey and Lindeman's perspectives. Then, linkages are made between experience and learning in adult learning theories and practices of andragogy, self-directed learning, and transformative learning. The second part of the chapter shifts to models of experiential learning, beginning with Kolb, followed by four models created by adult educators. Finally, the chapter introduces theories of reflective practice, action inquiry, situated cognition, and communities of practice according to their contributions to understanding the connection between experience and learning.

As a result of reading this chapter and completing the exercises, you, the reader, should be able to:

1. Recognize how characteristics of adult learners have implications for how they learn from and within experience.
2. Relate adult learning theories to life experience.
3. Explore models of experiential learning.
4. Examine theories of reflective practice, action inquiry, situated cognition, and communities of practice.
5. Apply your learning.

Adulthood plays out in a cyclical pattern, where learning leads to new experiences, and life experiences themselves become sources of learning. Imagine becoming a new parent. This life experience is difficult to comprehend until the child arrives, other than most expectant parents are prepared to love and care for their child. Suddenly, the new parent is responsible for the health and welfare of this tiny being. Parenting requires new learning about nutrition, sleep schedules, self-care, interacting, childcare, schooling, and being a positive role model. The new parent has engaged in **experiential learning,** defined by Beard and Wilson (2018) as:

> A sense-making process involving significant experiences that, to varying degrees, act as the source of learning for individuals, groups, and organizations. These experiences actively immerse and reflectively engage the inner world of learner(s) as whole beings (including physical-bodily, intellectually, emotionally, psychologically, and spiritually) with the intricate outer world of the learning environment, in places and spaces, within the social, cultural, and political milieu to create memorable, rich, and effective experiences for, and of learning. (p. 3)

The dynamic of experience and learning punctuates adulthood as adults engage in a continual flow of activities in daily life's private, public, and professional spheres. The heart of adult learning involves engaging in, reflecting upon, and making meaning of one's experiences, whether these experiences are primarily physical, emotional, cognitive, social, or spiritual. Prevailing understanding of adult learning includes the foundational work in andragogy, self-directed learning, and transformative learning. The life experiences and learning adults encounter serve as resources for lifelong learning. Much like the relationship between adult learning and change, experience and learning share a synergetic, mutual relationship. Box 10.2 identifies experiential learning practices.

 **Box 10.2 Tips and Tools for Teaching and Learning**

Best Practices for Facilitating Experiential Learning

Roberts and Welton (2022) and Mintz (2021) outlined key strategies for facilitating meaningful and impactful experiential learning:

1. **Frame learning experiences** by explaining the activity's purpose and context where appropriate.
2. **Consider alternatives to traditional class formats** such as off-campus learning (e.g., museums, performance venues, or businesses), studio courses, workshopping, clinical courses, or lab courses.
3. **Create solver communities** where learners analyze and debate wicked problems such as climate change, human rights abuses, inequities, migration, poverty, substance abuse, or other challenges.
4. **Create maker spaces**—collaborative workspaces where people can create, invent, and explore new ideas, share resources, and learn.
5. **Design for learner agency or choice** in topic selection and projects to promote ownership and empowerment in the learning environment.
6. **Align experiences with learning outcomes.** Consider what experiences resonate with the course purpose and learning objectives. For example, if you teach students instructional design, ensure they can go through the instructional design process with a topic of interest.
7. **Foster reflection** throughout the learning experience using multiple modalities such as written, visual narrative, interpersonal, and interpersonal reflection.
8. **Design for the relevance of application and meaning-making** by incorporating real-world experiences and applications of learning through projects, teamwork, and communication.
9. **Acknowledge the uncertainty and ambiguity** embedded in the learning process.
10. **Learn alongside your adult learners,** embodying the "guide on the side" ethos.
11. **Take a holistic approach** through group projects, community-based activities, or internships.
12. **Be flexible and value the role of serendipity in learning.** Giving up control and rigidly planned learning experiences opens up possibilities for new learning and ideas.

On the Relationship Between Experience and Learning

Philosophers as early as Aristotle contemplated the role of experience in learning. Aristotle sought to test all knowledge or theory in the real world of everyday experience: "Hence we ought to examine what has been said by applying it to what we do, and how we live; and if it harmonizes with what we do, we should accept it, but if it conflicts, we should count it [mere] words. (Aristotle NE:1179a20)" (cited in Dyke, 2009, p. 303). Still, the philosopher and educator John Dewey and his book *Experience and Education*, first published in 1938, proved to be the most influential on contemporary understanding of the role of experience in learning. Dewey (1963) viewed learning as a lifelong process of applying and adapting previous experience to new situations: "What [one] has learned in the way of knowledge and skill in one situation becomes an instrument of understanding and dealing effectively with the situations which follow. The process goes on as long as life and learning continue" (p. 44). Dewey called this the principle of **continuity,** in which what one is learning in the present is connected to past experiences and has potential future applications. For example, imagine you are an adult who enjoys gardening and have relocated from a northern to a southern climate. Learning what plants thrive in the new climate requires new learning, but simultaneously, you link this new learning to your gardening experiences in the previous setting. Of course, this new learning evolves with creative future applications.

Interestingly, Dewey (1963) recognized that not all experiences are "genuinely or equally educative" (p. 25). Some experiences can be "mis-educative" in that they have "the effect of arresting or distorting the growth of further experience" (Dewey, 1963, p. 25). Dewey explained: "An experience may be such as to engender callousness; it may produce lack of sensitivity and of responsiveness. Then the possibilities of having richer experience in the future are restricted" (pp. 25–26). He continued, "Wholly independent of desire or intent, every experience lives on in further experiences. Hence the central problem of an education based upon experience is to select the kind of present experiences that live fruitfully and creatively in subsequent experiences" (pp. 27–28). Mis-educative experiences can occur in real life or in the classroom. For example, a person who gets fired from their job and feels consumed with bitterness and anger will unlikely learn from the experience. In classrooms, activities such as simulations or teacher critiques might be so devastating as to inhibit future learning.

As adult educators, the role of experience in learning is also central to our understanding of *adult* learning. Lindeman (1961), an early adult educator and a contemporary of Dewey, famously wrote that "the whole of life is learning" and "the resource of highest value in adult education is the learner's experience"

 **Box 10.3 Tips and Tools for Teaching and Learning**

Paired Teaching and Learning

As an adult learner or educator, try this assignment to help adult learners experience shared teaching and learning. Invite adult learners to document their learning through a reflective paper, oral presentation, or multimedia event detailing the experience and what they learned. Steps:

1. Learners pair off and take turns teaching each other something they want to share.
2. Learners can teach a concept or skill they have mastered, such as how to play the guitar, cook an ethnic dish, operate a computer program, drive a motorcycle, appreciate opera, employ APA referencing style, and so on.
3. Plan the teaching and learning segments over at least two learning sessions so learners can reflect on the first session to improve instruction and learning in the second session.
4. Set up the learning event as a cognitive apprenticeship wherein the teacher verbalizes the cognitive process while simultaneously demonstrating the learning.
5. As the sessions proceed, the learner becomes more competent, thus reducing the need for "scaffolding" from the instructor.

(p. 6). He continued, "Experience is the adult learner's living textbook" (p. 7). Another feature of experience and learning is that most of your learning in adulthood occurs informally and incidentally as you go about your life, as you mostly learn outside formal educational settings. For example, getting lost and finding your path to your destination. Incidental learning—new knowledge as a byproduct of something else—also occurs when you are lost. You discover a new restaurant you want to try while navigating unknown streets. Box 10.3 offers an experiential teaching and learning strategy.

Andragogy and Experiential Learning

Knowles' (1980) formulation of andragogy (discussed in Chapter 7) centered on experience. A protégé of Lindeman, Knowles highlighted experience as one of andragogy's major assumptions in that an adult accumulates a growing reservoir of experience, a rich resource for learning (Knowles, 1980). As people age, they accumulate various life experiences to draw on in a learning situation. These experiences also stimulate the need for learning. For example, as a person learns to cook, their expanding knowledge fuels learning new recipes and cooking techniques. Thus, as adults, we not only connect with our past experiences to foster new learning, but our ongoing experiences also often require new learning. Experience is thus a resource and a stimulus for learning. However, Knowles acknowledged that an adult's prior experiences can also obstruct new learning: "But the fact of greater experience also has some potentially negative effects. As we accumulate experience, we tend to develop mental habits, biases, and presuppositions that tend to cause us to close our minds to new ideas, fresh perceptions, and alternative ways of thinking" (Knowles et al., 2011, p. 65). For instance, resistance to change is fueled by notions of how things were done in the past, obstructing new learning about the change.

In an interesting linking of andragogy and experiential learning, O'Bannon and McFadden (2008) proposed a model of **"experiential andragogy"** for use with nontraditional adult experiential education programs (e.g., service-oriented programs, educational travel, outdoor adventure-based programs). Their model has six stages: motivation, orientation, involvement, activity, reflection, and adaptation. "A learner must be intrinsically motivated to participate and learn, become actively engaged in the experience, reflect individually or in a group, and "consider how they will apply what they have learned to future experiences" (O'Bannon & McFadden, 2008, p. 27). In their model, "it is the process, the interaction between stages, which makes learning possible" (O'Bannon & McFadden, 2008, p. 25). King (2017) advocated the key characteristics of andragogy are suited to adults learning how to cope with the digital age. Bowling and Hensche (2021) concluded that andragogy is an unfinished theory with growth potential, particularly in online and non-formal education.

Self-directed and Experiential Learning

Experience is also significant in two other conceptualizations of adult learning—self-directed learning and transformative learning. Self-directed learning is about taking control of your own learning as an adult (see Chapter 4), where you determine what you wish to learn, how you go about it, and assess whether it was effective. For example, rising gas prices and concerns about climate change have motivated many people to become more conservation-minded and fuel-efficient. Many have researched and purchased hybrid or electric vehicles. This learning might involve investigating fuel-efficient or electric cars or adopting driving strategies and other practices that reduce fuel consumption, such as car-pooling, public transportation, driving a scooter, or riding a bicycle whenever possible.

Transformative and Experiential Learning

Additionally, transformative learning (see Chapter 11) is embedded in life experience. The process begins with an experience causing adults to question their assumptions about how the world works or how life is. Often, there is a disjuncture between an adult's experience and how they understand it. Dewey noted that learning initiates when previous experience fails to explain a present situation. Dewey:

> regarded non-reflective experience based on habits as a dominant form of experience. The reflective experience, mediated by intelligence and knowledge, grows out from the inadequacy and contradictions of the habitual experience and ways of action. For Dewey, the basis of, and reason for reflection was the necessity of solving problems faced in habitual ways of action. (Miettinen, 2000, p. 61)

Recall, as an adult learner or educator, how your previous beliefs, attitudes, or habits failed to accommodate a present experience. When that occurred, you likely found new ways of thinking about and dealing with the problem. Transformative learning occurs when, as adults, the way we understand an experience changes; that is, our meaning-making process has become more accommodating of our real-world experience. Returning to the fuel efficiency example, Rodríguez Aboytes and Barth (2020) conducted a systemic literature review to understand how transformative learning transpires in sustainable development education and how it might support experiential learning. Given the rising concern about climate change, the current environmental context provides a rich experiential learning ground about sustainability. They concluded that the sustainability context provides an empirical grounding to understand social learning, the role of experience, and the development of sustainability competencies as part of transformative learning.

Models of Experiential Learning

Several writers have mapped out the relationship between life experience and learning. The section begins with Kolb's experiential learning cycle, which has influenced several subsequent models. Next, four models developed by adult educators will be briefly presented, including Jarvis's types of learning model, Tennant and Pogson's four levels of experiential learning, Fenwick's five perspectives on experiential learning, and finally, Beard and Wilson's ecological and holistic learning. It is important to note that these writers use the term "experiential learning," meaning various conceptualizations of the relationship between experience and learning. Experiential learning also refers to using specific instructional strategies and programs familiar to adult educators designed to make learning as authentic and real-life as possible. Finally, "experiential learning" also refers to an adult's previous life experiences that can be reflected upon and documented for academic credit (see the National Society for Experiential Education, www.nsee.org, and the Council for Adult and Experiential Learning, www.cael.org). Our focus in this chapter is on understanding the reciprocal relationship between learning and life experiences as adults.

Kolb's Experiential Learning Cycle

A good place to begin a discussion of Kolb's Learning Cycle, now called the Kolb Experiential Learning Profile (KELP), is his definition of learning. "Learning," Kolb (1984) wrote, "is the process whereby knowledge is created through the transformation of experience" (p. 38). Experience is at the heart of his understanding of learning. Kolb (1984) offered six propositions defining experiential learning in his book *Experiential Learning: Experience as the Source of Learning and Development*:

1. Learning is best conceived as a process, not in terms of outcomes.
2. All learning is relearning.
3. Learning requires the resolution of conflicts between dialectically opposed models of adaptation to the world.
4. Learning is a holistic process of adaptation to the world.
5. Learning results from synergistic transactions between the person and the environment.
6. Learning is the process of creating knowledge. (Kolb et al., 2014, p. 212)

Kolb's learning model consists of four learning stages of: concrete experience, reflective observation, abstract conceptualization, and active experimentation. See Figure 10.1.

According to Kolb (1984), learners can engage each aspect of the model:

Learners, if they are to be effective, need four different kinds of abilities—*concrete experience abilities* (CE), *reflective observation abilities* (RO), *abstract conceptualizing abilities* (AC) and *active experimentation abilities* (AE). That is, they must be able to involve themselves fully, openly and without

FIGURE 10.1 KOLB'S EXPERIENTIAL LEARNING CYCLE

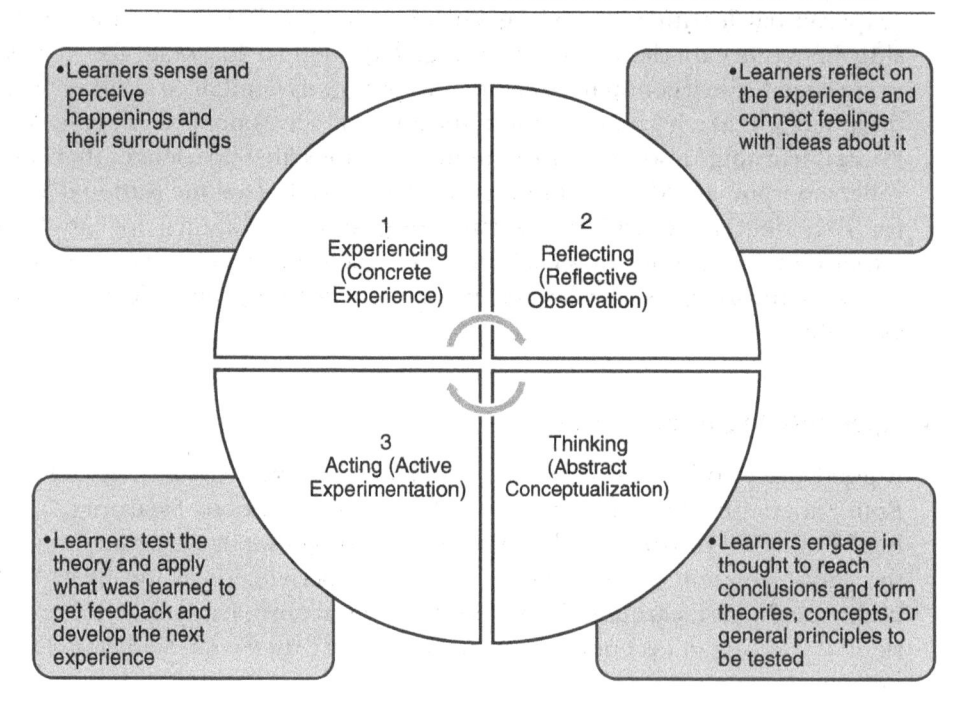

bias in new experiences (CE). They must be able to reflect on and observe their experiences from many perspectives (RO). They must be able to create concepts that integrate their observations into logically sound theories (AC) and they must be able to use these theories to make decisions and solve problems (AE). (p. 30)

For example, having a *concrete experience* means you, as an adult learner, need to tune into the senses of touch, sound, sight, and smell. For *reflective observation,* you need to consider your thoughts and actions. For *abstract conceptualization,* you can question assumptions. Finally, for *active experimentation,* you can ask questions of genuine curiosity of others.

Applications of Kolb's Model. The Kolb Learning Cycle has been used to help medical students prepare for their transition to practice by structuring seminars according to the cycle of concrete experience, reflective observation, abstract conceptualization, and active experimentation (Wijnen-Meijer et al., 2022).

Additionally, it has been applied in occupational therapy education, incorporating peer-assisted learning and combining clinical placement, labs, didactic presentations, simulation exercises, and reflection sessions (Barker et al., 2016). Williams (2023) noted the rise of **high-impact practices** (HIPs) (Kuh, 2008), which are educational experiences that immerse undergraduate university students in situations and contexts that prepare them for future careers and "help them make meaning of the world around them with the guidance of educational experts" (para. 3). HIPs include nontraditional classroom experiences like first-year seminars, learning communities, writing-intensive courses, service learning, undergraduate research, capstone experiences, internships, study abroad, and other immersive experiences.

Kolb Learning Cycle Instruments. To determine your preferred learning style as an adult learner or educator, Kolb has also developed an instrument, the Kolb Experiential Learning Profile (KELP). This instrument will help you identify your preferred learning modes and style. You can learn how to take the KELP in Box 10.4.

 ## Box 10.4 Tips and Tools for Teaching and Learning

Applying Kolb's Cycle to Learning

As an adult learner or educator, try these exercises to learn more about the Kolb Cycle:

1. Go to The Institute for Experiential Learning website and take the Kolb Experiential Learning Profile (KELP). Note there is a nominal fee: https://experientiallearninginstitute.org/the-kolb-experiential-learning-profile-kelp/
2. Next, trace a recent learning episode from the initiation to the completion of the learning. To what extent does your learning cycle reflect Kolb's cycle? How would you "adjust" Kolb's cycle to better accommodate your learning in Figure 10.2?
3. Review the experiential learning case studies at this link: https://experientiallearninginstitute.org/wp-content/uploads/2023/10/Individual-Benefits-Case-Studies-9.20.23.pdf

FIGURE 10.2 KOLB'S LEARNING CYCLE

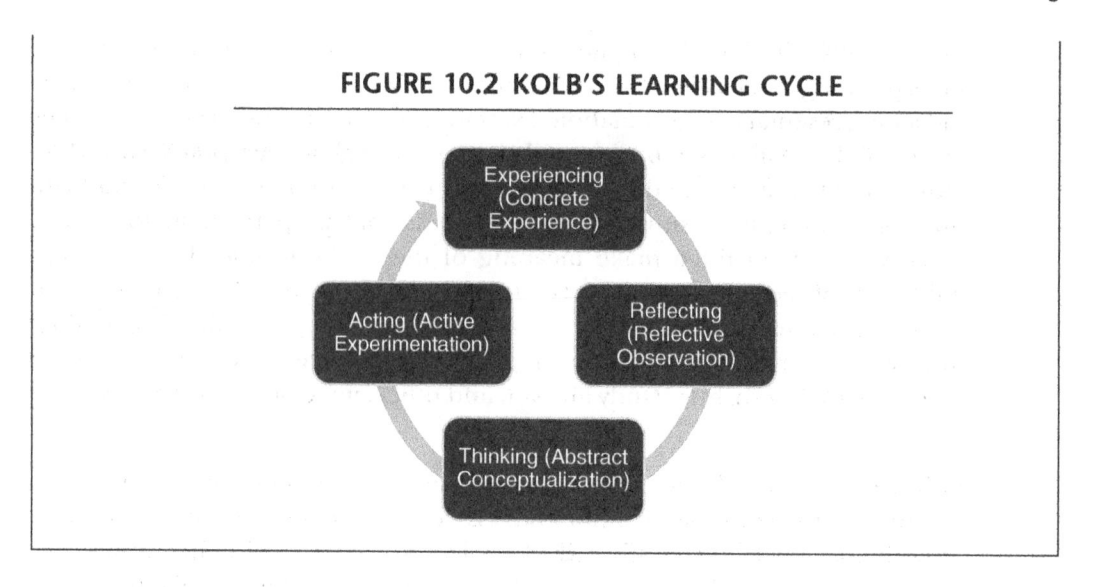

Critiques of Kolb's Model. Kolb's theory and KELP are not without their critics. The theory is context-free; that is, experience and reflection on that experience seem to occur in a vacuum unimpeded by power dynamics in any social context. One wonders, for example, how reflecting on experience and experimenting in a totalitarian regime might work out. Others suggest that some learners may not move through the process, as Kolb suggested. Instead, the model might "be viewed as a sparking chamber in which the learner makes contact with each point, but not in any specified mechanical order" (Dyke, 2006, p. 121). Still, others noted that novice facilitators are likely to teach using their own preferred style rather than teaching to relate to all styles. Finally, Bergsteiner et al. (2010), commenting that "issues of reliability and validity persist with the LSI," critiqued Kolb's model and LSI from a modeling perspective (p. 31).

Kolb's experiential learning model has been criticized for being eclectic, lacking sound theoretical and empirical foundations, and ignoring context (Coffield et al., 2004; Fenwick, 2003; Miettinen, 2000). Beard (2023) summarized the critiques as (1) being overly focused on cognition at the expense of other modes of experiencing such as semantically, emotionally, socially, and culturally; (2) viewing the learner as isolated in their work and sense-making; and (3) failing to recognize other modes of experiencing beyond the model. Morris (2019) responded to critiques that the Kolb model lacked clarity with a systematic literature review to examine "What constitutes a concrete experience and what is the nature of treatment of a concrete experience and experiential learning?" (p. 1064). They found five themes: (1) learners are involved, active participants; (2) knowledge is situated in place and time; (3) learners are exposed to novel experiences, which involve risk; (4) learning demands inquiry into specific real-world problems; and (5) critical reflection acts as a mediator of meaningful learning. Morris (2019) recommended revising the model labels to note that concrete experience should be contextually rich, reflective observation should be critical, abstract conceptualization should be context-specific, and active experimentation should be pragmatic.

The Kolb Educator Role Profile

Kolb et al. (2014) offered a model for matching educator roles, learner style, and subject matter when designing and facilitating educational programs known as the Kolb Educator Role Profile (KERP). Box 10.5 has information on taking the Kolb Educator Role Profile.

 ## Box 10.5 Tips and Tools for Teaching and Learning

Kolb Educator Role Profile (KERP)

Access the instrument at this link: https://experientiallearninginstitute.org/product/kolb-educator-role-profile-kerp/ for a nominal fee. There are also courses for a deeper exploration of the tool. The tool identifies roles educators use:

1. **Facilitator:** The adage "guide on the side" fits with this role, where the educator builds trusting relationship with learners and helps them reflect on and learn from personal experiences. Facilitators create open and welcoming learning environments that motivate learners through facilitating small discussions, supporting learner interests, and encouraging self-insight.
2. **Expert:** This role establishes the educator as subject matter authority. Expert educators help learners connect their experiences and insights with broader subject knowledge. Their approach tends to be authoritative and reflective, role modeling by encouraging critical thinking and analysis of the subject matter. Instructional strategies include lecture, textbook reading, and helping learners organize their thinking.
3. **Evaluator:** This role assumes an objective, results-oriented stance, helping learners master whatever they are learning against performance requirements. Evaluators outline requisite knowledge for quality performance and build their instructional design around assisting learners to understand it.

4. **Coach:** The coach partners with learners to help them apply their knowledge to achieve their personal goals. Assuming a collaborative and supportive approach, coaches tend to work one-on-one with learners, helping them create individual learning plans and giving them constructive feedback as they learn. Figure 10.2 illustrates the model.

Try taking the assessment or determine your preferred role as an adult educator based on the descriptions in Figure 10.3.

FIGURE 10.3 KOLB EDUCATOR ROLE PROFILE

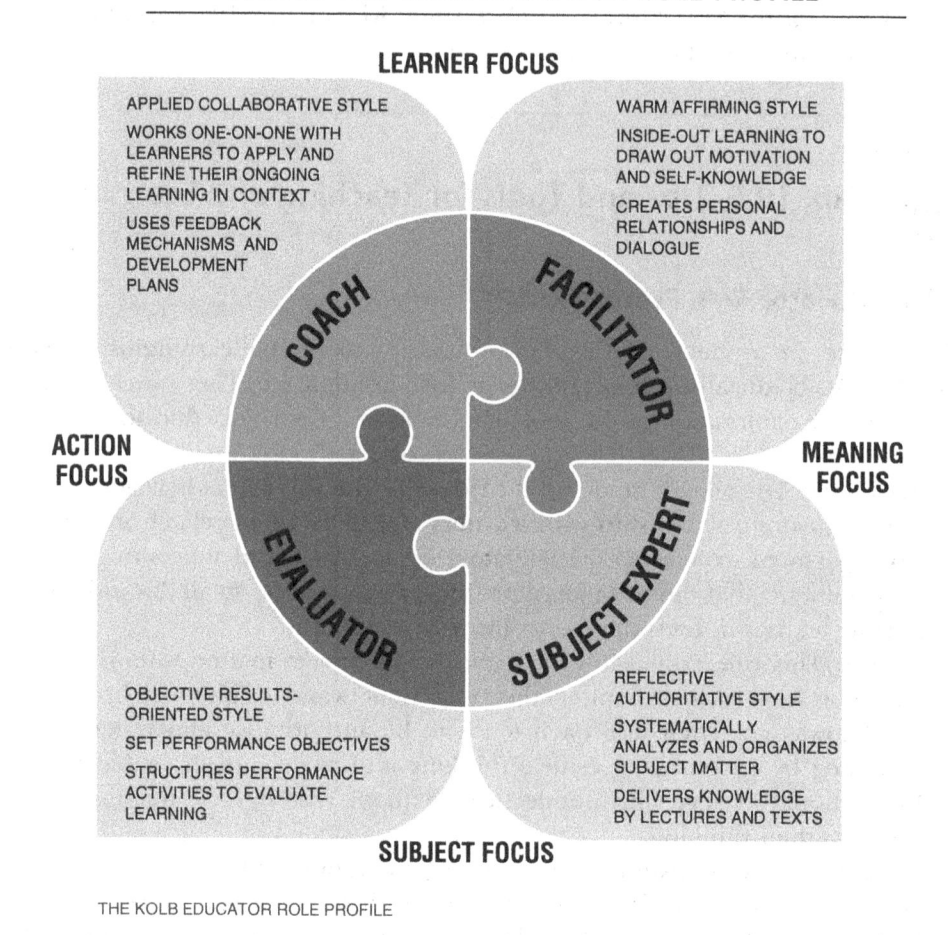

LEARNER FOCUS

APPLIED COLLABORATIVE STYLE

WORKS ONE-ON-ONE WITH LEARNERS TO APPLY AND REFINE THEIR ONGOING LEARNING IN CONTEXT

USES FEEDBACK MECHANISMS AND DEVELOPMENT PLANS

WARM AFFIRMING STYLE

INSIDE-OUT LEARNING TO DRAW OUT MOTIVATION AND SELF-KNOWLEDGE

CREATES PERSONAL RELATIONSHIPS AND DIALOGUE

COACH   FACILITATOR

ACTION FOCUS

MEANING FOCUS

EVALUATOR   SUBJECT EXPERT

OBJECTIVE RESULTS-ORIENTED STYLE

SET PERFORMANCE OBJECTIVES

STRUCTURES PERFORMANCE ACTIVITIES TO EVALUATE LEARNING

REFLECTIVE AUTHORITATIVE STYLE

SYSTEMATICALLY ANALYZES AND ORGANIZES SUBJECT MATTER

DELIVERS KNOWLEDGE BY LECTURES AND TEXTS

SUBJECT FOCUS

THE KOLB EDUCATOR ROLE PROFILE

The Kolb model has been influential for decades because it provides a relatable framework for understanding how adults learn through engagement with their world. Educators have applied the model to create more meaningful and applied lessons and design curricula, and it helps learners understand themselves as learners.

Four Models from Adult Educators

Perhaps because life experience is so central to understanding learning in adulthood, all those who write about adult learning consider the role of experience as Knowles did in proposing andragogy, or as can be found in the self-directed learning and transformative learning literature. The following section reviews four experiential learning models proposed by adult educators.

Jarvis's Model of Experiential Learning. In 1987, British adult educator Peter Jarvis published his learning model derived from participants in adult education workshops he invited to compare their learning "cycle" with Kolb's four-stage learning cycle. Experience is central to his model, and he defined learning as "the transformation of experience into knowledge, skills and attitudes" (Jarvis, 1987, p. 32). Jarvis's model is considerably more complex than Kolb's and consists of nine routes or types of learning. Three routes he labeled "non-learning," in which the individual either presumes to know already (presumption), decides not to consider the opportunity to learn (non-consideration), or outright rejects the chance to learn from the situation (rejection). The second three positions in his model constitute learning, but non-reflective learning (preconscious) involves basic skills through practice or memorization. He termed the final three routes "reflective learning." Here, an individual can contemplate an experience and "either accept or change it" (contemplation), "think about the situation and then act upon it, either confirming or innovating upon it" (reflective practice), or "think about the situation and agree or disagree with what they have experienced" (experimental learning) (Jarvis, 2006, p. 10).

In contrast to Jarvis's model, Kolb's experiential learning cycle seems rather simplistic and has been criticized along these lines, as has already been noted. Although Jarvis used Kolb's model as a touchstone for deriving his nine-stage model, his model continued to evolve, with Jarvis being its most ardent critic. He identified several strengths, such as "the centrality of experience in learning" and "an understanding of the interaction between the person and the social world as being significant for learning to occur" (Jarvis, 2006, p. 11). Points of criticism have to do with the learning process, types of learning, and his definition of learning. For example, Jarvis (2006) recognized that "learning through the emotions is much more significant than I originally realized" (p. 12). Further, while the transformation of experience is still central to his definition of human learning, he has expanded the definition. Now, it is the process in which the "whole person" engages in an experience that is processed "*cognitively, emotively or practically (or through any combination) and integrated into the person's individual biography resulting in a changed (or more experienced) person*" (Jarvis, 2006, p. 13, italics in original).

Tennant and Pogson's Model of Experiential Learning. Tennant and Pogson (1995) explained that experiential learning is not as much a process as Jarvis did, but it is a different way of leveraging experience as a learning resource. They proposed four "levels" or ways learners can think about experience by incorporating experience into instruction—prior experience, current experience, new experience, and learning from experience. As an adult learner, you can recall, mull, and link new learning to *previous experiences*. This strategy is reminiscent of Dewey's principle of continuity, discussed earlier, wherein new learning is connected to past experiences and foreshadows future learning. Say, for example, that you are attending a workshop on "Brain Power: Improving Your Memory." You recall when you learned and remember detailed information, such as steps in a computer program, the names of flowering plants, or a recipe for a popular dish. You would then examine *how* you remember this information to apply the strategy to future learning. Prior experience is also applicable to learning about yourself. Tennant (2012) emphasized the role of previous experience in learning about and knowing oneself: "Making sense of our past experiences to better understand our desires and interests is a route to self-knowledge" (p. 112).

A second category of experience is *current experience*. Here, learning activities connect to current experiences as an adult who is a family member, community member, or worker. Following the previous example, you might be running for a local town council or school board position. You strive to remember many people's names and positions. You immediately employ one of the memory strategies learned in the brain workshop. By embedding instruction in the immediate circumstances of an adult's life, theory becomes very practical and learning highly relevant.

A *new experience*, the third category, involves creating experiences through instructional techniques such as simulations, role-playing, internships, practicums, and other immersive activities that provide a base for new learning. Continuing with the memory example, numerous techniques and strategies for aiding your memory would be demonstrated and applied.

Their fourth category is *learning from experience*, by which Tennant and Pogson (1995) meant the critical examination of prior experience:

> Typically the meanings that learners attach to their experiences are subjected to critical scrutiny through the medium of the group. The adult educator may consciously set out to disrupt the learner's world view and stimulate uncertainty, ambiguity, and doubt about previously taken-for-granted interpretations of experience. (p. 151)

Again, using the memory workshop as an example, you and the other participants would explore previous experiences with memory to examine taken-for-granted assumptions about memory (such as it declines as people age). They summed up their model with the point that for learning to occur, "education must somehow stimulate learners to go beyond their experiences. . . . Indeed, experience has to be mediated and reconstructed (or transformed) by the student for learning to occur" (Tennant & Pogson, 1995, p. 151). Apply the model in Box 10.6.

Fenwick's Model of Experiential Learning. While Jarvis (2006) mapped the process of learning where experience is central, Tennant and Pogson (1995) considered experiential learning from an instructional perspective, and Fenwick (2003) proposed a more philosophical lens for viewing experiential learning. Fenwick conceptualized experiential learning from five perspectives, each drawing from a different theoretical paradigm. The first perspective is **constructivist,** where

---

 ## Box 10.6 Tips and Tools for Teaching and Learning

Applying Tennant and Pogson's Four Levels of Experience

Using the memory workshop discussed in this section as an example, select a topic and consider how you might design instruction to address each of the four levels of experience outlined by Tennant and Pogson:

1. Prior experience
2. Current experience
3. New experience
4. Learning from experience

learning creates meaning through engaging in and reflecting upon experience. This view underlies much of the experiential learning literature already covered in this chapter. For example, an adult recently diagnosed with diabetes would reflect upon their experience with the disease and learn what lifestyle and treatment options are best.

A second perspective is **situative,** wherein knowing or learning occurs in doing or practice: "Learning is rooted in the situation in which the person participates, not in the head of that person as intellectual concepts produced by reflection" (Fenwick, 2003, p. 25). From this perspective, the person diagnosed with diabetes would be tuned into their body, learning when blood sugar levels are high or low and adjusting accordingly.

Fenwick's (2003) third perspective is **psychoanalytic** and involves connecting with unconscious desires and fears. People's unconscious can interfere with their conscious desires and affect learning. Following the example of being diagnosed with diabetes, unconsciously, the person may deny they have the disease as it may conflict with their self-image as a healthy, active person. Such an unconscious fear might interfere with learning.

A fourth lens is what Fenwick (2003) called the **critical cultural perspective,** in which "dominant norms of experience" are critically questioned and resisted (p. 38). From this perspective, the person with diabetes might resist or challenge some of the assumptions about people with diabetes held by many (for example, that it is their "fault" for contracting the disease).

The fifth perspective is lodged in complexity theory and is labeled **"ecological."** Here, the focus is on "the *relationships* binding humans and non-humans (persons, material objects, mediating tools, environments, ideas) together in multiple fluctuations in complex systems" (Fenwick, 2004, p. 51). From a complexity theory perspective, learning is "the continuous improvisation of alternate actions and responses to new possibilities and changing circumstances that emerge, undertaken by the system's parts" (Fenwick, 2004, p. 53). The person with diabetes may decide to form a support group for dealing with the disease. This group is a system with a shared objective, but each member brings experiences from their own lives, healthcare systems, etc. Learning evolves as these systems interact.

Beard and Wilson's Seven Modes of Experiencing

Beard (2023) argued that critiques of experiential learning in the 21st century urged theorists to broaden notions of experiential learning, respecting Dewey's imploring that a philosophy of experience was needed that respected life's complexity as humans experience it. Beard and Wilson (2018) developed an ecological, holistic model of experiential learning that captures the complex interactions between belonging, doing, sensing, feeling, knowing, and being in the world. Beard (2023) emphasized a distinguishing feature of this model is that it does not neglect extra-human beings, including the physical, natural world of living species and spiritual aspects. The essence of their model was that individuals, groups, and organizations "exist in a state of *becoming*, always changing, always an interactional process of remaking the self and/or the world" (Beard, 2023, p. 205, italics in original).

There are many ways to think about the connection between life experience and learning. This section reviewed four models proposed by adult educators. Jarvis (2006) took Kolb's cycle as a starting point and devised a learning model from experience with nine possible pathways. Tennant and Pogson (1995) viewed experiential learning from a pedagogical perspective and proposed four ways of accessing experience in learning. Fenwick (2003) differentiated among five philosophical conceptions of experiential learning. Finally, Beard and Wilson (2018) attempted to meet Dewey's challenge of expanding the understanding of adult learning in complexity.

Reflective Practice and Action Inquiry

The relationship between adult learning and life experience is so intermingled that imagining any learning isolated from experience is difficult. Whether, as the reader, you reflect on one of the adult learning theories covered in previous chapters, holistic conceptions of learning involving body, emotions, and spirit, or even traditional learning theories such as behaviorism or cognitive psychology, all understandings of learning involve your experiences. Of course, learning designers can create classroom experiences to illustrate a lesson or invite learners to relate concepts to their everyday experiences where they attend to, think about, process, and construct meaning. In addition to the models already reviewed in this chapter, there are others that we feel as authors resonate particularly well with *adult* learning—reflective practice, action inquiry, situated cognition, and communities of practice. This section discusses reflective practice and action inquiry. Both approaches are frameworks for learning and improving practice but differ in focus, methodology, and application.

Reflective Practice

Reflective practice, or **practice-based learning,** is learning acquired through contemplation on or in experience. An adult learner considers their experiences and insights gained to guide their future learning and action. For instance, after a meeting, a person might replay the interpersonal dynamics and how they engaged with their team. They may assess what worked and what did not and determine a different approach for the next meeting.

The "practice" arena in reflective practice is whatever job or field you work in as an adult, and thus, there is much emphasis on reflecting on and improving your practice. Continuing professional education, in particular, has adopted reflective practice as an organizing concept. Reflective practice became very popular in education and other social science professions through Donald Schon's books *The Reflective Practitioner* (1983) and *Educating the Reflective Practitioner* (1987). Indeed, many professional preparation programs strive to develop "reflective practitioners" who take time to consider their experience and how to improve it. Schon's basic premise was that the real world of practice is messy and that your "technical" preparation for this world is merely a starting point. It is in practice itself that beneficial learning occurs. For example, an adult who takes a cooking class does not immediately become an outstanding cook. They learn by trying recipes, assessing what did and did not work, tasting, trial and error, consulting other cooks or information, and practicing.

Reflection-on-action and reflection-in-action are two key concepts in reflective practice. **Reflection-on-action** likely comes to mind when considering your experiential learning as an adult—you have an experience and consciously think about it after it has happened. For instance, you might have approached a problematic work colleague in a new way, experimented with artificial intelligence, or confided in a friend about a health issue. If you contemplated any of these experiences after you did them, you would have engaged in reflection-on-action. In evaluating these experiences, you perhaps decided to do something similar or different in your future "practice."

Reflection-in-action is distinguishable from reflection-on-action because the contemplation coincides with the person's engagement in the experience, synchronizing it with practice. This reflection "reshapes what we are doing while we are doing it" (Schon, 1987, p. 26). Reflection-in-action is what distinguishes the more expert practitioner from the novice. It characterizes the practitioners who "think on their feet," who experiment, change direction, and immediately respond to a changing context of practice. Reflection-in-action aligns with knowing-in-action or tacit knowing—as adults, we know what to do without articulating it. For example, minutes before one of the authors (Sharan) presented her research at a conference, the allocated time slot was cut by 15 minutes. Instead of rushing through the slides and talking quickly, she deleted the least essential component of the presentation, which for this group of practitioners was the jargon related to the research methodology. Experienced practitioners, whether educators, health practitioners, administrators, support staff, or rank-and-file workers, adjust their practice as they reflect-in-action.

You can engage in reflective practice as an adult learner or educator by analyzing your espoused theories versus your theories-in-use (Argyris & Schon, 1974). **Espoused theories** are those ideas and beliefs you hold about your practice, while theories-in-use are what you actually *do* in practice. As defined by Argyris and Schon,

> When someone is asked how he [sic] would behave under certain circumstances, the answer he [sic] usually gives is his [sic] espoused theory of action for that situation. This is the theory of action to which he [sic] gives allegiance, and which, upon request, he [sic] communicates to others. However the theory that actually governs his [sic] actions is his [sic] theory-in-use, which may or may not be compatible with his [sic] espoused theory; furthermore, the individual may or may not be aware of incompatibility of the two theories. (pp. 6–7)

For example, as adult educators, we can believe that adults learn differently from children and that their life experiences are a resource for learning—our espoused theory. However, once in the classroom, we may teach adults the same way we teach children, which is our theory-in-use. Another example is the administrator who espouses a participatory management style but actually employs a top-down, authoritarian style. What we believe about our practice may not be the same as what we actually do in practice. Box 10.7 outlines a study on exploring these concepts.

 ## Box 10.7 Reflective Practice

Study Espoused Versus Theory-in-use

Conduct a pilot study on espoused theory versus theories-in-use by interviewing a practitioner about some aspect of their practice (what they believe and think they do), then observe the person in practice. Compare their espoused theory with their theory-in-use. Try this exercise with a colleague in your field of practice (education, health, administration, and so on) and/or with a skill-based activity with which you are familiar, such as a sport or hobby.

While Schon's work is considered central to theorizing about reflective practice, several other writers have elaborated on various aspects of reflective practice. Fenwick (2004), for example, acknowledged that practice-based learning "recognizes and celebrates knowledge generated outside institutions" (p. 43), challenges "expert" knowledge, and values personal experience. However, "experiences also can reproduce structural inequities and reinforce entrenched beliefs or traditions of practice that may be harmful or repressive" (p. 44). This problem may be particularly troublesome for "educators who typically practice in isolation," dimming the potential for "systemic change" (p. 44). She proposed a more complex reflective practice model that sees learning as embodied within complex systems.

Reflective practice/experiential learning has also been connected to the characterization of work-based learning (WBL), applying the theoretical frame of experiential to workplace learning:

> What needs to be considered is how the learning processes take place in "work"-related environments and how, by understanding the mechanisms of learning, the work-based environment can be formalized as an authentic learning environment and thus accepted as comparable but nevertheless different from the traditional on-campus one. (Chisholm et al., 2009, p. 319).

Others have assumed a more postmodern, critical stance on reflective practice (Brookfield, 1991; Dyke, 2009; Mezirow, 2000; Usher et al., 1997). Key to this perspective is that learning from one's experience involves not just reflection but *critical* reflection (see Chapter 3 on Critical Perspectives). For example, Brookfield proposed three phases of critical reflection:

1. The identification of "the assumptions that underlie our thoughts and actions"
2. The scrutiny of "the accuracy and validity of these assumptions in terms of how they connect to, or are discrepant with, our experience of reality"
3. The reconstituting of these assumptions "to make them more inclusive and integrative" (Brookfield, 1991, p. 177)

Popularized by Schon, the notion of reflective practice has taken hold in adult education, human resource development, other areas of education, and many applied fields. His ideas and subsequent thinking are popular because they resonate with what adults know to be true about their learning. Adult learning is rooted in practice and experience, even if the experience is one of formal education, and for learning to occur, adults need to reflect on or in the experience.

Reflective practice tends to be individually focused. It can be retrospective, as in focusing on past events and results, but it can also be in the moment when an adult engages in an experience. Reflective practice can be guided, but it is often informal and iterative for adult learners. The following reflective approach is more collaborative.

Action Inquiry

As an adult learner or educator, you have daily life and work experiences available as a learning repository, but do you use them? You take actions—doing things with particular aims in mind—multiple times daily. Perhaps you think about your actions, although probably not as a general rule or in a structured way. **Inquiry** seeks information or meaning where you can be "simultaneously productive and self-assessing" (Torbert, 2004, p. 13). How often do you seek meaning around your actions? Likely, you do when something goes wrong, but engaging in this type of learning is always available. Action inquiry is a powerful approach to engaging in learning from life. Torbert (2004) defined **action inquiry** as "a way of simultaneously conducting action and inquiry as a disciplined leadership practice that increases the wider effectiveness of our actions" (p. 1). Action inquiry is a more systemic and collaborative approach than reflective practice and seeks to integrate action, reflection, and inquiry simultaneously.

The value of action inquiry is it is free, always available, and anyone can do it. Torbert continued, "Action inquiry becomes a moment-to-moment way of living whereby we attune ourselves through inquiry to acting in an increasingly timely and wise fashion for the overall development of the families, teams, and organizations in which we participate" (pp. 1–2). Torbert (2004) urged "conscious living" by paying careful attention to our interactions "from the inside-out to the experience we have, hoping to learn from them and modify our actions and even our way of thinking as a result" (p. 4). Another way to think about it is as a reflexive practice of correcting errors while engaging with others in your life and work. This practice demands that you be highly aware of the present situation and respond accordingly.

As an adult learner or educator, you will find it beneficial to inquire about your experiences and actions to promote life and career learning. **Inquiry** is engagement in reflection, listening, speaking, and leading with mindfulness and integrity. Having a coach, mentor, or friend who can help you inquire into your mindsets, emotions, and ideas and debrief with you when things go awry is helpful. **Action** takes the results of your inquiry (reflections, learning, mistakes, and consultations with others) to take the next step or work toward a desired outcome. Ideally, it is a mindful, timely, and just response to the activities and ideas you have been reflecting on. Reflecting on action and change helps ensure life events within your control are constructive.

Systems theory language names learning from the system known as single-, double-, and triple-loop learning or feedback. **Single-loop learning** is implementing incremental actions toward a goal and assessing how effectively they work—considered "doing things right" since it focuses on improving current processes and actions. It is an opportunity to assess outcomes and determine if mindsets, thoughts, or actions need to change. If the career goal was to develop as a leader, a person might continue to practice positive leadership behaviors like listening actively, giving constructive feedback, and expressing empathy. Single-loop learning might also be a case of doing the same thing and expecting different results. Torbert (2004) defined it as feedback about results in the outside world that require people to change their behaviors to achieve their goals more effectively.

Double-loop learning pauses to assess the goal attainment strategy, perhaps rethink it, and create a substantive change in the process. Returning to the leader example would involve more consideration of leadership strategies, how well they were working, and reflecting on one's assumptions about leadership and whether they are consistent with their actions. People might ask themselves how effective their strategies have been or what they believe about leadership. A person might adjust their leadership strategies or shift their thoughts as a leader. Torbert explained double-loop feedback as goals and strategies that may need to be changed to become more effective.

Triple-loop learning involves not only rethinking strategy but also rethinking purpose or the *why* of doing something for the self, others, and the system. Torbert (2004) viewed it as becoming present to the self in the moment and explained it "highlights the present relationship between our effects on the outside world and (1) our action, (2) our strategy, and (3) our attention itself" (p. 18). The learner might need to consider their actions, what is important to them, and how their behavior affects the people they live and work with and the broader context. Or they might notice their leadership values are in disharmony with the organizational culture and decide in the moment how to manage that tension. The triple loop only occurs when sitting with the situation and attempting to learn from the learning processes of oneself, the group, or the system. Torbert defined triple-loop feedback as focused on the quality of ongoing awareness people need to develop to embrace the forward territories of experience and test the legitimacy and integrity of their actions.

Torbert (2004) asked how people can "become more aware of, and less constrained by, [their] own implicit and often untested assumptions about situations [they] find [themselves] in?" (p. 21). He suggested the first step is to practice noticing—realize how limited the human attention and awareness span is. The next step is to exercise awareness in new ways amid challenges. Torbert recommended reflective practice as an essential tool to recognize the limits of ordinary attention by journaling about significant personal, professional, or community incidents, people, and unsatisfactory outcomes. Practice noticing in Box 10.8.

Action inquiry combines reflection and action in real time for either individuals or collectives. The iterative process can help align individual and collective development and growth. The beauty of action inquiry is it foregrounds learning as a key process for change, interpersonal collaboration, and growth.

 ## Box 10.8 Reflective Practice

Strategies to Practice Noticing

Torbert (2004, p. 56) offered strategies for recognizing the limits of ordinary attention and awareness. Practice noticing these things as you go about your day as a career explorer, sustainer, or changer.

1. Set an alarm to go off every 60 minutes. When your alarm rings, spend 30 seconds noticing how you feel mentally, emotionally, and physically when the alarm goes off, including irritation by the alarm's interruption.
2. When you transition from one activity to another, focus on the transition and notice how you feel about ending the previous activity and beginning the next one.
3. Check-in with yourself periodically every day, for example, at mealtime or bedtime, to identify the most satisfying moment since the last check-in. Stop to recognize what was least satisfying since the previous check-in and why. Reflect on whether you were aware of these reactions when the events occurred.
4. Develop a habit of noticing how you feel after each meaningful interaction with other people.

Situated Cognition and Communities of Practice

Just as "reflective practice" signifies learning that occurs with reflection on or in practice, "situated cognition," also known as "contextual learning," acknowledges the importance of *where* learning happens; that is, *the context itself shapes the learning*. Communities of practice represent groups of people sharing an interest who learn collectively and create a collective support and knowledge sharing group. Both are discussed in this section.

Situated Cognition

Reflective practice is viewed as reflecting *on* experience or practice, while **situated cognition** is more akin to learning *in* practice within a context, similar to reflection-in-action. Here, the spotlight shifts from the individual to the context. Learning occurs as people interact with others in a particular context with the tools at hand (such as objects, language, symbols, and so on). For example, on a trip to Singapore, one of the authors (Sharan) set out to learn about the public transportation system. The context was Singapore's bus and train system; the tools consisted of a transit pass, maps, and the trains and buses themselves, and it was socially interactive as she and her husband "figured out" the system with the occasional help of a passenger or employee of the system.

The previous example is reminiscent of several famous examples from research by Jean Lave, who is considered the major architect of this theory. In one study, adults were given math problems and sent to a grocery store to work with the objects in the store to solve the problems. They got 98% correct. Given the same problems in a paper-and-pencil test, they got 59% correct (Lave, 1988). In another example, Kim and Merriam (2010) studied how context, tools, and social interaction shaped the learning of older Korean adults taking computer classes. The physical setting of the classroom, the "tools" of computer terminals and teacher's notes, which were copied by the students, and Korean cultural values worked in concert to shape the learning that took place. Sun et al. (2024) conducted a case study to explore the learning of Chinese and Chinese American adults who formed a care group during the repercussions of the COVID-19 pandemic in the United States. They found how group members created meaning out of daily life, reformed their identity, and increased their visibility, concluding that situated learning can potentially generate collective transformative action with individual and collective growth in identity formation, community engagement, and social development through communities of practice.

Viewing learning from a situated cognition perspective removes learning from what only occurs within the person's mind and highlights the importance of context and social interaction as determinants of learning. And context and social interactions are culturally and politically defined. For example, in the study cited above on Korean elderly learning computers, the nature of the interaction between teacher and students and among the students themselves was culturally defined; that is, respect for teachers in this culture precluded informal or spontaneous exchanges that one might see in a Western classroom. Further, respect for age, even among a group of all older adults, meant that older students felt uncomfortable asking younger ones for assistance.

Communities of Practice

Communities of practice (CoPs), or learning communities, are adult learners who come together to learn about a shared interest. CoPs are yet another manifestation of a situated cognition perspective on how learning resides in learners' context, tools, and social interaction. Wenger (1998, 2000; Wenger & Snyder, 2000) is often associated with this concept. Communities of practice are everywhere as people informally come together around some common interest. We all belong to multiple communities of practice—our family is one, as is our workplace, professional association, a civic organization we might belong to, and social websites such as Facebook. As Wenger (1998) pointed out,

> Communities of practice are an integral part of our daily lives. . . .
> Although the term may be new, the experience is not. Most communities
> of practice do not have a name and do not issue membership cards. Yet, if
> we care to consider our own life from that perspective for a moment, we
> can all construct a fairly good picture of the communities of practice we
> belong to now, those we belonged to in the past, and those we would like
> to belong to in the future. . . . Furthermore, we can probably distinguish a
> few communities of practice in which we are core members from a larger
> number of communities in which we have a more peripheral kind of
> membership. (p. 7)

Communities of practice are composed of learners with varying levels of understanding and mastery of the group's knowledge, behaviors, attitudes, and norms. Some know more than others; however, "mastery resides not in the master but in the organization of the community of practice of which the master is a part" (Lave & Wenger, 1991, p. 95). Newcomers engage with others in the community, learn what they need to know to move from the periphery to the center of practice, and become more engaged and active over time. As a learner, consider your graduate studies program for which you might be reading this textbook. After enrolling in the program, you attended your first course; you were on the periphery of this community of practice. You became more central to the community as you interacted with fellow students, instructors, and others associated with the program, attended conferences, and learned some practices, procedures, and jargon. After several semesters, you become an "old timer" and can mentor new students in the community.

Learning is central to these communities because learning happens daily as adults, where we continually move between and among various communities. These communities of practice have "*shared histories of learning*" (Wenger, 1998, p. 86). The communities of practice and learning communities literature distinguishes between learning itself and designing for it to occur. "Learning cannot be designed," according to Wenger (1998, p. 225). "Ultimately, it belongs to the realm of experience and practice. It follows the negotiation of meaning; it moves on its own terms. It slips through the cracks; it creates its own cracks. Learning happens, design or no design. And yet there are few more urgent tasks than to design social infrastructures that foster learning" (Wenger, 1998, p. 225). In his theory, a community of practice becomes a learning community when learning is "not only a matter of course in the history of its practice, but at the very core of its enterprise" (Wenger, 1998, pp. 214–215).

There is now a relatively large literature on communities of practice and learning communities. Though there is no rigorous division, communities of practice are most often studied and implemented in organizational settings, sometimes linking to the concept of the learning organization (Senge, 1990). Fenwick (2008), for example, examined workplace learning from a community of practice perspective:

> Learning is viewed as the ongoing refinement of practices and emerging knowledge embodied in the specific action of a particular community. Individuals learn *as* they participate in everyday activity within a community (with its history, assumptions and cultural values, rules, and patterns of relationship), with the tools at hand (including objects, technology, language). (pp. 19–20, italics in original)

In education and community-based organizations, communities of practice and learning communities are terms often used interchangeably. When referring to online environments, learning community seems to be the preferred term. Sites of community and social movements are the spaces and places where activists learn through socialization with one another by learning in "communities of practice" (Lave & Wenger, 1991, p. 31). "Learning in activism is a naturally social process; through time, and the opportunity to observe and interact with others, activists become more expert at what they do" (Lave & Wenger, 1991, p. 246).

Reflective practice, situated cognition, and communities of practice represent other ways to think about the connection between experience and learning. Reflective practice, widely adopted in adult education, especially in continuing professional education, posits that learning occurs when reflecting on and in our experiences as adults (our "practice"). The more we engage in reflective practice, the more expert we become. Situated cognition is yet another way of looking at experience and learning. In this perspective, the context in which the learning occurs is critical to understanding and facilitating learning. Communities of practice, direct outgrowths of this perspective, can be employed as instructional strategies to foster learning from and in experience. Regardless of the approach to experiential education, experiential learning brings experience to life. Box 10.9 offers some active experiential learning facilitation methods.

 ## Box 10.9 Tips and Tools for Teaching and Learning

Teaching Around the Kolb Circle

Reflect on a subject or course you teach and list the different activities you use. Now compare it to Figure 10.4 and see if you are tending to the quadrants of the Kolb Learning Cycle. Next, revise your course to incorporate at least one strategy from each quadrant around the circle. By ensuring various active learning strategies that relate to a range of learning styles, you will create more powerful, compelling learning experiences for adults.

FIGURE 10.4 TEACHING AROUND THE CIRCLE

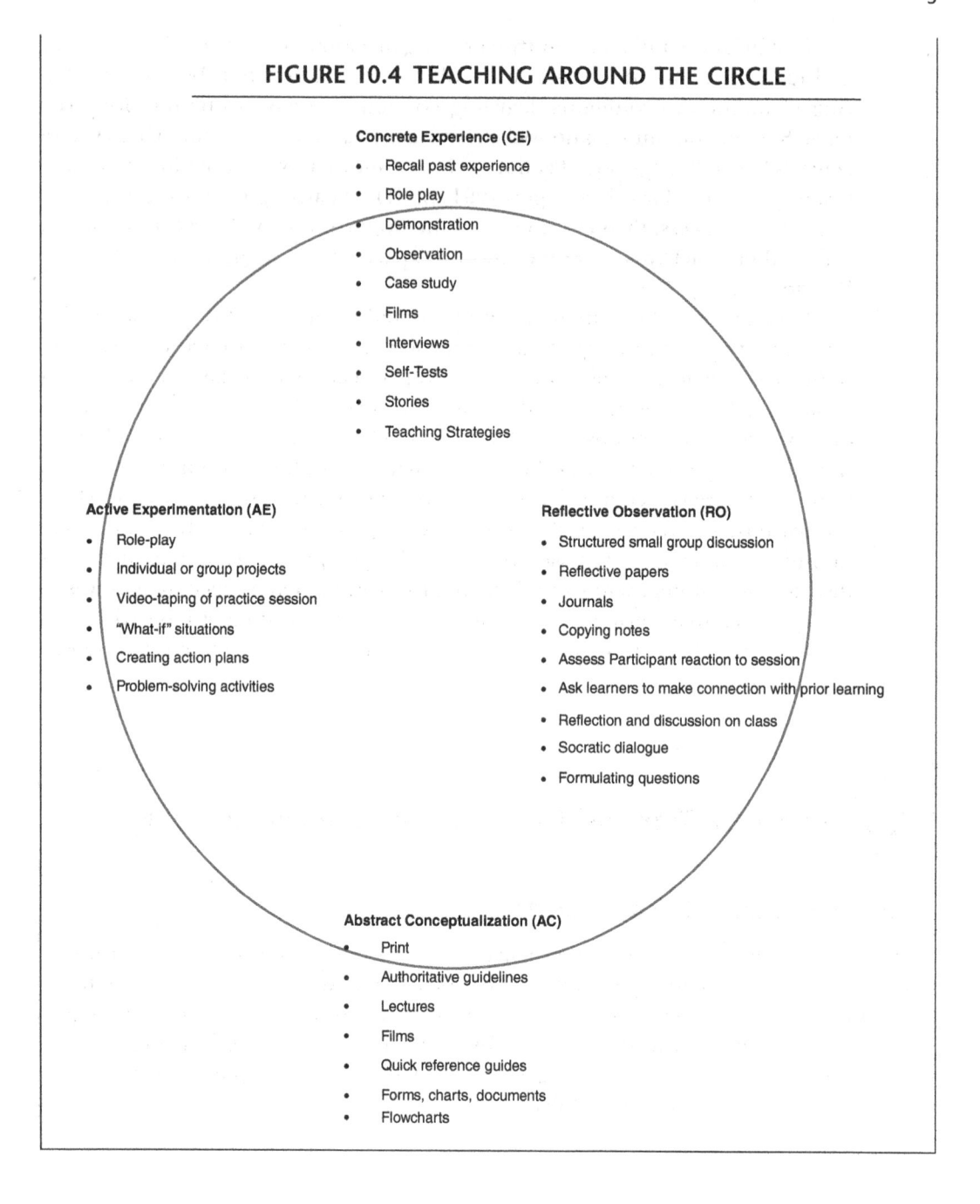

Concrete Experience (CE)

- Recall past experience
- Role play
- Demonstration
- Observation
- Case study
- Films
- Interviews
- Self-Tests
- Stories
- Teaching Strategies

Active Experimentation (AE)

- Role-play
- Individual or group projects
- Video-taping of practice session
- "What-if" situations
- Creating action plans
- Problem-solving activities

Reflective Observation (RO)

- Structured small group discussion
- Reflective papers
- Journals
- Copying notes
- Assess Participant reaction to session
- Ask learners to make connection with prior learning
- Reflection and discussion on class
- Socratic dialogue
- Formulating questions

Abstract Conceptualization (AC)

- Print
- Authoritative guidelines
- Lectures
- Films
- Quick reference guides
- Forms, charts, documents
- Flowcharts

Chapter Summary

Chapter 10 delved into the interconnectedness of life experience and learning. Adults are immersed in experiences filled with learning potential, whether at work, school, home, or community. This learning often leads adults to new experiences, and the iterative cycle continues. This chapter explored how scholars and the fields of adult education and human resource development have conceptualized this learning and experience relationship. First, Dewey's formative work was introduced, followed by Lindeman's. Explanations were presented, describing how an adult's life experience is recognized in andragogy, self-directed learning, and transformative learning theories. The second part of the chapter presented Kolb's model of experiential learning, followed by four models developed by adult educators. Each of these models describes a different aspect of experiential learning, including the process (Jarvis), types of experiential learning and their instructional implications (Tennant & Pogson), philosophical orientations (Fenwick), and ecological and holistic experiential learning (Beard & Wilson). Finally, the theories of reflective practice, action inquiry, situated cognition, and communities of practice were reviewed to highlight their contributions to understanding the connection between experience and learning.

Key Points

- The connection between experience and learning has been well documented, from Greek philosophers to Dewey and Lindeman.
- Andragogy, self-directed learning, and transformative learning all have life experience as a central component of understanding learning.
- The most well-known model of experiential learning is Kolb's experiential learning cycle; adult educators Jarvis, Tennant, Pogson, Fenwick, Beard, and Wilson have all advanced models of experiential learning focusing on adult learners.
- Reflective practice, or practice-based learning, is learning acquired through reflection on or in practice (experience). Schon has written extensively about reflection on and in practice and espoused theories versus theories in use.
- The theory of situated cognition posits that learning is embedded in the context where it occurs, with the tools of that context, and through social interaction. Communities of practice enable this form of experiential learning.

References

Antrim, M. T. (1902). Naked truth and veiled allusions. Henry Altemus.

Argyris, C. & Schon, D. A. (1974). *Theory in practice: Increasing professional effectiveness*. Jossey-Bass.

Barker, D. J., Lencucha, J., & Anderson, R. (2016). Kolb's learning cycle as a framework for early fieldwork learning. *World Federation of Occupational Therapists Bulletin, 72*(1), 28–34. https://doi.org/10.1080/14473828.2016.1162373.

Beard, C. (2023). Experiential learning. In A. Belzer, & B. Dashew (Eds.). *Understanding the adult learner: Perspectives and practices* (pp. 193–211). Taylor & Francis Group.

Beard, C., & Wilson, J. P. (2018). *Experiential learning: A practical guide for training, coaching and education* (4th ed.). Routledge.

Bergsteiner, H., Avery, G. C., & Neumann, R. (2010). Kolb's experiential learning model: Critique from a modeling perspective. *Studies in Continuing Education, 32*(1), 29–46. https://doi.org/10.1080/01580370903534355.

Bowling, J., & Hensche, J. A. (2021). Pedagogy and andragogy. In T. Rocco, M. C. Smith, R. C. Mizzi, L. R. Merriweather, & J. D. Hawley (Eds.), *The handbook of adult and continuing education* (pp. 158–167). Stylus Publishing.

Brookfield, S. (1991). Using critical incidents to explore learners' assumptions. In J. Mezirow & Associates (Eds.), *Fostering critical reflection in adulthood* (pp. 177–193). Jossey-Bass.

Chisholm, C. U., Harris, M. S. G., Horthwood, D. O. & Johrendt, J. L. (2009). The characterisation of work-based learning by consideration of the theories of experiential learning. *European Journal of Education, 44*(3), 319–337. https://www.jstor.org/stable/27743176.

Coffield, F., Moseley, D., Hall, E., & Ecclestone, K. (2004). *Learning styles and pedagogy in post-16 learning. A systematic and critical review*. Learning and Skills Research Centre. http://www.leerbeleving.nl/wp-content/uploads/2011/09/learning-styles.pdf.

Cornelius, S., & Macdonald, J. (2008). Online informal professional development for distance tutors: Experiences from The Open University in Scotland. *Open Learning, 23*(1), 43–55. https://doi.org/10.1080/02680510701815319.

Dewey, J. (1938/1963). *Experience and education*. Collier Books.

Dewey, J. (1963). *Liberalism and social action* (vol. 74). New York: Capricorn Books.

Dyke, M. (2006). The role of the "Other" in reflection, knowledge formation and action in late modernity. *International Journal of Lifelong Education, 25*(2), 105–123. https://doi.org/10.1080/02601370500510728.

Dyke, M. (2009). An enabling framework for reflexive learning: Experiential learning and reflexivity in contemporary modernity. *International Journal of Lifelong Education, 28*(3), 289–310. https://doi.org/10.1080/02601370902798913.

Fenwick, T. (2003). *Learning through experience: Troubling assumptions and intersecting Questions*. Krieger.

Fenwick, T. J. (2004). The practice-based learning of educators: A co-emergent perspective. *Scholar-Practitioner Quarterly, 2*(4), 43–59. https://eric.ed.gov/?id=EJ796130.

Fenwick, T. (2008). Workplace learning: Emerging trends and new perspectives. In S.B. Merriam (ed.), *Third Update on Adult Learning Theory* (pp. 17–20). New Directions for Adult and Continuing Education, no. 119. Jossey-Bass.

Jarvis, P. (1987). *Adult learning in the social context*. Croom Helm.

Jarvis, P. (2006). *Towards a comprehensive theory of human learning.* Routledge.

Kim, Y. S. & Merriam, S. B. (2010). Situated learning and identity development in a Korean older adults' computer classroom. *Adult Education Quarterly, 60*(5), 438–455. https://doi.org/10.1177/0741713610363019.

King, K. P. (2017). *Technology and innovation in adult learning.* John Wiley & Sons.

Knowles, M. S. (1980). *The modern practice of adult education: From pedagogy to andragogy* (2nd ed.). Cambridge Books.

Knowles, M. S., Holton, E. F. III, & Swanson, R. A. (2011). *The adult learner* (6th ed.). Gulf Publishing.

Kolb, D. A. (1984). *Experiential learning: Experience as the source of learning and development.* Prentice Hall.

Kolb, A. Y., Kolb, D. A., Passarelli, A., & Sharma, G. (2014). On becoming an experiential educator: The educator role profile. *Simulation & Gaming, 45*(2), 204–234. https://doi.org/10.1177/1046878114534383.

Kuh, G. D. (2008). High-impact educational practices. *Peer Review, 10*(4), 30–31. https://link.gale.com/apps/doc/A203770127/AONE?u=uga&sid=googleScholar&xid=e3c8ece9.

Lave, J. (1988). *Cognition in practice: Mind, mathematics, and culture in everyday life.* Cambridge University Press.

Lave, J. & Wenger, E. (1991). *Situated learning: Legitimate peripheral participation.* Cambridge University Press.

Lindeman, E. C. (1961). *The meaning of adult education in the United States.* Harvest House.

Mezirow, J. (2000). Learning to think like an adult: Core concepts of transformation theory. In J. Mezirow & Associates (Eds.), *Learning as transformation: Critical perspectives on a theory in progress* (pp. 3–33). Jossey-Bass.

Miettinen, R. (2000). The concept of experiential learning and John Dewey's theory of reflective thought and action. *International Journal of Lifelong Education, 19*(1), 54–72. https://doi.org/10.1080/026013700293458.

Mintz, S. (2021, July 26). *Seize the power of experiential learning.* Inside Higher Ed. https://www.insidehighered.com/blogs/higher-ed-gamma/seize-power-experiential-learning.

Morris, T. H. (2019). Experiential learning—A systematic review and revision of Kolb's model. *Interactive Learning Environments, 28*(8), 1064–1077. https://doi.org/10.1080/10494820.2019.1570279.

O'Bannon, T. & McFadden, C. (2008). Model of experiential andragogy: Development of a nontraditional experiential learning program model. *Journal of Unconventional Parks, Tourism & Recreation Research, 1*(1), 23–28.

Ollis, T. (2010). The pedagogy of activism: Learning to change the world. *The International Journal of Learning, 17*(8), 239–249. https://dro.deakin.edu.au/articles/journal_contribution/The_pedagogy_of_activism_learning_to_change_the_world/20968996.

Palloff, R. M. & Pratt, K. (2009) *Building learning communities in cyberspace: Effective strategies for the online classroom* (2nd ed.). Jossey-Bass.

Roberts, J., & Welton, A. (2022, August 2). *The 10 commandments of experiential learning.* Inside Higher Education. https://www.insidehighered.com/advice/2022/08/03/foundational-best-practices-experiential-learning-opinion.

Rodríguez Aboytes, J. G., & Barth, M. (2020). Transformative learning in the field of sustainability: A systematic literature review (1999–2019). *International Journal of Sustainability in Higher Education, 21*(5), 993–1013. https://doi.org/10.1108/IJSHE-05-2019-0168.

Schön, D. A. (1983). *The reflective practitioner: How professionals think in action.* Basic Books.

Schon, D. A. (1987). *Educating the reflective practitioner.* Basic Books.

Senge, P. M. (1990). *The fifth discipline: The art and practice of the learning organization.* Currency/Doubleday.

Sherer, P. D., Shea, T. P., & Kristensen, E. (2003). Online communities of practice: A catalyst for faculty development. *Innovative Higher Education, 27*(3), 183–194. https://doi.org/10.1023/A:1022355226924.

Stock, K. L., & Kolb, D. (2021). The experiencing scale: An experiential learning gauge of engagement in learning. *Experiential Learning & Teaching in Higher Education, 4*(1), 3–21. https://doi.org/10.1177/1046878114534383.

Sun, Q., Lin, X., Zhang, X., & Rui, R. (2024). Situated learning for community engagement: Chinese and Chinese Americans transformative action for identity reformation in the context of the politicized COVID-19 Pandemic. *Adult Education Quarterly, 74*(4), 321–340. https://doi.org/10.1177/07417136241246737.

Tennant, M. (2012). *The learning self: Understanding the potential for transformation.* Jossey-Bass.

Tennant, M. & Pogson, P. (1995). *Learning and change in the adult years.* Jossey-Bass.

Torbert, W. R. (2004). *Action inquiry: The secret of timely and transforming leadership.* Berrett-Koehler.

Usher, R., Bryant, I., & Johnston, R. (1997). *Adult education and the post-modern challenge: Learning beyond the limits.* Routledge.

Wenger, E. (1998). *Communities of practice: Learning, meaning, and identity.* Cambridge University Press.

Wenger, E. (2000). Communities of practice and social learning systems. *Organization, 7*(2), 225–246. https://doi.org/10.1177/135050840072002.

Wenger, E. & Snyder, W. M. (2000). Communities of practice: The organizational frontier. *Harvard Business Review, 78*(1), 139–145. https://hbr.org/2000/01/communities-of-practice-the-organizational-frontier.

Wijnen-Meijer, M., Brandhuber, T., Schneider, A., & Berberat, P. O. (2022). Implementing Kolb´s Experiential Learning Cycle by linking real experience, case-based discussion and simulation. *Journal of Medical Education and Curricular Development, 9.* https://doi.org/10.1177/23821205221091511.

Williams, K. (2023, October 17). *Transforming the classroom through experiential learning.* Times Higher Education. https://www.timeshighereducation.com/campus/transforming-classroom-through-experiential-learning.

CHAPTER ELEVEN

LEARNING FOR TRANSFORMATION

 **Box 11.1 Chapter Overview and Learning Objectives**

Kafka & Corngold, in a mesmerizing story of transformation, wrote:

> "One morning, when Gregor Samsa woke from troubled dreams, he found himself transformed in his bed into a horrible vermin" (*The Metamorphosis*, 1915, p. 6).

Kafka's story chronicled the physical change that took place in traveling salesman Gregor Samsa's imagination, functioning to capture the longer process of his metamorphosis from a human being, brother, and son to a worker bee whose existence had become bug-like, scuttling to and from work as the sole support for his non-working family. While Gregor Samsa's transformation is not something anyone would want to emulate, it is a dramatic metaphor for transformation and the learning that creates one. Although interesting, Kafka's story implies a negative transformation, which adult education scholars debate. Generally, most transformations studied and written about are positive changes leading to more inclusive and discriminating worldviews.

This chapter explores learning for transformation (L4T) by defining it and exploring its role for individuals, groups, organizations, communities, and social systems. It discusses transformative learning (TL), beginning with Mezirow's foundational work, examining its shortcomings, and considering evolutions in the theory. Generative knowledge, a relatively new theory of learning for transformation, is introduced. The chapter concludes with a discussion of ways to promote L4T.

As a result of reading this chapter and completing the exercise boxes, you, the reader, should be able to:

1. Define learning for transformation.
2. Describe the tenets of transformative learning.
3. Understand newer approaches to transformative learning.
4. Critique shortcomings of transformative learning.
5. Understand generative knowledge.
6. Apply strategies to foster L4T.

Learning for transformation (L4T) describes how you, as an adult, make meaning from your life experiences and develop greater consciousness about yourself and your beliefs, relationships, and the world in which you live in ways that can be perspective-altering and life-changing, known as a **perspective transformation.** L4T requires that you have or develop awareness about your assumptions and beliefs, question them, and consider alternative beliefs that might change your perspective about yourself or the world. For example, suppose you experience a serious life event such as an illness or the death of a loved one. In that case, you might reexamine your priorities and values and better align your thinking and actions with them by making changes to promote health or spending quality time with loved ones. The COVID-19 pandemic provided a serious global event that caused many people to reexamine their priorities when the world locked down in quarantine. The learning from this crisis resulted in phenomena such as "the great resignation," rising demand for remote and hybrid work, and for some adults, taking new jobs, launching new careers, or traveling more that better aligned with their values and desire for life balance. Box 11.2 invites you to reflect on transformations in your life.

Learning for Transformation (L4T)

Learning for transformation (L4T) is essential for adults' ongoing learning, development, and sense-making about their life experiences. This type of learning is not concerned with learning new knowledge or concepts but rather

Box 11.2 Reflective Practice

Identifying Your Transformations

As an adult learner or educator, identify a significant event provoking transformation in your thinking about some aspect of your life and reflect on the following questions:

1. What precipitated this transformation?
2. What steps or stages did you go through in the process?
3. What role, if any, did other people, including perhaps educators, play in your transformation?
4. How have you acted on your new perspective?

Variations:

Alternatively, you could identify and interview someone who has experienced a change in their perspective on life due to a disorienting dilemma such as divorce, the death of a loved one, or surviving a major disaster or other crisis, mapping it according to the questions in the first part of this box.

Seek to experience what Hathaway (2018, 2022) called **"reorienting connections,"** which involves seeking a "profound connection with the more-than-human world" (p. 280). This approach to transformative learning is more favorable than Kafka's, as presented in Box 11.1. Adults can develop reorienting connections by wandering through nature, taking in natural wonders or beauty, or experiencing other moments that inspire a sense of awe and gratitude that help you feel as though you are part of something larger than yourself and inspire care for other beings.

Discussing this activity with another person and comparing your transformations and learning might also be helpful.

assessing and reassessing your values and assumptions as an adult learner or educator. Sometimes, engaging in reflection about deeply held beliefs helps you see yourself or your beliefs in a new way. When you experience a shift in self-concept or beliefs, it does not change the content of what you know but how you make meaning of that content and how you see yourself in the world. For example, as an educator, you have professional knowledge about effectively facilitating adult learning. By reflecting on your efficacy with learners and your assumptions about teaching, you could change how you make sense of your subject matter, possibly questioning long-held assumptions and considering changing what is most relevant for students to learn. As well you could change your assumptions about teaching and learning. Shifting views about education is a common transformative learning experience for faculty who discover active learning after a career of lecturing students that leaves learners bored, tired, and minimally able to apply concepts. By shifting to an active learning pedagogy, the educator has altered their beliefs about teaching, not their subject knowledge. L4T can happen in any setting, as described in the following sections.

Sites of Learning for Transformation

Learning for transformation (L4T) has been promoted and studied in various contexts, from individuals to classrooms, organizations, workplaces, and communities. L4T begins with the individual, the first "site" explored in this chapter. Other sites are the classroom and online, workplace, and community. Within these sites, learning for transformation can be engaged through self-directed, experiential, or formal activities.

Individual. As an individual learner, you are at the heart of the learning for transformation (L4T) process. It is learners themselves whose attention turns to questioning and examining long-held assumptions about the self and the world in which they live. Even if changing society is the ultimate goal, as in the social change perspective of Freire and other activists, the process begins with individuals questioning and ultimately altering how they see themselves in the world. As Freire (1970) wrote in *Pedagogy of the Oppressed*:

> The point of departure of the movement lies in the people themselves.
> But since people do not exist apart from the world, apart from reality,
> the movement must begin with the human-world relationship.
> Accordingly, the point of departure must always be with men and women
> in the "here and now," which constitutes the situation within which they
> are submerged, from which they emerge, and in which they intervene.
> Only by starting from this situation—which determines their perception
> of it—can they begin to move. (pp. 72–73)

As learners and educators engaged in facilitating learning in myriad settings and institutions, most of our efforts focus on learning subject matter or skills. Some learning is about change in perspective, usually at the individual level, but sometimes with an added goal of changing an organization or society itself.

This section looks more closely at several sites where L4T is studied—the classroom, online, the workplace, and community or society.

The Classroom and Online. As a learning site, classrooms of adult students can be found everywhere, including colleges and universities, online, corporate training centers, churches, museums, social service agencies, and elsewhere. These classrooms are usually institutionally sponsored formal learning environments with a planned curriculum and an educator who structures the learning activities. There is typically some assessment, outcome, or closure to the experience. Students are there to learn something, and rarely is it to change how they see themselves or their world. However, perspective transformations sometimes occur, and some educators actively engage in practices to promote this type of learning along with their other content-based learning objectives, as will be discussed at the end of this chapter.

The most studied classroom setting is in higher education. Rose et al. (2024) emphasized that adult students are central to learning and education. They apply vast experience from their lives, relationships, and roles in various social contexts to their education. Bergman (2021) noted that adult learners comprised nearly 40% of higher education enrollment in 2018, and Rose et al. (2024) reported over 25% of undergraduates are adults beyond the "traditional" college age of 18–24 years. L4T is "foundational to teaching adults enrolled in colleges and universities" (Rose et al., 2024, p. 106). Mezirow's (1978) development of transformative learning theory, discussed in the next part of this chapter, focused on women's return to school experiences in college reentry programs. Kasworm and Bowles (2012) reviewed 250 published reports on transformative learning in credit and noncredit higher education settings. The authors noted that higher education is a natural site for transformative learning because "ideally, higher education offers an *invitation* to think, to be, and to act in new and enhanced ways. . . . These learning environments sometimes challenge individuals to move beyond their comfort zone of the known, of self and others" (p. 389, italics in original).

Janssens et al. (2022) analyzed quality assurance frameworks in the European higher education area to determine whether they support learning for transformation for sustainable development. They took a qualitative approach and found little support for L4T in most quality assurance frameworks, except the UK framework, which includes guidance on education for sustainable development and mentions transformative learning.

Some authors have recommended shifting to a **transformative pedagogy** (TP) incorporating learner-centered teaching practices that encourage students to surface and assess their beliefs, values, and assumptions, as Paulo Freire advocated (1970). Cappiali (2023) suggested that TP addresses social justice, critical thinking, challenging power structures, and well-being and offers a framework that holistically includes cognitive, practical, and affective dimensions in what she calls "a transformative-emancipatory pedagogy" (p. 7).

Gravett et al. (2024) advocated adopting mattering pedagogies by using a posthuman approach to rethink relational pedagogies within higher education that consider curriculum, teaching and learning, and assessment. **Relational pedagogies** are teaching methods that emphasize building healthy, collaborative relationships among educators and students that incorporate an ethic of care and critical pedagogy (Bovill, 2020). Rose et al. (2024) concluded in their book *Creating a Place for Adult Learners in Higher Education* that it is not enough for higher education institutions to promote a sense of belonging among adult students but that it is also:

> Important to understand that higher education can transform the ways that individuals see themselves, their families, their work, and their society. Students must integrate into the college, but then they also must reintegrate into their families and communities as they recognize the ways they have changed. (p. 242)

Higher education often changes learners in ways they did not expect, and this is particularly true for adults as they have a lifetime of experience on which to base their learning.

Workplace. Adults spend much of their lives in work-related activities, whether preparing for work, looking for work, or working. The workplace is a significant context for formal and informal or incidental learning. In some scholars' thinking, the way to address some of the rigidity, inequities, and oppressive practices common in workplaces is by first getting workers to critically examine their role, perhaps inadvertently, in perpetuating such practices. With critical reflection at the heart of the process, the enormity of the task of doing this regarding one's role as a worker and of the workplace itself is daunting. As Brookfield (2009) noted,

> Encouraging the practice of critical reflection seems at best highly problematic, at worst doomed to failure, if critical reflection is defined . . . as the process by which people learn to challenge dominant ideologies of capitalism, white supremacy, homophobia, and patriarchy and how hegemony encourages workers to collude in their own oppression. Few working as educators or process consultants are hired to

root out hegemony and challenge capitalism, since such projects are directly in opposition to the interests of boards of directors and shareholders. (p. 127)

Brookfield and others hoped to open up the possibility of improving workplaces by getting people to question and reflect on work practices and their role in them. For example, instead of accepting the dismissive "That is just the way things are done around here," something as simple as asking *why* something is done the way it is can begin the process. See Bierema et al. (2024) for a complete discussion of applying critical perspectives in organizations.

Transformative learning in the workplace is similar to **transformative organizational change**—a dramatic evolution or revolution of the organization's structure, culture, processes, or business. Both are change processes. However, as is the focus of this chapter, learning for transformation is usually about individual change. In contrast, transformative organizational change is "typically focused on system-wide, instrumental goals" (Marsick et al., 2012, p. 375). The two foci can, of course, be brought together as the change process for an organization involves individuals, and "individuals who are transformed make changes in the environment that enable others likewise to transform and together act on the environment to move toward desired goals" (p. 376).

Critical human resource development (HRD) emerged in the 2000s, intending to transform HRD theory and practice (Bierema, 2010; Bierema et al., 2024; Stewart et al., 2007). Traditional HRD tends to privilege management and shareholder interests over workers and other stakeholder interests. Both transformative learning and organizational change apply to critical HRD concerning individual, group, organization, and system transformation.

Community or Societal. Finally, a community itself can be the site for transformation. Community activists and social activists in the tradition of Highlander Folk School, #MeToo, Civil Rights Movements, Black Lives Matter, decolonization, LBGTQIA+ movements, labor movements, environmental activist groups, and many others seek a transformation at the community or societal level. Presumably, individuals engaged in these activities have undergone perspective transformations, seeking to effect change in the larger socio-political context. Formenti and Hoggan-Kloubert (2023) suggested that learning for transformation is promising for addressing wicked social problems such as civic education, sustainability and ecology, and migration with conceptual and practical tools. However, human agency is a consideration of relational, emotional, and political aspects of transformation.

Jubas (2023) chronicled the pedagogical function of the #MeToo movement and what it might teach about gendered mistreatment and mainstream feminism. She concluded that this particular social movement was characterized by *pedagogies of confession*—testimonials to experiencing or witnessing harm in a public forum, such as posting about experiencing harassment, discrimination, or abuse on social media; *feminist snap*—a breaking point when people feel compelled to respond to injustice rather than remaining silent. Jubas concluded that the #MeToo movement offered lessons for adult educators interested in socially transformative education in the way it destigmatized survivorship, created opportunities for individual healing, and, for some, opened the potential to create political change. She also troubled the smothering of the originator of the #MeToo movement, Tarana Burke, whose contributions were suppressed by what Jubas described as celebrity-driven #activism centered on White women's experiences and complaints, particularly in Western society.

Exploration of sites of transformative learning, including the self, the classroom, online, the workplace, and the community, uncovers more about the process and identifies some of the strategies used to foster this type of learning. Although organizations and other social systems can transform, these changes depend on individual learning that stimulates a desire to address challenges and problems within a social context. The following section turns to a more detailed discussion of transformative learning theory.

Transformative Learning

The chapter began recounting Kafka's story of metamorphosis, which, in Greek, means a change in form or structure, "a special change that transcends the form from within the form itself" (Nicolaides & Eschenbacher, 2022, p. 5). Nicolaides and Eschenbacher (2022) described the phenomenon of transformation as multifaceted across disciplines, yet familiar to all definitions is the understanding that "transformation denotes significant change" (p. 5). They described the VUCA context of events such as the COVID-19 pandemic, the Black Lives Matter movement spurred by the violent murders of Black and Brown people in the United States, and political, environmental, and social unrest as "times of liquid modernity" (p. 8), where adults find themselves embroiled in a series of personal, societal, and environmental crises. Given these contextual challenges, they advocated that individuals, groups, organizations, and societies expand the capacity for learning to navigate this unwieldy context effectively. Transformative learning is a key response to these conditions.

Defining Transformative Learning

Simply defined, **"transformational learning** shapes people; they are different afterward, in ways both they and others can recognize" (Clark, 1993, p. 47). Merriam and Baumgartner (2020) declared, "Transformative or transformational learning is about change—dramatic, fundamental change in the way we see ourselves and the world in which we live" (p. 166). You can probably recall, as a learner, how you have changed your mind, discovered new ways to do things, or found something distressing that caused you to assess your assumptions. Transformative or transformational learning (terms used interchangeably in the literature) has become the most studied and written about adult learning theory since Knowles proposed andragogy in the 1970s (see Chapter 7). Transformative learning (TL) has "replaced andragogy as the dominant educational philosophy of adult education, offering teaching practices grounded in empirical research and supported by sound theoretical assumptions" (Taylor, 2008, p. 12).

Perhaps because it is considered a form of learning by adults, not children, "transformative learning theory has brought a new and exciting identity to the field of adult education" (Cranton & Taylor, 2012, p.16). *The Palgrave Handbook of Learning and Transformation* (Nicolaides et al., 2022) indicates the development of scholarship and practice in this theoretical area of adult education over 50 years. There is a previous handbook (Taylor et al., 2012), a journal devoted to this type of learning (*Journal of Transformative Education*), and a bi-annual International Transformative Learning Conference (ITLC). Given the plethora of resources and approaches to TL theory, it is challenging to capture the essence of this theory in one short chapter. To that end, we (the authors) have organized the TL discussion into the following sections—How does TL occur? Mezirow's contributions, critiques of TL, and emerging theoretical perspectives.

How Does Transformative Learning Occur?

As learners and educators, we can think of "learning" as both a verb—"I am learning about this theory"—and a noun—"I have acquired knowledge (more learning) about this theory," similar to how Kegan (2000) differentiated between *"informational learning,"* that learning that adds to *"what we know,"* and is cumulative, and **transformational learning**—learning that "changes . . . *how we know"* (Kegan, 2000, p. 49, italics in original). While much of adult learning is additive, we know more about many things as we move through life, and that occasional, often dramatic life experience causes us to stop and examine how we think about something. Learning you have a life-threatening disease, being the first in your family to earn an advanced degree, winning a lottery, being caught in random violence, or other formative experiences may lead to questioning some of our assumptions about ourselves and the world. The **transformative learning process** is then set in motion, a

> Process by which we transform our taken-for-granted frames of reference (meaning schemes, habits of mind, mindsets) to make them more inclusive, discriminating, open, emotionally capable of change, and reflective so that they may generate beliefs and opinions that will prove more true or justified to guide actions. (Mezirow, 2000, p. 8)

Mezirow's Contributions to Transformative Learning Theory

Mezirow (1978) was the first to identify transformative learning as a cognitive, rational process in his study of women in community college reentry programs. He found that the experience caused them to examine their assumptions about who they were and how they were products of sociocultural expectations of women at that time. Mezirow (1991) described the transformative learning process as follows:

> Transformative learning involves an enhanced level of awareness of the context of one's beliefs and feelings, a critique of their assumptions and particularly premises, an assessment of alternative perspectives, a decision to negate an old perspective in favor of a new one or to make a synthesis of old and new, an ability to take action based upon the new perspective, and a desire to fit the new perspective into the broader context of one's life. (p. 161)

Mezirow's (1978) early description of transformational learning included 10 phases, beginning with "a disorienting dilemma." A **disorienting dilemma** occurs when a significant personal life event precipitates a crisis in our lives as learners, such as the death of a loved one, being a victim of a crime, job loss, and other defining moments. Subsequent research suggests that while a disorienting dilemma triggers the process, there can also be an accumulation of experiences over time that eventually come together to foster a transformation. For example, after numerous incidents of sexist treatment in the workplace, a woman employee begins to question her assumptions about equality in the workplace—this **questioning,** or self-examination, is the second phase in the process, followed by the third phase of **critically assessing the assumptions** which one has been living with *before* the initiation of this process (that is, that men and women are treated equally in the workplace). The subsequent phases include **"recognition that one's discontent and the process of transformation are shared"** (there are other women who have experienced sexist treatment and want to do something about it), **"exploration of options for new roles, relationships, and actions,"** and **"planning a course of action"** (forming a women's network, bringing sexist practices to the attention of management, and other steps to improve workplace equity) (Mezirow, 1991, p. 22). The remaining four phases include **"acquiring knowledge and skills for implementing one's plans,"** **"trying out new roles,"** which includes **"building competence and self-confidence in new roles and relationships,"** and finally, **"reintegrating the new perspective into one's life"** (p. 22). Box 11.3 offers an opportunity to apply Mezirow's 10 phases of TL.

Since the first presentation of his theory in the late 1970s, Mezirow refined and expanded it, taking into account theoretical critiques and empirical research. He also clarified the notion of reflection, saying it could involve three types: **"content reflection**—reflection on *what* we perceive, think, feel, or act upon as learners. **Process reflection** is an examination of *how* we perform these functions of perceiving, thinking, feeling, or acting" (Mezirow, 1991, pp. 107–108, emphasis in original). **Premise reflection** is going deeper, asking "*why* we perceive, think, feel, or act as we do" (p. 108). Premise reflection is the only one of the three that leads to a perspective transformation. Let's take the example above of the woman employee who experienced sexism in the workplace. Content reflection might be her thinking about an incident in a meeting where her men co-workers ignored her suggestions. Content reflection might cause her to ask herself, "What happened in that meeting?" Through process reflection, she might wonder if colleagues ignored her because the information she shared was unclear or confusing. Premise reflection would involve asking *why* colleagues ignored her. Was it because a woman made the suggestions? Such a question can potentially set in motion a perspective change about the role of women in the workplace.

Hoggan and Kasl (2023) identified key processes occurring in TL with increasing levels of complexity: (1) elaborating existing meaning schemes (reflecting on how you currently think about something), (2) learning new meaning schemes (seeing something in a new way), (3) transforming meaning schemes (shifting how you see something), and (4) transforming meaning perspectives (altering your viewpoints).

In light of a growing body of research on his theory, Mezirow acknowledged that emotions, intuition, context, and relationships play a role in the transformational learning process. However, they are still secondary to the critical cognitive aspects (Baumgartner, 2012). He also clarified his view on the relationship of perspective transformation to social action. The action itself, the final component

 **Box 11.3 Reflective Practice**

Comparing Your Transformative Learning to Mezirow's 10 Phases

This box focuses on defining transformations across the lifespan. This activity invites you, as an adult learner, to compare your transformations against Mezirow's (1991) phases of transformative learning outlined as follows:

1. A disorienting dilemma occurs, such as a crisis, illness, or death of a loved one, being a victim of a crime, job loss, or other life challenges. Such occurrences are often triggering, but they can also build gradually over time, such as realizing your values no longer align with what your parents taught you.
2. You begin a process of questioning or self-examination.
3. Before initiating this process, you critically assess the assumptions that guided your thoughts and actions.
4. You recognize that others share your new perspective or discontent with the old one.
5. You explore options for new roles, relationships, and actions.
6. You plan a course of action.
7. You acquire new knowledge and skills for implementing your plans.
8. You try out new roles.
9. You build competence and self-confidence into new roles and relationships.
10. You reintegrate the new perspective into your life (Mezirow, 1991, p. 22).

Since the first presentation of his theory in the late 1970s, Mezirow has refined and expanded his theory, taking into account theoretical critiques and empirical research. He also clarified the notion of reflection, saying it could involve "*content reflection*—reflection on *what* we perceive, think, feel, or act upon."

Questions for Reflection:

1. How closely did your journey align with the 10 phases outlined by Mezirow?
2. If your phases differed, how?
3. What are the shortcomings of the 10 phases?

of the process, can be in terms of "immediate action, delayed action or reasoned reaffirmation of an existing pattern of action" (Mezirow, 2000, p. 24). In his view, social action is not the goal of transformative learning; rather, personal transformation "leads to alliances with others of like mind," which can lead to social action (1992, p. 252). Box 11.4 highlights strategies for implementing TL.

 **Box 11.4 Tips and Tools for Teaching and Learning**

Implementing Transformative Learning

Hoggan and Kasl (2023) offered guidelines for implementing transformative learning according to key distinguishing elements they suggested are grounded in Mezirow's view of TL. This box describes them and gives definitions of each to consider as an adult learner or educator.

Element of Implementing TL and Questions Educators Can Ask Themselves	Definition
Consider the learning context. Where is the learning situated? What are the cultural and social expectations?	Learning contexts may be formal or informal. Formal learning tends to occur in institutions or organizations such as educational or community institutions or the workplace. Less formal settings might be field trips or meetings.
Determine what you hope to accomplish. What is the focus and intended goal of the learning?	Verifying the key purpose and desired learning outcome or outcomes sought for learners.
Decide what learners need to experience to accomplish the learning outcome or outcomes. What do you want learners to think or do due to the learning?	Clarifying the learning processes to be followed during the learning that include exploration of learner assumptions and expectations and how they influence their action in the world
Develop a plan to facilitate the learning. What do I, as the educator, need to create to promote effective learning?	Establishing the pedagogical strategies applied during the learning, such as critical reflection, dialogue, demonstration, modeling, or other approaches.
Engage in activities to implement the pedagogical strategy.	Implement the pedagogical activities that foster transformative learning, including surfacing and discussing assumptions, taking assessments, and experiencing active learning.

Critiques of TL

Marsick et al. (2022) pointed out in their Foreword to the 2022 *Palgrave Handbook of Learning and Transformation* (Nicolaides et al., 2022) that research on this theory "has been constricted by the homogeneity of the scholars theorizing and researching transformative learning. To date, our scholarship is dominated by the experiences of western, educated, industrialized, rich, and democratic or weird populations (Muthukrishna et al., 2020)" (p. x). Newman (2012), for example, startled the adult education world with an essay questioning the very existence of transformative learning. In his view the theory has become "all things to all people" (p. 49) and is unsubstantiated, ambiguous, and unwieldy. He proposed "we strike the phrase *transformative learning* from the educational lexicon altogether" and instead talk about "*good learning*" (p. 51, italics in original). One of his main reasons for doubting its existence is that "transformations can only be verified by the learners themselves" (p. 39). Even in telling their "stories" of transformation, stories "contain invention as well as record" (p. 40).

Hoggan (2016) raised what he described as a "significant problem" with transformative learning (TL) theory being "that it is increasingly being used to refer to almost any instance of learning" (p. 57). Given the vast array of definitions, frameworks, and theories of transformative learning, he suggested that an organizational scheme is needed to summarize this material. One approach is to proceed historically, according to Gunnlaugson (2008), who divided the literature into "first" and "second wave" theories. TL's first wave centers on Mezirow's groundbreaking work and includes his refinements and research building on and critiquing the theory. The second wave consists of those who departed from Mezirow's rationalistic perspective and expanded transformative learning to include holistic, extrarational, and integrative perspectives. For example, Dirkx (1998) proposed four lenses for understanding transformative learning—emancipatory, cognitive, developmental, and spiritual-integrative, and Taylor (2008) suggested that Mezirow's psychocritical approach would benefit from the addition of neurobiological, cultural-spiritual, race-centric, and planetary conceptions.

Hoggan (2016), recognizing that transformative learning theory had gone through what Gunnlaugson (2008) defined as first-wave theories (specific views on defining TL and its process) and second-wave theories (integrated concepts of TL drawing on multiple perspectives), concluded there was rationale for regarding TL as a **metatheory** (an overarching paradigm that synthesizes common components of TL theories). Taylor (2008) organized theoretical TL perspectives into seven categories: psychocritical, psychoanalytic, emancipatory, psychodevelopmental, spiritual or transformational, planetary, and race-centric. Hoggan and Kasl (2023) modified Taylor's categories, adding Illeris's (2014) discussion of identity. Table 11.1 summarizes these TL perspectives.

TABLE 11.1 TAYLOR'S SUMMARY OF TRANSFORMATIVE LEARNING'S THEORETICAL PERSPECTIVES

Approach to TL	Description	Example	Scholars
Psychocritical	TL is concerned with how adults make meaning of life experiences. These incorporate **"habits of mind,"** or one's interpretation of the world based on their background, experience, personality, and culture, and **"point of view,"** or how an adult expresses their habit of mind through beliefs, feelings, value judgments, or attitudes influencing thinking and action. Mezirow's 10 phases of TL were profiled earlier in this chapter, and according to Merriam and Baumgartner (2020), they can be classified into four main components: experience, critical reflection, reflective discourse, and action.	Mezirow (1978) interviewed women who decided to return to college after time away from their formal studies, and their experiences of life challenges, self-doubt, and hesitancy at returning to school were initially barriers. Still, through critical reflection and progress in their studies, they developed new ways of thinking about themselves and their capabilities, transforming their identity and views of themselves as capable of completing their studies, growing, and contributing to society.	Mezirow (1978) Cranton (2016) Merriam & Baumgartner (2020)
Psychoanalytic	TL is an internal self-discovery process grounded in soul work, emotion, imagery, fantasy, and other inner thoughts. "Education must adapt the end-in-view of helping individuals work towards acknowledging and understanding the dynamics between their inner and outer worlds. For the learner, this means the expansion of consciousness and working toward a meaningful integrated life as evidenced in authentic relationships with self and others" (Boyd & Myers, 1988, p. 261).	Dirkx (1997) observed that people tend to independently look for logic and reason when faced with disorienting dilemmas rather than looking for images and meaning within the soul or how they engage with the broader world. For example, a grieving spouse might reason, "I should be feeling better by now. My spouse has been gone for almost a year." Yet, when they turn toward their relationships with others to process the death of their partner and see connections between their heart and mind, a new capacity emerges to help them process their grief and support other grieving family members.	Boyd & Myers (1988) Dirkx (1997)

(Continued)

TABLE 11.1 (*Continued*)

Approach to TL	Description	Example	Scholars
Emancipatory	Questions the dominant structure of social context, including the political, economic, cultural, social, educational, and other entities (Freire, 1970; Habermas, 1985; Honneth, 2014). The goal is change that promotes social justice.	Learners visit a homeless shelter and help prepare and serve food. The experience has an indelible impact on how they view homelessness and the social dynamics that create it.	Freire (1970) Habermas (1985) Honneth (2014)
Psycho-developmental	Transformation involves developing more complex cognitive and psychosocial capacities by understanding the "form that transforms" (Kegan, 1982, 1998) or shifts in how a person constructs knowledge and meaning. The idea is that levels of development move from simple to more complex.	Belenky (1986) described women's development in their book *Women's Ways of Knowing*, which examined how women develop "voice" in a hierarchy of self-concept concerning knowledge and how they develop capacity as knowers or capability to construct their knowledge without relying on external authority. Daloz and Cross (1986) and Daloz (2012) chronicled how adults achieve higher levels of development through relationships with mentors and social action.	Belenky (1986) Daloz and Cross (1986), Daloz (2012) Kegan (1982, 1998)
Spiritual or Transformational	TL is fostered by recognizing connections larger than the self (Ferrer et al., 2005). Hart (2001) advocated holistic learning and chronicled how knowing and learning unfold through six interconnected levels of information, knowledge, intelligence, understanding, system, and transformation. Tolliver and Tisdell (2006) advocated expanding understanding of TL as learners incorporated seeing themselves in exchange with the world, engaging multiple dimensions of being, including rational, practical, spiritual, imaginative, somatic, and sociocultural domains.	After a near-death experience, a person feels a connection to the universe and embarks on a spiritual practice such as meditation, mindfulness, or yoga, reassessing their priorities and values in life.	Hart (2001) Ferrer et al. (2005) Tolliver & Tisdell (2006)

Identity	Identity differentiates transformation from other types of learning, whereby TL shifts how people experience themselves and how they want to be experienced by others (Illeris, 2014). Tennant (2005) advocated what he called "technologies of the self" to help adult learners shape their formation and change as (1) knowing oneself, (2) controlling oneself, (3) caring for oneself, and (4) recreating oneself.	After being dedicated to their work, a person loses their job or has a significant career setback that causes a reassessment of how they want to spend their career years and a decision to align their work more closely with their values and capacity to make a positive difference in the world.	Illeris (2014) Tennant (2005)
Planetary	Learners realize that living with a sense of connection rather than domination over the world is preferable, including valuing the interconnectedness of all life on earth. This view advocates environmental sustainability, values Indigenous knowledge, and assumes an ecological perspective (Hathaway, 2018, 2022; O'Sullivan, 2002). Lange (2018) advocated for an ontology of relationality, or considering the relationships between entities more essential than the entities themselves.	After attending a lecture on climate change, a person who never paid much attention to the issue has a new sense of urgency and needs to devote energy to promoting more ecological sustainability in their personal life, helping others become more aware, and ensuring their actions protect all living beings.	Hathaway (2018) Lange (2018) O'Sullivan (2002)
Race Centric	Helping learners question and challenge White supremacy and ensuring all learners have a voice and feel valued in learning settings, particularly those from historically excluded and underrepresented racial groups. Johnson-Bailey and Alfred (2006) wrote about promoting empowerment, inclusion, and intellectual growth, especially for students who have been silent due to racial marginalization. Centering marginalized voices in educational settings and promoting changes to racist structures and society is primary in this approach. Sheared (1994), and Sheared et al. (2010) advocated for a womanist perspective and giving voice to those traditionally silenced.	A faculty member teaches their students how to use dialogue and develops ground rules for respectful conversation that ensures everyone is heard and shares their experience. The instructor monitors the discussion to ensure privileged students do not dominate the conversation. Another example might be when a White person attends a workshop on White supremacy and how unconscious bias and systemic racism create injustice and inequity in society and begins to see their role in addressing systemic racism and White supremacy in their work and life.	Johnson-Bailey & Alfred (2006) Sheared (1994) Sheared et al. (2010)

The section on transformative learning defined the concept, summarized Mezirow's contributions to developing theory, raised critiques, and featured emerging theoretical perspectives. The next section focuses on a newer area of theory that speaks to learning for transformation.

Generative Knowing

Generative knowing is an emerging theory of adult learning that explores how adults create knowledge in complicated and ambiguous situations where answers and solutions are lacking. For example, the COVID-19 pandemic threw the globe into a frightening time of inability to predict health and safety or knowing how long the world might be on lockdown and offered unique learning opportunities. This section defines generative knowing and explores facilitation strategies.

Defining Generative Knowing

Marsick et al. (2014) advocated reimagining modern adult learning theory to help individuals, groups, and organizations more effectively cope with the world's VUCA (volatile, uncertain, complex, and ambiguous) context. Nicolaides (2022) introduced her theory of generative knowing as one strategy for responding to and living with uncertainty and unknowing based on her assertion that adult education is "grappling with how adults learn in a world being recomposed by a global pandemic and the *Ruptures* that have emerged from its influence" (p. 8, italics in the original). She proposed generative learning in response to the "need for a new learning theory that can keep up with the rapid rate of change . . . [it is] learning *to be, learning to become*" (Nicolaides, 2022, p. 8). According to Nicolaides, generative knowing has three phases: ruptures, in-scending, and awaring.

Ruptures are when adults meet the unknown with learning. Recall, as a learner, what you did during the COVID-19 pandemic. The globe was trying to make sense of a foreboding, strange, complicated, and uncertain situation. Yet, the global lockdown created space for some adults to question their assumptions and reflect on how they could approach their lives and work differently. Others clung to "the way it used to be" and experienced little if any learning or growth from the experience. As the pandemic waned and vaccines became widely distributed, some adults maintained their life changes and new outlook.

In contrast, others reverted to old habits, perhaps hinting at those who are generative learners and those who are not. A glaring example is how some CEOs have handled remote work versus return-to-work edicts. Donald Trump, on the first day of his second term in office, mandated that federal workers return to their offices five days a week to end the remote work culture that emerged during the pandemic. He threatened to fire federal workers who refused to comply with the order. Such unilateral actions show little regard for the lessons learned during the pandemic or how work might be smarter and more balanced for people. One clear thing is that not all leaders experienced learning for transformation due to the pandemic.

The next aspect of generative knowing is in-scending, which follows rupture. Nicolaides (2022) explained **in-scending** as:

> The intentional movement of inquiry that follows the sensations of the experience [of rupture] in order to undergo it, listen from the inside of the at-first darkness that is the side beneath . . . experience. This aspect of generative knowing, to *In-scend*, is a practice of inquiry into the ontology of experience. (p. 9, italics in the original)

What does in-scending mean for you as a learner? Rather than fretting about the unknown, you might approach it with curiosity to see what you can understand or learn. It involves inquiring about the situation and asking yourself, "What am I sensing or feeling?" "What do I not comprehend?" "How can I respond according to my ethics and values?" Nora Bateson (2016) wrote about knowledge and complexity and explained the dilemma of unknowing as: "the problem of authorizing uncertain, unacademic, unknowable, and unanswered knowledge. Being wrong and not knowing our assets. These traits are not dismissals of serious study but instead offer an invitation to the diversity of perspectives within a diversity of contexts" (p. 41). She further mused about the problem with problem-solving and how people expect solutions will be endpoints. However, she emphasized, "There are no end points in complex systems, only tendrils that diffuse and reorganize situations ... compensations come in crooked streams and don't end up where you thought they would" (p. 40). She noted that complex problems and their temporary solutions often worsen the problems, such as DDT killing pesky insects but creating multiple other problems or teaching to the test but failing to educate the learner. Perhaps this quest to problem-solve is due to humans' discomfort with uncertainty and the need to find a neat solution even when one does not exist.

Awaring is when new learning drives action. Workers reassessed their life balance during the pandemic. They made new choices, including leaving careers, switching organizations, and often opting to improve their life balance with options for remote or hybrid work structures. Nicolaides (2022) implored, "To facilitate generative learning, you have to create spaces of possibility" (p. 129).

Promoting Generative Knowing

As an adult educator, how do you create learning spaces that provide possibilities for learning? Nicolaides recommended three steps to help engage yourself and others in generative learning: (1) practicing **resonant inquiry** or committing to learning through inquiry; (2) showing **courageous vulnerability** by questioning ways of knowing, doing, and being with humility; and (3) **being flexible** when new learning leads to change and letting it surprise you rather than incapacitate you. Nicolaides also called for **spaces of possibility** characterized by suspending judgment, fostering authentic dialogue, appreciating neurodiversity, and acknowledging interdependence among the self, others, and the larger community.

Promoting Learning for Transformation

This chapter has defined learning for transformation (L4T) and explored Mezirow's transformative learning (TL) theory and newer approaches to understanding the phenomenon. It also introduced generative knowing. All of these approaches strive to promote learning through transformation. How might we, as adult educators, facilitate such learning? Box 11.5 summarizes three orientations for implementing L4T.

McClain (2024) noted that interest in fostering transformative learning emerged in the 2000s because educators realized how TL encourages learner change and provokes critical examination of their beliefs and actions. Mezirow (1990) outlined conditions for facilitating TL, including creating a safe learning environment, being student-centered, providing accurate information, engaging in problem-solving, and fostering critical reflection. Merriam and Baumgartner (2020) recommended fostering TL through a holistic approach or "teaching engaging students' minds, feelings, bodies, and spirits" (p. 191) or embodied learning and building genuine relationships based on trust and mutuality. Although many educators hope to inspire transformation, it is unpredictable and cannot be forced. Optimal conditions depend not only on a learning community of support among learners and educators but also on learner readiness and receptivity. Educators must also exercise care not to influence a learner's transformation process or determine when one has occurred (Cranton & Kasl, 2012; McClain, 2024).

Mezirow (2000) maintained the goal of adult education is "to help adults realize their potential for becoming more liberated, socially responsible, and autonomous learners—that is, to make more informed choices by becoming more critically reflective as 'dialogic thinkers' (Basseches, 1984) in their engagement in a given social context" (p. 30). Facilitating learning for transformation (L4T) is central for those who share Mezirow's vision of the goal of adult

 **Box 11.5 Tips and Tools for Teaching and Learning**

Three Orientations for Implementing L4T

Hoggan and Kloubert (2020) offered three orientations toward implementing learning for transformation (L4T) as: prescriptive, process-oriented, and adaptive.

1. **Prescriptive L4T** tends to be teacher-centered in that educators determine how learners should transform, including the worldview and the pedagogy. Hogan and Kloubert cautioned against this approach due to its educator-centric approach and ethical challenges that could leave the impression of indoctrination rather than liberatory or developmental learning.
2. **Process-oriented L4T** is pragmatic and focused on helping learners build skills and habits necessary in their lives and work. This approach does not attempt to teach a particular worldview but rather fosters the development of skills that help learners articulate their views and values and surface unexplored assumptions.
3. **Adaptive L4T** is the third orientation appropriate for the VUCA context, where challenges people face are conducive to transformative learning. For instance, consider the social and emotional challenges people faced during the COVID-19 pandemic and the learning types needed when faced with ambiguous problems and uncertainty, as described in Nicolaides's generative knowledge model.

As a learner or educator, which orientations have you experienced?

education. Although specific instructional L4T strategies have already been alluded to in this chapter, there are numerous strategies discussed in the literature (see especially Cranton, 2006; Mezirow et al., 2009; Nicolaides et al., 2022; and Taylor et al., 2012). This section explores underlying components and strategies of instruction necessary to create the conditions for transformation, including creating safe and brave learning spaces, fostering critical reflection, engaging in dialogue and meaningful conversation, using appropriate pedagogy, and integrating strategies of narrative, embodiment, and spirituality.

Creating Safe, Brave Learning Spaces

A theme that spans accounts of fostering L4T is that educators need to create space where such learning might occur. Although most adult educators value fostering critical reflection, it is far less common for educators to have as their primary goal affecting perspective transformations among their adult learners. Instead, this might be an outcome for some students as they learn the course's prescribed content. For this to occur, students must have space to reflect, discuss, and engage in activities that draw upon their life experiences. Vella (2000) advocated creating learning spaces that were "sacred," where learners listen to others' experiences without judgment. Creating safe, brave spaces has emerged as one strategy for promoting learning.

A **safe space** is a trusting learning environment where adults feel physically and emotionally protected and will not be judged, harassed, or discriminated against. Self-expression and community building are encouraged. **Brave spaces** also enable learners to share their experiences and perspectives, openly acknowledging they might be troubling or challenging. There is more empowerment for risk-taking, mistake-making, and collective learning. Co-creating ground rules and expectations is essential for educators and learners to establish environments that foster TL and generative knowing.

Drawing on narrative research in executive action learning, Corlett et al. (2021) defined a safe space where people can be vulnerable and truthful with others about their identities and perhaps challenges in an environment characterized by openness, honesty, and mutual support. Doornbosch et al. (2024) found through the analysis of community intergroup dialogue on divisive issues, learning behaviors promoting safe, brave environments included personal engagement through self-disclosure and risk-taking, and interpersonal engagement like validating others.

Fostering Critical Reflection

Critical reflection is crucial to promoting L4T. Although some suggest a transformation of perspective can occur through non-cognitive means such as a spiritual or intense emotional experience, creating such conditions in an educational environment is challenging. In instructional settings, the tools at our disposal as adult educators are to model and enable students to examine and critically assess their assumptions about themselves, the world, and their place. Brookfield (2012) has written extensively about engaging students in this process. Conscientization and critical reflection are two approaches.

Conscientization. As introduced in Chapter 2, educators can help adults raise their awareness about how values, rhetoric, beliefs, products, or social forces influence them. Freire (1973) defined this as **conscientization**, or how people acquire critical awareness through reflection, assumption testing, and action. For example, workplace affinity groups involve representatives of historically underrepresented or marginalized workers (e.g., women, LBGTQIA+, race, or other identities). As members of affinity groups discuss workplace issues, they critically assess structural and systemic issues that create inequities for their identity group and become more keenly aware of the issues and injustices. They organize to share feedback and advocate for policy, culture, and organization culture changes to address their issues.

Critical Reflection. Schön (1983) defined **reflection** as learning from experience and developing awareness of implicit knowledge. According to Mezirow (2012), critical reflection on premise (examining assumptions, beliefs, and values) can be transformative. Critical reflection enables adults to correct distortions in their beliefs and errors in problem-solving and involves critiquing presuppositions on which beliefs have been built (Mezirow, 2003). Schön (1983) wrote about **"knowing-in-action"** and how adults reflect on action (what happened at the meeting?) and **reflection-in-action** (during the meeting, a person considers, "How can I intervene to move this conversation toward resolution?"). Other ways to reflect include journaling and engaging in dialogue with others. Brookfield (2011) suggested that critical thinking involves (1) identifying assumptions framing thinking and action, (2) checking their accuracy and validity, (3) examining ideas and decisions from different vantage points, and (4) taking informed action.

Promoting Constructive Conversation

Cutting across the research on fostering L4T in practice is the theme of learning through conversation. This section focuses on dialogue and giving voice.

Dialogue. **Dialogue** is listening deeply, reflecting on one's reactions, examining one's assumptions, and speaking to be understood instead of defending (DeTemple & Sarrouf, 2017). Paulo Freire's definition of dialogue is featured in Chapter 3 (see Box 3.9), which is a conversation where people name the world. Dialogue involves adults listening to create new understandings or meanings about the issue grounded in mutuality, challenging existing social structures, and co-creating knowledge. Freire believed conscientization transpired in dialogue where "we find two dimensions, reflection, and action, in such radical interaction that if one is sacrificed—even in part—the other immediately suffers" (Freire, 2014, p. 88.). Mezirow (1997) asserted comparably that through dialogue, people "learn together by analyzing the related experiences of others to arrive at a common understanding that holds until new evidence or arguments present themselves" (p. 7).

Giving Voice. Sheared (2023) explained, "**Giving voice** seeks to undo the manner in which the traditional educator-learner paradigm has silenced voices, however unintentionally, and it recognizes that we must acknowledge the different ways in which reality is interpreted within a learning community" (p. 23). Giving voice as an educator involves creating space where learners acknowledge different realities and understand other ways of interpreting reality. It involves engaging learners and dialoguing where people listen and understand how each learner authors their world and affirms their intersectional identities such as culture, race, and gender. Grounded in Afrocentric feminist epistemology, Sheared (1994) offered four tenets: (1) concrete experience is used as a criterion of meaning, typically shared through narrative or story; (2) dialogue is the basis for assessing knowledge claims where students explore alternative ways of viewing the world; (3) an ethic of caring emphasizes the uniqueness of individuals, elicits appropriate emotion from the dialogue and recognizes empathetic understanding; and where participants become interconnected through call and response with each other that requires trust and care; and (4) an ethic of personal accountability guides both teaching and learning making everyone responsible for the process.

Using Appropriate Pedagogy

Pedagogy, or teaching method, is vital to consider in fostering T4L. This section features four approaches: learner-centeredness, experiential learning, womanist approaches, and intersectionality.

Learner-centered Pedagogy. Learner-centered teaching gives students some decision-making authority over course content and engages them in teaching the content to each other, along with some control over how they will learn course material, the pace of learning, and engagement and self and peer assessment activities (Weimer, 2012). Weimer suggested designing learner-focused activities and assignments to increase the propensity for transformative experiences for adults. They offered examples of how this might work by posing questions encouraging learners to find information or answers to promote critical reflection. Journaling is another activity that can prompt questioning and feedback and encourage learners to "discover reasons behind the reasons" (p. 448).

Experiential Learning Chapter 10 defined **experiential learning** as a sense-making process through engaging in, reflecting on, and making meaning of the events in one's life, whether cognitive, physical, emotional, social, or spiritual. Dillard et al. (2024) advocated that experiential learning theory needs to become more interdisciplinary, integrating digital tools, considering sociopolitical context, and fostering collaboration. **Transformative experiential learning** is revising one's interpretation of prior experience, occurring when there is a disconnection between an adult's experience and how they make sense of it. For example, imagine a leader whose identity is defined by being an effective builder of teams and someone who gets results. However, their team fails to deliver the expected result. The experience causes the leader to question their leadership ability, compounded by receiving feedback that they are not listening to or delegating effectively with their team.

Womanist Methodology and Polyrhythmic Realities. **Womanist methodology** holistically gives voice to people historically silenced in education due to traditional and unidimensional instructional methods (Sheared, 1994, 2023). **Polyrhythmic realities** recognize that people experience intersecting identities and truths, which makes them move in multiple directions simultaneously. Sharing and exposing differences and similarities that people experience and learning settings due to skin color, language, economic status, and personal experiences, and how they relate to individuals' historical, cultural, social, and political identities of themselves concerning others. Sheared's (2023) polyrhythmic reality chart is an exercise to help learners reflect critically on their identity, particularly in learning contexts (p. 31).

Intersectional Pedagogy. "Intersectional pedagogy (IP) is an educational intervention to help learners develop a social justice consciousness about interlocking systems of oppression that create injustice at the individual group and societal levels" (Sim & Bierema, 2023, p. 1). Sim and Bierema (2023) offered seven principles for implementing intersectional pedagogy with adult learners that have the potential for fostering learning for transformation: (1) raise intersectional consciousness; (2) share positionality and open vulnerability as the instructor; and (3) incorporate context and history. Challenge the social norms by unpacking power dynamics in society. Address both privilege and oppression. Deconstruct existing theories and practices. Connect to social change. Box 11.6 shares strategies for emancipatory pedagogy.

Box 11.6 Tips and Tools for Teaching and Learning

The Five E's of Emancipatory Pedagogy and Courageous Resistance

Thalhammer et al. (2007) published a report indicating that a sense of helplessness and lack of compassion and empathy toward others prevents people from acting on social injustice. Tan (2009) offered the Five E's of emancipatory pedagogy as an alternative to dehumanizing teaching and learning and as a framework to help learners take meaningful and timely action on issues of injustice. Each "E" is defined in this box with examples for facilitating adult learning that draw on Thalhammer et al.'s (2007) pedagogy of "courageous resistance" that involved six steps of (1) engaging in activities that allow bonding between learners, (2) practicing empathy, (3) practicing care, (4) diversifying from individual experience with people different from oneself, (5) networking with other groups for access to resources services and support, and (6) practicing new skills.

"E's"	Definitions drawing on Tan (2009)	Adult Learning Example drawing on Courageous Resistance (Thalhammer et al., 2007)
Engage	The educator builds trust, respect, and buy-in with learners, their stakeholders, and communities and helps learners connect their experiences to the new information.	Learners discover social inequities in their community and identify one issue that interests them.
Educate	The educator helps learners develop academic and critical competencies by providing relevant learning tools and information to help them understand the situation. This combines academic skills and critical analysis of social justice and injustice issues.	Learners identify causes of oppression in their area of interest or concern.
Experience	The educator exposes learners to the concepts being learned beyond the classroom by creating opportunities to act on their learning through social action that promotes peace, social accountability (e.g., law enforcement), immigrant rights, worker's rights, or educational justice.	Learners seek an experience related to their interest or concern, such as volunteering at a homeless or women's shelter, visiting an underprivileged school district, or other environment not part of their regular interactions. They journal about the experience.
Empower	The educator helps learners realize their worth and potential agency to address the issues they are studying in ways that embolden emancipatory action.	Learners identify ways they can help address the issue of interest or concern through their actions and agency.

"E's"	Definitions drawing on Tan (2009)	Adult Learning Example drawing on Courageous Resistance (Thalhammer et al., 2007)
Enact	Helping learners take meaningful and timely action using their new knowledge and perspective on issues they care about.	Learners develop a plan for how they want to take current and future action on the issue of interest or concern.

Narrative

In addition to fostering transformative learning from the cognitive strategy of critical reflection, many other writers have suggested using non-rational mediums such as **storytelling** or narrative, where learners retell experiences, reflect on them, create new meaning, and perhaps change perspective or behavior (Clark, 2012; Lawrence & Paige, 2016; Nicolaides et al., 2022): this section profiles storytelling and the imaginal method.

Storytelling. Engaging with experiences, values, perspectives, and emotions through a narrative can transform adults to see situations and allow them to reexamine the situation and prevailing perspectives. Anderson Sathe et al. (2022) offered a structure for storytelling through an accessible listening protocol (p. 435), and Muthayan (2022) outlined a 10-step storytelling through regression method (p. 542) designed for post-colonial contexts to involve learners in the co-creation of curriculum that responds to their specific developmental needs and social context. An excellent example of the power of stories is through the US National Public Radio's StoryCorps (see https://www.npr.org/series/4516989/storycorps). StoryCorps has archived nearly 700,000 stories, many reflecting transformative learning. Children's stories are also powerful pedagogical tools like Yamada's (2021) *What Do You Do with an Idea?* Or Yamada et al.'s (2013) *What Do You Do with a Problem?* Reading and discussing them aloud or having adults write and share their stories can be powerful learning experiences.

The Imaginal Method. Dirkx and Schlegel (2023) observed "emotional-laden experiences" in learning situations where intense emotions learners engage with content, peers, educators, or the broader social and cultural context. This learning activity helps learners gain insight into the self, typically through an iterative process of independent reflection and independent journaling. Dirkx and Schlegel offered the **imaginal method** to enable understanding of and working with emotion-laden experiences in adult learning contexts. The imaginal method has four steps to include (1) description (recalling an emotion-laden experience and the feelings it unearths and the images it evokes to make observations about how it feels, what happened, or who was involved), (2) association (making associations between the images that emerged during the emotion-laden experience and similar life experiences), (3) amplification (transcending the personal experience by asking what figures are images in the learner's cultural context remind them of the emotional and experience for instance for mythology, literature, theater, movies, or fairy tales; next, learners attempt to connect their own experience with more universal themes), and (4) animation (taking the image or figure that emerged in the previous description phase and bringing it to life in the moment). Box 11.7 offers additional approaches to using storytelling.

Box 11.7 Tips and Tools for Teaching and Learning

Exploring Transformative Learning Through Storytelling

Create service-learning experiences where learners engage in community issues through interviewing stakeholders, joining protests, meeting government officials, or taking field trips that will challenge learners' experiences and/or worldviews.

One example is to have students write a very linear account of their problem or issue on an index card by

1. Writing one sentence completing this statement: "My issue/problem is _____."
2. Next, they complete this statement: "The prescribed solution is _____."
3. Next, they set the card aside and are assigned the task of writing a story about the problem that begins with "Once upon a time" and ends with "The End." about their problem, embellishing as they see fit.
4. Once they finish the story, they read it to a partner, who then begins to identify and question assumptions they are hearing in the story.
5. After back-and-forth dialogue, learners compare their linear problem/prescription index card with the story and insights gained from writing about it and sharing dialogue.

Embodiment

Another type of learning is **embodied knowing,** where the mind-body connection is considered in teaching and learning, or what Nguyen and Larson (2015) described as unifying the body and mind in constructing knowledge. Maiese (2017) critiqued Mezirow's approach as relying heavily on critical reflection, questioning of assumptions and beliefs, and metacognitive reasoning. They noted broadly held assumptions that "cognition and thought are abstract, intellectual, disembodied processes that occur separately from emotion and affect" (p. 198). Maiese offered embodiment and enactivism as alternative ways of conceptualizing learning for transformation. **Enactivism** is the "embodied action and engagement of a living organism within its world" (p. 199). Embodiment incorporates arts-based learning and embodied cognition.

Arts-based Learning. L4T taps into the intuitive, emotional, and spiritual experiences of learners. While these are more challenging to prepare for, most who write about non-rational forms of transformative learning suggest using music, poetry, art, photography, literature, dreams, drama, fiction, and film to stimulate this type of learning (Butterwick & Lawrence, 2023; Klein, 2024; Lawrence, 2024). Lawrence (2024) viewed arts-based learning as embodied, seeing it as "a mechanism for uncovering unconscious knowledge and bringing important topics to the forefront of discussion. . . . [and] to provoke emotion and empathy to promote learning at cognitive, affective, and visceral levels" (p. 247). Two ways of promoting embodied learning are through the arts and embodied cognition.

Learning activities use artistic approaches to help adults learn through painting, storytelling, sculpting, improvisation, poetry, drawing, singing, or playing instruments. Holloway and Gouthro (2024) conducted a national study of arts-based adult education, finding that adult learners, "arts-based approaches can potentially infuse the work of adult educators to engage adult learners in inclusive pedagogy and active citizenship" (p. 12).

Showing films or film clips to illustrate the content of conflicting ideas, creating artistic representations of concepts with collages or sculpture, or writing a play or song to represent assumptions and critical assessment of them. Lawrence (2024) discussed integrating multiple art forms into teaching poetry, digital stories, photography, and witnessing art. Klein (2024) connected art-based learning with reflective and reflexive practice with questions for learners such as, "How does this [art] challenge your assumptions?" or "How does this image call you to respond or take action?" (p. 207).

Embodied Cognition. **Embodied cognition** is the notion that cognitive processing is rooted in motor behavior. Rowlands (2010) offered the four E's of cognition as embodied, embedded, enacted, and extended. An embodiment of learning, for example, might be gesturing when speaking as a way of constructing meaning, visual processing, mirroring others' bodily movements, or using the body to perform cognitive tasks, like counting a to-do list on one's fingers. Embodied cognition can be promoted through physical activity, engaging the senses, manipulating objects, repeating physical movements, using immersive digital technologies, or promoting mega-cognition through movement, such as having students engage their bodies with cognitive tasks.

Carter (2024) endeavored to build on Mezirow's (1978) TL theory and Mälkki's (2019) theory of reflection by understanding how embodied cognition supported adults' ability to make meaning and personally transform after the process of perspective transformation was interrupted and stalled. Through interviews, she found that "when sensory, emotional, or intellectual experiences are perceived as unbearable or unacceptable, resistance to them can lock down embodied cognition, creating a barrier to transformative learning" (p. 1). Adults may refuse to accept or deny the disorienting dilemma, and Carter found Kübler-Ross's grief (1970) process a helpful framework for helping people unlock a disorienting dilemma and open up new learning.

Spirituality

Spirituality involves nurturing and sharing the spirit of deep questioning and meaning making people engage in throughout their lives (Kroth et al., 2024). Carr-Chellman et al. (2021) found that most spirituality and adult education discussions occur outside the religious context. They advocated for reconnecting the two since both create space for learners to explore meaning and purpose in life. Kroth et al. (2024) encouraged spirituality as central to lifelong learning. They lamented that spiritual issues such as death, life purpose, moments of wonder and awe, grief, suffering, joy, and love are rarely discussed in the field's literature. They proposed a new proposition about adult learners: "All people are spiritual beings from birth to death who innately seek to understand and experience a life of meaning, purpose, death, and connection to that which is beyond themselves" (p. 39). Activities to tap into spirituality and TL involve reflecting on one's life purpose and making sense of life experiences through critical reflection, journaling, dialogue, consciousness development, meditation, spiritual and religious practices, and other activities to inspire awe and wonder.

Noting the absence of spirituality in Mezirow's definition of TL, Tisdell and Swartz (2022) explored it in the context of **pilgrimage**—metaphorically representing life's journey or a pathway that can also be literal travel on foot or by other means beyond the known and comfortable and engaging in self-reflection and potentially transformation. Tisdell and Swartz also drew parallels to Mezirow's 10 phases of TL. Tisdell and Swartz (2022) defined **Transformative pilgrimage learning** (TPL) as:

> A specific form of transformative learning in that it has to do with literal pilgrimage with its particular components, namely the sense of sacred place, the sense of movement, and its connection to the body, and to the spiritual world that is often deeply rooted to or brings us back to nature. (p. 204)

Drawing on Cousineau's (1999) discussion of pilgrimage, they highlighted the seven phases of spiritual pilgrimage as: (1) longing to move toward a new way of being, (2) feeling called to listen to one's inner drivers, (3) departing on the actual journey, (4) making the journey itself, (5) experiencing the labyrinth or following one's inner journey as well as taking the outward walk, (6) arriving at a particular physical location, and (7) returning home and integrating the experience into one's life. Learners can take a major pilgrimage or attempt to find a shorter place to move and engage with nature near home, such as parks, labyrinths, hiking, and other ways to move and reflect. Box 11.8 suggests exploring L4T through books and cinema.

 ## Box 11.8 Recommendations for Further Learning

Read a Book or Watch a Movie About Life Changes

Although you have experienced transformations as an adult learner, learning about others' learning journeys can be helpful. Try reading a biography, autobiography, or fictional account of someone who significantly changed their life. Some good examples include:

- Nelson Mandela's Autobiography, *The Long Walk to Freedom*
- Ed Husain's *The Islamist*

- Kafka's *Metamorphosis*
- Ibsen's *A Doll's House*
- *A Christmas Carol*
- *Schindler's List*
- *The Secret Life of Walter Mitty*
- *The King's Speech*

Movies are also a great way to learn about others' transformative learning, such as:

- *Educating Rita*
- *The Doctor*
- *Norma Rae*
- *Groundhog Day*
- *The Truman Show*
- *The Intern*
- *A Man Called Ove*
- *The Matrix*
- *The Bucket List*

Consider analyzing the transformation process and its outcome.

Chapter Summary

Chapter 11, "Learning for Transformation" (L4T), explored how adult learning can evoke significant personal change through learning, which involves critical reflection, dialogue, and self-awareness to challenge and potentially alter one's worldview. L4T helps individuals, groups, and societies navigate personal and societal crises like the COVID-19 pandemic, which prompted many to reevaluate life priorities. The wisdom of Jiddu Krishnamurti (2001) captures the beauty and potential of L4T: "If you begin to understand what you are without trying to change it, then what you are undergoes a transformation" (p. 8)

Key Points

- Learning for transformation (L4T) is about change in an adult's perspective and place in the larger social context.
- Sites of L4T can be the individual, the classroom, online, the workplace, and the community or society.

- Mezirow introduced transformative learning to describe L4T, and the theory has expanded beyond its initial cognitive rationality.
- Generative knowing is an emerging learning theory that describes how adults cope and learn in uncertain, shifting contexts.
- Instructional strategies promoting T4L include creating safe and brave learning spaces, fostering critical reflection, engaging in dialogue and meaningful conversation, using appropriate pedagogy, and integrating narrative, embodiment, and spirituality strategies.

References

Anderson Sathe, L., Cotter Zakrzewski, T., Romano, A., Longmore, A. L., & Kramlich, D. J. (2022). Transformative listening across global contexts: Fostering authentic connection to self, other and community. In A. Nicolaides, S. Eschenbacher, P. T. Buergelt, Y. Gilpin-Jackson, M. Welch, M. Misawa (Eds.), *The Palgrave Handbook of Learning for Transformation* (pp. 429–446). Palgrave Macmillan.

Basseches, M. (1984). *Dialectical thinking and adult development*. Ablex.

Bateson, N. (2016). *Small arcs of larger circles*. Triarchy Press.

Baumgartner, L. M. (2012). Mezirow's theory of transformative learning from 1975 to present. In E. W. Taylor & P. Cranton (Eds.), *The handbook of transformative learning* (pp. 99–115). Jossey-Bass.

Belenky, M. F. (1986). *Women's ways of knowing: The development of self, voice, and mind*. Basic Books.

Bergman, M. Adult learners and higher education. (2021). In T. S. Rocco, M. C. Smith, R. C. Mizzi, L. R. Merriweather, & J. D. Hawley, (Eds.). (2023). *The handbook of adult and continuing education* (pp. 266–274). Taylor & Francis.

Bierema, L. L. (2010). *Implementing a critical approach to organization development*. Kruger.

Bierema, L. L., Callahan, J. L., Elliott, C. J., Greer, T. W., & Collins, J. C. (2024). *Human resource development: Critical perspectives and practices*. Routledge.

Bovill, C. (2020). *Co-creating learning and teaching: Towards relational pedagogy in higher education*. Critical Publishing.

Boyd, R. D., & Myers, J. G. (1988). Transformative education. *International Journal of Lifelong Education, 7*(4), 261–284. https://doi.org/10.1080/0260137880070403.

Brookfield, S. (2009). Engaging critical reflection in corporate America. In J. Mezirow, E. W. Taylor, & Associates (Eds.), *Transformative learning in practice* (pp. 125–135). Jossey-Bass.

Brookfield, S. D. (2011). *Teaching for critical thinking: Tools and techniques to help students question their assumptions*. John Wiley & Sons.

Brookfield, S. D. (2012). Critical theory and transformative learning. In E. W. Taylor & P. Cranton (Eds.), *The handbook of transformative learning* (pp. 131–146). Jossey-Bass.

Butterwick, S., & Lawrence, R. L. (2023). Stories of hope, imagination, and transformative learning: A dialogue. *New Directions for Adult and Continuing Education, 2023*(177), 51–60. https://doi.org/10.1002/ace.20478.

Cappiali, T. M. (2023). A paradigm shift for a more inclusive, equal, and just academia? Towards a transformative-emancipatory pedagogy. *Education Sciences, 13*(9), 876. https://doi.org/10.3390/educsci13090876.

Carr-Chellman, D., Kroth, M., & Rogers-Shaw, C. (2021). Adult education for human flourishing: A religious and spiritual framework. In T. S. Rocco, M. C. Smith, R. C. Mizzi, L. R. Merriweather, & J. D. Hawley, (Eds.), *The handbook of adult and continuing education* (pp. 297–304). Taylor & Francis.

Carter, P. L. (2024). *Unlocking Embodied Cognition in Transformative Learning: Navigating Edge-Emotions Captured by a Disorienting Dilemma* (Doctoral dissertation, University of Georgia).

Clark, M. C. (1993). Transformational learning. In S. B. Merriam (Ed.), *An update on adult learning theory* (pp. 47–56). New Directions for Adult and Continuing Education, no. 57. San Francisco: Jossey-Bass. https://doi.org/10.1002/ace.36719935707.

Clark, M. C. (2012). Transformation as embodied narrative. In E. W. Taylor & P. Cranton (Eds.), *The handbook of transformative learning* (pp. 425–438). Jossey-Bass.

Corlett, S., Ruane, M., & Mavin, S. (2021). Learning (not) to be different: The value of vulnerability in trusted and safe identity work spaces. *Management Learning, 52*(4), 424–441. https://doi.org/10.1177/1350507621995816.

Cousineau, P. (1999). *A arte da peregrinação*. Grupo Editorial Summus.

Cranton, P. (2006). *Understanding and promoting transformative learning: A guide for educators of adults* (2nd ed.). Jossey-Bass.

Cranton, P. (2016). *Understanding and promoting transformative learning: A guide to theory and practice*. Stylus Publishing.

Cranton, P., & Kasl, E. (2012). A response to Michael Newman's "Calling transformative learning into question: Some mutinous thoughts," *Adult Education Quarterly, 62*(4), 393–398. https://doi.org/10.1177/0741713612456418.

Cranton, P. & Taylor, E. W. (2012). Transformative learning theory: Seeking a more unified theory. In E. W. Taylor & P. Cranton (Eds.), *The handbook of transformative learning* (pp. 3–20). Jossey-Bass.

Daloz, L. A. (2012). *Mentor: Guiding the journey of adult learners (with new foreword, introduction, and afterword)*. John Wiley & Sons.

Daloz, L. A., & Cross, K. P. (1986). *Effective teaching and mentoring*. Jossey-Bass.

DeTemple, J., & Sarrouf, J. (2017). Disruption, dialogue, and swerve: Reflective structured dialogue in religious studies classrooms. *Teaching Theology & Religion, 20*(3), 283–292. https://doi.org/10.1111/teth.12490.

Dillard, N., Sisco, S., & Collins, J. C. (2024). Expanding experiential learning in contemporary adult education: Embracing technology, interdisciplinarity, and cultural responsiveness. *New Directions for Adult and Continuing Education*. https://doi.org/10.1002/ace.20539.

Dirkx, J. M. (1997). Nurturing soul in adult learning. In P. Cranton (Ed.) *Best practices teaching ESL: a lifelong learning approach*. New Directions for Adult and Continuing Education, no. 74, pp. 79–88. https://doi.org/10.1002/ace.7409.

Dirkx, J. M. (1998). Transformative learning theory in the practice of adult education: An overview. *PAACE journal of lifelong learning, 7*, 1–14.

Dirkx, J., & Schlegel, S. (2023). The role of emotion-laden experiences in self-formation. In A. Belzer, & B. Dashew (Eds.), *Understanding the adult learner: Perspectives and practices* (pp. 99–116). Routledge.

Doornbosch, L. M., van Vuuren, M., & de Jong, M. D. (2024). Brave conversations within safe spaces: Exploring participant behavior in community dialogues. *Small Group Research*, 1046496241302071. https://doi.org/10.1177/104649642413020.

Ferrer, J. N., Romero, M. T., & Albareda, R. V. (2005). Integral transformative education: A participatory proposal. *Journal of Transformative Education, 3*(4), 306–330. https://doi.org/10.1177/1541344605279175.

Formenti, L., & Hoggan-Kloubert, T. (2023). Transformative learning as societal learning. *New Directions for Adult and Continuing Education, 2023*(177), 105–118. https://doi.org/10.1002/ace.20482.

Freire, P. (1970). *Pedagogy of the oppressed.* Seabury Press.

Freire, P. (1973). By learning they can teach. *Convergence, 6*(1), 78.

Freire, P. (2014). *Pedagogy of the oppressed: 30ᵗʰ anniversary edition.* Bloomsbury Academic & Professional. https://ebookcentral.proquest.com/lib/ugalib/reader.action?docID=1745456.

Gravett, K., Taylor, C. A., & Fairchild, N., (2024). Pedagogies of mattering: Reconceptualizing relational pedagogies in higher education. *Teaching in Higher Education, 29*(2), 388–403. https://doi.org/10.1080/13562517.2021.1989580.

Gunnlaugson, O. (2008). Metatheoretical prospects for the field of transformative learning. *Journal of Transformative Education, 6*(2), 124–135. https://doi.org/10.1177/1541344608323387.

Habermas, J. (1985). *The theory of communicative action: Volume 2: Lifeword and system: A critique of functionalist reason* (vol. 2). Beacon Press.

Hart, T. (2001). *From information to transformation: Education for the evolution of consciousness.* Peter Lang.

Hathaway, M. D. (2018). *Cultivating ecological wisdom: Worldviews, transformative learning, and engagement for sustainability.* University of Toronto (Canada).

Hathaway, M. (2022). Reorienting connections via ecological practices. In A. Nicolaides, S. Eschenbacher, P. T. Buergelt, Y. Gilpin-Jackson, M. Welch, & M. Misawa (Eds.), *The Palgrave handbook of learning for transformation* (pp. 279–300). Palgrave.

Hoggan, C. D. (2016). Transformative learning as a metatheory: Definition, criteria, and typology. *Adult Education Quarterly, 66*(1), 57–75. https://doi.org/10.1177/0741713615611216.

Hoggan, C., & Kasl, E. (2023). Transformative learning: Evolving theory for understanding change. In A. Blezer & B. Dashew (Eds.), *Understanding the adult learner* (pp. 213–233). Routledge.

Hoggan, C., & Kloubert, T. (2020). Transformative learning in theory and practice. *Adult Education Quarterly, 70*(3), 295–307. https://doi.org/10.1177/0741713620918510.

Holloway, S. M., & Gouthro, P. (2024). Multimodal adult learning through arts-based organisations. *Australian Journal of Adult Learning, 64*(1), 12–32. https://files.eric.ed.gov/fulltext/EJ1425252.pdf.

Honneth, A. (2014). *The I in we: Studies in the theory of recognition.* John Wiley & Sons.

Illeris, K. (2014). Transformative learning re-defined: As changes in elements of the identity. *International Journal of Lifelong Education, 33*(5), 573–586. https://doi.org/10.1080/02601370.2014.917128.

Janssens, L., Kuppens, T., Mulà, I., Staniskiene, E. & Zimmermann, A. B. (2022). Do European quality assurance frameworks support integration of transformative learning for sustainable development in higher education? *International Journal of Sustainability in Higher Education, 23*(8), 148–173. https://doi.org/10.1108/IJSHE-07-2021-0273.

Johnson-Bailey, J., & Alfred, M. V. (2006). Transformational teaching and the practices of black women adult educators. *New Directions for Adult and Continuing Education, 2006*(109), 49–58. https://doi.org/10.1002/ace.207.

Jubas, K. (2023). More than a monfessional Mo (ve) ment?# MeToo's pedagogical tensions. *Adult Education Quarterly, 73*(2), 133–149. https://doi.org/10.1177/07417136221134782.

Kafka, F., & Corngold, S. (1915). The metamorphosis: Translation, backgrounds and contexts, criticism. *(No Title)*.

Kasworm, C. E., & Bowles, T. A. (2012). Fostering transformative learning in higher education settings. In E. W. Taylor and P. Crnton (Eds.), *The handbook of transformative learning: Theory, research, and practice* (p. 388–422). John Wiley & Sons.

Kegan, R. (1982). *The evolving self: Problem and process in human development.* Harvard University Press.

Kegan, R. (1998). *In over our heads: The mental demands of modern life.* Harvard University Press.

Kegan, R. (2000). What "form" transforms? A constructive-developmental perspective on Transformational learning. In J. Mezirow & Associates (Eds.), *Learning as transformation: Critical perspectives on a theory in progress* (pp. 35–70). Jossey-Bass.

Klein, M. (2024). Reflective learning and reflexive practice. In J. Coryell, L. M. Baumgartner, & J. W. Bohonos (Eds.), *Methods for Facilitating Adult Learning* (pp. 200–214). Routledge.

Krishnamurti, J. (2001). *The book of life: Daily meditations with Krishnamurti.* Penguin Books India.

Kroth, M., Carr-Chellman, D., & Rogers-Shaw, C. (2024). Spirituality as the center of lifelong learning. *New Directions for Adult and Continuing Education, 184,* 39–45. https://doi.org/10.1002/ace.20543.

Kübler-Ross, E. (1970). *On death & dying.* Macmillan Co.

Lange, E. A. (2018). Transforming transformative education through ontologies of relationality. *Journal of Transformative Education, 16*(4), 280–301. https://doi.org/10.1177/1541344618786452.

Lawrence, R. L. (2024). Multiple ways of knowing: Facilitating arts-based and embodied learning in adult education. In J. Coryell, L. M. Baumgartner, & J. W. Bohonos (Eds.), *Methods for facilitating adult learning* (pp. 233–249). Routledge.

Lawrence, R. L., & Paige, D. S. (2016). What our ancestors knew: Teaching and learning through storytelling. *New Directions for Adult and Continuing Education, 149*(Spring), 63–72. https://doi.org/10.1002/ace.20177.

Maiese, M. (2017). Transformative learning, enactivism, and affectivity. *Studies in Philosophy and Education, 36*(2), 197–216. https://doi.org/10.1007/s11217-015-9506-z.

Mälkki, K. (2019). Coming to grips with edge-emotions: The gateway to critical reflection and transformative learning. In T. Fleming, A. Kokkos, & F. F. Finnegan (Eds.), *European perspectives on transformative theory* (pp. 59–73). Springer. https://doi.org/10.1007/978-3-030-19159-7_5.

Marsick. V. J., Watkins, K. E., & Faller, P. G. (2012). Transformative learning in the workplace: Leading learning for self and organizational change. In E. W Talyor, & P. Cranton (Eds.), *The handbook of transformative learning: Theory research and practice* (pp. 355–372). Jossey-Bass.

Marsick, V. J., Nicolaides, A., & Watkins, K. E. (2014). Adult learning theory and application in HRD. In N. E. Chalofsky, T. S. Rocco, & M. L Morris (Eds.), *Handbook of human resource development* (pp. 40–61). Wiley.

Marsick, V. J., Kasl, E., & Watkins, K. E. (2022). Looking back, looking forward. In A. Nicolaides, S. Eschenbacher, P. T. Buergelt, Y. Gilpin-Jackson, M. Welch, & M. Misawa (Eds.), *The Palgrave handbook of learning for transformation.* (pp. v–xiii). Palgrave.

McClain, A. L. (2024). New developments in transformative learning. *New Directions for Adult and Continuing Education, 184,* 20–29. https://doi.org/10.1002/ace.20540.

Merriam, S. B., & Baumgartner, L. M. (2020). *Learning in adulthood: A comprehensive guide.* John Wiley & Sons.

Mezirow, J. (1978). *Education for perspective transformation: Women's re-entry programs in community colleges.* New York: Teachers College, Columbia University.

Mezirow, J. (1990). How critical reflection triggers transformative learning. In. J. Mezirow & Associates (Eds.), *Fostering critical reflection in adulthood* (pp. 1–20). Jossey-Bass.

Mezirow, J. (1991). *Transformative dimensions of adult learning.* Jossey-Bass.

Mezirow, J. (1992). Transformation theory: Critique and confusion. *Adult Education Quarterly, 42*(4), 250–252. https://doi.org/10.1177/074171369204200404.

Mezirow, J. (1997). *Transformative learning: Theory to practice.* In *Update on adult learning theory.* (New Directions for Adult and Continuing Education, no. 74, pp. 5–12). Jossey-Bass. https://doi.org/10.1002/ace.7401.

Mezirow, J. (2000). Learning to think like an adult: Core concepts of transformation theory. J. Mezirow & Associates, *Learning as transformation: Critical perspectives on a theory in progress* (pp. 3-33). Jossey-Bass.

Mezirow, J. (2003). How critical reflection triggers transformative learning. *Adult and Continuing Education: Teaching, learning and research, 4,* 199–213.

Mezirow, J. (2012). Learning to think like an adult: Core concepts of Transformation Theory. In E. Taylor, P. Cranton, & Associates (Eds.). *The handbook of transformative learning: Theory, research, and practice* (pp. 73–96). John Wiley & Sons.

Mezirow, J., Taylor, E. W. & Associates. (2009). *Transformative learning in practice.* Jossey-Bass.

Muthayan, S. (2022). Pedagogy for transformative learning in post-colonial contexts. In A. Nicolaides, S. Eschenbacher, P. T. Buergelt, Y. Gilpin-Jackson, M. Welch, & M. Misawa (Eds.), *The Palgrave handbook of learning for transformation* (pp. 537–446). Palgrave Macmillan, Cham.

Muthukrishna, M., Bell, A. V., Henrich, J., Curtin, C. M., Gedranovich, A., McInerney, J., & Thue, B. (2020). Beyond western, educated, industrial, rich, and democratic (WEIRD) psychology: Measuring and mapping scales of cultural and psychological distance. *Psychological science, 31*(6), 678–701. https://doi.org/10.1177/0956797620916782.

Newman, M. (2012). Calling transformative learning into question: Some mutinous thoughts. *Adult Education Quarterly, 62*(1), 36–55. https://doi.org/10.1177/0741713610392768.

Nguyen, D. J., & Larson, J. B. (2015). Don't forget about the body: Exploring the curricular possibilities of embodied pedagogy. *Innovative Higher Education, 40,* 331–344. https://doi.org/10.1007/s10755-015-9319-6.

Nicolaides, A., & Eschenbacher, S. (2022). The many terms of transformation creating new vocabularies for transformative learning. In A. Nicolaides, S. Eschenbacher, P. T. Buergelt, Y. Gilpin-Jackson, M. Welch, & M. Misawa (Eds.), *The Palgrave handbook of learning for transformation* (pp. 1–22). Palgrave.

Nicolaides, A., Eschenbacher, S., Buergelt, P. T., Gilpin-Jackson, Y., Welch, M., & Misawa, M. (Eds.). (2022). *The Palgrave handbook of learning for transformation.* Palgrave.

O'Sullivan, E. (2002). The project and vision of transformative education: Integral transformative learning. In *Expanding the boundaries of transformative learning: Essays on theory and praxis* (pp. 1–12). Palgrave Macmillan US.

Rose, A. D., Ross-Gordon, J. M., & Kasworm, C. E. (2024). *Creating a place for adult learners in higher education: Challenges and opportunities.*

Rowlands, M. (2010). *The new science of the mind: From extended mind to embodied phenomenology.* MIT Press.

Schön, D. A. (1983). *The reflective practitioner: How professionals think in action.* Basic Books.

Sheared, V. (1994). Giving voice: An inclusive model of instruction—A womanist perspective. *New Directions for Adult and Continuing Education, 1994*(61), 27–37. https://doi.org/10.1002/ace.36719946105.

Sheared, V. (2023). Creating inclusive learning spaces for a diverse world: The womanist perspective. In A. Belzer, & B. Dashew (Eds.), *Understanding the adult learner: Perspectives and practices* (pp. 21–38). Routledge.

Sheared, V., Johnson-Bailey, J., Colin, S. A. J., Peterson, E., & Brookfield, S. D. (Eds.). (2010). *The handbook of race and adult education: A resource for dialogue on racism.* John Wiley & Sons.

Sim, E., & Bierema, L. L. (2023). Infusing intersectional pedagogy into adult education and human resource development graduate education. *Adult Education Quarterly.* https://doi.org/10.1177/07417136231198049.

Stewart, J., Rigg, C., & Trehan, K. (2007). *Critical human resource development: Beyond orthodoxy.* Prentice Hall.

Tan, L. (2009). The 5 E's of emancipatory pedagogy: The rehumanizing approach to teaching and learning with inner-city youth. In W. Ayers, T. M. Quinn, D. Stovall (Eds.), *Handbook of social justice in education* (pp. 485–496). Routledge.

Taylor, E. W. (2008). Transformative learning theory. *New Directions for Adult and Continuing Education, 119*, 5–15. https://doi.org/10.1002/ace.301.

Taylor, E. W., Cranton, P., & Associates. (2012). *The handbook of transformative learning: Theory, research and practice.* Jossey-Bass.

Tennant, M. (2005). Transforming selves. *Journal of Transformative Education, 3*(2), 102–115. https://doi.org/10.1177/1541344604273421.

Thalhammer, K. E., O'Loughlin, P. L., Glazer, M. P., Glazer, P. M., McFarland, S., Shepela, S. T., & Stoltzfus, N. (Eds.) (2007). *Courageous resistance: The power of ordinary people.* Palgrave MacMillan.

Tisdell, E. J., & Swartz, A. L. (2022).Transformative pilgrimage learning and the big questions in the COVD-19 era—Love, death, and legacy: Implications for lifelong learning and nursing education. In A. Nicolaides, S. Eschenbacher, P. T. Buergelt, Y. Gilpin-Jackson, M. Welch, & M. Misawa (Eds.), *The Palgrave handbook of learning for transformation* (pp. 199–216). Palgrave.

Tolliver, D. E., & Tisdell, E. J. (2006). Engaging spirituality in the transformative higher education classroom. *New Directions for Adult & Continuing Education, 2006*(109). https://doi.org/10.1002/ace.206.

Vella, J. (2000). A spirited epistemology: Honoring the adult learner as subject. *New Directions for Adult and Continuing Education, 85*, 7-16. https://doi.org/https://doi.org/10.1002/ace.8501

Weimer, M. (2012). Learner-centered teaching and transformative learning. In E. Taylor & P. Cranton (Eds.), *The handbook of transformative learning: Theory, research, and practice* (pp. 439–454). John Wiley & Sons.

Yamada, K. (2021). *What do you do with a problem?* Library Ideas, LLC.

Yamada, K., Forster, S., & Flahiff, J. (2013). *What do you do with an idea?* Seattle, WA: Compendium Kids.

CHAPTER TWELVE

CONNECTING NEUROSCIENCE AND ADULT LEARNING

 **Box 12.1 Chapter Overview and Learning Objectives**

Italian Renaissance polymath Leonardo da Vinci's life exemplified how wisdom arises from curiosity, interdisciplinary knowledge and collaboration, observation, and courage to explore the unknown. Although he is best known for his art masterpieces, da Vinci was also an inventor and left a legacy in the disciplines he mastered (art, cartography, anatomy, engineering, and scientific research) throughout his life. Wisdom is the culmination of the brain's ability to learn, remember, know, question, ponder, solve problems, and relate. da Vinci's motto captures this wise spirit:

"Leonardo da Vinci Ostinato Rigore" (Bianci, n.d., para. 14).

Translated to English, *ostinato rigore* means "obstinate rigor" (Bianci, n.d., para. 14). Bianci noted the motto was a "way of life" for da Vinci:

His dogged determination to pursue accuracy, precision, and in-depth understanding is well documented in his numerous sketches, detailed notes, and of course, his exceptional artwork and inventions. An example is his masterpiece *The Last Supper*. The painting is more than a beautiful representation of this biblical event. He painstakingly studied the dynamics of human emotion and group interaction, resulting in a masterpiece that captures the tumultuous scene with unparalleled realism and depth. His obstinate rigor truly shines through. (para. 15)

Wisdom is often viewed as the culmination of learning from experience that transcends intelligence (the capacity for learning, reasoning, and understanding) since wisdom is the ability to grasp human nature and think and act with soundness and integrity. This chapter discusses adult learning and the brain, including the development of intelligence and wisdom. The chapter begins with a discussion of neuromyths and their hold on education. Next, this chapter explores memory and learning, different understandings of intelligence, the development of cognition and wisdom, and the chapter concludes with how to design and facilitate educational programs with neuroscience in mind. Wary that adults live in the age of "VUCA," where the world is volatile, uncertain, complex, and ambiguous (Elkington et al., 2017), understanding the brain can lead to more effective coping and learning.

As a result of reading this chapter and completing the exercise boxes, you should be able to:

1. Define neuroscience and how it applies to learning.
2. Uncover neuro myths about learning.
3. Explore the role of memory in learning and aging
4. Discover normal signs of aging and tips for maintaining brain health.
5. Consider constructs of intelligence.
6. Examine cognitive development and wisdom.
7. Apply neuroscience-informed strategies to educational design and facilitation.

In 1996, at the age of 37, brain scientist Jill Bolte Taylor had a massive stroke, leaving her unable to walk, talk, read, or write. Over eight years, she re-taught her brain; today, she lives an everyday life and researches the human brain. She gave a TED talk, "My Stroke of Insight," about surviving the experience in 2008, and it was the first ever TED talk to go viral on the Internet. In her 2009 book, Taylor detailed the morning of her stroke, "*Wow, how many scientists have the opportunity to study their own brain function and mental deterioration from the inside out?*" (p. 44, italics in original). More recently, she published *Whole Brain Living* (Taylor, 2021) to help people face life challenges by considering brain anatomy.

Her work is a testimony to "the beauty and resiliency of our human brain because of its innate ability to adapt to change and recover function constantly" (Taylor, 2009, p. xv). Box 12.2 offers more information on the life and work of Dr. Bolte Taylor. Indeed, as a learner, your brain is an amazing organ in your body that changes as you learn.

This chapter is about neuroscience, the brain, and learning. **Neuroscience** studies the structure and function of the nervous system and brain. Neuroscientists research the brain and its impact on behavior and cognitive processing. They are concerned not only with healthy and normal functioning nervous systems but also with what happens when people have brain disorders. **Educational neuroscience** strives to develop and test educational programs and techniques (Feiler & Stabio, 2018).

The **brain** is an organ found in vertebrates made up of soft tissue and housed in the skull, attaching to the spinal cord and functioning as the control center of animal life. Taylor and Marienau (2023) noted that "the brain's prime directive is to help us survive and function" (p. 80). As humans, this control center constantly monitors all functions within our bodies, such as heart rate and breathing, as well as what is going on immediately around the body.

Box 12.2 Tips and Tools for Teaching and Learning

Dr. Jill Bolte Taylor's Stroke of Insight

Dr. Jill Bolte Taylor is a Harvard University–trained neuroscientist who had a severe left hemispheric brain hemorrhage that affected her ability to function or recall any of her life. Her 2009 memoir, *My Stroke of Insight*, documented the experience and eight-year recovery and spent 63 weeks on the *New York Times* nonfiction bestseller list. You can learn more about her work and life by viewing her famous TED talk, which was viewed over 27.5 million times:

https://www.ted.com/talks/jill_bolte_taylor_my_stroke_of_insight?subtitle=en

Due to her notoriety, *Time* magazine named her one of the "100 Most Influential People in the World" in 2008, and she was the premiere guest on Oprah Winfrey's *Soul Series* webcast. You can learn more about her work at her website: https://www.drjilltaylor.com/

External data flow into the body through our senses—seeing, hearing, touching, tasting, and smelling. The brain continually processes all this data, making adjustments as necessary, keeping us out of danger, and responding appropriately to incoming data. Box 12.3 highlights features of the human brain with basic facts and research findings.

 ## Box 12.3 Adult Learning by the Numbers

The Human Brain

The human brain is a complex organ that controls your thoughts, memory, emotions, touch, motor skills, vision, breathing, temperature, hunger, and other processes that regulate the body. This box highlights some features of the extraordinary human brain.

- The adult brain weighs approximately three pounds, and the average adult's brain is about 60% fat. The remaining 40% combines water, protein, carbohydrates, and salts (Johns Hopkins Medicine, n.d.).
- Every time your heart beats, your arteries carry 20–25% of your blood to the brain (Piedmont, n.d.).
- The brain is comprised of gray matter and white matter, composing different regions of the central nervous system. Gray matter is a darker outer portion of the brain composed primarily of neuron somas (round central cell bodies). White matter is the lighter intersection underneath gray matter in the brain made up of axons (long stem cells connecting neurons) wrapped in myelin (protective coating). Gray matter processes and interprets information, while white matter transmits the information elsewhere in the nervous system (John Hopkins Medicine, n.d.).
- The brain has 100,000 miles of blood vessels. The distance around the world at the equator is 24,900 miles (Piedmont, n.d.).
- The brain is the only object that can contemplate itself (Cleveland Clinic, n.d.-a.).
- The brain contains about 100 billion neurons or nerve cells that transmit sensory and other information. These neurons are connected by trillions of connections called synapses (a. Clinic, n.d.).
- The brain generates enough electricity to power a 25-watt light bulb. It is also faster and more powerful than a supercomputer (National Geographic, n.d.).

- The brain contains about 100 billion microscopic cells called neurons—so many it would take over 3,000 years to count them all (National Geographic, n.d.).
- Neurons send info to your brain at over 150 miles (240 kilometers) per hour (National Geographic, n.d.).
- Learning changes the brain's structure, and exercise makes you more intelligent (National Geographic, n.d.).
- The brain creates new connectivity throughout life (Cleveland Clinic, n.d.-a.).
- Adults who participate in mind-challenging activities are 63% less likely to develop dementia (Su et al., 2022). However, there are many other possible explanations, so it may not indicate causality.
- A Swedish longitudinal study found that women with high levels of physical fitness are 90% less likely to develop dementia than women who are moderately physically fit (Hörder et al., 2018).

The brain constantly sends and receives chemical and electrical signals throughout the body. As Taylor and Marienau (2016) explained, "In addition to continuously analyzing all body systems and states, your brain also responds instantly when those readings are out of whack, working to put things back in balance, called *homeostasis*" (p. 3, italics in original). They observed further, "The words we commonly use to name what the brain does—*think, identify, feel, understand, imagine, decide, know, plan, distinguish, believe, remember*—are descriptions of what we experience when vast networks of neurons are activated and ever-changing patterns of connection" (p. 10, italics in original). These signals control different processes, each interpreted by the brain. Messages may be tiredness, pain, or emotion.

Learning is acquiring knowledge, skills, and attitudes developed through life experience, study, or formal education. Learning can result in behavioral and attitudinal changes that are often permanent. Learning changes the brain's structure as the brain's neural pathways structure and restructure as new information is stored. This chapter presents an introductory discussion of the brain for adult learners and educators. Brain anatomy is fascinating; however, it is not the focus of this chapter, which is concerned with how neuroscience and the brain affect learning. For a more comprehensive neuroscience examination, consult Kandel et al.'s (2014) *Principles of Neural Science* and Squire et al.'s (2012) *Fundamental Neuroscience.* For a complete discussion of the brain and adult learning, see Taylor and Marienau's (2016) *Facilitating Learning with the Adult Brain in Mind: A Conceptual and Practical Guide.*

Neuromyths

Before this chapter delves into adult learning and the brain, we, the authors, feel it is important to dispel some popular, persistent neuromyths. A **neuromyth** is a misconception or oversimplified belief about the brain and brain function attributed to misinterpretations of research or outdated theory (Dekker et al., 2012; Ferrero et al., 2016; Grospietsch & Lins, 2021; Torrijos-Muelas et al., 2021; Waterhouse, 2023). "Neuroscience has been described as *seductive* when offered as a potential explanation for challenging problems, and teachers and educators are not immune" (Sullivan et al., 2021, p. 232, italics in original). Research and theory on the brain have impacted education and fueled the rise of the neuroeducation field. Yet, the Organization for Economic Cooperation and Development (OECD) began warning about neuromyths among teachers in 2002. Torrijos-Muelas et al. (2021) systematically reviewed 20 years of publications on neuromyths among in-service or prospective teachers. Neuromyths persist due to a lack of scientific knowledge, communication gaps between scientists and teachers, and low-quality information sources often consulted by teachers. Neuromyths are prevalent across the globe. Two persistent and incorrect ideas about the brain are the three-part triune brain and the two-part hemispheric brain that gave rise to belief in right or left brain dominance. Each will be discussed and critiqued.

The Three-part Triune Brain

The triune brain is a theory of brain development by Paul MacLean (1990), first introduced in the 1960s as evolving into three different layers over time. Taylor and Marienau (2016) criticized MacLean's model as overly simplistic. However, they noted it became well-known as it seemed to explain human nature and how people sometimes think and act in primitive and civilized ways. The triune brain was described as composed of three areas: (1) the reptilian brain, (2) limbic system, and (c) neocortex, each having a different function in the processing of information. The "reptilian brain" was labeled as such because it was believed to be the oldest, most primitive part of the brain and is found in reptiles, birds, and mammals. This innermost part of the brain was said to react instinctively—the so-called "fight or flight" response to perceived danger. The second part of the triune brain, **the limbic system,** which wraps around the reptilian brain, was thought to have developed as mammals evolved from reptiles, taking in sensory data and converting these data into units for processing in the neocortex. The **neocortex** is the third part of the brain that was considered distinct to primates and humans. It extends over the top of the brain and covers the limbic system. The neocortex would be the closest candidate if you tried to locate the "mind" as a learner.

Although widely accepted for generations, neuroscientist Lisa Feldman Barrett (2020) explained, "The triune brain idea is one of the most successful and widespread errors in all of science" (pp. 15–16). She mused about why the myth of the triune brain persists, why textbooks still depict it, and why executive education teaches CEOs how to regulate their "lizard brains." In part, it is because scientists need better public relations.

> But mostly it's because the triune brain is a story that comes with its own cheering section. With our unique capacity for rational thought, the story goes, we triumphed over our animal nature and now rule the planet. To believe in the triune brain is to award ourselves a first prize trophy for Best Species. (Barrett, 2020, p. 25)

Rather than the theory that evolution gradually added layers to brain anatomy, brains became larger over evolutionary time. Yet human brains did not emerge from reptile brains through evolution for emotion and rationality. Barrett noted that the brains of vertebrates look different from one another due to shorter or longer durations of brain development. "So the human brain has no new parts. The neurons in your brain can be found in the brains of other mammals and, likely, other vertebrates. This discovery undermines the evolutionary foundations of the triune brain story" (Barrett, 2020, p. 22).

The Two-part Hemispheric Brain and Right or Left Brain Dominance

Taylor and Marienau (2016) set one issue straight in their book *Facilitating Learning with the Adult Brain in Mind* regarding the left and right hemispheric differences: "According to the cliches, the left brain is analytical and word focused, whereas the right is emotional and sense focused; in essence, so this goes, the left thinks and the right feels. Not so!" (p. 69). They further noted that capacities people tend to attribute to one hemisphere or the other (for example, imagination versus rationality) are inaccurate. Both hemispheres work in tandem and continually communicate in a healthy brain.

The brain is divided into two similar-looking halves, and the belief is that people with right-brain hemispheric dominance were intuitive, creative, and free thinkers. In contrast, those with left-brain dominance were considered more quantitative, logical, and analytical. An estimated 77% of the US population believes this "right brain versus left brain" neuromyth (Rim, 2019); however, it is not valid, as the two halves of the brain work in tandem. Nielsen et al.

(2013) conducted magnetic resonance imaging of 1,000 people and disproved this theory by finding humans do not favor a particular side.

Awareness of neuromyths can affect how you approach teaching and learning as an adult educator or learner. Neuromyths are problematic because they can cause educators and learners to pass on or use incorrect content or ineffective learning strategies. Neuromyths can also waste educational resources, depriving teachers and learners of more effective methods and theories (Grospietsch & Lins, 2021). Box 12.4 summarizes common neuromyths to help you be a more informed educator and learner.

 ## Box 12.4 SoTL: The Scholarship of Teaching and Learning

Common Neuromyths in Education

This box features some common neuromyths that serve neither learners nor teachers well.

1. **People only use 10% of their brains, and if they could unlock the entire brain, they would have extraordinary ability.** The myth has persisted for more than a century (James, 1907), standing as the most enduring neuromyth. In Torrijos-Muelas et al.'s (2021) words, "Scientific research shows how improbable this assertion may be, just taking into consideration that no one single brain area is '100% out of work,' even when sleeping (Centre for Educational Research and Innovation and OECD, 2007)" (p. 2).

2. **People are right-brained (creative and artistic) or left-brained (logical and analytical).** According to research, both hemispheres are responsible for human function. They are in continual communication even though they differ in their functions (Ansari, 2008), countering myths about brain side dominance and multiple intelligences (Torrijos-Muelas et al., 2021). According to research, learners, rather than brain hemispheres, possess different strengths and weaknesses rooted in their intelligence, learning strategies, interest, motivation, attention, and other factors (Gruber, 2018).

3. **People prefer visual, auditory, or kinesthetic (VAK) learning styles.** Torrijos-Muelas et al. (2021) described VAKs as "one of the most deeply rooted and widely believed neuro myths . . . [that] is widely considered a fact, even more than that of the hemispheric preference" (p. 2). Rim (2019) reported that according to

one survey, 97% of respondents believed this myth. Still, the lack of evidence for VAK learning styles is well established (Pashler et al., 2008; Riener & Willingham, 2010; Willingham et al., 2015). This neuromyth has at least three implications for teaching and learning: (1) that people differ in preference for receival mode of information (VAK), (2) people learn better and more effectively when instruction matches their preferred learning style, and (3) educators should diagnose students' learning styles and adjust instruction accordingly.

4. **There are critical periods for learning specific skills like language linked to age, with the human brain being mainly developed by age three.** Although the number of neural connections in the brain increases significantly in the first years of life, this notion has been refuted by several researchers, and early age development was not found related to greater lifelong learning capacity and therefore assuming people are capable of lifelong learning is a more accurate approach to teaching and learning (Michael, 2021).

5. **Multiple Intelligences.** Gardner (2008) proposed that humans have independent brain-based intelligences for the following cognitive abilities: linguistic, logical-mathematical, spatial, body-kinesthetic, musical, interpersonal, intrapersonal, and naturalist. Several scholars have critiqued it as a neuromyth, and Waterhouse (2023) summarized them as lacking evidence to show a basis for multiple intelligences.

What educational myths have influenced your teaching and learning?

Now that you understand neuromyths as an adult educator or learner, the chapter will focus on theory and practice, considering adult learners and the brain.

Neuroplasticity

Enabled by new techniques that allow neuroscientists to study the brains of living persons, "Learning leads to changes in brain function . . . and brain structure" (Brault Foisy et al., 2020, p. 415). The human brain continually forms new connections through learning. This process, called **neuroplasticity** or **brain or neural plasticity,** is rooted in the Greek word *plastikos* (*plastica* in Italian) and means "to mold" or "to form." Plasticity refers to the brain's creation of new pathways or its ability to rewire or expand its neural networks through learning new things, enhancing existing cognitive capacities, recovering from brain injuries such as strokes, strengthening areas where function is lost or has declined, and improving brain fitness (Kaczmarek, 2020; Voss et al., 2017). Barrett (2020) explained, "Anytime you learn something—a new friend's name or an interesting fact from the news—the experience becomes encoded in your wiring so you can remember it, and over time, these encodings can change that wiring" (p. 37). Eliadis (2024) illuminated, "Neuroplasticity is the brain's ability to rewire itself, and, in that way, remain sharp" (p. 512). Forget and Le Pertel (2024) explained plasticity as the brain's lifelong adaptive nature, enabling it to alter structure and functionality according to new experiences, inputs, and damage. Brault Foisy et al. (2020) suggested the idea of a bidirectional relationship between learning and the brain. Chen and Goodwill (2022) discussed adult learning through the lens of neuroplasticity, offering ample evidence that expertise development through training and practice alters the structure and function of the adult brain and adults' capacity for continued neuroplasticity throughout their lifespan. New information enters the brain through electrical impulses; these impulses form neural networks, connecting with other networks, and the stronger and more numerous the networks, the greater the learning. Stanford University brain researcher David Eagleman put it this way:

> We often say the brain has plasticity, meaning it can be moulded like plastic. But I feel the term plasticity isn't big enough to capture the way the whole system is moving. Instead, I use the term "livewired" to represent that you have billions of neurons reconfiguring their circuitry every second. The connections between them are changing their strength and unplugging and re-plugging in elsewhere. (Wilson, 2021, para. 6)

The brain learns when challenged, and although aging causes it to lose neurons, neuroplasticity allows it to form new connections (Cavanaugh & Blanchard-Fields, 2017; Eliadis, 2024). Box 12.5 provides resources on plasticity.

Memory

As with the other cognitive functions discussed in this chapter, memory is one of the brain's activities, and neuroplasticity supports learning and memory. Learning helps adults acquire new knowledge, mindsets, or skills, while memory involves storing and retrieving prior learning (Forget & Le Pertel, 2024). According to Taylor and Marienau (2016), memory is not something stored whole in the brain that can be recalled later.

 **Box 12.5 For Further Learning**

Ted Talks on Brain Plasticity

Beginning with Michael Merzenich, there have been a few TED talks over the years discussing the power of the human brain:

Michael Merzenich: Growing Evidence of Brain Plasticity
https://www.ted.com/talks/michael_merzenich_growing_evidence_of_brain_plasticity?subtitle=en

Dr. Kelly Lambert: Improving our Neuroplasticity.
https://www.youtube.com/watch?v=gOJL3gjc8ak

Kristen Meisenheiner: Rewiring Revolution: Neuroplasticity's Impact on Well-being.
https://www.ted.com/talks/kristen_meisenheimer_rewiring_revolution_neuroplasticity_s_impact_on_well_being?subtitle=en

Lara Boyd: After Watching This, Your Brain Will Not Be The Same.
https://www.youtube.com/watch?v=LNHBMFCzznE

> Memory is neither a discrete thing, nor does it occupy a particular space in the brain; it is a process, not merely a subject of retrieval. By the time we become aware of, or intentionally bring to mind, that which we call *a* memory, the brain has been busily associating various prior and current *memory traces* located in far-flung neural networks. (p. 46, italics in original)

Information coming into the brain is processed and put into memory in the neocortex. Taylor and Marienau (2016) emphasized that the neocortex makes up 80–90% of the weight of the adult brain and functions to create thoughts and actions considered uniquely human, including spoken and written language, rational analysis, imagination, and self-understanding. They reflected how "these capacities give rise to art and science; they also enable us to review the past in ways that change over time and to imagine a future rich with possibilities" (p. 16).

However, what we process as adult learners and remember may depend on our feelings. People first react with their senses and emotions to stimuli before processing these data meaningfully. Further, because no two persons share exact prior experiences, each person attends to, processes, and remembers information differently from the next person. This diversity helps explain why several people can witness the same car accident or purse snatching, for example, but when asked to recall the event, remember it slightly differently, which is known as the "Rashōmon effect," after Kurosawa's (1950) classic film in which a murder is described in four contradictory ways by witnesses.

Historically, memory compares to a systems model or computer in which information is first entered (input), stored, and, at some later point, retrieved (output). More commonly, memory is divided into sensory, working, and long-term memory, all processes in the brain. These three memory components will be discussed first, followed by a review of current understandings about memory, aging, and memory and learning.

For us, as adult learners or educators, to remember something, that "something" has to enter through our senses. We must attend to something we see, hear, taste, smell, or touch. Adults experience constant sensory bombardment by stimuli to their senses, especially sight and hearing, and must consciously select what to remember. Say you are at a social event and are introduced to someone. If you do not hear their name clearly, there is no chance you will remember it later. Even if you listen to it but make no effort to remember it, you will likely forget it. You must hear and attend to the name to move from sensory to working to long-term memory. As people age, they often think they are losing their memory, which is likely a sign of normal aging. Chen and Goodwill (2022) noted,

> Life course experiences such as continued education, social engagement, sociocultural knowledge, cognitive stimulation, physical activity, diet, and stress could all have a profound impact on how effectively the brain can compensate for age-related neurobiological changes over the lifespan and maintain cognitive functions pertinent for lifelong learning. (p. 3)

Table 12.1 contrasts normal aging with symptoms that warrant seeking medical advice.

Working memory, located in the neocortex, is where the information you attend to as a learner is processed. Working memory is remembering what you need to buy at the grocery store as you shop or deciding which way home is the fastest during rush hour. Angelopoulou and Drigas (2021) defined **working memory** (WM) as "the ability to maintain and manipulate information, necessary for an action, for short periods in the order of seconds" (p. 2). They emphasized the intertwining of working memory and attention mainly due to the growth of cognitive neuroscience and neuroimaging studies.

TABLE 12.1 NORMAL SIGNS OF AGING AND SYMPTOMS WARRANTING MEDICAL ADVICE

Normal Signs of Aging	Symptoms Warranting Seeking Medical Advice
You sometimes search for the right words.	You use the wrong words—"stove" instead of "table."
You cannot find your car keys.	You forget how to drive or navigate.
When in a noisy environment, you must focus more on conversations.	You have difficulty following conversations when there is background noise or distraction.
You lose your temper more easily during arguments.	You scream at your partner often and for no reason.
You misplace your house keys periodically.	You constantly misplace your keys and other everyday items and find them in odd places like the refrigerator.
You forget what you had for dinner last night but remember when you get a hint.	You forget what you ate for dinner last night; no reminders can jog your memory.
You have trouble deciding which entree to choose at a restaurant, but ultimately, you must decide.	You find it impossible to decide what to eat, wear, or make other daily decisions.
You drive more slowly than you used to.	You are very slow to react behind the wheel and often miss stop signs or red lights.
It takes you a little longer to answer the phone.	You failed to recognize when the phone is ringing and that you need to answer it.

Source: Adapted from Harvard Medical School (2017).

Attention is the ability to focus on specific stimuli or locations. For example, a pilot would have many stimuli competing for their attention in an airplane cockpit and have to decide where to place their awareness (Angelopoulou & Drigas, 2021). Working memory differs from short-term memory as each has different cognitive functions. **Short-term memory (STM)** temporarily stores information for brief periods—a few seconds to a few minutes—such as remembering a telephone number. It differs from working memory, which handles information during a complex cognitive process, such as remembering numbers while reading. Before a learner can store something in long-term memory, it must be first in STM. Functions of STM include focusing the learner's attention on something in the environment and recognizing connections between what is stored in the brain and what is new (Cleveland Clinic, n.d.-b.).

Working memory can move between **sensory memory**—brief storage of sensory information such as sight, smell, hearing, taste, and touch that helps the learner process environmental cues—for more information, and **long-term memory** (LTM)—where information is stored and retrieved to make STM permanent. Information processed in working memory enters long-term memory and is stored for future use. As learners, we contrast working memory and long-term memory as the difference between the top of your desk (WM) and the file cabinet next to your desk (LTM). Decisions are made about items that come across your desk—do you discard the item, set it aside to deal with later, or attend to it, that is, process it so it can be filed in your file cabinet? The desktop is your working memory. Once we move to the file cabinet (LTM), we have **explicit or declarative memory**—memories consciously available that are episodic and semantic, and **implicit memory**—encoded memories that are unconscious and help you use objects and move the body (Tulving, 1985). Explicit episodic memory includes memories of past events or experiences that are recalled with the sights, sounds, and feelings of the original experience (Tulving, 2002). For example, you might remember some early school experience where you felt embarrassed or humiliated, an experience that comes to mind when you are in an educational situation as an adult. These episodic memories of earlier school experiences sometimes impede adults from pursuing learning later in life. **Semantic memories** involve knowledge, facts, understanding, and meaning you have acquired due to life experiences and learning. Most adults know who George Washington was, where China is located, and what it means to love someone and experience loss. Implicit **procedural or habitual activities** have to do with cognitive and motor skills you have learned, like how to read, play cards, play golf, mow the lawn, drive a car, and ride a bike.

Getting memories into long-term memory involves encoding, meaning the strategies we use as learners to place information into long-term memory. Finding the memory, or **retrieval,** is the other primary process in memory activity. In some research, older adults show some decline in the ability to recall or retrieve memories, but it must also be kept in mind that as we age, we accumulate thousands of memories. A 70-year-old trying to recall a particular birthday celebration or trip to the beach has many more memories to sort through than a 20-year-old asked to do the same thing. There is also a difference in whether adults are asked to recall information (as in an essay exam, for example) or recognize information (as in a multiple-choice exercise where one answer is correct). There is little difference between younger and older adults in recognition activities, although it might take older adults longer to recognize an answer. Box 12.6 offers some tips for brain health.

 ## Box 12.6 Tips and Tools for Teaching and Learning

Tips to Keep Your Brain Healthy

According to the Cleveland Clinic (2022) and Harvard Medical School (2022), some lifestyle habits promote brain health, including:

- Sleeping at least seven to eight hours nightly.
- Exercising consistently.
- Getting mental stimulation through taking new courses, doing puzzles or solving problems, and activities requiring manual dexterity and mental effort, such as drawing, painting, and other crafts.
- Drinking alcohol in moderation.
- Eating a diet full of vegetables, fruits, whole grains, lean protein, and healthy fats, such as the Mediterranean Diet.
- Lowering your blood pressure and cholesterol levels and controlling blood sugar levels.
- Practicing puzzles such as jigsaw puzzles, crosswords, or word searches.
- Being a non-smoker.
- Managing stress levels.
- Protecting your head from moderate to severe injuries by wearing appropriate safety gear and other precautions.
- Building social networks.

What do you need to do to improve your brain health?

Intelligence

As an adult learner or educator, have you ever wondered how you would answer the question, "What makes a person intelligent?" What would you say? Many might say an intelligent person is "smart" or "knows a lot." When related to school, people who learn easily and seem to remember lessons more readily than others might be viewed as intelligent. Others think of intelligence as scoring high on an intelligence test. These understandings represent the traditional perspective on intelligence, dominated by isolating and measuring aspects of intelligence. This section reviews the traditional perspective first, then considers some of the more recent models or "theories" of intelligence, all with an eye to how the brain, learning, and aging intersect with these understandings.

Scholars have lamented that the construct of adult intelligence has created perplexing problems for psychologists for almost 100 years, primarily due to their lack of real-life application (Ackerman, 2017; Halpern & Dunn, 2021). Early intelligence research is traceable to the first few decades of the 20th century when several researchers such as Wechsler, Spearman, and Binet sought to define and measure intelligence, first with children and then with adults (Foos & Clark, 2008). Spearman, in particular, proposed what he called a "general factor" of intelligence, commonly called the "g" factor. This "g" factor stands for one's general intellectual capacity, measured by scores on an intelligence test. The "g" factor is the same as what has come to be known as one's intelligence quotient or "IQ." The notion of a "g" factor or "IQ" is still in use in research today (Jensen, 2002). Box 12.7 provides some tools for reflecting on intelligence.

Fluid and Crystallized Intelligence

Thinking of intelligence as a single construct, such as the g factor, has proved problematic to those who see intelligence as a set of multiple abilities or dimensions. Thurstone (1938) was one of the first to take this position and developed the Primary Mental Abilities measure for understanding adult intelligence. This instrument had seven distinct measures: Spatial relations, reasoning, word

---

 ## Box 12.7 Tips and Tools for Teaching and Learning

Learning and Teaching About Intelligence

As an adult educator or learner, invite learners to begin a dialogue centering on intelligence:

1. Ask learners to write down their definition of "intelligence."
2. Compile these definitions into a list.
3. Ask learners to derive the commonalities across the definitions.
4. Weigh the components from the dialogue against key ideas about intelligence.

fluency, verbal meaning, numbers, perceptual speed, and memory. However, Cattell (1963) and then Horn and Cattell (1966) in the mid-1960s and their theory of fluid and crystallized intelligence had the most influence on thinking about intelligence, especially regarding aging. They reasoned that **fluid intelligence** is "hard-wired," dependent on the central nervous system, and involves abstract reasoning, pattern recognition, and response speed. **Crystallized intelligence** is dependent on life experience and education. "It consists of the set of skills and bits of knowledge that we each learn as part of growing up in any given culture, such as the ability to evaluate experience, the ability to reason about real-life problems, and technical skills learned for a job and other aspects of life" (Bjorklund, 2011, p. 106), for example, budgeting or conflict resolution. An example of a test item for fluid intelligence might be to determine what comes next in a series of shapes. One would have to recognize the logic of the pattern of the given shapes (the number of sides, amount of shading, and so on) to select the next logical shape. A test item for crystallized intelligence might be to choose a word that means the opposite of the given word.

Research suggests that as adults age, fluid intelligence decreases, perhaps due to the slowing down of response rate with age, while crystallized intelligence increases, giving a relatively stable measure of intelligence over time, as depicted in Figure 12.1. Combining the two measures of intelligence at a point in young adulthood, for example, will yield a similar average as combining a high crystallized score with a low fluid measure in older adulthood. Recent research on crystallized and fluid intelligence suggests that culture affects each of these components, and it is no longer assumed that the above pattern will hold (Zelinski & Kennison, 2007). Generational increases in fluid intelligence, for example, might be partially attributed to "changes in processing from more

FIGURE 12.1 FLUID AND CRYSTALLIZED INTELLIGENCE

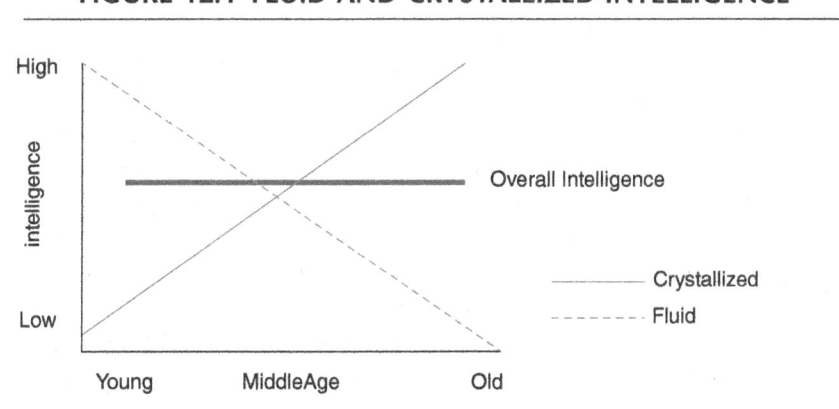

characteristically verbal to more iconic representations due to the rise of visually oriented modalities in film, television, computer games, and other media" (Zelinski & Kennison, 2007, p. 547). Thus, it is hypothesized that "larger cohort increases will be observed for the fluid-like cognitive skills that have been more emphasized in recent decades than previously, whereas crystallized skills that have been consistently emphasized over the past century would show less cohort change" (p. 547). Kovacs and Conway (2016) proposed Process Overlap Theory to explain how general and specific mental abilities interchange as people engage in cognitive tasks. For example, "People who perform above average on one kind of cognitive test (e.g., vocabulary) tend to perform above average on other kinds of cognitive tests as well (e.g., mental rotation)" (p. 151).

The notion that culture and context play a role in shaping what is considered "intelligent" behavior and that intelligence might be more than verbal and analytical reasoning underlies several other models of intelligence proposed within recent decades. There has also been the recognition that the West has so privileged the notion that intelligence is an individual, innate ability measurable by tests that other dimensions of what might be considered "intelligent" behavior in a real-world, multicultural context have been overlooked. The next section reviews three approaches to understanding intelligence that are more than what IQ tests measure: Sternberg's triarchic model and emotional intelligence.

Sternberg's Triarchic Theory of Intelligence

Another challenge to the traditional view of intelligence as a verbal and analytical, school-based measure comes from Sternberg et al. (2000), who alleged that "the problems faced in everyday life often have little relationship to the knowledge and skills acquired through formal education or the abilities used in classroom activities" (p. 32). **Sternberg's triarchic theory of intelligence** consists of three intelligence components—analytical, creative, and practical. **Analytical intelligence** is comparable to "general intelligence," typically measured by IQ tests and evidenced by the ability to complete academic tasks, solve problems, and reason abstractly. **Creative intelligence** is the capacity to solve problems with ingenuity that generates new approaches and unique solutions. **Practical intelligence** concerns how people deal with everyday experiences in real-world contexts. Practical intelligence involves acquiring and using **tacit knowledge**— understanding born through experience that adults rarely articulate because it becomes second nature, like riding a bicycle.

Sternberg and associates' work has been critiqued (e.g., Gottfredson, 2003) for "their bold claim that there exists a general factor of practical intelligence that is distinct from 'academic intelligence'" (Gottfredson, 2003, p. 343). The critique cites a lack of evidence, selective reporting of results, and correlates of tacit knowledge. Despite the critiques, the model has influenced the understanding of intelligence in adult education.

Social and Emotional Intelligence

Taylor and Marienau (2016) emphasized, "Without emotions, intelligence has no anchor. Without emotion, cognition has no grounding in values and social decision making is fatally flawed" (p. 56). Emotional intelligence (EI) is based on Thorndike's early 20th-century notion of **social intelligence**—the ability to function successfully in interpersonal situations. Gardner (1993) also described alternative forms of intelligence, including interpersonal and intrapersonal intelligence, similar to emotional intelligence in their content. Although interest in emotion began with Thorndike and Gardner, it was in 1990 when Salovey and Mayer coined the term **emotional intelligence**—"the ability to monitor one's own and other's feelings and emotions, to discriminate among them, and to use this information to guide one's thinking and action" (p. 189), which was popularized by Goleman.

Emotional intelligence (EI) is often associated with Goleman's (1995) trait-oriented definition: Knowing and managing emotions, motivating oneself, recognizing emotions in others, and handling relationships. Elsewhere, his definition incorporated self-awareness, impulse control, delayed gratification, managing stress and anxiety, and exhibiting empathy. Goleman broke his definition down into 25 different emotional competencies—causing some to argue that Goleman's all-inclusive definition is not scientific and describes personality traits rather than intelligence and/or ability (Mayer et al., 2000; Opengart & Bierema, 2015).

Mayer et al. (2000) posited that EI integrates psychological processes, including appraising and expressing emotions, assimilating emotions in thoughts, and understanding, regulating, and managing emotions. The authors distinguished their definition of EI as an ability versus a set of personality traits (Mayer & Salovey, 1997; Mayer et al., 2000; Salovey & Mayer, 1990, 1994). Bar-On (1997) depicted EI as "an array of noncognitive abilities, competencies, and skills that influence one's ability to succeed in coping with environmental demands and pressures" (p. 14). Debate is ongoing on whether EI is an ability or a collection of traits, and clarifying the definition is important to distinguish the pertinent research and determine validity (Mayer et al., 2008). Singh et al. (2022) contrasted three well-known and often referenced models of emotional intelligence (Bar-On, Mayer-Salovey, and Goleman), providing a thorough

TABLE 12.2 THREE DEFINITIONAL STREAMS OF EMOTIONAL INTELLIGENCE

Salovey and Mayer (1990) Ability model	Cherniss et al. (1998) Trait model	Bar-On (1997) Mixed model
Emotional Intelligence is: • The capacity to process information and reason with emotion • To perceive emotion • To integrate it into thought • To understand • To manage emotion	Emotional Intelligence is: • Self-awareness • Self-regulation • Self-motivation • Social awareness • Social skills	Emotional Intelligence is: • "An array of non-cognitive abilities, competencies, and skills" (p. 14) • Intrapersonal EQ • Interpersonal EQ • Adaptability EQ • Stress management EQ • General mood EQ

Source: Opengart (2005, p. 51).
Note: EQ = emotional quotient.

overview of existing models, assessment tools, and connections. They concluded that Mayer-Salovey places more emphasis on emotion. Table 12.2 illustrates the three streams of EI, as defined by the authors who first presented it within their framework of ability, trait, or a mixed-model definition of EI as organized by Opengart (2005).

Opengart and Bierema (2015) followed a mixed-model perspective of EI in a study of emotionally intelligent mentoring. Although some have argued that EI models are overly broad and have strayed from the core constructs of emotion and intelligence (Mayer et al., 2008), other research has indicated that the trait models have engaged in the bulk of such detours. Although the mixed model (EQi assessment; Bar-On, 1997) showed a significant correlation with personality variables, that does not necessarily reduce its validity and may be a reflection of it being a self-report assessment. Thus, the mixed-model approach can be valuable for understanding EI. This mixed-model perspective is appropriate because it incorporates previously identified elements critical to success in developmental relationships, which are important to learning, including emotional and social skills applied interpersonally and intrapersonally. Opengart and Bierema (2015) organized theoretical precepts of emotional intelligence into relational quadrants of EI and the self, EI and others, integration of EI into thought, and assimilation of EI into action, summarized in Table 12.3.

Although solid evidence still needs to be presented in support of emotional intelligence as a separate type of intelligence, this notion of emotional intelligence has resonated with educators and others who observe that there is more to success in life than just one's IQ. It may also help explain why some people are highly skilled at interpersonal relationships or how some become leaders. Several tests

TABLE 12.3 MIXED-MODEL PERSPECTIVE OF EI: EI AND THE SELF, EI AND OTHERS, EI AND THOUGHT, EI AND ACTION

EI and the self	EI and others	EI and thought	EI and action
• Develops self-awareness, regulation, and motivation • Adapts during emotional moments • Learns from social interactions • Uses emotions to improve social and interpersonal effectiveness	• Possesses self-awareness and management of emotions • Exhibits intrapersonal and interpersonal EI • Gages emotional states of others and adjusts behavior accordingly • Exhibits empathy toward others	• Able to reflect on emotions of self and others • Reasons with emotion • Perceives emotions • Understands emotions • Reflects on emotional states of self and others, both during and after social interaction • Uses insights from reflection on emotions to shape future social interactions • Learns from emotional interactions	• Manages emotions • Adapts to others' emotional states • Manages stress • Controls mood • Evaluates emotional situations and identifies effective responses • Uses situational judgment • Selects best responses during conflict • Maintains calm • Offers support to others • Helps others identify their emotional states

Source: Opengart and Bierema (2015).
Note: EI = emotional intelligence.

measure EQ, such as the Mayer-Salovey-Caruso Emotional Intelligence Test (MSCEIT) (see Bru-Luna et al. (2021) for a review of current EQ tests). It is fair to conclude that intelligence is a highly complex construct. Its relationship to the brain is evident in that general intelligence involves the intake and processing of information. This section reviewed some of the more common understandings of intelligence and how it relates to what we know about adult learning and adult functioning in an ever-changing world. See Box 12.8 for a focus on emotional intelligence and work.

Cognitive Development and Wisdom

As a learner, consider your family for clues about how thinking patterns change as people age. Babies who seem to put everything in their mouths are using their bodies and particularly their senses to learn about their world; teenagers often have rigid opinions as to what is right or wrong; the grandparent seen as "wise" has learned from life experience and weighs several factors before coming up with an insightful suggestion for dealing with a problem. Cognitive development is about how thinking patterns change as humans age.

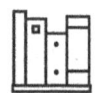 **Box 12.8 Recommendations for Further Learning**

Emotional Intelligence and Work

Ivcevic et al. (2021) conducted a national study of US workers across industries (N = 14,654), examining how emotionally intelligent supervisory behavior affected employee growth, affect, and creativity at work. Workers reported on their supervisors' display of emotionally intelligent behaviors, such as perceiving, using, understanding, and managing emotions, and self-reported their work experiences and creativity. They concluded that a supervisor's emotionally intelligent behavior links to creativity and innovation through its impact on employee growth opportunities. Despite the value of emotionally intelligent leadership for workers, it can also put them at risk.

Merve Emre (2021) published an article in *The New Yorker*, "The Repressive Politics of Emotional Intelligence," published in *The New Yorker* on April 19, 2021, critically examining Daniel Goleman's 1995 book, *Emotional Intelligence*, and its pervasive influence over the past 25 years. Emre argued that Goleman's work transformed the concept of emotional intelligence into a tool for corporate management, emphasizing self-control and adaptability to fit organizational norms. This shift, she warned, often suppresses genuine emotional expression and reinforces existing power structures by promoting conformity over individual authenticity. Emre contended that the widespread adoption of emotional intelligence in professional settings has led to emotional regulation that prioritizes productivity and compliance, potentially at the expense of personal well-being and authentic interpersonal relationships.

She also gave an informative interview on Adam Grant's (2021) Podcast *Worklife:* https://shows.acast.com/worklife-with-adam-grant/episodes/merve-emre-on-emotional-intelligence-as-corporate-control

Cognitive Development

There are numerous theories and models about cognitive development, and many begin with the foundational work of Jean Piaget (1966, 1972), whose four age-related stages of cognitive development are summarized in Table 12.4.

Think of these four stages as playing with a pack of cards: Infants would take hold of some cards and likely put them into their mouths. A 4-year-old could probably sort the kings, queens, and jacks into piles, a 10-year-old could play a

TABLE 12.4 PIAGET'S STAGES OF COGNITIVE DEVELOPMENT

Stage	Age	Characteristics
Sensory Motor	0–2	The child learns through the senses of sight, touch, sound, and taste.
Pre-operational stage	2–7	The child uses symbols, numbers, and words to represent objects.
Concrete operations	7–11	The child understands concepts, relationships, and formal operational concepts involving hypothetical reasoning and abstract thinking.
Formal operational thought	12+	The individual demonstrates abstract thinking, such as logic, reasoning, comparison, and classification.

simple card game using all the cards, and a young adult could play a sophisticated card game like poker or bridge.

Although the early theory of adult learning was concerned with ages, phases, or stages of life (e.g., Erikson, 1980; Levinson et al., 1978; Levinson, 1996), today, an understanding of adult development draws on constructive-developmental theories that focus on how adults make sense of their world through experience where they transition to higher levels of development. Adult development is not necessarily connected to age or stage. Instead, adults construct meaning from within rather than discovering an objective truth outside themselves. What does it mean to transition to higher levels of development as an adult learner?

1. Developing an independent sense of self—Not seeing yourself as your parents may have told you to see yourself (e.g., abiding by certain values, beliefs, or goals they expected from you), but rather forging an identity grounded in the values, beliefs, and goals that matter to you.
2. Showing self-awareness—Achieving a highly developed sense of the person you are (strengths and weaknesses) along with the emotional intelligence to monitor and adjust your emotions.
3. Controlling your behavior—Assuming responsibility for your thoughts and actions and exercising restraint in engaging with other individuals and groups.
4. Managing your relationships and social dynamics affecting you—Trusting and being trusted by others and mastering the resiliency to handle VUCA situations.
5. Becoming wise—Developing keen insights into the world and sound judgment in dealing with various individuals and situations.

There have been other models of development influenced by Piaget, such as Perry's (1999) stages of moral and ethical development, Kohlberg's (1981) stages of moral development, reflective thinking (King & Kitchener, 2004), ego development (Loevinger, 1976), faith development (Fowler, 1981), *Women's Ways of Knowing* (Belenky et al., 1986), and self-development (Kegan, 1982, 1994).

In addition to constructive meaning-making, adult learning is developmental because the capacity of adults to create meaning evolves to become more complex as they learn and change. Adult learning theory in this framework focuses on authority, responsibility, and the ability to tolerate ambiguity and complexity, which are difficult for many people to manage. This frame is increasingly relevant as adults live in the age of "VUCA," where the world is volatile, uncertain, complex, and ambiguous (Elkington et al., 2017). See Reio (2020) or Merriam and Baumgartner (2020) for a more extensive discussion of adult development.

Wisdom

Merriam and Baumgartner (2020) called wisdom "the hallmark of adult thinking" (p. 367). Although it might be assumed that adults automatically become wise with age, "becoming wise clearly requires more than 'just' growing old—accumulated life experience is an important foundation for wisdom, but not all highly wise individuals are old and many old individuals are not particularly wise" (Glück, 2024, n.p.). Wisdom represents the pinnacle of cognitive development since it represents how people *think* about real-life problems and issues. Wisdom is "expert-level knowledge in the fundamental pragmatics of life" (Baltes & Smith, 1990, p. 95) or "good judgment and advice in important but uncertain matters of life" (Baltes & Staudinger, 1993, p. 75). Sternberg (2003), whose triarchic theory of intelligence was reviewed earlier in this chapter, believed wisdom draws upon "practical" or "successful" intelligence and creativity and that wisdom is about "balancing various self-interests (intrapersonal) with the interests of others (interpersonal) and of other aspects of the context in which one lives (extrapersonal)" (p. 152). Box 12.9 offers some reflective activities for learning about wisdom.

Glück (2024) provided a topology of cognitive, personality, and developmental understandings of wisdom and aging, featured in Tables 12.5, 12.6, and 12.7. Glück (2024) classified **cognitive-focused models of wisdom** describing wise thinking as differentiated by awareness of certainty, unpredictability, and the limitations of one's knowledge, combined with recognizing the legitimacy of other people's perspectives and how differences in values and life experiences shape them. **Personality-focused models of wisdom** emphasize personality-related, affective, and motivational

 ## Box 12.9 Tips and Tools for Teaching and Learning

Learning and Teaching About Wisdom

As an adult educator or learner, invite learners to engage in an activity about wisdom:

1. Ask learners to think of someone they know or a public figure they call "wise."
2. Invite learners to list why they identified this person—what makes someone "wise."
3. Follow up the conversation by compiling the ages of these nominated wise people to explore the relationship between wisdom and age.

components, including curiosity, questioning one's beliefs or assumptions, empathy for others, having a sense of meaning, and experiencing awe. **Developmental models of wisdom** account for how wise adults develop and why some grow wiser than others across the lifespan. Although experience is necessary to acquire wisdom, it is not sufficient to become wise. Wisdom development depends on how people reflect on and learn from life experiences. Note that we, the authors, adapted the following tables and added the far-right column to focus on wisdom development implications for learning and teaching for Glück's cognitive, personality, and developmental models of wisdom.

One of the key questions about wisdom is its relationship to age. The cognitive, personality, and developmental understandings of wisdom and aging suggest that adults can develop mature cognitive functioning central to thinking and acting wisely. However, we also know that, as adult learners and educators, younger adults can be wise, and sometimes, we even say that children are "wise beyond their years." In 2005, Sternberg published a literature review on this very question. He concluded that perhaps due to the variation in how wisdom is defined and measured, there is no definitive answer to whether wisdom increases with age. However, Sternberg (2005) concluded that wisdom appears to be related to the situation rather than the person and that "cognitive variables, personality variables, and life experiences" are more important than age in the development of wisdom (p. 21). Sternberg (2005) pointed out that

> There is a joke about how many psychologists it takes to change a light bulb. The answer is it doesn't matter, so long as the light bulb wants to change. Similarly, people must want to develop their wisdom-related

TABLE 12.5 COGNITIVE-FOCUSED MODELS OF WISDOM

Model and Authors	Definition	Criteria and Components	Developmental Predictions	Empirical Relationships with Age	Implications for Adult Learning and Teaching
Berlin Wisdom Model (Baltes, 2000; Baltes & Smith, 2008)	Wisdom-related knowledge is a deep understanding of the fundamental, practical aspects of living a worthy and meaningful life.	1. Understanding basic facts about how life works, like relationships, health, and emotions; 2. Knowing how to handle life situations, such as solving problems, making decisions, and interacting with others. 3. Accepting that different people have different values and perspectives, there isn't always one "right" answer. 4. Understanding how life events fit into the bigger picture. 5. Realizing life is full of unknowns and learning to make good choices even when you cannot predict the outcome.	Wisdom develops with experience, but only for people who actively focus on learning and improving how they deal with life's significant challenges. It also depends on personal traits, specific skills, and life experiences.	Wisdom-related knowledge positively relates to age in adolescence and emerging adulthood (Pasupathi et al., 2001). In older age groups, no statistical relationship between wisdom-related knowledge and age was found (Staudinger, 1999).	Wisdom development is knowledge accumulated over a lifetime in a VUCA context. Therefore, education should encourage lifelong learning, reflection, and the ability to adapt and grow with experience. Teaching and learning should also be active in integrating real-world problem-solving and decision-making scenarios. Learners should also respect diverse perspectives, including empathy and cultural sensitivity toward people who are different from them.

Bremen Wisdom Model (Mickler & Standinger, 2008).	Self-related wisdom means having sound judgment and a deep understanding of how to handle challenging and uncertain situations in your own life.	1. Having a deep understanding of yourself, including your strengths, weaknesses, and what matters most to you. 2. Knowing simple, practical strategies to grow, improve, and keep on track. 3. Understanding how you connect and relate to others while balancing your needs and theirs. 4. Recognizing that your views and experiences aren't the only valid ones and being open to seeing things from other perspectives. 5. Being okay with uncertainty and not always having clear answers or outcomes.	Personal wisdom develops as expertise about yourself and your life but may be compromised by self-enhancement bias and dogmatism, especially in older age.	Old adults scored significantly lower in criteria 3–5 but slightly higher in self-knowledge than young adults. Controlling for openness to experience and fluid intelligence mediated part of these age differences.	Self-knowledge is key to wisdom. Guide learners to explore their values, strengths, weaknesses, and life goals, and learn how to self-monitor to grow. It is also essential to possess self-awareness and manage uncertainty. Key learning activities: Reflection, dialogue, self-awareness enhancing activities, goal setting, adaptability, collaborative problem solving, and resiliency with VUCA situations.
Wise Reasoning Model (Oakes et al., 2019; Grossmann et al., 2010).	Emphasizes the cognitive processes underlying wise decisions, such as intellectual humility—where learners acknowledge their limitations and develop openness to learning from others, perspective-taking, and recognizing uncertainty.	1. Cultivating intellectual humility. 2. Seeing others' perspectives. 3. Integrating different perspectives. 4. Recognizing uncertainty and change.	There are no theoretical predictions about development.	Older participants reasoned more wisely about intergroup and interpersonal conflicts than younger participants. Wise reasoning concerning specific real-life situations was negatively related to age below age 45 and positively associated with age above age 45 (Brienza et al., 2016).	This model focuses on promoting intellectual humility. Valuing multiple viewpoints is central to wise reasoning and embracing uncertainty. This model also encourages metacognition or thinking about one's thinking. Key pedagogies include assumption checking, reflection, dialogue, decision-making, and mindfulness.

TABLE 12.6 PERSONALITY-FOCUSED MODELS OF WISDOM

Model and Authors	Definition	Criteria and Components	Developmental Predictions	Empirical Relationships with Age	Implications for Adult Learning and Teaching
Self-Transcendence Model (Aldwin et al., 2019; Baltes & Smith, 1990)	Wisdom as self-transcendence involves self-definition independent of socially imposed labels or expectations and breaking down boundaries between the self and others to connect meaningfully.	1. Self-knowledge and self-integration 2. Peace of mind 3. Non-attachment 4. Self-transcendence 5. Presence in the here-and-now and growth (Koller et al., 2017).	1. Self-transcendence develops in people who rise beyond conventional limits and expectations by engaging in activities such as seeking insight or meditation through four developmental stages: (1) Self-knowledge, (2) Non-attachment, (3) Integration; (4) Self-transcendence (Levenson et al., 2005).	Older participants scored higher than young participants in peace of mind, non-attachment, and self-transcendence (Koller et al., 2017).	This approach can help create conditions for promoting transformative learning through encouraging interconnectedness between the learner and instructor, shifting away from competitive learning situations to focus on intrinsic growth, integrating reflective practices, encouraging transdisciplinary exploration of topics, emphasizing individual growth over grades, fostering an ethic of care and developing sensitivity to diversity, equity, and inclusion. Effective pedagogies include using portfolios, reflective journaling, and peer evaluations.

| Three-Dimensional Wisdom Model (Ardelt, 2003; Ardelt et al., 2018) | Wisdom is a combination of traits that help people empathize with others' viewpoints, question their assumptions, recognize their limitations, learn from experience, and show care and compassion toward others. | 1. Cognitive dimension
2. Reflective dimension
3. Compassionate dimension | The capacity to reflect and consider ideas from different perspectives is the foundation for developing other parts of wisdom. While mental sharpness (like problem-solving) may decrease with age, other qualities of wisdom, like emotional understanding and compassion, can grow at least into midlife. | Negative correlations with age were found, especially for the cognitive dimension (Ardelt 2003; Glück et al., 2013). More recent research found curvilinear trends, showing lower scores in the cognitive dimension of wisdom from midlife on but higher scores in the two other dimensions, especially in participants with higher educational levels (Ardelt et al., 2018). | The model highlights cognitive, reflective, and practical dimensions of learning, and therefore, the teaching should consider promoting critical thinking and analytical skills, helping learners develop curiosity and the ability to think deeply, considering concepts and situations from multiple viewpoints, and emphasizing teamwork, empathy, and collaboration. Pedagogy in this model might include problem-solving, dialogue, assumptions analysis, group projects, and service learning. |

TABLE 12.7 DEVELOPMENTAL MODELS OF WISDOM

Model and Authors	Definition	Criteria and Components	Developmental Predictions	Empirical Relationships with Age	Implications for Adult Learning and Teaching
HERO(E) Model of Wisdom (Webster, 2007; Webster et al., 2014)	Wisdom is applying insights from critical life experiences to facilitate the optimal development of the self and others.	1. Critical life experience 2. Openness 3. Emotional regulation 4. Reminiscence and reflectiveness 5. Humor	Wisdom develops through reminiscence and reflection on critical life experiences. Openness, emotional regulation, and humor support its development.	Middle-aged adults scored higher than younger and older adults on all wisdom components except reminiscence and reflectiveness.	Learning and teaching should focus on appreciating the humor in life experiences, developing emotional intelligence, reflecting on experience, receptiveness to new experiences, and learning from critical life experiences. Pedagogy might include storytelling, empathic listening, reflective journaling, dialogue, appreciation for diversity, equity, inclusion, and experiential learning such as service learning or real-world problem-solving activities.
MORE Life Experience Model (Glück & Bluck, 2013; Glück et al., 2019)	This model defines psychological resources that foster growth in wisdom as individuals reflect on life challenges and become competent at managing them.	1. Managing uncertainty and uncontrollability. 2. Being open to new perspectives and experiences. 3. Reflectivity. 4. Emotional sensitivity and emotion regulation.	Wisdom develops through reflection on challenging life experiences. Early-life predecessors of wisdom development include openness and emotional sensitivity. Later-life acquisition of awareness of uncertainty and uncontrollability helps wisdom development.	Wisdom resources were correlated with wisdom levels in a lifespan sample.	Learning and teaching should acknowledge the VUCA conditions of the environment and help learners develop a sense of control and competence in facing the demands of life. This outlook involves openness to new experiences and differing viewpoints, reflexivity, emotional intelligence, and empathy. Effective pedagogy in this model would include helping learners develop a growth mindset toward life's challenges, openness to new ideas and experiences, reflective practice including journaling and dialogue, stress management and resilience development, and collaborative learning projects.

skills in order for them actually to develop and then must adopt the attitudes toward life—openness to experience, reflectivity upon experience, and willingness to profit from experience—that will enable this development to occur. (p. 21)

Designing and Facilitating Educational Programs with Neuroscience in Mind

Advances in understanding memory and the brain have major applications to adult learning. We know, for example, that as learners, if we consciously attend to what we are trying to learn, the information will enter our working memory to be processed for long-term memory. "Formal and informal learning, which generates a long-term and accessible knowledge, is mediated by neuroplasticity to create adaptive structural and functional changes in brain networks" (Goldberg, 2022, p. 1). Scholars have recently offered strategies for cognitive development supporting learning and education (Goldberg, 2022; Leisman, 2022; Ruiz-Martín & Bybee, 2022). Brault Foisy et al. (2020) described teachers as "'orchestrators' of neuronal plasticity" (p. 422). They argued that the neuroplasticity concept links education and neuroscience and explained how learning results in changes in brain function. These issues occupy the fields of mind, brain, and education (MBE), neuroeducation, and educational neuroscience. MBE is concerned with (1) examining the biological processes supporting and constraining learning; (2) exploring the neural correlates of academic skills; and (3) investigating how teaching practices impact brain function and/or structure. Brault Foisy et al. (2020) also emphasized that brain architecture before learning influences how people learn. For example, if someone lives with dyslexia, specific brain regions may be impaired, creating learning challenges.

Neuroplasticity is also crucial for adults' workplace performance, career development, and advancement, helping them learn, develop, and adapt in dynamic, changing environments to advance (Forget & Le Pertel, 2024). Lifelong learning enhances neuroplasticity; effective training programs rouse it through multiple sensory stimulation. Neuroplasticity and cognitive agility develop through novel and challenging tasks that adults encounter in life and work.

Brault Foisy et al. (2020) offered key points for understanding teaching and the brain by exploring the efficacy of learning interventions for the same educational topic. They conducted a narrative review concluding that educators' pedagogical choices impact how people learn and retain information. When educators have an understanding of how their pedagogy influences learners' brains, they can use the following five educational practices to improve learning by keeping neuroscience in mind:

1. **Attention orienting:** When an educator directs a learner's attention to different features of the topic or lesson. For example, a teacher may say, "Pay attention to this concept as it will help you understand the next point." Other strategies might include using a hook or story to engage learners at the beginning of the lesson, posing questions related to the topic, or providing visual clues like pointing to a certain point on a diagram during discussion. Using verbal cues such as "Listen carefully" or "This is an important point" are simple orienting strategies. Attention orienting is also about keeping students engaged and focused throughout the lesson, which usually means varying the pace and activity level.

2. **Teaching particular strategies** involves teaching a specific tactic to achieve a solution, such as teaching math, for example, using a sequence of arithmetic operations versus memorizing the solution of a problem.

3. **Changing the level of cognitive engagement:** This occurs by adjusting the task's complexity level, for example, beginning a lesson by asking students to recall questions or knowledge about the topic and then progressing to more complex analysis and evaluation with activities such as comparing and contrasting different perspectives, justifying reasoning, or applying knowledge to case studies. Active learning also helps promote changing cognitive engagement levels with the subject.

4. **Modifying the educational context:** This strategy involves changing the learning environment. For example, in language learning, one context is a didactic classroom setting where students learn vocabulary, grammar, and history. However, effective language learning usually happens in more immersive settings where learners can practice the language, converse with native speakers, and conduct tasks of everyday life, such as shopping or going to a cafe. Examples include field trips, immersive technology or simulations, guest speakers, and project-based learning projects that help learners apply their knowledge in real-life situations.

5. **Interacting with the learner:** Although educators have multiple engagements with learners, how they interact can influence learning effectiveness. Important here is the learner's ability to receive feedback from the educator, practice, and adjust their behavior. Chapter 15 discusses learner-centered instruction and practices foundational to active learning.

Forget and Le Pertel (2024) recommended promoting brain health at work to support learning and memory in workplace performance. They recommended that organizations support their workforce's healthy lifestyles by encouraging exercise, healthy eating, and stress management. They suggested that training and development programs should incorporate active learning strategies, including problem-based and experiential learning because they encourage neural network development and improve the retention of new information. Cognitive training exercises help refine cognition, such as attention, memory, and problem-solving and are customizable according to job function. They also recommended mindfulness training as necessary for stress reduction.

Ruiz-Martín and Bybee (2022) linked cognitive principles of learning to the 5E model of instruction, developed by the Biological Sciences Curriculum Studies (BSCS) in 1987 and is a learning sequence model for teaching science, consisting of the five phases of engagement, exploration, explanation, elaboration, and evaluation. Table 12.8 describes these phases with implications for adult cognition and learning.

Goldberg (2022) conducted a review to apply neuroscience to key educational concepts of mindset, motivation, meaning-making, and attention and offered educators recommendations for learning content and educational design. Goldberg took Vygotsky's (1978) **zone of proximal development** model (ZPD)— the space between what a learner can and cannot do—and explored learning and development demands related to the model, as noted in Figure 12.2. The ZPD model characterized learning and development as dependent on balancing support and challenge of the learner, according to the individual learner's developmental needs. Decades later, Davidson and McEwen (2012) discovered brain neuroplasticity is affected by environmental conditions and the balance between learning demands or challenges and available resources or support. When learners are in their **comfort zone,** they tend to have ample resources to deal with demands placed on them and, therefore, do not need to engage in much learning to master tasks and information. The **stretch zone** is the optimal ZPD, where resources expand to meet the cognitive challenge. Resources and demands are balanced, creating the ideal environment for promoting effective adult learning. The **stress zone** is when learning demands exceed the resources available to the learner; thus, little or no learning will occur, meaning the learner's capacity to cope is severely limited by internal or external factors. Hence, educators should identify the stretch zone and provide learners appropriate resources to facilitate their learning. As Taylor and Marienau (2016) emphasized, "Brain-aware facilitation can also encourage adults to further develop their capacities for complexity as they seek to make more informed choices and act in more thoughtful and deliberate ways with regard to the greater good" (p. 287).

TABLE 12.8 THE 5E MODEL OF INSTRUCTION AND IMPLICATIONS FOR COGNITION AND LEARNING

Learning Phase	Definition	Implications for Cognition and Learning
Engage	Accessing the learner's prior knowledge and stimulating interest in the topic by helping learners connect past and present learning experiences and identifying prior understandings. This phase also serves to motivate learning.	Triggering recall or linking the topic to a relevant context helps learners draw on prior knowledge to integrate and retain new information. Learners build new knowledge on prior long-term memory. The key here is contextual and cognitive engagement. **Contextual engagement** helps learners connect the topic to real life, and **cognitive engagement** occurs when learners realize their current knowledge is insufficient for understanding the topic.
Explore	Providing learners with a common base of activities from which to access working memory and begin making inquiries about the new learning through inquiry, observation, and discussion with the guidance and scaffolding of the educator.	Promoting connections between prior knowledge and new information to be learned. The goal is sense-making about the learning topic or task. This phase is grounded in cognitive psychology and involves thinking about meaning based on the finding that people learn and remember better when they think about what they are learning and make connections with prior knowledge.
Explain	Providing teacher-led descriptions of the learning topic or task and allowing learners to articulate their understanding of it facilitates deeper understanding.	Formalizing concepts are grasped in the explorer stage, where the educator introduces new ideas and helps learners organize the information to facilitate encoding and later retrieval from memory. When learners have an organizational structure in which to fit new knowledge, they learn more effectively.
Elaborate	Challenging learners' conceptual and understanding skills by providing experiences to develop deeper and broader understanding and skill development through experiential learning.	Providing opportunities for learners to transfer their new knowledge to multiple contexts where they can practice applying the new concepts. This phase incorporates opportunities to practice the new knowledge.
Evaluate	Assessing learners' understanding and abilities related to the lesson content.	Assessing learners' knowledge and ability with the new content is essential throughout the learning engagement, and thus, formative and summative assessments are recommended. A key component of the evaluation stage is providing learner feedback so they can adjust their understanding or application and strengthen retrieval from long-term memory.

FIGURE 12.2 ZONE OF PROXIMAL DEVELOPMENT AND NEUROPLASTICITY

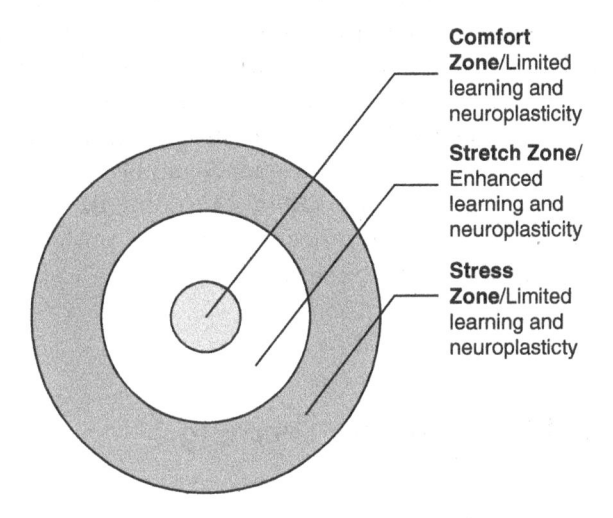

Comfort Zone/Limited learning and neuroplasticity

Stretch Zone/Enhanced learning and neuroplasticity

Stress Zone/Limited learning and neuroplasticty

Chapter Summary

Inspired by Leonardo da Vinci's pursuit of interdisciplinary knowledge, this chapter, "Connecting Neuroscience and Adult Learning," explored the interplay between brain function and adult education, offering insights into how neuroscience can enhance learning processes and emphasizing the brain's ability to adapt and develop wisdom. The chapter began with an overview of neuromyths, followed by a discussion of memory and learning. The chapter summarized different understandings of intelligence, explored the development of cognition and wisdom, and concluded with a discussion of neuroscience, learning, and teaching. Life experiences and learning play significant roles in all of these processes. As Leonardo da Vinci observed, "The noblest pleasure is the joy of understanding" (Bianci, n.d.).

Key Points

- Neuromyths were introduced, including those of the triune brain and dominant hemispheric brain.
- The chapter offered details on the stages of memory formation (sensory, working, and long-term memory) and normal aging effects versus concerning

symptoms, including tips for maintaining brain health, like mental stimulation, exercise, and healthy eating.

- Intelligence and emotional intelligence were discussed, including fluid and crystallized intelligence, Sternberg's triarchic theory, and emotional intelligence (EI).
- Cognitive development and wisdom were reviewed, including models of cognitive development and wisdom as a culmination of experience, self-awareness, and reflective thinking, with insights into its relationship with age.
- The chapter concluded with neuroscience implications for education design and facilitation, highlighting techniques to optimize memory and learning through active engagement, reflection, and real-world problem-solving. See Box 12.10 for further learning tips.

Box 12.10 For Further Learning

Resources and Web Links on Learning and the Brain

1. "The Mystery of Consciousness: Neuroscience Offers New Insights." This video is an illustrated talk by Antonio Damasio, a neuroscientist who explains how the brain, emotions, and consciousness are interrelated. www.ted.com/talks/lang/en/antonio_damasio_the_quest_ to _ understand_consciousness.html.
2. The Consortium for Research on EI (emotional intelligence) in Organizations. This website compiles information about emotional intelligence, such as the latest research, books on EI, EI tests, conferences dealing with EI, and so on. www.eiconsortium.org.
3. See the following websites for information and activities related to the brain and memory: Brain Metrix http://www.brainmetrix.com/; Luminosity http://www.lumosity.com/; PositScience http://www.positscience.com/.
4. David Eagleman podcast with Brene Brown's Unlocking Us on The Inside Story of the Ever-Changing Brain. https://brenebrown.com/podcast/brene-with-david-eagleman-on-the-inside-story-of-the-ever-changing-brain/.
5. Further, there are dozens of techniques we can use to improve our memory and many self-help websites (Cleveland Clinic's Healthy Brains, Luminosity, and BrainHQ to name just a few), and popular books we can access (see, for example, Joshua Foer's *Moonwalking with Einstein: The Art and Science of Remembering Everything* (2011), which combines research about memory and memory techniques; David Eagleman's (2022) *Livewired: The Inside Story of the Ever-changing Brain*; or Komblatt and Vega's (2022) *A Better Brain at Any Age*).

References

Ackerman, P. L. (2017). Adult intelligence: The construct and the criterion problem. *Perspectives on Psychological Science, 12*(6), 987–998. https://doi.org/10.1177/1745691617703437.

Aldwin, C. M., Igarashi, H., & Levenson, M. R. (2019). Wisdom as self-transcendence. In R. J. Sternberg & J. Glück (Eds.), *The Cambridge handbook of wisdom* (pp. 122–143). Cambridge University Press.

Angelopoulou, E., & Drigas, A. (2021). Working memory, attention and their relationship: A theoretical overview. *Research, Society and Development, 10*(5), e46410515288. https://doi.org/10.33448/rsd-v10i5.15288.

Ansari, D. (2008). Effects of development and enculturation on number representation in the brain. *Nature Reviews Neuroscience, 9*(4), 278–291. https://doi.org/10.1038/nrn2334.

Ardelt, M. (2003). Empirical assessment of a three-dimensional wisdom scale. *Research on Aging, 25*(3), 275–324. https://doi.org/10.1177/0164027503025003004.

Ardelt, M., Pridgen, S., & Nutter-Pridgen, K. L. (2018). The relation between age and three-dimensional wisdom: Variations by wisdom dimensions and education. *The Journals of Gerontology: Series B, 73*(8), 1339–1349. https://doi.org/10.1093/geronb/gbx182.

Baltes, P. B. (1990). *Toward a psychology of wisdom and its ontogenesis.* Cambridge University Press.

Baltes, P. B. & Smith, J. (1990). Toward a psychology of wisdom and its ontogenesis. In R. J. Sternberg (Ed.), *Wisdom: Its nature, origins, and development* (pp. 87–120). Cambridge University Press. 10.1017/cbo9781139173704.006.

Baltes, P. B., & Smith, J. (2008). The fascination of wisdom: Its nature, ontogeny, and function. *Perspectives on Psychological Science, 3*(1), 56–64. https://doi.org/10.1111/j.1745-6916.2008.00062.x.

Baltes, P. B., & Staudinger, U. M. (1993). The search for a psychology of wisdom. *Current Directions in Psychology Science, 2*, 75–80. https://doi.org/10.1111/1467-8721.ep10770914.

Baltes, P. B., & Staudinger, U. M. (2000). Wisdom: A metaheuristic (pragmatic) to orchestrate mind and virtue toward excellence. *American Psychologist, 55*(1), 122–136. https://psycnet.apa.org/buy/2000-13324-012.

Bar-On R. (1997). *Bar-on emotional quotient inventory (EQ-i): A test of emotional intelligence.* Toronto, Ontario, Canada: Multi-Health Systems.

Barrett, L. F. (2020). *Seven and a half lessons about the brain.* Houghton Mifflin.

Belenky, M. F., Clinchy, B. M., Goldberger, N. R., & Tarule, J. M. (1986). *Women's ways of knowing: The development of self, voice, and mind.* New York: Basic Books.

Bianci, L. (n.d.). *Leonardo da Vinci Quotes.* Leonardo da Vinci. https://www.leonardodavincisinventions.com/leonardo-da-vinci-quotes/.

Biological Sciences Curriculum Studies. (1987). *Biological sciences: An ecological approach* (6th ed.). Dubuque, IA: Kendall/Hunt.

Bjorklund, B. R. (2011). *The journey of adulthood* (7th ed.). Englewood Cliffs, NJ: Prentice Hall.

Brault Foisy, L. M., Matejko, A. A., Ansari, D., & Masson, S. (2020). Teachers as orchestrators of neuronal plasticity: Effects of teaching practices on the brain. *Mind, Brain, and Education, 14*(4), 415–428. https://doi.org/10.1111/mbe.12257.

Brienza, J. P., Kung, F., Santos, H., Bobocel, D. R., & Grossmann, I. (2016, December 28). Wisdom, bias, and balance: Toward a process-sensitive measurement of wisdom-related cognition. https://doi.org/10.31234/osf.io/p25c2.

Brookfield, S. (1986). *Understanding and facilitating adult learning: A comprehensive analysis of principles and effective practices.* McGraw-Hill Education (UK).

Bru-Luna, L. M., Martí-Vilar, M., Merino-Soto, C., & Cervera-Santiago, J. L. (2021). Emotional intelligence measures: A systematic review. *Healthcare, 9*(12), 1696. https://doi.org/10.3390/healthcare9121696.

Cattell, R. B. (1963). Theory of fluid and crystallized intelligence: A critical experiment. *Journal of Educational Psychology, 54,* 1–22.

Cavanaugh J. C. & Blanchard-Fields, F. (2017). *Adult development and aging.* (8th ed.). Cengage.

Centre for Educational Research and Innovation and Organization for Economic Co-operation and Development (OECD). (2007). *Understanding the brain: The birth of a learning science.* Paris: OECD.

Chen, S. A., & Goodwill, A. M. (2022). Neuroplasticity and adult learning. In K. Evans, W. O. Lee, J. Markowitsch, M. Zukas (Eds.), *Third international handbook of lifelong learning* (pp. 1–19). Cham: Springer International Publishing.

Cherniss C., Goleman D., Emmerling R., Cowan K., Adler M. (1998). *Bringing emotional intelligence to the workplace.* New Brunswick, NJ: Consortium for Research on Emotional Intelligence in Organizations, Rutgers University. https://www.eiconsortium.org/reports/technical_report.html.

Cleveland Clinic. (2022, March 30). *Brain.* Cleveland Clinic. https://my.clevelandclinic.org/health/body/22638-brain.

Cleveland Clinic. (n.d.-a). *Amazing facts you didn't know about your brain.* Cleveland Clinic. https://health.clevelandclinic.org/brain-teasers-infographic.

Cleveland Clinic. (n.d.-b). *Short-term memory.* Cleveland Clinic. https://my.clevelandclinic.org/health/articles/short-term-memory.

Davidson, R. J., & McEwen, B. S. (2012). Social influences on neuroplasticity: Stress and interventions to promote well-being. *Nature Neuroscience, 15*(5), 689–695. https://doi.org/10.1038/nn.3093.

Dekker, S., Lee, N. C., Howard-Jones, P., and Jolles, J. (2012). Neuromyths in education: Prevalence and predictors of misconceptions among teachers. *Frontiers in Psychology, 3,*429. https://doi.org/10.3389/fpsyg.2012.00429.

Duckworth, A. L., White, R. E., Matteucci, A. J., Shearer, A., & Gross, J. J. (2016). A stitch in time: Strategic self-control in high school and college students. *Journal of Educational Psychology, 108*(3), 329. https://psycnet.apa.org/doi/10.1037/edu0000062.

Dweck, C. S. (2006). *Mindset: The new psychology of success.* Random House.

Eagleman, D. (2022). *Livewired: The inside story of the ever-changing brain.* Vintage.

Eliadis, A. (2024). Neuroplasticity and adult learning: Can an old dog learn new tricks? *Educational Administration: Theory and Practice, 30*(11), 511–517. https://doi.org/10.53555/kuey.v30i11.8640ARTICLE.

Elkington, R., Van der Steege, M., & Glick-Smith, J. (2017). *Visionary leadership in a turbulent world: Thriving in the new VUCA context.* Emerald Publishing.

Emre, M. (2021, April 12). *The repressive politics of emotional intelligence.* The New Yorker. https://www.newyorker.com/magazine/2021/04/19/the-repressive-politics-of-emotional-intelligence.

Erikson, E. H. (1980). On the generational cycle. An address. *The International Journal of Psycho-Analysis, 61,* 213. https://www.proquest.com/scholarly-journals/on-generational-cycle-address/docview/1298182355/se-2.

Feiler, J. B., & Stabio, M. E. (2018). Three pillars of educational neuroscience from three decades of literature. *Trends in Neuroscience and Education, 13,* 17–25. https://doi.org/10.1016/j.tine.2018.11.001.

Ferrero, M., Garaizar, P., and Vadillo, M. A. (2016). Neuromyths in education: Prevalence among Spanish teachers and an exploration of cross-cultural variation. *Frontiers in Human Neuroscience, 10, 195467.* https://doi.org/10.3389/fnhum.2016.00496.

Foer, J. (2011). *Moonwalking with Einstein: The art and science of remembering everything.* Penguin Press.

Foos, P. W. & Clark, M. C. (2008). *Human aging.* Pearson.

Forget, M., & Le Pertel, N. (2024). Enhancing Neuroplasticity and Promoting Brain Health at Work: The Role of Learning and Memory in Workplace Performance. In *Learning and Memory-From Molecules and Cells to Mind and Behavior.* IntechOpen. https://www.intechopen.com/chapters/1153559.

Fowler, J. W. (1981). *Stages of faith: The psychology of human development and the quest for meaning.* HarperCollins.

Gardner, H. (1993). *Multiple intelligences: The theory in practice.* Basic Books.

Gardner, H. E. (2008). *Multiple intelligences: New horizons in theory and practice.* Basic books.

Gardner, H. & Moran, S. (2006). The science of multiple intelligences theory: A response to Lynn Waterhouse. *Educational Psychologist, 41*(4), 227–232. https://doi.org/10.1207/s15326985ep4104_2.

Glück, J. (2024). Wisdom and aging. *Current Opinion in Psychology, 55,* 101742. https://doi.org/10.1016/j.copsyc.2023.101742.

Glück, J., Bluck, S. (2013). The MORE life experience model: A theory of the development of personal wisdom. In: Ferrari, M., Weststrate, N. (Eds.). *The scientific study of personal wisdom.* Springer, Dordrecht. https://doi.org/10.1007/978-94-007-7987-7_4.

Glück, J., König, S., Naschenweng, K., Redzanowski, U., Dorner, L., Straßer, I., & Wiedermann, W. (2013). How to measure wisdom: Content, reliability, and validity of five measures. *Frontiers in Psychology, 4,* 405. https://doi.org/10.3389/fpsyg.2013.00405.

Glück, J., Bluck, S. & Weststrate, N. M. (2019). More on the MORE life experience model: What we have learned (so far). *The Journal of Value Inquiry, 53,* 349–370. https://doi.org/10.1007/s10790-018-9661-x.

Goldberg, H. (2022). Growing brains, nurturing minds—neuroscience as an educational tool to support students' development as life-long learners. *Brain Sciences, 12*(12), 1622. https://doi.org/10.3390/brainsci12121622.

Goleman, D. (1995). *Emotional intelligence: Why it can matter more than IQ.* Bantam Books.

Gottfredson, L. S. (2003). On Sternberg's "reply to Gottfredson." *Intelligence, 31*(4), 415–424. https://doi.org/10.1016/S0160-2896(03)00024-2.

Grant, A. (Host). (2021, June 8). Merve Emre on emotional intelligence as corporate control [Audio podcast episode]. In *WorkLife.* TED. https://shows.acast.com/worklife-with-adam-grant/episodes/merve-emre-on-emotional-intelligence-as-corporate-control.

Grospietsch, F., & Lins, I. (2021, July). Review on the prevalence and persistence of Neuromyths in education–where we stand and what is still needed. In *Frontiers in Education* (vol. 6, p. 665752). Frontiers Media SA. https://doi.org/10.3389/feduc.2021.665752.

Grossmann, I., Na, J., Varnum, M. E., Park, D. C., Kitayama, S., & Nisbett, R. E. (2010). Reasoning about social conflicts improves into old age. *Proceedings of the National Academy of Sciences, 107*(16), 7246–7250. https://doi.org/10.1073/pnas.1001715107.

Gruber, T. (2018). *Gedächtnis* (2nd ed.). Springer-Verlag. https://doi.org/10.1007/978-3-662-56362-5.

Halpern, D. F., & Dunn, D. S. (2021). Critical thinking: A model of intelligence for solving real-world problems. *Journal of Intelligence, 9*(2), 22. https://doi.org/10.3390/jintelligence9020022.

Harvard Medical School. (2017, August 30). *How memory and aging thinking ability change with age.* Harvard Health Publishing. https://www.health.harvard.edu/mind-and-mood/how-memory-and-thinking-ability-change-with-age.

Harvard Medical School. (2022, May 13). *12 ways to keep your brain young.* Harvard Health Publishing. https://www.health.harvard.edu/mind-and-mood/12-ways-to-keep-your-brain-young.

Hendricson, W. D., Andrieu, S. C., Chadwick, D. G., Chmar, J. E., Cole, J. R., et al. (2006). Educational strategies associated with development of problem-solving, critical thinking, and self-directed learning. *Journal of Dental Education, 70*(9), 925–936. 10.1002/j.0022-0337.2006.70.9.tb04163.x.

Hiemstra, R., & Brockett, R. G. (2012). Reframing the meaning of self-directed learning: An updated model. *Adult Education Research Conference*, pp. 155–162. https://newprairiepress.org/aerc/2012/papers/22.

Hörder, H., Johansson, L., Guo, X., Grimby, G., Kern, S., Östling, S., & Skoog, I. (2018). Midlife cardiovascular fitness and dementia: A 44-year longitudinal population study in women. *Neurology, 90*(15), e1298–e1305. https://doi.org/10.1212/WNL.0000000000005290.

Horn, J. L. & Cattell, R. B. (1966). Refinement and test of the theory of fluid and crystallized intelligence. *Journal of Educational Psychology, 57*, 253–270.

Ivcevic, Z., Moeller, J., Menges, J., & Brackett, M. (2021). Supervisor emotionally intelligent behavior and employee creativity. *The Journal of Creative Behavior, 55*(1), 79–91. https://doi.org/10.1002/jocb.436.

James, W. (1907). The energies of men. *Science 25*, 321–332. https://doi.org/10.1126/science.25.635.321.

Jensen, A. R. (2002). Psychometric g: Definition and substantiation. In R. J. Sternberg & E. L. Grigorenko (Eds.), *The general factor of intelligence: How general is it?* (pp. 39–53). Lawrence Erlbaum Associates.

John Hopkins Medicine. (n.d.). *Brain anatomy and how the brain works.* Johns Hopkins Medicine. https://www.hopkinsmedicine.org/health/conditions-and-diseases/anatomy-of-the-brain.

Kaczmarek, B. L. (2020). Current views on neuroplasticity: What is new and what is old? *Acta Neuropsychologica, 18*, 1–14. https://bibliotekanauki.pl/articles/2106004.pdf.

Kandel, E. R., Schwartz, J. H., Jessell, T. M., Siegelbaum, S. A., & Hudspeth, A. J. (2014). *Principles of neural science.* McGraw-Hill Education.

Kegan, R. (1982). *The evolving self: Problem and processes in human development.* Harvard University Press.

Kegan, R. (1994). *In over our heads: The mental demands of modern life.* Harvard University Press.

King, P. M., & Kitchener, K.S. (2004). Reflective judgment: Theory and research on the development of epistemic assumptions through adulthood. *Educational Psychologist, 39*(1), 5–18. https://doi.org/10.1207/s15326985ep3901_2.

Knowles, M. S. (1975). *Self-directed learning: A guide for learners and teachers.* Association Free Press.

Kohlberg, L. (1981). *The philosophy of moral development: Moral stages and the idea of justice.* HarperSanFrancisco.

Koller, I., Levenson, M. R., & Glück, J. (2017). What do you think you are measuring? A mixed-methods procedure for assessing the content validity of test items and theory-based scaling. *Frontiers in Psychology, 8*, 126. https://doi.org/10.3389/fpsyg.2017.00126.

Kornblatt, S., & Vega, F. (2022). *A better brain at any age: The holistic way to improve your memory, reduce stress, and sharpen your wits.* Conari Press.

Kovacs, K., & Conway, A. R. A. (2016). Process overlap theory: A unified account of the general factor of intelligence. *Psychological Inquiry, 27*(3), 151–177. https://doi.org/10.1080/1047840X.2016.1153946.

Kurosawa, A. (Director). (1950). Rashōmon [Film]. Daiei Film.

Lee, H. J. (2012). Rocky road: East Asian international students' experience of adaptation to critical thinking way of learning at U.S. universities. In J. Buban & D. Ramdeholl (Eds.), *Proceedings of the 53rd Annual Adult Education Research Conference* (pp. 395–397). SUNY Empire State College.

Leisman, G. (2022). On the application of developmental cognitive neuroscience in educational environments. *Brain Sciences, 12*(11), 1501. https://doi.org/10.3390/brainsci12111501.

Levenson, M. R., Jennings, P. A., Aldwin, C. M., & Shiraishi, R. W. (2005). Self-transcendence: Conceptualization and measurement. *The International Journal of Aging and Human Development, 60*(2), 127–143. https://doi.org/10.2190/XRXM-FYRA-7U0X-GRC0.

Levinson, D. J. (1996). *The seasons of a woman's life.* Alfred A. Knopf.

Levinson, D., Darrow, C. N., Klein, E. B., Levinson, M. H., & McKee, B. (1978). *The seasons of a man's life.* Ballantine.

Loevinger, J. (1976). *Ego development.* Jossey-Bass.

MacLean, P. (1990). *The triune brain in evolution: Role in paleocerebral function.* Plenum Press.

Mayer J. D., Salovey P. (1997). What is emotional intelligence? In P. Salovey, D. J. Sluyter (Eds.), *Emotional development and emotional intelligence: Educational implications* (pp. 3–31). Basic Books.

Mayer J. D., Salovey P., Caruso D. R. (2000). Emotional intelligence as zeitgeist, as personality, and as a mental ability. In R. Bar-On, J. Parker (Eds.), *The handbook of emotional intelligence* (pp. 92–117). Jossey-Bass.

Mayer J. D., Salovey P., Caruso D. R. (2008). Emotional intelligence: New ability or eclectic traits? *American Psychologist, 63*, 503. https://psycnet.apa.org/doi/10.1037/0003-066X.63.6.503.

Merriam, S. B., & Baumgartner, L. M. (2020). *Learning in adulthood: A comprehensive guide.* John Wiley & Sons.

Michael, D. (2021). *Neuromyths and adult learning.* EPALE - Elektronische Plattform für Erwachsenenbildung in Europa. https://epale.ec.europa.eu/de/node/305857.

Mickler, C., & Staudinger, U. M. (2008). Personal wisdom: Validation and age-related differences of a performance measure. *Psychology and Aging, 23*(4), 787. https://psycnet.apa.org/doi/10.1037/a0013928.

National Geographic. (n.d.). *Your amazing brain.* National Geographic Kids. https://kids.nationalgeographic.com/science/article/your-amazing-brain.

Nielsen, J. A., Zielinski, B. A., Ferguson, M. A., Lainhart, J. E., & Anderson, J. S. (2013). An evaluation of the left-brain vs. right-brain hypothesis with resting state functional connectivity magnetic resonance imaging. *PloS one, 8*(8), e71275. https://doi.org/10.1371/journal.pone.0071275.

Oakes, H., Brienza, J. P., Elnakouri, A., & Grossmann, I. (2019). Wise reasoning: Converging evidence for the psychology of sound judgment. In R. J. Sternberg & J. Glück (Eds.), *The Cambridge handbook of wisdom* (pp. 202–225). Cambridge University Press.

Opengart R. (2005). Emotional intelligence and emotion work: Examining constructs from an interdisciplinary framework. *Human Resource Development Review, 4*, 49–62. https://doi.org/10.1177/1534484304273817.

Opengart, R., & Bierema, L. (2015). Emotionally intelligent mentoring: Reconceptualizing effective mentoring relationships. *Human Resource Development Review, 14*(3), 234–258. https://doi.org/10.1177/1534484315598434.

Organisation for Economic Co-operation and Development (OECD). (2002). *Understanding the brain towards a new learning science.* OECD Publishing.

Pashler, H., McDaniel, M., Rohrer, D., and Bjork, R. (2008). Learning styles. *Psychological Science in the Public Interest, 9*(3), 105–119. https://doi.org/10.1111/j.1539-6053.2009.01038.x.

Pasupathi, M., Staudinger, U. M., & Baltes, P. B. (2001). Seeds of wisdom: Adolescents' knowledge and judgment about difficult life problems. *Developmental Psychology, 37*(3), 351. https://psycnet.apa.org/doi/10.1037/0012-1649.37.3.351.

Perry, W. G. (1999). *Forms of intellectual and ethical development in the college years: A scheme.* Jossey-Bass.

Piaget, J. (1966). *The origins of intelligence in children.* International Universities Press.

Piaget, J. (1972). Intellectual evolution from adolescent to adulthood. *Human Development, 16,* 346–370.

Piedmont. (n.d.). *10 fun facts about your brain.* Piedmont. https://www.piedmont.org/living-real-change/10-fun-facts-about-your-brain.

Reio, T. G. (2020). Adult development. In T. Rocco et al., (Eds.), *The handbook of adult and continuing education* (pp. 81–90). Routledge.

Riener, C., & Willingham, D. (2010). The myth of learning styles. *Change: The Magazine of Higher Learning, 42*(5), 32–35. https://doi.org/10.1080/00091383.2010.503139.

Rim, C. (2019, September 13). *Majority of teachers believe outdated myths like being "left-" or "right-brained," survey finds.* Forbes. https://www.forbes.com/sites/christopherrim/2019/09/13/majority-of-teachers-believe-outdated-myths-like-being-left-or-right-brained-survey-finds/.

Rocco, T. S., Smith, M. C., Mizzi, R. C., Merriweather, L. R., & Hawley, J. D. (Eds.). (2023). *The handbook of adult and continuing education.* Taylor & Francis.

Ruiz-Martín, H., & Bybee, R. W. (2022). The cognitive principles of learning underlying the 5E model of Instruction. *International Journal of STEM Education, 9*(1), 21. https://doi.org/10.1186/s40594-022-00337-z.

Salovey P., Mayer J. D. (1990). Emotional intelligence. *Imagination, Cognition and Personality, 9,* 185–211. https://doi.org/10.2190/DUGG-P24E-52WK-6CDG.

Salovey P., Mayer J. D. (1994). Some final thoughts about personality and intelligence. In R. J. Sternberg, P. Ruzgis (Eds.), *Personality and intelligence* (pp. 303–318). New York: Cambridge University Press.

Singh, A., Prabhakar, R., & Kiran, J. S. (2022). Emotional intelligence: A literature review of its concept, models, and measures. *Journal of Positive School Psychology, 6*(10), 2254–2275.

Squire, L., Berg, D., Bloom, F. E., Du Lac, S., Ghosh, A., & Spitzer, N. C. (Eds.). (2012). *Fundamental neuroscience.* Academic Press.

Staudinger, U. M. (1999). Older and wiser? Integrating results on the relationship between age and wisdom-related performance. *International Journal of Behavioral Development, 23*(3), 641–664. https://doi.org/10.1080/016502599383739.

Sternberg, R. J. (1988). *The triarchic mind: A new theory of human intelligence.* Viking/Penguin.

Sternberg, R. J. (2003). *Wisdom, intelligence, and creativity synthesized.* Cambridge University Press.

Sternberg, R. J. (2005). Older but not wiser? The relationship between age and wisdom. *Ageing International, 30*(1), 5–26.

Sternberg, R. J., Forsythe, G. B., Hedlund, J., Horvath, J. A., Wagner, R. K., Williams, W. M., et al. (2000). *Practical intelligence in everyday life.* Cambridge University Press.

Su, S., Shi, L., Zheng, Y., Sun, Y., Huang, X., Zhang, A., et al. (2022). Leisure activities and the risk of dementia: A systematic review and meta-analysis. *Neurology, 99*(15), e1651–e1663. https://doi.org/10.1212/WNL.000000000020092.

Sullivan, K. A., Hughes, B., & Gilmore, L. (2021). Measuring educational Neuromyths: Lessons for future research. *Mind, Brain, and Education, 15*(3), 232–238. https://doi .org/10.1111/mbe.12294.

Taylor, J. B. (2009). *My stroke of insight.* New York: Plume/Penguin.

Taylor, J. B. (2021). *Whole brain living: The anatomy of choice and the four characters that drive our life.* Hay House, Inc.

Taylor, K., & Marienau, C. (2016). *Facilitating learning with the adult brain in mind: A conceptual and practical guide.* Jossey-Bass, a Wiley Brand.

Taylor, K., & Marienau, C. (2023). Minding the brain: The emotional foundations of adult learning. In A. Belzer, & B. Dashe (Eds.), *Understanding the adult learner: Perspectives and practices* (pp. 79–97). Stylus Publishing.

Taylor, T. A. H., Kemp, K., Mi, M., & Lerchenfeldt, S. (2023). Self-directed learning assessment practices in undergraduate health professions education: A systematic review. *Medical Education Online, 28*(1). 10.1080/10872981.2023.2189553.

Thurstone, L. L. (1938). *Primary mental abilities.* University of Chicago Press.

Torrijos-Muelas, M., González-Víllora, S., & Bodoque-Osma, A. R. (2021). The persistence of neuromyths in the educational settings: A systematic review. *Frontiers in Psychology, 11,* 591923. https://doi.org/10.3389/fpsyg.2020.591923.

Tulving, E. (1985). How many memory systems are there? *American Psychologist, 40,* 385–398.

Tulving, E. (2002). Episodic memory: From mind to brain. *Annual Review of Psychology, 53*(1), 1–25. https://doi.org/10.1146/annurev.psych.53.100901.135114.

Voss, P., Thomas, M. E., Cisneros-Franco, J. M., & de Villers-Sidani, É. (2017). Dynamic brains and the changing rules of neuroplasticity: Implications for learning and recovery. *Frontiers in Psychology, 8,* 1657. https://doi.org/10.3389/fpsyg.2017.01657.

Vygotsky, L. S. (1978). *Mind in society: The development of higher psychological processes.* Harvard University Press.

Waterhouse, L. (2023). Why multiple intelligences theory is a neuromyth. *Frontiers in Psychology, 14,* 1217288. https://doi.org/10.3389/fpsyg.2023.1217288.

Webster, D. J. (2007). Measuring the character strength of wisdom. *The International Journal of Aging and Human Development, 65*(2), 163–183. https://doi.org/10.2190/AG.65.2.d.

Webster, J. D., Westerhof, G. J., & Bohlmeijer, E. T. (2014). Wisdom and mental health across the lifespan. *Journals of Gerontology Series B: Psychological Sciences and Social Sciences, 69*(2), 209–218. https://doi.org/10.1093/geronb/gbs121.

Willingham, D. T., Hughes, E. M., and Dobolyi, D. G. (2015). The scientific status of learning styles theories. *Teaching of Psychology, 42*(3), 266–271. https://doi.org/10.1177/ 0098628315589505.

Wilson, C. (2021, May 15). *I'm interested in whether we can create new senses.* NewScientist, Science Direct. https://www.sciencedirect.com/science/article/pii/S0262407921008435?casa_ token=Pf0iJOCrk7AAAAAA:Vj0aTfGPaTR1YNtUhUEkceI3xFlLC8W0QO7rCmt6WrP9rb WYdJzbpBAmQPfxCdaUPvXhAIHnddE.

Zelinski, E. M. & Kennison, R. K. (2007). Not your parents' test scores: Cohort reduces psychometric aging effects. *Psychology and Aging, 22*(3), 546–557. https://doi.org/10.1037/ 0882-7974.22.3.546.

DEVELOPING AND DELIVERING ADULT LEARNING PROGRAMS—THE *WHAT*

*A*dult Learning: Linking Theory and Practice *is organized around a framework* to understand adult learning theory that considers the context, educator, learner, and learning process for adults. The *method* or design and facilitation of learning is the bridge between theory and practice in adult education. It is the moment we, as educators, must take our theories and concepts of adult learning and put them into practice to create relevant, timely, and engaging learning experiences for diverse learners. There is no formula for creating powerful programs to optimize learning. Yet, as discussed throughout this book, there are several things that educators can do to ensure that each participant has an opportunity to learn from the experience.

The final aspect of the framework is the *method* or *what* is required to effectively develop and deliver learning for adults by incorporating the *where, who,* and *how* of adult learning. Linking theory and practice is vital in creating compelling adult learning experiences. **Design** involves creating relevant, timely, and engaging learning experiences for diverse learners. **Delivery** is the real-time implementation of the learning (Bierema, 2019).

Section 5 consists of three chapters. Chapter 13, "Designing Adult Learning Experiences and Programs," equips adult educators and learners with the necessary understanding and tools to design adult learning experiences and programs and assess quality. Chapter 14, "Designing Effective Online Learning for Adults," examines the influence of the digital age on adult learning and education. Chapter 15, "Facilitating Active Adult Learning Programs," describes how to design and facilitate active adult learning programs.

Reference

Bierema, L. L. (2019). Adult learning theories and practices. In M. Fedeli, & L. L. Bierema (Eds.), *Connecting adult learning and knowledge management: Strategies for learning and change in higher education and organizations* (pp. 3–26). Springer.

CHAPTER THIRTEEN

DESIGNING ADULT LEARNING EXPERIENCES AND PROGRAMS

 **Box 13.1 Chapter Overview and Learning Objectives**

Daffron and Caffarella (2021) captured the essence of designing adult education experiences:

> Creativity in program planning allows adult educators to bring about issues relating to difficult environmental problems and social issues that threaten the very existence and stability of our planet. (p. 3)

This chapter equips you as an adult educator and learner with the necessary understanding and tools to design adult learning experiences and programs and assess quality. As a result of reading this chapter and completing the exercises, you, the reader, should be able to:

1. Understand the purposes of designing programs for adults.
2. Consider the components of designing for adult learning.
3. Identify the main factors related to the role of the educator in designing programs.
4. Plan learning experiences based on the characteristics of adult learners.

A dults learn throughout their lives in various situations—when starting new jobs, navigating relationships, making mistakes, changing careers, moving to new cities, traveling abroad, experiencing loss, and tackling new challenges (Bierema, 2019). Learning in adulthood is driven more by responsibility than by age. **Adult learning,** therefore, refers to learning undertaken by individuals with adult-like responsibilities, such as caring for dependents, managing a household, holding a job, or participating actively in the community. The following sections explore the core characteristics of designing adult learning experiences and programs.

The core of adult learning lies in the method—specifically, in designing programs that effectively integrate the "who," "how," and "where" of learning into cohesive and meaningful experiences, according to the framework discussed throughout this book. How can the delivery of these programs respect and enhance these framework elements? An effective design and facilitation approach bridges theory and practice, considering the roles of educators and learners and the context and learning processes. **Design** is crafting relevant, timely, and engaging learning experiences for diverse learners. At the same time, **delivery** is the real-time enactment of practices that respect learners as individuals and help them reflect on their experiences and new insights. There is no universal formula for creating impactful programs that optimize learning for everyone. However, as this book discusses, there are many strategies educators can use to ensure learners have opportunities to actively construct knowledge (Bierema, 2019). Box 13.2 summarizes influential theories and models on curriculum design.

Educators, organizations, and sponsors are involved in the training programs with different aims and trying to create the right conditions for adults to learn and for organizations to develop and grow. Being a planner in these VUCA times means navigating a rapidly evolving landscape with flexibility, innovation, and a deep understanding of adult learners' unique needs. Modern adult education planners are tasked with more than just creating curricula; they must design programs that are accessible, relevant, and engaging for diverse populations (Burns, 2020). Educational program design includes integrating digital tools and platforms that facilitate online and hybrid learning models and fostering a learning environment that supports adults balancing work, family, and education.

Effective planners proactively address societal changes—such as shifts in the labor market, technological advancements, and the growing demand for lifelong learning. They focus on immediately applicable and future-proof skills, preparing learners for careers that may evolve or emerge in the coming years. Creating relevant learning experiences requires planners to stay current with

Box 13.2 SoTL: The Scholarship of Teaching and Learning

Theory and Models on Curriculum Design and Development

Curriculum design involves determining what content to include and how to organize it to support effective learning (Button, 2021). Tyler (1949) introduced a foundational model emphasizing learning objectives, content selection, evaluation, and curriculum revision, later expanded by Bloom et al. (1956) with a taxonomy of educational objectives focused on cognitive, psychomotor, and affective domains.

In the 1960s, Mager (1962) emphasized writing behavioral objectives detailing performance expectations, conditions, and criteria while exploring motivational strategies. Ausubel (1962) introduced meaningful learning theory, advocating for curricula that connected new knowledge to prior learning using techniques like advanced organizers. Taba (1962) outlined a seven-step process for curriculum development, emphasizing learner-centered approaches and iterative evaluation.

Gagné (1965) proposed sequencing curriculum units hierarchically, ensuring learners acquire foundational skills before progressing. Bruner (1966) championed a spiral curriculum to revisit and deepen knowledge progressively. Stenhouse (1975) presented a process-oriented model emphasizing collaborative curriculum design, critical reflection, and problem-solving, viewing the curriculum as a testable hypothesis rather than a rigid framework.

As Biggs (2003) outlined, constructive alignment ensures teaching methods, learning activities, and assessments support learning outcomes. Biggs highlights the need for clear, actionable objectives (intended learning outcome, ILO) and coherent alignment across teaching and evaluation stages. Similarly, Fink's (2003) integrated course design incorporated learning goals, teaching activities, and feedback, underscoring the influence of situational factors such as course context and professional expectations.

---

trends, seek learner feedback, and continually refine their programs to ensure they remain relevant and impactful (Kinshuk et al., 2016).

Furthermore, being a planner today means embracing inclusivity and equity. Inclusive adult education program design accommodates learners from all walks of life, including those who may face barriers due to language, socioeconomic status, or disabilities. By prioritizing learner-centered approaches and fostering an environment that values each student's background and experience, planners can help create transformative learning experiences that empower adults to achieve their personal and professional goals. Being an adult education planner today requires a commitment to continuous improvement, a willingness to adapt, and dedication to making education meaningful and accessible.

Designing adult education programs should aim to organize the learning process more effectively and foster active involvement among participants to support individual and group learning. Effective adult education benefits individual learners, sparks organizational discussions, and influences society. Those who take on leadership roles in education promote learning and strategically plan for improved learning outcomes. Adult education and training programs are created with these primary purposes in mind, tailored for different audiences:

- Promoting the growth and development of individuals and organizations
- Addressing real-life issues and challenges people wish to confront
- Developing professional competencies relevant to the workforce
- Fostering positive change across various contexts
- Encouraging well-being and autonomy among individuals (Argyris, 2017; Merriam & Baumgartner, 2020)

Considering the change theories and practices presented in Chapter 9 helps planners follow Daffron and Caffarella's (2021) advice to foster growth, resilience, and adaptability in learners (Daffron & Caffarella, 2021).

The Principles of Effective Adult Learning Design

Effective adult learning design is rooted in principles that address adult learners' unique characteristics and needs. One of the most important principles is **engagement,** emphasizing participatory and collaborative approaches to keep learners actively involved. Adults learn best when directly involved in the process, so methods like group discussions, role-playing, case studies, and real-life simulations are invaluable. For example, in corporate training, learners might work in teams to solve a realistic problem, mimicking workplace challenges. These strategies promote interaction and make learning enjoyable and socially enriching. Research indicates that active learning techniques significantly enhance the retention and application of knowledge among adults, allowing learners to connect theory with practice meaningfully (Riegnell & Bulthuis, 2022; Williams, 2024).

Equally critical is **relevance,** which ensures the learning material directly applies to the adult learner's personal or professional goals. Adults are highly motivated when they see the immediate value of their learning. For instance, a workshop on leadership skills should include scenarios directly related to managing teams, resolving conflicts, or strategic planning, as these are directly applicable to workplace situations. By relating lessons to their lived experiences, learners can connect new knowledge to what they already know, reinforcing retention and applicability. Studies have shown that when adult learners perceive course content as relevant to their current or future roles, their engagement and satisfaction levels increase significantly (Palis & Quiros, 2014). Dondi et al. (2021) surveyed 18,000 people in 15 countries to understand how workers could "future-proof" their skills in "a labor market that is more automated, digital, and dynamic" (p. 2) where workers need to add value beyond technology, demonstrate digital literacy, and be adaptive to change and emerging occupations. The study identified 56 foundational skills to help adults thrive in the workplace, organized into four cognitive, interpersonal, self-leadership, and digital categories.

Another vital principle is **active learning,** which involves adults in the learning process rather than having them passively receive information. Hands-on activities like building prototypes, conducting experiments, or engaging in practice-based exercises promote "learning by doing." For example, in a training program for healthcare professionals, participants could practice clinical skills through simulations or role-playing to ensure competency and confidence in real-world situations. Various educational theories have supported this experiential approach, emphasizing learning through experience and reflection (Hasanah, 2023; Palis & Quiros, 2014).

Feedback serves as a cornerstone for effective adult learning by providing opportunities for growth and improvement. Constructive feedback, delivered in real-time, helps learners identify strengths and areas for development. For instance, learners could receive detailed feedback from peers and instructors after presenting a group project, fostering a deeper understanding of the subject matter. Positive reinforcement during feedback also builds confidence and encourages continued engagement. Research highlights that timely feedback enhances learning outcomes and promotes a culture of continuous improvement among adult learners (Griffin, 2023; Williams, 2024).

These principles, when combined, create a **holistic learning environment** tailored to adult learners. They address adults' intrinsic need for autonomy, relevance, and practical application while fostering a sense of accomplishment and personal growth. By designing experiences that are engaging, relevant, hands-on, and feedback-rich, educators and facilitators can ensure adult learners achieve meaningful, lasting outcomes in their learning journey.

Moreover, incorporating elements such as **flexibility** in learning paths allows adults to tailor their educational experiences according to their needs and circumstances. This adaptability is particularly crucial given the diverse backgrounds of adult learners who may face various life challenges that affect their ability to engage with traditional educational formats (Outwitly, 2022). Box 13.3 showcases practical design principles.

 Box 13.3 SoTL: The Scholarship of Teaching and Learning

Principles of Learning Design

Bound and Chia (2020) created a practical guide to design learning highlighting six main principles to help educators design learning programs and experiences. The central dimension behind their approach is **learner-centered learning** (Weimer, 2013), which recognizes the value of the experience for learning (Kolb & Kolb, 2009). The six principles are: Authenticity, Alignment, Holistic, Feedback, Judgment, and Future Orientation.

1. **Authenticity** in learning emphasizes realistic engagement, making it crucial for effective performance in real-world settings. Key elements of authentic learning include active learner engagement and a focus on the unique complexities of specific works, including interdisciplinary aspects.
2. John Biggs (2003) described **"constructive alignment"** as addressing all course design elements—learning goals, outcomes, assessments, and activities—that should work together harmoniously. For instance, if a course aims to develop report-writing skills, an aligned assessment would involve writing a report for a real audience, not answering multiple-choice questions. This approach ensures that learning and assessment are relevant and realistic.
3. **Holistic** learning combines knowledge, action, thought, and emotion, blending theory with practice and technical skills with broader learning abilities. It engages multiple senses and aims to incorporate the ethics and values of a profession. This integrated approach connects learning deeply to the learner, merging what is learned with who the learner becomes, emphasizing the essence of the learner's identity.
4. **Feedback** is essential to understand how learning is progressing. Learners should actively participate in giving and receiving feedback from peers, educators, and supervisors and in self-assessment. This feedback loop, involving multiple perspectives, helps improve performance by creating opportunities for learners to discuss and apply feedback for growth.

5. **Judgment** is the skill that enables learners to evaluate their learning effectively. It's crucial for understanding their performance and aligning it with expectations. This process is closely linked with feedback, as both require active learner involvement to support growth and self-awareness (Boud & Molloy, 2013).

6. **Future orientation** refers to a learner's ability to address new and unpredictable challenges beyond the scope of their immediate training. It encompasses 21st-century skills such as critical thinking, creativity, and lifelong learning. A deep understanding of a subject—developed through exposure to diverse perspectives and the ability to evaluate evidence—empowers learners to solve problems effectively in unfamiliar contexts. Future orientation also includes inquiry skills: knowing the right questions, gathering relevant information, and applying big-picture thinking to interpret findings (Bound & Chia, 2020).

Reflecting on these various principles can help you, both as an adult educator and as a learner, to think about your design or learning experiences more consciously.

As you reflect on these principles, what have you considered when designing adult learning programs and experiences? How have these principles influenced you and your activity as an educator and adult learning planner?

Effective adult learning design prioritizes engagement through active participation, ensures relevance by connecting content to real-world applications, promotes active learning through hands-on experiences, and provides constructive feedback to facilitate growth. By implementing these principles within educational programs, facilitators can create impactful learning experiences that empower adults to succeed personally and professionally.

Designing an Effective Adult Learning Program

Designing effective programs begins with a meticulous **needs assessment,** which identifies the learners' specific characteristics, challenges, and goals. This process starts by clearly defining the target audience (Daffron & Caffarella, 2021). For instance, if the program is for mid-career professionals in the healthcare industry, facilitators might determine that participants need to improve skills in patient communication, time management, or advanced clinical procedures. **Collecting broad feedback** is recommended to pinpoint learning needs by conducting surveys, interviews, or focus groups to reveal common themes or shared struggles among participants (Daffron & Caffarella, 2021). For example, if a focus group highlights a lack of confidence in handling emergency cases, the program can prioritize modules addressing critical decision-making under pressure. By tailoring the program to the precise needs of the learners, facilitators ensure the content is both relevant and impactful. The scientific literature emphasizes that a robust needs assessment is crucial for aligning educational programs with learner expectations and requirements, thus enhancing overall effectiveness (Hunt, 1986; Ślósarz et al., 2022).

The next step is to **define learning objectives** that align with the identified needs and provide a clear roadmap for the program. Biggs (2003) suggested indicating the objectives through a verb indicating the level of learning required, accompanied by the object of the action (such as *know, solve problems, synthesize*). These objectives should follow the **SMART framework**: Specific, Measurable, Achievable, Relevant, and Time-bound. For instance, instead of a vague goal like "Enhance communication skills," a SMART objective might state: "By the end of the second session, participants will demonstrate the ability to effectively de-escalate a patient's concerns using three specific active listening techniques." Box 13.4 further elaborates on this concept.

Creating precise learning objectives ensures that both the facilitator and the learners understand the desired outcome and can objectively assess progress. Well-defined objectives clarify expectations and enhance motivation by connecting learning to personal and professional goals (Atkinson, 2024). For example, after practicing role-play scenarios, evaluate learners' ability to maintain eye contact, paraphrase the patient's concerns, and propose empathetic solutions. With objectives established, the curriculum developer focuses on designing a logical and engaging structure that builds knowledge progressively (Dirkx & Prenger, 1997).

Developing awareness about your teaching philosophy, approaches, values, and beliefs helps you find helpful support in existing learning theories and research about role distribution among the educator and learners and apply practical ideas about designing and distributing tasks (Rothwell, 2008). Generally, the curriculum should be modular, with each session reinforcing and expanding upon the last. For example, in a leadership program, the first module might focus on identifying personal leadership styles using tools like the DiSC assessment. The second module could then address how to adapt those styles to different team dynamics, and the final module might involve real-world simulations where learners practice leading diverse teams under various scenarios. The curriculum should integrate multiple methods of

 ## Box 13.4 Tips and Tools for Teaching and Learning

How to Write SMART Objectives

Elaborating on Hey's (2024) directions, this box focuses on writing SMART objectives using the case of an online course focused on active learning in adult education.

Specific: It clearly defines what you want to achieve, answering the questions of what, why, where, when, and how of the goals.

"By the end of Week 2, participants will identify and describe at least three active learning strategies that can be implemented in their teaching practice."

Measurable: A method to measure whether the objective has been achieved is needed; it answers the question, "How will I know when it is accomplished?" It is good to identify quantifiable criteria to measure the objective's progress.

"By the conclusion of the course, participants will design and present a lesson plan that incorporates at least two active learning techniques, evaluated through peer feedback and instructor assessment."

Achievable: The objective should be realistic and attainable within the available resources, and an appropriate time frame should be set.

"Within four weeks, participants will demonstrate their ability to facilitate an active learning session by leading a 15-minute group activity during a live online class."

Relevant: The objective should be based on and aligned with the participants' goals, long-term growth, and values. If it does not matter to the learner in some way, it's not relevant. It should bring value to their personal or professional life and move them toward their ambitions.

"By the end of the course, participants will articulate how incorporating active learning strategies can enhance learner engagement and retention in their specific educational contexts."

Time-bound: Having a deadline helps create urgency and prompt action. A detailed action plan with tasks and timelines to achieve the objective is beneficial.

"Participants will complete a reflective journal entry by the end of each week, documenting their experiences and insights gained from implementing active learning strategies in their teaching, for a total of four entries by the course's conclusion."

These objectives are designed to ensure learners have clear targets to meet throughout the course, allowing instructors and participants to gauge progress effectively. Each objective aligns with the principles of the SMART framework, ensuring they are specific, measurable, achievable, relevant, and time-bound.

For more examples, you can visit the Teachers Helping Teachers Blog: https://www.midwestteachersinstitute.org/99-amazing-examples-of-smart-goals-for-teachers/

instruction to address different learning preferences. A module could start with a short lecture introducing theoretical concepts, followed by a group workshop to encourage discussion and collaboration, and conclude with hands-on activities such as creating a team management plan or practicing leadership in role-play exercises. For instance, learners in a project management program might use software to simulate planning a project, assigning tasks, and addressing unforeseen challenges. Incorporating active learning techniques has been shown to enhance engagement and retention among adult learners significantly (James et al., 2024; McDonough, 2014).

By combining a precise needs assessment with SMART objectives and a structured, multifaceted curriculum, facilitators can ensure the program is aligned with learner goals and delivers measurable outcomes. This approach guarantees that each component of the learning experience, whether theoretical or practical, empowers participants to apply their newfound skills and knowledge effectively in real-world settings. Furthermore, integrating continuous feedback mechanisms throughout the program facilitates ongoing improvement and adaptation based on learner experiences (Bash, 2005).

Instructional Strategies for Designing Learning for Adults

Designing instructional strategies for adult learners requires a thoughtful approach that leverages their unique characteristics, such as self-direction, life experience, and a strong desire for practical application. Effective instructional strategies not only engage adult learners but also ensure that they achieve meaningful and measurable learning outcomes. This section features key instructional strategies tailored for adult learning design, including experiential learning, problem-based learning, interactive and collaborative learning, self-directed learning, case studies, blended learning, scaffolded instruction, feedback and assessment, and gamification.

Experiential Learning

Adults bring a wealth of prior knowledge and experiences to the learning environment. Instructional strategies should leverage this by incorporating **experiential learning** activities where participants actively solve problems or complete tasks (Brown & Harvey, 2006). For instance, in a training session for project managers, learners could work in small groups to create project plans based on real-world scenarios, allowing them to apply their knowledge and skills in a controlled, practical environment. Reflection is a key component of experiential learning, so learners should be encouraged to analyze and discuss their performance to deepen understanding. Research indicates that experiential learning enhances the retention and application of knowledge by connecting theoretical concepts with practical experiences (Carlson McCall et al., 2018). See Chapter 10 for a complete discussion of experiential learning.

Problem-Based Learning (PBL)

Adults are often motivated by learning that addresses real-life challenges. **Problem-based learning** engages learners by presenting them with complex, realistic problems without clear solutions. For example, in a workshop for healthcare professionals, participants might be tasked with designing a care plan for a patient with multiple chronic conditions. Facilitators guide the learners in analyzing the problem, exploring solutions, and applying their findings. This strategy fosters critical thinking, collaboration, and practical application of knowledge. Research indicates that PBL can significantly enhance critical thinking skills among adult learners, as it encourages them to engage deeply with the material and collaborate with peers to find solutions (Pashchenko, 2024).

Interactive and Collaborative Learning

Adult learners thrive in interactive environments where they can share and learn from peers. Group discussions, role-playing, and collaborative projects are excellent strategies to enhance interaction and deepen learning. Role-play requires learners to practice new knowledge and skills in small groups (Bergquist & Phillips, 1975; Fedeli & Taylor, 2024). For instance, participants could role-play conflict resolution or negotiation in a leadership training program. Pairing or grouping learners with diverse perspectives enhances the richness of discussions and helps learners understand and apply concepts in varied contexts (Agosti, 2006; Brookfield, 2013). The "Un-meeting" approach has been shown to stimulate collaborative adult learning by creating a space for open discussion and brainstorming among experienced professionals, fostering an environment conducive to shared knowledge creation (Jones et al., 2021).

Self-Directed Learning

As described in Chapter 8, adults value autonomy in their learning process. Instructional strategies encouraging learners to take ownership of their learning through self-directed approaches resonate with most learners (Guglielmino, 1977; Piskurich, 1994). For example, facilitators can provide curated resources such as videos, articles, and case studies that learners can explore independently. Incorporating technology, such as online modules or interactive learning platforms, enables learners to customize their experience based on their needs and goals.

Use of Case Studies and Real-world Scenarios

Case studies are powerful tools for adult learning because they connect theoretical knowledge to practical application (Hequet, 1995; Schmidt, 2024). Facilitators can present detailed scenarios that mirror real-world situations relevant to the learners' professional or personal lives (Marsick, 2004). For example, in a corporate setting, a case study might involve analyzing the root causes of a failed product launch and proposing strategies for improvement. This approach enhances problem-solving skills and ensures learners see the relevance of their learning (Gust, 2006). Similar approaches include community-based service learning (Stewart et al., 2024) and field experiences (Zarestky & Vilen, 2024).

Blended Learning and Technology Integration

As further elaborated in Chapter 14, **blended learning** combines face-to-face and online learning to offer flexibility and variety. This strategy is particularly effective for adults with busy schedules, as it allows them to balance learning with other responsibilities. Online components can include video lectures, discussion forums, or interactive quizzes, while in-person sessions focus on hands-on activities or group work. For example, a professional development course could include online modules for foundational concepts, followed by in-person workshops for practical application. Blended learning improves learner satisfaction by providing personalized experiences that cater to the diverse needs of adult learners (Singh, 2021). See Coryell et al. (2024) for further discussion on technology-enhanced teaching and learning.

Scaffolded Instruction. **Scaffolding** involves breaking learning into manageable chunks and providing support as learners progress (Luckritz Marquis, 2021; Wood et al., 1976). This strategy is crucial for adult learners who may feel overwhelmed by new or complex information. For example, in a technology training program, participants could first learn the basic functions of a software application through guided tutorials. As they gain confidence, they could move on to advanced features, with opportunities to practice each step. Gradually removing the support ensures learners gain independence.

Immediate Feedback and Assessment

Adults benefit from **immediate and constructive feedback,** allowing them to recognize their strengths and areas for improvement (Hattie & Yates, 2013; Mondal et al., 2024). Instructional strategies should include frequent opportunities for feedback, such as quizzes, peer evaluations, or instructor reviews (Race, 2001). For instance, in a writing workshop, learners could receive real-time feedback on drafts during collaborative editing sessions. This approach reinforces learning and keeps learners engaged and motivated (Hattie, 2012).

Gamification

Gamification involves incorporating game elements, such as points, levels, or rewards, to enhance engagement. While often associated with younger learners, gamification can be equally effective for adults when used appropriately. For example, a sales training program might include a competitive leaderboard for completing modules or mastering new skills. Adults appreciate challenges that are goal-oriented and tied to measurable achievements. The integration of gamification strategies increases motivation and engagement among adult learners by tapping into their intrinsic motivations (Huang & Huang, 2024; Por et al., 2024)

By combining these strategies, facilitators can design learning experiences that resonate with adult learners' needs and preferences. Each strategy emphasizes active participation, practical application, and opportunities for reflection, ensuring that the learning process is engaging, meaningful, and transformative. Ultimately, effective instructional strategies empower adult learners to apply their new knowledge and skills in real-world contexts, driving personal and professional growth.

The Facilitator's Role in Adult Learning Program

The role of the **facilitator** in adult learning is pivotal to the success of the learning experience, as they act not only as instructors but also as guides, mentors, and catalysts for engagement and growth. Unlike traditional teaching, where the instructor often dominates the learning environment, facilitators in adult education adopt a learner-centered approach, tailoring their methods to the participant's unique needs, experiences, and goals (Fedeli & Bierema, 2019). This shift toward facilitation is supported by research indicating that effective adult learning facilitators enhance the quality of educational programs through their ability to create supportive environments and adapt to diverse learner needs (Zagir & Dorner, 2022).

One of the primary responsibilities of a facilitator is to **create an inclusive and supportive environment** where learners feel valued and respected. Adults come to the learning process with diverse experiences, and a skilled facilitator leverages these experiences as valuable contributions to the discussion. For example, during a professional development workshop, the facilitator might encourage participants to share their workplace challenges, creating opportunities for peer-to-peer learning and exchanging best practices. This practice aligns with findings emphasizing the importance of fostering a sense of belonging among learners, significantly enhancing engagement and motivation (Miyazawa, 2024; Zagir & Dorner, 2021).

Facilitators also play a critical role in **maintaining learner engagement.** By employing interactive strategies such as open-ended questioning, group discussions, and hands-on activities, they ensure that learners remain active participants rather than passive recipients of information (Fedeli & Bierema, 2019). For instance, in a leadership training session, a facilitator might use role-playing exercises to simulate real-world decision-making scenarios, encouraging participants to reflect on their choices and learn from each other's perspectives. Research indicates experiential learning methods enhance retention and foster deeper understanding by connecting theoretical concepts with practical applications (Miyazawa, 2024; Zagir & Dorner, 2021).

Additionally, facilitators must **adapt to the varying needs of their learners,** modifying their approach as necessary to accommodate different learning styles, skill levels, ages, or cultural backgrounds (Rothwell, 2008). This flexibility requires keen observation and active listening, allowing the facilitator to identify when learners may need additional support or when a particular method is not resonating with the group. Studies highlight that effective facilitators possess competencies that enable them to assess group dynamics and adjust their strategies accordingly, ensuring that all voices are heard and valued within the learning environment (Moiso, 2024; Zagir & Mandel, 2020).

Another essential role of the facilitator is to **provide timely and constructive feedback** (Fedeli & Bierema, 2019). Adults value practical, actionable insights that they can immediately apply, whether improving their skills or deepening their understanding of a concept. A facilitator might, for example, observe a group activity and provide specific feedback on what worked well and where there is room for improvement. This process reinforces learning, builds confidence, and fosters a growth mindset among participants. Moreover, facilitators act as motivators, helping learners overcome self-doubt or fear of failure by emphasizing progress and celebrating small wins throughout the learning journey (Zagir & Dorner, 2021, 2022).

Equally important is the facilitator's ability to connect the learning material and the real-world applications that are most relevant to the participants. Adults are goal-oriented learners who are often more motivated when they can see the immediate benefits of their learning. A skilled facilitator will constantly bridge theory and practice, using examples, case studies, and simulations that align with the learners' personal or professional contexts. For instance, in a digital marketing course, the facilitator might guide learners through creating a campaign strategy for a hypothetical client, mirroring the challenges they will likely face in their workplaces (Miyazawa, 2024; Moiso, 2024).

Lastly, the facilitator serves as a **guide** rather than an authority figure, encouraging self-directed learning while providing learners with the structure and resources to succeed. They empower participants by fostering autonomy, enabling them to take responsibility for their own learning. For instance, in a blended learning environment, the facilitator might provide learners with curated materials and tools for independent study while using in-person sessions to deepen understanding through discussion and collaboration. This approach respects the independence of adult learners while still offering the support needed to achieve their goals (Moiso, 2024; Zagir & Mandel, 2020).

The facilitator's role is multifaceted and dynamic, requiring a blend of empathy, adaptability, and expertise. By creating a safe, engaging, and relevant learning environment, facilitators inspire adults to explore, grow, and apply their learning effectively in their personal and professional lives. Their ability to guide rather than dictate, motivate rather than mandate, and connect rather than command sets them apart as indispensable contributors to the success of adult learning programs.

Assessment and Evaluation of Adult Education Programs

Assessment and evaluation of adult learning programs are critical components for ensuring their effectiveness, relevance, and alignment with the needs of learners and stakeholders. Adult learning programs typically cater to diverse groups with varying backgrounds, experiences, and goals. Therefore, the assessment and evaluation processes must be comprehensive, inclusive, and flexible to capture the nuances of adult education.

Assessment involves measuring the learning outcomes of individual participants, focusing on their acquisition of knowledge, skills, and competencies. Learning evaluation can be achieved through a variety of tools, such as formative assessments (e.g., quizzes, peer reviews, self-assessments) and summative assessments (e.g., final projects, presentations, certification tests) (Sambell et al., 2012). These tools should be tailored to adult learners, often emphasizing real-world applications, reflective practices, and problem-solving abilities rather than rote memorization (Sambell et al., 2012). Recent literature emphasizes the importance of "assessment for learning" over "assessment of learning," advocating for learning-oriented assessment (LOA) that prepares adult learners for future responsibilities and decision-making (Mubayrik, 2020).

Evaluation, on the other hand, assesses the program's overall effectiveness. It involves analyzing multiple dimensions, such as curriculum relevance, instructional methods, resource allocation, and learner satisfaction. Evaluations may use frameworks such as Kirkpatrick's (2006) Four Levels of Training Evaluation, which examine participant reaction, learning, behavior changes, and long-term results. Mixed-method approaches combining qualitative data (e.g., focus groups, interviews, open-ended surveys) with quantitative metrics (e.g., test scores, completion rates, retention statistics) are particularly effective in capturing a holistic view of program success (Hill, 2023).

A key consideration in adult learning program evaluation is the **alignment** of program objectives with the participants' needs and the broader societal or organizational goals. Adults often seek learning opportunities to enhance professional skills, fulfill personal development goals, or adapt to changing life circumstances. As such, program evaluation must gauge how well the curriculum addresses these aspirations while remaining responsive to emerging trends and challenges in adult education. The evolving landscape necessitates evaluations assessing current effectiveness and adapting to learner demographics and societal demands (Olesen & Vincze, 2018).

Additionally, adult learners bring diverse experiences, learning styles, and preferences into the educational setting. Assessments and evaluations must, therefore, adopt a learner-centered approach, integrating flexibility and adaptability. For example, competency-based assessments allow learners to demonstrate mastery at their own pace, while portfolios and reflective journals provide insights into their learning journeys and achievements over time. This adaptability is crucial in accommodating various learner needs and fostering an inclusive educational environment (Mubayrik, 2020).

Another critical aspect is the role of feedback in both assessment and evaluation (Sambell et al., 2012). **Constructive feedback** fosters continuous improvement for both learners and program facilitators. For learners, it provides actionable insights to guide their progress and align efforts with objectives. Feedback highlights program developers' and educators' strengths and weaknesses, offering a roadmap for enhancing content delivery, engagement strategies, and resource allocation. Integrating immediate feedback mechanisms is essential for improving teaching practices and learner outcomes (Agency for Vocational Education and Training and Adult Education, n.d.; Hill, 2023).

In sum, effective assessment and evaluation of adult learning programs require a systematic and inclusive approach that considers the unique characteristics of adult learners. By focusing on measurable outcomes, continuous improvement, and alignment with real-world contexts, these processes ensure that adult education initiatives remain impactful, equitable, and relevant in an ever-changing educational landscape. Emphasizing a culture of assessment within adult education not only enhances program quality but also supports lifelong learning objectives among diverse populations (Olesen & Vincze, 2018; The Tertiary Education Commission, 2024).

Challenges in Designing Adult Learning Programs

Designing adult learning programs involves navigating complex challenges from adult learners' unique needs, characteristics, and circumstances. One of the foremost challenges is accommodating the vast diversity among adult learners. Adult learners bring varying prior knowledge, skills, and experiences, which can create disparities in readiness and confidence within a single program. For instance, findings from studies show that adult learners' challenges vary based on age, gender, knowledge, and skills, highlighting the need for instructional designers to consider these factors when creating educational environments (Kara et al., 2019). Unlike traditional students, adult learners are typically goal-oriented and seek education that addresses their personal or professional aspirations (Cercone, 2008; Knowles, 1996). However, this diversity can make it challenging to design one-size-fits-all programs, requiring a flexible, personalized approach that caters to both individual goals and the collective objectives of the program. Some may seek professional advancement, while others may aim for personal development or skill acquisition for everyday life. This diversity necessitates flexible, personalized learning experiences that align with individual and group objectives. Recognizing this diversity is crucial for effective program design, as it allows for the integration of various learning styles and experiences into the curriculum (OECD, 2023; Six Red Marbles, 2023) and fosters a tailored approach to meet varied learning needs effectively (Kara et al., 2019).

It is important to create an engaging and accessible learning environment that resonates with adult learners. Many adults prefer practical, real-world applications of knowledge over theoretical approaches. Incorporating experiential learning opportunities, such as case studies, simulations, and collaborative projects, is essential but requires thoughtful integration to ensure relevance and effectiveness. Active learning strategies that promote problem-solving exercises and group collaboration can enhance engagement by making content more relatable (Johnson et al., 2018).

Motivating adult learners poses a unique challenge, as detailed in Chapter 6. Adults tend to value education directly relevant to real-world experiences, but maintaining engagement in the face of competing priorities can be difficult. Program designers must incorporate active learning strategies, such as problem-solving exercises, group collaboration, and case-based learning, which make content more relatable and foster a sense of accomplishment. Furthermore, embedding opportunities for immediate application of skills, such as workplace projects or internships, can help bridge the gap between theoretical knowledge and practical use (Knowles et al., 2005).

Moreover, adult learners often favor self-directed learning, which demands program designers to balance structure with autonomy, offering guidance while allowing learners to take ownership of their education. However, this self-directed approach can lead to challenges in maintaining engagement over time, particularly in self-paced or online programs. Innovative strategies such as gamification and regular feedback mechanisms are necessary to motivate learners (De Paepe et al., 2018).

Technological integration is another critical consideration, and Chapter 14 fully explores the topic, including challenges related to adopting digital tools. Other design concerns include language barriers, literacy levels, and cultural diversity among learners. All add complexity to program design, requiring sensitivity to inclusivity and equity. Materials should reflect diverse perspectives and experiences while creating safe, brave spaces where learners feel valued and understood (Kimaro et al., 2022; Thompson & Porto, 2014).

Another significant hurdle is balancing the competing demands in the lives of adult learners. Many adult learners must juggle responsibilities such as full-time jobs, family care, and community commitments, leaving them with limited time and energy for learning. As a result, adult learning programs must prioritize accessibility and flexibility, offering asynchronous and modular formats that allow learners to progress at their own pace. Balancing the depth and breadth of content within these time constraints is a delicate task (Martinez, 2003). However, creating such adaptable structures while maintaining a coherent and effective curriculum requires careful planning and significant resources. Time management is further complicated by the need to integrate rich, meaningful content within limited windows of availability, all while ensuring that learners stay motivated and engaged throughout the program (OECD, 2023).

Finally, assessing and evaluating adult learning outcomes presents its challenges. Traditional assessment methods may not capture the practical, application-oriented learning typical of adult education. Developing authentic assessments that reflect real-world scenarios and allow learners to demonstrate competencies meaningfully is crucial but can be resource-intensive (Willging & Johnson, 2009).

In summary, designing effective adult learning programs demands a nuanced understanding of adult learners' needs and challenges, requiring flexibility, inclusivity, and a learner-centered approach. It involves balancing diverse learning goals, leveraging technology responsibly, and fostering an environment that promotes engagement and practical application. Effectively addressing these challenges can lead to transformative learning experiences that empower adults to achieve their personal and professional aspirations. Overcoming these challenges enhances the quality of adult education, creating impactful programs that foster lifelong learning among adults (Miller, 1993) and empowers learners to achieve their goals and make meaningful contributions to their personal and professional environments (OECD, 2023). Box 13.5 provides a program planning case study.

 **Box 13.5 Adult Learning and Teaching Cases**

Planning an Adult Learning Program for Workforce Upskilling in Technology

Background

A mid-sized technology company, TechAdvancers Inc., faces challenges adapting to rapid advancements in Artificial Intelligence (AI) and Data Analytics. The organization realizes that a significant portion of its workforce lacks the necessary skills to effectively integrate these technologies into daily tasks. To address this, the company has implemented an *Adult Learning Program for Workforce Upskilling* to equip employees with essential AI and data analytics skills.

Target Audience: Learners are employees aged 25–55 with varying levels of education and professional experience.

Groups: Entry-level employees, mid-career professionals, and senior managers.

Characteristics:

- Diverse educational backgrounds (some with no formal training in technology).
- Busy schedules due to full-time work and family responsibilities.
- Different levels of comfort with digital tools and online learning.

Program Goals:

- Equip employees with a foundational knowledge of AI and data analytics.
- Enable participants to apply AI tools to improve their workflow.
- Foster a culture of continuous learning and innovation.

Key Challenges:

- Diverse levels of prior knowledge and technical skills.
- Limited time availability due to employees' full-time work commitments.
- Varied learning preferences and styles (e.g., hands-on learners vs. theory-oriented learners).
- Resistance to change is felt by some employees who feel intimidated by new technology.

Program Design Process:

1. **Step 1: Needs Assessment** TechAdvancers Inc. conducts surveys, focus groups, and interviews to identify skill gaps and employee expectations. Key findings:

- 70% of employees want real-world, job-relevant training.
- 50% prefer flexible, self-paced learning due to time constraints.
- 30% express anxiety about using new technology and prefer in-person guidance.

2. **Step 2: Program Structure** Based on the needs assessment, the program is designed with the following features:

- Modular Structure: Divided into three levels (Beginner, Intermediate, Advanced) to cater to different skill levels.

- Blended Learning Model: Combines online learning (self-paced modules) with in-person workshops for practical application.
- Flexible Schedule: Offers evening and weekend sessions and on-demand recordings for self-paced learning.

3. **Step 3: Content Development** Content is developed with input from industry experts and instructional designers:

- Beginner Module: Fundamentals of AI and Data Analytics, designed with minimal technical jargon.
- Intermediate Module: Application of AI tools in common workflows (e.g., using predictive analytics for sales forecasting).
- Advanced Module: Advanced AI techniques and project-based learning (e.g., building AI models to solve workplace problems).

4. **Step 4: Engaging Delivery Methods** To ensure participant engagement:

- Interactive Content: Videos, quizzes, and interactive simulations.
- Collaborative Activities: Peer-to-peer projects and group problem-solving exercises.
- Real-World Applications: Case studies and workplace scenarios for immediate application.
- Gamification: Rewards such as badges for completing modules and recognition in company meetings.

5. **Step 5: Support Systems** To address employee anxieties and foster a positive learning experience:

- Tech Support: A helpdesk to assist with technical challenges during online sessions.
- Mentorship: Senior employees trained as mentors to guide participants through the program.
- Feedback Loops: Regular surveys and check-ins to assess learner progress and satisfaction.

6. **Step 6: Evaluation and Assessment**

- Formative Assessment: Ongoing quizzes and assignments to monitor understanding.
- Summative Assessment: A capstone project where participants solve a real-world problem using AI tools.
- Program Evaluation: Post-program surveys and performance reviews are used to measure the impact on workplace efficiency.

Outcomes:

- Employee Learning: Over 85% of participants report increased confidence in using AI tools.
- Productivity Gains: Teams using predictive analytics report a 20% improvement in workflow efficiency.
- Cultural Shift: The program fosters a culture of collaboration and innovation, with employees sharing ideas and solutions more frequently.
- Retention: Employees express increased job satisfaction, with a noticeable reduction in turnover rates.

Reflections and Lessons Learned

- Success Factors:
  - Flexibility in delivery (self-paced modules and live workshops) made the program accessible.
  - Real-world applications ensured immediate relevance.
  - Support systems reduced learner anxiety and fostered a positive environment.
- Areas for Improvement:
  - More customization for advanced learners to keep them challenged.
  - Additional resources for participants struggling with the technical aspects.

This case study illustrates how thoughtful program design, grounded in a clear understanding of learners' needs, can address the challenges of adult education while achieving impactful outcomes for both learners and organizations.

Future Trends

The main trend in designing effective adult learning experiences is to widen access through diversification and flexibility, considering traditional, adult, and lifelong learning paths. Providing access to diverse populations, addressing evolving learning needs, and ensuring flexibility in learning opportunities are the primary goals of adult education and lifelong learning. When planning and designing educational experiences, the relevant UNESCO & Shanghai Open University (2023) Research Report outlines various models that incorporate and integrate technology. As an educator and adult learner, you can consider these approaches to enhance the design and planning of effective learning experiences. Among the most used methods, it highlights live online lectures and seminars, increased use of blended and hybrid learning, lectures available as video and podcast, use of social video and mobile technology, MOOC and open educational resources, E-portfolio, adaptive learning, and artificial intelligence (UNESCO & Shanghai Open University, 2023, p. 49).

As the education landscape continues to evolve, adult learning and lifelong education are experiencing transformative changes driven by technology, societal shifts, and the needs of a dynamic workforce, as highlighted in Chapter 2. These trends point to a future that emphasizes flexibility, inclusivity, and personalized learning experiences. From integrating adaptive technologies to the growing focus on mental health and sustainability, the following innovations are shaping the future of adult education, ensuring it remains relevant and impactful for diverse learners. The following table summarizes some of the most significant trends supported by current research and industry developments (Table 13.1).

Personalization and Adaptive Learning

The future of adult education lies in highly personalized learning experiences. Advances in Artificial Intelligence (AI) and machine learning are enabling adaptive learning platforms that can analyze a learner's performance in real-time and tailor content, pace, and assessments to their individual needs. This level of personalization ensures that learners receive targeted support, making education more effective and engaging. For instance, AI-driven systems can identify when a learner struggles with a concept and provide additional resources, such as video tutorials or practice exercises tailored to their learning style (UNESCO & Shanghai Open University, 2023). Big data and analytics will be more significant in designing and refining adult learning programs. By tracking learner behaviors, preferences, and outcomes, educators can make data-informed decisions to improve program effectiveness. Predictive analytics can also help identify at-risk learners early and provide targeted interventions to keep them on track (Al-Zahrani & Alasmari, 2023; Ikegwu et al., 2022; Kurilovas, 2020).

Microlearning, Modular Formats, and Lifelong Learning

Busy adult learners increasingly favor microlearning—short, focused learning units consumable in small timeframes. Programs designed in bite-sized modules enable learners to acquire specific skills or knowledge quickly and effectively. The World Economic Forum (2020) supported this format, where microlearning addresses the time constraints of modern learners, offering flexibility and skill-focused modules. It particularly appeals to professionals who want to improve their skills without committing to lengthy courses. Furthermore, as career paths become less linear, lifelong learning will become a norm rather

TABLE 13.1 SUMMARY OF THE RECENT TRENDS IN ADULT EDUCATION

Trend	Definition	Example	Sources
Personalization and Adaptive Learning	Using analytics to refine learning experiences and interventions.	AI and predictive analytics can identify and support at-risk learners, providing tailored additional resources, video tutorials, or exercises.	Al-Zahrani and Alasmari (2023); Ikegwu et al. (2022); Kurilovas (2020); UNESCO and Shanghai Open University (2023)
Microlearning, Modular Formats, and Lifelong Learning	Short, focused learning units are designed for time-constrained learners and continuous skill development.	Professionals take stackable modules to earn certifications and micro-credentials for professional growth.	Council of the European Union (2022); World Economic Forum (2020)
Gamification and Immersive Technologies	Game-like elements and immersive tools enhance engagement and learning outcomes.	VR (Virtual Reality) simulations for medical training, AR (Augmented Reality) for hands-on skill development.	Callwood (2024); Li et al. (2023)
Focus on Soft Skills and Emotional Intelligence	Training in communication, critical thinking, and adaptability alongside technical skills.	Role-playing and collaborative projects to enhance teamwork and resilience.	Hasanah (2024); Richardson (2023)
Inclusivity and Equity in Design	Programs designed for accessibility and cultural sensitivity.	Universal Design for Learning (UDL) fosters equal opportunities.	UNESCO (2021)
Integration of Work-Based Learning	Aligning learning with real-world work experiences.	Apprenticeships and internships are integrated into academic programs.	OECD (2022)
Sustainability and Green Learning Practices	Environmentally conscious education strategies.	Online training to reduce carbon footprints and introducing sustainability topics in curricula.	United Nations (2015)
Emphasis on Mental Health and Well-being	Integrating mental health strategies into education.	Mindfulness-based programs (MBPs) to reduce stress and enhance learning.	Galante et al. (2021); Henning (2018)
Social and Peer-Learning Platforms	Community-based learning through digital platforms.	Peer-to-peer collaboration for networking and knowledge sharing.	Hasanah (2024)

than an exception. Adult learning programs will increasingly offer modular, stackable credentials that learners can earn throughout their careers. Digital badges, micro-credentials, and competency-based certifications will provide tangible evidence of skills acquisition, making it easier for learners to showcase their capabilities to employers. The Council of the European Union (2022) endorsed stackable credentials and digital badges, reshaping how adults engage in continuous professional development.

Gamification and Immersive Technologies

Gamification is becoming a powerful tool for increasing learner engagement and motivation. Adult learning programs can create a sense of accomplishment and healthy competition among participants by incorporating game-like elements such as leaderboards, achievements, and rewards. Recent meta-analyses have shown that gamification can significantly improve student motivation, engagement, and learning outcomes, with an overall effect size of $g = 0.822$ across various studies (Li et al., 2023). This approach makes learning more enjoyable and encourages active participation, which is crucial for effective adult education. Moreover, immersive technologies like Virtual Reality (VR) and Augmented Reality (AR) revolutionize experiential learning. These technologies allow learners to practice real-world scenarios in safe, simulated environments. For instance, VR simulations enliven medical training, enabling healthcare professionals to practice procedures without risk to patients (Callwood, 2024). The interactive nature of AR tools also enhances hands-on technical skills training by providing immediate feedback and contextual learning experiences. As these technologies become more accessible and affordable, their integration into educational curricula will likely expand significantly.

Focus on Soft Skills and Emotional Intelligence

In an era where automation and artificial intelligence are reshaping the workforce, the demand for **human-centric skills**—such as emotional intelligence, creativity, critical thinking, and adaptability—is surging. Future adult learning programs will increasingly prioritize the development of these soft skills, often embedding them within technical training to cultivate well-rounded professionals. Research indicates that soft skills are essential for employability; employers highly value qualities like communication, teamwork, and adaptability (Hasanah, 2024; Richardson, 2023).

Integrating soft skill development into educational programs is accomplished by adopting role-playing, collaborative projects, and reflective practices. These strategies enhance learners' interpersonal skills and promote self-confidence and resilience—indispensable qualities in today's dynamic work environments. Furthermore, fostering emotional intelligence can improve learners' relationships and conflict-resolution abilities (Richardson, 2023).

Inclusivity and Equity in Design

As diversity becomes a central focus in education, programs will increasingly integrate inclusive content and activities, for example, by addressing accessibility for learners with disabilities, offering multi-language support, and considering cultural sensitivities in content and delivery. UNESCO's Global Education Monitoring Report (2021) emphasizes the implementation of Universal Design for Learning (UDL). These principles will guide program creation, ensuring all learners have equal opportunities to participate and succeed. Box 13.6 features culturally responsive teaching.

 **Box 13.6 Tips and Tools for Teaching and Learning**

Culturally Responsive Teaching

Culturally Responsive Teaching emerged from Gloria Ladson-Billing's (1994) culturally relevant pedagogy framework that recognizes the role of culture in shaping how learners see themselves and the world around them. Rhodes (2018) pointed out that much of the teaching research is theoretically responsive and has focused on K–12 settings. Guy (1999) advocated embracing culturally responsive teaching to create more effective learning environments for adult learners from minority backgrounds, emphasizing that culture is at the heart of everything in education. Key assumptions of culturally responsive learning for adults highlighted in Rhodes's (2018) work:

1. Learners and educators bring their cultural identities into the learning setting (Guy, 2009).
2. Cultural strategies people bring to the learning environment may or may not serve learners well, depending on the learning activity.

3. The learner is at the core of the learning process and draws on their cultural knowledge, prior experiences, frames of reference, and performance styles (Gay, 2010; in Rhodes, 2018).

4. Historically excluded or marginalized learners due to cultural identity and experience may encounter a cultural mismatch between their culture and the culture of the learning environment, especially when dominant cultures stigmatize their culture's group norms and values.

5. Culturally relevant pedagogy addresses the mismatch by centering learners and their values, beliefs, and experiences in the learning process.

6. The Motivational Framework for Culturally Responsive Teaching (Ginsberg & Wlodkowski, 2009; Wlodkowski, 2004; Woldkowski & Ginsberg, 2017) "dynamically combines the essential motivational conditions that are intrinsically motivating for adults in culturally diverse learning environments" (Woldkowski & Ginsberg, 2017, p. 97). Here are the components of the framework with questions posed by Woldkowski & Ginsberg (2017, pp. 100–101):

   a. **Establish inclusion** by creating norms of respect and connection among learners that value the co-construction of knowledge using strategies like jigsaw or peer teaching activities (Rhodes, 2018). When planning the lesson, ask, "How do we create or affirm a learning atmosphere in which we feel respected and connected?"

   b. **Develop attitude** by addressing the *relevance and creation of student volition* in the learning environment (emphasis in the original, Rhodes, 2018, p. 35) by having learners create classroom norms for problematic terms and labels and invite student input into the formulation of course goals and outcomes. Learning assessment invites problem-solving activities that yield a variety of possible solutions. When planning the lesson, ask, "How do we create or affirm a favorable disposition toward learning through personal relevance and learner volition?"

   c. **Enhance meaning** by inviting deep reflection and critical inquiry into issues related to the course content, such as simulations, role-playing, or games (Rhodes, 2018). Ask throughout the lesson, "How do we create engaging and challenging learning experiences that include learners' perspectives and values?"

   d. **Engender competence** using assessments sensitive to learner backgrounds with multiple ways of demonstrating learning. These might include reflective learner self-assessments, dialogue, focused reflections, or journals (Rhodes, 2018). Ask throughout and at the end of the lesson, "How do we create or affirm an understanding that learners have effectively learned something they value and perceive as authentic to their real world?"

Consider the points and strategies as an adult learner or educator.

1. What have you experienced or integrated into your teaching?
2. How might this information change how you approach learning and teaching in the future?

Integration of Work-Based Learning

The future will see a stronger integration of learning with workplace practices. Work-based learning models, such as apprenticeships, internships, and cooperative education, will become more prominent. Program designs will likely align closely with industry needs, enabling learners to apply real-life skills while earning credentials. Partnerships between educational institutions and employers will play a key role in shaping these programs. As the OECD (2022) report outlines, industry-aligned learning bridges the gap between academic knowledge and practical application.

Sustainability and Green Learning Practices

With the increasing emphasis on sustainability, adult learning programs will adopt environmentally conscious practices. The United Nations' (2015) Sustainable Development Goals (SDG 4) champion a focus on eco-friendly education practices, including reducing the use of physical materials, integrating sustainability topics into curricula, and utilizing virtual platforms to reduce the carbon footprint of training events. Programs may also focus on equipping learners with skills to drive sustainability initiatives within their industries.

Emphasis on Mental Health and Well-being

Integrating mental health and well-being strategies into adult education is crucial for creating supportive learning environments. A study published in *PLOS Medicine* found that mindfulness-based programs (MBPs) effectively promote mental health and reduce stress among participants. The research suggests incorporating MBPs into educational settings can enhance learners' well-being and create a positive learning atmosphere (Galante et al., 2021; Henning et al., 2018).

Social and Peer-Learning Platforms

Community-based learning remains a fundamental aspect of adult education. Social learning platforms that promote peer-to-peer collaboration, networking, and knowledge sharing are expected to gain traction in future educational frameworks. These platforms create vibrant learning communities where participants can interact meaningfully, share insights, and support one another throughout their educational journeys. Integrating social learning elements into adult education programs fosters a sense of belonging among learners. This communal approach can enhance motivation and retention rates while providing opportunities for collaborative problem-solving—increasingly vital skills in modern workplaces (Hasanah, 2024). By embracing these social platforms, educational institutions can create more engaging and supportive environments conducive to lifelong learning.

By adopting these trends, educators and organizations can create transformative learning experiences that empower adults to thrive in an ever-changing world. These innovations will ensure that adult education remains relevant, accessible, and impactful for learners from all walks of life.

Summary

Designing effective adult learning programs requires a deep understanding of adult learners' unique characteristics, motivations, and challenges. Chapter 13 emphasized the importance of aligning learning experiences with adult responsibilities by incorporating experiential learning, real-world applications, and problem-solving strategies. Effective program design integrates structured yet flexible approaches like blended learning, gamification, and scaffolded instruction. Adult educators take a facilitative approach, playing a crucial role in fostering engagement, providing feedback, and creating inclusive environments that empower learners. Assessment and evaluation should be incorporated throughout, ensuring that programs meet learners' needs with relevance and impact. Design and facilitation challenges include honoring learner diversity, equity, and inclusion, balancing engagement with flexibility, and integrating appropriate technology. Future trends like AI-driven personalization, microlearning, and a focus on soft skills signal a shift toward more adaptive and inclusive adult education programming. Embracing these principles helps educators and organizations create transformative learning environments that support lifelong learning and professional growth.

Chapter Highlights

- Adult Learning Programs serve multiple purposes, including facilitating personal and professional development, addressing real-world issues, and encouraging lifelong learning and adaptability.
- Core Elements of Program Design include aligning learning experiences with adult learners' responsibilities and motivations, creating inclusive and supportive learning environments, integrating experiential learning, real-world applications, and problem-solving, and using inclusive and flexible designs to accommodate diverse learners.
- Key active adult instructional strategies include experiential learning, problem-based learning, blended learning, scaffolded learning, and gamification and immersive technology.
- Effective adult learning facilitators create inclusive and supportive learning environments, foster engagement through active learning, provide timely and constructive feedback, and encourage learner autonomy and self-direction.

References

Agency for Vocational Education and Training and Adult Education. (n.d.). *Development of a quality assurance system in Adult Education—ASOO.* https://www.asoo.hr/en/quality-assurance/adult-education/project-development-of-a-qa-system-in-adult-education/.

Agosti, A. (2006). *Gruppo di lavoro e lavoro di gruppo: spetti pedagogici e didattici.* FrancoAngeli.

Al-Zahrani, A. M. & Alasmari, T. (2023). Learning analytics for data-driven decision making: Enhancing instructional personalization and student engagement in online higher education. *International journal of online pedagogy and course design (IJOPCD), 13*(1), 1–18. https://doi.org/10.4018/IJOPCD.331751.

Argyris, C. (2017). *Integrating the individual and the organization.* Routledge.

Atkinson J. (2024, January 10). *10 High impact teaching strategies for adult learners.* Training Industry. https://trainingindustry.com/articles/strategy-alignment-and-planning/10-high-impact-teaching-strategies-for-adult-learners/.

Ausubel, D. P. (1962). A subsumption theory of meaningful verbal learning and retention. *The Journal of General Psychology, 66,* 213–224. https://doi.org/10.1080/00221309.1962.9711837.

Bash, L. (2005). *Best practices in adult learning.* Anker.

Bergquist, W. H., & Phillips, S. R. (1975). *A handbook for faculty development.* The council for the advancement of small colleges.

Bierema, L. L. (2019). Adult learning theories and practices. In Fedeli, M., & Bierema, L. L. *Connecting adult learning and knowledge management* (pp. 3–25). Springer.

Biggs, J. (2003). Aligning teaching for constructing learning. *Education, 94*(11), 112106. https://doi.org/10.1063/1.3100776.

Bloom, B. S., Engelhart, M. D., Furst, E. J., Hill, W. H., & Krathwohl, D. R. (1956). *Taxonomy of educational objectives: The classification of educational goals; Handbook I, Cognitive domain.* David Mckay.

Boud, D., & Molloy, E. (2013). Rethinking models of feedback for learning: The challenge of design. *Assessment & Evaluation in Higher Education, 38*(6), 698–712. https://doi.org/10.1080/02602938.2012.691462.

Bound, H., & Chia, A. (2020). *The six principles of learning design. Designing learning for performance—a practice note.* Institute for Adult Learning. https://doi.org/10.13140/RG.2.2.29378.61127.

Brookfield, S. D. (2013). *Powerful techniques for teaching adults.* John Wiley & Sons.

Brown, D. R., & Harvey, D. (2006). *An experiential approach to organization development* (7th ed.). Pearson Education.

Bruner, J. (1966). *Toward a theory of instruction.* Harvard University Press.

Burns, R. (2020). *Adult learner at work: The challenges of lifelong education in the new millenium.* Routledge.

Button, L. (2021). *Curriculum essentials: A journey.* Pressbooks. https://oer.pressbooks.pub/curriculumessentials/.

Callwood, K. (2024, November 10). *Immersive learning predictions: 2023 Trends & Insights.* Hyperspace^mv—the Metaverse for Business Platform. https://hyperspace.mv/immersive-learning-predictions-2023-trends-insights/.

Carlson McCall, R., Padron, K., & Andrews, C. (2018). Evidence-based instructional strategies for adult learners: A review of the literature. *Codex: the Journal of the Louisiana Chapter of the ACRL, 4*(4). 29–47. ISSN 2150-086X.

Cercone, K. (2008). Characteristics of adult learners with implications for online learning design. *AACE Journal, 16*(2), 137–159. https://www.learntechlib.org/primary/p/24286.

Coryell, J. E., Baumgartner, L. M., & Bohonos, J. W. (Eds.). (2024). *Methods for facilitating adult learning: Strategies for enhancing instruction and instructor effectiveness.* Routledge.

Council of the European Union. (2022). Council recommendation on a European approach to micro-credentials for lifelong learning and employability, 2022/C 243/02. Official journal of the European Union.

Daffron, S. R., & Caffarella, R. S. (2021). *Planning programs for adult learners: A practical guide.* John Wiley & Sons.

De Paepe, L., Zhu, C., & DePryck, K. (2018). Drop-out, retention, satisfaction and attainment of online learners of Dutch in adult education. *International Journal on E-Learning, 17*(3), 303–323. https://www.learntechlib.org/primary/p/174173.

Dirkx, J. M., & Prenger, S. M. (1997). *A guide for planning and implementing instruction for adults. A theme-based approach.* Jossey-Bass.

Dondi, M., Klier, J., Panier, F., & Schubert, J. (2021). Defining the skills citizens will need in the future world of work. *McKinsey & Company, 25,* 1–19. https://hrday.nl/wp-content/uploads/2022/10/JTB.pdf.

Fedeli, M., & Bierema, L. L. (2019). *Connecting adult learning and knowledge management.* Springer.

Fedeli, M., & Taylor, E. W. (2024). Collaborative learning and group work. In. J. E. Coryell, L. M. Baumgartner, & J. W. Bohonos (Eds.), *Methods for facilitating adult learning: Strategies for enhancing instruction and instructor effectiveness* (pp. 117–131). Routledge.

Fink, L. D. (2003). *Creating significant learning experiences. An integrated approach to designing college courses.* Jossey-Bass.

Gagné, R.M. (1965). *The conditions of learning.* Holt, Rinehart & Winston.

Galante J., Friedrich C., Dawson AF, Modrego-Alarción M., Gebbing P., Delgado-Suárez, I., Gupta, R., Dean, L., Dalgleish, T., White, I.R. and Jones, P.B., (2021). Mindfulness-based programmes for mental health promotion in adults in nonclinical settings: A systematic review and meta-analysis of randomised controlled trials. *PLoS Med, 18*(1): e1003481. https://doi.org/10.1371/journal. pmed.1003481.

Gay, G. (2010). *Culturally responsive teaching: Theory, research, and practice.* Teachers College Press.

Ginsberg, M., & Wlodkowski, R. (2009). *Diversity and motivation: Culturally responsive teaching in college.* Jossey-Bass.

Griffin D. (2023, June 26). *Effective adult learning strategies for 2023: Unlocking success in the digital age: Analysis Prime University.* https://www.analysisprimeuniversity.com/effective-adult-learning-strategies-for-2023-unlocking-success-in-the-digital-age/.

Guglielmino, L. M. (1977). *Development of the Self-Directed Learning Readiness Scale.* Doctoral Dissertation. University of Georgia.

Gust, K. J. (2006). Teaching with Tiffany's: A "go-lightly" approach to information literacy instruction for adults and senior learners. *Reference Services Review, 34*(4), 557–569. https://doi.org/10.1108/00907320610716440.

Guy, T. (1999). Culture as context for adult education: The need for culturally relevant adult education. In T. C. Guy (Ed.), *Providing culturally relevant adult education* (pp. 5-18). Jossey-Bass.

Guy, T. (2009). Culturally relevant curriculum development for teachers of adults: The importance of identity, positionality, and classroom dynamics. In V. C. X. Wang (Ed.), *Curriculum development for adult learners in the global community* (pp. 9–38). Krieger.

Hasanah, S. (2023, October 2). *Top 7 Effective teaching methods for adult learning.* Digiformag. https://www.digiformag.com/en/teaching-methods/top-7-effective-teaching-methods-for-adult-learning/.

Hasanah, S. (2024, February 14). *Is adult learning important? Here's how it's empowering the future workforce.* Digiformag. https://www.digiformag.com/en/professional-training/is-adult-learning-important-heres-how-its-empowering-the-future-workforce/.

Hattie J. (2012). *Visible learning for teachers: Maximizing impact on learning.* Routledge.

Hattie J., & Yates G. C. (2013). *Visible learning and the science of how we learn.* Routledge. http://www.lonestar.edu/multimedia/SevenPrinciples.pdf.

Henning, M., Krägeloh, C., Dryer, R., Moir, F., Billington, R., & Hill, A. (2018). *Wellbeing in higher education.* Routledge.

Hequet, M. (1995). Games that teach. *Training, 32*(7), 53–58.

Hey A. (2024, August 3). 6 smart learning objectives examples you need to know | Coursebox AI. https://www.coursebox.ai/blog/smart-learning-objectives-examples.

Hill, L. H. (2023). *Assessment, evaluation, and accountability in adult education.* Routledge.

Huang, W. D., & Huang, J. (2024). Gamification of learning for adult learners. In. J. E. Coryell, L. M. Baumgartner, & J. W. Bohonos (Eds.), *Methods for facilitating adult learning: Strategies for enhancing instruction and instructor effectiveness* (pp. 285–303). Routledge.

Hunt, G. (1986). Needs assessment in adult education: Tactical and strategic considerations. *Instructional Science, 15*(1), 287–296. https://doi.org/10.1007/BF00139616

Ikegwu, A. C., Nweke, H. F., Anikwe, C. V., Alo, U. R., & Okonkwo, O. R. (2022). Big data analytics for data driven industry: A review of data sources, tools, challenges, solutions, and research directions. *Cluster Computing, 25*(5), 3343–3387. https://doi.org/10.1007/s10586-022-03568-5.

James, W., Oates, G., & Schonfeldt, N. (2024). Improving retention while enhancing student engagement and learning outcomes using gamified mobile technology. *Accounting Education*, 1–21. https://doi.org/10.1080/09639284.2024.2326009.

Johnson, E., Morwane, R., Dada, S., Pretorius, G., & Lotriet, M. (2018). Adult learners' perspectives on their engagement in a hybrid learning postgraduate programme. *The Journal of Continuing Higher Education, 66*(2), 88–105. https://doi.org/10.1080/07377363.2018.1469071.

Jones, C. T., Lane, A., Shah, A., Carter, K., Lackey, R., & Kolb, R. (2021). The Un-meeting approach to stimulate collaborative adult learning: An application for clinical research professionals. *Journal of Clinical and Translational Science, 5*(1), e162. https://doi.org/10.1017/cts.2021.821.

Kara, M., Erdoğdu, F., Kokoç, M., & Cagiltay, K. (2019). Challenges faced by adult learners in online distance education: A literature review. *Open Praxis, 11*(1), 5. https://doi.org/10.5944/openpraxis.11.1.929.

Kimaro, E., Machumu, H., Kalimasi, P., & Heikkinen, A. (2022). Challenges of adult education provision towards social sustainability at the institute of adult education Morogoro campus. *Journal of Institute of Adult Education, 24*.

Kinshuk Chen, N. S., Cheng, I. L., & Chew, S. W. (2016). Evolution is not enough: Revolutionizing current learning environments to smart learning environments. *International journal of artificial intelligence in education, 26*, 561–581. https://doi.org/10.1007/s40593-016-0108-x.

Kirkpatrick, D., & Kirkpatrick, J. (2006). *Evaluating training programs: The four levels*. Berrett-Koehler.

Knowles, M. (1996). Adult learning. In R. L. Craig (Ed.), *The ASTD training and development handbook* (pp. 253–264). McGraw-Hill.

Knowles, M., Holton, E., & Swanson, R. (2005). *The adult learner: The definitive classic in adult education and human resource development* (6th ed.). Elsevier.

Kolb, A. Y., & Kolb, D. A. (2009). Experiential learning theory: A dynamic, holistic approach to management learning, education and development. In S. J. Armstrong & C. V. Fukami (Eds.), *The SAGE handbook of management learning, education and development* (pp. 42–68). SAGE Publications Ltd.

Kurilovas, E. (2020). On data-driven decision-making for quality education. *Computers in Human Behavior, 107*, 105774. https://doi.org/10.1016/j.chb.2018.11.003.

Ladson-Billings, G. (1994). *The dreamkeepers. Culturally responsive teaching*. Jossey-Bass.

Li, M., Ma, S., & Shi, Y. (2023). Examining the effectiveness of gamification as a tool promoting teaching and learning in educational settings: A meta-analysis. *Frontiers in Psychology, 14*, 1253549. https://doi.org/10.3389/fpsyg.2023.1253549.

Luckritz Marquis, T. (2021). Formative assessment and scaffolding online learning. *New Directions for Adult and Continuing Education, 169*, 51–60. https://doi.org/10.1002/ace.20413.

Mager, R.F. (1962). *Preparing instructional objectives*. Fearon.

Marsick, V. (2004). Case study. In M. W. Galbraith, *Adult learning methods: A guide for effective instruction* (pp. 383–404). Krieger.

Martinez, M. (2003). High attrition rates in e-learning: Challenges, predictors and solutions. *The E-Learning Developers' Journal*. https://www.elearningguild.com/pdf/2/071403 MGT-L.pdf.

McDonough, D. (2014). Providing deep learning through active engagement of adult learners in blended courses. *Journal of Learning in Higher Education, 10*(1), 9–16. https://eric.ed.gov/?id=EJ1143328.

Merriam, S. B., & Baumgartner, L. M. (2020). *Learning in adulthood: A comprehensive guide.* John Wiley & Sons.

Miller, M. T. (1993). Barriers to adult education training programs: Challenges for the adult educator. https://eric.ed.gov/?id=ED365795.

Miyazawa, M. (2024). The role of a facilitator in multidisciplinary collaboration and student's experienced-based learning. *European Conference on Knowledge Management, 25*(1), 1043–1050. https://doi.org/10.34190/eckm.25.1.2527.

Moiso, D. R. (2024, November 7). *What is a facilitator and what do they do? | SessionLab.* SessionLab. https://www.sessionlab.com/blog/what-is-a-facilitator/.

Mondal, H., Mondal, S., & Juhi, A. (2024). Adult learners: Assessment strategies. In T. McGlashing Tarbutton, & L. B. Doyle (Eds.), *Adjunct faculty in online higher education: Best practices for teaching adult learners* (pp. 311–331). IGI Global.

Mubayrik, H. F. B. (2020). New Trends in Formative-Summative Evaluations for Adult Education. *SAGE Open, 10*(3). Advance online publication. https://doi.org/10.1177/2158244020941006.

OECD. (2022). Education at a glance: OECD indicators, OECD Publishing, https://doi.org/10.1787/3197152b-en.

OECD. (2023). *Flexible adult learning provision: What it is, why it matters, and how to make it work.* OECD.

Olesen L. A., & Vincze Z. (2018). *Budapest Evaluation of Adult Education and Training activities.* Erasmus+ Strategic Partnership "Designing, monitoring and evaluating adult learning classes: Supporting quality in adult learning" (DEMAL).

Outwitly. (2022, April 21). *Reimagining the adult education experience.* Outwitly. https://outwitly.com/case-study/reimagining-the-adult-education-experience/.

Palis, A. G., & Quiros, P. A. (2014). Adult learning principles and presentation pearls. *Middle East African Journal of Ophthalmology, 21*(2), 114–122. https://doi.org/10.4103/0974-9233.129748.

Pashchenko, T. V. (2024). Critical thinking development in adult learners through problem-based learning in an online setting. *Voprosy Obrazovaniya/Educational Studies Moscow, 2,* 226–250. https://doi.org/10.17323/vo-2024-16699.

Piskurich, G. M. (1994). Developing self-directed learning. *Training & Development, 48*(3), 30–36. https://link.gale.com/apps/doc/A15317745/AONE?u=nysl_me_lenox&sid=googleScholar&xid=070c7878.

Por, F. P., Ong, C. S. B., Ng, S. K., & Eak, A. D. (2024). A bibliometric analysis on gamifying adult learning: Past, present and future trends of learner-centered pedagogies. *Interactive technology and smart education.* Advance online publication. https://doi.org/10.1108/itse-11-2023-0226.

Race P. (2001). *Using feedback to help students learn.* The Higher Education Academy.

Rhodes, C. M. (2018). Culturally responsive teaching with adult learners: A review of the literature. *International Journal of Adult Vocational Education and Technology (IJAVET), 9*(4), 33-41. https://doi.org/https://doi.org/10.4018/IJAVET.2018100103.

Richardson, S. (2023, October 13). *Soft skills: why they matter and resources to teach them.* Adult Learning Alliance of Arkansas. https://arkansasliteracy.org/tutor-resources/soft-skills-why-they-matter-and-resources-to-teach-them/.

Riegnell, J., & Bulthuis, S. (2022). *Successful adult learning principles.* Lund University

Rothwell, W. J. (2008). *Adult learning basics.* ASTD Press.

Sambell, K., McDowell, L., & Montgomery, C. (2012). *Assessment for learning in higher education.* Routledge.

Schmidt, S. W. (2024). Case studies estimate/case stories. In. J. E. Coryell, L. M. Baumgartner, & J. W. Bohonos (Eds.), *Methods for facilitating adult learning: Strategies for enhancing instruction and instructor effectiveness* (pp. 104–116). Routledge.

Singh, H. (2021). Building effective blended learning programs. Educational technology. In B. H. Khan, S. Affouneh, S. H. Salha, Z. N. Khlaif (Eds.), *Challenges and opportunities for the global implementation of e-learning frameworks* (pp. 15–23). IGI Global Scientific Publishing https://doi.org/10.4018/978-1-7998-7607-6.ch002.

Six Red Marbles. (2023, May 17). *Ask an Expert: Six key questions to help adult learners thrive in 2023.* Six Red Marbles. https://www.sixredmarbles.com/blog-red/ask-an-expert-six-key-questions-to-help-adult-learners-thrive-in-2023/.

Ślósarz, L., Błaszczyński, K., Švecová, M., & Kobylarek, A. (2022). Adult education needs inventory: Construction and application. *Frontiers in Psychology, 13.* https://doi.org/10.3389/fpsyg.2022.1035283.

Stenhouse, L. (1975). *An introduction to curriculum research and development.* Heineman.

Stewart, T., Mitchell, T. D., Perry, L., & O'Steen, B. (2024). Community based service learning as engaged andragogy. In J. E. Coryell, L. M. Baumgartner, & J. W. Bohonos (Eds.), *Methods for facilitating adult learning: Strategies for enhancing instruction and instructor effectiveness,* 217–232. Routledge.

Taba, H. (1962). *Curriculum development: Theory and practice.* Harcourt, Brace & World.

The Tertiary Education Commission. (2024). *Guidelines for using the literacy and numeracy for adults assessment tool 2024.* The Tertiary Education Commission Te Amorangi Mātauranga Matua. https://www.tec.govt.nz/assets/Forms-templates-and-guides/Guidelines-for-using-the-Literacy-and-Numeracy-for-Adults-Assessment-Tool-v2.pdf.

Thompson, J., & Porto, S. (2014). Supporting wellness in adult online education. *Open Praxis, 6*(1), 17–28. https://doi.org/10.5944/openpraxis.6.1.100.

Tyler, R. W. (1949). *Basic principles of curriculum and instruction.* The University of Chicago Press.

UNESCO. (2021). *Global Education Monitoring Report 2021: Central and Eastern Europe, the Caucasus and Central Asia—Inclusion and education: All means all.*

UNESCO & Shanghai Open University. (2023). *International trends of lifelong learning in higher education: Research report.* UNESCO eBooks. https://doi.org/10.54675/dczr7108.

United Nations. (2015). Transforming our world: The 2030 Agenda for Sustainable Development. A/RES/70/1.

Weimer, M. (2013). *Learner-centered teaching: Five key changes to practice.* John Wiley & Sons.

Willging, P. A. & Johnson, S. D. (2009). Factors that influence students' decision to dropout of online courses. *Journal of Asynchronous Learning Networks, 13*(3), 115–127. https://files.eric.ed.gov/fulltext/EJ862360.pdf.

Williams, B. (2024, November 12). *Instructional design principles for adults: Best practices.* Insight7—AI Tool for Interview Analysis & Market Research. https://insight7.io/instructional-design-principles-for-adults-best-practices/.

Wlodkowski, R. (2004). Creating motivational learning environments. In M. W. Galbraith, *Adult learning methods: A guide for effective instruction,* 3rd ed. (pp. 141–164). Krieger.

Wlodkowski, R. J., & Ginsberg, M. B. (2017). *Enhancing adult motivation to learn: A comprehensive guide for teaching all adults.* John Wiley & Sons.

Wood, D., Bruner, J. S., & Ross, G. (1976). The role of tutoring in problem solving. *Journal of Child Psychology and Psychiatry, 17*(2), 89–100.

World Economic Forum. (2020). *The future of jobs report 2020.* World Economic Forum. https://www.weforum.org/publications/the-future-of-jobs-report-2020/.

Zagir, T., & Dorner, H. (2021). Revisiting competences of adult learning facilitators: Perspectives from the Mongolian context. *Journal of Adult and Continuing Education, 28*(1), 184–207. https://doi.org/10.1177/14779714211003100.

Zagir, T., & Dorner, H. (2022). Adult learning facilitators' professional identity: An exploratory review based on a selection of empirical studies. *Journal of Adult Learning, Knowledge and Innovation, 4*(2), 44–51. https://doi.org/10.1556/2059.2021.00045.

Zagir, T., & Mandel, K. M. (2020). Competences of adult learning facilitators in Europe: Analyses of five European research projects. *Hungarian Educational Research Journal, 10*(2), 155–171. https://doi.org/10.1556/063.2020.00016.

Zarestky, J., & Vilen, L. (2024). Field-based experiences and C*Sci training for adults. In. J. E. Coryell, L. M. Baumgartner, & J. W. Bohonos (Eds.), *Methods for facilitating adult learning: Strategies for enhancing instruction and instructor effectiveness* (pp. 250–267). Routledge.

CHAPTER FOURTEEN

DESIGNING EFFECTIVE ONLINE LEARNING FOR ADULTS

 **Box 14.1 Chapter Overview and Learning Objectives**

The adage "Arriving at one goal is the starting point to another" is attributed to John Dewey, and it speaks to how the context of adult learning is constantly shifting, especially with technological advances. Manca (2020) observed that social media plays a significant role in modern education by facilitating informal digital learning. It allows students to collaborate in knowledge construction, participate in real-time discussions, and access various educational resources beyond traditional classroom boundaries.

Chapter 14 examines the influence of digital media on adult learning and education. It begins by addressing how technology shapes various dimensions of life, including work, family, and community. The discussion then transitions to the digital transformations within higher education institutions and the experiences of adult learners, focusing on their engagement with technology and how they navigate the challenges of a highly interconnected world. Finally, the chapter evaluates the role of technology in supporting education, assessing its effectiveness and considering the complexities and limitations associated with its use.

As a result of reading this chapter and completing the exercises, you, the reader, should be able to:

1. Understand the change that digital media provokes in our society and people's life.
2. Know some of the most important political strategies in the United States and Europe to enhance digital transformation.
3. Reflect on the main factors that influence the planning of online learning.
4. Understand the challenge of online teaching and learning.

As an adult, think of the last news story you scanned, purchase you made, book you read, bank transaction you performed, information you looked up, or friend you contacted. Chances are some or all these activities were **computer-mediated**—enabled by a computer rather than human-to-human contact. Technology is a significant variable affecting adult learning, like other topics addressed in this book, including learner characteristics, motivation, experience, self-directedness, and brain function. These characteristics, as do social, political, and technological contexts, affect learning. Increasingly, learners are turning to the World Wide Web, whether to access information or take a course immediately. We live in the **Digital Age** (or the Information Age or Computer Age), where we freely exchange and have instant access to information. The ability to search the Internet has changed our access to and relationship with information. Information is now at our fingertips 24/7, which previously would have required a trip to the library or consultation with an expert. Say you want to install tile in your bathroom. Just a few years ago, you might have gone to your public library, local bookstore, or home improvement center to learn how to do it. Or, you might have sought advice from an expert tile installer. Today, you can google "tile installation" and have immediate access to blogs, instructional videos, product information, patterns, photos, and step-by-step instructions, often curated by generative artificial intelligence (GAI).

Adults' ability to access information has facilitated learning in a significant way: It is just-in-time, relevant, and self-directed. It can also be overwhelming, inaccurate, and misguided. The Digital Age is a shift from the Industrial Age, where information and manipulation have replaced manual labor and manufacturing. With the emergence of the Digital Age, new challenges have come: training and recruiting knowledge workers, bridging cultural and economic divides created by increased mobility, and addressing cultural conflict and misunderstanding (Bennett & Bell, 2010). The implications of using technology in adult learning in formal, informal, and non-formal settings impact our professional and personal lives (Billett, 2018). We live in a world where technology is present in all elements of adult activities (Poquet & De Laat, 2021).

Adults live in a world where it is difficult to "unplug" from being constantly tethered to devices such as smartphones, email and social media accounts, social networking pages, and blogs linking to information. This "plugged-in" life has created an environment that permeates all others: "Technology is not just a device useful as a tool. Rather, technology has infused every aspect of society to essentially change the thought process in learning" (Parker, 2013, p. 55). Box 14.2 highlights the demography of adults' digitized lives. Later, the chapter explores how being connected to adult learners renews the demand for eLearning and troubles issues of access created by the Digital Divide.

 ## Box 14.2 Adult Learning by the Numbers

The Connected Adult Learner

This box provides key information about the global spread of technology and Internet access. As a reader and an adult educator, this data encourages you to reflect on how these advancements transform adult learning. It also prompts you to consider the challenges and limitations of integrating these tools into education.

Internet Usage

- More than 66% of all the people on Earth now use the Internet, with the latest data putting global users at 5.35 billion. Internet users have grown by 1.8% over the past 12 months, thanks to 97 million new users since the start of 2023. But despite these impressive figures, more than 2.7 billion people remain offline worldwide, with India alone home to more than 680 million of the world's "unconnected." Nine countries still contend with Internet saturation rates below 20%, while 54 countries and territories out of 233 where data exist suffer from Internet saturation rates below 50% (Kemp, 2024).
- Today, typical Internet users spend 6 hours and 40 minutes online daily. At the upper end of the scale, South Africans still spend the greatest amount of time online, with the typical user reporting an average of 9 hours and 24 minutes daily using the Internet. Japanese people report spending an average of less than 4 hours per day using the Internet, over an hour *less* than any other nation in GWI's survey (Kemp, 2024).

Social Media Usage

- Active social media users' identities have passed the 5 billion mark, with the latest user figure equivalent to 62.3% of the world's population. The global total has increased by 5.6%, meaning the world averaged 8.4 new social media users per second over the past year. The adoption rate accelerated further in the last three months of 2023, reaching an average of 9.4 new users every second (Kemp, 2024).

- Countries along the Persian Gulf's western edge see the highest ratio of social media users to population. On the other hand, North Korea still suffers from the lowest levels of social media adoption in the world, probably because the country's government continues to impose a total digital blockade that prevents the country's citizens from accessing the Internet (Kemp, 2024).

- People worldwide spend a considerable amount of *time* using social media. The "typical" social media user spends 2 hours and 23 minutes daily using social media. Social media remains the most popular connected pastime, with more than 97% of working-age Internet users accessing social networks or messaging platforms monthly. Across all ages, chat and messaging apps are the slightly more popular choice, with 94.7% of all Internet users aged 16–64 reported using at least one of these platforms in the past 30 days. Social networks lag slightly, with 94.3% of the same cohort saying they have used at least one of these services in the past month. Search engines rank third, with just over 4 in 5 survey respondents (80.7%) using services like Google and Bing monthly (Kemp, 2024).

Policies for Digitalization and COVID-19 as an Academic Accelerating Effect

Not surprisingly, the intersection of education and technology has garnered growing political interest and remains central to discussions and initiatives. In educational contexts, technology functions as a cognitive partner that supports the activation of complex cognitive processes (Angeli & Valanides, 2015). Beyond increasing classroom productivity and updating pedagogical paradigms, technology has proven effective in delivering high-quality education in underserved areas such as rural regions or developing countries (Bianchi et al., 2022).

The National Educational Technology Plan (NETP), first introduced in 1996, is the federal blueprint for leveraging technology in education. The plan is updated periodically, with the 2024 iteration emphasizing bridging digital divides in access, design, and use that hinder equitable educational outcomes. The plan provides actionable strategies for improving access to devices and connectivity, investing in educator training, and fostering innovative pedagogies through technology. By aligning national goals with actionable recommendations for state and institutional adoption, the NETP underscored the importance of technology in enhancing student learning experiences (OECD, 2023a; US Department of Education, 2024).

The Office of Educational Technology (OET) serves as the federal agency overseeing the strategic implementation of digital tools in education. Its initiatives emphasize research-backed approaches to technology integration, professional development for educators, and ensuring equity in access. By promoting inclusive policies, the OET strives to level the playing field for students from diverse socioeconomic backgrounds, facilitating widespread adoption of effective digital learning practices (OECD, 2023a, US Department of Education, 2021).

Higher education institutions are vital in translating federal goals into localized action. Institutional policies often focus on:

- Creating Inclusive Digital Learning Environments: Universities aim to design courses and platforms that accommodate diverse learners, including people with disabilities.
- Equipping Faculty for Digital Instruction: Professional development programs ensure educators can effectively incorporate technology into teaching.
- Data Governance and Analytics: Institutions prioritize safeguarding student data while leveraging analytics for improved decision-making (Tandet, 2024).

The federal Digital Government Strategy (2021) aligns closely with the goals of educational digitization, focusing on enhancing transparency, innovation, and accessibility in public services. The COVID-19 pandemic significantly accelerated digitization efforts within higher education. Institutions rapidly adopted online learning platforms and hybrid models to ensure continuity of education during lockdowns. In response, federal initiatives have increasingly prioritized funding for digital infrastructure improvements, such as broadband access and student device provision (OECD, 2023a; Tandet, 2024; US Department of Education, 2024).

Also, the European Union has actively promoted the digitalization of higher education institutions for several decades. At the start of the 2000s, the European Commission began developing policies and initiatives to enhance the use of digital technologies in education and training. The Life-long Learning Memorandum recognized the growing impact of technology on citizens' lives, including its role in transforming how people learn, and emphasized informal learning (Commission of the European Communi-ties, 2000). This document also acknowledged the economic, cultural, and social changes characterizing knowledge-era countries. It highlighted the need to ensure universal access to new skills and competencies, including information technology, to promote active societal participation. The European Higher Education Area (EHEA), a pan-European initiative that fosters cooperation and harmonization in higher education policies, has encouraged the adoption of digital technologies in learning and teaching since the early 2000s. It also supports e-learning and open learning as cross-cutting functions of its objectives.

The potential of technologies in education and research were priorities under Horizon 2020 (2014–2020), the EU's research and innovation program, which included support for the digitalization of higher education. The program funded projects and initiatives to leverage digital technologies to improve learn-ing, develop new digital tools and resources, and promote accessibility and inclusion in higher education.

In 2018, the European Commission issued the "Communication on Build-ing a European Education Area," aimed at creating a more effective and effi-cient education system in Europe through digital technologies (European Commission, 2018a). Highlighting that technology adoption in education lagged behind technological advancements, the European Commission launched the Digital Education Action Plan, focusing on three priorities: improving the use of digital technology in teaching and learning, developing digital skills for digital transformation, and enhancing education through better data analysis and foresight (European Commission, 2018b).

The year 2020 saw a renewal of the Digital Education Action Plan for 2021–2027. Acknowledging the digital divide, particularly between rural and urban areas, and the acceleration of digitalization brought about by the COVID-19 pandemic, the plan emphasized the potential of digital technolo-gies in promoting high-quality education and the need to move beyond the physical classroom (European Commission, 2020).

These efforts also align with the EU's Digital Compass 2030 and the Digital Europe Program, aimed at fostering societal digitalization. Other initiatives, such as DIGI-HE (2020–2022), the European Open Science Cloud (EOSC), and the BLOOM Hub, continue to support the digital transformation of higher education by promoting best practices, fostering open access to data, and devel-oping resources for blended and online learning.

Digital Literacy in Teaching and Learning Environments

Although promoting the digital transformation of education and training systems, enhancing digital skills, and online learning are the priorities of recent policies, some researchers believe that little guidance is available to higher education institutions regarding developing digital competencies. Ilomäki et al. (2016) explained:

> It is generally assumed that the basic competences that are important for every citizen, including digital competence, should be acquired at school. In vocational education, work-related competences are more specific, including particular competences for using technologies, although policy papers seldom focus on this level. Higher education is less bound by policy regulations, and it is often more independent from the national authorities. Digital competence is not a central topic of the curriculum at this level. It appears, furthermore, that the school level is the main object for policymakers when it comes to learning and teaching digital competence. (p. 657)

Tømte et al. (2019) also reported a lack of policies and strategies in higher education related to technological infrastructure development and curricular re-organization toward online learning adoption. As a result, teachers have basic digital skills. Although students are digital natives and know how to use technological devices quite easily, many cannot use them properly, manage the amount of information they can access, and create knowledge independently (León-Pérez et al., 2020). Moreover, other studies see students as self-learners in digital literacy, primarily developing competencies outside formal educational settings (Cappuccio, 2015; Liotino et al., 2023). In addition, as reported by Liotino et al. (2023), there is confusion about definitions and terms related to digital competencies, skills, and digital literacy.

We, the authors of this book, use the term **digital skills** to refer to the practical and technical actions involved in using digital tools and devices, considering them as sub-elements of digital competence (Ilomäki et al., 2016). Van Laar et al. (2020) conducted a study based on a literature review to define the 21st-century digital skills essential for workers. Their research identified six key digital skills: information skills, communication skills, collaboration skills, critical thinking skills, creative skills, and problem-solving skills (Van Laar et al., 2020, p. 3). These skills are crucial for professionals to effectively engage with software and digital devices in their work environments. Given the rapid evolution of technology, digital skills require continuous updating. As new tools and devices emerge, professionals must adapt and expand their competencies to remain effective.

The term **digital competencies** merges with the definition used by the *Digital Competence Framework for Citizens of the European Commission,* considering them "as the confident, critical and creative use of ICT to achieve goals related to work, employability, learning, leisure, inclusion and/or participation in society" (Vuorikari et al., 2022, p. 2). **Digital literacy** is a set of competencies ranging from cognition to practice to reflection that come into play when humans use technology (Gilster, 1997). Further expanding this definition, Martin (2008) described digital literacy as a higher level of digital competencies, the result of using technology contextualized to the professional or disciplinary sphere, and digital transformation through innovation and creativity.

In teaching-learning environments, **technology-enhanced learning** (TEL) employs digital technologies to support, enhance, and improve learning (European Commission, 2018a), including assessment, tutoring, and teaching processes (UNESCO, 2016). TEL might include the use of digital tools on the web, on computers, and/or in virtual classrooms, such as learning platforms, educational games, videos, e-books, and other means to make learning more engaging, collaborative, personalized, and accessible (Jisc, 2017, UNESCO, 2016). Other terms used synonymously are **e-learning** or **digital learning,** which use technology to improve educational processes (UNESCO, 2016).

A key step in the process of implementing digital learning environments is to provide space for reflection on users' needs, which is why initiatives that encourage the co-construction of such contexts seem to be more successful (Aydin et al., 2024; Laurillard et al., 2009). Indeed, the incorporation of partially finished artifacts within a community adapts them to the interests and needs of the community, the artifact thus becoming the result of a process of participation and negotiation between those who develop it and those who use it (Laurillard et al., 2009; McQueen et al., 2024). As Wenger (1999) confirmed, when introducing a new artifact into a group, it must go through a meaning-making process before integrating it into practice.

Laurillard et al. (2009) advocated a holistic, systemic approach to TEL adoption. Key considerations include understanding the professional context, which shapes curriculum, pedagogy, and assessment. Consistency between educators' values and innovations is crucial, allowing time for reflection on teaching beliefs. Co-developing TEL products fosters ownership and highlights researcher-user collaboration. Effective TEL use requires supporting teachers in shifting from institutional models toward radical change. Finally, educators should collaborate in designing technology-integrated lessons or activities (Laurillard et al., 2009). The previously referenced TDC-S study revealed that teachers with robust digital competencies are better equipped to innovate curricula and foster student engagement, particularly when institutional support prioritizes continuous professional development (Aydin et al., 2024).

The COVID-19 pandemic exponentially accelerated the digitization of teaching-learning processes and teachers' and students' acquisition of digital skills (Bolisani et al., 2020; Liotino et al., 2023). The pandemic stimulated the abrupt and unexpected introduction of digital teaching, and in some cases, educators did not even have time to redesign teaching-learning activities (Ulla & Perales, 2022). Since then, blended and hybrid learning has gained increasing attention. **Blended learning** is "a thoughtful integration of classroom face-to-face learning experiences with online learning experiences" (Garrison & Kanuka, 2004, p. 96). **Hybrid learning** is:

> An approach to teaching that not only integrates technology in the teaching process but also combines students who are inside a physical classroom and students from online. In other words, hybrid teaching is synchronous teaching of students in the classroom and online using an online platform. (Ulla & Perales, 2022, p. 2)

Teachers must relate the pedagogical affordances of technologies to their own pedagogical and disciplinary approaches to realize a specific form of professional digital competence so that technologies are effectively integrated into teaching practice (Angeli & Valanides, 2015; Starkey, 2020). Some scholars have identified **professional digital competence** as the highest level (Redecker, 2017; Starkey, 2020). It includes technological competence, pedagogical compatibility of technologies, and social awareness. Most importantly, **social awareness** refers to the teacher's ability to interact in the context of digitized education at a systemic level (Starkey, 2020) and encompasses a complex set of skills and knowledge that includes using technologies for teaching, critically evaluating instructional decisions with technologies, and designing and implementing pathways for digital learners. These three aspects are complemented by managing digitized, face-to-face, and online learning environments, contextualizing one's teaching role using data management/monitoring and analysis systems, and participating in professional digital communities (Starkey, 2020).

Adult Education in the Time of Generative Artificial Intelligence

When generative artificial intelligence (GAI) tools first appeared, education focused on upgrading institutional technology and developing digital skills. However, artificial intelligence (AI) has since transformed educational contexts and practices, reshaping teaching, learning, administration, and research. One of the most significant impacts of AI has been on teaching and learning. By enabling personalized education, AI allows tailoring instructional methods to individual students' needs. Tools like adaptive learning platforms and intelligent tutoring systems adjust content based on a student's progress and performance, creating a more customized learning experience (Al-Zahrani & Alasmari, 2024; Slimi, 2023).

Furthermore, AI has enhanced student engagement through chatbots and virtual assistants, which provide immediate feedback and support. This responsiveness has enriched the learning process and made it more interactive (Al-Zahrani & Alasmari, 2024; Slimi, 2023). On the administrative side, AI automates routine tasks such as grading and managing enrollments. This automation saves time and allows educators to devote more attention to teaching and mentoring students (Al-Zahrani & Alasmari, 2024; Slimi, 2023). Additionally, AI has revolutionized assessments by introducing tools that evaluate the originality and quality of student submissions while offering detailed feedback. These innovations streamline the grading process and enhance student learning (Lee et al., 2024; Slimi, 2023).

Despite these benefits, the introduction of AI has also brought significant challenges. The widespread use of generative AI tools has raised concerns about plagiarism and the authenticity of student work, creating new dilemmas for academic integrity. Institutions are now grappling with managing these issues while leveraging AI's advantages (Butson & Spronken-Smith, 2024; Lee et al., 2024). Additionally, there is an ongoing concern about equity in education. The digital divide means not all students have equal access to AI technologies, and without careful planning, this disparity could worsen existing educational inequalities (Butson & Spronken-Smith, 2024; Lee et al., 2024).

Looking to the future, researchers emphasize the need for higher education institutions to integrate AI more comprehensively into their curricula. Doing so will prepare students for a workforce where AI is becoming increasingly important (Lee et al., 2024; Slimi, 2023). Equally crucial is the development of AI literacy among educators, students, and administrators. Understanding the technical capabilities of AI and its ethical implications is essential for making informed decisions about its use in education (Al-Zahrani & Alasmari, 2024; Slimi, 2023).

The advancement of AI is significantly transforming the workplace, influencing how individuals experience their professional environments and daily lives (Poquet & de Laat, 2021). Workplaces increasingly adopt digital technologies to enhance learning, streamline operations, and improve performance (Ng & Poquet, 2020). In this context, lifelong learning must evolve to integrate AI and emerging technologies into professional development pathways, ensuring that workers and employees can adapt and grow alongside these advancements.

Designing Online Pedagogy

Designing online pedagogy for adults requires specific knowledge of adult learning principles, theories, and practices and new teaching and learning techniques to develop and maintain learner engagement. The instructor usually acts as a guide who can provide presence and availability during the learning process (Bloomberg, 2021). The offer of online courses has tremendously increased, and educators have to be prepared for these innovative teaching methods and understand when and how to apply online teaching strategies. Educators must establish their presence in the online context, promote learning using online strategies, engage students, and promote interaction and participation (Archambault et al., 2022). Box 14.3 summarizes a helpful framework for online instructors.

 Box 14.3 SoTL: The Scholarship of Teaching and Learning

Five Pillars of Online Pedagogy

The Five Pillars of Online Pedagogy (Archambault et al., 2022)

This box outlines the five key pillars of effective online teaching, providing educators with strategies to enhance learner engagement and understanding.

1. **Incorporate Active Learning**

   Effective adult learning is an active, dynamic process. Instructors should engage learners through interactive strategies like simulations, problem-solving activities, inquiry-based learning, and real-world tasks. These methods capture attention and encourage hands-on participation, fostering a more profound understanding.

2. **Build Relationships and Learning Community**

   Learning thrives on collaboration. Educators can enhance engagement and support by creating opportunities for meaningful connections—both formal

---

and informal. Activities encouraging sharing, collaboration, and teamwork help learners build strong relationships, foster a sense of belonging, and develop peer support networks. This sense of community empowers learners to form a shared identity and work effectively in groups.

3. **Leverage Learner Agency**

    Learning is not just about acquiring facts—it is a transformative process that shapes beliefs, practices, and personal identity. Educators should promote autonomy by encouraging self-directed learning, giving learners control over their goals, and nurturing engagement in communities of practice where learning evolves organically.

4. **Embrace Mastery Learning**

    Mastery learning focuses on achieving a deep, thorough understanding of the subject. Educators can guide learners to develop skills that allow for upskilling and reskilling while emphasizing the application of knowledge in real-world contexts. This approach helps learners connect theoretical concepts to practical, professional use.

5. **Personalize the Learning Journey**

    Learning is most effective when tailored to the individual. Educators should build on learners' prior experiences and knowledge, adapting instruction to meet their unique needs. This personalized approach enables learners to construct new knowledge meaningfully, with applications that extend to academic and professional settings.

By integrating these five pillars—active learning, community building, learner agency, mastery learning, and personalization—educators can create online learning experiences that are engaging, supportive, and impactful. These principles enhance learning outcomes and empower learners to thrive in educational and professional environments.

Engaging, well-sequenced learning with ongoing feedback is key to effective online learning. Incorporating active learning in online design is one of the keys to success (Archambault et al., 2022). Facilitating effective online learning involves building good relationships between the educator and the learner and among the learners as a learning community that has healthy levels of cognitive, social, and teaching presence (Archambault et al., 2022; Stavredes, 2011). Developing and cultivating an online presence is fundamental for learning. It is based on the educator's ability to interact and connect online with the learners, encouraging them to become a learning community (Kaufmann & Vallade, 2020).

Social presence is the capacity for learners to develop interpersonal relationships that support engaged learning. Teaching presence is the instructor's capacity to support learners' cognitive and social presence. Promoting an active learning experience online is the key to engaging learners cognitively and socially. Throughout this book, we, the authors, have offered strategies to involve learners, and Chapter 15 is devoted to active learning. Activities that promote critical reflection and thinking are particularly effective in facilitating online learning. These strategies allow adult learners to engage with their workplaces and communities through service learning activities.

Creating Online Learning Communities

Recent research highlights the importance of collaborative tools and regular interaction in fostering online learning communities. For instance, utilizing platforms like Google Workspace or Microsoft Teams enhances real-time collaboration among students, mitigating communication delays and fostering a sense of belonging (Lindsay-Finan, 2024). Furthermore, regular interaction through synchronous activities such as live webinars or virtual office hours significantly improves student engagement and satisfaction in online courses (Huang et al., 2023; Lindsay-Finan, 2024).

The significance of inclusivity is echoed in contemporary literature, emphasizing the need for accessible course materials and accommodating diverse learning styles within online environments (Eden et al., 2024; Evanick, 2023). Creating supportive spaces where all learners feel valued is crucial for fostering collaboration and mutual respect among participants. Moreover, integrating collaborative learning activities such as group projects can enhance engagement by allowing students to share resources and learn from one another (Huang et al., 2023; Lindsay-Finan, 2024).

Developing a strong learning community starts with teaching learners the principles of dialogical conversation—how to actively listen and engage in discussions, even when faced with differing viewpoints. Establishing clear guidelines for small group interactions and class processes is vital to building a supportive and collaborative environment.

Dr. Bob Hill (personal communication) has designed an innovative approach called "Reading Circles," where small student groups create their own "safe talking guidelines." Within these circles, students rotate roles such as discussion director, reading passage master, illustrator, vocabulary builder, creative connector, question collector, process checker, devil's advocate, and even a humorous, reflective role called the freeloader. The groups discuss responses to pre-assigned questions, recording their thoughts and insights in "Reading Circle Portfolios." This approach encourages collaborative learning while respecting individual contributions. At the start of the semester, students complete an active listening inventory to assess their listening skills. They learn the importance of having their assumptions challenged and practice techniques for bringing conversations to a respectful and non-coercive close. These strategies help foster deeper engagement while creating a sense of belonging and mutual respect within the learning community.

Collaborative learning activities build community and are good adult education practices. Opportunities for small group and one-on-one peer learning activities also help promote community development and deepen learning. Using **peer feedback** mechanisms such as peer reviews fosters accountability among learners while enhancing their understanding of course material (Eden et al., 2024; Huang et al., 2023). Establishing shared goals within these communities is also essential; clearly defined objectives help align learners' efforts toward collective achievements.

Developing a sense of community in cyberspace requires a multifaceted approach encompassing educators' active facilitation, inclusive instructional design principles, collaborative tools for interaction, and opportunities for meaningful peer engagement. By integrating these strategies into online courses, educators can create vibrant learning communities that enhance educational outcomes and foster a sense of belonging among diverse learners (Abedini et al., 2021; Jesionkowska, 2020; Pesare et al., 2017). The following paragraphs briefly describe technological media widely used today as applied to learning.

Web 3.0

The third generation of the World Wide Web (WWW), often called Web 3.0 or Web3, is the next generation of the Internet. It began gaining traction in 2015, with significant contributions from figures like Gavin Wood, co-founder of Ethereum. Although **"Semantic Web"** was originally coined by Tim Berners-Lee et al. (2001), it has evolved to encompass broader ideas about decentralization and user empowerment in the digital space. While elements of Web 3.0 have been emerging since then, it remains largely in development today (Chirag, 2024; Essex et al., 2023). Key features of Web 3.0 are:

- **Decentralization:** Unlike Web 2.0, which relies on centralized servers and databases, Web 3.0 uses decentralized networks to store and manage data.

This shift lets users maintain data ownership and engage in peer-to-peer transactions without intermediaries.

- **Semantic Web:** This aspect improves how machines understand and process information, enabling more intelligent search results and interactions based on context rather than just keywords.
- **Artificial Intelligence:** AI plays a significant role in Web 3.0 by enhancing the ability of applications to learn from user behavior and provide personalized experiences.
- **Blockchain Technology:** This technology underpins the decentralization of data, ensuring security and transparency through distributed ledgers.
- **Ubiquitous Connectivity:** Web 3.0 aims for seamless access across devices, allowing users to interact with applications anytime and anywhere.
- **3D Graphics:** Enhanced visual experiences are integrated into applications, making them more engaging and immersive (Burdova, 2024; Essex et al., 2023).

While Web 2.0 focuses on user interaction and content creation within a centralized framework, Web 3.0 emphasizes decentralization, user control over data, and intelligent interactions facilitated by advanced technologies like AI and blockchain (Geroni, 2023; Jha, 2024; Sutherland, 2024).

Social Media

Social media are web-based Internet sites that support social exchanges, including Facebook, Twitter (officially known as X since 2023), and YouTube; these three media alone have attracted over five billion people worldwide, and the numbers will continue increasing (Statista, 2020). Social media are undergoing a process of transformation in terms of the number of users, changing the landscape of education as well (Barrot, 2021; Chugh & Ruhi, 2018). Barrot (2021) conducted a literature review of 2,215 Scopus-indexed journal articles on social media in education from 2007 to 2019. Research output grew significantly, with North America (39.59%) leading, followed by Asia (24.20%) and Europe (23.88%). Australia and Oceania (8.80%), Africa (2.57%), and South America (0.95%) contributed less. Journal articles dominated (95.67%), and higher education was the primary research setting (85%), with fewer studies on secondary (9%) and primary/professional education (6%). The study highlights the expansion of social media research in education and its uneven global distribution.

Social media potentially support the creation and sharing of information and may improve learner dialogue and collaboration, informal learning, and community building. Many educators eschew social media as something they have no desire to use or time to learn. Yet, the reality is that educators must become literate with technology and multiple means of reaching learners, including social media. Chugh and Ruhi (2019) asserted, "Technology has facilitated the rediscovery of traditional teaching methods, by incorporating pedagogically useful futures in multidimensional environment . . . a dominant social interaction technology that has a plethora of uses" (p. 1). Statista (2017) argued that people spend 188 minutes daily using social media; 90% of college students worldwide report using social media as an academic resource, and 85% of higher education institutions use it for academic and professional purposes (Khaled, 2024).

Educators cannot avoid using social media for educational purposes: "By committing to be a social media participant, you will be better able to understand the media characteristics and pedagogical potential in the classroom" (Joosten, 2012, p. 16). Recent studies confirm that social media can create a more engaging, interactive, and student-centered learning environment, transforming static teaching into dynamic, participatory education (Alles, 2023; Hortigüela-Alcalá et al., 2019; Manca, 2020). Moreover, these platforms facilitate access to a wealth of resources and information that can enrich the learning experience (Mirza, 2024).

Although some educators may hesitate to embrace social media due to concerns about distractions or privacy issues, its potential to enhance education and learning deserves educators' attention. Educators can foster a more connected and engaged learning environment that reflects contemporary student behaviors and preferences by integrating social media thoughtfully into teaching strategies—whether through communication platforms like Facebook and Twitter or collaborative tools like wikis. The challenge lies not in resisting these tools but in harnessing their power responsibly to enrich educational experiences.

Social Video Sites, Social Sharing, and Social Bookmarking

Social media takes various forms, including video-sharing sites, wikis, photo-sharing platforms, and social bookmarking tools, which enable users to connect and share content (Chugh & Ruhi, 2019). Social bookmarking tools, such as Diigo, Delicious, and Google Bookmarks, enable users to collect, save, and share links to articles, news, or web pages in one centralized location; those tools provide educators and students with opportunities to manage resources related to course content easily.

Social media fosters valuable connections between students and teachers, enhancing teaching and learning experiences while improving student performance in higher education (Balakrishnan et al., 2017; Chugh & Ruhi, 2018).

A vast range of educational videos is available on nearly any topic, making learning more engaging. Flickr, for example, allows users to curate and organize images and videos, which are shareable via a simple URL. Educators can also assign students to search for specific images or videos to support their learning. Many learning management systems also integrate bookmarking features, allowing students and instructors to efficiently store and access relevant resources (Hölterhof & Heinen, 2014; Scerbakov et al., 2018).

Learning Networks

Learning networks are a subset of social media, as described above. Informal learning networks play a fundamental role in society, serving as dynamic systems that support knowledge exchange and adaptation (Van Dijk, 2020). These networks transcend specific environments, distinguishing them from formal learning networks operating in designated educational settings (Richter et al., 2011). Some of these learning networks arose during COVID-19 to facilitate the exchange of challenges among people facing similar work difficulties. A study by Rehm et al. (2020) highlighted the role of a learning network among school leaders. At that time, they could share information and provide insights into their challenges with students, teachers, and families. Informal learning networks are highly flexible, collaborative, and responsive, making them an invaluable resource for school leaders and educators, especially in rapidly changing educational landscapes (Rehm et al., 2020).

Flipped Classroom

The **flipped classroom** has gained significant traction recently, particularly during and after the COVID-19 pandemic. While there is no single definition, Garner and Shank (2024) noted in their literature review that there is general agreement on key techniques used in this approach. These include providing students with learning materials in advance and using classroom time for discussions, group work, and other interactive activities.

The flipped classroom is a student-centered method that fosters greater ownership of learning. In this model, the instructor acts as a facilitator, guiding students, supporting their learning process in the classroom, and preparing necessary materials and resources (Garner & Shank, 2024). Numerous studies have demonstrated that the flipped classroom enhances **learning outcomes,** increases **student engagement,** and fosters higher motivation to learn (Akçayır & Akçayır, 2018; Green, 2015; Shi et al., 2020).

Podcasting

Podcasts are audio recordings of lecture material accessible online and downloadable onto mobile devices or computers. They are increasingly recognized as valuable learning resources, with studies showing students' favorable attitudes toward podcast use in learning, appreciating their flexibility and accessibility as effective supplements to traditional teaching methods (Gunderson & Cumming, 2023). These qualities enhance engagement and comprehension, making podcasts useful in higher education.

Gunderson and Cumming (2023) conducted a study exploring how educators integrate audio podcasting into teaching using the principles of universal design. Their findings suggest that this approach fosters a more inclusive learning environment, particularly benefiting students with disabilities. From their literature review, several key benefits of podcasts in education emerged. For example, using podcasts as summative assessments (Forbes & Khoo, 2015; Powel & Robson, 2014) improves both teaching and learning (Bamanger & Alhassan, 2015) and serves as supplementary instructional tools across various learning environments (Muller & Wergin, 2014).

Massive Open Online Courses (MOOCs)

"Massive open online courses are one of the important outputs of connectivism," and there have been several generations more and less related to the main learning theories (Mattar, 2018, p. 210). The first-generation MOOCs or cMOOCs emphasized the integration between "connectivity of social networking, the facilitation of an acknowledged expert in a field of study, and a collection of freely accessible online resources" (McAuley, 2010, p. 4) and consist in creating and sharing resources among the participants in the network (Apoki, & Crisan, 2019; García-Peñalvo et al., 2018; Mattar, 2018). Later, xMOOCs emerged, whereby teachers generate and organize activities in modules to be completed by the learners in a platform according to behaviorism principles (Apoki & Crisan, 2019; García-Peñalvo et al., 2018).

Another model combines the principles of constructivism and connectivism: the hMOOC (García-Peñalvo et al., 2018). Specifically, MOOCs designed according to constructivism principles (Lave & Wenger, 1991; Mattar, 2018; Peck et al., 1999) offer opportunities for cooperative learning (Johnson & Johnson, 2008) through a collection of activities (e.g., online forums, group works to carry out projects, case analysis and panel discussions, peer assessment activities, dedicated spaces for questions and answers) (Abeer & Miri, 2014; Chen, 2016).

Support agents are usually involved in stimulating participant collaboration and interaction (Apoki & Crisan, 2019) to create communities of inquiry (Kaul et al., 2018; Kovanović et al., 2018). This kind of MOOC promotes active learning (Bonwell & Eison, 1991; Fedeli & Bierema, 2019; Prince, 2004) by supporting learning through ongoing quizzes and real-life learning applications (Bali, 2014). Previously mentioned activities advocate giving prompt feedback to learners (Bali, 2014; Chen, 2016). Moreover, they provide various resources to "address the diversity of learners" (Bali, 2014, p. 49). Following the same intent, they allow integration through group or individual offline activities (Chen, 2016), equip learners with short videos and summaries related to the content of the course (Apoki & Crisan, 2019; Chen, 2016), and analyze learners' behaviors and preferences to create personalized quizzes (Apoki & Crisan, 2019). There has been growing international interest in using MOOCs in blended curricula (Bralić & Divjak, 2018; Kloos et al., 2015). Indeed, MOOCs harness the potential of blended learning, combining the mainly online content and activities of the MOOC with face-to-face classroom learning (Deng et al., 2017; Fedeli et al., 2022).

Effectiveness of Online Learning

Online learning has demonstrated sustained effectiveness in higher education, particularly when leveraging structured collaboration and learner-centered design. A systematic review by Meng et al. (2024) confirmed its efficacy across diverse learner demographics, emphasizing its adaptability for adult education through asynchronous formats and blended models that balance professional and academic commitments. For instance, courses integrating collaborative tasks—such as problem-based learning or instructor-facilitated discussions—yielded superior outcomes compared to purely self-directed approaches. A 2024 study of 298 undergraduate students revealed that structured group activities in asynchronous environments enhanced cognitive engagement and relational interaction quality, correlating with higher self-reported learning gains and satisfaction (Bach & Thiel, 2024). Also, collaborative e-learning strategies improve critical thinking by 25% compared to traditional methods (Bach & Thiel, 2024).

The role of **learner agency** in online environments is pivotal. Allowing students to control media interactions fosters self-monitoring and reflection, as learning analytics research shows that timely feedback based on behavioral data improves metacognitive skills (Meng et al., 2024). However, success in self-directed learning (SDL) depends on institutional scaffolding. A 2024 MOOC analysis highlighted that SDL thrives when paired with cooperative strategies and formative assessments rather than unstructured independence (Bach & Thiel, 2024).

Social connectedness remains a cornerstone of retention. Learners who perceive strong peer and instructor rapport are 30% more likely to persist, as collaborative environments foster accountability and reduce isolation (Bach & Thiel, 2024; Nepal et al., 2024). As with adults in traditional classrooms, online learners face similar challenges in their participation. Hachey et al. (2023) highlighted that learners who feel connected to their peers and instructors are likelier to persist in their courses.

Team-based learning (TBL) models exemplify persistence, where structured peer interactions—whether online or in-person—enhance academic performance by promoting active engagement and personalized feedback (Bach & Thiel, 2024). For example, the study on team-based learning (TBL) from Shen et al. (2024) revealed that online and in-class TBL methodologies resulted in superior academic performance compared to traditional methods, emphasizing the importance of structured interaction and engagement in learning. Moreover, the study underscored that learner control over media interactions fosters reflection, activity, and self-monitoring—critical components of effective adult education practice. However, it also noted that one-on-one feedback is more effective than group-level guidance, reinforcing the need for personalized support in online learning environments (Pan et al., 2024; The US Department of Education, 2021).

Factors influencing persistence include demographic variables such as age and gender and essential skills like computer literacy, time management, and effective communication (Ho & Phan, 2024; Shaikh & Asif, 2022). External constraints—such as financial pressures and family obligations—also play a critical role in learners' ability to remain enrolled (Nepal et al., 2024; Shaikh & Asif, 2022). Box 14.4 synthesizes what the scientific literature reports as the advantages of online learning.

We, the authors of this book, do not want to convince everyone to use these teaching and learning tools but rather to stimulate reflection on the appropriateness of the medium for achieving teaching and learning objectives. Teachers and learners should scrutinize the strengths and limitations of their learning tools and strategies. Indeed, the following section explores challenges and constraints from the literature.

Box 14.4 SoTL: The Scholarship of Teaching and Learning

Advantages of Online Learning in Adult Education

Expanding on what is already shared by Instructional Design Australia (2024), this box contains summaries of available studies on the advantages of e-learning in adult education. Indeed, eLearning plays a pivotal role in adult education by offering flexibility, diverse resources, personalized experiences, enhanced engagement, and cost efficiency. As the landscape of education continues to evolve with technological advancements, these advantages position eLearning as a vital component in supporting adult learners' educational journeys.

Flexibility and Convenience: eLearning enables adult learners to access materials and participate in asynchronous activities, accommodating irregular schedules and geographic constraints. Studies demonstrate that this adaptability is critical for adults balancing work, caregiving, and education, as seen in Latvia's rapid adoption of digital tools during the pandemic, which increased participation rates by allowing learners from rural and international regions to engage (Jekabsone & Gudele, 2023). The 24/7 availability of online platforms further supports self-paced learning, aligning with adult learners' preference for autonomy (Hoon, 2018).

Access to Diverse Resources: eLearning provides adult learners access to an extensive array of resources, including multimedia materials, interactive modules, and online libraries. This rich variety facilitates the exploration of diverse perspectives and engagement with current information. The availability of up-to-date content is particularly beneficial for adult learners seeking to enhance their knowledge in rapidly evolving fields (Laouris & Eteokleous, 2005; Seismic, 2022). Cross-cultural collaboration in online classrooms—such as peer interactions between learners in diverse regions—enriches problem-solving approaches and mirrors globalized workplace dynamics (Hoon, 2018).

Personalized Learning Experience: One of the standout features of eLearning is its ability to provide customized learning experiences. Adaptive technologies and online assessments can evaluate learners' knowledge and deliver targeted feedback tailored to individual needs and preferences. This customization enhances the learning process by allowing adults to focus on areas where they require more support or challenge themselves in areas where they excel (Gibson, 2008; Pipi Learning, 2024). Modular systems further personalize pacing, allowing adults to "stack" micro-credentials over time without rigid deadlines (OECD, 2023b).

Enhanced Engagement and Interactivity: Designing eLearning platforms with interactive features such as discussion forums, multimedia presentations, and simulations significantly enhance learner engagement. These tools foster peer collaboration and promote critical thinking and problem-solving skills essential for adult learners in professional settings (Fullstack Academy, 2024; Tu et al., 2005).

Cost and Time Efficiency: By eliminating physical infrastructure and travel costs, eLearning reduces financial barriers. Institutions in Latvia expanded their reach cost-effectively during the pandemic, attracting learners who previously faced geographic or economic constraints (Jekabsone & Gudele, 2023). Bite-sized, asynchronous modules minimize time away from work, making continuous education feasible for busy professionals (OECD, 2023b).

Challenging Aspects of Online Learning

Although online learning has democratized access to education by offering unprecedented flexibility and convenience, it presents unique challenges that require thoughtful intervention. Addressing psychological barriers such as motivation, anxiety, and stress is critical, as is tackling social and instructional limitations like isolation and delayed feedback. Efforts to enhance digital literacy, redesign courses for better engagement, foster meaningful social interactions, and establish robust support systems are vital in creating a more effective and inclusive online learning environment for adult learners. These challenges are technical, psychological, social, and instructional issues.

The **Digital Divide** refers to the differences between those who have access to the Internet and those who do not. As of 2022, approximately 2.7 billion people remain unconnected worldwide, with significant gaps in Internet penetration across different regions (Kemp, 2024; Signé, 2023;). For instance, while Europe boasts an Internet saturation rate of 89%, Africa lags significantly behind at just 40% (Signé, 2023). This divide is not merely a matter of access; it encompasses various dimensions, including digital literacy, affordability, and the availability of infrastructure. In developed countries, vulnerable groups such as low-income individuals, older adults, racial and ethnic minorities, and people with disabilities are particularly affected by these barriers (Raihan et al., 2024). The gender gap in Internet access prevents equitable access. In 2022, an estimated 264 million fewer women than men were accessing the Internet globally, with women being 7% less likely to own a mobile phone and 16% less likely to use mobile Internet than men (Signé, 2023). This gap worsens in regions like sub-Saharan Africa, where nearly 45% fewer women than men have access to the Internet. Significant disparities persist even in rapidly developing economies; for example, in South Asia and the Middle East, nearly 35% fewer women than men are online (Raihan et al., 2024).

This non-use is particularly prevalent among senior citizens, individuals with lower educational attainment, and those living in low-income households, as confirmed by the National Telecommunications and Information Administration (2024). Also, the reasons for remaining offline often relate to the perceived irrelevance of the Internet to their lives; nearly half of non-users cited this as their primary reason for not engaging online (National Telecommunications and Information Administration, 2024).

The digital divide significantly impacts people with disabilities, creating barriers that hinder their access to essential technology and information. Exacerbating this divide are disparities in Internet access and digital literacy, which are critical for full participation in modern society. One of the main challenges faced by people with disabilities is related to the accessibility of technology. Many devices and applications are not designed with accessibility, making it difficult for individuals with physical, sensory, or cognitive disabilities to use them effectively. For instance, websites may lack compatibility with screen readers or may not accommodate users who require alternative input methods due to mobility impairments (Comunicacion Equipo, 2024; Community Tech Network, 2023). Costs can also be barriers: the high cost of assistive technologies and home Internet services presents a significant barrier. Many individuals with disabilities face economic disadvantages, including higher unemployment rates, further limiting their ability to afford necessary technology (Community Tech Network, 2023; Johansson et al., 2020). Moreover, there is often a shortage of training programs tailored specifically for people with disabilities. Support staff may have inadequate preparation to assist individuals in navigating digital tools, which can hinder their ability to gain digital skills (Community Tech Network, 2023; Johansson et al., 2020).

The COVID-19 pandemic further highlighted these disparities as more activities shifted online. While there was a notable increase in first-time Internet users—466 million in 2020 alone—the overall access challenges remain critical. The pandemic underscored how essential digital connectivity is for economic and social participation (Signé, 2023). The urban–rural divide also remains significant; in 2023, urban residents worldwide had an Internet usage rate of 81%, while rural residents lagged at just 50% (Lucidity Insights Research Team, 2024).

Bridging the digital divide remains a pressing global issue that requires coordinated efforts across various sectors. Addressing barriers related to age, income, education, and gender will be crucial for fostering equitable access to digital resources and ensuring that all individuals can participate fully in an increasingly connected world.

Psychological Challenges

One of the primary psychological challenges associated with online learning is the need for heightened motivation and self-regulation. Unlike traditional classroom settings that provide structured schedules and direct supervision, online learning demands self-discipline and intrinsic motivation (Rahmani et al., 2024). Consequently, fostering robust time-management skills becomes essential. As Gay and Betts (2020) observed, such skills are integral to enhancing persistence and ensuring the success of online learning activities. Box 14.5 advises self-motivation in digital learning environments.

 **Box 14.5 Tips and Tools for Teaching and Learning**

Mental Contrasting and Implementation Intentions

This box offers a simple tool to foster self-motivation in online settings. Indeed, Winger (2024) created a mental contrasting and implementation intentions (MCII) exercise for weekly monitoring to foster self-motivation (Table 14.1). Since the practice helps students identify benefits and barriers while creating an action plan, a student is more vested in altruistic reasons for completing the task and prepared for obstacles that may arise, hopefully generating motivation and resulting in higher retention rates.

By integrating the MCII exercise into your practices and classes, educators can cultivate an environment that promotes self-regulation, resilience, and sustained engagement among learners, ultimately leading to better educational outcomes.

The psychological toll of online learning extends beyond motivation, manifesting in increased anxiety and stress. The transition to a virtual learning environment is associated with heightened uncertainty, particularly regarding technology-related issues and the demands of self-directed learning (Fiorini et al., 2022; Winger, 2024).

TABLE 14.1 MENTAL CONTRASTING AND IMPLEMENTATION INTENTIONS (MCII) EXERCISE AS PROPOSED BY WINGER (2024)

Mental contrasting and implementation intentions exercise
Week 1 Objective
Benefits
Barriers
Action Plan

For many students, the home environment—intended to serve as a learning space—introduces additional complications. Competing responsibilities, household distractions, and blurring personal and academic boundaries exacerbate stress levels, often impeding effective study routines (Fiorini et al., 2022).

Social Challenges

The lack of direct, in-person interaction is another significant hurdle in online education. While virtual platforms allow for communication, they often fail to replicate the immediacy and depth of face-to-face exchanges. This absence can weaken the formation of social connections between students and instructors—connections vital for fostering motivation, engagement, and a sense of belonging (Rosenberg, 2001; Winger, 2024). The isolation inherent in many online learning experiences may leave learners feeling disconnected, undermining their overall satisfaction and commitment to the educational process.

Compounding this issue are the family responsibilities many adult learners must navigate, with women frequently facing disproportionate caregiving burdens. These dual roles of student and caregiver can make it particularly challenging for learners to allocate adequate time and attention to their studies (Fiorini et al., 2022; Winger, 2024). For some, this juggling act creates an overwhelming sense of pressure, which diminishes their ability to engage with coursework and may lead to burnout.

Instructional Challenges

The instructional aspects of online learning are not without their limitations, particularly regarding feedback mechanisms. Unlike in-person environments, where students can seek clarification and receive immediate responses, online platforms often introduce delays in communication. Feedback from instructors may lack the timeliness or personalization needed to address learners' doubts effectively, potentially impairing their understanding of course material and hindering progress (Cho & Heron, 2015; Winger, 2024). These limitations highlight the importance of refining online pedagogical strategies to ensure learners feel adequately supported. The following box contains reflective activities and offers a chance to pause and analyze the practices already implemented in your online teaching activities. Box 14.6 summarizes incremental online teaching practices that are easy to implement.

Box 14.6 Reflective Practice

Inventory of Small Online Teaching Practices

The *Inventory of Small Online Teaching Practices* is a detailed guide for evaluating and enhancing online teaching strategies, developed by Bierema (2021) and based on Darby and Lang's (2019) *Small Online Teaching*. It includes nine categories focusing on specific teaching practices to support effective online education:

1. **Designing for Learning:** Encourages backward course design, explicit communication of activity and assignment purposes, connection between early and later course activities, and student reflection on learning objectives and progress.
2. **Guiding Learner Engagement:** Focuses on breaking tasks into smaller steps, releasing content strategically, providing frequent feedback, and highlighting key discussion points.
3. **Using Media and Technology Tools:** Promotes accessibility, creating short videos, engaging learners with interactive content, using relevant media, and aligning technology choices with learning objectives.
4. **Building Community:** Stresses the importance of cognitive, social, and teaching presence, fostering cultural inclusivity, showing instructor personality, and creating a supportive and empathetic learning environment.
5. **Giving Feedback:** Advocates timely, meaningful, and empathetic feedback through various channels, including personalized and media-based comments.
6. **Fostering Student Persistence and Success:** Emphasizes structured learning, personal outreach, scaffolding assignments, and encouraging self-assessment through non-consequential quizzes and mastery-oriented tasks.
7. **Creating Autonomy:** Encourages offering learners choices, fostering self-directed learning, and engaging students in syllabus co-design and community agreements.

8. **Making Connections:** Highlights activating prior knowledge, embedding frameworks like concept maps, relating content to personal experiences, and encouraging students to connect learning with real-world contexts.
9. **Developing as an Online Instructor:** Encourages ongoing professional development, self-evaluation, engagement with exemplary practices, certification, and sharing knowledge with peers.

This inventory is a comprehensive framework for online educators to reflect on and enhance their teaching practices, ensuring learner engagement, inclusivity, and success.

Chapter Summary

Technology has become part of everyday life. Also, because of the positive effects of its use for learning, policymakers urge its introduction in higher education institutions. However, more attention is needed to develop digital literacy and related competencies and skills to facilitate technology adoption in teaching-learning processes. As set out in Chapter 14, designing effective online learning for adults involves addressing diverse challenges and leveraging targeted strategies to foster engagement, inclusivity, and success. The digital divide remains a significant barrier, disproportionately affecting seniors, low-income households, and individuals with disabilities. Key obstacles include limited access to technology, lack of digital literacy, and insufficient accessibility features. Tailored solutions, such as community-led training and partnerships, can mitigate these gaps.

Instructional challenges include providing timely, personalized feedback and ensuring interactive, accessible course design. The Inventory of Small Online Teaching Practices offers a comprehensive framework to enhance teaching strategies, emphasizing clear communication, scaffolding assignments, fostering autonomy, and aligning content with learners' real-world contexts.

By addressing these barriers and implementing inclusive, adaptive approaches, educators can create equitable and effective online learning environments that support adult learners' diverse needs and empower them for success.

Key Points

- Technology's Impact on Adult Learning—Digital tools and platforms reshape how adults access, engage with, and apply knowledge in formal and informal settings.
- The Digital Divide and Accessibility Challenges—While internet access is widespread, disparities remain, affecting learners from low-income backgrounds, rural areas, and those with disabilities.
- Blended and Hybrid Learning Models—A mix of online and in-person instruction is becoming the norm, requiring educators to adapt their teaching strategies for engagement and inclusivity.
- Social Media in Education—Platforms like Facebook, Twitter, and YouTube facilitate informal learning and collaboration but raise concerns about misinformation and distraction.
- AI and Online Learning—Generative AI tools are revolutionizing education by personalizing learning experiences, automating assessments, and enhancing student support.
- The Role of Digital Literacy—Both learners and educators need strong digital skills, including information evaluation, communication, and critical thinking, to navigate online education effectively.
- Building Online Learning Communities—Fostering interaction and collaboration through discussion forums, group projects, and real-time communication tools enhances student engagement and retention.
- Challenges of Online Learning—While digital education offers flexibility, it also presents issues like isolation, self-motivation struggles, and the need for effective instructional design.

References

Abedini, A., Abedin, B., & Zowghi, D. (2021). Adult learning in online communities of practice: A systematic review. *British Journal of Educational Technology, 52,* 1663–1694. https://doi.org/10.1111/bjet.13120.

Abeer, W., & Miri, B. (2014). Students' preferences and views about learning in a MOOC. *Procedia-Social and Behavioral Sciences, 152,* 318–323. https://doi.org/10.1016/j.sbspro.2014.09.203.

Akçayır, G., & Akçayır, M. (2018). The flipped classroom: A review of its advantages and challenges. *Computers and Education, 126,* 334–345. https://doi.org/10.1016/j.compedu.2018.07.021.

Alles, S. (2023). Social media in education. *INTED Proceedings.* https://doi.org/10.21125/inted.2023.1987.

Al-Zahrani, A. M., & Alasmari, T. M. (2024). Exploring the impact of artificial intelligence on higher education: The dynamics of ethical, social, and educational implications. *Humanities and Social Sciences Communications*, *11*(1), 1–12. https://doi.org/10.1057/s41599-024-03432-4.

Angeli, C., & Valanides, N. (2015). *Technological pedagogical content knowledge. Exploring, developing, and assessing TPCK.* Springer. ISBN: 978-1-4899-8080-9.

Apoki, U. C., & Crisan, G. C. (2019, June). Employing software agents and constructivism to make massive open online courses more student-oriented. In *2019 11th International Conference on Electronics, Computers and Artificial Intelligence (ECAI)*, 1–8. IEEE.

Archambault, L., Leary, H., & Rice, K. (2022). Pillars of online pedagogy: A framework for teaching in online learning environments, *Educational Psychologist*, *57*(3), 178–191. https://doi.org/10.1080/00461520.2022.2051513.

Aydin, M. K., Yildirim, T., & Kus, M. (2024). Teachers' digital competences: A scale construction and validation study. *Frontiers in Psychology*, *15* 1356573. https://doi.org/10.3389/fpsyg.2024.1356573.

Bach, A., & Thiel, F. (2024). Collaborative online learning in higher education—quality of digital interaction and associations with individual and group-related factors. *Frontiers in Education*, *9* 1356271. https://doi.org/10.3389/feduc.2024.1356271.

Balakrishnan, V., Teoh, K. K., Pourshafie, T., & Liew, T. K. (2017). Social media and their use in learning: A comparative analysis between Australia and Malaysia from the learners' perspectives. *Australasian Journal of Educational Technology*, *33*(1), 81–97. https://doi.org/10.14742/ajet.2469.

Bali, M. (2014). MOOC pedagogy: Gleaning good practice from existing MOOCs. *Journal of Online Learning and Teaching*, *10*(1), 44–56.

Bamanger, E. M., & Alhassan, R. A. (2015). Exploring podcasting in English as a foreign language learners' writing performance. *Journal of Education and Practice*, *6*(11), 63–74. ISSN 2222-1735.

Barrot, J. S. (2021). Scientific mapping of social media in education: A decade of exponential growth. *Journal of Educational Computing Research*, *59*(4), 645–668. https://doi.org/10.1177/0735633120972010.

Bennett, E. E., & Bell, A. A. (2010). Paradox and promise in the knowledge society. In C. K. Kasworm, A. D. Rose & J. M. Ross-Gordon (Eds.), *Handbook of adult and continuing education* (pp. 411–420). SAGE.

Berners-Lee, T., Hendler, J., & Lassila, O. (2001). The semantic web: A new form of web content that is meaningful to computers will unleash a revolution of new possibilities. ScientificAmerican.com.

Bianchi, N., Lu, Y., & Song, H. (2022). The effect of computer-assisted learning on students' long-term development. *Journal of Development Economics*, *158*, 102919. https://doi.org/10.1016/j.jdeveco.2022.102919.

Bierema, L. L. (2021). *Inventory of small online teaching practices.* [Unpublished manuscript]. The University of Georgia.

Billett, S. (2018). Distinguishing lifelong learning from lifelong education. *Journal of Adult Learning, Knowledge and Innovation*, *2*(1), 1–7. https://doi.org/10.1556/2059.01.2017.3.

Bloomberg, L. D. (2021). Designing and delivering effective online instructions. In *How to engage adult learners* (1st ed.). Teachers College Press.

Bolisani, E., Fedeli, M., De Marchi, V., & Bierema, L. (2020). Together we win: Communities of practices to face the COVID crisis in higher education. In A. Wensley & M. Evans.

17th International Conference on Intellectual Capital, Knowledge Management & Organizational Learning. https://books.google.it/books?id=T4MIEAAAQBAJ.

Bonwell, C. C., & Eison, J. A. (1991). *Active learning: Creating excitement in the classroom. 1991 ASHE-ERIC higher education reports.* ERIC Clearinghouse on Higher Education, The George Washington University, DC 20036-1183.

Bralić, A., & Divjak, B. (2018). Integrating MOOCs in traditionally taught courses: Achieving learning outcomes with blended learning. *International Journal of Educational Technology in Higher Education, 15,* 1–16. https://doi.org/10.1186/s41239-017-0085-7.

Burdova, C. (2024, November 14). *What is Web 3.0 (Web3 definition)?* https://www.avast.com/c-web-3-0.

Butson, R., & Spronken-Smith, R. (2024). AI and its implications for research in higher education: A critical dialogue. *Higher Education Research & Development, 43*(3), 563–577. https://doi.org/10.1080/07294360.2023.2280200.

Cappuccio, G. (2015). La competenza digitale all'università per la progettazione di percorsi di media education. *Giornale Italiano della Ricerca Educativa, 8*(14), 67–82. ISSN 2038-9744.

Chen, M. (2016, March). Study of instructional model for information technology fundamental courses under MOOC environment. In *2015 1st International Conference on Information Technologies in Education and Learning (icitel-15)* (pp. 5–10). Atlantis Press. https://doi.org/10.2991/icitel-15.2016.2.

Chirag. (2024, April 9). Web 3.0 vs. Web 2.0—Why and How it matters for businesses? *Appinventiv.* https://appinventiv.com/blog/web3-0-vs-web2-0/.

Cho, K. M., & Heron, M. L. (2015). How students perceive e-learning in higher education: An Exploration of actors that promote and inhibit perceived learning. *International Journal of E-Learning & Distance Education, 30*(2), 1–17.

Chugh, R. & Ruhi, U. (2018). Social media in higher education: A literature review of Facebook. *Education and Information Technologies, 23*(2), 605–616, https://doi.org/10.1007/s10639-017-9621-2.

Chugh, R., & Ruhi, U. (2019). Social media for tertiary education. In A. Tatnall (Ed.), *Encyclopedia of education and information technologies.* Springer. https://doi.org/10.1007/978-3-319-60013-0_202-1.

Commission of the European Communities. (2000). A Memorandum on Lifelong Learning. *Commission Staff Working Paper.* Brussels, 30.10.2000 (SEC2000 1832).

Community Tech Network. (2023, July 14). *Digital inclusion for people with disabilities: Bridging the accessibility gap.* Community Tech Network. https://communitytechnetwork.org/blog/digital-inclusion-for-people-with-disabilities-bridging-the-accessibility-gap/.

Comunicacion Equipo. (2024, April 23). *How does the digital divide affect people with disabilities?* Pasiona Consulting. https://pasiona.com/en/how-does-the-digital-divide-affect-people-with-disabilities/.

Darby, F., & Lang, J. M. (2019). *Small teaching online: Applying learning science in online classes.* John Wiley & Sons.

Deng, R., Benckendorff, P., & Gannaway, D. (2017). Understanding learning and teaching in MOOCs from the perspectives of students and instructors: A review of literature from 2014 to 2016. *Digital Education: Out to the World and Back to the Campus: 5th European MOOCs Stakeholders Summit, EMOOCs 2017, Madrid, Spain, May 22–26, 2017, Proceedings 5, 176–181.*

Eden, C. A., Chisom, O. N., & Adeniyi, I. S. (2024). Online learning and community engagement: Strategies for promoting inclusivity and collaboration in education. *World Journal of Advanced Research and Reviews, 21*(3), 232–239. https://doi.org/10.30574/wjarr.2024.21.3.0693.

Essex, D., Kerner, S. M., & Gillis, A. S. (2023, September 9). *What is Web 3.0 (Web3)? Definition, guide and history.* https://www.techtarget.com/whatis/definition/Web-30.

European Commission. (2018a). *Communication on Building a European Education Area.* https://ec.europa.eu/info/publications/communication-building-european-education-area-reforming-education-and-training-policies_en.

European Commission. (2018b). *Communication on the Digital Education Action Plan.* https://eur-lex.europa.eu/legal-content/EN/TXT/?uri=COM:2018:22:FIN.

European Commission. (2020). *Digital Education Action Plan 2021–2027.* https://eur-lex.europa.eu/legal-content/EN/TXT/?uri=CELEX%3A52020DC0624.

Evanick, J. (2023, December 18). *Digital inclusivity: Creating equitable online learning environments.* eLearning Industry. https://elearningindustry.com/digital-inclusivity-creating-equitable-online-learning-environments.

Fedeli, M., & Bierema, L. L. (2019). *Connecting adult learning and knowledge management.* Springer.

Fedeli, M., Liotino, M., Taylor, E. W., Araneta, M. G. (2022). Enhancing learning in higher education using mooc: The experience of the University of Padua. In G. Casalino, M. Cimitile, P. Ducange, N. P. Zea, R. Pecori, P. Picerno & P. Raviolo (Eds.), *Higher Education Learning Methodologies and Technologies Online.* HELMeTO 2021. Communications in Computer and Information Science, vol. 1542. Springer. https://doi.org/10.1007/978-3-030-96060-5_16.

Fiorini, L. A., Borg, A., & Debono, M. (2022). Part-time adult students' satisfaction with online learning during the COVID-19 pandemic. *Journal of Adult and Continuing Education, 28*(2), 354–377. https://doi.org/10.1177/14779714221082691.

Forbes, D., & Khoo, E. (2015). Voice over distance: A case of podcasting for learning in online teacher education. *Distance Education, 36*(3), 335–350. https://doi.org/10.1080/01587919.2015.1084074.

Fullstack Academy. (2024, November 21). 5 ways adult students benefit from online learning. *Fullstack Academy.* https://www.fullstackacademy.com/blog/5-ways-adult-students-benefit-from-online-learning.

García-Peñalvo, F. J., Fidalgo-Blanco, Á., & Sein-Echaluce, M. L. (2018). An adaptive hybrid MOOC model: Disrupting the MOOC concept in higher education. *Telematics and Informatics, 35*(4), 1018–1030. https://doi.org/10.1016/j.tele.2017.09.012.

Garner, B., & Shank, N. (2024). Using adult learning theory to explore student perceptions of the flipped class method. *Journal of Marketing Education, 46*(3), 198–213. https://doi.org/10.1177/02734753231196501.

Garrison, D. R., & Kanuka, H. (2004). Blended learning: Uncovering its transformative potential in higher education. *The Internet and Higher Education, 7*(2), 95–105. https://doi.org/10.1016/j.iheduc.2004.02.001.

Gay, G. H., & Betts, K. (2020). From discussion forums to eMeetings: Integrating high touch strategies to increase student engagement, academic performance, and retention in large online courses. *Online Learning, 24*(1), 92–117. https://doi.org/10.24059/olj.v24i1.1984.

Geroni, D. (2023, May 1). *Difference between Web 2.0 and Web 3.0.* 101 Blockchains. https://101blockchains.com/web-2-0-and-web-3-0/.

Gibson, S. (2008). Online assessment: Essential considerations for selecting measures for adult learning. *Journal of Continuing Education in the Health Professions, 28*(4), 222–228.

Gilster, P. (1997). *Digital literacy.* John Wiley & Sons.

Green, T. (2015). Flipped classrooms: An agenda for innovative marketing education in the digital era. *Marketing Education Review, 25*(3), 179–191. https://doi.org/10.1080/10528008.2015.1044851.

Gunderson, J. L., & Cumming, T. M. (2023). Podcasting in higher education as a component of Universal Design for Learning: A systematic review of the literature. *Innovations in Education and Teaching International, 60*(4), 591–601. https://doi.org/10.1080/14703297.2022.2075430.

Hachey, A. C., Wladis, C., & Conway, K. M. (2023). Investigating online versus face-to-face course dropout: Why do students say they are leaving? *Education Sciences, 13*(11), 1122. https://doi.org/10.3390/educsci13111122.

Ho, D. P. K., & Phan, T. N. T. (2024). Student persistence in online learning: A literature review. *VNU Journal of Foreign Studies, 40*(1), 76–102. https://doi.org/10.63023/2525-2445/jfs.ulis.5211.

Hölterhof, T., & Heinen, R. (2014). Bridging Personal learning Environments: Interfacing personal environments and learning management systems: The example of a bookmarking tool. In I. Buchem, *THE PLE CONFERENCE 2013* (pp. 52–67).

Hoon, S. (2018). Adult learning and the advantages of the online learning experience. *Westcliff International Journal of Applied Research, 2*(2), 31–36.

Hortigüela-Alcalá, D., Sánchez-Santamaría, J., Pérez-Pueyo, Á. & Abella-García, V. (2019). Social networks to promote motivation and learning in higher education from the students' perspective. *Innovations in Education and Teaching International, 56*(4), 412–422. https://doi.org/10.1080/14703297.2019.1579665.

Huang, X., Li, H., Huang, L., & Jiang, T. (2023). Research on the development and innovation of online education based on digital knowledge sharing community. *BMC Psychology, 11*(1). https://doi.org/10.1186/s40359-023-01337-6.

Ilomäki, L., Paavola, S., Lakkala, M., & Kantosalo, A. (2016). Digital competence–an emergent boundary concept for policy and educational research. *Education and Information Technologies, 21*(3), 655–679. https://doi.org/10.1007/s10639-014-9346-4.

Instructional Design Australia. (2024, March 13). *The role of eLearning in Adult Education.* https://instructionaldesign.com.au/the-role-of-elearning-in-adult-education-pros-cons-and-best-practices/.

Jekabsone, I., & Gudele, I. (2023). Online adult education for sustainable development: The analysis of the consequences of the COVID-19 pandemic in latvia. *Journal of Teacher Education for Sustainability, 25*(1), 155–167. https://doi.org/10.2478/jtes-2023-0010.

Jesionkowska, J. (2020). Designing online environment for collaborative learning in a scientific community of practice. *Advances in Intelligent Systems and Computing, 916*, 176–185. https://doi.org/10.1007/978-3-030-11932-4_18.

Jha, S. (2024, September 4). *Web 3.0 explained: A comprehensive guide.* Simplilearn.com. https://www.simplilearn.com/tutorials/blockchain-tutorial/what-is-web-3-0.

Jisc. (2017). *Technology enhanced learning.* https://www.jisc.ac.uk/guides/technology-enhanced-learning.

Johansson, S., Gulliksen, J., & Gustavsson, C. (2020). Disability digital divide: The use of the Internet, smartphones, computers and tablets among people with disabilities in Sweden. *Universal Access in the Information Society, 20*(1), 105–120. https://doi.org/10.1007/s10209-020-00714-x.

Johnson, R. T., & Johnson, D. W. (2008). Active learning: Cooperation in the classroom. *The Annual Report of Educational Psychology in Japan, 47*, 29–30. https://doi.org/10.5926/arepj1962.47.0_29.

Joosten, T. (2012). *Social media for educators: Strategies and best practices.* Jossey-Bass.

Kaufmann, R., & Vallade, J. I. (2020). Exploring connections in the online learning environment: Student perceptions of rapport, climate, and loneliness. *Interactive Learning Environments.* Advance online publication. https://doi.org/10.1080/10494820.2020.1749670.

Kaul, M., Aksela, M., & Wu, X. (2018). Dynamics of the community of inquiry (CoI) within a massive open online course (MOOC) for in-service teachers in environmental education. *Education Sciences, 8*(2), 40. https://doi.org/10.3390/educsci8020040.

Kemp, S. (2024, January 31). *Digital 2024: Global Overview Report—DataReportal—Global Digital Insights.* DataReportal—Global Digital Insights. https://datareportal.com/reports/digital-2024-global-overview-report.

Khaled, M. (2024, June 4). Social media and education: Exploring the pros and cons with surprising statistics in 2024 | ProfileTree. *ProfileTree Web Design and Digital Marketing.* https://profiletree.com/social-media-and-education-exploring-statistics/.

Kloos, C. D., Muñoz-Merino, P. J., Alario-Hoyos, C., Ayres, I. E., & Fernández-Panadero, C. (2015, March). Mixing and blending MOOC Technologies with face-to-face pedagogies. In *2015 IEEE Global Engineering Education Conference (EDUCON)* (pp. 967–971). IEEE. https://doi.org/10.1109/EDUCON.2015.7096090.

Kovanović, V., Joksimović, S., Poquet, O., Hennis, T., Čukić, I., De Vries, P., et al. (2018). Exploring communities of inquiry in massive open online courses. *Computers & Education, 119*, 44–58. https://doi.org/10.1016/j.compedu.2017.11.010.

van Laar, E., van Deursen, A. J. A. M., van Dijk, J. A. G. M., & de Haan, J. (2020). Determinants of 21st-century skills and 21st-century digital skills for workers: A systematic literature review. *Sage Open, 10*(1). https://doi.org/10.1177/2158244019900176.

Laouris, Y., & Eteokleous, N. (2005). Digital divide among adult learners: An empirical study. *Journal of Digital Learning in Teacher Education, 21*(1), 4–11.

Laurillard, D., Oliver, M., Wasson, B., Hoppe, U. (2009). Implementing technology-enhanced learning. In N. Balacheff, S. Ludvigsen, T. de Jong, A. Lazonder, S. Barnes, (Eds.), *Technology-enhanced learning.* Springer. https://doi.org/10.1007/978-1-4020-9827-7_17.

Lave, J., & Wenger, E. (1991). *Situated learning: Legitimate peripheral participation.* Cambridge University Press.

Lee, D., Arnold, M., Srivastava, A., Plastow, K., Strelan, P., Ploeckl, F., Lekkas, D., & Palmer, E. (2024). The impact of generative AI on higher education learning and teaching: A study of educators' perspectives. *Computers and Education Artificial Intelligence, 6*, 100221. https://doi.org/10.1016/j.caeai.2024.100221.

León-Pérez, F., Bas, M. C., & Escudero-Nahón, A. (2020). Self-perception about emerging digital skills in higher education students. *Comunicar: Media Education Research Journal, 28*(62), 89–98. https://doi.org/10.3916/C62-2020-08.

Lindsay-Finan J., (2024, September 30). *Building effective learning communities online | InSync Insights.* https://blog.insynctraining.com/online-learning-communities.

Liotino M., Costa J.P., Rocha Bicalho D., da Cruz L., Hassinger H. (2023). Digital competence development in higher education: Political influence and student experiences in Portugal and Italy. In L. Breitschwerdt, J. Schwarz, & S. Schmidt-Lauff (Eds.), *Comparative Research in Adult Education Global Perspectives on Participation, Sustainability and Digitalisation.* Wbv Publikation (pp. 143–161). ISBN 978-3-7639-7169-5.

Lucidity Insights Research Team. (2024, February 6). *Digital divide: Urban vs rural internet access varies greatly by income groups and regions.* https://lucidityinsights.com/infobytes/percentage-of-individuals-using-the-internet-in-urban-and-rural-areas-2023.

Manca, S. (2020). Snapping, pinning, liking or texting: Investigating social media in higher education beyond Facebook. *The Internet and Higher Education, 44,* 100707. https://doi.org/10.1016/j.iheduc.2019.100707.

Martin, A. (2008). Digital literacy and the "digital society." *Digital literacies: Concepts, policies and practices, 30*(151), 1029–1055.

Mattar, J. (2018). Constructivism and connectivism in education technology: Active, situated, authentic, experiential, and anchored learning. *RIED-Revista Iberoamericana de Educación a Distancia, 21*(2). https://doi.org/http://dx.doi.org/10.5944/ried.21.2.20055.

McAuley, A., Stewart, B., Siemens, G., & Cormier, D. (2010). *The MOOC model for digital practice.* University of Prince Edward Island.

McQueen, R., Pullen, M., Chapman, S., Hann, S., Beauchamp, G., Crick, T., Davies, O., Hughes, C., Lewis, C., & Owen, K. L. (2024). Co-designing learning spaces with learners: Lessons from a Welsh primary school classroom. *Cylchgrawn Addysg Cymru/Wales Journal of Education.* https://doi.org/10.16922/wje.p4.

Meng, W., Yu, L., Liu, C., Pan, N., Pang, X., & Zhu, Y. (2024). A systematic review of the effectiveness of online learning in higher education during the COVID-19 pandemic period. *Frontiers in Education, 8.* https://doi.org/10.3389/feduc.2023.1334153.

Mirza, E. (2024, November 25). *The role of social media in education.* SocialBu Blog. https://socialbu.com/blog/role-of-social-media-in-education.

Muller, R., & Wergin, R. (2014). A test of learning concepts: Teaching business integration to the freshmen business student learner via podcasting. *Journal of Learning in Higher Education, 10*(1), 45–51.

National Telecommunications and Information Administration. (2024, April 30). *Office of Internet Connectivity and Growth 2023 Annual Report.* https://www.ntia.gov/report/2024/office-internet-connectivity-and-growth-2023-annual-report.

Nepal, R. M., Khadka, B., Guragain, S., & Ghimire, J. (2024). Interest and motivation of disadvantaged students toward online learning during the COVID-19 pandemic in Nepal. *Frontiers in Education, 9.* https://doi.org/10.3389/feduc.2024.1356279.

Ng, W., & Poquet, O. (2020). *Exploratory study of analytics-based technologies used for corporate learning and development* (Technical Report). Institute for Adult Learning.

OECD. (2023a). *Country digital education ecosystems and governance: A companion to digital education outlook 2023.* OECD Publishing. https://doi.org/10.1787/906134d4-en.

OECD. (2023b). *Flexible adult learning provision: What it is, why it matters, and how to make it work.*

Pan, G., Mao, Y., Song, Z., & Nie, H. (2024). Research on the influencing factors of adult learners' intent to use online education platforms based on expectation confirmation theory. *Scientific Reports, 14*(1), 12762. https://doi.org/10.1038/s41598-024-63747-9.

Parker, J. E. (2013). Examining adult learning assumptions and theories in technology-infused communities and professions. In V. C. Bryan & V. C. X. Wang (Eds.), *Technology use and research applications for community education and professional development* (pp. 53–65). IGI Global.

Peck, K. L., Jonassen, D. H., Wilson, B. G. (1999). *Learning with technology: A constructivist perspective.* Merrill.

Pesare, E., Roselli, T., & Rossano, V. (2017). Engagement in social learning: Detecting engagement in OCOP. In *Advances in human factors, business management, training and education,* 151–158. Springer.

Pipi Learning. (2024, February 22). *Does eLearning work for adult learners?* https://pipilearning.co.nz/blog/does-elearning-work-for-adult-learners.

Poquet, O., & De Laat, M. (2021). Developing capabilities: Lifelong learning in the age of AI. *British Journal of Educational Technology, 52*(4), 1695–1708. https://doi.org/10.1111/bjet.13123.

Powell, L., & Robson, F. (2014). Learner-generated podcasts: A useful approach to assessment. *Innovations in Education & Teaching International, 51*(3), 326–337. https://doi.org/10.1080/14703297.2013.796710.

Prince, M. (2004). Does active learning work? A review of the research. *Journal of Engineering Education, 93*(3), 223–231. https://doi.org/10.1002/j.2168-9830.2004.tb00809.x.

Rahmani, A. M., Groot, W., & Rahmani, H. (2024). Dropout in online higher education: A systematic literature review. *International Journal of Educational Technology in Higher Education, 21*(1), 19. https://doi.org/10.1186/s41239-024-00450-9.

Raihan, M. M., Subroto, S., Chowdhury, N., Koch, K., Ruttan, E., & Turin, T. C. (2024). Dimensions and barriers for digital (in)equity and digital divide: A systematic integrative review. *Digital Transformation and Society.* https://doi.org/10.1108/dts-04-2024-0054.

Redecker, C. (2017). European Framework for the Digital Competence of Educators: DigCompEdu. In Y. Punie (Ed.), *European framework for the digital competence of educators.* Publications Office of the European Union.

Rehm, M., Moukarzel, S., Daly, A. J., & del Fresno, M. (2020). Exploring online social networks of school leaders in times of COVID-19. *British Journal of Educational Technology 52*(4), 1414–1433. https://doi.org/10.1111/bjet.13099.

Richter, D., Kunter, M., Klusmann, U., Lüdtke, O., & Baumert, J. (2011). Professional development across the teaching career: Teachers' uptake of formal and informal learning opportunities. *Teaching and Teacher Education, 27*(1), 116–126. https://doi.org/10.1016/j.tate.2010.07.008.

Rosenberg, M. J. (2001). *E-Learning: Strategies for delivering knowledge in the digital age.* McGraw-Hill.

Scerbakov, N., Kappe, F. & Schukin, A. (2018). Social Bookmarking as a Component of E-Learning. In T. Bastiaens, J. Van Braak, M. Brown, & O. Zawacki-Richter (Eds.), *Proceedings of EdMedia: World Conference on Educational Media and Technology* (pp. 108–115). Amsterdam, Netherlands: Association for the Advancement of Computing in Education (AACE). https://www.learntechlib.org/primary/p/184187/.

Seismic. (2022, October 6). *The benefits of online learning | Seismic.* https://seismic.com/enablement-explainers/the-benefits-of-online-learning-for-adults/.

Shaikh, U. U., & Asif, Z. (2022). Persistence and dropout in higher online education: Review and categorization of factors. *Frontiers in Psychology, 13*, 902070. https://doi.org/10.3389/fpsyg.2022.902070.

Shen, J., Qi, H., Mei, R., & Sun, C. (2024). A comparative study on the effectiveness of online and in-class team-based learning on student performance and perceptions in virtual simulation experiments. *BMC Medical Education, 24*(1), 135. https://doi.org/10.1186/s12909-024-05080-3.

Shi, Y., Ma, Y., MacLeod, J., & Yang, H. H. (2020). College students' cognitive learning outcomes in flipped classroom instruction: A meta-analysis of the empirical literature. *Journal of Computers in Education, 7*(1), 79–103. https://doi.org/10.1007/s40692-019-00142-8.

Signé, L. (2023, July 5). Fixing the global digital divide and digital access gap. *Brookings.* https://www.brookings.edu/articles/fixing-the-global-digital-divide-and-digital-access-gap/.

Slimi, Z. (2023). The impact of artificial intelligence on higher education: An empirical study. *European Journal of Educational Sciences, 10*(1), 17–33. https://doi.org/10.19044/ejes.v10no1a17.

Starkey, L. (2020). A review of research exploring teacher preparation for the digital age. *Cambridge Journal of Education, 50*(1), 37–56. https://doi.org/10.1080/0305764X.2019.1625867.

Statista. (2017). *Average daily time spent on social media among teens and young adults worldwide from 1st quarter to 3rd quarter 2017, by region (in minutes).* https://www.statista.com/statistics/800821/average-daily-timespent-social-media-teens-young-adults/.

Statista. (2020, April 1). *Number of global social network users 2010–2023.* https://www.statista.com/statistics/278414/number-of-worldwide-social-network-users/.

Stavredes, T. (2011). *Effective online teaching: Foundations and strategies for student success.* Jossey-Bass.

Sutherland. (2024, June 26). *What Is Web 3.0—a definition and history.* Sutherland. https://www.sutherlandglobal.com/insights/glossary/what-is-web3.

Tandet J. (2024, April 8). *Understanding digital transformation in higher education.* https://moderncampus.com/blog/digital-transformation-in-higher-education.html.

Tømte, C. E., Fossland, T., Aamodt, P. O., & Degn, L. (2019). Digitalisation in higher education: mapping institutional approaches for teaching and learning. *Quality in Higher Education, 25*(1), 98–114. https://doi.org/10.1080/13538322.2019.1603611.

Tu, C. H., Blocher, M., & Havitz, M. E. (2005). Predicting learner satisfaction and performance in an e-learning environment: An examination of uncertainty, image, and media richness. *MIS Quarterly, 29*(4), 649–669.

Ulla, M. B., & Perales, W. F. (2022). Hybrid teaching: Conceptualization through practice for the post COVID19 Pandemic education. *Frontiers in Education, 7.* https://doi.org/10.3389/feduc.2022.924594.

UNESCO. (2016, May 23). *Technology-enhanced learning.* UNESCO International Bureau of Education. https://www.ibe.unesco.org/en/glossary-curriculum-terminology/t/technology-enhanced-learning.

US Department of Education. (2021). *Digital Government Strategy Report.* https://www.ed.gov/about/ed-initiatives/digital-government-strategy.

US Department of Education. (2024, January 30). *US Department of Education releases 2024 National Educational Technology Plan.* https://www.ed.gov/about/news/press-release/us-department-of-education-releases-2024-national-educational-technology.

Van Dijk, J. (2020). *The network society* (2nd ed.). Sage.

Vuorikari, R., Kluzer, S. & Punie, Y. (2022). *DigComp 2.2: The Digital Competence Framework for Citizens—With new examples of knowledge, skills and attitudes.* JRC Publications Repository. https://doi.org/10.2760/115376.

Wenger, E. (1999). *Communities of practice: Learning, meaning, and identity.* Cambridge University Press.

Winger, A. (2024, July 15). *Overcoming challenges in online learning: retention factors and prime persistence practices.* Faculty Focus | Higher Ed Teaching & Learning. https://www.facultyfocus.com/articles/online-education/overcoming-challenges-in-online-learning-retention-factors-and-prime-persistence-practices/.

CHAPTER 15

FACILITATING ACTIVE ADULT LEARNING PROGRAMS

Box 15.1 Chapter Overview and Learning Objectives

Bierema (2019) shared this anecdote lamenting boring lectures:

Anyone, anyone?

The 1986 US hit teen comedy film, Ferris Bueller's Day Off, *written, co-produced, and directed by John Hughes, and co-produced by Tom Jacobson, featured the antics of star Matthew Broderick as Ferris Bueller, a high school slacker who skips school, with hilarious, disastrous consequences. One of the most famous scenes was actor-teacher Ben Stein's monotonous lecture about the Smoot–Hawley Tariff Act where he drones on to the class asking questions, followed by a quick, "Anyone, anyone?" pleading for student participation, before swiftly moving on to the next point, only to repeat the process over and over again. It is painful to watch the actor pleading "Anyone, anyone?" as students dozed, drooled on their desks, chewed gum, and goofed off during the lecture. Stein was quite proud of his acting moment to perfectly portray a boring professor. Perhaps you have been that instructor, asking "Anyone, anyone?" to a silent room filled with glazed-over eyes?* (Courtesy of Bierema, 2019, p. 27)

Chapter 15 describes active learning (AL) in adult educational programs. Effective learning engages learners in talking, moving, and doing in ways that help them apply the concepts and principles they are learning. This chapter begins with an overview of passive learning and its shortcomings. It describes AL approaches, including interactive lectures and multiple strategies for shifting away from lectures as a primary instructional method. As a result of reading this chapter and completing the exercise boxes, you, the reader, should be able to:

1. Recognize the shortcomings of lecture as an instructional method.
2. Apply techniques to make lectures interactive.
3. Incorporate active learning strategies into your teaching repertoire.

As an adult educator or learner, you have undoubtedly suffered through a lecture in school, church, the workplace, or community that left you bored, daydreaming, and fidgeting. Yet, lecture has prevailed for centuries as a preferred mode of teaching and public speaking, even though most people dislike giving and listening to them. Educators tend to over-rely on lectures, possibly because it was how they were taught. Gulick's (1908) sentiment toward lectures remains pertinent more than 100 years later:

> We have all seen—and alas, been an integral part of—some audience
> that was trying to endure the last half hour of an unendurable speech.
> Everybody was shifting his [sic] position, crossing one leg over the other
> or back again, moving the fingers, playing with watch-charms or chains,
> yawning, twitching, folding programs, wiping eye-glasses, twisting
> moustaches. Those were all fatigue signs. (p. 96)

Audiences lament lectures, described as mind-numbing and sleep-inducing. W. H. Auden offered this disparaging description of a professor: "A person who talks in other people's sleep" (Mendelson, 2013). The widely experienced and chagrined lecture is the oldest instructional method known to humankind.

The Traditional Lecture

A **traditional lecture, or direct instruction,** involves an instructor talking while learners listen. If you lecture regularly as an educator, you will rarely be interrupted and notice learners lose interest in as little as 10–15 minutes. Donald

Swinehart (in Dickson, 1980) keenly observed: "The lecture is that procedure whereby the material in the notes of the professor is transferred to the notes of the students without passing through the mind of either" (p. 211). Another reality of the lecture is that "the individuals learning the most in this classroom are the professors. They have reserved for themselves the very conditions that promote learning: actively seeking new information, organizing it in a meaningful way, and having the chance to explain it to others" (Huba & Freed, 2000, p. 35).

The lecture is "an instructional technique through which an agent presents an oral discourse on a particular subject" (Verner & Dickinson, 1967, p. 85). Others have more cynical accounts:

> A single instructor lectures and lectures and lectures fairly large groups of business and professional people, who sit for long hours in an audiovisual twilight, making never-to-be-read notes at rows of narrow tables covered with green baize and appointed with fat binders and sweating pitchers of ice water. (Nowlen, 1988, as cited in Cervero 1992, p. 91)

Also known as a speech, sermon, talk, address, oration, panel, symposium, and forum, the lecture is an ancient teaching mode, likely invented as soon as humans developed the ability to talk. It was a hallmark of the ancient Greeks, Roman educators, and the great universities of the Middle Ages. Despite the inventions of the printing press and social media, the lecture has survived despite its derision. Although lectures can be appropriate methods, a key problem is they require learners to be passive recipients of information, leaving them little opportunity to share experiences, discuss the concepts, or apply their knowledge. As an adult educator or learner, you can probably recall good and bad lectures, and Box 15.2 provides an opportunity for this consideration.

Coryell (2024) explained that although lecture is an effective method for transmitting information, students do not always acquire the desired understanding from this pedagogy. She also criticized its lack of interactivity and feedback. As an educator, it is helpful to periodically critique your teaching methods, particularly lectures, to assess what is serving learners well.

What occurs in an effective lecture? Learners are engaged in reflection, conversation, and sharing with classmates. The instructor invites learners to participate, perhaps breaking up the lecture by short, engaging activities. Effective lectures are a combination of "small lectures that present information in short doses, usually 10–15 minutes maximum, inviting learners to react and interact with activities. Strong lecturers engage in ongoing assessment of their learning community to ensure learning. Have yours?" (Bierema, 2019, p. 28). Box 15.3 presents data on the fallibility of lectures.

 **Box 15.2 Reflective Practice**

Pros and Cons of Lecture

A common refrain in adult education is that, as an educator, you can either be the "sage on the stage," typical in a teacher-centered traditional lecturer, or the "guide on the side," common in an active, learner-centered, facilitative teaching approach. Lecture has negative and positive attributes. This box summarizes them and raises questions for reflection.

Advantages of Lecture

- Time efficiency.
- Cost-effectiveness.
- Provides access to instructors' expertise.
- Offers equal contact with the same information, assuming learners are listening.

Disadvantages of Lecture

- The instructor speaks at length, often without visual prompts, characterized by instructor-centricity.
- Learner interaction only occurs when they raise their hands and wait to be called on by the instructor.
- Student talk is discouraged. Instead, they listen passively and take notes independently.
- Few opportunities exist for the instructor to correct learners' misunderstandings and errors.
- Individual learners may not have their learning needs met.
- Learning transfer is variable.

As you can see, the disadvantages outweigh the advantages of lecture, so if you incorporate lectures into your educational repertoire as an adult educator, using an interactive lecture approach incorporating active learning is recommended and discussed in the next section.

Reflective Questions on Lecture

Reflect on a notable lecture you have experienced (good or bad) as an adult educator or learner. What do you remember? What made the lecture notable? How might you improve upon it? How do you use lecture in your practice? How would students rate yours (be honest!)?

 ## Box 15.3 Adult Learning by the Numbers

Data on Lectures

Over the years, researchers have documented the shortcomings of lectures. This box features a sampling.

- Penner (1984) synthesized 30 years of lecture research in the 1980s and concluded that the average student's attention span was 10–20 minutes and that concentration faded after about 10–20 minutes. Other sources support this figure, although the attention span for using a digital device is less than one minute.
- According to one study, about 18% of learners paid attention at any given time, listening in 45-second increments, and less than 1% retained anything after 6 months (Reilly, 1992, p. 696).
- Lectures fail about 80% of the time (Medina, 2009).
- The traditional lecture format often leads to high student absenteeism, and the instructor's ability to assess student comprehension and ability to apply learning is minimal (Eison, 2010).
- Freeman et al. (2014) conducted a meta-analysis examining 225 studies of undergraduate STEM teaching methods. They found that undergraduate students in classes with traditional stand-and-deliver lectures are 1.5 times more likely to fail than students in classes that use more stimulating, active learning methods, concluding "active learning leads to increases in examination performance that would raise average grades by half a letter, and that failure rates under traditional lecturing increased by 55% over the rates observed under active learning" (p. 8410) and concluded that STEM education would benefit in part by abandoning the traditional lecture in favor of active learning.
- A 2018 study of over 2,000 college classes in STEM monitored nearly 550 faculty teaching over 700 courses at 25 institutions across the United States and Canada. Stains et al. (2018) concluded that 55% of STEM classroom interactions consisted mainly of conventional lecturing. Another 27% featured interactive lectures. Only 18% emphasized a student-centered style using active learning. The researchers recommended that colleges and universities focus more on training faculty members and active teaching methods to shift STEM teaching in higher education.

Fedeli and Taylor (2024) summed up the shortcomings of the lecture:

> Lecturing does not offer an effective means for learning; What is needed is the opportunity to experiment, experience, and apply knowledge to authentic real-world context. From this perspective, the focus necessarily shifts from teacher to student, from content to process, and from summative to ongoing assessment that promotes better learning and success. Most significant is that learners at times learn more in a classroom when they are learning in relationship to others. (p. 120)

The following section introduces an alternative to ineffective lectures.

Active Learning

The National Research Council (NRC, 1997, 2003) and the National Science Foundation (1996) urged the adoption of active learning strategies and other alternatives to uninterrupted lectures to model the methods and mindsets of scientific inquiry and for students to experience real-world application of principles and learn practical, employable skills (Allen & Tanner, 2005). **Active learning** (AL) is a pedagogical strategy that engages adult learners with each other and the instructor in mutual conversation, application, and creation about the topic under study. Also known as **guided instruction,** AL has roots in constructivist education and views learners as authors of their meaning and knowledge about the world. Given the low efficacy of lecture, AL is more effective since it does not simply tell learners what to think or do; it engages them in co-creating knowledge with other learners and applying it to real-world problems.

Unlike direct instruction or lecture-type activities, AL shifts centrality away from the instructor giving monotonous lectures to focusing on learners' understanding and learning. Hallmarks of AL include that learners are moving, talking, and thinking in a fast-paced, engaging atmosphere. Although learners do most of the work during an AL session, it is the instructor's thoughtful, advance design of an engaging lesson that frees them to facilitate interaction during class. This section discusses considerations for implementing active learning and offers guidance for interactive lecturing and AL activities.

Considerations for Active Learning Implementation

Although this chapter and book advocate active adult learning, you might feel trepidation as an educator if you have not tried it before. Consider Lang's (2021) advice in Box 15.4 for taking a slow incremental approach to AL. Once you begin planning for AL, there are additional considerations for implementing AL.

Implementing Active Learning

Børte et al. (2020) reanalyzed two systemic reviews to understand barriers to student active learning in higher education. They recommended the following prerequisites for student active learning (AL) to succeed: (1) aligning research and teaching practices, (2) supporting infrastructure for research and teaching,

Box 15.4 SoTL: The Scholarship of Teaching and Learning

Lang's *Small Teaching*

Small Teaching by James M. Lang (2021) offers practical, research-based techniques to incorporate into teaching without requiring major overhauls. Lang emphasized that **small, intentional changes can significantly impact student learning and engagement.** Here are the key points:

Make Incremental Changes. Rather than overhauling entire courses, Lang advocated for slight adjustments in teaching practices grounded in cognitive science. These small changes can cumulatively improve learning outcomes.

Build on Cognitive Science. Lang drew on research in cognitive psychology, especially findings on memory, attention, and the science of learning. He discussed how small techniques can help students retain information better, connect new knowledge with prior learning, and deepen their understanding.

Adopt Key Teaching Practices:

1. **Retrieval Practice:** Incorporate frequent, low-stakes testing or recall activities to help students reinforce and retain information.
2. **Prediction:** Encourage students to foretell answers or outcomes before learning new content to prime their engagement and critical thinking.
3. **Connect Prior Knowledge:** Begin new lessons by helping students link current content to previously learned material to build a foundation for deeper understanding.
4. **Tap into Motivation and Emotions:** Use small gestures to positively impact motivation and engagement, like expressing genuine enthusiasm for the subject and showing empathy toward students.

Follow a Framework for Implementation:

1. **Before Class:** Spend a few minutes reviewing the previous class's content or prompting students to recall key points. Consider asking students to make predictions about the day's lesson.
2. **During Class:** Incorporate short, active learning activities (like peer discussions or brief quizzes) to break up lectures and reinforce material.
3. **After Class:** Encourage students to reflect on what they learned or self-test.

Long-Term Learning Benefits. Small changes in teaching can support long-term learning by moving knowledge from short-term to long-term memory and fostering skills that enable students to apply knowledge in new contexts.

In summary, Lang's "small teaching" approach focuses on manageable, evidence-based strategies to improve learning and engagement that faculty can gradually incorporate into any teaching practice.

and (3) providing staff and professional development. The University of Padova, Italy (UNIPD), is implementing these steps, creating the most important faculty development program ever realized in Italian universities, to date training 1,400 faculty members in AL principles. Fedeli (2019), the program's original director, described the program:

> Teaching4Learning@UNIPD started in early 2016, and it represented the first step for UNIPD to foster innovative teaching in response to the aforementioned national survey results and European recommendations (European Commission, 2011, 2013). Specifically, it encouraged faculty to experiment and discover new teaching strategies: [It]involved students and promoted their active participation in educational activities; de-privatized teaching; and progressively increased the number of faculty learning communities by building on relationships with interested colleagues. It was initiated by faculty who self-selected to participate and who had significant inclination to improve their approach to teaching and learning. (p. 53)

UNIPD has built the capacity to support the implementation by developing 60 change agents to promote the adoption of AL across the university. Fedeli and Taylor (2023) sought to understand the impact of the program, including student satisfaction and program effectiveness, concluding, "The findings indicated that trained faculty increased student satisfaction in specific disciplines, especially in face-to-face settings, consistent with existing literature relating to active learning and student satisfaction" (p. 169). This chapter offers theoretical and practical active learning approaches, including interactive lecturing and active learning design and facilitation.

Interactive Lecturing

Interactive lecturing (IL) is a type of active learning or guided instruction that intersperses activities with periods of **micro-lecturing** or **micro-learning**—short lectures lasting 5–15 minutes that break educational material down into smaller units (De Gagne et al., 2019; Roesler & Dreaver-Charles, 2018). Coryell (2024) defined IL as,

> An updated form of the lecture method that takes advantage of the efficiency of information transmission yet also incorporates active learning pauses (Rice, 2018). Active learning activities are those that engage adults in purposefully reflecting, conceptualizing, practicing/experimenting, and applying new knowledge in meaningful and more personalized engagement with the learning content. (p. 22)

It occurs when "Students interact with the instructor in two-way communication, asking questions and engaging in discussion" (Abeysekera, 2008, p. 192), recognized as "a social event where the lecturer can enhance (student) participation" (Morell, 2004, p. 326). For example, the instructor begins a class by helping learners prepare to learn, as noted in Box 15.4. This approach uses the first five minutes to facilitate a small group discussion about a question posed before class started. Next, the instructor offers a micro-lecture, an activity, another micro-lecture, and so on. Micro-lectures also help avoid what Bob Pike called "audio bombardment" by shifting activities approximately every eight minutes (Pike, 2003, as cited in Silberman, 2006, p. 3) and including opportunities for brief dialogue, free writing, or assessment. See Box 15.5 for more tips.

Interactive lectures also give learners visual scaffolding by integrating slides, demonstrations, or other visual cues to supplement the auditory. Incorporating visual stimuli aligns with the reality that 80–90% of information processed by the brain is visual, and it can improve retention and content mastery by 14–38% (Silberman, 2006). Further, visual cues improve vocabulary proficiency by up to 200% and decrease the time required to present a concept by up to 40% (Silberman, 2006, p. 3).

For example, imagine a 55-minute class introducing adult learning. The session might go something like the agenda featured in Table 15.1. Interactive lectures are

Box 15.5 SoTL: The Scholarship of Teaching and Learning

Lang's *Small Teaching Tools*

Although throwing out your current nonactive learning practices as an adult educator might be tempting or overwhelming, you might want to consider Lang's (2021) advice from his book, *Small Teaching*, offering solid evidence for integrating active learning into your teaching in small increments. Lang discouraged educators from completely dumping their curriculum and radically reforming their teaching approach. Instead, Lang encouraged minor adjustments with significant impact, such as slightly altering course design, shifting student communication patterns, or adjusting feedback practices. Lang offered specific practices in the book according to four broad instructional moments that incorporate brief 5–10-minute classroom learning activities that provide speedy occasions for learner action, mainly when introducing or concluding topics:

1. **Preparing to Learn:** Arrive early to chat with and get to know students, use pre- and post-testing to assess learning, or offer study tips to students.
2. **The First Five Minutes of Class:** Post reflection questions for consideration before the class starts, administer low-stakes assessments, or ask students to write minute papers about their topic knowledge.
3. **Hitting Pause:** Stop at multiple points during the class to ask for feedback, use peer review and peer instruction, or use a think-pair-share activity.
4. **Last Five Minutes of Class:** Ask students to write down the most important concepts they heard, invite them to predict the next class session's topics, or request that students tie the day's lesson to contexts outside the classroom.

Darby and Lang (2019) published *Small Teaching Online* to apply similar principles to virtual context.

effective strategies for promoting learner engagement and opportunities for learners to talk and compare experiences during face-to-face or online classes.

Using Interactive Lectures in Large Classes

Faculty who teach large classes are often the first to disavow active learning because they view it as incompatible with large class sizes. This view is mistaken.

TABLE 15.1 SAMPLE INTERACTIVE LECTURE AGENDA

Minutes Allotted	Activity	Description
:05	Preparing to Learn	Before class begins, the instructor posts reflection questions such as: • Who is an adult learner? • What motivates you to learn?
:05	The First Five Minutes of Class	Ask learners to free write about one of the questions from the "preparing to learn" activity.
:15	Micro-lecture	The instructor shares a brief lecture on defining adult learning. The presentation includes slides and a short video for maximum visual stimulation.
:15	Hitting Pause Plus Debrief	Learners join small groups based on which question they wrote about and then discuss their reflections for 10 minutes. Next, debrief the small group discussions with the entire class.
:15	Micro-lecture	The instructor continues the lecture on the adult learner, delving into motivation to learn.
:05	Last Five Minutes of Class	Invite learners to tie what they learned to their own life experiences.

Active learning and interactive lecture strategies work regardless of class size. Occasionally, instructors need to lecture to explain a new concept or describe a series of sequential steps, and when done well, IL is effective. Afrasiabifar and Asadolah (2019) explored outcomes in a nursing program when the traditional lecture was replaced with IL, discovering an increase in mean test scores and higher reported satisfaction with the learning experience. Ploetzner (2022) conducted a meta-analysis of interactive videos in online learning (using videos with **enhanced interaction features** that require the learner to play and pause buttons, navigate materials, take quizzes, and collaborate). They found when educational videos used enhanced interaction features, they were significantly more effective than video learning without the features. Sözmen et al. (2021) explored that when medical students engaged in regular microlearning during the COVID-19 pandemic, they developed higher self-confidence and achieved higher final grades. Box 15.6 features ways to integrate AL into large classes.

The Flipped Classroom

A **flipped classroom** (FC) shifts (or flips) lectures outside scheduled classroom time, where faculty record lectures in advance, and learners view them independently outside the regular class period. Learners may also engage in online

 **Box 15.6 Tips and Tools for Teaching and Learning**

Facilitating Large Lectures Using Active Learning

Large classes often discourage faculty from trying active learning strategies due to the sheer size and prospect of facilitating an unwieldy audience. If you, as an educator, teach large classes, you can use active learning principles. Why should you? Active learning in large lectures reduces anonymity, increases student accountability, engages learners, and enhances learning. Here are some proven strategies:

Get To Know Your Students

1. Compile a photo roster.
2. Create small groups and give them folders where they can affix photos. You keep the folder and only distribute it during class. Use the folders for collecting assessments and assignments or distributing information.
3. Use your learning management system (LMS) to have students create profiles with photos.
4. Collect electronic student bios with photos and review them before meeting with students.
5. When speaking with students, ask for their names and use them in that interaction.
6. Enable the "change name" feature in Zoom or your meeting platform.
7. Hold smaller group meetings either in person or virtually outside class.

Engage Learners

1. Use dyads, triads, and small groups for activities.
2. Use think-pair-share or write-pair-share activities.
3. Provide group time in class for project work.
4. Flip the classroom (put content online and engage in interactive exercises during class).
5. Use your online space to foster interaction through assignments, a "social lounge" for sharing non-class-related items, and a class-related help thread where students can ask each other questions about the course (helpful if the professor chimes in occasionally).

Practice Effective Care of the Learner

1. Begin the session with an active way of engaging learners with the content and each other. Use interactive techniques.
2. Divide the content and activities into manageable segments or modules with different modes of delivery (e.g., video; panel discussion, like charette; small group discussion; guest speakers; application exercises; demonstration; and paired discussions).
3. Incorporate regular breaks.
4. Manage time effectively.
5. Do not sacrifice processing time for content.

For additional examples and tools, see Allen & Tanner (2017), Elliott et al. (2017), Ndebele & Maphosa (2013).

discussions, research, or other activities outside class. Militsa Nechkina (1984), a member of the USSR Academy of Pedagogical Sciences, first proposed the idea of a flipped classroom, which was embraced in Russian education. Harvard professor Eric Mazur (2013) began advocating the method in 1997 and has been a leading AL voice in higher education. Özbay and Çınar (2021) systematically reviewed nursing education studies of the FC from 2013 to 2020, concluding it improved the quality of teaching and supported effective learning, advocating for more use of the FC model. What can you do if you, as an adult educator, want to make your lectures interactive? Table 15.2 summarizes some strategies to engage adult learners, whether lecturing or applying active learning methodology.

Active Learning Design and Facilitation

Although interactive lecture is highly recommended for engaging learners, as an educator, you may wish to amplify opportunities for learners to be more active than an interactive lecture format allows. The next step is to shift to active learning or guided instruction. Active learning (AL) was defined earlier in this chapter as engaging learners with the topic and each other through conversation,

TABLE 15.2 INTERACTIVE LECTURE STRATEGIES

Interactive Lecture Strategy	Description	Pedagogical Considerations	Examples
Demonstration	A demonstration is teaching by showing instead of telling. It uses visual tools, including posters, flip charts, videos, or other means to describe concepts or steps. Instead of only talking about a topic, demonstrations show learners how to do something. Demonstrations often result in a final product, like learning how to use a computer program, fill out a form, do an experiment, or complete a task.	1. When giving a demonstration, ensure it relates to the topic. 2. Assemble the needed materials, plan the steps, and practice explaining each step. 3. Prepare any visuals you will use.	• Cooking shows teach viewers step-by-step techniques of following a recipe, such as measuring, sautéing, or baking. • Job interview role-playing. • A home improvement workshop on gardening or painting.
Question Posing	Asking good questions involves raising inquiries about the topic and is essential to effective learning (Chin & Osborne, 2008). Questions spark learner interest, confirm what students already know, challenge their thinking, help them remember information, focus on key ideas, encourage deeper thinking, assess learning progress, and help students think critically and comprehend the lesson more effectively. Questions can also help educators assess learner proficiency.	A challenge for educators is that learners may be reluctant to ask or answer questions (Almeida & Teixeira-Dias, 2012). Still, questions can serve multiple purposes, such as to pique interest, assess prior knowledge, challenge worldviews, stimulate recall or previous knowledge, focus on key theories or ideas, extend thinking, promote reflection and critical thinking, and assess learning. Educators can diminish learners' reluctance to ask challenging questions by posing provoking questions for class discussion.	• Avoid closed questions answerable with a *"yes"* or *"no,"* such as *"Do you agree with this idea?"* • A better question is an open question that requires a response such as: a. *"What about this idea is confusing to you?"* b. *"What aspects of this idea do you agree/disagree with?"* c. *"What else would you like to know about the topic?"* • Open questions help learners review information and participate by asking questions.

Learner Polling	Technology is available to facilitate learner response through questions, polls, word clouds, and other tools during class using keyboards or smartphones. Research shows that anonymous responses encourage more participation (Freeman et al., 2006). There are free or low-cost apps that can help make lessons more interactive, easily found with an internet search.	1. Although increasingly accessible and free, technology is not necessary for learner polling. 2. A simple show of hands works quite well with questions like, *"Who has heard of this idea?"* or *"Who agrees/disagrees?"* 3. Another low-tech option is using multi-color cards to show opinions that learners hold up, for example: a. **Green** =Agree b. **Yellow** =Not sure c. **Red** =Disagree 4. You can also make polling more active by placing different answers or ideas around the room and having students stand near the one they agree with. For example, in a leadership lesson, students could stand by a quote that best represents their beliefs and discuss why with the class.	Use polling to: • Track attendance • Assess learning • Administer quizzes • Query stances on emotionally or politically charged issues • Solicit feedback • Manage question and answer periods • Play games
Small Group Discussions	Adults tend to be reluctant to speak in front of the class due to fears of making mistakes. Conversations in small groups create lower-stakes engagement and are easy to involve learners. Incorporating small group discussions is a practical active learning approach, regardless of class size.	Here are some strategies for using small groups in teaching, regardless of class size: • Establish groups that work together for the whole semester. • Assign group projects and create temporary groups for the duration of the project. • Create discussion groups that change with every class or perhaps use multiple discretion groups in a single class, depending on the duration. • Creatively break learners into groups (do not ask learners to count off because people forget their numbers and class time is lost). Try creating groups using playing cards, assorted candy, birth months, or color-coded folders.	• Assign all groups the same or different questions about various issues appropriate for the lesson. • Debrief small group conversations with the entire class to entertain key insights, controversies, and questions. • Pair students with one person before moving them into a larger group discussion. This small "warm-up" conversation primes the conversation with the larger, more challenging group. • Brookfield and Preskill (2012) have written a comprehensive guide to using discussion as a pedagogy, and their book is an excellent resource.

movement, and application without relying on long-winded, passive lectures. Incorporating AL does not mean you entirely abandon lectures or must transform your teaching repertoire. Major (2020) noted the term "active learning" gained traction after Bonwell and Eison (1991) published a report on the topic, defining AL as "anything that involves students in doing things and thinking about the things they are doing" (p. 19). Continuing, Major explained, "True active learning requires students to be dynamic participants in their own learning, regardless of the particular activity in which the students are to engage" (p. 20). AL invites collaborative learning, enabling learners to assume responsibility for their learning and critical thinking (Hacisalihoglu et al., 2018), and improves retention, engagement, and overall student success (Allsop et al., 2020). This section focuses on the theory and practice of integrating AL fully into educational pedagogy.

Active Learning Design

Munna and Kalam (2021) conducted a literature review of teaching effectiveness research in higher education settings, finding AL improves inclusivity and faculty and student performance. Theobald et al. (2020) compared exam scores and failure rates in STEM courses between traditional lecture and active learning in classes taught by the same instructor. On average, AL reduced achievement gaps for underrepresented undergraduate students, and they concluded that broad implementation of high-quality AL potentially reduces or eliminates achievement gaps in stem courses and increases equitable higher education. Nardo et al. (2022) reported similar findings in a first-year chemistry course. Box 15.7 summarizes a study of AL design and facilitation strategies.

 Box 15.7 SoTL: The Scholarship of Teaching and Learning

A Systematic Literature Review of Active Learning Strategies

Nguyen et al. (2021) conducted a systematic literature review of 29 active learning (AL) studies examining affective and behavioral student responses that recommended at least one AL strategy. Most AL activities involve in-class problem-solving within a traditional lecture-based course. They discovered generally positive affective and behavioral outcomes for students' self-reports of learning, class participation, and course satisfaction. They synthesized AL into three categories incorporating eight strategies, summarized as follows.

1. **Planning Strategies** are ways educators work outside the class to improve the active learning experience, representing the bulk of activities:
   a. Designing Appropriate Activities: Creating learning activities that engage and invite learner participation, balancing learning goals within class time and format constraints.
   b. Developing Group Policies: Developing guidelines to ensure effective group and team processes, including suggesting appropriate roles, ground rules, and assigning groups.
   c. Aligning the Course: Calibrating learning with course goals, topics, assignments, and other types of assessment, and ensuring appropriate timing of activities.
   d. Reviewing Student Feedback: Soliciting and acting on learner feedback on learning activities and using the information to adjust and improve the course.

2. **Explanation Strategies** provide students with clarifications and rationale for using active learning and used strategies of:
   a. Establishing Expectations: Explaining course design and AL expectations, including setting the tone and routine for the course and active learning tasks, which are particularly useful at the beginning of the semester, the start of class, and before beginning an active learning activity.
   b. Explaining the Purpose: Articulating the rationale and value of AL tasks.

3. **Facilitation Strategies** involve working with students to ensure that the learning activity proceeds as intended and that students remain engaged and active throughout the semester:
   a. Approaching Learners: Offering learners feedback during the activity and monitoring progress by approaching teams who need help during the activity.
   b. Encouraging Learners: Reassuring learners as they engage in the activity about their progress and showing care for their success, community building, and sustaining a respectful, supportive learning environment.

Michael (2006) examined pedagogical studies in the sciences to uncover the best available evidence, concluding, "There IS evidence that active learning, student-centered approaches to teaching physiology work, and they work better than more passive approaches" (p. 165). They offered five active learning conclusions: (1) Learners actively construct meaning (p. 160); (2) Learning facts ("what"—declarative knowledge) and learning to do something ("how"—procedural knowledge) are distinct processes (p. 161); (3) Learning may be specific to the domain or context (subject matter or course), or more readily transferred to other domains (p. 161); (4) People are more likely to learn collaboratively than individually (p. 161); and (5) Learning is enhanced when learners have to explain concepts whether to self, peers, or teachers (p. 162).

In addition to following Lang's (2021) small teaching advice about making incremental changes to pedagogy, varying the activity level is also vital to keep students engaged and not exhaust them with activity after activity. Table 15.3 summarizes several active learning strategies for low, medium, and high activity levels.

Facilitating Active Learning Exercises. Whether presenting an interactive lecture or more active approaches, facilitating an active learning (AL) exercise involves the educator's planning and active facilitation during the event. Key considerations for effective AL include facilitating effectively, incorporating ample wait time, integrating quick interactive exercises throughout the class period, and moderating activity levels.

Effective AL Exercise Facilitation. Achieving effective AL requires planning and intention. As noted in this chapter, instructors appear to do less work during an active learning session. However, they have spent time before the class developing activities that engage students and are easy to implement during the class period. In addition to planning, active learning works most effectively when the learning environment is safe and brave, as discussed in Chapter 12. Learners also need scaffolding and prompts to ensure the exercise proceeds as planned and has easy-to-follow steps. Smooth exercise facilitation requires providing clear, visible instructions to the learners, prompting questions for reflection and discussion, and adapting as needed during the exercise. Table 15.4 offers tips for ensuring effective management of AL exercises.

After finishing an AL exercise, as an educator spend a few minutes debriefing it with learners to assess how well the activity's purpose and objectives were met and acknowledge learners' engagement. Solicit reactions to both the activity and new insights. Ask how the activity might be improved or applied to learners' lives and work.

Wait Time. A common mistake educators make when posing questions is not lingering long enough for learners to ponder a meaningful answer. This period

TABLE 15.3 INSTRUCTIONAL TECHNIQUE BY ACTIVITY LEVEL

Activity Level of Instructional Techniques

High	Medium	Low
Group Discussion Have small groups discuss course material and field questions from learners in their audience.	**Reaction Panel** A group of experts presents short presentations, and a moderator guides the discussion and elicits questions from the audience.	**Lecture** An educational talk to an audience. Generally passive.
Buzz Group A small group of people is divided from a larger group to talk about ideas and solutions to problems for a short period.	**Screened Speech/Video** Watch or listen to a speech or video and discuss. Give prompts to listen or watch for (e.g., What was the key question/point?).	**Panel** A group of people who answer questions, give advice or opinions, or take part in a discussion for an audience.
Case Study Learners collaborate to learn course concepts and develop key skills and competencies while focusing on real-life problems.	**Listening Group** Learners listen to each other's work and discuss it.	**Symposium** A collection of essays or papers on a particular subject presented by several contributors.
Game Create or use a web-based game platform to review lessons.	**Behavior Modeling** Show learners how to do something and guide them through imitating the modeled behavior.	**Demonstration** A practical exhibition and explanation of how something works or is performed.
Simulation, Application Learners and/or faculty perform specific roles for demonstration purposes. Include guiding principles, specific rules, and structured relationships.	**Role Playing** Acting out a phenomenon relevant to the lesson.	**Self-assessment** Evaluation of oneself or one's actions and attitudes related to the performance of a job or learning task against an objective standard.
In-basket An assessment tool to evaluate how well learners can make decisions related to content.	**Storytelling** Tell stories about the topic to spark interest, aid the flow of lectures, make the material memorable, and build rapport.	**Quiz** A test of knowledge, especially a brief, informal test, is given to learners.
Structured Learning Experience—SLE An experiential, supervised, in-depth learning activity that allows learners to experience the concept (i.e., work-based learning).	**Silence** Often underrated, silence can make space for reflection, demonstration, collaboration, and concentration.	**Voting or Polling** A low-stakes, real-time engagement of learners around course content through reflection, opinion assessment, knowledge or skill evaluation, and/or skills in real-time and with low or no stakes.

(Continued)

TABLE 15.3 (*Continued*)

Activity Level of Instructional Techniques

High	Medium	Low
Critical Incident Learners identify situations where they have experienced effective, exceptional, challenging, or personally meaningful outcomes.	**Observation** Learning by watching the behaviors and interactions of other people and then mimicking, critiquing, or analyzing them.	**Reading** Learners read silently or read passages aloud to the class.
Trial and Error A problem-solving method where learners make multiple attempts to reach a solution.	**Reflective Practice** Examining one's underlying beliefs and assumptions about a topic or concept.	**Video** Showing film clips to learners that relate to the course content.
Jigsaw/Peer Teaching A team-based activity where each member/team becomes a subject matter expert in course material and teaches their subject to their team members. Learners teach each other basic/intermediate levels of course materials or needed skills.	**Dialogue** Communication that prioritizes meaning-making over idea advocacy, where participants suspend judgment and ask questions of genuine curiosity.	**Audio** Playing audible content for learners to listen and react to (e.g., speeches, poetry, music, literature).
Categorization Grouping objects or ideas according to criteria that describe common features or the relationships among all members of the concept.	**1-Minute Paper/Writing** Short writing tasks ask learners to focus on one term or concept from a lesson. The writing can be helpful for assessment or reflection.	
Walking, Movement Adults learn better through movement. Try stretch breaks, or short walks with a partner to discuss the topic and retain material.	**Concept Mapping** Visual representations of information include charts, graphic organizers, tables, flowcharts, Venn Diagrams, timelines, or T-charts.	
	Think-Pair-Share Short individual reflection or writing to a prompt or question; *then* a paired discussion with a partner; *then* larger group sharing.	

TABLE 15.4 TEN STRATEGIES FOR FACILITATING GROUP EXERCISES

1. Explain the **purpose** or **why** behind the exercise. Share objectives and benefits.
2. Specify **what** participants are supposed to do. Provide visual backup and demonstrate where needed.
3. Indicate **who** will do what.
4. Direct participants to **where** the activity will take place.
5. Indicate **when** the activity will end.
6. **Summarize** instructions (or ask a participant to do this).
7. **Observe**, monitor, and adjust (to time and other unanticipated variables), and keep activity energized.
8. Conduct **process** and **time checks** with groups.
9. **Debrief** exercise for key points, feelings, insights, and learning.
10. Establish **So whats** and summarize the highlights.

Courtesy of Bierema (2019), p. 46

is known as **"wait time,"** or moments of silence after an instructor asks a question to give learners time to answer (Rowe, 1972, 1987). Rowe, who invented the term, discovered that educators wait approximately 1.5 seconds after asking learners questions, giving learners insufficient time to formulate a meaningful response. Further, simply doubling the wait time to three seconds yielded better responses. Not surprisingly, waiting even longer than 3 seconds increased the proportion of correct answers, bolstered learner participation, and improved test scores. Stahl (1990, 1994) revised the terminology to **"think time"** to more accurately reflect this silent period for learners to process information, assess feelings, compose an oral response, or take action. Irving and Garling (n.d.) explained:

> It is necessary to give students some time to think about the questions and formulate a response. Even though it can feel like you have been waiting forever for an answer, or even just some small sign that they heard you, in reality it was probably less than one second. On average, teachers only wait between 0.7 and 1.4 seconds after asking a question (Stahl, 1994). Try counting to at least three in your mind (one mis-sis-sip-pi, two mis-sis-sip-pi, etc.) before repeating the question or rewording it. Nobody wants to turn into the economics teacher in *Ferris Bueller's Day Off.* (n.p.)

More complicated questions require even longer "think time" for learners to formulate a meaningful reply. Ingram and Elliott (2016) advocated that extending wait time can potentially shift classroom interaction patterns. They discouraged adopting a standard three-second wait time since it focuses educators' attention on the length of wait rather than pausing long enough for the desired student interactions. Shiau et al. (2024) conducted a systematic review to synthesize and update research on the role of wait time when questioning children. They concluded that most research on this concept is in education and that although "natural wait time is short . . . extended wait time yields significant benefits for both child and adult talk" (p. 3341). One of the studies they reviewed found a 10-second waiting time to be more productive than shorter pauses. Try integrating wait time into your teaching and conversation as an educator or learner. You might be surprised at what emerges.

Integrating Quick Active Learning Exercises. As an educator, you may wish to take a lead from Lang's *Small Teaching* (2021) and integrate active learning strategies incrementally. Box 15.8 outlines quick and easy techniques to engage learners

---

 ## Box 15.8 Tips and Tools for Teaching and Learning

Quick Strategies for Bolstering Participation in an Interactive Lecture

Focused Listing

Inviting individual learners to brainstorm by creating lists related to their learning or asking learners to brainstorm independently and then discuss their answers with a partner or small group. Here are examples of focused listening questions you can pose. Remember to give learners a visual prompt by putting the task on a slide or:

1. Create a list of terms or ideas related to . . .
2. List five things you know about [the topic].
3. List three things that are unclear about . . .

Generate Real-life Examples

Invite learners to identify real-world examples of the topic of the lesson. For example, if you are studying diversity, equity, and inclusion, you might ask learners to identify instances of discrimination or harassment in the news or their workplace or community. Once learners generate examples, they have some juicy topics for dialogue in pairs or small groups.

Finish the Sentence

Introduce a topic or question for reflection and then prompt learners to complete one of the following sentences:

An alternative way of thinking about this would be _____.

A point I agree/disagree with is _____.

A variation is to introduce or conclude a topic with a sentence completion. For example, when you are introducing a topic, you might ask:

My challenge with [topic] is _____.

My excitement about [topic] is _____.

When you conclude an interactive lecture, you might try one or more of these sentences for learners to complete:

I didn't know that _____.

The thing about [topic] that isn't clear is _____.

Next, I will try _____.

This experience has made me think _____.

and enliven your teaching. These strategies work equally well for interactive lectures or more active classes.

Simple ways of engaging learners are almost endless, and your learners will be delighted to feel more engaged in the experience.

Active Learning Approaches

In addition to interactive lecturing, Bierema (2019) offered three ways to engage adult learners in active learning, including (1) reflective practice;

(2) information seeking, analysis, and synthesis; and (3) group inquiry. This section discusses each approach with specific activities.

Reflective Practice. **Reflective practice**—analyzing one's mindsets, thoughts, and actions—has been featured throughout this book as an effective development process for adult learners. Schön (1983), in his research of professionals' learning, recognized that having technical knowledge was inadequate for them to excel in their careers and that they needed to continually engage in cycles of reflection in and on and action to adapt to shifting dynamics, as discussed in Chapter 1 and throughout the book. As an educator, you can foster reflection by encouraging individual or collective assessment of thought or action at any point during a class period or assign reflective activities outside class. Table 15.5 summarizes reflective AL activities.

Reflective practice gives learners a moment to pause and ponder—something they may neglect daily.

Information Seeking, Analysis, and Synthesis. The lecture adequately conveys information to students but is not the only way; it often falls short of giving learners opportunities to find, scrutinize, and integrate information that more AL approaches promote. Enlisting learners and searching for information is a more constructivist pedagogy in that learners co-create meaning about the subject. Table 15.6 highlights these strategies.

Group Inquiry. Group inquiry involves two or more individuals engaging in reflective practice and assumption questioning about the lesson. Collective inquiry allows learners to tap into their experiences and share their thoughts and assumptions about the topic. Opportunities for people to engage in collective exploration help them tie new knowledge to existing knowledge, retain information, apply new learning, promote peer-to-peer learning and coaching, and develop capacity for real-world application. Box 15.9 details how to conduct the highly interactive jigsaw activity.

Finding creative ways for learners to make queries into the learning topics are engaging antidotes to traditional lectures. Table 15.7 summarizes additional group inquiry approaches—and Box 15.10 makes recommendations for further learning.

TABLE 15.5 REFLECTIVE PRACTICE ACTIVITIES

Strategy	Description	Example
Reflective Pause	Building in time for learners to ponder a question or prompt (Rice, 2018, 2023).	Ask learners to Think-Pair-Share: 1. *Think* about a question or prompt. 2. *Pair* with another learner. 3. *Share* thoughts, insights, or questions after reflecting on the prompt. This activity can be done relatively quickly, and the class size is not an issue.
Observation	Learners view a phenomenon or activity during or outside class to understand how it unfolds.	• Peer Observations: Group the learners into triads and ask persons 1 and 2 to engage in an activity such as discussing the topic or a role play. Person 3 observes and then shares observations after persons 1 and 2 complete the activity. If time allows, learners can reverse roles. • Critique: For example, students learning to teach adults might observe and critique a training activity during class or at their workplace.

Writing Tasks	Brief or prolonged opportunities for learners to write about a topic help them organize their learning. Whittard (2015) suggested writing activities show respect and build trust with learners.	The Minute Paper (Cross & Angelo, 1988).
		1. Give learners a prompt such as:
		  a. "What is the key insight you are taking away from today's class?" or
		  b. "What do you need to understand better to master this topic?"
		2. Gives learners one minute to write their thoughts.
		3. Discuss what learners wrote or use the papers for learning assessment.

Mind or Concept Mapping	A visual organization or representation of a thinking process or idea. The map begins with a central idea, such as "adult learning," and other ideas are connected to the main idea, "branching," to show relationships, such as "experience" or "transformation." Mapping helps learners reflect on and make connections about the topic. Daley and Torre (2010) scrutinized 35 concept map studies, concluding four uses: (1) promoting meaningful learning, (2) serving as an additional learning resource, (3) enabling educator feedback, and (4) assessing learning and performance.	1. Give learners a topic or ask them to identify one related to the lesson. 2. Learners can draw the maps by hand or use a digital interface like Canva or Google Mind Maps. 3. Have learners share their maps. 4. Students can also map collectively.

TABLE 15.6 INFORMATION SEEKING, ANALYSIS, AND SYNTHESIS ACTIVITIES

Strategy	Description	Example
Information Search	Individuals or small groups hunt for information and present it to a small group or class.	• Learners seek out professionals in their field and conduct informational interviews. • The instructor creates a scavenger hunt about a topic (Von Lau & Gopalai, 2022). Alternatively, learners could develop the activity. • Learners conduct searches using generative artificial intelligence (GAI). • Learners search in a library or examine current events on their learning topic (Stark et al., 2021).
Study Group	Collaborative learning groups engage in tasks and dialogues about the course content or complete homework. This approach can achieve various goals, including developing critical thinking, enhancing understanding and comprehension, fostering dialogical skills, and building collaboration capacity. Learners can submit written summaries of their work for assessment and feedback.	• Typical study group tasks might include taking nonconsequential quizzes, developing chronologies or timelines, defining terms, analyzing texts, or giving feedback on written work. • Writing circles are particularly effective for students developing theses and dissertations (Hass, 2011; Hsaio & Rajagopal, 2023; Rajagopal et al., 2021; Sridharan et al., 2023).
Debate	Formal and civil discussion of a topic from multiple viewpoints (Litan, 2020) that promotes perspective-taking, appreciates diverse perspectives, furthers empathy and open-mindedness, develops confidence, improves communication, fosters active listening skills, and encourages civic engagement and participation in a healthy democracy (Baines et al., 2023).	Darby (2007) offered the following advice on setting up a debate where learners: 1. Work individually or collectively to research the topic. 2. Develop and present logical arguments, usually before an audience. 3. Actively listen to the differing perspectives and attempt to differentiate between subjective and objective information. 4. Develop question-asking ability, discernment, empathy, and poise, and ultimately formulate their own opinions after assessing the evidence presented.
Application Exercise	Individuals or small groups apply a concept to real or hypothetical situations to improve their capacity for effective future performance. It is also known as "deliberative practice" (Campitelli & Gobet, 2011; Clear, n.d.).	• Accounting students create profit and loss statements. • Medical students practice taking blood pressure or medical histories on each other. • Cooking recipes repeatedly to perfect the method or dish. • Practicing music or sports.

 ## Box 15.9 Tips and Tools for Teaching and Learning

The Jigsaw

The Jigsaw (Aronson, 1975, 1978) is a collaborative learning activity. Building on the metaphor of a jigsaw puzzle, each piece—the learner's contribution—is vital to completing the activity. The activity involves two different groups. The first or original group should have enough members to cover the learning tasks involved, and the second group can be larger as each second group focuses on one of the learning tasks. For example, the following table shows a jigsaw structure based on 12 students:

Original Grouping	Second Grouping	Original Grouping
Four groups of three members who will separate into new, larger groups to address three unique learning tasks.	The four groups move into four new, larger groups and receive a unique teaching task that they will bring back to their original group.	The original groups reunite. Each member was in a different group (A, B, C) and shares their lesson with the original group. So, group number 1 is paired with learning tasks A, B, or C, and so on.
Group 1: 1, 1 ,1 **Group 2:** 2, 2, 2 **Group 3:** 3, 3, 3 **Group 4:** 4, 4, 4	**Group A:** 1, 2, 3, 4 **Group B:** 1, 2, 3, 4 **Group C:** 1, 2, 3, 4	**Group 1:** 1A, 1B, 1C **Group 2:** 2A, 2B, 2C **Group 3:** 3A, 3B, 3C **Group 4:** 4A, 4B, 4C

Steps:

1. Create "original groups." Group size depends on the topic and how many second groups you will need. Complete this step before class time to allow some flexibility if there are absences, such as having more than one person from the original group join the second group.
2. Once the original groups are established, explain that each group member will be moved to a new "second group," where they will work collectively on a learning task shared with the original group. For instance, if the topic were learning theory, each second group would receive a learning theory (e.g., Group A: Andragogy, Group B: Self-directed learning, Group C: Transformational learning, and so forth.). The second group now has the task of learning their topic and creating a teaching plan to bring back to their original group. Best practice

involves giving each group the content you wish to cover and inviting them to use other resources to develop their lesson.

3. Once the learning task is completed, second group members return to their original group. Like a puzzle that started put together, it is taken apart and then reassembled as they present their lessons.

The Jigsaw is beneficial because it is an interactive, egalitarian, effective, and efficient activity that encourages listening, engagement, and empathy by giving each group member an essential part of the process. The jigsaw builds a learning community and enhances interaction among all learners as they contribute to the collective learning task.

Adapted from Bierema (2019, pp. 39–40)

TABLE 15.7 GROUP INQUIRY ACTIVITIES

Group Inquiry	Description	Example
Case Study	Learners address a hypothetical or real-world scenario that they need to investigate, discuss, analyze, and attempt to solve. Learners can work on the same or different cases, and then small groups can present their analyses to each other.	• Take a current event and use that as the case for analysis. • Use pre-developed case studies such as *Harvard Business Review*, available by subscription, or use field-specific case study textbooks. • Identify a topic and have learners develop a learning plan or intervention.
Games and Simulations	Learners practice course concepts using highly interactive activities incorporating structure or rules such as a board game, quiz show, or simulated real-life situation. Murillo-Zamorano et al. (2021) studied gamification using control and experimental groups in a 132-student economics course. They found strong evidence that creating an interactive and engaging gameful experience enhances learner involvement without lowering academic performance. This approach also helps learners develop essential skills needed for career success.	Tay et al. (2022) conducted a systematic literature review examining digital game-based learning, analyzing 30 articles and deriving 3 themes for using games and simulations: 1. Integrate real-world context, problems, or knowledge into the game and provide adequate hints. 2. Maximize game design elements to motivate and sustain learner engagement through points or goal accumulation and the learner's ability to control the learning process within and beyond the game. 3. Consider how learning during the game will be transferred to real life.

Learning Tournaments	A learning tournament uses a game or simulation format, and small groups contend with each other to see who can demonstrate knowledge with the most accuracy and speed.	A popular format is to play a form of a US game show called *Jeopardy*, where students have to guess questions to answers flashed on a screen. Fisher (2023) reviewed nine free customizable Jeopardy templates for instructional use, and additional resources are readily available via a Google search.
Role Play	Learners assume the roles of individuals or groups and act out planned or improvised scenarios to simulate real-life situations.	For example, students could role-play how to and how not to do something (e.g., a procedure, interview, or social interaction). The amount of structure for the role play can vary, depending on purpose and educational objectives. Role plays effectively teach attitudes and interpersonal skills and provide practice on course objectives while enhancing the transfer of learning to the real world.

 ## Box 15.10 Recommendations for Further Learning

This box contains recommended reading and videos on active learning.

Reading

Keengwe, J. (Ed.). (2022). *Handbook of Research on Active Learning and Student Engagement in Higher Education*. IGI Global.

Sukackė, V., Guerra, A. O. P. D. C., Ellinger, D., Carlos, V., Petronienė, S., Gaižiūnienė, L., et al. (2022). Towards active evidence-based learning in engineering education: A systematic literature review of PBL, PjBL, and CBL. *Sustainability, 14*(21), 13955. https://doi.org/10.3390/su142113955

Video Resources

Mazur Interactive Lecture: https://youtu.be/wont2v_LZ1E
Dr. Richard Felder: https://youtu.be/1J1URbdisYE
Video: *Ferris Bueller's Day Off*. https://www.youtube.com/watch?v=uhiCFdWeQfA&feature=youtu.be

Chapter Summary

Active learning is a proven approach for enhancing learner engagement and understanding. As Lang (2021) advocated in the small learning model, even slight, incremental changes to your teaching and courses can yield significant results for you as an adult educator that have a lasting impact on your learners. Presumably, you do not want your classes to mimic the droning lecture in the film *Ferris Bueller's Day Off*, with the professor's protracted attempts to foster engagement of zoned-out learners by pleading, "Anyone, anyone?" With active learning strategies, you will avoid being *that* instructor. The following section concludes the book with key points embedded in Table 15.8.

Book Summary

This book provides a framework for embracing and applying adult learning theory—whether you are an educator seeking to ignite change or a learner striving for growth. By carefully considering the adult learning context, the adult educator's role, the adult learner's needs, and the learning process itself, you can design experiences that empower adults to thrive in life, contribute meaningfully to their communities, and excel in their careers. With this framework, you can also assess your learning experiences to design learning and assess quality. As you plan or reflect on learning experiences, use the questions in Table 15.8 as a reflective guide to the content of this book—helping you craft meaningful, engaging, and life-changing learning journeys.

Learning is the breath of life for you as an adult learner and educator—it fuels growth, expands possibilities, and empowers us to fully engage in the private, public, and professional spheres of life. It challenges us, enriches our knowledge, and strengthens our ability to navigate an ever-evolving world. Teaching, in turn, is a profound responsibility that calls for deep self-awareness, genuine care for learners, and the ability to link theory with practice in truly resonating ways. To teach well is to inspire, guide, and create opportunities for transformation. It is our hope, as authors, that the second edition of *Adult Learning: Linking Theory and Practice* provides you with a road map to facilitate meaningful, active learning in your life as an adult educator or adult learner, considering myriad ways you can promote excellent learning and teaching.

TABLE 15.8 BRINGING THE ADULT LEARNING FRAMEWORK TOGETHER IN ADULT LEARNING AND EDUCATION

Frame Aspect	Reflective Questions
Context	• How can I create a safe yet challenging learning environment? • How are VUCA issues impacting the content and learning processes? • How can learners claim their voices in the current social context? • What positionalities are at play in the classroom? How do learners experience me? Themselves? Each other? • How can I maximize learning in a digital environment? • How is equity being promoted or obstructed in learning?
Educator	• How do I define myself as an adult educator? • How am I showing up as an educator? • What are my teaching values, beliefs, and philosophies? • How resilient, flexible, and open am I? • What is my teaching philosophy? Have I written it down? Shared it with learners? • What is my teaching orientation? How does it help and hurt my teaching? • How balanced and centered am I? What can I do better? • How am I doing at cultivating the four crucial mindsets distinguishing excellent teachers of adults: (1) cultivating a global, adaptive stance; (2) thinking critically about your work as an adult educator; (3) committing to equity and justice; and (4) becoming an adult learning leader?
Learner	• What are my characteristics as a learner? • What motivates me to learn? • How is my learning relevant to my life? • How self-directed am I in my learning? • How are my diverse learner needs being honored? • How equitable is the learning environment?
Process	• How can I honor learners' experiences? • How can I foster reflection and critical reflection? • How are learning and change related to my experience? • How do I leverage experience for learning? • How does learning for transformation affect my life and learning? • How well do learners' espoused theories match their theories-in-use? • How can I incorporate learning that speaks to learners' narratives, spirituality, embodiment, or transformative experiences? • How can I learn or create instruction with neuroscience in mind?
Method	• How can I bridge theory and practice in my work as an adult learner or educator? • How should adult learning be designed to create relevant, engaging, and timely learning experiences for diverse learners? • What design considerations must I make for in-person, hybrid, and online learning environments? • What tools do I want to use or learn to facilitate adult learning more effectively? • How can I become a more active learning facilitator of adult learning?

References

Abeysekera, I. (2008). Preferred learning methods: A comparison between international and domestic accounting students. *Accounting Education: An International Journal, 17*(2), 187–198. https://doi.org/10.1080/09639280701220236.

Afrasiabifar, A., & Asadolah, M. (2019). Effectiveness of shifting traditional lecture to interactive lecture to teach nursing students. *Investigacion & Educacion En Enfermeria, 37*(1), e07. https://doi-org.proxy-remote.galib.uga.edu/10.17533/udea.iee.v37n1a07.

Allen, D., & Tanner, K. (2005). Infusing active learning into the large-enrollment biology class: Seven strategies, from the simple to complex. *Cell Biology Education, 4*(4), 262–268. https://doi.org/10.1187/cbe.05-08-0113.

Allsop, J., Young, S. J., Nelson, E. J., Piatt, J., & Knapp, D. (2020). Examining the benefits associated with implementing an active learning classroom among undergraduate students. *International Journal of Teaching and Learning in Higher Education, 32*(3), 418–426.

Almeida, P. A., & Teixeira-Dias, J. J. (2012). Aligning teaching, learning and assessment in a first-year chemistry course. *International Journal of Learning, 18*(4), 143–158. https://doi.org/10.18848/1447-9494/CGP/v18i04/47583.

Aronson, E. (1975). The jigsaw route to learning and liking. *Psychology Today,* 43–59.

Aronson, E. (1978). *The jigsaw classroom.* Thousand Oaks, CA: Sage.

Baines, A., Medina, D., & Healy, C. (2023, January 26). *Using debate as an educational tool.* Edutopia. https://www.edutopia.org/article/using-debate-educational-tool/.

Bierema, L. L. (2019). Adult learning theories and practices. In Fedeli, M., & Bierema, L. L. *Connecting adult learning and knowledge management.* Springer.

Bonwell, C. C., & Eison, J. A. (1991). *Active learning: Creating excitement in the classroom. 1991 ASHE-ERIC higher education reports.* ERIC Clearinghouse on Higher Education, The George Washington University, One Dupont Circle, Suite 630, Washington, DC 20036-1183.

Børte, K., Nesje, K., & Lillejord, S. (2020). Barriers to student active learning in higher education. *Teaching in Higher Education, 28*(3), 597–615. https://doi.org/10.1080/13562517.2020.1839746.

Brookfield, S. D., & Preskill, S. (2012). *Discussion as a way of teaching: Tools and techniques for democratic classrooms.* San Francisco: John Wiley & Sons.

Campitelli, G., & Gobet, F. (2011). Deliberate practice: Necessary but not sufficient. *Current Directions in Psychological Science, 20*(5), 280–285.

Cervero, R. (1992). Professional practice, learning, and continuing education: An integrated perspective. *International Journal of Lifelong Education, 11*(2), 91–101.

Chin, C. & Osborne, J. (2008). Student's questions: A potential resource for teaching and learning science. *Studies in Science Education, 44*(1), 1–39.

Clear, J. (n.d.). *The beginners guide to deliberative practice.* https://jamesclear.com/beginners-guide-deliberative-practice.

Coryell, J. E. (2024). Interactive lecture: Engaging active learning interactive teaching and learning with lecture. In J. E. Coryell, L. M. Baumgartner, & J. W. Bohonos (Eds.), *Methods for facilitating adult learning: Strategies for enhancing instruction and instructor effectiveness* (pp. 21–37). Routledge.

Cross, K. P., & Angelo, T. A. (1988). *Classroom assessment techniques. A handbook for faculty.* Jossey-Bass.

Daley, B. J., & Torre, D. M. (2010). Concept maps in medical education: An analytical literature review. *Medical Education, 44*(5), 440–448. https://doi.org/10.1111/j.1365-2923.2010.03628.x.

Darby, M. (2007). Debate: A teaching-learning strategy for developing competence in communication and critical thinking. *American Dental Hygienists' Association, 81*(4), 78–78.

Darby, F., & Lang, J. M. (2019). *Small teaching online: Applying learning science in online classes.* John Wiley & Sons.

De Gagne, J. C., Park, H. K., Hall, K., Woodward, A., Yamane, S., & Kim, S. S. (2019). Microlearning in health professions education: Scoping review. *JMIR Medical Education, 5*(2), e13997. https://doi.org/10.2196/13997.

Eison, J. (2010). Using active learning instructional strategies to create excitement and enhance learning. *Jurnal Pendidikantentang Strategi Pembelajaran Aktif (Active Learning) Books, 2*(1), 1–10.

Elliott, S., Combs, S., Huelskamp, A., & Hritz, N. (2017). Engaging students in large health classes with active learning strategies. *Journal of Physical Education, Recreation & Dance, 88*(6), 38–43. https://doi.org/10.1080/07303084.2017.1330163.

European Commission. (2011). *Supporting growth and jobs: an agenda for the modernisation of Europe's higher education systems: Communication from the commission to the European parliament, the council, the European economic and social committee and the committee of the regions.* Publications Office. https://data.europa.eu/doi/10.2766/17689.

European Commission. (2013). *High Level Group on the Modernisation of Higher Education: Report to the European Commission on improving the quality of teaching and learning in Europe's higher education institutions.* Publications Office. https://data.europa.eu/doi/10.2766/42468.

Fedeli, M. (2019). Linking faculty development to organizational development: Teaching4Learning@Unipd. In M. Fedeli & L. L. Bierema (Eds.), *Connecting adult learning and knowledge management* (pp. 51–68). Springer.

Fedeli, M., & Taylor, W. E. (2023). The impact of an active learning designed development program: A students' perspective of an Italian University. *Tuning Journal for Higher Education, 1*(4), 151-174. https://doi.org/10.18543/tjhe1112023.

Fedeli, M., & Taylor, E. W. (2024). Collaborative learning and group work. In. J. E. Coryell, L. M. Baumgartner, & J. W. Bohonos (Eds.), *Methods for facilitating adult learning: Strategies for enhancing instruction and instructor effectiveness* (pp. 117-1131). Routledge.

Fisher, S. (2023, August 30). 9 best free Jeopardy templates. *Lifewire.* https://www.lifewire.com/free-jeopardy-powerpoint-templates-1358186.

Freeman, M., Blayney, P., & Ginns, P. (2006). Anonymity and in class learning: The case for electronic response systems. *Australasian Journal of Educational Technology, 22*(4), 568. https://doi.org/10.14742/ajet.1286.

Freeman, S., Eddy, S. L., McDonough, M., Smith, M. K., Okoroafor, N., Jordt, H., & Wenderoth, M. P. (2014). Active learning increases student performance in science, engineering, and mathematics. *Proceedings of the National Academy of Sciences, 111*(23), 8410–8415. https://doi.org/10.1073/pnas.1319030111.

Gulick, L. H. (1908). *Mind and Work.* Doubleday.

Haas, S. (2014). Pick-n-Mix: A typology of writers' groups in use. In C. Aitchison & C. Guerin *Writing groups for doctoral education and beyond* (pp. 46–64). Routledge.

Hacisalihoglu, G., Stephens, D., Johnson, L., & Edington, M. (2018). The use of an active learning approach in a SCALE-UP learning space improves academic performance in undergraduate General Biology. *PloS One, 13*(5), e0197916. https://doi.org/10.1371/journal.pone.0197916.

Hsaio, Y. P., & Rajagopal, K. (2023). Support student integration of multiple peer feedback on research writing in thesis circles. In O. Noroozi & B. DeWever (Eds.), *The power of peer learning: Fostering students' learning processes and outcomes* (pp. 47–70). Springer.

Huba, M. E., & Freed, J. E. (2000). *Learner-centered assessment on college campuses: Shifting the focus from teaching to learning.* Allyn and Bacon.

Ingram, J., & Elliott, V. (2016). A critical analysis of the role of wait time in classroom interactions and the effects on student and teacher interactional behaviours. *Cambridge Journal of Education, 46*(1), 37–53. https://doi.org/10.1080/0305764X.2015.1009365.

Irving, A., & Garling, B. (n.d.). Wait time. *Classroom.* https://questioninganddiscussionforteaching.wordpress.com/wait-time/.

Lang, J. M. (2021). *Small teaching: Everyday lessons from the science of learning.* John Wiley & Sons.

Litan, R. (2020). *Resolved: Debate can revolutionize education and help save our democracy.* Brookings Institution Press.

Major, C. (2020). Collaborative learning: A tried and true active learning method for the college classroom. *New Directions for Teaching and Learning, 2020*(164), 19–28. https://doi.org/10.1002/tl.20420.

Mazur, E. (2013). Peer instruction. *A User's Manual. [Kindle Edition].* Retrieved from Amazon.com.

Medina, J. (2009) *Brain rules: 12 principles for surviving and thriving at work, home and school.* Seattle: Pear Press.

Mendelson, E. (2013). *Who wrote Auden's definition of a professor?* The W. H. Auden Society. http://audensociety.org/definition.html.

Michael, J. (2006). Where's the evidence that active learning works? *Advances In Physiology Education, 30*(4), 159–167. https://doi.org/10.1152/advan.00053.2006.

Morell, T. (2004). Interactive lecture discourse for university EFL students. *English for Specific Purposes, 23*(3), 325–338. https://doi.org/10.1016/S0889-4906(03)00029-2.

Munna, A. S., & Kalam, M. A. (2021). Teaching and learning process to enhance teaching effectiveness: A literature review. *International Journal of Humanities and Innovation (IJHI), 4*(1), 1–4. https://doi.org/10.33750/ijhi.v4i1.102.

Murillo-Zamorano, L. R., López Sánchez, J. Á., Godoy-Caballero, A. L., & Bueno Muñoz, C. (2021). Gamification and active learning in higher education: Is it possible to match digital society, academia and students' interests? *International Journal of Educational Technology in Higher Education, 18*, 1–27. https://doi.org/10.1186/s41239-021-0024.

Nardo, J. E., Chapman, N. C., Shi, E. Y., Wieman, C., & Salehi, S. (2022). Perspectives on active learning: Challenges for equitable active learning implementation. *Journal of Chemical Education, 99*(4), 1691–1699. https://doi.org/10.1021/acs.jchemed.1c01233.

National Research Council, Committee on Undergraduate Science Education. (1997). *Science teaching reconsidered: A handbook.* Washington, DC: National Academies Press.

National Research Council, Committee on Undergraduate Science Education. (2003). *Improving undergraduate instruction in science, technology, engineering and mathematics: Report of a workshop.* Washington, DC: National Academies Press.

National Science Foundation. (1996). *Shaping the Future: New Experiences for Undergraduate Education in Science, Mathematics, Engineering and Technology. Report of the Advisory Committee to the NSF Directorate for Education and Human Resources.* Washington, DC.

Ndebele, C., & Maphosa, C. (2013). Promoting active learning in large class university teaching: Prospects and challenges. *Journal of Social Sciences, 35*(3), 251–262. https://doi.org/10.31901/24566756.2013/35.03.06.

Nechkina, M. (1984). Increasing the effectiveness of a lesson. *Communist, 2,* 51.

Nguyen, K. A., Borrego, M., Finelli, C. J., DeMonbrun, M., Crockett, C., Tharayil, S., et al. (2021). Instructor strategies to aid implementation of active learning: A systematic literature review. *International Journal of STEM Education, 8*, 1–18. https://doi.org/10.1186/s40594-021-00270-7.

Nowlen, P. M., (1988). *A new approach to continuing education for business and the professions: The performance model.* Macmillan.

Özbay, Ö., & Çınar, S. (2021). Effectiveness of flipped classroom teaching models in nursing education: A systematic review. *Nurse Education Today, 102*, 104922. https://doi.org/10.1016/j.nedt.2021.104922.

Penner, J. G. (1984). *Why Many College Teachers Cannot Lecture.* Springfield, IL: Thomas.

Pike, R. W. (2003). *Creative training techniques handbook: Tips, tactics, and how-to's for delivering effective training.* Human Resource Development.

Ploetzner, R. (2022). The effectiveness of enhanced interaction features in educational videos: A meta-analysis. *Interactive Learning Environments, 32*(5), 1597–1612. https://doi.org/10.1080/10494820.2022.2123002.

Rajagopal, K., Vrieling-Teunter, E., Hsiao, Y. P., Van Seggelen-Damen, I., & Verjans, S. (2021). Guiding thesis circles in higher education: Towards a typology. *Professional Development in Education, 50* (2): 315–332. https://doi.org/10.1080/19415257.2021.1973072.

Reilly, R. F. (1992, September 1). The erosion of trust, a speech delivered to the Juniata College Annual Spring Awards Convocation, Huntington Pennsylvania, April 20, 1992. In *Vital Speeches of the Day* (vol. LVIII, No. 22).

Rice, G. T. (2018). *Hitting pause: 65 lecture breaks to refresh and reinforce learning.* Stylus.

Rice, G. T. (2023). *Hitting pause: 65 lecture breaks to refresh and reinforce learning.* Taylor & Francis.

Roesler, W. J., & Dreaver-Charles, K. (2018). Responsive eLearning exercises to enhance student interaction with metabolic pathways. *Biochemistry and Molecular Biology Education, 46*(3), 223–229. https://doi.org/10.1002/bmb.21112.

Rowe, M. B. (1972). *Wait-time and rewards as instructional variables, their influence in language, logic, and fate control.* Paper presented at the National Association for Research in Science Teaching, Chicago, IL, 1972. ED 061 103. ERIC Resource Center. www.eric.ed.gov http://eric.ed.gov/?id=ED061103.

Rowe, M. B. (1987). Wait time: Slowing down may be a way of speeding up. *American Educator 11*(2), 38–43. https://doi.org/10.1177/002248718603700110.

Schön, D. A. (1983). *The reflective practitioner: How professionals think in action.* Temple Smith.

Shiau, A. Y. A., McWilliams, K., & Williams, S. (2024). The role of wait time during the questioning of children: A systematic review. *Trauma, Violence, & Abuse, 25*(5), 3441–3456. https://doi.org/10.1177/15248380241246793.

Silberman, M. (2006). *Active training: A handbook of techniques, designs, case examples and tips.* San Francisco: Wiley.

Sözmen, E. Y., Karaca, O., & Batı, A. H. (2021). The effectiveness of interactive training and microlearning approaches on motivation and independent learning of medical students during the COVID-19 pandemic. *Innovations in Education and Teaching International, 60*(1), 70–79. https://doi.org/10.1080/14703297.2021.1966488.

Sridharan, B., McKay, J., & Boud, D. (2023). The four pillars of peer assessment for collaborative teamwork in higher education. In O. Noroozi & B. DeWever (Eds.), *The power of peer learning: Fostering students' learning processes and outcomes* (pp. 3–24). Springer.

Stahl, R. J. (1990). *Using "think-time" behaviors to promote students' information processing, learning, and on-task participation. an instructional module.* Tempe, AZ: Arizona State University.

Stahl, R. J. (1994). *Using "think-time" and "wait-time" skillfully in the classroom.* ERIC Clearinghouse. https://files.eric.ed.gov/fulltext/ED370885.pdf.

Stains, M., Harshman, J., Barker, M. K., Chasteen, S. V., Cole, R., DeChenne-Peters, S. E., et al. (2018). Anatomy of STEM teaching in North American universities. *Science, 359*(6383), 1468–1470. https://doi.org/10.1126/science.aap8892.

Stark, R. K., Opuda, E., McElfresh, J., & Kauffroath, K. (2021). Scavenging for evidence: A systematic review of scavenger hunts in academic libraries. *The Journal of Academic Librarianship, 47*(3), 102345. https://doi.org/10.1016/j.acalib.2021.102345.

Swinehart, D. F. (1980). "Swinehart's Definition," in *The Official Explanations* by P. Dickson. New York: Dell.

Tay, J., Goh, Y. M., Safiena, S., & Bound, H. (2022). Designing digital game-based learning for professional upskilling: A systematic literature review. *Computers & Education, 184*, 104518. https://doi.org/10.1016/j.compedu.2022.104518.

Theobald, E. J., Hill, M. J., Tran, E., Agrawal, S., Arroyo, E. N., Behling, S., et al. (2020). Active learning narrows achievement gaps for underrepresented students in undergraduate science, technology, engineering, and math. *Proceedings of the National Academy of Sciences, 117*(12), 6476–6483. https://doi.org/10.1073/pnas.1916903117.

Verner C. & Dickenson, G. (1967). The Lecture: An analysis and review of research. *Adult Education, 17* (2), 85–100.

Von Lau, E., Gopalai, A. A. (2022). Scavenger hunt activity to reinforce engineering fundamentals. In C. Chang-Tik, G. Kidman, M.Y. Tee (Eds.), *Collaborative Active Learning.* Palgrave Macmillan, Singapore. https://doi.org/10.1007/978-981-19-4383-6_7.

Whittard, D. (2015). Reflections on the one-minute paper. *International Review of Economics Education, 20*, 1–12. https://doi.org/10.1016/j.iree.2015.06.002.

NAME INDEX

SUBJECT INDEX